HANDBOOK OF HUMAN PERFORMANCE

VOLUME 2

HEALTH AND PERFORMANCE

Edited by

A.P. Smith & D.M. Jones

ACADEMIC PRESS

Harcourt Brace Jovanovich, Publishers

LONDON   SAN DIEGO   NEW YORK   BOSTON   SYDNEY   TOKYO   TORONTO

HANDBOOK OF
HUMAN PERFORMANCE

VOLUME 2

HEALTH AND PERFORMANCE

ACADEMIC PRESS LIMITED
24–28 Oval Road
London NW1 7DX

United States Edition published by
ACADEMIC PRESS INC.
San Diego, CA 92101

A catalogue record for this book is available from the British Library
ISBN 0-12-650352-4

Typeset by P&R Typesetters Ltd, Salisbury, Wilts
and printed in Great Britain by Hartnolls Ltd., Bodmin, Cornwall.

Contents

Contributors   vii
General Preface   ix
Volume Preface   xi
List of Contents for Volumes 1, 2 & 3   xiii

1 Meals and Performance   1
A.P. SMITH and A.M. KENDRICK

2 Vitamin and Mineral Intake and Human Behaviour   25
D. BENTON

3 Caffeine   49
H.R. LIEBERMAN

4 The Effects of Alcohol on Performance   73
F. FINNIGAN and R. HAMMERSLEY

5 Smoking, Nicotine and Human Performance   127
K.A. WESNES and A.C. PARROTT

6 Cannabis   169
J.F. GOLDING

7 Colds, Influenza and Performance   197
A.P. SMITH

8 HIV and AIDS   219
V. EGAN and G. GOODWIN

9 Diabetes, Hypoglycaemia and Cognitive Performance   243
I.J. DEARY

10 Chronic Fatigue Syndrome and Performance   261
A.P. SMITH

11 Prescribed Psychotropic Drugs: the Major and Minor Tranquillizers   279
L.R. HARTLEY

12 Antidepressant Drugs, Cognitive Function and Human Performance   319
H.V. CURRAN

13 The Effects of Anaesthetic and Analgesic Drugs   337
K. MILLAR

Subject Index   387

Author Index   393

Contributors

D. Benton, Department of Psychology, University College, Swansea, SA2 8PP, UK

H.V. Curran, Institute of Psychiatry, De Crespigny Park, London, SE5 8AF, UK

I.J. Deary, Department of Psychology, University of Edinburgh, 7 George Square, Edinburgh, EH8 9JZ, UK

V. Egan, Infectious Diseases Unit, Ward 7a, City Hospital, Greenbank Drive, Edinburgh, EH10 5AJ, UK

F. Finnigan, Behavioural Sciences Group, 4 Lilybank Gardens, University of Glasgow, G12 8QQ, UK

J.F. Golding, Royal Air Force Institute of Aviation Medicine, Farnborough, Hampshire, GU14 6SZ, UK.

G. Goodwin, MRC Brain Metabolism Unit, Royal Edinburgh Hospital, Morningside Park, Edinburgh, EH10 5HA, UK

R. Hammersley, Behavioural Sciences Group, 4 Lilybank Gardens, University of Glasgow, G12 8QQ, UK

L.R. Hartley, Department of Psychology, Murdoch University, Western Australia 6150, Australia

A.M. Kendrick, Health Psychology Research Unit, School of Psychology, University of Wales College of Cardiff, Cardiff, CF1 3YG, UK

H.R. Lieberman, Military Performance and Neuroscience Division, US Army Research Institute of Environmental Medicine, Natick, Ma. 01760-5007, USA

K. Millar, Behavioural Sciences Group, 4 Lilybank Gardens, University of Glasgow, Glasgow, G12 8QQ, UK

A.C. Parrott, Department of Psychology, Polytechnic of East London, London, E15 4LZ, UK

A.P. Smith, Health Psychology Research Unit, School of Psychology, University of Wales College of Cardiff, Cardiff, CF1 3YG, UK

K.A. Wesnes, Cognitive Drug Research, 13 The Grove, Reading, RG1 4RB, UK

General Preface

In this three volume series, the effects of different states and environments on performance are examined. That contemporary research in this area could not be encompassed in one volume marks not just the diversity of effects which now come under this rubric but also its maturity as a subject area. Twenty years ago, this would have been a slim volume indeed!

What are the factors which caused the growth of interest which led to the book? No single factor can be identified, rather the interplay of several factors seems to be responsible. Initially, interest centred on the use of task-performance as measures of central nervous system efficiency and as indices which by-passed the difficulty of obtaining objective measures of the person's state. Models of human performance became more refined in the decades after the Second World War, because the judicious selection of tasks meant that a more analytic approach could be used. This approach yielded more than a simple index of performance to represent overall efficiency. Rather, using a battery of tasks or by careful analysis of the microstructure of individual tasks (often focusing on the interplay of several measures), qualitative judgements could be made about the action of the agent. The term 'efficiency' in this context is somewhat misleading because it seems to imply that the main interest is in loss of efficiency and in obtaining some single quantitative index of the person's state. Although this might be part of the motivation, particularly for the early studies, latterly much more interest has centred upon discerning different classes of response. This helps to further our understanding of the physiological basis for each of the effects and the likely interplay of factors.

The increasing portability and cheapness of microprocessors has also played a role in the increasing scope of work. By using microprocessors, field observations may now be made with the accuracy that was hitherto only possible in laboratories. We can now judge the effect of a particular factor at the place of work and moreover for extended periods of time. In each of the contributions, authors have provided an up-to-date account of the empirical work in the area. Where possible, findings are presented from both laboratory and field settings and in each case discussion of methodological issues will also be found. Some work is still in the very early stages and hence highly developed and integrated theories are not always the rule. The volumes provide, in their breadth and depth, a cross-section of interesting work in the area of human performance.

The three volumes reflect the division of work in the area into three distinct but often interacting domains. Volume 1 has its roots in occupational health and work psychology. It contains some of the longest established areas of interest: noise, heat, distraction and vibration. New industrial processes and machines have introduced new concerns such as the increasing use of solvents in the chemical industry, the concern about hyperbaric environments in the search for oil and the behavioural effects of electrical fields and ionization in the distribution of electricity. The contents of Volume 1 also reflect the fact that much more work is now undertaken in offices than in factories (at least in the Western world). Visual display units, once a rarity, now seem ubiquitous. Although the settings in which they are used are by and large more hospitable in some respects than the traditional shop-floor, the pace, content and organization of work will still have consequences on efficiency.

Volume 2 contains research which is very much less traditional and which has been marked by enormous growth in the last decade. Here the emphasis is on the relationship between health and behaviour. Three complementary approaches can be discerned. First, there is growing evidence and concern about the effect of behaviours such as smoking and alcohol consumption on performance and well-being. Second, the behavioural consequences of illness (acute and chronic, mental and physical) in terms of the effects on performance are examined. Third, and perhaps the longest recognized, is the interest in psychological side-effects of treatment both on mental and physical health.

Volume 3 continues to regard the state of the person, but its scope is in terms of chronic, long term, slowly-changing effects of state. This volume also takes up the theme of chronic and acute change in state by setting aside a section to the study of individual differences in state and trait. The periodicity of the day—night cycle has implications for efficiency because alertness varies with the time of day, the nature and, more particularly, the length of work. Even when undisturbed, these factors produce a change in efficiency. When disturbed, by shiftwork or emergencies, the consequences are normally much more dramatic. There is obvious practical interest in knowing what effects new patterns of work will have on the person both in the short term for efficiency and in the long term, for health.

Preface to Volume 2

There has been considerable recent interest in the relationship between health and behaviour. Much of the research has been concerned with the role of psychological characteristics in susceptibility to illness. Other studies have concentrated on the effects of behaviour, such as nutrition, smoking, alcohol consumption and exercise on health. In addition, psychologists have also examined both acute and chronic illnesses, and have been involved in the treatment of both physical and mental disorders. The present volume aims to complement these approaches by considering in detail the relationship between health and performance efficiency.

The volume consists of four sections. The first is concerned with nutrition and performance, with Chapter 1 reviewing the effects of meals, and Chapter 2 the effects of micro-nutrients. The second section of the volume describes the effects of habitual substance use on performance. Chapters 3 and 4 review the effects of two psychoactive substances found in drinks, namely caffeine and alcohol. Following this, Chapters 5 and 6 describe our current knowledge of the effects of smoking, nicotine and cannabis on performance.

The third part of the volume considers the effects of illness on performance. Two of the chapters are concerned with the impact of viral illnesses, with Chapter 7 describing recent research on influenza, colds and performance, and Chapter 8, HIV infection and the neuropsychological sequelae of AIDS. Two chronic conditions are covered in the next two chapters, with Chapter 9 discussing diabetes and performance, and Chapter 10 describing the behavioural effects associated with the chronic fatigue syndrome.

The final section of the volume considers the effects of pharmacological treatment and possible adverse effects associated with medical procedures. Chapter 11 reviews the effects of major and minor tranquillisers on performance, and Chapter 12 evaluates the extent to which anti-depressants influence performance. The final chapter, Chapter 13, covers recent research on the effects of anaesthetics, analgesics and performance.

Overall, the chapters in the volume provide wide ranging coverage of many different aspects of the relationship between health and performance. However, all chapters provide both detailed descriptions of the area of research, and also critical evaluations of the methodology, theory and practical implications of the findings. We believe that this volume has achieved the aim of integrating a range of topics to produce a detailed profile of health and performance. We would like to thank the authors for their contributions and also thank everyone else who has helped us in the various stages of our editorial duties.

Andrew Smith and Dylan Jones

List of Contents for Volumes 1, 2 & 3

VOLUME 1

THE PHYSICAL ENVIRONMENT

Contributors
General Preface
Volume Preface
List of Contents for Volumes 1, 2 & 3

1 Noise and Performance
A.P. SMITH and D.M. JONES

2 Irrelevant Speech and Cognition
D.M. JONES and N. MORRIS

3 Vibration
M.J. GRIFFIN

4 Heat and Performance
S. HYGGE

5 Cold
S. BROOKE and H. ELLIS

6 Air Pollution and Behaviour
S.M. HORVATH and D.M. DRECHSLER-PARKS

7 Organic Solvents
B. STOLLERY

8 Hyperbaric Environments
S. BROOKE and H. ELLIS

9 Electrical Fields
B. STOLLERY

10 Ionization
E.W. FARMER

11 The Visual Environment
E. MEGAW

12 Visual Display Units
A.J. TATTERSALL

VOLUME 2

HEALTH AND PERFORMANCE

Contributors
General Preface
Volume Preface
List of Contents for Volumes 1, 2 & 3

1 Meals and Performance
A.P. SMITH and A.M. KENDRICK

2 Vitamin and Mineral Intake and Human Behaviour
D. BENTON

3 Caffeine
H.R. LIEBERMAN

4 The Effects of Alcohol on Performance
F. FINNIGAN and R. HAMMERSLEY

5 Smoking, Nicotine and Human Performance
K.A. WESNES and A.C. PARROTT

6 Cannabis
J.F. GOLDING

7 Colds, Influenza and Performance
A.P. SMITH

8 HIV and AIDS
V. EGAN and G. GOODWIN

9 Diabetes, Hypoglycaemia and Cognitive Performance
I.J. DEARY

10 Chronic Fatigue Syndrome and Performance
A.P. SMITH

11 Prescribed Psychotropic Drugs: the Major and Minor Tranquillizers
L.R. HARTLEY

12 Antidepressant Drugs, Cognitive Function and Human Performance
H.V. CURRAN

13 The Effects of Anaesthetic and Analgesic Drugs
K. MILLAR

VOLUME 3
STATE AND TRAIT

Contributors
General Preface
Volume Preface
List of Contents for Volumes 1, 2 & 3

1 Intelligence
M. ANDERSON

2 Aging and Human Performance
D.R. DAVIES, A. TAYLOR and L. DORN

3 Sex Differences in Performance: Fact, Fiction or Fantasy?
J. USSHER

4 Extraversion
G. MATTHEWS

5 Anxiety and Performance
J.H. MUELLER

6 Mood
G. MATTHEWS

7 Effects of Sleep and Circadian Rhythms on Performance
S.S. CAMPBELL

8 Time of Day and Performance
A.P. SMITH

9 Sleep Deprivation
A. TILLEY and S. BROWN

10 Vigilance
F. NACHREINER and K. HÄNECKE

11 Symptoms of Acute and Chronic Fatigue
A. CRAIG and R.E. COOPER

1

Meals and Performance

A.P. SMITH & A.M. KENDRICK

INTRODUCTION

The association between meals and performance is a complex one, with many factors playing important roles: factors which need to be taken into account when attempting to interpret the link between meals and performance include the timing of the meal, the nature of the meal (in terms of nutrient composition, size and bulk), characteristics of the person eating the meal and the nature of the activity being carried out (type of performance task). In addition, the modifying effects of antecedent and post-meal factors must also be considered.

POST-LUNCH DIP IN PERFORMANCE

There are few data on the effects of meals on subsequent performance, with the majority of studies concentrating on the effects of lunch on laboratory-based tasks. Real-life performance has, however, also been shown to be subject to post-lunch deficits in performance. Monk and Folkard (1985) review a series of six studies investigating diurnal variation in real-life tasks. These tasks ranged from speed of answering a switchboard (Browne, 1949) to the frequency of minor accidents in hospital (Folkard *et al.*, 1978), and demonstrated that performance in real-life situations varied during the day and, in addition, certain tasks showed clear evidence of a post-lunch dip in performance (see Figure 1.1). The impairments most frequently observed after consumption of lunch were lapses of attention (frequency of nodding off

HANDBOOK OF HUMAN PERFORMANCE
VOLUME 2 ISBN 0-12-650352-4

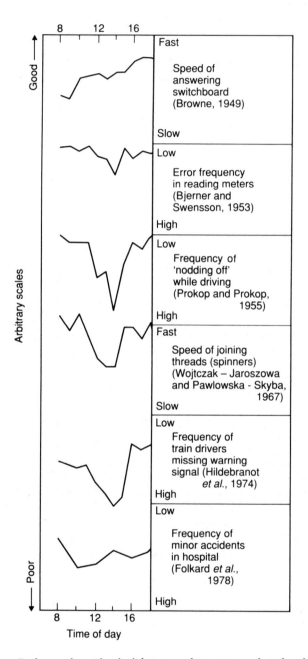

Figure 1.1 Evidence of post-lunch deficit in performance in selected real-life tasks. (From Folkard and Monk, 1985.)

Table 1.1 Effects of lunch on a variety of performance tasks

Task	Pre-lunch (10.30 a.m.)	Post-lunch I (1.00 p.m.)	Post-lunch II (3.30 p.m.)
5-Choice reaction time			
Correct (no.)	2669	2649	2747
Errors (no.)	28.3	35.4	28.5
Gaps (no.)	13.3	20.0	12.1
Vigilance			
Correct detections (%)	62.5	58.3	62.5
False reports (no.)	8.0	9.2	10.6
Card sorting			
Time for 2 categories (s)	61.9	62.2	62.9
Time for 8 categories (s)	85.2	86.1	86.0
Letter cancellation			
Output (no.)	1675	1598	1673
Error (%)	1.40	1.67	1.58
Time estimation			
10 s	10.01	10.82	9.53
120 s	121.00	124.14	111.52
Digit span (actual)	7.98	7.79	7.74
Reaction time (ms/actual)	320	330	315
Calculations			
Number done	350	338	340
Percentage error	2.87	2.79	2.31

From Blake, 1967.

during driving, frequency of train drivers missing warning signals, and accuracy errors in reading meters).

Further support for the existence of a post-lunch dip in performance comes from controlled, laboratory experiments such as the one by Blake (1971) who reported a decrement in performance following lunch on a number of tasks including vigilance, card sorting, serial reaction, calculations and reaction time (see Table 1.1).

Meals or circadian variations?

The foregoing studies, while supporting the existence of a post-lunch dip in performance, do not address the question of whether or not this phenomena is directly related to the consumption of food or is simply a reflection of underlying endogenous changes in performance (see Campbell, 1992). This can only be achieved by comparing the early afternoon performance in subjects who consume a meal with those who do not.

Several of the early laboratory studies which contrasted lunch and no-lunch conditions failed to show a strong effect of consuming a meal on post-lunch performance. Simonson *et al.* (1948) used a letter recognition task and failed to demonstrate significant differences between lunch and no-lunch conditions. King *et al.* (1945) conducted a study on altitude tolerance comparing the performance of pilots in lunch and no-lunch conditions. It was found that performance of a psychomotor task (block placement) was worse when lunch was not consumed, than when it was. It has been suggested, however, that this is more likely to be due to the length of time since the last meal than to the consumption of lunch *per se* (Craig, 1986).

More recently, Christie and McBrearty (1979) used letter cancellation, handwriting speed, a tracking task and rate of tapping to compare the post-lunch performance of a group who received lunch with a group who did not. No clear evidence of a post-lunch performance deficit was seen. Similarly, Blake (reported in Colquhoun, 1971) failed to demonstrate a difference between lunch and no-lunch conditions on a letter cancellation task.

From these studies it would appear that the post-lunch dip in performance is simply reflecting changes in endogenous rhythms and is unrelated to the consumption of a meal. A number of recent studies, however, provide data which suggest that the post-lunch dip has both endogenous and exogenous components. Craig *et al.* (1981) compared perceptual discrimination when lunch was eaten with when it was not. The task required subjects to determine which of two equiprobable signals was present on any trial, the signal being a white disc on a black background. One of the discs (A) was 10 per cent larger than the other (B). Forty subjects (mean age twenty-three years) were randomly assigned to 'lunch' or 'no-lunch' conditions. Lunch consisted of a standard three-course refectory meal (no further details given), with consumption of coffee also being allowed. Performance was assessed one hour before and one hour after the consumption of the meal. Clear discrepancies were seen between the lunch and no-lunch conditions, with those subjects who had been given lunch showing an impairment in their ability to discriminate between events. Since no such decrement was seen in those who had not eaten lunch, it seems likely that the effect was due to the direct effect of eating lunch and not to endogenous factors, such as circadian rhythms, alone.

Similarly, Smith and Miles (1986a) contrasted early afternoon vigilance performance in subjects who had eaten lunch with those who had not. Two tasks were employed: detection of repeated numbers and a proportion estimation task. The detection of repeated numbers task involved subjects monitoring a sequence of three-digit numbers presented on a computer screen and the subject had to respond when the number presented was identical to the one preceding it. The outcome measures for this task were the numbers of hits (correct identification of target) and false alarms (incorrect identification). The estimation task involved estimating the percentage of letters in a continuously presented stream of single letters and single digits. Forty-eight students (thirty female, eighteen male) participated. In the lunch condition, a standard meal was provided (a three-course meal chosen by the subjects from the university refectory) and testing took place one hour prior to the meal and again one hour following the meal. The no-lunch condition followed the same procedure but no meal was consumed during the lunch period. The main findings were: firstly, the consumption of lunch produced a performance deficit on the detection of repeated numbers task not seen in those who did not eat lunch (see Figure 1.2); secondly, the estimation task showed an afternoon performance deficit irrespective of lunch condition.

Further evidence of differences in performance between lunch and no-lunch conditions is provided by a study of Smith and Miles (1986b). This study compared late morning and early afternoon performance in forty-eight subjects who either had lunch or abstained from eating. Performance on a serial self-paced choice reaction time task and the Stroop colour–word task (a test of selective attention) were assessed prior to and following lunch. Two measures were derived from the reaction time task: (1) time taken to detect and respond to a target (reaction time), and (2) time taken to return to a home key (movement time). The results showed that consumption of lunch impaired detection performance (reaction times) on the choice reaction time task (see Figure 1.3).

In contrast to this, movement time was significantly slower in the early afternoon than in the morning, and this effect was independent of the consumption of a meal. The Stroop task involves the completion of four conditions: (1) reading a list of colour names printed in black ink, (2) naming patches of coloured ink, (3) naming the colour of ink in which incongruent colour names are printed, (4) reading colour names printed in incongruent coloured ink. The outcome measure was the time to complete each condition, and the results showed that none of the Stroop conditions were influenced by the consumption of lunch.

Such findings suggest that the post-lunch dip has both exogenous and endogenous components and that these are related to some extent to the

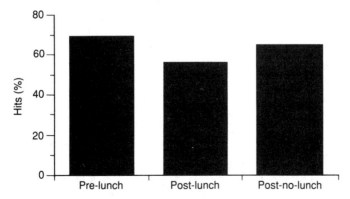

Figure 1.2 Post-lunch deficit in performance on detection of repeated numbers task. (From Smith and Miles, 1986a.)

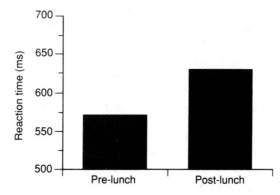

Figure 1.3 Effects of lunch on serial self-paced choice reaction time task. (From Smith and Miles, 1986b.)

nature of the performance task. Thus, certain tasks will show an early afternoon drop in performance which is due to circadian changes only and unrelated to the consumption of food, while other tasks will only show a performance deficit following the consumption of a meal. Tasks which typically show a meal effect are those requiring sustained attention, and short tasks do not generally show an effect of meals, unless they are part of a longer battery. Indeed, short tasks may show a post-lunch improvement. For example, Folkard and Monk (1985) describe post-lunch increments in performance on two verbal reasoning tasks and prose recall. Similarly, Millar *et al.* (in press) found that the ingestion of food improved performance on the secondary reaction time component of a dual task (duration five minutes) and on a choice reaction time task (duration three minutes).

Not only is the nature of the task important, but within-task components are differently affected by the consumption of a meal. Thus, for example, in the Smith and Miles (1986b) study reported earlier, response times on a choice reaction time task were subject to meal effects, but movement times were not.

In summary, the post-lunch dip in performance appears to be produced by both endogenous and exogenous factors. It has been demonstrated that consumption of a meal impairs early afternoon performance, although the nature of the activity being performed is important in determing whether or not this post-lunch dip is observed or not. The existence of performance differences between late morning / early afternoon which can be attributed to endogenous rhythms is less clear-cut. Indeed, it has been suggested that the 'endogenous' components may simply be a reflection of a conditioned response to rhythmic behaviour, for example the regularity of meal breaks (Smith and Miles, 1986b). The strongest test of the existence of endogenous rhythms is to minimize the influences of exogenous factors (for example, the sleep–wake cycle, outside stimuli) through 'isolation studies' (see Campbell,

1992). These involve isolating the subject from any cues relating to the passage of time, generally by placing the subject in a specially constructed isolation unit (Folkard and Monk, 1985). Subjects are allowed to eat and sleep when they wish, uninfluenced by outside factors such as day/night or time of day. Such studies indicate a drop in performance, similar to the post-lunch dip which is unassociated with meal regularity, but is also seen in measures of body temperature. It is proposed that at least part of the post-lunch dip is due, not to the ingestion of a meal, but is controlled by endogenous rhythms (Wever, 1985).

FACTORS INFLUENCING THE POST-LUNCH DIP

The previous section demonstrated that the nature of the activity being carried out is important in determining whether or not a post-lunch dip in performance is seen. The next section considers the extent to which characteristics of the person eating the meal and the nature of the meal itself are important to the occurrence and extent of the post-lunch dip in performance.

Introversion, neuroticism, anxiety

There is some evidence to suggest that the post-lunch dip in performance is mediated by personality factors. Of particular importance appear to be introversion, neuroticism and level of anxiety. Craig *et al.* (1981) found that scores on the extraversion and neuroticism scores of the Eysenck personality inventory correlated 0.4 and −0.38 respectively with an observed post-lunch dip in perceptual sensitivity (i.e. stable extraverts demonstrated a larger post-lunch dip in performance on this task than did neurotic introverts). This finding was substantiated in a study by Smith and Miles (1986c) in which a cognitive vigilance task was used. This task involved monitoring a series of digits, responding to either three consecutive odd or three consecutive even digits. Three outcome measures were derived: number of hits, number of false alarms and reaction times (for correct responses). Twenty-four university students participated in the study. Personality was assessed using the Eysenck personality inventory. In addition, state anxiety scores (Spielberger *et al.*, 1970) were collected at both the pre- and post-lunch sessions. Pre/post lunch differences in hit rate correlated 0.44 with extraversion scores and −0.47 with neuroticism scores. In addition, a correlation of 0.83 was seen between pre/post-lunch state anxiety scores and pre/post-lunch performance anxiety differences on the vigilance task (hit rate). This latter finding is of interest as it has been postulated that the differences in performance between stable extraverts and neurotic introverts may be due to differing levels of anxiety, with stable extraverts generally being thought to have low anxiety levels.

Sex differences

Gender also appears to play a role in the development and extent of post-lunch performance deficits. Although Christie and McBrearty (1979) found no evidence of a general dip in performance following lunch, a sex-by-meal effect was seen for a letter cancellation task with significant differences being seen between the lunch and no-lunch conditions for males only.

In contrast, Spring *et al.* (1983) examined post-meal performance on auditory reaction time and a dichotic shadowing task (a measure of selective and sustained attention) in 184 subjects (aged 18–65) receiving either a high protein or a high carbohydrate meal. Mood and performance testing was conducted two hours after the consumption of the meal. No effect of gender was seen on the performance tasks; however, gender effects were evident in the mood data. The consumption of a high carbohydrate meal produced more reports of 'sleepiness' in females, while males reported more feelings of 'calmness'.

Nature of the meal

A number of studies have manipulated the nature of the meal to examine the extent to which this influences the post-lunch dip. The first manipulation considered here is the nutrient composition, and then the size of the meal (both in terms of calorific intake and bulk) is discussed.

NUTRIENT COMPOSITION

Simonson *et al.* (1948) found a high carbohydrate meal reduced accuracy on a fast-paced letter recognition task in comparison with a 'standard' lunch or a high fat lunch. Spring *et al.* (1983) found differences between high carbohydrate and high protein meals on performance tasks. No effect of meal type was evident on a reaction time task, but several parameters of a dichotic listening task (accuracy, errors of omission) were influenced by the nutrient composition of the meal. Impaired performance was seen on this task following a high carbohydrate lunch, but not a high protein lunch. However, an interaction with age was also seen, with the effect of a carbohydrate meal on post-lunch performance being seen only in subjects over the age of forty. Reduced accuracy was independent of the presence or absence of distractors and thus the authors conclude that meal composition influences sustained, as opposed to selective, attention.

An impairment of performance following carbohydrate intake was also demonstrated in a study by Smith *et al.* (1988) who investigated the effect of meal composition on two attention tasks, one involving focused attention and the other categoric search (Broadbent *et al.*, 1986). In the focused attention task, either the letter A or the letter B appeared at the centre of a computer screen. On some occasions just the letter was presented, while on others distractors were also present (one on either side of the target letter). The distractors were either asterisks or letters (A or B), and were either close to or far from the target letter. The search task again involved responding to either the letter A or B, but the subject did not know in which of two locations the letter would appear. On some trials the two locations were close together in the centre of the screen and on others they were further apart (i.e. in the periphery). Performance following the consumption of either a high starch, a high protein or a high sugar meal were compared in twelve subjects (mean age 29.4 years). On the search task, reaction times to stimuli presented in the periphery were slower after carbohydrate meals (high starch and high sugar) (see Figure 1.4a). In contrast, the high protein meal was associated with greater distraction from stimuli close to the target in the focused attention task (see Figure 1.4b). It thus appears that protein and carbohydrate meals affect different aspects of attention.

In summary, the nutrient composition of the meal appears to be an important factor in the extent and nature of the post-lunch dip. It should be noted, however, that these studies have only examined the acute effects of meals. Further studies are needed to examine the effects of nutrients on performance later in the day and over a longer time period (days as opposed to hours).

SIZE OF MEAL

The size of the meal is usually calculated in terms of calorific content. It is generally believed that the larger the meal the more likely that post-lunch effects on performance are to be demonstrated. Although Smith and Miles (1986c) demonstrated post-meal impairments with a small, sandwich-based meal, most studies demonstrating post-lunch performance deficits have employed three-course meals (Craig *et al.*, 1981, Smith and Miles, 1987, Smith *et al.*, 1988). In most studies, however, subjects have been studied in an uncontrolled eating situation, i.e. they are allowed to eat what they want. Studies in which the calorific content of the meal is systematically manipulated are needed to determine the extent to which the calorific content of the meal alters post-meal performance. One such study has been reported (Smith *et al.*, 1991) in which the meal size (calorific content) was controlled according to the metabolic rate of individual subjects. Thirty-five female subjects (mean age 25.9 years, range 19−39) took part in the study. Three meal sizes were contrasted: a normal-sized lunch defined as providing one-third of the daily requirement for each individual; a large lunch designed to provide 40 per cent more energy than the normal lunch; a small lunch containing 40 per cent less energy than the normal lunch. The nutrient composition of the three lunches was equivalent (55 per cent carbohydrate, 15 per cent protein,

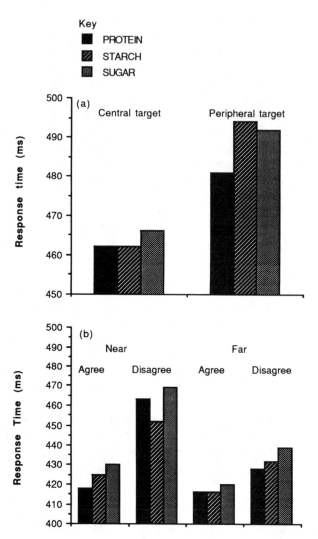

Figure 1.4 Effect of meal type on response times on: (a) categoric search task, and (b) focused attention task. (From Smith *et al.*, 1988.)

30 per cent fat). Performance on two attention tasks (focused attention and search task) was assessed before and $1\frac{1}{2}$ hours after lunch. Meal size did not affect response time on either of the attention tasks, but accuracy on the search task was significantly reduced following the large meal. Accuracy was also lower on the focused attention task following the large meal, but this failed to reach significance. It thus appears that changes in meal size increase 'momentary inefficiency' or 'lapses of attention', rather than altering the average speed of responding.

The effect of size of meal has been shown to interact with the normal eating habits of the individual, with a larger than normal lunch resulting in a greater dip in post-lunch performance than a normal size lunch (Craig and Richardson, unpublished data cited in Craig, 1986). Craig and Richardson found that accuracy in a letter cancellation task was significantly influenced by the size of the lunch normally consumed by the subjects. Subjects received either a heavy meal (1000 kcal, three-course meal) or a small meal (less than 300 kcal, sandwich). Subjects receiving a heavier than normal meal had increased errors, while those receiving a smaller than usual meal made fewer errors.

In conclusion, nutrient composition appears to influence different types of attention, whereas increasing the size of meal produces more momentary lapses of attention. While effects of factors relating to the meal itself have been demonstrated, it should be remembered that, in general, these effects are small and one must therefore consider whether other factors produce a more dramatic effect on the post-lunch dip.

The influence of stimulants

The role of stimulants in alleviating the post-lunch performance deficits is of theoretical and practical interest. At the theoretical level, it links in with theories of arousal and performance and can help us understand which mechanisms may be involved in producing this drop in performance. At the practical level, the determination of means of reducing the post-lunch dip will be of obvious practical value in the work environment.

Smith and Miles (1986c) demonstrated the beneficial effects of noise, which is often considered to increase arousal, on post-lunch performance. Continuous free-field noise was used, with a sound level of 75 dB(A) in the noise condition and a level of 40 dB(A) in the quiet condition. The task used was a variation of the Bakan vigilance task (as used by Wesnes and Warburton, 1984) in which a series of digits are presented on monitors, the task of the subject being to respond when they detect a sequence of either three consecutive odd or three consecutive even digits. Numbers of hits and false alarms and response times were recorded. All subjects received a lunch consisting of soup, two sandwiches, a fruit pie and some fruit. A post-lunch dip in number of targets correctly detected (hits) was seen in the quiet condition, but not in the noise condition. It thus appears that noise reduced the effect of the post-meal impairment. A similar effect was seen for the response time data; noise reduced the slowing of response times seen following lunch in the quiet condition.

Smith and Miles (1987) investigated performance on two search and memory tasks (SAM) with differing memory loads. These tasks involved scanning lines of capital letters for either one (low memory load) or five (high memory load) possible targets. The time taken to complete each task and accuracy of detection was recorded. Subjects were tested before and after

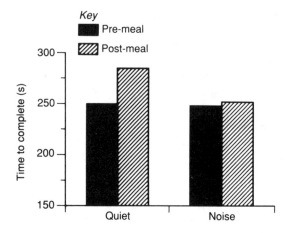

Figure 1.5 Effect of noise on search and memory task. (From Smith and Miles, 1987.)

lunch and in the presence and absence of noise. No effects of meal or noise was seen for the simpler task (detection of one letter). The more complex task (detection of five letters), however, demonstrated a post-meal decrease in response time. This decrease was less in the group performing in the presence of noise, suggesting that the post-meal impairment in performance was reduced by noise (see Figure 1.5).

Smith *et al.* (1990) examined the influence of another stimulant, caffeine, on the post-lunch dip in performance. A sustained attention (Bakan vigilance task) and a mental rotation task were used. A double-blind, within-subject design was employed to compare caffeine and no caffeine conditions in thirty-two students. Caffeine removed the post-lunch decline in performance on the sustained attention task, and this was evident both for speed (see Figure 1.6a) and accuracy scores (see Figure 1.6b). Caffeine also reduced the slowing of responses in the mental rotation task seen following lunch, but only for the most difficult condition of the task. Accuracy on the mental rotation task was unaffected by either lunch or caffeine.

Sedatives

From the previous section it seems that stimulants can, in some circumstances, reduce the post-lunch impairment in performance. If this is so, then it may be the case that sedatives increase post-lunch deficits. Few studies have considered the effects of lowering arousal on post-lunch performance. However, there is now some data on lunch and alcohol, and lunch and sleep deprivation and this is reviewed below. Millar *et al.* (in press) provide some data suggesting a link between the effects of food and alcohol on performance. This study was primarily interested in the mitigating effects of food on known

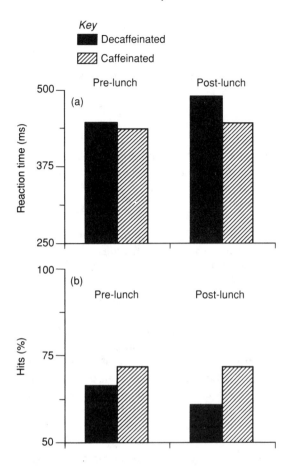

Figure 1.6 Effect of caffeine on (a) speed of responding and (b) accuracy on Bakan vigilance task. (From Smith *et al.*, 1990.)

performance deficits attributable to alcohol and thus performance tasks were chosen to reflect abilities known to be sensitive to alcohol: dual performance (primary tracking, secondary visual reaction time), short-term memory, choice reaction time (decision time and movement times) and critical flicker frequency (CFF). A total of 133 male subjects participated in the study (age range 18–46). A between-subject design was employed with subjects randomly assigned to one of eight groups formed by the combination of four alcohol doses (zero–placebo, low, medium and high) and two food conditions (standard lunch versus fasting). The low, medium and high alcohol levels related to peak blood alcohol levels (BAL) of 20, 40 and 80 mg 100 ml^{-1}. Performance was assessed prior to the consumption of lunch and again after peak blood alcohol levels had been reached (approximately one hour post-meal). Alcohol was given immediately after lunch. The findings indicate that alcohol-related performance deficits are reduced by the prior consumption of food, suggesting an interaction between food, alcohol and performance.

Another situation where arousal is reduced is when the person is sleep deprived. Smith and Maben (in preparation) compared the performance of sleep-deprived and non-sleep-deprived subjects before and after lunch. A number of functions were assessed including logical reasoning, sustained, focused and selective attention. A standard 1000 kcal lunch was eaten by all subjects and testing took place $1\frac{1}{2}$ hours following the consumption of the meal. A post-lunch dip in performance on the accuracy component of the focused attention task was evident for the sleep-deprived group but not the non-sleep-deprived group. This finding suggests that sleep deprivation may influence the extent of the post-lunch dip and further studies investigating this topic are now required.

True comparisons of the effects of stimulants and sedatives on performance can only be achieved by including both types of agents in the same study. Smith *et al.* (in preparation, a) considered the effects of both caffeine (a stimulant) and alcohol (a sedative) on post-meal performance in fifty-nine university students. A between-subjects design was employed with random allocation of subjects to one of eight groups formed by combining lunch (no lunch versus lunch), caffeine (no caffeine versus caffeine) and alcohol (no alcohol versus alcohol). Lunch was a standard, 1000 kcal, three-course meal. Performance measures included: detection of repeated numbers (sustained attention), focused attention, search task (selective attention) and a logical reasoning task. Testing was carried out prior to lunch and again $1\frac{1}{2}$ hours following consumption (or not) of the meal. From the findings, caffeine and alcohol in isolation appear to have different effects in line with their stimulant/sedative properties. In addition, speed of responding on the search task (a measure of selective attention) demonstrated an interaction between consumption of lunch and alcohol intake, with the negative effects of alcohol being reduced by eating lunch.

In summary, the influence of sedatives on the post-lunch dip requires further, controlled studies in which tasks known to be susceptible to post-lunch deficits in performance are studied in the presence and absence of sedatives.

POSSIBLE MECHANISMS

A number of mechanisms have been proposed as underlying the phenomena of the post-lunch dip in performance, good reviews of which are given by Spring *et al.* (1983) and Spring (1986).

One mechanism which has been suggested relates to variations in levels of the amino acid, tryptophan, by the nutrients present in a meal. Data from animal work demonstrates that the intake of a high carbohydrate meal after a period of fasting decreases plasma levels of large neutral amino acids (LNAA) by 40–60 per cent, but does not alter levels of tryptophan. These large neutral amino acids and tryptophan compete for common transport sites to the central nervous system and thus a decrease in LNAA will elevate brain levels of tryptophan. The neurotransmitter serotonin (a derivative of tryptophan) will be affected by rising levels of tryptophan as increased synthesis of tryptophan will increase the release of serotonin. It is thus suggested that behaviour and phenomena associated with serotoninergic neurotransmission will be affected by the consumption of carbohydrate-rich meals (Spring *et al.*, 1983). In contrast, protein reduces levels of serotonin and thus different effects on performance would be expected.

In addition, alterations by food on brain levels of tyrosine (elevated by protein) and choline (elevated by lecithin) and their subsequent effects on the synthesis of the catecholamines (dopamine, norepinephrine) have been proposed as possible mechanisms in the explanation of the influence of food on performance.

Another proposed mechanism suggests that behavioural differences are due to a state of hypoglycaemia. It is postulated that following the consumption of a meal, blood glucose levels fall resulting in a hypoglycaemic state which results in impaired performance. Thus, Karlan and Cohn (1946) in attempting to explain post-meal feelings of lassitude suggested that a sharp rise in glucose post-prandially initiates an insulin surge leading to a hypoglycaemic state, which produces alterations in mood. Another suggestion is that it is not the existence of a hypoglycaemic state as such but rather the rate of change which impairs performance. Christie and McBrearty (1979) measured performance, mood and several physiological measures including heart rate and blood capillary glucose levels (CBG). Performance data provided no evidence of a post-lunch change in performance, but mood scores of 'activation' and 'deactivation' appeared to be susceptible to a meal-related effect. The CBG data suggest that there is no evidence that mood swings were accompanied by a hypoglycaemic state, however, the mood changes were accompanied by the largest change in CBG levels. It was thus hypothesized that post-prandial lassitude is related not to hypoglycaemia but to a parasympathetic vagal initiation of the surge, as described by Woods and Porte (1974).

In summary, a number of mechanisms may be involved in the production of post-lunch impairments in performance. Alterations in the synthesis of neurotransmitters and plasma glucose levels may all be contributory factors.

THE POST-LUNCH DIP IN PERFORMANCE: SUMMARY AND RECOMMENDATIONS

Recent studies have clearly demonstrated that performance efficiency changes after lunch. However, it has been shown that the link between food and behaviour is a complex one and a number of factors involved have been highlighted. These include the nature of the meal itself, the type of activity being carried out and individual differences in the people being studied. Further work is required to aid our understanding of the separate and combined roles of these factors. The majority of studies to date have concentrated on the acute effects of meals, and thus our knowledge of the long-term effects of eating or not eating certain types of meal is limited. Well-planned, controlled longitudinal studies conducted both in the laboratory and in 'real-life' situations are needed to answer this gap in our knowledge. Another area of interest is that of the role of antecendent and post-lunch activities on the post-lunch dip. Again, this requires the initiation of studies in which these factors are carefully controlled.

MEALS OTHER THAN LUNCH

The previous sections have concentrated on the effects of lunch on performance. Work in this field has tended to concentrate on the effects of lunch as this is the meal most commonly eaten during working hours and which may influence an employee's ability to perform their job. The next section considers breakfast and meals eaten at other times of day and their relation to performance. Such studies are of relevance to educational settings (do children eating breakfast perform better at school than those who do not?) and in areas of employment where shift work is in operation.

Breakfast

Despite the popular belief that breakfast is the most important meal of the day, there are few published studies in which the effects of breakfast on performance have been studied. In a recent review, Dickie and Bender (1982a) found fewer than thirty papers relating to this topic. While research on the effects of lunch on early afternoon performance has focused on adults, concern about the effects of breakfast appear to centre mainly on the effects of skipping breakfast on school performance in children.

   The role of breakfast on subsequent performance remains a matter for debate. It is popularly believed that consumption of breakfast enhances performance, a suggestion which has arisen largely from a series of studies by Tuttle and colleagues over the past thirty years, collectively known as the Iowa breakfast studies. The main aim of these studies was to evaluate the effects of varying breakfast regimens on physiological performance. A number of the studies also included some tests of mental performance, although these were limited mainly to reaction time tasks. The findings of these studies suggest that mental and physical performance deteriorates following the consumption of breakfast. Tuttle *et al.* (1949) in the first experiment of the series, compared the effects of four breakfast regimens: (1) a heavy breakfast, 800 calories, (2) a light breakfast, 400 calories, (3) no breakfast, and (4) coffee only, 60 calories. In addition to a range of physiological measures, simple and choice reaction time were tested in six females aged between twenty-two and twenty-seven years. Results indicate that in the no-breakfast condition, there was a tendency towards slower reaction times. This finding was substantiated when the experiment was repeated in the same group of subjects. Five out of six females showed a significant increase in simple reaction time in the no-breakfast condition, while three out of six showed a significant increase in choice reaction time in the same condition.

Tuttle *et al.* (1950) conducted a similar experiment in ten males aged twenty-one to twenty-eight years, comparing a 'basic' breakfast of 750 calories to a no-breakfast condition. Testing took place three hours following the consumption (or not) of breakfast. The findings were mixed: six of the ten subjects showed no change in reaction time in the no-breakfast condition (as compared with the 'basic' breakfast), three showed a significant increase in reaction times, while one subject increased his reaction time significantly during the no-breakfast condition.

No effect of breakfast on reaction times was found in a study by Tuttle *et al.* (1952) in which three breakfast conditions were compared: (1) bacon, egg and milk breakfast, (2) no breakfast, (3) cereal and milk breakfast. Ten men aged sixty to eighty-three years participated in the study, which was conducted over a period of thirteen weeks. Subjects received the bacon, egg and milk breakfast for the first five weeks, followed by four weeks on no breakfast and four weeks on cereal and milk. It was found that for seven out of the eight subjects no change in reaction times was seen during the course of the experiment.

Tuttle *et al.* (1954) examined the scholastic achievements and attitudes of schoolboys aged twelve to fourteen years. These were based on subjective assessments by schoolmasters. A cereal and milk breakfast was compared with omitting breakfast. The results suggested that consumption of breakfast had a favourable effect on attitude and school performance. However, objective assessments of choice reaction time were not affected by missing breakfast.

A deterioration in performance associated with omitting breakfast has been noted by other researchers. King *et al.* (1945) assessed visual and motor functioning two to three hours following the consumption or omission of breakfast. They noted that these functions were impaired when breakfast was not eaten compared with when it was. Similarly, Pollit *et al.* (1981, 1982/1983) in a study of the performance of schoolchildren found an impairment on a task of picture identification (matching familiar figures test). Children who had not eaten breakfast were more likely to make errors on this task than children who had eaten breakfast. However, performance on a test of attentional ability (continuous performance task) was not affected by the consumption or not of breakfast. This finding is in keeping with the results reported by Conners and Blouin (1983).

These early studies have been criticized for having small group numbers, for producing inconsistent findings and for the use of subjective assessments (Dickie and Bender, 1982a). In addition, the range of performance measures used was small, being limited mainly to reaction time tasks.

More recently, Richards (1972) compared a standard 450 calorie breakfast with a no-breakfast condition. In the no-breakfast situation, coffee was allowed (40 calories). The eighteen subjects were chosen so that half habitually ate breakfast and half habitually skipped breakfast. A range of performance measures were employed: a visual search test, a short-term memory test, an error vigilance test and a coding test. Testing was carried out between noon and 1.00 p.m. Subjects were tested on five occasions: once following their normal breakfast (learning session), twice following the standard breakfast and twice following no breakfast. A modified Latin-square design was used. No change in performance associated with the consumption or omission of breakfast was seen. Of interest is the finding that in three of the tests, performance was worst when subjects deviated from their normal meal. The author suggests that 'the occasional omission of breakfast is more deleterious than the constant omission'.

Dickie and Bender (1982b) report two studies in which mental performance was assessed in secondary school children. The first study compared the performance of children who habitually ate breakfast with those who did not. A total of 227 first-year (mean age 12.5 years) and 260 fourth-year (mean age 15.3 years) pupils completed a letter cancellation task before and after lunch. It was hypothesized that if lack of breakfast affected late morning performance that this would be expected to disappear following the midday meal. The children were placed into four groups depending on what food they had consumed that day: (1) breakfast and mid-morning snack, (2) breakfast and no mid-morning snack, (3) no breakfast and mid-morning snack, (4) no breakfast and no mid-morning snack. The results indicate no difference between those who ate breakfast and those who did not on either speed or accuracy in completing the cancellation task. The second experiment used two short-term memory tasks (with different memory loadings), a simple addition test and an attention task (logical reasoning) to compare breakfast and no breakfast conditions in a group of school children who habitually ate breakfast. Fifty-five children (mean age 17 years) completed the short-term memory and simple addition tasks and 53 children (mean age 16.2 years completed the logical reasoning task. Testing took place over two weeks: on week 1 all subjects ate breakfast as normal and were tested at 11.00–11.30 a.m. for three consecutive days; on week 2 the same procedure was followed with an experimental group not receiving breakfast. No evidence of any change in mental performance relating to the omission of breakfast was seen.

Benton and Sargent (in press) assessed the effects of no breakfast versus a high protein drink on two memory tasks: spatial memory and immediate recall of a word list. Time to complete the task and number of errors were recorded for both tests. Thirty-three subjects aged nineteen to twenty-eight years participated in the study. Half were habitual breakfast eaters and half were not. Consumption of the high protein drink increased the speed with which both memory tasks were completed. This is in contrast to the study by Dickie and Bender (1982b) in which breakfast did not influence performance on a number of tasks including memory. However, the two studies differ in a number of ways, for example differences in tasks employed and breakfasts consumed, which may account for the discrepancies in the findings.

A recent study by Smith *et al.* (in preparation, b) failed to find an effect of breakfast on mid-morning performance of sustained attention tasks. Forty-eight university students were randomly assigned to receive either a light breakfast (cereal and toast, 470 kcal), a cooked breakfast (bacon, scrambled egg and toast, 470 kcal) or no breakfast. Subjects were assessed prior to the consumption of breakfast and again one and two hours following the meal. No effect of breakfast was seen on simple reaction time, choice reaction time or sustained attention. Some effects on mood were seen, however, with the group receiving the cooked breakfast rating themselves as less discontented, less bored, more sociable and more outward-going than either the light breakfast or no-breakfast groups.

Another study by the same group (Smith *et al.*, in preparation, c) used a similar study design but expanded the performance tasks to include the assessment of memory. The consumption of breakfast significantly improved performance on a free recall task (see Figure 1.7). Performance on this task was unaffected by the ingestion of caffeine and, in addition, no interaction

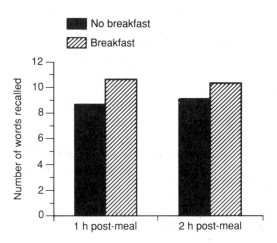

Figure 1.7 Influence of breakfast on recall memory. (From Smith *et al.*, unpublished data.)

between caffeine and breakfast was seen. Recognition memory performance was also improved by the consumption of breakfast with the group receiving breakfast having a lower false alarm rate on this task than the no-breakfast group.

A possible mechanism for the role of breakfast in mediating memory ability has been proposed by Benton and Sargent (in press). They suggest that memory processes are linked to the availability of glucose to the brain, which may be metabolized through pyruvate to acetyl-Co-A (a substrate for acetylcholine synthesis). However, the link between circulating glucose levels and neurotransmitter synthesis remains a matter of debate.

In summary, the few studies which have looked at the effects of breakfast on performance have produced discrepant findings. On balance, it seems that breakfast in isolation has minimal effects on subsequent performance of many tasks, although there is some support for a beneficial role of breakfast on memory abilities. Given that breakfast itself has little influence on subsequent performance, one must ask whether consumption of breakfast modifies the effects of lunch. This question has yet to be addressed.

Meals in the middle of the night

The effect of meals consumed during the night on subsequent performance is of particular relevance to industries in which shift work is the norm. While deficits following a meal consumed at midday have been demonstrated, it is not possible to extrapolate these results to the effects of a similar meal consumed at a different time of day. Smith and Miles (1986c) investigated the effects of a standard meal consumed either during the day (12.30–1.30 p.m.) or during the night (1.30–2.30 a.m.). A cognitive vigilance task in which a series of digits is presented on a computer screen and the subject is required to detect series of three consecutive odd or even numbers was employed. The outcome measures were number of hits, number of false alarms and response times. This task was chosen as cognitive tasks with high memory loads are not thought to show a night-time decrement in performance. Twenty-four subjects were tested on four occasions: at 9.40 a.m., 11.50 a.m., 2.10 p.m. and 4.20 p.m. during the day and 10.40 p.m., 00.50 a.m., 3.10 a.m. and 5.20 a.m. during the night. Post-meal impairments in the number of targets detected (hits) were evident at the test session immediately following the consumption of the meal both during the day and at night. No post-meal decrement was seen for false alarms or response times.

There were, however, some differences between performance during the day and at night. Hit rate increased by the second post-meal session (4.20 p.m. during day and 5.20 a.m. at night) in the day group, while the night group showed a continuing decline. In addition, response times were slower following the meal in the day, but were not influenced by the same meal at night. The effect of a stimulant, noise, also produced different day and night-time results: noise alleviated the post-meal performance deficit during the day but not at night. These findings suggest that the effects of meals on performance during the day and at night are qualitatively different.

It thus seems that the effects of meals may be related to the time of day at which the meal is consumed, but this is conditional upon the type of task used. Post-meal effects on performance of attention and memory tasks differ depending on whether one is considering breakfast, lunch or night-time meals. The extent to which this is due to the time of consumption or due to differences in the size and composition of the meals needs to be examined.

CONCLUSIONS

The effects of lunch on performance are well established and the factors influencing the nature of this effect have been well documented. In summary: sustained attention tasks are the most susceptible to this effect; the nutrient composition and size of the meal have slight effects; stimulants such as caffeine and noise reduce the size of the post-lunch dip in sustained attention; and low anxiety subjects show a greater post-lunch decline in performance than high anxiety subjects.

The effects of breakfast on subsequent performance are less clear-cut, partly due to a paucity of large, well-designed studies. Early reports of a detrimental effect of breakfast on mental and physical performance have been unsubstantiated by recent studies. A positive role of breakfast on memory performance is suggested by recent studies and this needs to be considered in more detail in future experiments.

There are a number of unanswered questions regarding the link between nutrition and performance. What are the effects of meals eaten in the evening on performance? How do snacks influence performance? What are the long-term effects of meals on performance and how does a change in dietary regime affect performance? What contextual factors influence the relationship between nutrition and performance?

This topic is of practical importance because impairments following lunch are often large and the individual may be unaware of the possible decline in performance efficiency. Such deficits are of obvious importance in the work environment and answers to the above questions are needed to clarify our understanding of the link between what we eat and how we perform. Meals are also likely to produce many different physiological effects. Future studies must determine which are the crucial mechanisms involved in meal/performance effects.

REFERENCES

Benton, D. and Sargent, J. (in press). Breakfast, blood glucose and memory.

Blake, M.F.J. (1967). Time of day effects on performance in a range of tasks. *Psychonomic Science* **9**: 345–50.

Blake, M.J.F. (1971). Temperament and time of day. In *Biological Rhythms and Human Performance*, edited by W.P. Colquhoun. New York and London: Academic Press.

Broadbent, D.A., Broadbent, M.H.P. and Jones, D.L. (1986). Performance correlates of self-reported cognitive failure and obsessionality. *British Journal of Clinical Psychology* **25**: 285–99.

Browne, R.C. (1949). The day and night performance of teleprinter switch board operators. *Occupational Psychology* **23**: 121–6.

Campbell, S.S. (1992) Effects of sleep and circadian rhythms performance. In *Handbook of Human Performance*, Vol. 3, *State and Trait*, edited by A.P. Smith and D.M. Jones. London: Academic Press.

Christie, M.J. and McBrearty, E.M.T. (1979). Psychophysiological investigations of post-lunch state in male and female subjects. *Ergonomics* **22**: 307–23.

Colquhoun, W.P. (1971). Circadian variation in mental efficiency. In *Biological Rhythms and Human Performance*, edited by W.P. Colquhoun. New York and London: Academic Press.

Conners, C.K. and Blouin, A.G. (1983). Nutritional effects on behaviour of children. *Journal of Psychiatric Research* **17**: 193–201.

Craig, A. (1986). Acute effects of meals on perceptual and cognitive efficiency. *Nutrition Reviews Supplement* **44**: 163–71.

Craig, A., Baer, K. and Diekmann, A. (1981). The effects of lunch on sensory-perceptual functioning in man. *International Archives of Occupational and Environmental Health* **49**: 105–14.

Dickie, N.H. and Bender, A.E. (1982a). Breakfast and performance. *Human Nutrition: Applied Nutrition* **36A**: 46–56.

Dickie, N.H. and Bender, A.E. (1982b). Breakfast and performance in schoolchildren. *British Journal of Nutrition* **48**: 483–96.

Folkard, S. and Monk, T.H. (eds) (1985). *Hours of Work: Temporal Factors in Work Scheduling.* Chichester: Wiley.

Folkard, S., Monk, T.H. and Lobban, M.C. (1978). Short- and long-term adjustment of circadian rhythms in 'permanent' night nurses. *Ergonomics* **21**: 785–99.

Karlan, S.C. and Cohn, C. (1946). Hypoglycaemic fatigue. *Journal of the American Medical Association* **130**: 553–5.

King, C.G., Bickerman, H.A., Bouvet, W., Harrer, C.J., Oyler, J.R. and Seitz, C.P. (1945). Effects of pre-flight and in-flight meals of varying composition with respect to carbohydrate, protein or fat. *Journal of Aviation Medicine* **16**: 69–84.

Millar, K., Hammersley, R. and Finnigan, F. (in press). Reduction of alcohol-induced performance impairment by prior ingestion of food. *British Journal of Psychology.*

Monk, T.H. and Folkard, S. (1985). Shiftwork and performance. In *Hours of Work: Temporal Factors in Work-scheduling*, edited by S. Folkard and T.H. Monk. Chichester: Wiley.

Pollitt, E., Liebel, R.L. and Greenfield, D. (1981). Brief fasting, stress and cognition in children. *American Journal of Clinical Nutrition* **34**: 1526–33.

Pollitt, E., Lewis, N.L., Garza, C. and Shulman, R.J. (1982/83). Fasting and cognitive performance. *Journal of Psychiatric Research* **17**: 169–74.

Richards, M.M.K. (1972). Studies on breakfast and mental performance. *Nutrition* **26**: 219–23.

Simonson, E., Brozek, J. and Keys, A. (1948). Effects of meals on visual performance and fatigue. *Journal of Applied Physiology,* **1**: 270–8.

Smith, A.P. and Maben, A. (in preparation). The effects of sleep deprivation and lunch on mood, cardiovascular function and performance.

Smith, A.P. and Miles, C. (1986a). The effects of lunch on cognitive vigilance tasks. *Ergonomics* **29**: 1251–61.

Smith, A.P. and Miles, C. (1986b). Effects of lunch on selective and sustained attention. *Neuropsychobiology* **16**: 117–20.

Smith, A.P. and Miles, C. (1986c). Acute effects of meals, noise and nightwork. *British Journal of Psychology* **77**: 377–87.

Smith, A.P. and Miles, C. (1987). The combined effects of occupational health hazards: an experimental investigation of the effects of noise, nightwork and meals. *International Archives of Occupational and Environmental Health* **59**: 83–9.

Smith, A.P., Kendrick, A.M. and Maben, A. (in preparation, a). The influence of caffeine and alcohol on post-lunch performance.

Smith, A.P., Kendrick, A.M. and Maben, A. (in preparation, b). Influence of breakfast on mood, cardiovascular function and performance.

Smith, A.P., Kendrick, A.M. and Maben, A. (in preparation, c). Breakfast effects on memory ability.

Smith, A., Leekam, S., Ralph, A. and McNeill, G. (1988). The influence of meal composition on post-lunch changes in performance efficiency and mood. *Appetite* **10**: 195–203.

Smith, A., Rusted, J.M., Eaton-Williams, P., Savory, M. and Leathwood, P. (1990). Effects of caffeine given before and after lunch on sustained attention. *Neuropsychobiology* **23**: 160–3.

Smith, A., Ralph, A. and McNeill, G. (1991). Influences of meal size on post-lunch changes in performance efficiency, mood and cardiovascular function. *Appetite* **16**: 85–91.

Spielberger, C.D., Gorsuch, R.E. and Lushene, R.E. (1970). *The State–Trait Anxiety Inventory (STAI) Test Manual.* Palo Alto, CA: Consulting Psychologists Press.

Spring, B. (1986). Effects of food and nutrients on the behaviour of normal individuals. In *Nutrition and the Brain*, edited by R.J. Wurtman and J.J. Wurtman. New York: Raven Press.

Spring, B., Maller, O., Wurtman, J., Digman, L. and Cozolino, L. (1983). Effects of protein and carbohydrate meals on mood and performance: interactions with sex and age. *Journal of Psychiatric Research* **17**: 155–67.

Tuttle, W.W., Wilson, M. and Daum, K. (1949). Effect of altered breakfast habits on physiologic response. *Journal of Applied Physiology* **1**: 545.

Tuttle, W.W., Daum, K., Myers, L. and Martin, C. (1950). Effect of omitting breakfast on the physiologic response of men. *Journal of the American Dietary Association* **26**: 332–5.

Tuttle, W.W., Daum, K., Imig, C.J., Randall, B. and Schumacher, M.T. (1952). Effect of omitting breakfast on the physiologic response of the aged. *Journal of the American Dietary Association* **28**: 117.

Tuttle, W.W., Daum, K., Larsen, R., Salzano, J. and Roloff, L. (1954). Effect on schoolboys of omitting breakfast: physiologic responses, attitudes and scholastic attainments. *Journal of the American Dietary Association* **30**: 674–7.

Wesnes, K. and Warburton, D.M. (1984). Effects of scopolamine and nicotine on human rapid information processing performance. *Psychopharmacology* **82**: 147–50.

Wever, R.A. (1985). Man in temporal isolation: basic principles of the circadian system. In *Hours of Work: Temporal Factors in Work-scheduling*, edited by S. Folkard and T.H. Monk. Chichester, Wiley.

Woods, S.C. and Porte, D. (1974). Neural control of the endocrine pancreas. *Physiological Reviews* **54**: 596–619.

2

Vitamin and Mineral Intake and Human Behaviour

D. BENTON

INTRODUCTION

In the late twentieth century relatively little effort is being made to examine the association between the intake of vitamins and minerals and psychological functioning. This lack of interest is derived from a pervading nutritional wisdom that does not allow the intake of micro-nutrients to be a matter for concern for the vast majority of the population. It is argued in this chapter that there is growing evidence to support the assertion that, for some of the population, a sub-clinical deficiency of micro-nutrients exists to the extent that psychological efficiency is disrupted. In addition, the psychological concomitants of clinical and experimentally-induced deficiencies are reviewed.

Psychological measures have been used only infrequently to study the adequacy of diet. However, cognitive functions involve the collective activity of many billions of neurones, and countless biochemical pathways and their associated enzymes. It may well be that small dietary deficiencies, that are dismissed as causing only minor changes to the activity of a single enzyme, will, along with many other similar minor effects, have a measurable and potentially important cumulative influence on cerebral functioning.

MULTI-VITAMIN AND MINERAL SUPPLEMENTATION

Supplementation of children

In a double-blind cross-over study, Boggs et al. (1965) studied nine pre-school children of low intelligence on a Headstart program, who were given

HANDBOOK OF HUMAN PERFORMANCE
VOLUME 2 ISBN 0-12-650352-4

vitamin/mineral supplements. They found that the supplements significantly improved both the teachers' ($p < 0.0001$) and parents' ratings of the children's behaviour ($p < 0.04$). The increase in intelligence scores approached significance. The extent to which these findings reflect a carefully selected sample is unclear.

Interest in the impact of mineral and vitamin supplements on cognitive functioning has been stimulated more recently by the report that their administration was associated with increased non-verbal intelligence in twelve-year-old schoolchildren (Benton and Roberts, 1988). In this study, using a double-blind procedure, sixty children were randomly given either a supplement containing a wide range of vitamins and minerals or a placebo. Figure 2.1 illustrates these findings. The scores on the Calvert non-verbal test of those taking the supplement increased markedly, on average they were nine IQ points more than those receiving the placebo ($p < 0.001$). Verbal intelligence was not significantly influenced.

At the same time Schoenthaler *et al.* (1991a) randomly allocated twenty-six delinquent juveniles, aged between thirteen and sixteen years, to groups receiving either a placebo or a supplement for thirteen weeks. No significant

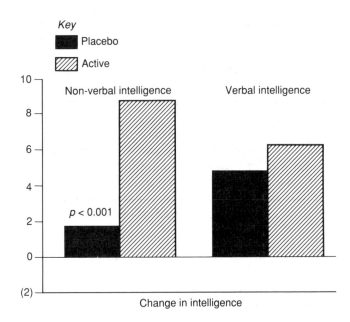

Figure 2.1 The impact of vitamin/mineral supplements on the non-verbal intelligence of Welsh schoolchildren. Sixty twelve-year-old children took either a vitamin/mineral supplement or a placebo each day for nine months. The taking of the active tablet was associated with significant increase in scores on a non-verbal but not verbal intelligence. (Data from Benton and Roberts, 1988.)

change in verbal scores resulted. When taking the placebo the non-verbal intelligence scores of those receiving the placebo decreased by an average of 1 point, whereas when taking the supplement it increased by 6 points ($p < 0.05$). Blood samples were taken before and after taking the tablets and the intelligence tests: the levels of ten vitamins and seven minerals were analysed. Individuals were distinguished whose levels of blood nutrients had or had not increased. The non-verbal intelligence of those whose blood micro-nutrients status had not changed decreased by an average of 2.7 points, whereas in those whose blood status had improved there was an increase of 11.6 points ($p < 0.001$).

The Benton and Roberts (1988) study stimulated several attempts to replicate the findings; although some of the resulting data are negative it can be argued that a consistent picture is emerging. Nelson *et al.* (1990) examined 227 children, aged seven to twelve years, who took a vitamin/mineral supplement for four weeks. This double-blind placebo study found no evidence that supplementation induced changes in intelligence scores. The Nelson *et al.* (1990) study cannot be seen as a replication study as it differs from the original in many ways: the tests, the composition of the tablets, and the time for which they were taken. In particular, such a short duration of administration makes this study difficult to interpret.

In contrast, Crombie *et al.* (1990) went to great trouble to replicate the Benton and Roberts (1988) design using the same tests and tablets. In this double-blind study Crombie *et al.* (1990) studied 86 children from one school and found that a small, but insignificant, advantage of 2.4 points on the Calvert non-verbal test for those taking the supplement as opposed to the placebo.

Under double-blind conditions Benton and Buts (1990) gave 167 Belgian schoolchildren either a supplement or placebo for five months. Based on a fifteen day dietary diary, the intake of eleven minerals and vitamins was calculated. In 45 per cent of the sample the intake of eleven vitamins and minerals was less than 50 per cent of the US recommended daily allowance (RDA) in six or more instances (a group described as consuming a poor diet). Figure 2.2 shows that the boys who were eating the poorer diet scored significantly better on the Calvert non-verbal test following vitamin/mineral supplementation for five months ($p < 0.02$). A similar finding resulted when boys were divided into those attending schools for the more academically gifted, as opposed to those attending technical/manual schools. The less academic boys who received a supplement scored significantly better on the non-verbal test when compared with those who received a placebo ($p < 0.02$), although this was not true for girls. It may well be that the impact of nutrition subtly interacts with background and the immediate environment.

Most of the studies so far described have examined children in their early teenage years. Benton and Cook (1991a) argued that if children existed whose diet was deficient in mineral and vitamins then a younger group would offer

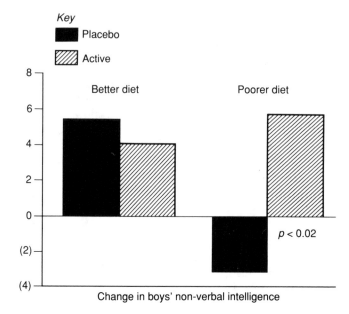

Figure 2.2 The relationship between the quality of the diet and the reaction to vitamin/mineral supplementation. On the basis of a 15 day diary, 103 Belgian boys were distinguished as consuming diets with greater or lesser levels of vitamins and minerals. In the third, described as having a poorer diet, the taking of vitamin/mineral supplements for five months was associated with significantly higher non-verbal intelligence scores. (Data from Benton and Buts, 1990.)

a high-risk group. They therefore examined forty-seven children, of six years of age, who were given four subtests of the British Ability Scale that could be combined to give an intelligence score. In a double-blind study the tests were given before and after taking either a vitamin/mineral supplement, or a placebo for six or eight weeks. Figure 2.3 illustrates the results. The scores of the children receiving the active tablets increased by 7.6 points whereas the scores of those receiving the placebo decreased by 1.6 points ($p < 0.001$). Again it was the non-verbal, rather than the verbal scores that were stimulated by the taking of vitamin/mineral supplements.

Schoenthaler *et al.* (1991b) reported by far the largest study on this topic. In California, six hundred and fifteen children took a placebo, or a tablet containing twenty-three micro-nutrients at the US RDA, half the RDA or twice the RDA, each day for twelve weeks. Using the Wechsler intelligence scale, the non-verbal rather than verbal intelligence scores of those taking the active supplement significantly improved. The non-verbal scores of those taking the placebo increased by 8.9 points whereas the increase was 12.6 points when the 100 per cent RDA tablets were taken. 'Responders' were defined as those whose intelligence scores had increased by 15 points

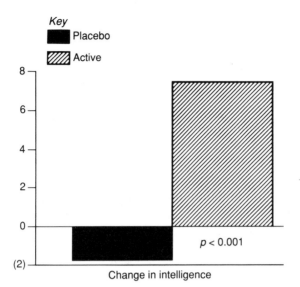

Figure 2.3 The influence of taking vitamin/mineral supplements on the intelligence of six-year-old children. The intelligence of 47 children was measured before and after taking vitamin/mineral supplements for either six or eight weeks. The taking of the placebo was not associated with a change of scores although when taking the active tablet the scores increased significantly. (Data from Benton and Cook, 1991a.)

or more, whereas those whose scores increased by 7 points or less were labelled 'non-responders'. By this definition, 45 per cent of those taking the 100 per cent RDA tablets were responders and 55 per cent non-responders.

Evaluation of studies examining supplementation and intelligence

Unlike many suggestions that vitamin supplements improve an aspect of either physical or psychological functioning, this area is unusual in that the assertion is based on a series of well designed double-blind studies. Of the eight studies described, six report positive findings: a consistency that suggests that there is a phenomenon worthy of further study.

Any inconsistency in this area can be explained by the assumption that not all children respond to supplementation, rather there is a subgroup of children, whose diet offers insufficient vitamins and minerals, that benefit. In fact the evidence from Crombie *et al.* (1990), Nelson *et al.* (1990) and Benton and Buts (1990) is that most children do not respond. The subgroup of boys who responded in the Benton and Buts study had a significantly lower intake of calcium, iron, magnesium, zinc, phosphorus and vitamins A, B1, B2, B6 and nicotinic acid than the boys who failed to respond. The diets of the boys in both the Nelson *et al.* (1990) and Crombie *et al.* (1990) studies were significantly better than those eaten by the Belgian boys who responded to supplementation (Benton and Buts, 1990). So far, two studies have described a subsample with a poor diet that responded to supplementation (Schoenthaler et al., 1991a; Benton and Buts, 1990). Other researchers reporting beneficial responses have chosen their sample either on the basis of dietary problems (Benton and Cook, 1991a), or social disadvantage such that nutritional deficiencies may have existed (Boggs et al., 1965). Benton and Cook (1991a) found that the more the parents reported that their child ate food containing sugar, the more the performance on an intelligence test improved when vitamin/mineral supplements were consumed. The obvious explanation is that the taking of a large proportion of their calories as refined sugar resulted in a deficiency of micro-nutrients.

Both Benton and Roberts (1988) and Schoenthaler et al. (1991b) pointed to the theoretical importance of the finding that the supplement-induced improvements were in non-verbal rather than verbal intelligence. Verbal tests are largely measures of 'crystallized intelligence' (Cattell, 1943) and to a large extent reflect experience. In contrast, non-verbal tests are a measure of 'fluid intelligence' and reflect biological potential. With this analysis one would expect any supplement-induced improvement in brain biochemistry to stimulate non-verbal rather than verbal measures.

When the taking of vitamins/mineral supplements is associated with better intelligence scores, the performance of those taking the placebo decline, or at least do not improve as might be expected. Such a pattern has been found on four occasions (Benton and Roberts, 1988; Schoenthaler et al., 1991a; Benton and Buts, 1990; Benton and Cook, 1991a). As an improvement in performance on taking an intelligence test for the second time is a robust finding, the repeated failure to observe this phenomenon led Benton (1991) to suggest that the children were not concentrating or were not able to sustain attention.

To date, Benton and Cook (1991a) are the only researchers who have examined the influence of supplementation on attention. Having asked their sample of six-year-old children to perform a computer game that was so difficult that failure was inevitable, Benton and Cook monitored the extent to which the children continued to concentrate on the task. The children who had taken a vitamin/mineral supplement were more likely to concentrate on the task than those receiving the placebo.

An alternative explanation is offered by the finding of Benton and Cook (1991a): when faced with a difficult task not only were children less likely to concentrate but also less likely to fidget. In adults, at least, there is good evidence that supplementation improves the mood of those with an inadequate diet (Heseker et al., 1990), and fidgeting may be a reflection of irritability.

The pattern of response in Schoenthaler et al. (1991b) differed from previous studies in that the taking of the placebo was not associated with a decreased performance on the non-verbal tests. A possible explanation is that the demands of individual testing in Schoenthaler et al. (1991b) made not paying attention less likely; the previous studies had tended to use group administered tests. If this explanation is valid then a diet deficient in vitamins and minerals is influencing both attention and intellectual performance.

Any suggestion that vitamin and mineral supplementation improves children's performance is bound to be viewed sceptically as it implies that their diets are marginally deficient in vitamins and minerals. This view so radically conflicts with the conventional assumption that the intake of minerals and vitamins is adequate in the majority of the population, that a substantial body of data will be required before it is commonly accepted. However, the existing data support the view that it is profitable to examine further the hypothesis that there is a subgroup of children, with a diet low in vitamins and minerals. It seems unlikely that a subclinical deficiency of vitamins and minerals will influence non-verbal intelligence exclusively: future studies will need to explore the impact on mood and attention as well as other aspects of psychological functioning.

Supplementation and the behavioural problems of children

There are several clinical reports that the administration of large doses of vitamin and mineral supplements benefit children with learning disabilities. Cott (1972) reported that he had successfully treated five hundred children who had varying degrees of learning disabilities with high doses of vitamins C (1 gm/day), B6 (200–400 mg/day), niacin (1–2 gm/day) and calcium pantothenate (400–600 mg/day). Although sometimes dramatic improvements in learning ability were claimed, these were uncontrolled rather than experimental observations. Green (1970) similarly reported the successful treatment, using the orthomolecular approach, of a ten-year-old who had difficulties with reading and spelling, although he was of normal intelligence.

Although Thiessen and Mills (1975) claimed to have followed up these clinical observations with a controlled study, the study was not double-blind, the treatments were not randomly allocated, there was no statistical analysis and the control group was studied for less than half the time of the experimental group. These workers gave children with severe reading and spelling difficulties 3 g vitamin C, 3 g niacinamide, 250 mg vitamin B6 and 250 mg pantothenic acid, on a daily basis for nine to eighteen months. They concluded that reading and spelling were not altered, although hyperactivity, sleep disturbances and some perceptual dysfunctions improved. Such uncontrolled studies at best suggest hypotheses that deserve to be more systematically examined.

In a well controlled study, Kershner and Hawke (1979) gave twenty learning disabled children large doses of vitamins B6, C, niacinamide and calcium pantothenate for six months. The addition of these vitamins to the diet failed to improve intellectual, perceptual and behavioural measures. The authors caution, however, that the sweeping generalization that megavitamins are ineffective is not warranted. Learning disabilities can be the reflection of a range of aberrant mechanisms, and many more well-designed studies are needed to establish the efficacy or otherwise of supplementing particular subgroups with micro-nutrients. Children need to be carefully described in terms of both behavioural and biochemical parameters, as it is improbable that all will respond equally.

Coleman et al. (1979) studied a group of six hyperkinetic children with low levels of blood serotonin given either methylphenidate or pyridoxine. The treatments just failed to produce statistically significant results, maybe because of the small sample size. The trend was for both methylphenidate and pyridoxine to be better than a placebo, a finding that should be further examined.

Hard evidence that children with behavioural problems will benefit from vitamin supplementation does not exist. There are, however, sufficient clinical reports of improvements that it is unwise simply to dismiss the possibility that benefits will result when vitamin/mineral supplements are given to carefully selected groups of children. The reports that large doses of some vitamins may have adverse effects suggest that studies should be carried out only by those familiar with possible side-effects.

VITAMIN STATUS AND ADULT BEHAVIOUR

With vitamin deficiency, psychological symptoms such as depression, hysteria and hypochondria may appear earlier than the symptoms of an outright deficiency disease. This has been observed in the cases of thiamin (Brazek, 1957), riboflavin (Sterner and Price, 1973), and vitamin C but not vitamin A deficiency (Kinsman and Hood, 1971).

The elderly

The elderly as a group have a higher risk of micro-nutrient deficiency than young adults (Exton-Smith and Scott, 1968). The high risk of deficiency results from a number of factors, first among which is that a declining calorie intake decreases the opportunity to obtain micro-nutrients. Other contributing factors may include a shortage of money; physical disabilities that makes shopping and the preparation of food difficult; the loss of teeth and a decreased sense of taste may be associated with a poor appetite; the ability to absorb nutrients may decline with age. In their review of nutrition in the elderly Worthington-Roberts and Hazzard (1982) comment that frank vitamin deficiencies are rarely seen in the United States, although it is not uncommon to find dietary intakes of water-soluble vitamins below the recommended levels.

Goodwin et al. (1983) correlated biochemical indices of vitamin status and cognitive functioning in the elderly. They reported significant correlations between folate, riboflavin, vitamins C and B12 statuses and memory capacity. The levels of riboflavin and folate were also positively related to the ability to think abstractly. Taylor (1968) found that 90 per cent of an elderly population had low levels of serum B1 and C: the administering of a complex of B vitamins and vitamin C produced significant improvements in both physical and mental abilities although in some cases they took up to a year to develop. Chome *et al.* (1986) followed up these findings and compared elderly having a deficiency of at least one vitamin, with those who did not. The deficient group produced poorer scores in tests of mood; however, supplementation failed to alter psychological functioning, although the authors suggest that this may have reflected a small sample size.

Mood

Schoenthaler (1987) studied young offenders guilty of serious crimes in two penal institutions. He used a seven-day dietary diary to distinguish those who were well nourished (43 per cent) from those with deficiencies (57 per cent) of minerals and vitamins. A multi-vitamin and mineral supplement was given for three months to all offenders, irrespective of the quality of their diet: it was argued that those with a poor diet would respond, while the well nourished would not. In one institution a mood scale was administered and it was found that, when compared with those eating an adequate diet, the mood of those with a poor diet improved over the course of the experiment ($p < 0.01$). In a second penal institution, the taking of a supplement decreased misbehaviour in those having a poor diet by 69 per cent ($p < 0.05$).

Heseker *et al.* (1990) screened 1228 male subjects aged 17–29 years for low levels of blood vitamins and selected 197 to receive supplements or a placebo for eight weeks under a double-blind procedure. The taking of the supplement was associated with improvement on several indices of mood. The results of this study show that psychological parameters are capable of measuring differences between those who receive adequate and borderline nutrition.

THE ROLE OF PARTICULAR MICRO-NUTRIENTS

Thiamin

Thiamin is necessary for the release of energy from carbohydrate; thus the bodily requirement for thiamin is regulated to the amount of carbohydrate in the diet. When the eating of polished rice became widespread in the Far East severe memory problems became widespread and were labelled 'beri-beri amnesia'. De Wardener and Lennox (1947) studied British soldiers who became prisoners of the Japanese and were suddenly subjected to a diet low in thiamin. Within six weeks the first symptoms were noticed: loss of appetite was followed by uncontrolled eye movements, sleeplessness and anxiety. Loss of memory occurred in 62 per cent of the subjects: it was the ability to store new information that was disrupted rather than the ability to recall information stored long before. The importance of thiamin was demonstrated on the occasions when supplies of the vitamin were available: the response was dramatic and in the majority of cases the symptoms improved within forty-eight hours when given 2 mg a day. These workers equated cerebral beri-beri and Wernicke's encephalopathy.

Wernicke's disease is a neurological disorder due to thiamin deficiency, that is characterized by nystagmus, ataxia, confusion and recent memory loss. Treatment with B vitamins may result in complete recovery (Escobar et al., 1983). However, Korsakoff's dementia, in which new long-term memories are not formed, often persists after treatment or spontaneous recovery from Wernicke's disease. The nutritional complications associated with alcoholism are the most common aetiology of Korsakoff's dementia in developed countries. There are, however, reports that Wernicke's disease can be induced by intravenous feeding in hospital (Nadel and Burger, 1976). In such cases the body stores of thiamin are depleted as it is needed to metabolize carbohydrate.

It may well be that thiamin as such is not specifically involved in memory function. Gibson et al. (1982) pointed to the similarities in the symptoms of various metabolic encephalopathies including hypoxia, hypoglycaemia, hyper-ammonemia, heavy metal intoxication and thiamin deficiency; all are associated with a decreased alertness and the inability to sustain attention that progresses to disorientation, problems of memory, and finally stupor and death. Gibson et al. (1982) proposed that an impairment of cholinergic functioning was the common link in all these disorders. The synthesis of acetylcholine involves the thiamin-dependent metabolism of glucose, and thiamin deficiency is associated with decreased acetylcholine synthesis.

The feeding of a restricted diet allows the role of a vitamin to be ascertained. Brozek (1957) fed young men diets that offered either 0.61, 1.01 or 1.81 mg of thiamin a day for 24 weeks, followed by an acute period of total thiamin deprivation for 15–27 days; this was followed by supplementation. The development of anorexia, muscular weakness and increased irritability and depression were the first signs of deprivation. On the Minnesota Multiphasic Personality Inventory there was a marked deterioration of the psychoneurotic triad of hypochondriasis, depression and hysteria. Tests of intellectual functioning remained stable although psychomotor skills and complex reaction times were disrupted. In the final stage when 5 mg a day was administered as a supplement, the changes were dramatic both in terms of the speed and degree of change: in particular appetite was rapidly restored and personality changed for the better. Brozek (1957) concluded that 0.6 mg thiamin a day was suboptimal for adult men consuming 3000 calories, and even raising the thiamin intake about 1.0 mg a day added only a few days of protection against a diet completely lacking thiamin.

Thiamin and children

Harrell (1946) examined 120 orphans who lived together on a farm. They ate the same diet that, following analysis at Columbia University, was estimated to supply 1 mg of thiamin a day. The WHO recommended daily allowance for children aged 10–12 years is 1 mg a day for boys, and 0.9 mg for girls, so the diet would have been thought to supply an adequate amount of thiamin. A range of tests were taken before and after the taking of either a placebo or 2 mg thiamin each day for a year. There were remarkable improvements in those taking the thiamin rather than the placebo; they were significantly taller, had better eyesight, quicker reaction times, and scored better on tests of memory and intelligence.

Vitamin B12 and folate

Numerous investigators have reported associations between deficiencies of vitamins B12 and folate and psychiatric syndromes including depression and dementia (Hunter *et al.*, 1967; Botez *et al.*, 1977; Carney and Sheffield, 1978; Abou-Saleh and Coppen, 1986; Hector and Burton, 1988; Sommer and Wolkowitz, 1988). Some workers have hypothesized that cognitive impairment and organic psychosis are often associated with B12 deficiency (Hector and Burton, 1988), whereas depression is associated with folate deficiency (Carney and Sheffield, 1978; Shorvon *et al.*, 1980). Bell *et al.* (1990) examined geriatric patients of whom only 3.7 per cent were B12 and 1.3 per cent folate deficient. Nevertheless, those with below median levels of both vitamins had poorer mental state scores compared with those with the level of one of these vitamins above the median value. The severity of depression was negatively correlated with folate level, whereas those with an organic psychosis, and a family history of the disorder, had lower B12 levels. Botez *et al.* (1984) selected a group of forty-nine patients with low folate levels. After seven to eleven months of folate supplementation the patients were less easily fatigued and distracted and the scores on all the subtests of the Wechsler intelligence scale increased, particularly those measuring non-verbal rather than verbal skills.

Vitamin C

The clinical description of scurvy includes behavioural symptoms such as listlessness, lassitude and weakness, although it is difficult to exclude the possibility that such naturalistic observations reflect a deficiency of nutrients other than vitamin C. Farmer (1944) experimentally induced scurvy and found increased error rates on a choice reaction time task. Severe fatigue was reported late in a seven month deprivation period. In a more systematic study, Kinsman and Hood (1971) reported that experimentally-induced scurvy was initially associated with changes in personality scores on the neurotic triad of the Minnesota Multiphasic Personality Inventory (hypochondriasis, depression and hysteria scales). Personality changes preceded decrements in psychomotor performance that were said to reflect reduced arousal and poorer motivation.

There have been many suggestions that daily intake of large doses of vitamin C may decrease the likelihood of contracting a range of human disorders, for example the common cold. *In vitro* studies find that ascorbic acid blocks dopamine receptors (Kayaalp *et al.*, 1981) which suggests the hypothesis that large doses may have behavioural influences, a view supported by the report that oral doses of 1 or 3 g of vitamin C caused changes in EEG recordings (Pfeiffer *et al.*, 1968). Naylor and Smith (1981) found that a single 3 g dose of vitamin C improved both manic and depressed patients. Kubala and Katz (1960) used biochemical assays of blood ascorbic acid levels to distinguish those with higher and lower levels of the vitamin: those with higher levels produced better intelligence scores. The scores of those with low levels of vitamin C in the blood improved when they were supplemented with orange juice.

Benton (1981) reported that an hour and a half after taking 1 or 2 g of vitamin C reaction times and psychomotor co-ordination were poorer. The failure of Pascoe and Stone (1984) to replicate this finding may reflect the use of only six subjects. Miller *et al.* (1978) examined the chronic administration of vitamin C over a five month period but found no effects when using tests of motor control and reaction time.

Zinc

The concentration of zinc in the neonate is similar to that in the adult, but unlike other minerals such as iron, the newborn does not have a substantial reserve of zinc. Walravens and Hambidge (1976), in a double-blind study, examined the impact of supplementing a popular infant milk formula with zinc for six months (1.8 mg zinc per litre in control and 5.8 mg per litre in supplemented formula). Those who received the supplemented formula had significantly higher levels of plasma zinc at both three and six months. The speed of growth of boys receiving the zinc supplement was increased to the extent that at six months the average height was 2.1 cm, and the average weight was 535 grams, greater than the controls. It was concluded that the low zinc content of the usual formula was to some extent limiting growth: a conclusion made more important as all infants in this study were normal healthy neonates, born at term. Naturally, the zinc level in the milk powder was increased, but when babies fail to thrive, particularly if their appetite is poor, then the possibility of a shortage of zinc should be explored.

There may be a risk of suboptimal zinc nutrition in the United States (Sandstead, 1973). A study in Denver (Hambidge *et al.*, 1972) used hair levels as an index of zinc status and found low levels (less than 70 mcg zinc per gram hair) more commonly in pre-school children than older children from middle income homes. The children with low zinc levels were small for their age and had a history of poor appetite. The incidence of low zinc levels was higher in low income pre-school children, selected for low height, who were enrolled in the Headstart program. The supplementation of children with low hair zinc resulted in a significantly faster rate of growth (Hambidge, 1977).

It has become fashionable in some quarters to relate a low intake of dietary zinc to a range of children's problems. The general proposition that low levels of dietary zinc can be expected to have psychological concomitants is made fairly easily. A specific attempt to relate zinc to a particular disorder is a much more difficult task, and the evidence much less compelling.

Pfeiffer and Braverman (1982) reviewed the evidence that zinc plays an important role in the central nervous system; in fact, after iron, zinc is the most prevalent trace element. The hippocampus has both the highest levels and the highest turnover of zinc in the brain, and unlike many other areas, the levels of zinc are higher than iron (Hamilton, 1979). The high concentration in the hippocampus suggests a role in particular psychological functions, for example memory. The role of zinc in nucleic acid metabolism may explain its importance in brain development. Pfeiffer and Braverman (1982) concluded that in the rat, zinc deficiency during the critical period during which brain growth takes place causes permanent adverse effects to brain function.

ZINC AND BEHAVIOUR

Experimentally-induced zinc deficiency is associated with apathy, lethargy, depression, amnesia and mental retardation (Prasad *et al.*, 1978). Acrodermatitis enteropathica, a human hereditary dysfunction of zinc absorption is associated with similar symptoms that are zinc-responsive (Walravens *et al.*, 1981). Henkin *et al.* (1973) gave large oral doses of histidine, an amino acid that complexes with zinc and is then excreted in the urine. Experimentally-induced zinc deficiency in these subjects was associated with anorexia and impairment of the senses of taste and smell. Those with dysfunctions of olfaction and the sense of taste have been found to have low concentrations of zinc in both serum (Henkin *et al.*, 1973) and saliva (Henkin *et al.*, 1975). Aamodt *et al.* (1979) found that one-third of those complaining of problems of taste and the sense of smell had significantly impaired zinc absorption.

There are various clinical reports that girls suffering with anorexia nervosa respond to zinc supplementation by gaining weight, although those who advocate this approach see the origin of the disorder in social and psychological events. Paradoxically, starvation increases the urinary excretion of zinc and thus exacerbates the effects of a low dietary intake. The impairment of the zinc-dependent senses of taste and smell further reduces the desire for food (Bryce-Smith and Simpson, 1984). In addition, the serum levels of zinc, following a zinc supplemented meal, have been found to be lower in anorexics than in those not suffering with the disorder (Dinsmore et al., 1985). It seems possible that the intestinal mucosa, by virtue of its high rate of cellular proliferation, might be particularly susceptible to the adverse effect of zinc deficiency, producing a vicious circle in which the absorption of zinc is further depressed. Given the possibility that any improvement in anorexia that follows zinc supplementation may be a placebo response, a double-blind study is needed in this area.

Grant et al. (1988) measured the concentration of zinc in the sweat and hair of dyslexic children. Compared with controls, children suffering with dyslexia had a much lower level of zinc in their sweat, but not hair. Ward et al. (1987) found highly positive correlations between the zinc levels in the placenta and head circumference among those having normal births. In animals, zinc deficiency during pregnancy is associated with learning difficulties in adult life (Caldwell et al., 1976). After reviewing the association between the level of minerals in hair and behaviour, Rimland and Larson (1983) concluded that intelligent individuals tended to have higher levels of zinc in their hair.

Although the suggestion has been frequently made that zinc deficiency, either pre-natally or at some later stage, may be associated with psychological problems, many of the data are correlational in nature. There have been few attempts to monitor psychological functioning while manipulating zinc levels. An exception is Tucker and Sandstead (1984) who fed nine volunteers a zinc deficient diet for about four months, and then gave zinc supplements for about three weeks. After monitoring cognitive functioning they concluded that 'there were no cognitive deficits that could be related to the zinc status ... over the course of the zinc depletion'.

Selenium

There are varying levels of the essential trace element selenium in soils throughout the world. As the level of soil selenium varies so does the amount in the food chain and the human body (Burk, 1976). In areas such as New Zealand, United Kingdom, and parts of China, Scandinavia and the United States, the levels of selenium in food are so low as to suggest the possibility of a subclinical deficiency. Benton and Cook (1990, 1991b) argued that if a subclinical deficiency existed, it would be associated with only minor biochemical changes that might be expressed in terms of reported well-being or mood. Using a double-blind procedure, in a cross-over trial with a six month washout, they found selenium therapy to be associated with a marked improvement in mood (Figure 2.4).

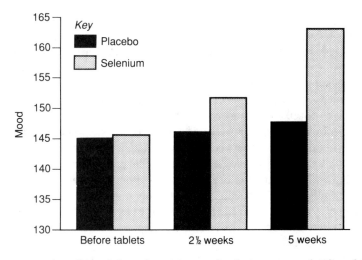

Figure 2.4 The influence of supplementation with selenium on mood. Fifty subjects took either 100 mcg selenium a day or a placebo for five weeks in a cross-over study with six months washout. The taking of selenium was associated with a marked improvement in mood; higher scores are associated with feeling less depressed and anxious. (Data from Benton and Cook, 1991b.)

The question arises as to the origin of this response. An obvious suggestion is that it may be a reflection of a subclinical intake of selenium. In 1978 the average British diet was calculated to provide approximately 60 mcg of selenium per day (Thorn *et al.*, 1978). More recently it was calculated selenium intake had decreased to 43 mcg per day (Barclay and MacPherson, 1986) as the wheat used for flour-making is increasingly grown in the United Kingdom rather than imported from Canada. The fact that people eat less bread now than previously is another reason for the decreasing intake of selenium. Although there is no British standard, an intake of 43 mcg per day fails to meet the US RDA of 70 mcg per day for men and 55 mcg per day for women (US Food and Nutrition Board, 1989).

There are several reports that supplements containing selenium, amongst other substances, have beneficial effects in geriatric patients. Tolonen *et al.* (1985) gave a combination of selenium and vitamin E to geriatric patients for a year, arguing that the anti-oxidant properties may alleviate the ageing process. A significant improvement was observed in terms of anxiety, depression, mental alertness and other measures. In a similar but larger study, Clausen *et al.* (1989) gave an anti-oxidant cocktail containing selenium, gamma-linolenic acid and vitamins A, C and E for a year; improvements on ratings on a scale for demential syndromes approached statistical significance. Van Rhijn *et al.* (1990) studied elderly subjects with a history of memory impairment and examined the influence of a mixture of zinc, selenium and evening primrose oil. After twenty weeks, mood and some indices of cognitive functioning were improved. Although these studies of geriatic decline have all emphasized the anti-oxidant nature of selenium and related micro-nutrients, selenium is unevenly distributed in the brain (Hock *et al.*, 1975; Larsen *et al.*, 1979) suggesting the possibility of a yet to be established neural function.

If the Benton and Cook (1990, 1991b) findings can be shown to be typical of the general population, then psychological measures will have given the first unequivocal evidence of a subclinical deficiency in the general population. Good health is a relative rather than absolute state and was defined by Dubos (1959) not in terms of physiology but as the ability of individuals to function in a manner acceptable to themselves and to others in the group of which they are members. It is probable that if individuals were aware that the treatment of a dietary deficiency could decrease feelings of anxiety and depression, even if these are not perceived as particular causes of problems, then treatment would be demanded.

Although an essential element, in excess, selenium is toxic; there is no suggestion that supplementation would be beneficial if the diet already provides adequate amounts. In all probability, the response shown in Figure 2.4 will have significance only in those parts of the world with low soil selenium: north-eastern, pacific north-western and extreme south-eastern United States; north-central and eastern Canada; eastern Finland; New Zealand; parts of Australia; and much of the People's Republic of China (Combs and Combs, 1984).

Iron

Iron is the most abundant trace element in the body and is distributed in an uneven manner suggesting roles other than in metabolism. When reviewing the topic, Yehuda and Youdim (1988) concluded that: 'Iron deficiency and anaemia are the most prevalent nutritional disorders in the world. The behavioural changes induced by iron deficiency in adults includes unusual lethargy, irritability, apathy, listlessness, fatigue, inability to concentrate, pagophagia, pica, inattention, hypoactivity and sometimes a decreased IQ level.'

When reviewing the studies that relate iron deficient anaemia to children's development Pollitt and Kim (1988) concluded that there is: 'an impressive consistency ... between iron deficiency anaemia and comparatively low performance in the Bayley scale of mental development. Improvement in performance is observed following an iron therapeutic intervention.' Pollitt and Leibel (1976) had previously concluded that iron deficiency affected the ability to sustain attention.

THE ADEQUACY OF WESTERN DIET

Any reader unfamiliar with nutritional studies should not assume that dietary problems are necessarily widespread: in fact, clinical deficiencies are rare in industrialized countries. For the majority of nutritionists the argument goes that if the diet supplies sufficient protein and calories, then all the necessary vitamins and minerals come associated with the protein and calories. There is no completely satisfactory way of assessing the adequacy of diet, although biochemical parameters are considered to be better measures of vitamin status than those calculated from a dietary diary.

Greenwood and Richardson (1979) reviewed the literature dealing with the diets of adolescents and concluded that 'specific nutrient deficiencies have been identified in a significant proportion of the adolescent population. They include iron, calcium, vitamin A, vitamin C . . .'. When a large sample of British schoolchildren recorded their diets for a week there was evidence of low intakes of iron, calcium and riboflavin in teenage girls, and a generally low intake of vitamin B6 (DHSS, 1989). Where the average intake for particular nutrients reached acceptable levels there were wide variations in individual consumption. While the average intake appeared to be acceptable, there were some children who ate less than 70, or even 50 per cent of the recommended daily amount (DHSS, 1989). It is important to appreciate the status of recommended daily amounts (RDA). As the need for micro-nutrients varies from person to person, and from time to time depending on life events, an RDA is a statistic that aims to include the needs of two standard deviations of the population. Many people will find an intake of less than 100 per cent of the RDA perfectly adequate. All that can be said of such data is that the lower the percentage of the RDA taken by an individual, the greater the probability that their intake is inadequate. Sometimes an intake of less than 70 per cent of the RDA is said to cause concern.

Using conventional biochemical definitions, there is a consistent picture that the vitamin intakes of only a small minority of individuals are deficient (Arab *et al.*, 1982; Lemoine *et al.*, 1986; Sabry *et al.*, 1974). Vitamin B1 is a cause of some concern since about 5 per cent of the population are typically found to be deficient and about 25 per cent have borderline intakes. A similar if not slightly worse position is found when folate is examined. In other tests, such as those for vitamins A and E, even borderline deficiency is rare. It is clear, judging by these biochemical assays, that the majority of the population do not give cause for concern.

Although surveys of the vitamin status of the general population produces evidence that only a small minority of the population is deficient, the possibility exists that the incidence may be higher in subpopulations. Surveys typically find the incidence of riboflavin deficiency to be low, being a problem in less than 1 or 2 per cent of the population. However, Lopez *et al.* (1980)

found a 26.6 per cent incidence of deficiency in a group of 210 New York adolescents from low-income backgrounds. Sandstead *et al.* (1971) studied the nutritional status of pre-school children from economically depressed areas. Biochemical data gave grounds for concern in 96 per cent of the children in the case of vitamin A, 35 per cent for iron, 17 per cent for folic acid and 13 per cent for vitamin B1. Malvy *et al.* (1989) assayed the serum of 392 healthy French schoolchildren for vitamins A and E and found 5 per cent to be at risk of deficiency for one or other of the vitamins. Although their biochemical data were suggestive of a problem in a minority of children, Malvy *et al.* (1989) comment that in the absence of a health problem the children cannot be viewed as being at risk, but rather reflect recent decreases in supply or increases in demand.

Lonsdale (1988) tested 1011 patients who approached a practice in Ohio specializing in nutritional correction and found that 28 per cent were thiamin deficient. Carney *et al.* (1982) examined 172 successive admissions to a psychiatric hospital and, based on biochemical assays for vitamins B1, B2 and B6, found that 53 per cent were deficient in at least one vitamin. Young and Ghadirian (1989) reviewed the evidence that the incidence of folic acid deficiency is high in patients with various psychiatric diagnoses including dementia, depression and schizophrenia.

CONCLUSIONS

This brief review of nutritional status gives support to the view that sections of Western society may be subclinically deficient. While biochemical and other approaches suggests that we should be looking for evidence of subclinical deficiency, without evidence of associated functional problems we should not conclude that a problem necessarily exists. The acid test is to demonstrate that functioning is improved following supplementation. The repeated findings in double-blind studies that vitamin supplementation improves psychological function, are reviewed above. The tentative conclusion is unavoidable: that subclinical deficiencies of vitamins may exist in some sections of the population. The nature, extent and implications of the existence of subclinical vitamin deficiencies are topics that await psychological research.

In case studies, and studies that induced a clinical deficiency by feeding diets low in particular nutrients, psychological symptoms are often amongst the first observed. Although space precludes a comprehensive discussion, the chapter reviews some of the increasing number of well designed studies that have found that vitamin and mineral supplements benefit psychological functioning. The critical evidence needed to demonstrate a subclinical deficiency is that the provision of additional amounts of the nutrient can be shown to be of benefit in well controlled studies. Accepting that the existence of subclinical deficiencies conflicts with established views, a conservative conclusion is that the data justify further exploration of the topic. The extent of such problems is unclear. A way forward may be to examine high-risk groups distinguished in terms of their age, social background or psychological problems. Both children and the elderly are groups who may be particularly at risk, although for different reasons.

The question of isolating the nutrients responsible for particular responses has hardly been addressed. It can be argued that, with the exception of iron, it is unlikely that a deficiency of a specific nutrient will occur, except under special circumstances such as the absence of a mineral in the soil, or the choice of a restricted diet. Attempts to establish the role of a particular nutrient is made difficult by the many interactions between micro-nutrients. For example, vitamin E and selenium act synergistically; vitamin C facilitates the uptake of iron; a large intake of zinc results in a deficiency of copper and other trace elements. It is likely that a poor diet will result in a general deficiency of micro-nutrients so that a varied diet, or a broadly based supplement, is likely to yield greater benefit.

The common assertion that the Western diet is adequate in terms of vitamins and minerals may reflect the biological methods that have been used to judge vitamin status. Although nutritionists have not traditionally used psychological measures to monitor nutritional status, it may be argued if subclinical deficiencies exist then psychological changes may be one of the first indications. It seems that psychology may have techniques to offer nutrition; in turn nutritional manipulations may complement the treatment of some psychological problems.

REFERENCES

Aamodt, R.L., Rumble, W.F., Johnston, G.S. and Henkin, R.I. (1979). Malabsorption of zinc and hyposmia: a new syndrome. *Clinical Research* **27**: 244A.

Abou-Saleh, M.T. and Coppen, C. (1986). The biology of folate in depression: implications for nutritional hypotheses of the psychoses. *Journal of Psychiatric Research* **20**: 91–101.

Arab, L., Schelenburg, B. and Schlierf, G. (1982). Nutrition and health. A survey of young men and women in Heidelberg. *Annals of Nutrition and Metabolism* **26** (Supplement 1): 1–244

Barclay, M.I. and MacPherson, A. (1986). Selenium content of wheat flour used in the UK. *Journal of the Science of Food and Agriculture* **37**: 1133–8.

Bell, I.R., Edman, J.S., Marby, D.W., Satlin, A., Dreier, T., Liptzin, B. and Cole, J.O. (1990). Vitamin B12 and folate status in acute geropsychiatric inpatients: affective and cognitive characteristics of a vitamin nondeficient population. *Biological Psychiatry* **27**: 125–37

Benton, D. (1981). The influence of large doses of Vitamin C on psychological functioning. *Psychopharmacology* **75**: 98–9.

Benton, D. (1991). Vitamin and mineral intake and cognitive functioning. In *Micronutrients in Health and the Prevention of Disease*, edited by A. Bendich and C.E. Butterworth. New York: Marcel Dekker, pp. 219–32.

Benton, D. and Buts, J-P. (1990). Vitamin/mineral supplementation and intelligence. *Lancet* **335**: 1158–60.

Benton, D. and Cook, R. (1990). Selenium supplementation improves mood in a double-blind crossover trial. *Psychopharmacology* **102**: 549–50.

Benton, D. and Cook, R. (1991a). Vitamin and mineral supplements improve the intelligence scores and concentration of six year children. *Personality and Individual Differences* **12**: 1151–1158.

Benton, D. and Cook, R. (1991b). The impact of selenium supplementation on mood. *Biological Psychiatry* **29**: 1092–8.

Benton, D. and Roberts, G. (1988). Effect of vitamin and mineral supplementation on intelligence of a sample of schoolchildren. *Lancet* **i**: 140–3.

Boggs, U.R., Scheaf, A., Santoro, D. and Ritzman, R. (1965). The effects of nutrient supplements on the biological and psychological characteristics of low IQ preschool children. *Journal of Orthomolecular Psychiatry* **14**: 97–127.

Botez, M.I., Fontaine, F., Botez, T. and Bachevalier, J. (1977). Folate-responsive neurological and mental disorders: Report of 16 cases. *European Neurology* **16**: 230–46.

Botez, M.I., Botez, T. and Maag, U. (1984). The Wechsler subtests in mild organic brain damage associated with folate deficiency. *Psychological Medicine* **14**: 431–437.

Brozek, J. (1957). Psychological effects of thiamine restriction and deprivation in normal young men. *American Journal of Clinical Nutrition* **5**: 109–18.

Bryce-Smith, D. and Simpson, R.I.D. (1984). Cases of anorexia responding to zinc sulphate. *Lancet* **i**: 350.

Burk, R.F. (1976). Selenium in man. In *Trace Elements in Human Health and Disease*, Vol. 2, edited by A.S. Prasad. New York and London: Academic Press, pp. 105–33.

Caldwell, D.F., Oberleas, D. and Prasad, A.S. (1976). Psychobiological changes in zinc deficiency. In *Trace Element in Human Health and Disease*, Vol. 1, edited by A.S. Prasad. New York and London: Academic Press, pp. 311–325.

Carney, M.W.P. and Sheffield, M.T. (1978). Serum folic acid and B[12] in 272 psychiatric inpatients. *Psychological Medicine* **8**: 139–44.

Carney, M.W.P., Ravindran, A., Rinsler, M. and Williams, D.G. (1982). Thiamine, riboflavin and pyridoxine deficiency in psychiatric patients. *British Journal of Psychiatry* **135**: 249–54.

Cattell, R.B. (1943). The measurement of adult intelligence. *Psychological Bulletin* **40**: 153–193

Chome, J., Paul, T., Pudel, V., Bleyl, H., Heseker, H., Huppe, R. and Kubler, W. (1986). Effects of suboptimal vitamin status on behavior. *Bibliotheca Nutritio et Dieta* **38**: 94–104.

Clausen, J., Nielsen, S.A. and Kristensen, M. (1989). Biochemical and clinical effects of an antioxidant supplementation of geriatric patients. *Biological Trace Element Research* **20**: 135–51.

Coleman, M., Steinberg, G., Tippett, J., Bhagavan, H.N., Coursin, D.B., Cross, M., Lewis, C. and DeVeau, L. (1979). A preliminary study of the effect of pyridoxine administration in a subgroup of hyperkinetic children: a double-blind crossover comparison with methylphenidate. *Biological Psychiatry* **14**: 741–51.

Combs, G.F. and Combs, S.B. (1984). The nutritional biochemistry of selenium. *Annual Review of Nutrition* **4**: 257–80.

Cott, A. (1972). Megavitamins: the orthomolecular approach to behaviour disorders and learning disabilities. *Academic Therapy* **VII**: 245–58.

Crombie, I.K., Todman, J., McNeill, G., Florey, C. Du V., Menzies, I. and Kennedy, R.A. (1990). Effect of vitamin and mineral supplementation on verbal and non-verbal reasoning of schoolchildren. *Lancet* **335**: 744–7.

DHSS (1989). *The Diets of British Schoolchildren*. London: HMSO.

de Wardener, H.E. and Lennox, B. (1947). Cerebral beriberi. *Lancet,* 12–17.

Dinsmore, W.W., Alderrice, J.T., McMaster, D., Adams, C.E.A. and Love, A.H.G. (1985). Zinc absorption in anorexia nervosa. *Lancet,* **ii**: 1041–2.

Dubos, R. (1959). *Mirage of Health: Utopias Progress and Biological Change*. New York: Harper and Row.

Escobar, A., Aruffo, C. and Rodriguez-Carbajal, J. (1983). Wernicke's encephalopathy: a case report with neurophysiologic and CT-scan studies. *Acta Vitaminologica et Enzymologica* **5**: 125−31.

Exton-Smith, A.N. and Scott, D.L. (eds) (1968). *Vitamins in the Elderly.* Bristol: John Wright.

Farmer, C.J. (1944). Some aspects of vitamin C metabolism. *Federation Proceedings* **3**: 179.

Gibson, G., Barclay, L. and Blass, J. (1982). The role of the cholinergic system in thiamin deficiency. *Annals of the New York Academy of Sciences* **378**: 382−403.

Goodwin, J.S., Goodwin, J.M. and Garry, P.J. (1983). Association between nutritional status and cognitive functioning in a healthy elderly population. *Journal of the American Medical Association* **249**: 2917−21.

Grant, E.C.G., Howard, J.M., Davies, S., Chasty, H., Hornsby, B. and Galbraith, J. (1988). Zinc deficiency in children with dyslexia: concentrations of zinc and other minerals in sweat and hair. *British Medical Journal* **296**: 607−9.

Green, G. (1970). *Treatise on Subclinical Pellagra.* Canadian Schizophrenia Foundation.

Greenwood, C.T. and Richardson, D.P. (1979). Nutrition during adolescence. *World Reviews of Nutrition and Dietetics* **33**: 1−41.

Hambidge, K.M. (1977). The role of zinc and other trace metals in pediatric nutrition and health. *Pediatric Clinics of North America* **24**: 95−106.

Hambidge, K.M., Hambidge, C., Jacobs, M. and Baum, J.D. (1972). Low levels of zinc in hair anorexia poor growth and hypogeusia in children. *Pediatric Research* **6**: 868−74.

Hamilton, E. (1979). *The Chemical Elements and Man.* New York: C.C. Thomas.

Harrell, R.F. (1946) Mental responses to added thiamine. *Journal of Nutrition* **31**: 283−98.

Hector, M. and Burton, J.R. (1988). What are the psychiatric manifestations of vitamin B^{12} deficiency? *Journal of the American Geriatric Society* **36**: 1105−12.

Henkin, R.I., Patten, B.M., Re, P.K. and Bronzert, D.A. (1973). A syndrome of acute zinc loss: cerebellar dysfunction, mental changes, anorexia and taste and smell dysfunction. *Archives of Neurology* **32**: 745−51

Henkin, R.I., Mueller, C. and Wolf, R. (1975). Estimation of zinc concentration of parotid saliva by flameless atomic absorption spectrophotometry in normal subjects and in patients with idiopathic hypogeusia. *Journal of Laboratory Clinical Medicine* **86**: 175.

Heseker, H., Kubler, W., Westenhofer, J. and Pudel, V. (1990). Psychische Veranderungen als Fruhzeichen einer suboptimalen Vitaminversorgung. *Ernahrungs-Umschau* **37**: 87−94.

Hock, A., Demmel, U., Schicha, H., Kasperek, K., Feinendegen, L.E. (1975). Trace element concentration in human brain. *Brain* **98**: 49−64.

Hunter, R., Jones, M., Jones, T.G. and Matthews, D.M. (1967). Serum B^{12} and folate concentrations in mental patients. *British Journal of Psychiatry* **113**: 1291−5.

Kayaalp, S.O., Rubenstein, J.S. and Neff, N.H. (1981). Inhibition of dopamine D-1 and D-2 binding sites in neuronal tissue by ascorbate. *Neuropharmacology* **20**: 409−10.

Kershner, J. and Hawke, W. (1979). Megavitamins and learning disorders: a controlled double-blind experiment. *Journal of Nutrition* **109**: 819−26.

Kinsman, R.H. and Hood, J. (1971). Some behavioral effects of ascorbic acid deficiency. *American Journal of Clinical Nutrition* **24**: 455−64.

Kubula, A.L. and Katz, M.M. (1960). Nutritional factors in psychological test behavior. *Journal of Genetic Psychology* **96**: 343−52.

Larsen, N.A., Pakkenberg, H., Damsgaard, E. and Heydorn, K. (1979). Topographical distribution of arsenic manganese and selenium in the normal human brain. *Journal of Neurological Sciences* **42**: 407−16.

Lemoine, A., Le Devehat, C. and Herbeth, B. (1986). Vitamin status in three groups of French adults. *Annals of Nutrition and Metabolism* **30** (Supplement 1): 1−94.

Lonsdale, D. (1988). Red cell transketolase studies in a private practice specializing in nutritional correction. *Journal of the American College of Nutrition* **7**: 61−7.

Lopez, C., Schwartz, J.V. and Cooperman, J.M. (1980). Riboflavin deficiency in an adolescent population in New York City. *American Journal of Clinical Nutrition* **33**: 205−11.

Malvy, J.M.D., Mourey, M.S., Carlier, C., Caces, P., Dostalova, L., Montagnon, B. and

Amedee-Manesme, O. (1989). Retinol, β-carotene and α-tocopherol status in a French population of healthy children. *International Journal of Vitamin and Nutritional Research* **59**: 29–34.

Miller, J.Z., Nance, W.E. and Kang, K. (1978). A co-twin control study of the effect of vitamin C. *Twin Research: Clinical Studies*, 151–6.

Nadel, A. and Burger, P.C. (1976). Wernicke Encephalopalopathy following prolonged intravenous therapy. *Journal of the American Medical Association* **235**: 2403–5.

Naylor, G.J. and Smith, A.H.W. (1981). Vanadium: a possible aetiological factor in manic depressive illness. *Psychological Medicine* **11**: 249–56.

Nelson, M., Naismith, D.J., Burley, V., Gatenby, S. and Geddes, N. (1990). Nutrient intake vitamin/mineral supplementation and intelligence in British schoolchildren. *British Journal of Nutrition* **64**: 13–22.

Pascoe, P.A. and Stone, B.M. (1984). Ascorbic acid and performance in man. *Psycopharmacology* **83**: 376–7.

Pfeiffer, C.C. and Braverman, E.R. (1982). Zinc the brain and behavior. *Biological Psychiatry* **17**: 513–32.

Pfeiffer, C.C., Goldstein, L., Murphree, H.B. and Nicols, R.C. (1968). A critical survey of possible biochemical stimulants. In *Psychopharmacology: A Review of Progress*, edited by D.H. Efron. Washington, DC: Department of Health Education and Welfare, pp. 693–9.

Pollitt, E. and Kim, I. (1988). Learning and achievement among iron-deficient children. In *Brain Iron: Neurochemical and Behavioural Aspects*, edited by M.B.H. Youdim. London: Taylor and Francis, pp. 115–44.

Pollitt, E. and Leibel, R.L. (1976). Iron deficiency and behavior. *Journal of Pediatrics* **88**: 372–81.

Prasad, A.S., Rabbani, P. and Abbash, A. (1978). Experimental zinc deficiency in humans. *Annals of Internal Medicine* **89**: 483–90

Pueschel, S.M., Reed, R.B., Cronk, C.E. and Goldstein, B.I. (1980). 5-hydroxytryptophan and pyridoxine. *American Journal of Disorders of Children* **134**: 838–44.

Rimland, B. and Larson, G.E. (1983). Hair mineral analysis and behavior: an analysis of 51 studies. *Journal of Learning Disabilities* **16**: 279–85.

Sabry, Z.I., Campbell, J.A., Campbell, M.E. and Forbes, A.L. (1974). Nutrition Canada. *Nutrition Today* January/February, 5–13.

Sandstead, H.H. (1973). Zinc nutrition in the United States. *American Journal of Clinical Nutrition* **26**: 1251–60.

Sandstead, H.H., Carter, J.P., House, F.R., McConnell, F., Horton, K.B. and Van der Zwaag, R. (1971). Nutritional deficiencies in disadvantaged preschool children. *American Journal of Disorders of Children* **121**: 455–63.

Schoenthaler, S. (1987). Malnutrition and maladaptive behavior: two correlational analyses and a double-blind placebo-controlled challenge in five states. In *Nutrients and Brain Function*, edited by W.B. Essman. Basel: Karger, pp. 198–218.

Schoenthaler, S.J., Amos, S.P., Doraz, W.E., Kelly, M.A. and Wakefield, J. (1991a). Controlled trial of vitamin–mineral supplementation on intelligence and brain function. *Personality and Individual Differences* **12**: 343–50.

Schoenthaler, S.J., Amos, S.P., Eysenck, H.J., Peritz, E. and Yudkin, J. (1991b). Controlled trial of vitamin–mineral supplementation: effects on intelligence and performance. *Personality and Individual Differences* **12**: 351–62.

Shorvon, S.D., Carney, M.W.P., Chanarin, I. and Reynolds, E.H. (1980). The neuropsychiatry of megaloblastic anaemia. *British Medical Journal* **281**: 1036–8.

Sommer, B.R. and Wolkowitz, O.M. (1988). RBC folic acid levels and cognitive performance in elderly patients: a preliminary report. *Biological Psychiatry* **24**: 352–4.

Sterner, R.T. and Price, R.W. (1973). Restricted riboflavin: within subject behavioral effects in humans. *American Journal of Clinical Nutrition* **26**: 150–60.

Taylor, G.F. (1968). A clinical survey of elderly people from a nutritional standpoint. In

Vitamins in the Elderly, edited by A.N. Exton-Smith and D.L. Scott. Bristol: John Wright, pp. 51–6.

Thiessen, I. and Mills, L. (1975). The use of megavitamin treatment in children with learning disabilities. *Orthomolecular Psychiatry* **4**: 228–96.

Thorn, J., Robertson, J. and Buss, D.H. (1978). Trace nutrients: selenium in British food. *British Journal of Nutrition* **39**: 391–6.

Tolonen, M., Halme, M. and Sarna, S. (1985). Vitamin E and selenium supplementation in geriatric patients. *Biological Trace Element Research* **7**: 161–8.

Tucker, D.M. and Sandstead, H.M. (1984). Neuropsychological function in experimental zinc deficiency in humans. In *The Neurobiology of Zinc. Part B: Deficiency Toxicity and Pathology*, edited by C.J. Frederickson, G.A. Howell and E.J. Kasarskis. New York: Alan Liss, pp. 139–52.

US Food and Nutrition Board (1989). *Recommended Dietary Allowances* (10th edn). Washington, DC: National Academy Press.

Van Rhijn, A.G., Prior, C.A. and Corrigan, F.M. (1990). Dietary supplementation with zinc sulphate, sodium selenite and fatty acids in early dementia of Alzheimer's type. *Journal of Nutritional Medicine* **1**: 259–66.

Walravens, P.A. and Hambidge, K.M. (1976). Growth of infants fed a zinc supplemented formula. *American Journal of Clinical Nutrition* **29**: 1114–21.

Walravens, P.A., Van Doornick, W.J. and Hambidge, K.M. (1981). Metals and mental function. *Journal of Pediatrics* **93**: 535.

Ward, N.I., Watson, R. and Bryce-Smith, D. (1987). Placental elemental levels in relation to fetal development for obstetrically normal births: a study of 37 elements. Evidence for effects of cadmium, lead and zinc on fetal growth and for smoking as a source of cadmium. *Journal of Biosocial Research* **9**: 63–81.

Williams, R.J. (1956). *Biochemical Individuality*. New York: Wiley.

Worthington-Roberts, B.S. and Hazzard, W.R. (1982). Nutrition and aging. *Annual Review of Gerontology and Geriatrics* **3**: 297–328.

Yehuda, S. and Youdim, M.B.H. (1988). Brain iron deficiency: biochemistry and behaviour. In *Brain Iron: Neurochemical and Behavioural Aspects*, edited by M.B.H. Youdim. London: Taylor and Francis, pp. 89–114.

Young, S.N. and Ghadirian, M. (1989). Folic acid and psychopathology. *Progress in Neuro-Psychopharmacology and Biological Psychiatry* **13**: 841–63.

3

Caffeine

H.R. LIEBERMAN

INTRODUCTION

Caffeine occurs naturally in a number of foods, is employed as a food additive and is used as a drug. When administered in the doses found in these substances it has measurable effects on specific types of human behaviour. No other substance has its combination of uses nor is as widely consumed. Each day, hundreds of millions of people ingest behaviourally active quantities of caffeine in various forms. In many Asian countries, tea is the caffeine-containing beverage of choice, although coffee is becoming popular in Japan. In most of Europe and North America, coffee is the major dietary source of caffeine. Cola beverages and a few other soft drinks also contain caffeine and are popular throughout the world. In addition, caffeine is available in most pharmacies and supermarkets in the United States for use as a stimulant. It is also sold in combination with aspirin in certain popular analgesics and, until recently, was included as an adjuvant in a number of popular weight-loss preparations. In spite of such widespread use, published behavioural research on caffeine is limited and difficult to interpret. Controversies concerning the behavioural effects of caffeine abound.

The nature of caffeine's behavioural effects, the doses that produce effects, whether its consumption is addictive and the underlying reason for its popularity all remain unresolved. Any conclusions regarding the public health

The views, opinions and/or findings contained in this report are those of the author and should not be construed as an official Department of the Army position, policy or decision, unless so designated by other official documentation. I thank Dr Barnard Fine and Maj. Mary Mays, PhD for their helpful comments on earlier versions of this review.

implications of its consumption are further complicated by the numerous controversies that exist in the epidemiological literature. For example, reports have appeared suggesting that caffeine consumption is associated with heart disease and cancer, although such claims are controversial. The nature, extent and practical implications of using caffeine to alter specific psychologic parameters, such as performance and mood-state, as well as its abuse potential, are of critical importance for the public health. If caffeine improves performance, and thereby prevents accidents and increases productivity, its risk-to-benefit ratio will be shifted toward acceptance. However, if caffeine lacks beneficial effects when consumed in doses contained in common foods and drugs, there is little reason for it to be ingested by so many individuals throughout the world.

CAFFEINE IN FOODS AND DRUGS

The earliest documented use of caffeine-containing beverages dates to the Tang Dynasty of China (AD 618–907) where tea was a popular drink believed to prolong life. In spite of its widespread popularity in the orient, tea did not reach Europe until about 1600 (Roberts and Barone, 1983). The use of the coffee bean as a food probably originated in Ethiopia, and cultivation may have begun as early as the sixth century AD, although the first written reference is attributed to an Arab physician of the tenth century. It was introduced throughout Europe in the seventeenth century. At that time, a writer stated that it 'prevents those who consume it from feeling drowsy. For that reason, students who wish to read into the late hours are fond of it' (Pietro della Valle cited in Tannahill, 1989).

Caffeine (1,3,7-trimethylxanthine) is one member of a class of naturally occurring substances termed methylxanthines. Two other members of this class of compounds are found in food and drugs, one is theobromine (3,7-dimethylxanthine) and the other is theophylline (1,3-dimethylxanthine). Their structural formulae are shown in Figure 3.1. Caffeine is by far the most

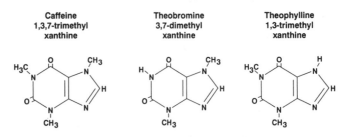

Figure 3.1 Structural formulae of the three methylxanthines found in foods and drugs.

important of these substances since it is consumed in much larger quantities than the other two (Gilbert *et al.*, 1976). Theobromine is found in significant quantities in cocoa. It is considered to be the least active xanthine, and may not be of consequence with respect to behavioural effects, although additional studies to confirm this conclusion are needed (Rall, 1980; Hirsh, 1984). Theophylline, in spite of many reports in the popular press to the contrary, is not the primary xanthine contained in tea; caffeine is much more abundant. Tea leaves contain only 0.03 per cent theophylline by weight but 3.23 per cent caffeine. Theophylline is also found in trace amounts in coffee and cocoa. However, it is a minor metabolite of caffeine in man and therefore may be found *in vivo* following consumption of caffeine. Kola nuts, which are used to flavour colas, contain some caffeine but most of the caffeine found in these beverages is added (Hirsh, 1984).

Because caffeine and related compounds occur naturally in coffee, tea and chocolate, their actual concentration in these foods before preparation will vary depending on growing conditions, plant variety, processing and storage. The method of preparation also greatly increases the variability in caffeine concentration of the final beverage. A weakly brewed cup of tea or a cup of coffee made with a smaller quantity of beans will obviously contain less caffeine. The method of preparation appears to be especially critical for coffee. Coffee prepared using the drip method contains, on average, the most caffeine, about 110 mg per cup, while instant (soluble) contains considerably less, about 60 mg per cup on average (Burg, 1975a; Hirsh, 1984): see Table 3.1. However, the actual level of caffeine contained in each type of coffee can vary tremendously. Roasted and ground coffee has been reported to contain from 40–150 mg per cup while instant coffee has from 40–108 mg per cup (Graham, 1978; Gilbert *et al.*, 1976; Roberts and Barone, 1983; Institute of Food Technologists' Expert Panel, 1987). Higher quality coffee beans, the arabica varieties, contain substantially less caffeine than the lower quality robusta beans. Tea, as well as most colas and other beverages, typically contain less caffeine per serving than coffee. A cup of tea contains about 40 mg of caffeine and most colas 30–40 mg per 12 oz serving (see Table 3.1).

In the United States, coffee accounts for the majority of caffeine consumption: 72 per cent (Barone and Roberts, 1984; Hirsh, 1984). It has been estimated that total per capita caffeine intake in the United States is 195 mg per day, total daily theobromine intake is 39 mg and total theophylline intake is only 0.14 mg per day. This surprisingly high daily theobromine intake, obtained mainly from cocoa products, suggests that animal and human neurochemical and behavioural studies with this compound are needed, particularly given the surprisingly low doses of caffeine that can affect performance and mood (Lieberman *et al.*, 1987a; Griffiths *et al.*, 1990).

To interpret properly the behavioural literature on caffeine, it is essential that data on the caffeine content of foods (Table 3.1) and daily caffeine intake levels be considered. For any study to be relevant to typical human behaviour,

Table 3.1 Caffeine content of selected beverages and foods

Item	Caffeine content[a] (mg)
Coffee (5 oz cup)	
Drip method	90–150
Percolated	64–124
Instant	40–108
Decaffeinated	2–5
Instant decaffeinated	2
Tea, loose or bags (5 oz cup)	
1-minute brew	9–33
3-minute brew	20–46
5-minute brew	20–50
Tea products	
Instant (5 oz cup)	12–28
Iced tea (12 oz can)	22–36
Chocolate products	
Hot cocoa (6 oz)	2–8
Dry cocoa (1 oz)	6
Milk chocolate (1 oz)	1–15
Baking chocolate (1 oz)	35
Sweet dark chocolate (1 oz)	5–35
Chocolate milk (8 oz)	2–7
Chocolate-flavoured syrup (2 tbsp)	4
Cola beverages (12 oz)	
Coca-Cola Classic	46
Pepsi	38
Coke	46
RC Cola	36
Diet Pepsi	36
Diet Coke	46
Diet RC Cola	48
TAB	46
Other soft drinks	
Dr Pepper	41
Diet Dr Pepper	41
Mountain Dew	54
Mellow Yellow	52
Diet Mellow Yellow	12
Mr Pibb	40

[a] Institute of Food Technologists' Expert Panel, 1987; Consumer Reports, 1991.

it must employ appropriate doses of caffeine. Pharmacologists study drugs in a wide range of doses, focusing on those doses which produce effects on the parameter of interest. However, if the objective is to study the effects of a food constituent on human behaviour, doses that produce caffeine levels in the same general range as the diet should be used. This applies not only to human behavioural studies but also to neuropharmacologic and behavioural studies with animals, particularly if these are to be generalized to human caffeine use. Hirsh (1984) estimates that the appropriate range is from a fraction of a mg per kg per day up to 20–30 mg per kg per day. A daily dose of 200 mg per day for an average sized human would be a dose of approximately 3 mg per kg per day. The National Research Council estimated that fewer than 0.1 per cent of the US population consumes more than 11 mg per kg per day of caffeine (NRC, 1977). For an insightful and thorough discussion of these issues, and a detailed review of the neuropharmacology of caffeine, see Hirsh (1984).

As noted above, caffeine is also found in certain over-the-counter (OTC) drugs and several prescription medications. Two tablets of Anacin^{TM} (the recommended dose) contain aspirin and 64 mg of caffeine. Caffeine tablets, for use as a stimulant, can be purchased in most pharmacies in the United States. The recommended dose is 100–200 mg. Some prescription migraine headache preparations also contain caffeine. Theophylline, often in very high doses, is widely used to treat asthma. Overall, drugs probably only provide a small part of the total xanthine intake in the United States because so much of these compounds is consumed in foods. However, it is important to keep this potential source of caffeine in mind, both with respect to individuals who may be consuming higher doses than they realize, and for research studies where the accurate assessment of baseline levels of caffeine consumption can be critical.

PHYSIOLOGICAL FACTORS THAT GOVERN CAFFEINE'S BEHAVIOURAL EFFECTS

Mechanisms of action

There is overwhelming evidence that the methylxanthines, at levels found in the diet, act by blocking the effects of the naturally occurring neuromodulator adenosine (Snyder, 1984). The structural formulae of caffeine and adenosine are illustrated in Figure 3.2. The similarities between the two substances are readily apparent. Adenosine is widely distributed in the brain and periphery, as are receptors with selective affinity for it. Several classes of such receptors have been isolated, including the A_1 and A_2 subtypes (Daly *et al.*, 1981). In a number of electrophysiological, biochemical and behavioural studies, adenosine has been found to have potent inhibitory actions (Hirsh, 1984).

The methylxanthines appear to act *in vivo* by inhibiting the binding of endogenously released adenosine to its receptor sites. This produces a net increase in central nervous system (CNS) activity, because the inhibitory action of adenosine is blocked. The *in vitro* affinity of various xanthines for adenosine receptors is highly correlated with the behavioural potency of these

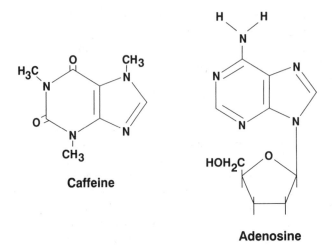

Figure 3.2 The structural formulae of caffeine and adenosine.

compounds: strong evidence that these receptors are the endogenous site of action of the xanthines (Snyder *et al.*, 1981; Daly *et al.*, 1981). Although it initially appeared that the behavioural effects of the methylxanthines were mediated by the A_1 receptors, it is now thought that it is through the A_2 receptors that these substances exert their influence on the brain and behaviour (Griebel *et al.*, 1991).

Until it was discovered that the xanthines acted via adenosine receptors, a variety of other mechanisms of action were advanced to explain their behavioural effects. Three of the most widely entertained were: calcium mobilization, phosphodiesterase inhibition, and prostaglandin antagonism. However, caffeine's effects on adenosine receptors occur at much lower concentrations than those produced by any of the other mechanisms. These other mechanisms may account for some of the toxic effects caffeine can have at higher doses because they become relevant only when caffeine is administered in doses that are at least twenty to thirty times higher than those found in foods (Rall, 1982; Hirsh, 1984; Snyder, 1984).

Metabolism

The chemical structures of the three xanthines found in foods are shown in Figure 3.1. Caffeine is moderately soluble in water, but is hydrophobic enough to cross the blood–brain barrier easily. As a result, caffeine is rapidly absorbed, even after oral administration, and is completely distributed throughout the body (Hirsh, 1984; Burg, 1975b). In humans, peak plasma levels of caffeine generally occur 15–45 minutes after ingestion and its plasma half-life is 5–6 hours (Bonati *et al.*, 1982; Von Borstel, 1983). Because of its ability to permeate biological membranes, little caffeine is excreted by the kidney, and its elimination depends on conversion to metabolites that are excreted in urine. Most of this biotransformation occurs in the liver.

Different mammals utilize different pathways to metabolize caffeine. In humans, about 70 per cent is metabolized to paraxanthine. In several non-human primates, theophylline is the predominant metabolite. However, theobromine is the principal product in mice and rats. Since different metabolites have different pharmacological properties, species differences in responsiveness to caffeine can be expected based on metabolic factors alone. *In vitro*, paraxanthine and theophylline appear to be more potent than caffeine, while theobromine tends to be less active (Rall, 1980; Daly *et al.*, 1981; Von Borstel, 1983).

A variety of factors significantly modify the rate of caffeine's elimination in man. In pregnant women, caffeine's half-life has been reported to increase to eighteen hours. Oral contraceptive use appears to increase caffeine half-life to approximately eleven hours. On the other hand, in cigarette smokers caffeine's half-life is 3–4 hours (Von Borstel, 1983). Such individual differences must be considered when behavioural and other studies are conducted because equal doses of caffeine will not be physiologically equivalent.

BEHAVIOURAL CONSEQUENCES OF CAFFEINE CONSUMPTION

As discussed above, a great deal of information is available describing the pharmacological properties of caffeine. In addition, a scientific consensus exists regarding many of its physiological effects and its mechanism of action. However, there appears to be considerably less agreement among scientists with respect to the behavioural effects of caffeine. In fact, a survey of the scientific literature, including several of the most recent review papers, would lead the reader to believe that caffeine's effects on behaviour are highly variable and the subject of considerable controversy (Sawyer *et al.*, 1982; Dews, 1984). Ironically, most consumers of caffeine are less circumspect, regarding it as a mild stimulant when consumed in moderate doses, just as Pietro della Valle (cited in Tannahill, 1989) recognized four hundred years ago.

In one of the more recent reviews of the behavioural effects of caffeine on humans, Dews (1984) notes that caffeine has been studied extensively for a variety of reasons including: it is readily available; it is generally recognized as safe; it has a rapid onset of action, and it is active when taken by mouth. However, he notes that a disadvantage of its use is that when administered in the doses found in foods, its effects are 'so slight and subtle that the investigator is usually glad to be able to detect them'.

The reasons for the confusing state of the scientific literature on the behavioural effects of caffeine are numerous and are discussed in detail below. One overriding problem is the great variability in the experimental approaches that behavioural scientists have applied to testing caffeine, particularly with regard to the selection of behaviour tests. In addition, many investigators have failed to consider critical confounding variables, such as baseline caffeine use, in the design of their studies. Furthermore, a key principle – the statistical power of a study, which must be considered when the results of negative studies are interpreted – is often ignored.

In general, there is lack of agreement among psychologists regarding appropriate methods to employ to detect behavioural effects of drugs, foods and environmental manipulations (Lieberman *et al.*, 1986; Lieberman, 1987). This is a problem not only for studies of caffeine but also for psychopharmacology and neuropsychology in general. That the behavioural effects of a substance like caffeine, which has generated so many research studies and is so widely used, remains controversial is unfortunate.

Test selection

The selection of appropriate behavioural tasks to detect the effects of foods, drugs or other treatments on human behaviour is one of the most crucial aspects of the design of such studies (Lieberman *et al.*, 1986). If the behavioural tasks employed are insensitive to the effects of the treatment being evaluated, no effects will be detected even if all other aspects of a study are conducted flawlessly. Unfortunately, although many standardized behavioural tasks are available, the choice of the most appropriate to test a specific parameter, such as memory, vigilance or learning, is largely a matter of the investigator's personal preference. In addition, tests that are typically employed to assess a particular cognitive function, such as 'learning' invariably have a multifactorial substrate. Nearly all 'learning' tasks will require sensory processing, memory and motor output. To complicate matters further, even variations in the manner in which a particular test is employed can be of critical importance with regard to the likelihood of detecting an effect. Undoubtedly, in many studies of caffeine, the effect size is quite marginal with respect to the normal variability of the behaviour being assessed, which is certain to result in variability in results across similar studies.

STATISTICAL CONSIDERATIONS

Classically, in psychology and in many other experimental sciences, one of the most sacrosanct statistical principles is protection against the type I error. This type of statistical error is the likelihood of inferring that an effect is present when such a conclusion is not warranted. By convention, the type I error protection level for a specific dependent measure in a study is set at

5 per cent. Therefore, a null hypothesis will be rejected only if there is less than a one-in-twenty chance of this type of an 'incorrect' conclusion. Until recently, the probability of the other type of statistical error — a type II error — was largely ignored. A type II error is the probability of failing to detect an effect that is actually present. Even when formally considered, it is often set at 20 per cent, and many published studies actually have much higher type II error levels, sometimes as high as 50 or 60 per cent. Consequently, and somewhat counterintuitively, a positive study that is conducted using exactly the same methods and with the same size sample, is more likely to represent the 'true' state of affairs than is an identical negative study.

CONFOUNDING FACTORS

When a substance which appears to have relatively subtle and specific effects on behaviour is evaluated using methods that are less than ideal, the results are likely to be inconclusive and ambiguous. A number of factors, if not properly controlled, can obscure the results of what would otherwise appear to be well designed studies of the behavioural effects of caffeine. One of these factors is the baseline level of caffeine consumption of the participants. Another is the uncontrolled use of caffeine immediately prior to testing.

Baseline consumption of caffeine by participants in caffeine studies is of great importance, because regular heavy use of caffeine appears to produce tolerance to its behavioural effects (Goldstein *et al.*, 1969). Individuals who normally consume high levels of caffeine are less sensitive to the effects of the substance. In addition, some individuals choose to abstain from using caffeine because they believe they are inherently over-sensitive to it. In fact, studies of children's patterns of caffeine consumption suggest that differences in sensitivity to caffeine may be due to inherent physiological characteristics of the individual and not just a consequence of tolerance, withdrawal or subject selection (Rapoport *et al.*, 1984).

In addition, certain personal characteristics can directly affect caffeine's metabolism, and must be considered in behavioural studies of caffeine. Smokers metabolize caffeine almost twice as rapidly as do non-smokers. Other factors, notably pregnancy, liver disease and the use of certain types of oral contraceptive, can decrease the rate at which caffeine is metabolized (Von Borstel, 1983). Individuals with any of these personal characteristics are likely to have considerably different behavioural responses to caffeine administration from the general population.

Effects of caffeine on basis behavioural functions

A detailed and complete picture of caffeine's effects on simple sensory and motor functions is not currently available. Comprehensive studies of caffeine's effects on sensory function have never been conducted. At present, there is no evidence to suggest that moderate doses of caffeine have direct effects on sensory function, although well controlled studies using state-of-the-art methods have not been conducted. One simple measure of visual function which is often employed in psychopharmacological studies – critical flicker fusion – does not appear to be altered by caffeine administration (File *et al.*, 1982; Swift and Tiplady, 1988). There is considerable evidence that caffeine can affect overall responsiveness to external stimuli, both auditory and visual, but the effects appear to be related to the maintenance of vigilance, as discussed below, rather than to the sensory components of the task.

Many studies have investigated the effects of caffeine on simple and complex reaction time. The results tend to be equivocal: some negative reports have appeared in the literature, but positive reports have also been published. Clubley *et al.* (1979) found that simple auditory reaction time was significantly shortened after 75 and 150 mg of caffeine were administered at 9.00 a.m. and testing was conducted later that morning. Smith *et al.* (1977) observed a small but statistically significant decrease in choice reaction time when 200 mg of caffeine was administered to male university students who were heavy cigarette smokers and caffeine consumers. On the other hand, Kuznicki and Turner (1986) found no effect of caffeine in doses of 20–160 mg on visual choice reaction time.

In a study discussed in greater detail below, Lieberman *et al.* (1987a) observed a dose-related reduction in response latency as a consequence of caffeine administration (32–256 mg) using a four-choice visual reaction time task (Figure 3.3). No increase in error rate was observed on this or other tasks when caffeine was administered. In a subsequent study, using a similar experimental design, significant effects of 64 mg of caffeine (the only dose tested) were observed on simple auditory reaction time but not on four-choice visual reaction time (Lieberman *et al.*, 1987b). In both studies, only individuals who consumed less than 400 mg of caffeine per day were participants.

In a study conducted by Roache and Griffiths (1987) using 200, 400 and 600 mg of caffeine, choice reaction time improved most when either 200 or 400 mg were administered. The 600 mg dose produced effects that were intermediate between placebo and the other doses. Therefore, high doses of caffeine may have less of a positive effect on reaction time than moderate doses. Complex interactions between caffeine, subject age and baseline caffeine use also have been observed. Swift and Tiplady (1988) reported that visual choice reaction time was reduced by 200 mg of caffeine in elderly but not young volunteers. Childs (1978) found that scanning performance was slowed in individuals who normally consume about two cups of coffee per week, but was faster among individuals who consume, on average, nine and a half cups per week. These effects were observed when 400 mg of caffeine was administered but not 200 mg.

Overall, it appears that when caffeine is administered in moderate doses it may have positive effects on simple and complex reaction time. However,

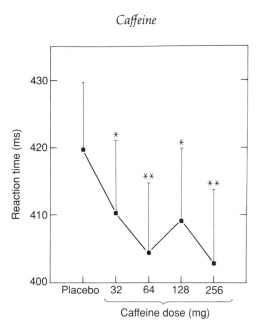

Figure 3.3 Four-choice visual reaction time (mean ± SEM) after administration of caffeine and placebo (* indicates $p < 0.05$ compared to placebo; ** indicates $p < 0.005$ compared with placebo on *post hoc* tests).

such effects are difficult to detect consistently because of their modest size, non-monotonic nature and what may be a complex relationship between dose administered and the caffeine-consumption history of the subjects.

Effects of caffeine on sustained vigilance

Several papers have appeared indicating that caffeine in moderate doses will increase vigilance (Regina *et al.*, 1974; Clubley *et al.*, 1979). However, other investigators have failed to detect such effects (Loke and Meliska, 1984). In an effort to document the effects of caffeine on behaviour of normal individuals, Lieberman *et al.* (1987a) developed a standardized testing paradigm that has consistently detected effects of caffeine on vigilance. In an initial study, several vigilance tests were compared and one – the Wilkinson vigilance test (Wilkinson, 1970) – was found to be sensitive to a wide range of caffeine doses. This test assesses sustained auditory vigilance. Every 2 s for a 1 h time period a 400 ms tone is presented via headphones. To mask out extraneous stimuli, white noise is continuously presented in the background. Forty of the tones are approximately 70 ms shorter than the rest and the subject must correctly identify these infrequent signal tones by responding on a computer keyboard. Unlike Wilkinson's original version, task difficulty is equated from subject to subject by varying slightly the duration of the test stimuli. This is accomplished during a practice session by adjusting each subject's performance level to a criterion of approximately 50 per cent correct (Lieberman *et al.*, 1987b). In addition to correct responses, false alarms (that is, responding when a signal tone has not been presented) are also recorded.

Twenty healthy males (mean age 28.1 years) participated in the initial double-blind, cross-over study (Lieberman *et al.*, 1987a). Smokers and individuals who consumed more than 400 mg of caffeine per day were excluded, and caffeine consumption was restricted for twelve hours before testing. Caffeine was administered in capsule form at 8.00 a.m. in doses of 32, 64, 128 and 256 mg. Testing was conducted from 8.40–11.00 a.m. All four doses of caffeine significantly improved detection rate as assessed by the modified Wilkinson vigilance task without any change in error rate (Figure 3.4). Particularly surprising was a significant effect of caffeine at 32 mg – a dose not typically considered to be behaviourally active. In subsequent studies Lieberman *et al.* have consistently documented effects of caffeine with the modified Wilkinson task, in some instances using a briefer (30 minute)

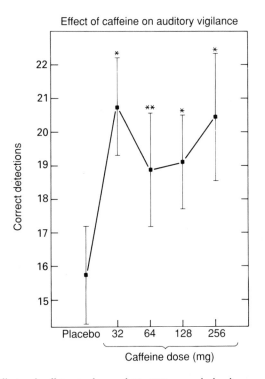

Figure 3.4 Effects of caffeine in doses of 32–256 mg and placebo on mean (±SEM) number of correct detections on the Wilkinson auditory vigilance task (* indicates $p < 0.005$ compared to placebo; ** indicates $p < 0.01$ compared with placebo on *post hoc* tests).

version. In one study it was found that caffeine alone (64 mg) and caffeine (64 and 128 mg) in combination with aspirin, improved vigilance (Lieberman *et al.*, 1987b). In a subsequent study we replicated our original findings using 64 and 128 mg of caffeine (Lieberman, 1988). These effects have also been observed in women and elderly volunteers (Lieberman *et al.*, unpublished observations), again using doses of 64, 128 and 256 mg. The effects of caffeine on vigilance were not related to the baseline caffeine consumption levels of the subjects, probably because heavy caffeine consumers (defined as daily intake of more than 400 mg) were not enrolled in the studies. In addition, since the effects were of equal magnitude in low and moderate consumers, it is unlikely that they were attributable to the fact that the volunteers were required to abstain from caffeine use for twelve hours prior to testing. Thus, it appears that caffeine can increase vigilance when a sensitive test is employed in an appropriate testing paradigm.

Effects of caffeine on complex cognitive performance

Detecting effects of various manipulations on complex cognitive processes is invariably a difficult undertaking. Even when potent drugs are tested the results can be equivocal. Numerous investigators have attempted to document effects of caffeine on memory, learning and other types of complex cognitive function. No definitive conclusions can be drawn from these studies, and it would appear that, if such effects are present, they are not particularly robust.

Battig *et al.* (1984) assessed the effects of 300 mg of caffeine on a complex spatial learning task and did not observe any significant changes. Clubley and colleagues (1979) were unable to detect effects of 100 mg of caffeine on short-term verbal memory. File *et al.* (1982) did not observe any change in verbal learning following doses of 125–500 mg of caffeine citrate. In a study conducted by Loke *et al.*, (1985), caffeine, in doses of 3 and 6 mg kg^{-1}, had no effect on immediate and delayed recall and delayed recognition of word lists by moderate consumers of caffeine. In one of the few studies to report significant effects, Erikson *et al.* (1985) found that caffeine had a positive effect on retention of word lists when testing was conducted at a slow (but not at a fast) rate. However, the effect was of modest size and was present only in females. Roache and Griffiths (1987) did not observe any effects of caffeine on immediate recall or delayed recognition of word lists after 200, 400 or 600 mg of caffeine were administered. In a study discussed above, in which 64 and 128 mg of caffeine improved vigilance, significant effects on short- and long-term verbal memory and learning could not be detected (Lieberman, 1988). In that study special efforts were made to select learning and memory tasks that should be sensitive to caffeine. It should be noted that memory tasks generally produce data that are more variable than vigilance tasks, so to detect effects of caffeine on this function much larger sample sizes than are typically employed in such studies may be necessary. In addition, as discussed below, personality differences may interact with the effects of caffeine on complex cognitive tasks.

Changes in mood associated with caffeine consumption

The effects of caffeine on mood are more difficult to document consistently than are those on vigilance, at least when vigilance is assessed using the modified Wilkinson vigilance test. However, changes in mood state following moderate doses of caffeine are reasonably robust and are consistent with the effects that caffeine has on vigilance. A number of investigators have documented such effects.

As would be expected, caffeine appears to enhance alertness and reduce fatigue when these mood-states are assessed using appropriate methods, even when low and moderate doses are administered. Caffeine's effects on mood appear to be especially dose-dependent. As discussed below, it may actually have opposite effects on some mood-states, particularly anxiety, depending on dose.

Clubley et al. (1979) reported significant positive effects of caffeine on self-reported 'mental sedation' when it was administered in doses of 75, 150 and 300 mg. Leathwood and Pollet (1982) observed significant effects of 100 mg of caffeine on a series of bipolar analogue scales including: vigour/lethargy, wide awake/sleepy, and full-of-go/listless. Griffiths et al. (1990) observed significant positive effects of caffeine on alertness, well-being, concentration and a number of related states when 100 mg were administered. In an earlier study, Roache and Griffiths (1987) observed increased alertness, vigour and decreased fatigue when caffeine was administered in doses of 200, 400 and 600 mg. Loke (1988) observed that caffeine significantly decreased boredom in doses of 200 and 400 mg, but also increased ratings of anxiety and tension at a dose of 400 mg. The subjects were undergraduates who were tested between 3.00 and 6.00 p.m. Cole et al. (1978) also noted increased levels of anxiety after administration of a 300 mg dose of caffeine to volunteers who were known abusers of d-amphetamine. Roache and Griffiths (1987) observed a non-significant increase in tension following 400 and 600 mg of caffeine and no change following 200 mg. Only a few studies have failed to detect effects of caffeine on mood, including Svensson and his colleagues (1980) who found no significant effects of 100 mg of caffeine on the mood-state of twenty-three undergraduates.

In a study conducted to compare the effects of caffeine on young and elderly volunteers, young subjects reported feeling more alert, interested and steadier on caffeine (200 mg) but elderly volunteers did not (Swift and Tiplady, 1988). It was also observed that the younger volunteers felt calmer following caffeine administration. However, this study was conducted with only six volunteers in each group, and although it was a cross-over study, this is still a small sample size. In a study comparing twelve young and twelve elderly volunteers, who were all tested on 64, 128 and 256 mg of caffeine as well as placebo, Lieberman *et al.* were unable to document any differential effects of caffeine on the mood or performance of young versus elderly volunteers (Lieberman *et al.*, unpublished observations).

In a series of studies discussed above, in which a standardized testing paradigm was used, positive effects of caffeine at 64 and 128 mg on self-reported alertness, vigour and fatigue have typically been detected (Lieberman *et al.*, 1987b; Lieberman, 1988; Lieberman *et al.*, unpublished observations). This is in agreement with the results of most other investigators. In addition, in one of these studies, decreased anxiety was observed following both doses of caffeine. Since that study was conducted between 9.00 and 11.00 a.m. and required subjects to engage in a series of performance tests, these findings may reflect the time of day when testing was conducted and the demands made upon the subjects. Based on the literature reviewed above, it appears that caffeine can increase anxiety when administered in single bolus doses of 300 mg or higher, which is many times greater than the amount present in a single serving of a typical caffeine-containing beverage (Table 3.1). However, in lower doses it appears to have little effect on this mood-state or, under certain circumstances, it may even reduce anxiety levels. It has also been observed that caffeine reduces self-rated depression when administered in moderate doses (Lieberman, 1988; Lieberman, unpublished observations). This may be a secondary effect of caffeine resulting from its ability to facilitate performance, increase self-reported vigour and reduce fatigue.

Although a variety of questionnaires have been successfully employed to assess the effects of caffeine on self-reported mood-state, some appear to be better than others. Among those which seem to be most sensitive are the Profile of Mood States, POMS (McNair *et al.*, 1971) and the Nestlé analogue scale (Leathwood and Pollet, 1982).

Simulator studies

Surprisingly few studies have been conducted to determine whether caffeine will have beneficial or harmful effects in simulated or real work environments. In one of the few studies to address such issues, Regina *et al.* (1974) tested twenty-four young, well rested males in a realistic simulation of automobile driving. They administered 200 mg of caffeine or placebo orally and monitored certain aspects of driving behaviour for ninety minutes. Subjects were tested twice, once with and once without caffeine, in a counterbalanced order. Caffeine significantly improved several kinds of performance including response time to accelerations and decelerations of a lead car. In addition, performance on a visual vigilance task also improved significantly. This task required the subject to detect the automatic illumination of the full-beam indicator on the dashboard which occurred at random intervals throughout testing. After the first ninety minutes of testing and a ten-minute rest period, another 200 mg dose of caffeine was administered and driving performance was assessed for an additional ninety minutes. The second dose of caffeine also significantly improved performance, although, due to the nature of the experimental design, residual effects from the first dose cannot be excluded. Caffeine's beneficial effects were greater during the second test period compared with the first, although this difference was only statistically significant for one variable – response time to lead car accelerations. That the results of this study are similar to those investigating caffeine's effects on vigilance using laboratory tasks, especially the Wilkinson test, is reassuring.

In another simulator study, Johnson (in press) evaluated the effects of 200 mg of caffeine on marksmanship. Using a Weaponeer Rifle Marksmanship Simulator, which employs a modified M16A1 rifle, performance was assessed for three hours after administration of caffeine or placebo. The soldiers participating in the study were required to respond to the infrequent appearance of a target by picking up a rifle and aiming and firing as rapidly and as accurately as possible. Caffeine decreased detection time but did not significantly increase the total number of targets that were hit.

These studies would appear to have important practical implications. It seems that the use of caffeine in moderate doses can improve the performance of individuals who must drive automobiles for sustained periods of time. In addition, the performance of soldiers engaged in a simulation of a critical military task, sentry duty, clearly improved following caffeine administration. These beneficial effects may increase in situations where vigilance is reduced due to sleep loss, jet lag or circadian variations in arousal. The study of Walsh *et al.* (1990) discussed above, which demonstrated decreased sleep tendency following caffeine administration at night, strongly supports this conclusion. Future studies to replicate and extend these findings should be conducted in a variety of transportation and industrial simulators, and, when practical, in actual work environments. Epidemiological studies are also possible: for example, it would be of interest to assess the incidence of certain types of transportation accidents as a function of the operators' caffeine intake.

SLEEP

Since caffeine appears to improve ability to maintain vigilance and increase alertness, it is not surprising that it may interfere with sleep. Many individuals choose to abstain from caffeine consumption in the afternoon and evening because they have observed that caffeine will disrupt their night-time sleep.

However, other individuals report that they can consume caffeine-containing beverages before bedtime with no adverse impact on their sleep (Colton *et al.*, 1967; Levy and Zylber-Katz, 1983). These differences are, in all probability, attributable to individual variability in responsiveness to caffeine. Both innate differences in sensitivity to caffeine, as suggested by Rapoport *et al.* (1984), and acquired tolerance by individuals who consume substantial quantities of caffeine, probably contribute to these differences. Individuals who consume three to six cups of coffee per day appear to be less likely to report sleep-disturbances than those who drink less than one cup of coffee per day. This may be because heavy drinkers metabolize caffeine much more rapidly (Levy and Zylber-Katz, 1983).

Anecdotal reports that caffeine consumption will alter sleep are supported by the scientific literature. Walsh *et al.* (1990) observed that, in both low and high consumers of caffeine, administration of a high dose (4.0 mg kg^{-1}) at 10.20–10.50 p.m. reduced sleep tendency, as measured by the multiple sleep latency test. Based on these findings, the authors suggest that caffeine administration may improve the performance of nightshift workers. Dews (1982) reviewed three independent studies that evaluated the effects of caffeine administered thirty minutes before retiring, on self-reported sleep-latency. Effects were undetectable when caffeine was administered in doses below 80 mg but were substantial at higher doses. When volunteers ingested 300 mg, self-reported sleep latency increased by a factor of approximately 2.6 relative to placebo.

Caffeine has also been tested for its ability to reduce the next-day 'hangover' effects that occur when certain hypnotics are administered. For example, caffeine, in a dose of 250 mg, was found to reduce significantly next-day sleepiness following administration of flurazepam (30 mg) or triazolam (0.5 mg) (Johnson *et al.*, 1990). Caffeine also antagonizes the sedative effects of diazepam immediately after both are administered (File *et al.*, 1982; Roache and Griffiths, 1987).

PERSONALITY AND CAFFEINE

A substantial body of literature exists that relates personality to responsiveness to caffeine. For a recent review the reader should consult Revelle *et al.* (1987). Revelle and his colleagues (1980, 1987) have found, in a number of studies, that the impulsivity subscale of the Eysenck Personality Inventory, EPI (Eysenck and Eysenck, 1968) is related to responsiveness to caffeine, time of day and task difficulty. Specifically, they have observed when testing large groups of students that caffeine can facilitate the performance of impulsive individuals and impair the performance of non-impulsives taking complex cognitive tests in the morning. In the evening, the opposite appears to be the case. They also suggest that, on simple tasks, caffeine generally improves performance. On the other hand, some investigators have failed to detect any relationships between the EPI and caffeine consumption (Erikson *et al.*, 1985; Battig and Buzzi, 1986).

In a study discussed above, Lieberman *et al.* found self-reported 'Morning-ness—Eveningness', assessed by the questionnaire of Horne and Ostberg (1976), to be significantly correlated with responsiveness to caffeine (Lieberman *et al.*, submitted). Specifically, it was noted that morning types tended to be less sensitive to the positive effects of caffeine when testing was conducted in the morning, as would be expected. We did not observe a significant interaction between a subject's score on the extraversion scale or the impulsiveness subscale of the EPI and performance. However, there was a substantial but non-significant correlation between the extraversion scale and responsiveness to caffeine. These findings tend to support the work of Revelle *et al.* Many of the studies that do not find an interaction between caffeine and impulsiveness have used too few subjects to test for interaction effects.

Another personality dimension of interest to researchers is field inde-pendence/dependence (Witkin *et al.*, 1982). Using the Gottschaldt Hidden Shapes Test (Cattell, 1955) as a measure of field dependence, Fine and McCord (1991) have observed complex interactions between caffeine con-sumption, field dependence, oral contraceptive use and colour discrimination ability in female undergraduates. Interactions between caffeine intake and oral contraceptive use are consistent with reports that these drugs slow the rate at which caffeine is metabolized (Von Borstel, 1983). Future studies with caffeine should consider personality as assessed by the EPI, Morningness/ Eveningness and field dependence, as well as the time of day when testing is conducted, as important covariates.

ADVERSE BEHAVIOURAL EFFECTS OF CAFFEINE

Anxiety

Several papers have appeared which suggest that caffeine consumption can adversely affect individuals suffering from anxiety disorders. For example, Boulenger *et al.* (1984) observed that individuals with panic anxiety disorder had self-rated anxiety levels that correlated positively with their level of caffeine consumption. Lee *et al.* (1985) observed that patients with anxiety disorder consumed significantly less caffeine than a group of medical inpatients. They concluded that patients suffering from anxiety disorders were probably more sensitive to the anxiety-producing effects of caffeine than other individuals, leading them to decrease their caffeine consumption. It has also been suggested that consumption of more than 600 mg of caffeine per day may induce in normal individuals a syndrome known as 'caffeinism', which is characterized by anxiety, disturbed sleep and psychophysiological complaints similar to those seen among patients suffering from anxiety neurosis (Boulenger *et al.*, 1984).

Fine motor performance

Perhaps as a consequence of its effects on arousal level, caffeine has been associated, at least anecdotally, with impaired fine motor performance. When caffeine was administered to non-users in a dose of 160 mg, but not lower doses, it did appear to disrupt hand steadiness (Kuznicki and Turner, 1986). However, in the same study, no adverse effects of caffeine on hand steadiness of regular caffeine consumers were detected. There was no evidence that doses of 32–256 mg either facilitated or disrupted performance on several complex motor tasks when low and moderate users were tested (by Lieberman *et al.* (1987a)). Other investigators have also typically failed to find adverse effects of caffeine on various tests of motor performance.

Withdrawal

The sudden withdrawal of caffeine from a person's diet, if it has been consumed in substantial amounts on a regular basis, often appears to have adverse effects. Most notable is headache, which is relieved by consumption of caffeine. Caffeine-withdrawal headaches are also relieved by OTC analgesics and spontaneously remit after a few days of caffeine withdrawal (Hirsh, 1984). These headaches may be attributable to the withdrawal of caffeine from peripheral adenosine binding sites, thereby causing hypersensitivity to endogenous adenosine. Chronic administration of caffeine to animals increases the number of these binding sites on blood vessels and its withdrawal alters vascular tone. If adenosine binding sites are located in the blood vessels of the scalp and cranium in humans, the sudden elimination of caffeine from such sites could lead to excessive dilation and hyperaemia (excess blood flow and local fluid accumulation) producing headache (Heistad *et al.*, 1981). Adverse effects of caffeine on mood-state, such as increased fatigue, have also been reported following its sudden withdrawal from the diet of heavy users (Holtzman, 1990).

Based on such data, individuals who wish to reduce or eliminate caffeine from their diet should do so gradually. In addition, individuals who are heavy users of caffeine should be advised that its sudden withdrawal may produce a headache and adverse changes in mood-state.

Abuse potential

It has been suggested that caffeine is an addictive drug, with similarities to abused substances (Holtzman, 1990). The evidence for this association includes the adverse physical effects of caffeine withdrawal (for a review see Griffiths and Woodson, 1988), as well as animal and human studies of caffeine self-administration. Caffeine is a weak reinforcing stimulant in non-human primates, although the extent of responding to caffeine is far less than that maintained by stimulants like amphetamine. In addition, about half of human volunteers tested show a statistically significant preference for caffeine-containing preparations when these are repeatedly administered in disguised form (Holtzman, 1990). Hirsh (1984) has noted that addiction can best be defined as compulsion to use a drug, and specifically, involvement with the abused substances to the exclusion of other interests. The use of methyl-xanthines in foods and beverages would not appear to qualify as such behaviour (Hirsh, 1984; Sobotka, 1989). In addition, caffeine clearly has low abuse potential compared to more widely recognized drugs of abuse (Griffiths and Woodson, 1988). A thorough discussion of these issues would go beyond the scope of this chapter and would need to address a number of complex scientific, regulatory and philosophical issues.

CONCLUSIONS

Beneficial and adverse behavioural effects of caffeine

When caffeine is consumed in the range of doses found in many foods it improves the ability of individuals to perform tasks requiring sustained vigilance, including simulated automobile driving. In addition, when administered in this same dose range, caffeine increases self-reported alertness and decreases sleepiness. Firm conclusions regarding caffeine's effects on higher cognitive functions, such as learning and memory, cannot be reached at this time. Numerous attempts to document such effects have yielded inconclusive results, perhaps because of unassessed factors such as personality type.

Adverse behavioural effects occur when caffeine is consumed in excessive doses or by individuals who are overly sensitive to the substance. In high doses caffeine may increase anxiety; it also interferes with sleep when consumed by certain individuals at bedtime. Like many other drugs, regular caffeine consumption appears to produce tolerance to its behavioural effects. Sudden withdrawal of this substance from the diet will often lead to adverse symptoms such as headache and undesirable changes in mood-state. Some scientists believe that caffeine has properties similar to those exhibited by drugs of abuse.

Risks and benefits of caffeine consumption

Physicians, scientists, public health officials and government agencies must make judgements regarding the use of caffeine. Recommendations must be made to individuals regarding their personal use of caffeine and the public health must be protected from any possible adverse effects of such a widely used food constituent. Conversely, the public should be protected from unwarranted intrusion in their selection of foods based on unconfirmed recommendations of self-appointed nutrition experts, uninformed medical professionals and the press. In the United States, complex statutes and regulations govern the use of caffeine. Once caffeine is ingested and enters the circulation its source is of little importance physiologically; however US government agencies must regulate this substance based on the medium in which it is consumed. Caffeine that occurs naturally in foods is regulated in a different manner from the caffeine added to foods. Drugs that contain caffeine are subject to different regulations from foods. The multiple sources of caffeine can lead to peculiar consequences: for example, a large cup of coffee purchased at a local restaurant may contain more active drug than the recommended dose for an over-the-counter (OTC) stimulant. Also, an individual who believes he does not consume any caffeine may in fact be consuming it in soft-drinks or OTC drugs that are not usually thought of as containing caffeine.

At present, the risk-to-benefit ratio of caffeine use cannot be definitely ascertained. Positive behavioural consequences of caffeine consumption, such as increased ability to sustain vigilance, higher levels of self-reported alertness and other positive mood-states have been documented. These beneficial effects clearly generalize to simulations of automobile driving, and presumably other transportation and industrial operations. The use of caffeine in such circumstances could prevent accidents attributable to lapses of vigilance, such as falling asleep at the wheel, which are a significant cause of serious motor vehicle accidents in the United States. However, adverse effects of caffeine on sleep quality have been observed and some scientists believe that caffeine has many of the characteristics of an addictive drug. In addition, a large and complex literature exists concerning possible adverse effects of caffeine on the incidence of various diseases. Although many such controversies remain unresolved, no definitive data exist that link caffeine to any chronic disease. An expert panel recently concluded that: 'while questions about the ultimate safety of caffeine remain, there is a solid evidence supporting the view that moderate amounts are not harmful to the average healthy adult' (Institute of Food Technologists' Expert Panel, 1987). It would, therefore, appear that as long as definite health risks are not discovered, the behavioural effects of caffeine will determine its risk-to-benefit ratio. Behavioural scientists, policy-makers and regulatory officials will have to consider the documented beneficial and adverse effects of caffeine and draw conclusions that will result in the best overall outcome for the public.

REFERENCES

Barone, J.J. and Roberts, H. (1984). Human consumption of caffeine. In *Caffeine*, edited by P.B. Dews. New York: Springer, pp. 59–73.

Battig, K. and Buzzi, R. (1986). Effect of coffee on the speed of subject-paced information processing. *Neuropsychobiology* **16**: 126–30.

Battig, K., Buzzi, R., Martin, J.R. and Feierabend, J.M. (1984). The effects of caffeine on physiological functions and mental performance. *Experientia* **40**: 1218–23.

Bonati, M., Latini, R., Galletti, F., Young, J.F., Tognoni, G. and Garattini, S. (1982). Caffeine disposition after oral doses. *Clinical Pharmacology and Therapeutics* **32**(1): 98–106.

Boulenger, J.P., Uhde, T., Wolff, E.A. and Post, R.M. (1984). Increased sensitivity to caffeine in patients with panic disorders. *Archives of General Psychiatry* **41**: 1067–71.

Burg, A.W. (1975a). How much caffeine in the cup. *Tea Coffee Trade Journal* **147**(1): 40–2.

Burg, A.W. (1975b). Physiological disposition of caffeine. *Drug Metabolism Review* **4**: 199–228.

Cattell, R.B. (1955). *The Objective–Analytic Personality Factor Batteries*. Champaign, Ill.: Institute for Personality and Ability Testing.

Childs, J. (1978). Caffeine consumption and target scanning performance. *Human Factors* **20**: 91–6.

Clubley, M., Bye, C.E., Henson, T.A., Peck, A.W. and Riddington, C.J. (1979). Effects of caffeine and cyclizine alone and in combination on human performance, subjective effects and EEG activity. *British Journal of Clinical Pharmacology* **7**: 157–63.

Cole, J.O., Pope, H.G., LaBrie, R. and Ionescu-Pioggia, M. (1978). Assessing the subjective effects of stimulants in casual users. *Clinical Pharmacology and Therapeutics* **24**: 243–52.

Colton, T., Gosselin, R.E. and Smith, R.P. (1967). The tolerance of coffee drinkers to caffeine. *Clinical Pharmacology and Therapeutics* **9**(1): 31–9.

Consumer Reports (1991). **56**(8): 525.

Daly, J.W., Bruns, R.F. and Snyder, S.H. (1981). Adenosine receptors in the central nervous system relationship to the central actions of methylxanthines. *Life Sciences* **28**: 2083–97.

Dews, P.B. (1982). Caffeine. *Annual Review of Nutrition* **2**: 323–41.

Dews, P.B. (1984). Behavioral effects of caffeine. In *Caffeine*, edited by P.B. Dews. New York: Springer.

Erikson, G.C., Hager, L., Houseworth, C., Dungan, J., Petros, T. and Beckwith, B. (1985). The effects of caffeine on memory for word lists. *Physiology and Behavior* **35**: 47–51.

Eysenck, H.J. and Eysenck, S.B.G. (eds) (1968). *Manual for the Eysenck Personality Inventory*. San Diego: Educational and Industrial Testing Service.

File, S.A., Bond, A.J. and Lister, R.G. (1982). Interaction between effects of caffeine and lorazepam in performance tests and self-ratings. *Journal of Clinical Psychopharmacology* **2**: 102–6.

Fine, B.J. and McCord, L. (1991). Oral contraceptive use, caffeine consumption, field-dependence, and the discrimination of colors. *Perceptual and Motor Skills* **73**: 931–41.

Gilbert, R.M., Marshman, J.A., Schwieder, M. and Berg, R. (1976). Caffeine content of beverages as consumed. *Canadian Medical Association Journal* **114**: 205–8.

Goldstein, A., Kaizer, S. and Whitby, O. (1969). Psychotropic effects of caffeine in man. IV. Quantitative and qualitative differences associated with habituation to coffee. *Clinical Pharmacology and Therapeutics* **10**(4): 489–97.

Graham, D.M. (1978). Caffeine: its identity, dietary sources, intake and biological effects. *Nutrition Reviews* **36**: 97–102.

Griebel, G., Saffroy-Spittler, M., Misslin, R., Remmy, D., Vogel, E. and Bourguignon, J. (1991). Comparison of the behavioural effects of an adenosine A_1/A_2-receptor antagonist, CGS 15943A, and an A_1-selective antagonist, DPCPX. *Psychopharmacology* **103**: 541–4.

Griffiths, R.R. and Woodson, P.P. (1988). Caffeine physical dependence: a review of human and laboratory animal studies. *Psychopharmacology* **94**: 437–51.

Griffiths, R.R., Evans, S.M., Heisman, S.J., Preston, K.L., Sannerud, C.A., Wolf, B. and Woodson, P.P. (1990). Low-dose caffeine discrimination in humans. *Journal of Pharmacology and Experimental Therapeutics* **252**: 970–8.

Heistad, D.D., Marcus, M.L., Gourley, J.K. and Busija, D.W. (1981). Effect of adenosine and dipyridamole on cerebral blood flow. *American Journal of Physiology* **240**: H775–H780.

Hirsh, K. (1984). Central nervous system pharmacology of the dietary methylxanthines. In *The Methylxanthine Beverages and Foods: Chemistry, Consumption, and Health Effects*, edited by G.A. Spiller. New York: Allan R. Liss, Inc.

Holtzman, S.G. (1990). Caffeine as a model drug of abuse. *Trends in Pharmacological Sciences* **II**(9): 355–6.

Horne, J.A. and Ostberg, O. (1976). A self-assessment questionnaire to determine morningness–eveningness in human circadian rhythms. *International Journal of Chronobiology* **4**: 97–110.

Institute of Food Technologists' Expert Panel on Food Safety & Nutrition (1987). *Evaluation of Caffeine Safety*. Chicago: Institute of Food Technologists.

Johnson, R.F. (in press). Rifle-firing simulation: Effects of mood, heat and medications on marksmanship. In Proceedings of the 33rd Annual Conference of the Military Testing Association.

Johnson, L.C., Spinweber, C.L. and Gomez, S.Z. (1990). Benzodiazepines and caffeine: effect on daytime sleepiness, performance, and mood. *Psychopharmacology* **101**: 160–7.

Kuznicki, J.T. and Turner, L.S. (1986). The effects of caffeine on caffeine users and non-users. *Physiology and Behavior* **37**: 397–408.

Leathwood, P. and Pollet, P. (1982). Diet-induced mood changes in normal populations. *Journal of Psychiatric Research* **17**: 147–54.

Lee, M.A., Cameron, O.G. and Greden, J.F. (1985). Anxiety and caffeine consumption in people with anxiety disorders. *Psychiatric Research* **15**: 211–17.

Levy, M. and Zylber-Katz, E. (1983). Caffeine metabolism and coffee-attributed sleep disturbances. *Clinical Pharmacology and Therapeutics* **33**(6): 770–5.

Lieberman, H.R. (1987). The behavioral effects of foods. In *Chemical Composition and Sensory Properties of Foods and their Influence on Nutrition*, edited by J. Solms, D.A. Booth, R.M. Pangborn and O. Raunhardt. New York: Academic Press.

Lieberman, H.R. (1988). Beneficial effects of caffeine. In *Twelfth International Scientific Colloquium on Coffee*. Paris: ASIC.

Lieberman, H.R., Spring, B. and Garfield, G.S. (1986). The behavioral effects of food constituents: strategies used in studies of amino acids, protein, carbohydrates and caffeine. *Diet and Behavior: A Multidisciplinary Evaluation, Nutrition Reviews* **44** (supplement): 61–70.

Lieberman, H.R., Wurtman, R.J., Emde, G.G., Roberts, C. and Coviella, I.L.G. (1987a). The effects of low doses of caffeine on human performance and mood. *Psychopharmacology* **92**: 308–12.

Lieberman, H.R., Wurtman, R.J., Emde, G.G. and Coviella, I.L.G. (1987b). The effects of caffeine and aspirin on mood and performance. *Journal of Clinical Psychopharmacology* **7**(5): 315–20.

Lieberman, H.R., Gabrieli, J.D.E., Nader, T. and Wurtman, R.J. (submitted). Changes in mood, performance and memory induced by moderate doses of caffeine.

Loke, W.H. (1988). Effects of caffeine on mood and memory. *Physiology and Behavior* **44**: 367–72.

Loke, W.H. and Meliska, C.J. (1984). Effects of caffeine use and ingestion on a protracted visual vigilance task. *Psychopharmacology* **84**: 54–7.

Loke, W.H., Hinrichs, J.V. and Ghoneim, M.M. (1985). Caffeine and diazepam: Separate and combined effects on mood, memory, and psychomotor performance. *Psychopharmacology* **87**: 344–50.

McNair, D.M., Lorr, M. and Droppleman, L.F. (1971). *Profile of Mood States Manual*. San Diego: Educational and Industrial Testing Service.

National Research Council (1977). *Estimating Distribution of Daily Intakes of Caffeine. Committee on GRAS List Survey, Phase III*. Food and Nutrition Board, Division of Biological Sciences, Assembly of Life Sciences, National Research Council, National Academy of Sciences, Washington, DC.

Rall, T.W. (1980). Central nervous system stimulants. The xanthines. In *The Pharmacological Basis of Therapeutics* (6th edn), edited by A.G. Gillman, L. Goodman and A. Gilman. New York: Macmillan.

Rall, T.W. (1982). Evolution of the mechanism of action of methylxanthines: From calcium mobilizers to antagonists of adenosine receptors. *Pharmacologist* **24**: 277–87.

Rapoport, J.L., Berg, C.J., Ismond, D.R., Zahn, T.P. and Neims, A. (1984). Behavioral effects of caffeine in children. *Archives of General Psychiatry*, **41**: 1073–9.

Regina, E.G., Smith, G.M., Keiper, C.G. and McKelvey, R.K. (1974). Effects of caffeine on alertness in simulated automobile driving. *Journal of Applied Psychology* **59**: 483–9.

Revelle, W., Humphreys, M.S., Simon, L. and Gilliland, K. (1980). The interactive effect of personality, time of day, and caffeine: a test of the arousal model. *Journal of Experimental Psychology* **109**: 1–31.

Revelle, W., Anderson, K.J. and Humphreys, M.S. (1987). Empirical tests and theoretical extensions of arousal-based theories of personality. In *Personality Dimensions and Arousal*, edited by J. Strelau and H.J. Eysenck. London: Plenum Press.

Roache, J.D. and Griffiths, R.R. (1987). Interactions of diazepam and caffeine: behavioral and subjective dose effects in humans. *Pharmacology, Biochemistry and Behavior* **26**: 801–12.

Roberts, H.R. and Barone, J.J. (1983). Biological effects of caffeine: history and use. *Food Technology* **37**: 32–9.

Sawyer, D.A., Julia, H.L. and Turin, A.C. (1982). Caffeine and human behavior: arousal, anxiety, and performance effects. *Journal of Behavioral Medicine* **5**: 415–39.

Smith, D.L., Tong, J.E. and Leigh, G. (1977). Combined effects of tobacco and caffeine on the components of choice reaction time, heart rate, and hand steadiness. *Perceptual Motor Skills* **45**: 635–9.

Snyder, S.H. (1984). Adenosine as a mediator of the behavioral effects of xanthines. In *Caffeine*, edited by P.B. Dews. New York: Springer.

Snyder, S.H., Katims, J.J., Annau, Z., Bruns, R.F. and Daly, J.W. (1981). Adenosine receptors and behavioral actions of methylxanthines. *Proceedings of the National Academy of Science* **78**: 3260–4.

Sobotka, T.J. (1989). Neurobehavioral effects of prenatal caffeine. *Annals of the New York Academy of Sciences* **562**: 327–39.

Svensson, E., Persson, L. and Sjoberg, L. (1980). Mood effects of diazepam and caffeine. *Psychopharmacology* **67**: 73–80.

Swift, C.G. and Tiplady, B. (1988). The effect of age on the response to caffeine. *Psychopharmacology* **94**: 29–31.

Tannahill, R. (1989). *Food in History*. New York: Crown Publishers.

Von Borstel, R.W. (1983). Metabolism. *Food Technology* **37**(9): 40–6.

Walsh, J.K., Muehlbach, M.J., Humm, T.M., Dickins, Q.S., Sugerman, J.L. and Schweitzer, P.K. (1990). Effect of caffeine on physiological sleep tendency and ability to sustain wakefulness at night. *Psychopharmacology* **101**: 271–3.

Wilkinson, R.T. (1970). Methods for research on sleep deprivation and sleep function. In *Sleep and Dreaming*, edited by E. Hartmann. Boston: Little, Brown.

Witkin, H.A., Dyk, R.B., Faterson, H.F., Goodenough, D.R. and Karp, S.A. (1962). *Psychological Differentiation*. New York: Wiley.

4

The Effects of Alcohol on Performance

F. FINNIGAN & R. HAMMERSLEY

INTRODUCTION

The literature on the effects of alcohol on performance is so diverse that for caution's sake one can only conclude that *any* demanding performance may be impaired after any amount of alcohol. But studies are so varied and so often methodologically inadequate that it is impossible to specify exactly when, how and why performance will be impaired.

This review considers the acute effects of alcohol on human performance, concentrating on the literature of 1980–1991. Its orientation is cognitive rather than clinical or social. For brevity, it does not consider interactions between alcohol and other drugs, nor studies which examine the effects of alcohol on judgements about oneself, on actual (or judged) social interactions, or on emotional competence. Also excluded are studies of the effects of chronic alcohol use, for few of these have directly studied performance in an adequate fashion.

Prior to reviewing the literature in detail, it is necessary to be aware of some of the inconsistencies and difficulties which beset it. These difficulties are sufficiently extensive that it cannot be guaranteed that particular findings will generalize to other conditions. Space prevents a full study-by-study critique of methodological problems, although readers will be notified of the more glaring defects.

The authors are equally responsible for the content of this chapter. We are grateful to the Alcohol Education and Research Council for their funding of our research related to this chapter and to Keith Millar for his helpful advice and comments.

Modern research on the effects of alcohol is best characterized as being ambitious rather than rigorous. Many studies 'test' elaborate hypotheses about the cognitive and biological processes underlying the effects of alchohol while using tasks which have never been validated as acceptable measures of any aspect of performance. Furthermore, one must wonder about the fate of studies or measures of performance which completely fail to show significant effects of alcohol. One suspects that these are under-reported, especially as the consensus belief appears to be that alcohol impairs performance. We infer this belief because studies which use multiple tests of performance and only find effects of alcohol on one test, or even only on one aspect of one test, are usually written up as demonstrations of the adverse effects of alcohol; they might with equal justification be reported as evidence that alcohol is relatively benign. As will be seen, while ample evidence exists that alcohol is capable of impairing performance, even at low doses, it is premature to assume that it invariably does so.

This review concentrates on studies since 1980. Several reviews of earlier studies exist (Attwood *et al.*, 1980; Carpenter, 1962; Collins and Chiles, 1980; Levine *et al.*, 1975; Wait *et al.*, 1982) and a full review would exceed the space available here. In general, earlier studies are no more methodologically adequate than those reviewed here.

METHODOLOGICAL PROBLEMS

The measurement of alcohol dose

Alcohol can be administered as: (1) a fixed dose; (2) a dose of grams per kilogram of bodyweight, (3) a dose of grams per kilogram of lean body weight, which requires estimation of body fat, or (4) a dose of millilitres per litre of body water, which requires estimation of body water (Watson *et al.*, 1981). Dose can be reported as grams per kilogram, millilitres per kilogram of absolute alcohol, or $ml\,kg^{-1}$ of the alcoholic drink (usually vodka) administered. Not all studies then measure achieved blood alcohol (or breath alcohol, which is an acceptable, easier procedure). Not doing so risks achieved blood alcohol levels (BAL) which are markedly different from those intended, due to individual differences, subjects' failure to comply with fasting instructions and variations in the metabolism of alcohol (relevant literature is reviewed below). In studies with small numbers of subjects, uncontrolled variations in achieved blood alcohol may affect outcome significantly.

Studies which do measure blood or breath alcohol express their findings in a diversity of units, the most common of which is grams of absolute alcohol per some volume of blood, but measures of millilitres of absolute alcohol per volume of blood are also reported, as are various other weight/volume ratios. While it is mathematically trivial to translate one unit into another, this problem makes the immediate comparison of the results of different studies unnecessarily difficult. There is a need for alcohol research to adopt standards in these regards.

Where possible we have converted all doses of alcohol to grams of absolute alcohol per kilogram of body weight, and all measures of blood and breath alcohol to mg% (mg of alcohol per 100 ml of blood, although different authors use the % symbol differently). In converting from volume to weight, we have assumed that a millilitre of alcohol weighs 0.8 mg.

A further problem is that the observed effects of alcohol may be due in part to placebo or expectancy effects. Because of the proprioceptive changes caused by alcohol ingestion, it is difficult to keep subjects entirely blind concerning whether they are receiving alcohol or not, nonetheless non-blind conditions of testing should not be used except for special reasons. Subjects may not be blind where the alcohol dose is administered differently from the placebo, is detectable by sight, taste or smell alone, or alcohol and placebo are presented in a fixed order. Although subjects may detect the immediate physiological changes produced by alcohol ingestion, at least placebo subjects may also believe that they are drinking alcohol, making placebo and alcohol conditions as nearly comparable as possible.

Measurement over time

The preceding problems are compounded by the failure of many studies of performance to consider the dynamics of alcohol metabolism. In general, higher doses lead to higher blood alcohol levels for longer. Testing performance at a fixed time after alcohol consumption will not give results which necessarily represent performance over the period of hours when alcohol can affect performance. For example, after twenty minutes many subjects may have metabolized all of a small dose, so their performance may be unimpaired relative to a placebo group. With a higher dose, many subjects may not yet have peaked at twenty minutes, so their performance may also be unimpaired, but may nonetheless be impaired later on. Practice effects may also occur, so that subjects will become less impaired with time; alternatively, fatigue effects may occur, so that subjects may become more impaired with time.

Given the substantial practical importance which is attached to the effects of alcohol on performance, it is vital that these effects be studied over time. Demonstrating an impairment, or lack thereof, at a single point in time provides little information about the practical magnitude of that impairment: it might be the time when performance after alcohol was worst or best. And, because metabolism varies with dose and stomach contents, it is not possible to compare studies which have used different delays before testing (Lin *et al.*, 1976; Sedman *et al.*, 1976).

Tests of performance

The effects of alcohol most frequently have been studied on tracking, choice reaction time, complex reaction time, signal detection, memory, simulations of driving, divided attention tasks and decision-making tasks. The particular versions of these tasks used vary widely between studies, and a wide variety of other tasks have been used which are unique to particular studies. At worst, the tasks used seem to have sprung from the mind of Heath Robinson. The best standard in the literature seems to be that if one can cite a study where a task was used before (even for an entirely different purpose), then it can be used again. This is not good enough.

Many studies measure performance on more than one task and it is common for alcohol to affect performance on one task but not on another. When alcohol does not affect performance it is often difficult to ascertain whether this is because of a genuine null-effect or because the particular version of the particular task was insufficiently sensitive to the effects of alcohol. Ideally, the sensitivity of the task should be known, but sometimes the specific task version is devised for the specific experiment. More often, the task was originally designed for another purpose, such as neurological assessment or the measurement of individual differences. Normative data on the sensitivity of tasks to the effects of psychoactive drugs are sadly lacking.

Even assuming that most tasks have been adequately sensitive, the problem remains that every study (with the exception of a few series of experiments by the same researchers) uses a unique configuration of tasks and it is usually conceivable that results will only poorly transfer to other designs. Effects, such as fatigue, may differ markedly depending upon the set of tasks used.

Multiple comparisons

Studies that use multiple tests often use multiple univariate statistics to compare conditions without any correction for multiple comparisons. Thus impairment after alcohol may be found on one or two measures, but not found on several others. In the absence of a coherent theory to predict when impairment should or should not be found, a 'significant' difference on one or two measures out of several may be due to chance alone. Indeed, if a large number of tests have been used then there is a high probability of the vague hypothesis that alcohol impairs some aspect of performance being supported by chance alone. It may be the case, nonetheless, that alcohol selectively affects some aspects of performance, but demonstrating this convincingly is difficult.

Basic experimental design

Because of methodological and ethical considerations, running a subject in a study of the effects of alcohol is a laborious business. Many studies have used within-subjects designs and some, whether within- or between-subjects, have used only small numbers of subjects. While the data to allow accurate power calculations are not available, in preparing for our own research we concluded that the effects of small doses of alcohol (achieved BAL of < 80 mg%) on performance are probably difficult to detect with less than fifteen subjects.

There appear to be substantial individual variations in the metabolism of alcohol which are likely to affect performance. Performance itself is affected by individual differences. For both these reasons, the reliability and generality of many studies' findings is questionable (see below). In particular, the results of studies which do not both control for between-subject variations in baseline performance and use placebo conditions are difficult to interpret. Deviations from baseline alone may be due to practice or fatigue effects, especially in cross-over trials. In the absence of baseline measures, differences between placebo and alcohol may be due to accidental individual variations between groups.

Ecological validity

Alcohol is the most widely used drug in this society and from an early age people are given a great deal of knowledge about alcohol (e.g. Aitken *et al.*, 1988). Also, unlike prescription drugs, alcohol ingestion is under fairly precise personal control. Most drinkers drink gradually, to achieve and maintain a desired level of subjective intoxication, and they can judge intake moderately accurately (Russ *et al.*, 1986). They may also plan their alcohol ingestion to avoid conflicts with demanding tasks. On the other hand, they may sometimes drink to reduce the stress of demanding tasks (e.g. Young *et al.*, 1990). Additionally, alcohol is often drunk with food and taken only rarely after hours of fasting (see below). Lastly, behaviour after alcohol is saturated with social meaning: drinkers being likely to engage in qualitatively different behaviours, perhaps becoming rowdy or more extravert (e.g. MacAndrew and Edgerton, 1969). The pharmacological model of drug action, where alcohol simply affects normal behaviour, may be of little relevance to natural drinking.

In contrast, in the laboratory the pharmacological model is imposed on subjects, who cannot tell what they have drunk, have no control over the dose they ingest, have to drink alcohol in a fixed time period, are usually fasted prior to the alcohol dose and are then obliged to engage in tests of performance, whether they like it or not. Those tests are relatively meaningless activities. One can only speculate as to the relevance of performance under such conditions for everyday life. Natural intoxication may lead to more impairment, less impairment or different impairments.

CONSEQUENCES OF METHODOLOGICAL PROBLEMS

The problems outlined so far make an objective review of the literature difficult. Any attempt at meta-analysis or tabulation of different studies' findings is restricted by the fact that most studies are unique in terms of at least one of: (1) alcohol dosage, (2) methodology of testing, and (3) the specific tests of performance used. Thus, there is no good reason to expect that different studies should give consistent results. Furthermore, as many studies are small, and/or use within-subjects designs, and/or use uncorrected multiple univariate comparisons, their results may be unreliable anyway. We will not discuss methodology in detail except where it is pertinent to explaining conflicting or unusual findings. We have also chosen to review by task rather than by study. The disadvantage is a certain amount of redundancy and our neglecting the problem of interactions between tasks; the advantage is some semblance of consistent findings.

At minimum, future studies should encompass the following:

1. Take baseline measures of performance to allow for individual differences and practice effects.
2. Use between-subjects designs despite the psychopharmacological tradition of using within-subjects designs.
3. Use sufficient numbers of subjects. We suggest at least 15 per cell, or, preferably, the use of adequate statistical power estimation based on previous research.
4. Ensure, in so far as this is possible, that subjects cannot tell when they are consuming alcohol.
5. Include placebo alcohol conditions in the design.

Table 4.1 summarizes the basic design of most of the studies to be reviewed here. Excluded are studies purely of the chronic effects of alcohol abuse and studies of expectancies which ignore performance. The last column in the table rates the overall adequacy of the research design. Studies score 1 point for each use of: using baseline measures, between-subjects designs, fifteen or more subjects, using blind administration of alcohol and including placebo conditions. They can score 0.5 for seeming to get any of these points partly correct. Figure 4.1 summarizes how the studies rated. It can be seen that only 23 per cent rate 5. Studies which score 2 or less (23 per cent) are inadequate as studies of the effects of alcohol on performance, while studies which score 3 or 4 (45 per cent) should be interpreted with caution. Six studies are not rated because the design criteria used were inappropriate for their aims.

Table 4.1 Basic methodological adequacy of studies of the effects of alcohol on performance 1980–1991

Authors	Baseline measures used?	Design	N	Blind administration of alcohol	Placebo?	Rating (max. = 5)
Attwood et al., 1980	Yes, but discarded in analysis	Randomized cross-over	6	Not described	Yes	2
Baker et al., 1985	Yes	Randomized cross-over	31	Yes	Yes	4
Baylor et al., 1989	Controlled for practice	Fixed cross-over	5	Probably not	Yes	2
Beirness and Vogel-Sprott, 1984	Controlled for practice	Between-subjects	24	Yes, but not exactly	Yes	4
Bowden et al., 1988	No	Correlational study	40	Self-reported consumption	Not relevant	—
Breckenridge and Berger, 1990	Yes	Between-subjects	60	Yes	Yes	5
Brewer and Sandow, 1980	Not relevant	Real accident data	403	Not relevant	Yes	—
Collins and Chiles, 1980	No	Randomized cross-over	11	Yes	Yes	2
Connors and Maisto, 1980	Yes	Between-subjects	64	Yes	Yes	5
Fagan et al., 1987	Yes	Randomized cross-over	8	Yes	Yes	3
Farrimond, 1990	Yes	Within- and between-subjects	21	Not described	Yes	4
Golby, 1989	'Familiarization' but no baseline	Within-subjects, order unclear	48	Yes, but perhaps order cues	Yes	3
Gustafson, 1986a	No	Fixed cross-over	11	Yes	Yes	2
Gustafson, 1986b	No	Fixed cross-over	6	Yes, but order cues	Yes	2.5
Hockey et al., 1981	Subjects matched on baseline ability	Between-subjects	20	Yes	Yes	5
Jones and Jones, 1980	Yes	Between-subjects	32	No	No	3
Kent et al., 1986	Practice but no baseline	Randomized cross-over	12	Yes, but perhaps order cues (only two conditions)	Yes	1.5
Laberg and Löberg, 1989	Yes	Randomized cross-over	30	Yes (but expectancies manipulated)	Yes	4
Landauer and Howat, 1982	No	Randomized cross-over	26	Yes, probably	Yes	4
Lawrence et al., 1983	Practice but no baseline	Between-subjects, but all took alcohol	20	Not relevant	No	2

Table 4.1—continued

Authors	Baseline measures used?	Design	N	Blind administration of alcohol	Placebo?	Rating (max. = 5)
Lipscomb and Nathan, 1980	Yes	Within subjects there were 3 training sessions (aim was to compare different subject groups)	24	Yes	No	4
Lipscomb et al., 1980	Yes	Between-subjects	32	Yes	No	4
Linnoila et al., 1980	Practice, no correction for baseline	Randomized cross-over	20	Yes	Yes	4.5
MacCarthy and Tong, 1980	No	'Incomplete' within-subjects	14	Yes	Yes	2
McMillen and Wells-Parker, 1987	Yes	Between-subjects	39	Yes	Yes	5
McMillen et al., 1989	No	Between-subjects	96	Yes	Yes	4
McNamee et al., 1980	No	Within-subjects	17	Yes	Yes	3
Maylor and Rabbitt, 1987a	No	Randomized cross-over	40	Yes, but order cues	Yes	3.5
Maylor and Rabbitt, 1987b	No (but the study is of practice)	Within/between (several sessions varied between groups)	80	Yes	Yes	5
Maylor and Rabbitt, 1988	No (as for Maylor and Rabbitt, 1987b)	Within/between	80	Yes	Yes	5
Maylor et al., 1987	No	Randomized cross-over	36	No control of taste or smell cues	Yes	2
Maylor et al., 1989	No (as for Maylor and Rabbitt, 1987b)	Between	20	Yes	Yes	5
Maylor et al., 1990	No (as for Maylor and Rabbitt, 1987b)	Within/between	24	Yes	Yes	5
Millar et al., 1987	Yes	Between-subjects	36	Yes	Yes	5
Millar et al., 1992	Yes	Between-subjects	133	Yes	Yes	5

Study		Design	N	Control of cues		Rating
Mills and Bisgrove, 1983a	Yes	Randomized cross-over	24	No control of smell or taste cues	Yes	3
Mills and Bisgrove, 1983b	Yes	Randomized cross-over	40	Yes	Yes	4
McKinley et al., 1989	No	Between-subjects	88	No	Yes	3
McMillen and Wells-Parker, 1987	Yes	Between-subjects	39	Yes	Yes	5
McMillen et al., 1989	No	Between-subjects	96	Yes	Yes	4
Minocha et al., 1985	Yes	Within-subjects, not randomized	6	Yes	No	2
Misawa et al., 1983	Yes	Within-subjects	5	??	No	1–2
Mongrain and Standing, 1989	No	Between-subjects	72	Yes	Yes	4
Morrow et al., 1990	No	Partially randomized cross-over	14	Yes	Yes	2
Moskowitz et al., 1985	Yes	Within-subjects, probably randomized cross-over	10	Yes	Yes	3
Mueller et al., 1983	No (but perhaps not applicable)	Between-subjects	36	Yes	Yes	4.5
Niaura et al., 1987	Yes	Between-subjects (male vs female)	24	Probably (only one dose administered)	No	3.5
Nelson et al., 1986	No	Between-subjects	160	Yes	Yes	4
O'Malley and Maisto, 1984	Yes	Between-subjects	48	Yes	Yes	5
Parker et al., 1980a	Yes	Randomized cross-over	16	Yes but order cues	Yes	4
Parker et al., 1980b	Not relevant	Correlational	45	Not relevant	–	–
Parker et al., 1981	No	Randomized cross-over	16	Yes	Yes	4
Parker et al., 1983	Not relevant	Correlational	1367	Not relevant	–	–
Patel, 1988	No	Between-subjects	128	Probably	Yes	5
Parker and Noble, 1980	Not relevant	Correlational	102	Not relevant	–	–
Pollock et al., 1986	No	Between-subjects (sons of alcoholics vs normals)	71	No	No	2
Read and Yuille, in press	Not applicable	Between-subjects	142	Yes	Yes	5
Rohrbaugh et al., 1988	Practice, no baseline	Randomized cross-over	12	Yes	Yes	2.5

Table 4.1—continued

Authors	Baseline measures used?	Design	N	Blind administration of alcohol	Placebo?	Rating (max. = 5)
Ross and Pihl, 1988	No	Between-subjects	87	Yes	Yes	4
Schandler et al., 1984	No	Between-subjects	32	Yes	Yes	4
Shapiro and Nathan, 1986	Yes	Between-subjects	16	Yes	Yes	5
Taberner, 1980	Yes	Between-subjects	158	Yes	Maybe	4.5
Thomson and Newlin, 1988	No	Fixed cross-over	50	No	No	1
Tucker and Vuchinich, 1983	Yes	Between-subjects	48	Yes	Yes	5
Wait et al., 1982	Yes	Between-subjects	40	Not relevant	No	3
Wilson et al., 1984	Yes	Between-subjects	58	Yes, probably	Yes	5
Williams and Skinner, 1990	Not relevant	Between-subjects	38	Not relevant	–	–
Williams et al., 1981	No	Between-subjects	42	Yes	Yes	4
Yesavage and Leirer, 1986	No	Randomized cross-over	10	No (but not feasible)	No	2
Young and Pihl, 1982	Yes	Between-subjects	48	No	No	3

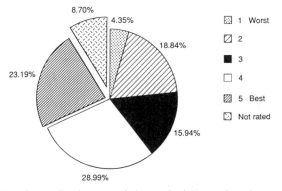

Figure 4.1 Rated overall adequacy of the methodology of studies summarized in Table 4.1.

It is worth looking at the most common defects of the studies shown in Table 4.1. Most studies (78 per cent) had at least fifteen subjects. However, the basic design varied, as shown in Figure 4.2. Half the studies used between-subjects designs. Next most popular were randomized cross-over designs, or at least quasi-randomized cross-over designs. Although these have problems (Millar, 1983), they are at least the best within-subjects design one can have. Fixed cross-over designs (9 per cent of the studies reviewed) are particularly undesirable because: (1) they confound practice with alcohol condition, and (2) when only either one dose of alcohol or placebo is administered subjects may not be blind to the nature of the second dose because they may be able to infer that it is 'the other one'. A similar problem may occur for the final testing session even when there are more conditions

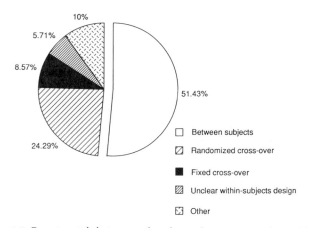

Figure 4.2 Experimental designs used in the studies summarized in Table 4.1.

in the design. A further 6 per cent of studies used some sort of within-subjects design, but it was not clearly described in the paper. Lastly, the 'other' category in Figure 4.2 includes both adequate and inadequate unusual designs.

Figure 4.3 shows methods of administering alcohol. Fifty-seven per cent administered alcohol in a blind fashion, including placebo conditions. An additional 16 per cent may not have been fully blind either because taste and smell cues were inadequately controlled or because of fixed cross-over designs. A further 13 per cent of studies should have used blind and placebo administration, but did not. Lastly, the design of 14 per cent of studies meant that it may not have mattered that subjects knew what they were drinking.

As shown in Figure 4.4, only 40 per cent of studies used baseline data. A further 10 per cent allowed subjects to practise the tests of performance before alcohol was administered, but 34 per cent only began testing after alcohol had been ingested. With such procedures, apparent effects of alcohol treatment may be due to pre-existing differences between subjects. The remainder (16 per cent) include studies which explicitly study the relationship between alcohol and practice, notably those by Maylor and colleagues (Maylor and Rabbitt, 1987a, 1987b, 1988; Maylor et al., 1987; Maylor et al., 1989, 1990).

One might hope that these methodological defects were becoming less common across the decade, or were restricted to some less stringent journals. As far as we could ascertain, this was not the case. Only about half the studies were adequate on each aspect of method reviewed, and only a quarter were fully adequate. Studies of the effects of alcohol which violate the simple rules we have laid out ought not to be published.

In addition to the five measures listed above, studies should also ideally:

1. Measure achieved blood or breath alcohol.
2. Measure performance and BAL (blood alcohol level) over time.
3. Show some agreement about which measures of psychomotor performance are 'fundamental' for alcohol research. (This would be helpful, although unlikely.)

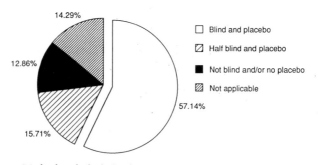

Figure 4.3 Methods of alcohol administration used in the studies summarized in Table 4.1.

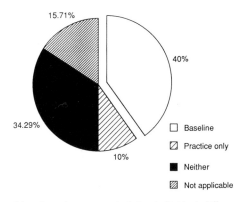

Figure 4.4 Use of baseline data to control for individual differences in the studies summarized in Table 4.1.

4. Following on from (3), more statistical sophistication should be employed in interpreting results.
5. Some study of the relevance of laboratory alcohol research for performance in everyday life would be welcome. In particular, we need to know the extent to which people can and do control their dose and hence their impairment.

It is perhaps premature to specify how to do any of these things.

MODELS OF THE PSYCHOPHARMACOLOGY OF ALCOHOL

Alcohol has quite straightforward effects on the CNS, which can provide a model of the effects which alcohol should have on performance. Alcohol is a general CNS depressant. As dose increases, so increasingly primitive brain functions are depressed (Tiplady, 1991). Firstly, higher cortical functions, such as planning, are likely to suffer, then perception and fine motor control, then memory and sensation, and finally breathing and other automatic functions. But, this general depressant function should not be confused with disinhibition: the folk psychology idea that alcohol uncovers 'more primitive' behaviours like violence. Alcohol is disinhibiting only in the sense that it initially acts as a general relaxant—which may improve performance among subjects who are aroused or anxious; it may also impair long-term planning and attention and, depending upon the precise state of the CNS, may increase some activities and decrease others (Tiplady, 1991). In other words, after a drink people may behave differently, perhaps speaking and acting without worrying as much as usual about the possible long-term consequences of their behaviour.

Additionally, they may ignore information, such as non-verbal signals that they are being boring or annoying, to which they would normally attend. But alcohol has no selective capacity to impair some CNS functions without impairing others. Thus, the simplest model of the effects of alcohol is 'the higher the dose the larger the impairment'.

Alcohol most impairs complex tasks

In practice, and as one would expect from the nature of the CNS, alcohol frequently appears to affect some tasks and not others. Three hypotheses have been proposed in this regard. Firstly, perhaps alcohol tends to have most impact on complex cognitive functions, such as decision-making, which should be more impaired than simpler functions, such as movement time (e.g. Baylor *et al.*, 1989; Landauer and Howat, 1982). A model of this is shown in Figure 4.5. Basically, the more performance there is to impair, the more impaired performance should be. To illustrate, imagine a drunk musician. She should be able to tap a simple rhythm, but be incapable of playing her second violin part along with the orchestra.

Alcohol most impairs simple tasks

Or, second, perhaps alcohol tends to have most impact on primitive psychological functions, which means that performance of complex tasks will

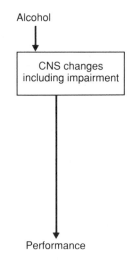

Figure 4.5 Alcohol impairs performance: the simplest model of the relationship.

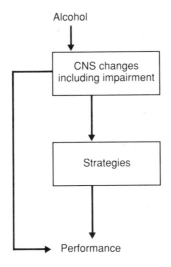

Figure 4.6 The alcohol performance relationship is mediated by strategy.

tend to be less impaired than performance of simple tasks (e.g. Moskowitz *et al.*, 1985). For, in complex tasks subjects may be able to adopt strategies to compensate for their impairment. A model of this is shown in Figure 4.6. Our drunk violinist may be impaired in tapping a simple rhythm but nonetheless capable of covering up her impairment in the orchestra, perhaps because her part is over-learned, or perhaps because her fellow musicians give her redundant rhythm cues, or perhaps even because she mimes the tricky bits without the conductor noticing.

The studies reviewed have found some evidence for both hypotheses. The explanation of this is that both hypotheses have confused *simple tasks* with *simple neuropsychological routines*. A conceptually simple task, say reaction time, is not necessarily simple in terms of the neuropsychological processing required. Indeed, it is remarkably difficult to find a psychomotor task which cannot be influenced by complex cognitive factors, such as expectancy. The distinction between simple and complex tasks is not a viable one. Instead, as with the study of brain damage, one needs to examine the pattern of deficit across a range of tasks before drawing conclusions (Maylor *et al.*, 1987).

Alcohol impairment is mediated by psychological factors

Thirdly, then, being able to compensate for an impairment and maintain performance does not mean that the basic, primitive impairment had vanished. In this regard, Maylor and Rabbitt (1987a, 1988; Maylor *et al.*, 1989) have shown that alcohol slows rate of processing, independently of practice or cognitive judgements and control over performance.

Steele and Josephs (1990) have argued that the seeming diversity of the social and cognitive effects of alcohol can be explained by 'alcohol myopia', which is the tendency for people to attend more to immediate, proximal information after imbibing alcohol and less to information distant in space, time or concept. While Steele and Josephs provide evidence that myopia is a common strategy for dealing with alcohol impairment, they have not demonstrated that other strategies, such as attending more to distal information and neglecting proximal information, are impossible. Thus myopia could just be a common way of coping with a general impairment. This strategy may not be special to alcohol nor directly caused by alcohol's specific neuro-psychological impact. In our opinion, this theory is too specific for the data available.

More generally, the basic impairment in neurological function caused by alcohol may show up in some tasks and not others, but there is not a clear taxonomy of tasks affected by alcohol and tasks not affected. In principle, it is likely that the effects of alcohol on performance will be mediated by cognitive and learning factors, but such factors will not necessarily have an effect on or will affect only tasks which appear to be cognitive. If it is measured accurately enough, the drunk violinist's timing will be impaired in both the tapping task and orchestral performance. It will depend upon her particular skills whether this deficit is noticeable or not.

This leads to the more complicated model shown in Fig. 4.7. According to this, performance after alcohol is much less predictable. If the drunk violinist

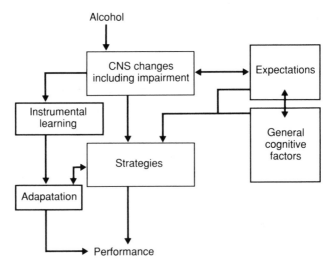

Figure 4.7 The effects of alcohol on performance depend upon past experience and current cognitive state.

expects to be impaired after alcohol, has not learned how to perform after alcohol and does not change strategy, then she is likely to be impaired on both tapping and her orchestral performance. But if her intoxication, expectations, learning and strategy are not all in concordance, then her performance may be impaired, unimpaired or perhaps even improved by alcohol. Performance after alcohol has as much to do with the general state of the person as with the particular effects of alcohol.

BASIC ACUTE EFFECTS

In this section we concentrate on the basic effects of alcohol, ignoring mediators of those effects. The complexities of studies cited here will be reviewed further in later sections. Where we quote descriptions of particular tasks without explanation, the paper reviewed provides no further explanation.

Motor skills

TRACKING

In tracking tasks, subjects are required to move some kind of pointer, keeping track of some kind of moving target, or tracing some kind of maze. The cognitive demands of different tracking tasks vary considerably in both overall difficulty and in the resources demanded by the task. For example, some tracking tasks require a steady hand, others do not. Also, some tracking tasks are undertaken in conjunction with a secondary reaction time task (such secondary tasks are reviewed below). Nonetheless, we have classified tracking as a motor skill because that is how many of the studies which use a tracking task classify it. Popular wisdom is that: (1) tracking is one of the skills involved in driving a car, and (2) alcohol impairs tracking.

Connors and Maisto (1980) found a significant difference on 'simple pursuit rotor tracking' between placebo conditions and conditions where subjects had achieved 40 mg% alcohol on the ascending limb of the blood alcohol curve.

Beirness and Vogel-Sprott (1984) also studied tracking after alcohol, using a 'Tracometer' although not using placebo control conditions. Tracking was impaired nonetheless.

Niaura *et al.* (1987) examined gender differences in acute response to alcohol. Subjects' tracking performance was more impaired when BAL was increasing towards peak than when it was decreasing after peak. The authors term this finding 'acute recovery function', but, in the absence of a control group, the effect may have been an improvement in tracking due to practice, rather than a recovery from the effects of alcohol.

Using a similar tracking task, Wilson et al. (1984), investigating behaviour sensitivity and acute behavioural tolerance to alcohol, administered alcohol to twenty-four pairs of biological brothers and placebo alcohol to a further five pairs. Further details of this study are described below. Subjects receiving alcohol performed less well than placebo subjects for at least 120 minutes after drinking a dose to achieve 100 mg%.

Maylor et al. (1990) studied the effects of practice and alcohol on tracking and simple reaction time, using both dual-task and single-task procedures. Tracking was not affected by alcohol, although performance was improved by practice and reduced by the use of a dual (rather than single) task procedure. Other findings are reviewed below.

Linnoila et al. (1980), in a repeated-measures design, studied the effects of alcohol on performance in two small groups of men, one aged 20–25, the other aged 35–45. Among other tasks reported below, they used a 'subcritical continuous tracking task'. Deviation from target increased with alcohol dose up to 100 mg%, and when the task was made hardest, older subjects performed less well in all conditions including zero alcohol.

Moskowitz et al. (1985), in a within-subjects design ($n = 10$), used a tracking task combined with a visual search task. Scrutiny of the means (no standard deviations are reported) suggests that performance did not differ across placebo and four doses of alcohol (maximum achieving 60 mg%), but results were converted into a single measure of performance for analysis, which found a main effect of alcohol. The combination of small n and five sessions means that sessions cannot have been randomized, so trial effects must contaminate these rather weak findings.

Using a visuo-motor integration task (actually a primitive video tennis game) which they report resembles tracking, Thomson and Newlin (1988) found that alcohol (0.5 g kg^{-1}) increased errors, the largest effect being found when subjects did not expect alcohol.

Turning to maze tracing, Pollock et al. (1986) found that the time to trace a maze and errors both increased after alcohol for up to 118 minutes after drinking a dose which achieved about 35 mg%.

Thus, as in previous research, in six out of nine studies alcohol has been shown to impair tracking in a variety of conditions. It is not possible, however, to infer that higher doses impair tracking more, nor to predict how tracking will be impaired over time. Another problem is that tracking tasks are rarely described in sufficient detail to understand what was actually required of the subject. Different tasks probably make different demands.

CO-ORDINATION

Since 1980 several studies have measured body sway (the extent to which a standing person sways from upright, either with eyes open or eyes closed) and found that alcohol increases body sway (Golby, 1989; Niaura et al., 1988;

Lipscomb and Nathan, 1980; Lipscomb *et al.*, 1980; Mills and Bisgrove, 1983a; O'Malley and Maisto, 1984; Wilson *et al.*, 1984; Shapiro and Nathan, 1986; Fagan *et al.*, 1987), sway increasing with alcohol dose, up to 70 mg% BAL (Lipscomb and Nathan, 1980; Mills and Bisgrove, 1983a; O'Malley and Maisto, 1984). In contrast, Golby (1989) found that sway was increased at 0.5 g kg^{-1}, but decreased to placebo levels at 1.0 g kg^{-1}. But in the within-subjects design used (counterbalancing of conditions is not reported) these differences could be due to practice effects. The effects of alcohol on sway are more obvious with the subject's eyes closed (O'Malley and Maisto, 1984). Subjects with a high tolerance to alcohol sway less (Lipscomb *et al.*, 1980). Somewhat perplexingly, Fagan *et al.* (1987) found no effects of alcohol on sway until $2\frac{1}{2}$ hours after drinking. But this study used only eight subjects and a within-subjects design, so this may have been due to some unusual mixture of practice, fatigue and asymmetrical transfer effects. Measuring body sway is not straightforward and varies considerably from study to study. Also (excepting Lipscomb *et al.*, 1980) none of these studies used baseline measures of sway, which introduces the additional problem of individual variation. Nonetheless, eight out of ten studies found body sway to increase with alcohol, the remaining two being less clear cut.

Other tasks with a component of co-ordination have also been used. Wait *et al.* (1982) studied the effects of alcohol on adaptation to prisms which displaced the field of vision by eleven degrees. Tasks were dart throwing, tracing a mirror image and pointing. Alcohol affected right-hand pointing, increasing the prism-induced rightwards bias compared to baseline and control conditions. Other tasks (including left-hand pointing) were unaffected by alcohol, probably because they were not sufficiently sensitive. The implications of this study are unclear: prismatic adaptation and alcohol make strange bedfellows.

Breckenridge and Berger (1990) used the Purdue pegboard as a measure of fine motor skills and found that performance was reduced after alcohol compared with placebo conditions.

Minocha *et al.* (1985) also used several measures of co-ordination, but in a within-subjects design on six subjects. This and other oddities of their method make their findings uninterpretable. For the record, they found slower pegboard performance after alcohol but no effect on a 'motor speed' task.

Among other tasks reviewed below, Golby (1989) used a soccer slalom test, where subjects had to dribble a ball around a fixed course of parking cones. He found few effects of alcohol, but compared with placebo, at a dose of 0.5 g kg^{-1} subjects completed the slalom faster and after a dose of 1 g kg^{-1} subjects completed the slalom slower than at 0.5 g kg^{-1} but faster than placebo. As reported for body sway, these differences could be due to practice effects. The task is interesting, but the results are difficult to interpret.

Along with body sway, Wilson *et al.* (1984) used other motor tasks including dowel balancing, rail walking and tapping. They first administered a dose achieving about 10 mg% and found deficits on both dowel balancing and rail walking for up to 120 minutes after drinking. When BAL reached half its peak value another half-dose of alcohol was administered. Sixty minutes later, rail walking was still impaired, dowel balancing was not. Tapping was never impaired.

Other studies purporting to measure motor skills have used tasks with an obvious cognitive component, such as reaction time tasks. These are reviewed below. To sum up, alcohol probably increases body sway in a dose-related fashion, but its other effects on co-ordination have yet to be studied adequately.

Simulations of driving

It is widely accepted that the risk of being involved in an automobile accident increases after alcohol, increases dramatically with higher doses, and measures to reduce drinking and driving reduce accident rates (Dunbar, 1985). It should be noted, however, that drinking does not occur randomly and neither do traffic accidents. For example, young males are more likely to drink more and, with or without alcohol, to have an automobile accident. It could be, to an extent, that accidents are a function of the people and settings of high alcohol use tending to be accident-prone for other reasons.

At minimum, the relationship between automobile accidents and alcohol is probably more complex than can be explained by alcohol's impact on simple psychomotor performance. More cognitive/emotional factors, such as risk-taking and para-suicidal behaviour, are probably also important. This said, several studies have examined relatively naturalistic driving behaviour.

McMillen and colleagues (McMillen and Wells-Parker, 1987; McMillen et al., 1989) have examined the impact of personality, expectancy and alcohol on risk-taking in a driving simulation. Findings are reviewed in the appropriate sections. Compared with placebo, there were no effects of alcohol dose on risk-taking, defined by amount of time spent at high speed and number of cars overtaken. Mongrain and Standing (1989), using a similar video game, found, in contrast, an effect of alcohol dose on risk-taking, defined by top speed and number of accidents, but no effects of alcohol dose on driving performance despite an unusually high maximum dose calculated to achieve a BAL of 160 mg% — twice the British legal limit. It has not been demonstrated that performance on a commercial video driving game will transfer to natural driving behaviour and, especially for risk-taking, this seems intrinsically unlikely; video controls are simpler, the action is faster, the visual field to be attended to is much smaller and the real risks are immeasurably less.

Turning to real driving, Brewer and Sandow (1980) examined whether the accident involvement of intoxicated drivers could be attributed to errors involving divided attention. Examining real accidents via witness and driver testimony and other evidence, it was found that drivers with BAL of at least 0.05 g per 100 cm^{-3} (which we think is a misprint because it is equivalent to 500,000 mg%, more probable is 50 mg%) were more likely to have been engaged in some secondary activity at the time of accident than drivers involved in accidents with BAL below that level. This suggests that one source of driving impairment after alcohol is a reduced ability to allocate cognitive resources to more than one task at a time.

Attwood et al. (1980) also examined a real driving task, although using only six male subjects in a within-subjects design. At different sessions subjects ingested placebo alcohol or doses to achieve BAL of 40, 80 and 100 mg%. It is not clear whether subjects were blind to the alcohol dose. Three driving tasks were used: driving at a constant speed, following a car moving at a variable speed and stopping the car. Several measures such as lane position, velocity and brake pressure were recorded for each task. Baseline 'familiarization' data were discarded. There were no differences between conditions on any one measure by t-tests, but this is not suprising as an n of six gives little power. Undeterred, the authors then entered various statistics derived from the measures, such as mean, standard deviation and interquartile range, into a stepwise discriminant function analysis which attempted to discriminate between zero alcohol and the highest dose conditions. For driving at a constant speed, a combination of the interquartile range of lane position, the variance in velocity, the range of steering and the variance in accelerator pressure could significantly discriminate between conditions. As there were eighty-nine variables which could have been entered into this analysis and only six subjects, the reliability of this finding is highly questionable. More doubts are raised by the fact that the equivalent analyses on the other driving tasks gave quite different results, which we see no purpose in detailing. At best, perhaps alcohol increased the variability of various aspects of driving performance. This sort of study would benefit greatly from a between-subjects design, a larger n and planned statistical comparisons. Even if the magnitude of the average driving impairment caused by alcohol is too small to be measured with six subjects, if a large number of people drink and drive then there will still be many excess accidents attributable in part to alcohol.

Excepting Brewer and Sandow (1980), these studies of 'driving' have not been well-designed and one cannot draw useful conclusions from them.

Perception

There have been few studies of the effects of alcohol on purely perceptual tasks. Wait et al.'s (1982) study was reviewed above, but the relevance of prismatic adaptation to everyday perception is not clear.

Farrimond (1990) examined changes in phenomenal regression (the tendency to perceive objects as closer to their 'ideal' shape than they would appear from the retinal image alone) after alcohol. Twenty-one subjects were run in three miniature experiments, one using a between-subjects design and two using within-subjects designs. Baseline measures were taken. It is not clear whether subjects were blind to alcohol administration. Notwithstanding these design problems, alcohol was found to decrease phenomenal regression. If this result applies outside the artificial psychophysical judgement setting used, then after alcohol people might have relative difficulty identifying familiar objects, or tend to over-estimate how far away they were.

McNamee *et al.* (1980) explored the effects of alcohol on various parameters of judgement of velocity in a task where subjects had to estimate the time of arrival of a moving light at a target. A within-subjects design was used, with baseline measures and blind administration of alcohol. No overall main effects of alcohol were found but planned comparisons between alcohol and placebo conditions showed a small reduction in over-estimation of time of arrival; that is, subjects improved slightly after alcohol. MacCarthy and Tong (1980) found a main effect of alcohol on the ability to discriminate between successively paired stimulus velocities. Comparing discrimination of fast versus slow velocity pairs, alcohol led to a larger impairment on the latter, harder, discriminations.

Tucker and Vuchinich (1983) studied the effects of alcohol on the rating of the emotions shown by photographs of faces and found some evidence that alcohol reduced rating accuracy. However, the effects were slight and subjects rated exactly the same set of photographs both before and after alcohol or placebo. Thus, the effect of alcohol might have been due to factors other than the complex information-processing deficit hypothesized by the authors. Among other possibilities, after alcohol subjects may have attended less to the second set of faces, or they may have been less able to use memory for the first session (see below) as an aid to rating.

Baker *et al.* (1985) used a test of tachistoscopic perception along with a battery of other tests reviewed below. Alcohol increased the number of errors in reproducing a simple pattern shown for 5 ms.

Moskowitz *et al.* (1985) (see tracking section), used another tachistoscopic task; letter recognition with backwards masking. Scrutiny of the means again suggests that alcohol did not affect performance. As previously noted, the methodology is unsatisfactory.

Wilson *et al.* (1984), amongst many tests, used the Colorado test of perceptual speed and the ETS card rotations (a test of spatial ability). Alcohol reduced the former twenty minutes after drinking (but not thereafter) and did not affect the latter. The major problem with this study is that it analysed seventeen measures across seven time points and results are reported as 119 univariate analyses. Although motor tasks were consistently impaired over time (see above), these perceptual tasks and the memory and decision-making tasks reported below were only impaired at one of seven time points. Such occasional 'significant' differences may be due to chance alone.

This portion of the literature is incoherent and no conclusions can be drawn.

CRITICAL FLICKER FUSION

The critical flicker fusion (CFF) frequency task assesses the subject's threshold to the fusion of a flickering light source. Low thresholds indicate CNS depression and pre-1980 studies found it to be lowered by alcohol, amongst other drugs (see Hindmarch, 1982). Several recent studies have included the CFF in their test battery (Baker *et al.*, 1985; Fagan *et al.*, 1987; Golby, 1989; Millar *et al.*, 1992; Misawa *et al.*, 1983), but none have found alcohol to affect CFF.

Wilson *et al.* (1984), along with many other tests, used a test of 'time simultaneity' similar to CFF, except that it was the relative onset of two lights which varied. This was affected by alcohol up to eighty minutes after drinking.

Memory

A number of pre-1980 studies have examined the effects of alcohol on memory, tending to find that alcohol has substantial effects on various aspects of memory performance. For example, Moskowitz and Murray (1976) showed that alcohol increased the time taken to transfer information from initial iconic memory to the short-term (working) memory system. Jones and Jones (1977) found a primacy effect in a list-learning paradigm (impaired performance on early and middle items). Weingartner and Murphy (1977) found an impairment of delayed recall.

Hockey *et al.* (1981) examined the effects of alcohol on a task with a component of processing load (subjects had to add a number to a letter of the alphabet and work out what letter the addition corresponded to (e.g. $J + 4 = N$) and processing load increased as the size of the number increased) and a component of memory load (subjects were required to work out a varying number of these problems before reporting the result (e.g. JVAT $+ 4 =$ NZEX) and memory load increased with the number of letters). Using a design where subjects were matched by their prior abilities at this task, processing was slowed by alcohol, which also increased transposition errors in memory. Alcohol did not affect the number of letters recalled nor the time it took to encode transformed letters.

Millar *et al.* (1987) examined the impact of the hormone vasopressin on alcohol-induced amnesia. They used an auditory short-term recall task (twelve words per list) and a long-term semantic recognition task. Alcohol significantly impaired short-term memory (and vasopressin reduced this impairment) but did not affect semantic recognition.

Millar *et al.* (1992) used the same short-term memory task as part of a battery of tests to examine the effects of food and alcohol on performance. In this experiment, alcohol had no impact on short-term memory, but the lists were administered spaced (one per test session over time) whereas Millar *et al.* (1987) administered them in blocked fashion, one after another. Spacing the lists may have reduced inter-list interference, increasing performance and making the test insensitive to alcohol.

Niaura *et al.* (1987) used two auditory supra-span 24-word lists per trial, with immediate recall after each list. They found greater impairment on the ascending limb of the BAL curve and that females' impairment decreased more slowly between the ascending and descending limb, but the study did not include a placebo group so no main effect of alcohol was observable. As noted above, these findings may have been due in part to practice.

Jones and Jones (1980), in a study of the effects of age and drinking history on the impact of alcohol on women, used a series of 12-word lists presented visually and tested both short-term recall immediately after each list (which they call 'immediate memory') and long-term recall of all words after six lists had been presented (which they incorrectly call 'short-term memory'). Short-term recall (normal terminology, not theirs) was unaffected by alcohol, age or drinking history. Long-term recall after alcohol was independently reduced by age and drinking history, but not by alcohol. Jones and Jones then calculate the ratio of long- to short-term memory, but this ignores several memory phenomena, including hypermnesia (recalling more items given more time), recall-as-rehearsal (What is the impact of short-term recall on long-term recall?), interference between lists (which may inhibit long-term recall rather than simply generating 'confusions') and, most problematically, the fewer words recalled short-term, the larger the ratio. Thus this ratio is not readily interpretable as 'a more sensitive measure of short-term memory' (by which they mean long-term memory). Nonetheless, alcohol consumption, age and drinking history were all related to this dubious ratio. Perhaps alcohol affected something, but one would need to replicate these findings using independent long-term and short-term memory tasks as well as placebo conditions, before drawing any conclusions.

Nelson *et al.* (1986) had subjects answer general knowledge questions after either alcohol of placebo. There were no expectancy effects or effects of alcohol on confidence, but alcohol did reduce the number of correct answers that subjects gave.

Minocha *et al.*'s (1985) considerably flawed study (see above) found that alcohol impaired both verbal and visual memory.

Maylor and Rabbitt (1987b) examined the effects of alcohol on rate of forgetting in a continuous recognition task where subjects repeatedly had to decide whether they had seen a word before, words being repeated after varying delays (between 1 and 49 items later) which encompassed both short- and long-term memory. The study was of randomized cross-over design, but order effects were controlled for. Alcohol significantly reduced recognition accuracy and there was an effect of session on accuracy (the second session leading to faster, less accurate responding). Alcohol also slowed responding, but equally across all numbers of intervening items, which suggested that alcohol made subjects more cautious in their recognition decisions. Lastly, alcohol reduced recognition accuracy more over longer delays, suggesting to the authors that alcohol increased the rate of forgetting.

In an intriguingly naturalistic procedure, Read and Yuille (in press) had subjects consume alcohol, no alcohol or placebo alcohol and then commit a theft from a professor's office, with 'Assurances that no harm would come to them if caught', but believing that others in the university were unaware of the research and would treat the theft as real. Arousal and expectancy were also manipulated. Compared with no alcohol conditions, alcohol reduced memory for details of the room, the physical appearance of an intruder who disturbed the theft and for the subject's own actions. In a second experiment using 80 mg% BAL instead of 110 mg% BAL, alcohol had no impact on memory for the room, but reduced recall of what the subject did. Only when arousal was low did alcohol reduce identification of the intruder, suggesting that arousal (which would have been at naturalistically high levels in this procedure) can reduce alcohol-related impairment. Also, those who had received alcohol performed better if they were told they had received placebo, whereas placebo subjects performed worse if told they had received placebo. The most interesting point to be taken from this study is that alcohol can affect some aspects of memory and not others. If, for example, an intoxicated person compensates by focusing on the central task in hand, then their memory for the task may be unimpaired, whereas their memory for peripheral details may be impaired. The issue of arousal is also important.

Wilson *et al.* (1984) used a test of iconic memory, among seventeen other tests. Iconic memory was not consistently impaired by alcohol.

Alcohol can reduce both short- and long-term memory performance, but the locus of the impairment is not clear. It is possible that alcohol can reduce the efficiency of both encoding and retrieval processes. As discussed in the section on models of the effects of alcohol, alcohol may alter the direction of attention, which would in turn affect which aspects of an event could be remembered.

ALCOHOL AFTER LEARNING IMPROVES RETENTION

It is fairly clear that memory is often impaired after alcohol. Perhaps more surprisingly, alcohol after learning appears to improve subsequent memory for the learned material. Parker *et al.* (1980, 1981) found in a within-subjects design that alcohol after exposure enhanced both forced-choice picture recognition and verbal recall. It is difficult to assess their results without between-subject data, particularly from the recognition tasks, which seem to have been unusually difficult. In a between-subject design, Meuller *et al.* (1983) found that alcohol after exposure enhanced verbal recall but did not enhance verbal recognition. With hindsight, it is regrettable that Meuller *et al.* (1983) did not use a picture recognition task which might at least have established alcohol's retroactive effect on picture memory. These findings are discussed in terms of alcohol facilitating memory consolidation, or alcohol reducing retroactive interference, probably by interfering with the retrieval of post-alcohol events. Meuller *et al.* (1983) interpret their results as favouring the latter explanation. There could be a variety of other explanations, depending upon one's preferred theory of memory. While these findings are intriguing, it would be premature to encourage post-learning alcohol consumption as a means of facilitating memory.

Kent *et al.* (1986) studied state-dependent recall in a small within-subjects design and found that recall for material learned after alcohol was generally better when alcohol was readministered. State-dependent learning is a well-known phenomenon and one can speculate that it is related to the phenomenon discussed in the previous paragraph.

Reaction time and decision-making tasks

Decision-making tasks of one sort or another have been the most frequently used in the study of the effects of alcohol on performance. We found twenty-nine studies during 1980–1990 which included such tasks. A common feature among the bewildering variety of tasks that have been studied was that the responses required are relatively trivial to learn and task difficulty essentially depends upon deciding which response to make when. This, in turn, varies depending upon the number of options available and upon the complexity of the decision involved. We therefore classify tasks along a continuum of decision complexity.

SIGNAL DETECTION TASKS

Signal detection tasks require subjects to respond every time that a particular stimulus occurs. Response is required within a time-frame, but not otherwise timed and is not supposed to be problematical. The difficulty of detecting the stimulus varies depending upon its prominence in the visual or other perceptual field, the regularity of its appearance and other factors. Signal detection errors consist of not detecting the stimulus and usually increase with the length of the task, due to boredom and other factors.

Fagan *et al.*, (1987) found that signal detection (spotting repetition in a long series of patterns) was impaired, but not until three hours after drinking 0.8 g kg^{-1}. The nature of the statistical analyses used is unclear and the *n* was only eight.

Linnoila *et al.* (1980) in a small within-subjects study (see tracking section) used a vigilance task lasting thirty minutes where subjects had to respond to illuminated dots 60 mm apart flashed randomly in a stream of dots 48 mm apart. Response time was slowed and errors were increased by alcohol in a dose-related fashion.

Maylor *et al.* (1987) used a within-subjects design and a visual search task where subjects had to locate digits on sheets containing 1300 characters. There was a main effect of alcohol on the number of targets missed and alcohol interacted with session to affect speed of search and false alarms. Although the findings are complicated by practice effects, there is evidence that the smaller dose (29 mg%) of alcohol reduced misses, while the large dose (130 mg%) increased misses.

Moskowitz *et al.* (1985) combined a tracking task with detection of the number 2 in a continually changing 24-digit array. As described in the tracking section, there appears to have been no effects of alcohol on this particular task but the method was inadequate.

As well as the video driving task already described, Mongrain and Standing (1989) used a task where subjects had to detect a briefly flashed letter X among a field of Z stimuli. This task lasted less than seven minutes, which is short for a vigilance task. Nonetheless, alcohol reduced hits and increased false alarms.

Patel (1988) administered alcohol (achieved 50–70 mg%) or placebo and had subjects perform in static noise at 85–90 dB, or normal 'semi-sound-proofed' conditions. The subjects' task was to sketch as many items as they liked which might be inside a domestic fridge-freezer. For reasons which escape us, Patel (1988) describes this as a vigilance task. Placebo subjects in noise drew fewer objects and spent less time on this task; presumably to evade the noise as soon as possible. Other conditions were roughly equal, so apparently noise did not affect performance if alcohol had been consumed. This might be improvement if one wants more work under noise, or decrement if one considers that after alcohol subjects acted less sensibly and remained in the noise longer.

Rohrbaugh *et al.* (1985) in a repeated measures design on twelve subjects, used a task where subjects had to attend to a rapidly changing series of blurred digits, pressing a button when 0 was seen. Placebo and three doses of alcohol (0.45, 0.80 and 1.05 g kg^{-1}) were administered. The hit rate decreased significantly after alcohol, and this effect increased over each vigilance session. Between the 325th and 486th digit, the placebo mean hit rate was about 77 per cent, the low dose about 72 per cent, the medium dose about 68 per cent and the high dose down to 56 per cent. False alarm rates were unaffected by alcohol. Reaction times were also slowed by alcohol, but the effect was smaller. Rohrbaugh *et al.* (1988) report that they counterbalanced alcohol condition across sessions. However there are twenty-four possible permutations of four conditions, so counterbalancing is impossible with twelve subjects. So it would have been useful if the data had been analysed for sessions effects, for there is an unknown component of practice and/or fatigue contaminating the above results.

Wilson *et al.* (1984) amongst 17 tests, had subjects locate and circle a target in rows of four letters. They call this 'simple reaction time', but it seems more like vigilance. It was unaffected by alcohol.

Although the tasks used are varied and not all studies are methodologically adequate, alcohol does appear to impair vigilance.

SIMPLE REACTION-TIME TASKS

Simple reaction-time tasks require a set response to a particular stimulus, but the stimulus is easy to detect and the response is required as rapidly as possible. The response is not supposed to be problematical and errors are few. Thus, simple reaction time is supposed to be a 'pure' measure of response speed. But, simple as such tasks may be, responding has at least two components: a component of 'decision time' where the stimulus is recognized and the response initiated, and a component of 'moving time' where the response is planned and executed. Both components can be influenced by complex cognitive factors, as well as by specific physical design of the apparatus used. The idea that simple reaction time measures some sort of elementary psychological (or even physiological) stimulus—response connection is mistaken (see Maylor and Rabbitt, 1987a).

Baylor *et al.* (1989) used a 'brake' and 'accelerator pedal' apparatus, combined with electromyographic recordings of muscle activity which allowed simple RT to be decomposed into pre-motor time and time to react, both of which were slowed by an alcohol dose achieving 170 mg% but not by a dose achieving 100 mg%. There were more errors in both alcohol conditions. Movement time (the time to move off the accelerator and hit the brake) was unaffected. These findings are limited by the small *n* (5) and within-subjects design. Subjects were unusually well-practiced at the task.

Gustafson (1986a) used a simple reaction to an auditory stimulus. Testing lasted for thirty minutes. After a dose achieving 88 mg%, reaction time slowed significantly across the thirty minute period. This did not happen in placebo conditions or after a dose achieving 22 mg%. Subjects in the 88 mg% condition also missed more stimuli. Unfortunately, eleven subjects were all tested in the order placebo, 22 mg%, 88 mg% across three sessions, so by the third session performance could contain a substantial component of boredom or fatigue. Unaware of this problem, Gustafson (1986b) reports a similar study, using the same design, even fewer subjects (six) and visual reaction time. As the author notes, this 'yielded almost identical results' to the previous study.

Linnoila *et al.* (1980) found that alcohol did not affect RT, despite its affecting other tasks (see above). This may have been due to lack of power in a small sample.

Millar *et al.* (1992) used an RT task as a secondary task with the tracking task already described. Alcohol slowed secondary RT. This finding is discussed further in the section on divided attention.

Taberner (1980) had subjects operate a hand-held push button with their thumb when a red light appeared. In a within-subjects design, a 0.76 g kg^{-1} dose significantly slowed RT, whereas a dose of 0.15 g kg^{-1} did not. This study is discussed further under gender.

Maylor *et al.* (1990) used a simple RT task either along with a tracking task or on its own. When the RT task was performed alone then it was impaired by alcohol (0.64 g kg^{-1}), but not as much as in dual-task conditions (see below). Practice did not reduce this impairment.

There is some evidence that simple RT is slowed by alcohol, but, as is discussed at the end of the next section, excepting Maylor *et al.* (1990) none of these studies is a fully adequate study of simple RT.

CHOICE REACTION TIME TASKS

Choice reaction time tasks are similar to simple reaction time tasks except that subjects have to make one of a fixed set of responses, depending upon which of a small, fixed set of stimuli occurs. Thus, both thinking time and moving time are usually longer than in simple reaction time tasks and there are more likely to be response errors.

In the small study reviewed under simple reaction time, Baylor *et al.* (1989) also examined choice reaction time (doing nothing at a green light versus braking at a red light). Choice RT was slower than simple RT. Results from both tasks seem to have been pooled in analysis, so presumably the effects (on pre-motor time and time to react but not on moving time) were the same.

Connors and Maisto (1980) used a three-choice RT task as a secondary task with tracking and found no effect of alcohol, although subjects who drank more quickly also reacted more quickly and improved over trials.

Fagan *et al.* (1987) used the six-choice RT task (six lights require six spatially analogous responses) from the Leeds psychomotor tester. Alcohol slowed choice RT but, as with their signal detection task, the effect was not significant until 150 minutes after drinking 0.8 g kg^{-1}.

Golby (1989) reports using two six-choice reaction time tasks, one using the Leeds psychomotor tester. The other task required gross body movements, six lights and response pads being arranged in a 2.5 m arc. Neither task was affected by alcohol.

Landauer and Howat (1982) used an eight-choice RT task where a numeral was displayed and subjects had to press the appropriate button. In a within-subjects design, decision time increased with alcohol dose up to 73 mg%, but movement time was unaffected.

Lawrence et al. (1983) examined circadian variation in the effects of alcohol (approximately 70 mg% achieved). They used a four-choice reaction time task which seems to have been otherwise similar to the Leeds psychomotor tester. No placebo conditions were used, but subjects who received alcohol at 9.00 a.m. made more errors and their performance was more variable than subjects who received alcohol at 6.00 p.m. In the morning, both errors and variation in performance increased with time up to ninety minutes after drinking, which was just after peak BAL.

Maylor et al. (1989) used a four-choice RT task where subjects had to press one of four adjacent computer keys labelled A, B, C or D when the corresponding letter appeared on the computer screen. Subjects were also required to indicate when they felt that they had made a particularly fast and accurate response by pressing another key. They were studying the effects of practice and alcohol (achieved 70 mg%) on performance across two sessions, the first session being placebo, and half the subjects receiving alcohol on the second session. Alcohol did not affect error rate but slowed RT by about 40 ms. Alcohol did not affect judgement of fast responses. Thus, this study suggests that alcohol simply slows response speed rather than altering subjects' control strategies.

Maylor et al. (1987) used a similar RT task, along with the visual search task reviewed above. They found large effects of alcohol on reaction time, which was slowed by the larger dose of alcohol (130 mg%) but not by the smaller (29 mg%). In contrast, the larger dose did not affect accuracy, whereas the smaller dose *increased* accuracy. Maylor et al. (1987) make the important point that the speed–accuracy trade-off in this study was different for the two tasks used and for the different doses of alcohol.

Millar et al. (1992) used a five-choice RT task designed to be an analogue of the Leeds psychomotor tester task, but using a VDU screen and computer keyboard. The use of a computer allowed the decomposition of RT into decision time and movement time. Alcohol did not affect the speed of either component or errors. However, fasted subjects (compared to those given lunch) had slower decision times and made more errors.

Minocha et al.'s (1985) flawed study found inconsistent results on a choice reaction time task. Insufficient detail is given to make sense of their findings.

Misawa et al.'s (1983) study used only five subjects who performed a choice reaction time task after placebo or 33.5, 67.0 or 134.0 ml of whisky (probably 40 per cent alcohol). Additionally, they performed this task alone, with either of two secondary tasks, or with both secondary tasks. Practice effects were not considered. The high dose of alcohol impaired performance between 30 and 180 minutes after drinking, while the lower doses do not appear to have impaired performance. We cannot be more specific because of the complex design.

The results for both simple and choice reaction time are inconsistent, alcohol sometimes affects performance and sometimes does not. Ignoring the generally weak design of some studies, we suggest that Maylor *et al.*'s (1987) point about strategy is important. If subjects can maintain speed by sacrificing accuracy or vice versa, then studies which do not measure both may miss a genuine impairment. Reaction time is not the result of a unitary process. Also, strategies may change over time or vary with alcohol dose. It is possible that this could explain why some studies have found effects at low doses, but not at higher ones.

COMPLEX REACTION TIME AND DECISION-MAKING TASKS

Complex reaction time and decision-making tasks are similar to the preceding tasks except that there is a more overt component of cognitive decision-making in the task. There are many different complex reaction time tasks, some with a substantial component of knowledge, others requiring less knowledge. Compared again with 'simpler' RT tasks, responding is likely to be slower and there are likely to be more errors.

Fagan *et al.* (1987) found no effects of alcohol on semantic decision-making, but the methodology may have been insufficiently sensitive (see above).

Hockey *et al.* (1981) used the task reported in the memory section. They found that, without memory load, time to do a mental transformation was slowed increasingly by alcohol as the size of the transformation increased.

Lawrence *et al.* (1983) used a reasoning task based on grammatical transformation. As described above, there was no placebo group. Subjects solved fewer problems after alcohol in the morning than in the evening.

Linnoila *et al.* (1980) found no effects of alcohol on a task where subjects had to respond to two successive odd or even numbers in a series of single digits changing every two seconds. As already noted, the lack of effect may have been due to small sample size. We did not put this in the vigilance section because the judgement 'odd' or 'even' is not purely perceptual.

Maylor and Rabbitt (1987) examined the effects of alcohol and practice on performance in two studies. They used a simple video game where subjects had to 'bomb' a 'tank' moving across a screen. The bomb launch position was fixed, but where the tank appeared varied, which varied the time available for decision. Across sessions, alcohol (achieving 63 mg%) did not affect mean performance but it increased variability and decreased accuracy. Practice improved performance more after alcohol, but there was more room for improvement.

In the same study Maylor and Rabbitt (1988) also examined the effects of practice and alcohol on a word categorization task where subjects had to choose which of three words was a member of a target category, and a visual search task where subjects had to search for either digits among letters or letters among digits. In both tasks there could be either consistent mapping (where targets stayed the same and automated processing could be learned, e.g. always digits) or varied mapping (where the targets varied and processing could not become automated, e.g. digits or letters). Alcohol increased error rates for both conditions of both tasks, but did not have a main effect on mean response time. Practice improved performance but did not reduce the impairment caused by alcohol, not did the level of automated processing possible.

Ross and Pihl (1988) had subjects assess the spelling of words presented on a VDU by pressing response keys. Ignoring the personality and expectancy variables discussed below, there was a main effect of alcohol (placebo or 1.06 g kg^{-1} alcohol) on slowing reaction time.

Wilson *et al.* (1984), along with the many other tasks already reviewed, had subjects do a logical sentence completion task, which was unaffected by alcohol. Finally, being unable to invent a test involving the kitchen sink, they also had subjects play the Apple II version of Space Invaders. Over time, this was impaired by alcohol in three out of seven trials, but there appears to have been considerable learning over the seven trials.

Generally, these studies provide some evidence that alcohol slows cognitive decision-making across a range of tasks.

DIVIDED-ATTENTION TASKS

Lastly, and outside the continuum, some studies use dual or multiple tasks where subjects are required to do two or more subtasks at once. All driving tasks are of this kind. When attention is divided it becomes possible for subjects to maintain performance on one task after alcohol by neglecting the other. One of the most common experimental procedures is to link a tracking task with a secondary reaction time task.

Connors and Maisto (1980) did just this and found a deficit on tracking but not on RT.

Millar *et al.* (1992) used a tracking task and an RT task together. They found that, after alcohol, subjects sacrificed their RT performance to maintain tracking performance, although a minority of subjects adopted the opposite strategy (Hammersley *et al.*, unpublished).

Mills and Bisgrove (1983a) used a divided attention task as well as measuring body sway. The central task was to attend to a display of changing digital information and respond when numbers exceeded one value or fell below another value. The secondary task was to respond to any change in two peripheral displays. Central and secondary performance were combined for analysis. Compared to placebo and baseline within subjects, a low dose of alcohol (0.37 g kg^{-1}) did not impair performance, but a higher dose (0.76 g kg^{-1}) did.

Using the same task, Mills and Bisgrove (1983b) found a linear relationship between BAL and impairment. Impairment was highest in a field study where mean achieved BAL was 95 mg%.

Niaura *et al.* (1987) included a divided attention task in the battery already reviewed. Subjects had to circle target characters on a sheet of characters and press a button as fast as possible whenever a light came on in the periphery of their vision. Subjects were more impaired on the ascending than on the descending limb of the BAL curve. As already noted, this may have been due to practice.

Maylor *et al.* (1990) included a divided attention combination of simple RT and tracking in the study already reviewed. Both tasks were impaired by being presented together. Alcohol impaired RT but not tracking. As Maylor and colleagues have found with various other tasks, practice did not reduce alcohol impairment.

Despite various methological difficulties and different tasks, all seven studies have found some evidence that alcohol impairs divided attention tasks.

To sum up studies of decision-making, a reasonable, simple hypothesis is that alcohol slows mental processing. Thus, depending on the task and given that the task is sufficiently sensitive to such slowing, subjects may either perform decision-making tasks more slowly or maintain speed by becoming less accurate or neglecting some other aspect of performance, such as a secondary task. It is difficult, even impossible, to prevent such strategy shifts, and studies which fail to measure all relevant aspects of performance or which collapse performance data across different measures, may miss genuine impairment.

Table 4.2 Effects of alcohol on various tasks, 1980–1991

	Some impairment	*No impairment / uncertain*
Tracking	6	3
Body sway	8	2
Risk-taking in driving video-game	1	1
Critical flicker fusion frequency	1	5
Memory	8	2
Decision-making tasks		
Signal detection	5	3
Simple RT	6	1
Choice RT	7	4
Complex RT	6	2
Divided attention	7	0
Total decision-making	31 (76%)	10 (24%)
Grand total	55 (71%)	23 (29%)

The numbers shown are numbers of *tasks*. Many studies have used multiple tasks and the table takes no account of methodological defects.

Ignoring the considerable methodological problems described above, Table 4.2 summarizes the findings of the studies reviewed. In our opinion there is little certainty both because publication is probably biased towards studies reporting effects of alcohol, and because there are too many flaws in most of the studies. Nonetheless, the best guess at this point would be that alcohol impairs a whole range of cognitive tasks. If one regards the tasks reviewed as a random sample of possible tasks and procedures then the odds are 7:3 that a given task will be impaired by alcohol.

MEDIATORS OF THE ALCOHOL–PERFORMANCE RELATIONSHIP

While alcohol can readily be shown to impair performance, it has too often been assumed that there is a simple correlation between dose or current BAL and impairment. In actuality several factors mediate this relationship and we now turn to these.

Food

It is well-established that food prior to drinking reduces subsequent BAL (e.g. Lin *et al.*, 1976; Sedman *et al.*, 1976; Welling *et al.*, 1977) and it has been assumed that this reduction would be associated with less impaired performance. Millar *et al.* (1992) explicitly tested this assumption and found that food reduced performance impairment on a secondary reaction time task but that performance was only modestly related to current BAL because of the other factors discussed below. In addition, fasting can impair performance (Fisher and Atkinson, 1979; Pollitt *et al.*, 1982), as can eating lunch (Craig *et al.*, 1981; Smith and Miles, 1986a, b, c; Spring *et al.*, 1983), although Christie *et al.* (1976) found no adverse effect of lunch. Consequently, the food–alcohol interaction may produce effects on performance other than a simple reduction in impairment due to reduced BAL.

Lastly, studies of the effects of alcohol using fasted subjects may give results which do not represent everyday life where few people consume alcohol after fasting for several hours or longer.

Time and hangover effects

Recording both performance and BAL over time, we have found that performance at a given time is not highly correlated with current blood alcohol (Hammersley *et al.*, 1990; Millar *et al.*, 1991). Instead, after a given dose of alcohol, impaired performance is relatively constant over time. For example, secondary reaction time was slowed to about 112 per cent of baseline after a dose of alcohol achieving a peak of about 40 mg% BAL, but this impairment did not improve as BAL reduced over time. By 120 minutes after drinking, performance was still at 115 per cent of baseline, whereas BAL had reduced to below 10 mg% from peak. Furthermore, performance could be better predicted from initial alcohol dose than from current BAL. Thus, a larger dose of alcohol had larger effects on performance which persisted while BAL was reducing. With smaller doses, some subjects were still impaired once BAL had returned virtually to zero.

Several studies of small numbers of pilots have examined effects of alcohol on performance after BAL has returned to zero. These studies are also notable because they use analogues of overlearned tasks. Pilots' deficits in flight simulators are not plausibly explicable in terms of alcohol impairing learning.

Morrow *et al.* (1990) examined the cumulative effects of alcohol and age on performance using young and more mature pilots in a flight simulator. They found that more mistakes were made in reporting heading and altitude over the radio on the descending limb of the BAL curve and that some performance decrement persisted for eight hours after drinking.

Collins and Chiles (1980) tested pilots during intoxication and the following morning and found circadian but no hangover effects. Their tests did not involve full flight simulation and may have been less sensitive than those used by Morrow *et al.* (1990). Two of eleven subjects (both female) felt ill after drinking (achieved BAL 99.3 mg%) and did not complete testing. The subjective state of the other subjects is not reported.

Yesavage and Leirer (1986) tested pilots in a flight simulator on two mornings fourteen hours after drinking (achieved BAL 100 mg%) and after abstaining from alcohol for forty-eight hours. Pilots were significantly impaired after alcohol. There was no relationship between subjective rating of performance and actual performance, which suggests that pilots could not judge their impairment. It is not reported whether or not they felt hungover.

Bowden *et al.* (1988) in a correlational study sought evidence for a relationship between alcohol consumption in the previous week and current cognitive deficit on some standard neuropsychological tests. Controlling for age and education, they found no such effects. However, the large standard errors in their data and the presence of effects which just miss significance for abstraction and vocabulary suggest that this was due to an insufficiently powerful procedure. With more subjects and/or more sensitive tests of performance, long-term hangover effects might have been found.

Thus, with the usual caveat about the use of different procedures in different studies, it appears that performance can remain impaired for considerable periods (up to fourteen hours or longer) after drinking alcohol. The doses studied have been sufficient to achieve BAL of about 100 mg%, which requires about 5 or 6 units to achieve, depending on sex and body weight. This quantity of alcohol is likely to be reached or exceeded by many individuals during a normal evening of drinking. It also seems likely that these 'hangover' effects can occur when people do not feel subjectively hung over, although this does not appear to have been explicitly studied. Lastly, the 'eight hour rule' imposed by many airlines may be insufficiently stringent. Eight hours after a large dose of alcohol some people may still have elevated BAL and even after a modest dose people may still be somewhat impaired. Low or zero current BAL some time after alcohol consumption does not indicate that performance ability has necessarily returned to normal levels.

Judgements of intoxication

People generally have control over their alcohol intake. It is sensible to assume that control over intake is based upon people's judgements about their current intoxication and their guesses about their future intoxication. Some people sometimes deliberately drink to extreme intoxication or even unconsciousness, but such drinking is rare and people will usually avoid demanding performance afterwards. Moreover, people attempt to limit their alcohol intake when performance is required. To do so, people must be able to judge their alcohol intake.

Radlow and Hurst (1985) examined the relationship between BAL and subjective intoxication over a two-hour period. Intoxication was judged by magnitude estimation. Subjects estimated that they reached peak intoxication faster than they actually did and then estimated that their BAL declined faster than it actually did. Thus, both the ascending and descending limbs of the subjective curve were steeper than those of the BAL curve and subjective peak was earlier than actual BAL peak.

Portans *et al.* (1989) found similar results, using a twenty-point rating scale. They also found that heavy drinkers estimated peak BAL to be lower and to occur earlier than did light drinkers, suggesting either tolerance or initial insensitivity to alcohol encouraging heavier consumption.

Lukas *et al.* (1986) varied alcohol dose and used both an eleven-point rating scale and the moving of a joystick to indicate subjective intoxication. They found that rating-scale responses did not discriminate between the two alcohol doses, although both differed from placebo. However, the joystick response discriminated between doses. Other than that, their findings over time are essentially the same as from the preceding studies.

Millar *et al.* (1992) again had similar findings, using a twenty-point rating scale. This study used placebo and three doses of alcohol, allowing the dose–subjective intoxication relationship to be examined. Despite subjects being poor at estimating the time course of their intoxication, there was a main effect of dose on subjective intoxication, indicating that subjects could subjectively discriminate between different doses, although estimates were insensitive to the effects of food in reducing BAL. This study also looked at individual differences (Hammersley *et al.*, unpublished), which were substantial. For example, of sixteen fasted subjects who received a dose of alcohol to achieve BAL of approximately 80 mg%, eight never rated themselves as significantly more intoxicated than did placebo subjects.

Subjective intoxication has not been measured consistently, or with a validated instrument, although this does not seem to make much difference to the basic findings: people are poor at estimating their subjective intoxication, tend to feel most intoxicated before BAL has peaked and then feel less intoxicated over time while BAL remains elevated. People cannot use internal cues to estimate their intoxication.

Mills and Bisgrove (1983b) measured subjective impairment on the divided attention task that subjects had just performed. In the laboratory there was a main effect of dose on subjective impairment, indicating that subjects could, to an extent, estimate their performance correctly. However, in a field study at a party this relationship was absent, perhaps in part because alcohol doses were higher. Related findings are discussed in the next section.

People with, or at risk of, alcohol problems tend to use external cues to estimate intoxication, such as the number of drinks consumed (Laberg, 1986; Pollock *et al.*, 1986; Shukit, 1984). Looking at normals, Russ *et al.* (1986) used a naturalistic procedure. At a fraternity party, beer consumption was discretely recorded. As subjects left they were asked how many cups of beer they had consumed and to estimate their BAL; BAL was also measured. *Post hoc*, subjects were divided into three groups on the basis of BAL. Fifty per cent of subjects achieving less than 50 mg% correctly estimated how many cups they had drunk. Subjects with higher BAL readings were less accurate; 60 per cent of those with BAL readings above 100 mg% under-estimated their consumption. Subjects were generally bad at guessing their BAL. Sixty-seven per cent of subjects with BAL readings below 100 mg% under-estimated their readings, whereas 85 per cent of those above that level over-estimated. Lastly, over 90 per cent of subjects achieving less than 100 mg% correctly said they were below the legal limit, but only 53 per cent of those over 100 mg% rated said they were above the limit. That is, the most intoxicated group under-estimated, despite over-estimating their BAL. Russ *et al.* (1986) do not discuss this disparity. Perhaps people cannot usefully estimate BAL at all. Furthermore, as common sense would suggest, as people drink more they are more likely to lose count or forget some drinks.

So, neither internal nor external cues to intoxication are used accurately. Larger doses of alcohol and longer delays since drinking probably increase under-estimation. Thus, people are unreliable judges of their own intoxication and unlikely to be skilled at avoiding impairment by drinking sufficiently little. On the basis of Mills and Bisgrove (1983b), people may be slightly better at judging how well they have just performed. In natural work or driving settings, this could well be too late.

Expectancy effects

Related to judging intoxication, people's beliefs and knowledge about what they are drinking have been shown to affect subsequent performance. At the risk of sounding like a broken record: much of this literature is methodologically inadequate. Various different approaches have been used.

EXPECTING TO RECEIVE ALCOHOL

The most basic approach is to manipulate whether or not the subjects expect to receive alcohol and also manipulate whether they receive alcohol or placebo. Ideally, this should occur in the 'balanced placebo' design (Marlatt and Rohsenow, 1980; Rohsenow and Marlatt, 1981) which is a between-subjects design with expectations and alcohol dose manipulated independently. Unfortunately, subjects can detect the physiological changes brought about by alcohol ingestion, which confounds the balanced placebo approach (Knight et al., 1986). In our own research, we have found that manipulating placebo subjects' expectations can lead some of them to believe that they have received either alcohol or placebo, but that most subjects who have received alcohol believe that they have received alcohol by the end of the experiment, whatever the expectancy manipulation. Not surprisingly, the probability of subjects correctly judging that they have received alcohol increases as the received dose increases. Despite this problem, the balanced placebo design is preferable to within-subjects designs or other approaches without complete controls or counterbalancing.

Two hypotheses have been proposed concerning the effects of expecting to receive alcohol. The more obvious is that placebo subjects who expect to receive alcohol should perform more like subjects who have actually received alcohol. That is, they should exhibit the classic placebo phenomena (e.g. Tucker and Vuchinich, 1983).

The alternative hypothesis is that, of subjects who receive alcohol, those who expect alcohol should be less impaired than those who do not expect to receive alcohol. The reason for this is that expecting alcohol allows subjects to adjust and compensate for the effects of alcohol. Compensating may occur both at the cognitive level (such as a change in strategy) and the physiological level, involving changes in basic physiological measures such as heart rate which are the opposite of those produced by alcohol (e.g. Newlin, 1986; Shapiro and Nathan, 1986).

There is evidence for the existence of both compensatory and placebo, or anticipatory, responses to alcohol and other drugs (see Laberg, 1990; Powell et al., 1990). It is not entirely clear, however, how these effects will affect performance. Table 4.3 summarizes how the two models ought to affect performance and also adds a combined model which assumes that both kinds of effect will occur at equal strength. But by now it should be obvious that

Table 4.3 Predictions about the effects of expectancy on performance

Condition	Placebo	Compensation	Combination
EA/RA	1	3	2 (4)
EA/RP	3	2	3 (5)
EP/RA	2	1	1 (3)
EP/RP	4	4	4 (8)

Higher numbers denote ranked better performance.
Figures in parentheses are the sum of placebo and compensation predictions.
EA = expect alcohol, EP = expect placebo, RA = receive alcohol, RP = receive placebo.

it is naive to hypothesize about effects on performance as if it were a single, easily measured phenomenon.

PERFORMANCE MEASURES

Williams *et al.* (1981) investigated expectancy versus pharmacological effects of alcohol (0.00, 0.54 or 1.08 g kg^{-1}). Neither expectancy nor alcohol had a significant influence on motor performance. Cognitive performance was impaired by alcohol and expectancy, but did not deteriorate with increasing alcohol dose, which is interpreted by the authors as being due to subjects psychologically and physiologically compensating for the effects of alcohol. Although the study did employ a balanced placebo design, it is flawed by the fact that the baseline performance data were not obtained before beverage consumption and, with only seven subjects per cell, their findings may be due to uncontrolled differences between subjects in the two expectancy conditions rather than a compensatory effect.

In contrast, Tucker and Vuchinich (1983), using the balanced placebo design, report a dose by expectancy interaction on perception of facial stimuli. Twenty-four males and twenty-four females were administered an alcoholic (0.5 g kg^{-1}) or a non-alcoholic beverage. The expect-alcohol, receive-alcohol group had significantly lower correct scores than did the expect-placebo, receive-alcohol group. An interaction showed that greater impairment occurred when subjects believed that they had consumed alcohol. The instructional set differentially influenced the responses of males and females. Expect-alcohol males had significantly lower correct scores than both expect-placebo males and expect-alcohol females. However, this study suffers the same methodological problems as above (six subjects per cell) which makes the findings difficult to generalize.

Ross and Pihl (1988) examined how public forms of self awareness interacted with alcohol dose (1.06 and 0.10 g kg^{-1}) and expectancy, to determine performance on a task in which subjects had to check the spelling of a series of words. Eighty-seven subjects participated in a modified balanced placebo design (a randomized double-blind procedure was used). They found that telling subjects that they had received a high dose of alcohol (irrespective of the actual amount of alcohol they had received) facilitated RT performance.

Young and Pihl (1982) used a factorial design to examine the amount of self-control forty-eight male subjects would choose to exert over their drunkenness. They found that subjects motivated to stay sober after ingestion of 1.06 g kg^{-1} of alcohol performed better on a RT task for visual stimuli than did non-motivated subjects.

Shapiro and Nathan (1986) demonstrated a conditioned tolerance response to alcohol (0.75 g kg^{-1}) on a coding vigilance task. The authors conclude that cues predicting alcohol consumption, and/or the expectation that alcohol would be received, induced the responses that reduced the detrimental effect of alcohol. Body sway, heart rate and pulse volume amplitude did not show this compensatory response. The major problem with this study was the small n of 13.

In contrast, Thomson and Newlin (1988) found no conditioned compensatory response under placebo, but found grossly impaired performance with 'disguised' alcohol after repeated sessions with alcohol. A second experiment in which all subjects received alcohol but half expected to receive tonic only, found no difference in performance when alcohol was expected from when it was disguised. The authors discuss their findings in terms of a 'situational specificity of tolerance'.

Connors and Maisto (1980) found no effect of an instruction regarding the content of the beverage on motor performance.

Wilson et al. (1984) found acute tolerance to alcohol on some of their tests by improved performance after dose 2 compared to performance after dose 1 when BAL levels were about equivalent. But, as already discussed, this study is problematical.

PHYSIOLOGICAL MEASURES

Newlin (1986) found a compensatory response to the effects of alcohol in fourteen male subjects. Group 1 was administered placebo in a distinctive drinking environment after being administered 0.5 g kg^{-1} of alcohol in two sessions in the same environment. Group 2 received distilled water in three sessions in the same experimental room. Some subjects who were given a placebo reported intoxication, they showed compensatory responses for pulse transit time and finger temperature. In a subsequent study using a similar methodology, Newlin (1989) examined placebo responding in thirty-nine female subjects randomly allocated to a control, placebo (non-alcohol beer) or real beer condition (24 oz of 5 per cent alcohol = 27 g absolute alcohol). Heart rate significantly increased in placebo subjects compared with controls and this response was in the same direction as the effect of alcohol. These findings were in the opposite direction to those of their male counterparts. As the alcohol beverage was different in the two studies and both studies used small samples, comparisons are impossible.

Staiger and White (1988) similarly found a conditioned compensatory response in nine male and three female volunteers. Subjects showed a decrease in heart rate and a slight decrease in skin temperature. However, unlike Newlin and Shapiro and Nathan's studies, conditioned heart rate response occurred irrespective of expectancy. Small sample size is again a problem.

Lipscomb *et al.* (1980) examined the effect of tolerance on the anxiety reducing function of a small (0.5 g kg^{-1}) and a large dose (1.0 g kg^{-1}) of alcohol. Heart rate increased more after the small dose. Further, heart rate of high tolerance subjects increased significantly more than that of low tolerance subjects. Lastly, measures of both skin conductance and heart rate showed significant dose by tolerance interactions. After the low dose, high tolerance subjects were more anxious in a stressful social interaction than were low tolerance subjects, but this difference disappeared after the high dose, suggesting that high tolerance subjects must consume more alcohol to achieve the reduction in anxiety. However, these findings may be due to some component of the 'anxiety provoking' situation other than anxiety and small sample size is again a problem.

In general, these studies are too small to produce clear results. Additionally, it is probable that the act of drinking itself, especially a calorific liquid like non-alcoholic beer, will produce physiological changes.

EXPECTANCY AND DEGREE OF DEPENDENCE

Several studies have shown that expectancy and response to alcohol varies according to degree of alcohol dependence. Berg *et al.* (1981) examined the role of expectancies in subjects differing in degree of alcohol dependence. Twelve alcoholics and twelve social drinkers, matched on age and education, were examined in a balanced placebo design. The results showed that expecting alcohol resulted in greater subjective and psychological responses in the more severely dependent groups, whereas the social drinkers tended to show more effects of the drug itself.

Laberg (1986) examined automatic arousal and responsivity to alcohol in ten severely, ten moderately and ten non-dependent subjects. Expectations of alcohol exerted greater influence on craving than the pharmacological effect of alcohol, with greater subjective and psychological responses elicited in the more severely dependent group than the other two groups.

In a subsequent study, Laberg and Löberg (1989), using a similar design to above, found that severely dependent subjects who were led to believe that they had consumed alcohol showed impairment of sensory-motor performance.

Beirness and Vogel-Sprott (1984) examined tolerance to alcohol and tracking performance as a function of different reinforcement contingencies. Four groups of six males were administered 0.67 g kg^{-1} of vodka under one of four contingency conditions. They found that the quickest development of tolerance (i.e. the fastest decline in impairment) was achieved by subjects who received information about performance and a monetary reward which was contingent on the display of non-impaired performance under alcohol. The design of the study did not contain a placebo control condition, and with an n of six per cell, the effect may be due to factors other than a compensatory response to alcohol.

In the study mentioned in the section on driving simulations, McMillen and Wells-Parker (1987) examined expectancy and the effect of alcohol in thirty-nine male and female (ratio not documented) subjects on risk-taking behaviour while driving. Subjects were randomly allocated to one of six treatment conditions, expect high alcohol/receive high alcohol (1.7 g kg^{-1}); expect high alcohol/receive moderate alcohol (0.58 g kg^{-1}); expect moderate alcohol/receive high alcohol; expect moderate alcohol/receive moderate alcohol; expect no alcohol/receive no alcohol; expect moderate alcohol/receive no alcohol (not a 3 × 3 factorial design). Subjects who were told that they had consumed a moderate amount of alcohol engaged in most risk-taking behaviour, regardless of the amount of alcohol they had consumed. As the study had only an n of six per cell, documented evidence regarding sex differences in alcohol metabolism were ignored and female hormonal influences on perceptual and motor abilities disregarded, it is unclear as to what these findings suggest.

In a subsequent study using a similar methodology, McMillen et al. (1989) again investigated the effects of alcohol on risk-taking behaviour with the focus this time on the influence of personality. Ninety-six subjects (64 male and 32 female), divided into high and low sensation seekers, were randomly assigned to an alcohol (1.7 g kg^{-1}) or no-alcohol condition and one of two levels of expectancy. Risk-taking behaviour was measured as in the previous study. The results showed that greater risk-taking behaviour was observed by high sensation seekers, and an interaction of sensation seeking and alcohol expectancy implied that high sensation seekers engaged in more risk-taking behaviour when they were led to believe that they had consumed alcohol. The opposite was true for low sensation seekers. Actual alcohol levels did not significantly influence behaviour. In spite of the fact that these findings cannot be extrapolated to natural driving, they do suggest the possible importance of personality in mediating the response to alcohol.

Mongrain and Standing (1989) also measured personality in their similar study of risk-taking in a driving simulation task. Top speed of driving decreased with neuroticism and anxiety and increased with sensation seeking. However, no alcohol–personality interactions were observed and the basic design of the study was flawed.

The effects of alcohol on performance on the Purdue pegboard (fine motor skills) as a function of locus of control and perceived alcohol ingestion were investigated by Breckenridge and Berger (1990). Thirty internal and thirty external scorers were assigned to a control (no alcohol expected/no alcohol received); an alcohol (alcohol expected/alcohol received) and a placebo group (alcohol expected/no alcohol received). The alcohol groups' (both internal and external locus scorers) performance was significantly impaired after alcohol. External placebo scorers did not differ from these two alcohol groups and showed significant impairment despite the fact that they had not ingested alcohol, suggesting that external locus of control scorers behave as if intoxicated when they believe that they have consumed alcohol.

Only an open verdict is currently possible about the effects of personality on performance after alcohol.

EFFECT OF SETTING ON DRINKING

Wigmore and Hinson (1991) explored the effect of expectancy and setting on consumption of alcohol. Using the balanced placebo design, 84 male volunteers were randomly allocated to a 'laboratory setting' or a 'bar-room' setting. They found that subjects in the laboratory setting consumed more when they believed that their beverage contained 'real beer' than when they believed that it contained no alcohol, irrespective of actual content. Also, those subjects, in either setting, who believed that they had ingested alcohol, regardless of the real content, rated themselves significantly more drunk than those subjects who believed that they had consumed no alcohol.

To sum up, it appears that under certain conditions, people may compensate for alcohol's effects. Studies have produced results consistent both with the placebo and the compensation accounts of expectancy. It may well be that differences in procedure and experimental design among studies may account for these contradictions. Until studies adopt a standard expectancy manipulation, use the balanced placebo design and test sufficient numbers of subjects, inconsistent findings will continue to be produced.

Individual differences

People vary extensively in their response to alcohol. However, the reasons for these variations are far from clear. One possibility is personality, which, as already reviewed, has been studied in conjunction with expectancy manipulations. Another explanation is individual variations in the quantities of the different liver enzymes which metabolize alcohol, and these are determined in part by genetic predisposition and in part by tolerance of alcohol (Bosron and Li, 1986). We do not review these variations here because they are, as yet, difficult to ascertain for an individual.

METABOLISM OF ALCOHOL

There are considerable individual differences in the metabolism of alcohol. Following a standard dose of alcohol, there is marked individual variation in both peak BAL and the time to achieve that peak. Similarly, there is marked variability in the rate elimination of alcohol from the blood. Such variability adds further complication to the interpretation of results. This presents a particularly serious methodological problem for studies which simply test performance at fixed intervals after drinking. For example, most studies measure performance after alcohol at a fixed period of time (on average half an hour after ingestion of alcohol) irrespective of alcohol dose. However, the BAL curve varies with dose (Rix, 1983) and after, for example, half an hour, at lower doses subjects may have virtually zero BAL, while at higher doses subjects may just be about to reach peak BAL. Additionally, there is a marked individual variation in how subjects metabolize alcohol. For example, Dubowski (1985) demonstrated that after a single dose of alcohol under controlled conditions he found a fourteenfold variation between absorption time BAL levels.

We have found similar individual differences in absorption and elimination of alcohol after a constant dose of alcohol, considering performance and subjective intoxication as a function of time (Hammersley et al., unpublished). Sixteen fasted subjects received an alcohol dose designed to achieve peak BAL of 80 mg%. Peak BAL varied from 47 to 81 mg%, time to reach peak varied from 20 to 60 minutes and elimination rate varied from 4 to 40 mg% per hour. None of these measures were well correlated with each other. Subjects were poor at estimating their current intoxication and rated themselves less drunk than was actually the case. Reaction time was impaired by alcohol but the magnitude of impairment over time was unpredictable and poorly related to current BAL.

Kent et al.'s (1986) study found individual differences in susceptibility to the state-dependent effects of alcohol in twelve 'healthy non-alcoholic' male volunteers. They found a significant positive correlation between frequency of word association, heavy drinking and alcohol-induced blackouts. However, it is difficult to evaluate their findings with this small within-subjects design. In addition, it is questionable if all people who suffered alcohol-induced blackouts should have been classified as 'healthy non-alcoholic'.

Sher (1985) used a balanced placebo design to assess individual differences in alcohol expectancies on subjective feelings following alcohol (1 g kg^{-1}) or placebo taking into consideration the influence of setting. Their findings suggest both main effects of alcohol for expectancies and setting and a complex interaction between these factors. The impact of these effects are dependent on the limb of the blood alcohol curve, setting and individual differences in expectancies.

GENDER

Men and women metabolize alcohol differently, women tending to peak more rapidly at a higher BAL, even when body size is taken into account in calculating dose (Dubowski, 1976). Furthermore, there are menstrual cycle effects on female alcohol metabolism (Jones and Jones, 1976): highest, fastest BAL tending to be achieved during the premenstrual phase. This variation and the ethical issue of the potential adverse effects of alcohol on early foetal development have led to many studies using only male subjects. Even when both sexes are used, many studies include relatively few females and do not mention sex differences; seemingly fewer females volunteer for alcohol research. There are, nonetheless, several studies of women's responses to alcohol, but most of these examine social or emotional tasks which are outside the present review.

Research on sex differences prior to 1980 generally found few differences. Taberner (1980) found that males' simple reaction time was significantly slowed from thirty to ninety minutes after drinking, whereas females' reaction time was only slowed at ninety minutes. However, the two groups did not differ significantly. The fact that males were significantly faster at baseline than the females may have determined this finding.

Wait *et al.*'s (1982) study of prismatic adaptation discussed above found no sex differences in the effects of alcohol on performance.

Mills and Bisgrove (1983a) also found no differences in performance on a divided attention task after a low dose of alcohol (0.37 g kg^{-1}), but larger impairment relative to baseline in females after a dose achieving about 0.76 g kg^{-1}. There were no sex differences in body sway. Rating their performance, females were less sensitive to the effects of alcohol than males. There were only twelve males and twelve females studied and the sexes were matched for alcohol consumption per kilo; assuming that a subject weighed about 60 kg, these 'light drinkers' were consuming on average over 100 g of alcohol (12.7 units) a week. Fewer females than males consume this amount (Wilson, 1980) and this control measure may have matched normal males with less normal females, biasing the results. A larger sample size is clearly required.

Jones and Jones (1980) used female subjects only and examined the impact of age and drinking experience on memory both before and after drinking alcohol. All subjects received the same dose of alcohol. As discussed above, the measures of memory used were idiosyncratic and of unknown reliability. Nonetheless, alcohol may have affected memory more among the middle-aged and among moderate rather than light drinkers.

Niaura et al. (1987) found that women attained higher BAL than men from 0.65 g kg^{-1} dose of alcohol. Females' memory was more impaired than males, who recovered memory performance more quickly. This may have been a practice effect. Tracking, body sway and divided attention task performance did not differ between the sexes, but it is not reported whether intoxicated performance measures differed significantly from baseline. This leads us to suspect that they did not, making observation of sex differences problematical.

At this point there is no clear evidence of sex differences in performance after alcohol when dose is administered by body weight. The shortcomings of studies to date make it impossible to guess whether the absence of a sex difference is a genuine null-effect or due to inadequate sensitivity. Future studies which examine sex differences need to consider drinking history and other personal characteristics of volunteer subjects as possible confounds with gender.

Another study has examined the impact of maternal drinking while breast feeding on infant development. Little et al. (1989), controlled for cannabis, tobacco and caffeine intake (none of which affected development). Using the Bayley scales for infant development, more maternal alcohol use (by self-report) was associated with slightly (but significantly) reduced motor development scores, but did not affect mental development. The rather low criterion employed for high alcohol use was more than 14.2 g of absolute alcohol per day (about 2 standard units).

EFFECTS OF AGE

Parker and Noble (1980) found a trend for older subjects (over 42 years) to drink more than younger subjects. Most surveys find the opposite (e.g. Wilson, 1980). Performance data on non-verbal tests of abstracting and problem-solving abilities suggested that the old were more affected by alcohol than the young.

Linnoila et al.'s (1980) rather weakly designed within-subjects study examined the combined effects of age and alcohol on performance in twenty male subjects matched on education level and drinking practices. Subjects, divided into young (between 20 and 25 years) and old (between 25 and 35 years) groups received four different doses of alcohol with a one-week interval between sessions. The results suggested to Linnoila et al. that age and a low dose of alcohol had an additive effect on performance on a continuous tracking task which bordered on statistical significance. Such a slight finding is not surprising since performance was not measured until sixty minutes after ingestion of alcohol irrespective of alcohol dose. In addition, although subjects were practised on the tasks, no baseline measures were obtained. Thus, the (non-significant) finding may be due to individual variation between subjects in task performance ability. As a result of these methodological inadequacies no conclusions can be drawn.

There is little evidence at this time that age or sex substantially affect performance after alcohol. However, the research fails to control adequately for drinking history and other possibly relevant variables. For example, as men in their late teens and early twenties tend to drink most (Wilson, 1980), a random sample of young males is likely to have a higher mean tolerance to alcohol than an older, or female, sample. Studies of the effects of drinking history on the response to alcohol are not reviewed here because they focus on the distinction between alcoholics and normal drinkers. Normal people differ in their response to alcohol, but to understand why, more studies of multivariate individual differences are required, as are more studies which link biochemistry with behaviour among normal drinkers.

CONCLUSIONS

Never mind the quality, feel the width: alcohol often impairs performance. In a diversity of tasks, it often: (1) impairs tracking, (2) increases bodysway, (3) reduces subsequent memory performance, and (4) slows decision-making and probably other thought processes. It is not clear that alcohol affects basic perceptual processes. Drinking also leaves a residual impairment on sober performance for at least fourteen hours and plausibly much longer after large doses. While it seems plausible that alcohol should adversely affect driving, and this conclusion is supported by accident statistics, the literature is not adequate to posit a convincing theory as to how and why alcohol impairs driving or other natural skilled performance. Development of such a theory is hindered by the methodological problems discussed at the beginning of this chapter. Even if these problems were corrected, several needs remain.

There is a need for more use of over-learned tasks. Most studies of 'performance' have really been studies of learning after alcohol, either from scratch or from some moderate level of practice. However, when tasks are well learned (notably in studies of pilot performance in flight simulators), alcohol can still impair performance.

There is a need to establish the basic facts about the effects of alcohol on performance under methodologically adequate conditions. The abundance of findings of impairments after alcohol does not guarantee the findings' accuracy. If, as is plausible, alcohol impairs learning then it could impair any task which is novel to the subjects, effectively masking any other impairment. There is a related need for more study of the relationship between alcohol ingestion and choice of task strategy.

Studies which find no effects of alcohol on some tasks are particularly problematic. In the absence of evidence that the tasks are generally sensitive to drug or other similar effects, the absence of an effect may always be due to the design of the study being insufficiently powerful to detect the effect. If enough people drive or work while impaired then a small impairment which is difficult to detect in an experiment may lead to substantial numbers of surplus accidents, even if no single person is impaired by more than a couple of per cent.

On the other hand, the effects of small doses of alcohol on performance seem to be of roughly the same magnitude as the effects of fatigue, boredom, hunger, eating, many commonly prescribed drugs and various other risk factors which are impossible to eliminate from everyday life. It would be a mistake to single out small doses of alcohol as a major problem.

There is a need for further study of individual indifferences in the response to alcohol. In this regard, there is also a need to consider the role of strategy in subjects' coping with impairment after alcohol. As with our violinist in the introduction, on some tasks impairment may be hidden by a strategy shift. We suspect, from pharmacological common-sense, that alcohol has consistent effects on the nervous system. Whether those effects manifest themselves as impairment depends upon what the criteria for impairment are. If, for example, a task requires few errors, but is untimed, then alcohol may not increase errors. Or, if peripheral tasks may safely be neglected then alcohol may not affect the central task. Nonetheless, there is evidence that alcohol can impair some tasks which resemble flying or driving.

Because of ethical considerations, recent work has usually, at most, administered alcohol to achieve BAL of up to 80 or 100 mg%, which are common legal limits for driving. Although impairment below those levels is modest, such legal limits nonetheless seem generous for four reasons. (1) Impairment sometimes occurs at lower levels and there is not sufficient data to plot accurately the relationship between dose and impairment. (2) It seems likely that impairment persists as BAL reduces, meaning that in practice current BAL will often under-estimate impairment: someone who at some point exceeded 100 mg%, but now has 10 or 20 mg% BAL may be more impaired than someone who is currently peaking at 20 mg%. (3) People are poor at estimating their intoxication. (4) Folk beliefs about the legal limit appear to be that more than one or two drinks an hour will take a normal person over it and that it thus represents an approximation of leisurely drinking. But, an average sized male actually has to drink at least four or five units of alcohol all at once on an empty stomach, or a larger amount more slowly, to exceed the limit. For all these reasons, the simple police message 'Don't drink and drive' should perhaps be reinforced with a simple legal limit which functionally prevents any consumption of alcohol for some time prior to driving. Because of measurement problems and the possibility that sugar may sometimes ferment to alcohol in the stomach, a limit of 20 mg% or thereabouts would seem sensible to us. Higher limits encourage: (1) driving while impaired, (2) not waiting long enough before driving after drinking, and (3) under-estimating the impact that one or two drinks can have on performance.

Turning to theory, at this point there is no clear evidence that alcohol impairs simple tasks, but spares more complex ones or vice versa. The simplest and most coherent explanation of the effects of alcohol on performance is that at modest doses alcohol slightly slows speed of mental processing. It is likely, but not demonstrated, that this slowing is dose-related. How this slowing affects performance depends upon tasks, strategy, expectations and person, as shown in Figure 4.7.

This review has come full circle: alcohol can impair performance. We look forward to future research beyond this basic fact, but for the moment more detailed claims should be viewed with caution.

REFERENCES

Aitken, P.P., Eadie, D.R., Leathar, D.S., McNeill, R.E.J. and Scott, A.C. (1988). Television advertisements for alcoholic drinks *do* reinforce under-age drinking. *British Journal of Addiction* **83**: 1399–419.

Attwood, D.A., Williams, R.D. and Madill, H.D. (1980). Effects of moderate blood alcohol concentration on closed-course driving performance. *Journal of Studies on Alcohol* **41**: 623–34.

Baker, S.J., Chrzan, G.J., Park, C.N. and Saunders, J.H. (1985). Validation of human behavioral tests using ethanol as a CNS depressant model. *Neurobehavioral Toxicology and Teratology* **7**: 257–61.

Baylor, A.M., Layne, C.S., Mayfield, R.D., Osborne, L. and Spirduso W.W. (1989). Effects of ethanol on human fractionated response times. *Drug and Alcohol Dependence* **23**: 31–40.

Beirness, D. and Vogel-Sprott, M. (1984). Alcohol tolerance in social drinkers: operant and classical conditioning effects. *Psychopharmacology* **84**: 393–7.

Berg, G., Laberg, J.C., Skutle, A. and Öhman, A. (1981). Instructed versus pharmacological effects of alcohol in alcoholics and social drinkers. *Behaviour, Research and Therapy* **19**: 55–66.

Bosron, W.F. and Li, T-K. (1986). Genetic polymorphism, human liver alcohol and aldehyde dehydrogenaises and their relationship to alcohol metabolism and alcoholism. *Hepatology* **6**: 502–10.

Bowden, S.C., Walton, N.H. and Walsh, K.W. (1988). The hangover hypothesis and the influence of moderate social drinking on mental ability. *Alcoholism: Clinical and Experimental Research* **12**: 25–9.

Breckenridge, R.L. and Berger, R.S. (1990). Locus of control and perceived alcohol ingestion in performance of a fine motor skill. *Psychological Reports* **66**: 179–85.

Brewer, N. and Sandow, B. (1980). Alcohol effects on driver performance under conditions of divided attention. *Ergonomics* **23**: 185–90.

Carpenter, J.A. (1962). Effects of alcohol on some psychological processes. *Quarterly Journal of Studies on Alcohol* **23**: 274–314.

Collins, W.E. and Chiles, W.D. (1980). Laboratory performance during acute alcohol intoxication and hangover. *Human Factors* **22**: 445–62.

Connors, G.J. and Maisto, S.A. (1980). Effects of alcohol, instruction and consumption rate on motor performance. *Journal of Studies on Alcohol* **41**: 509–17.

Craig, A., Baer, K. and Diekmann, A. (1981). The effects of lunch on sensory-perceptual functioning. *International Archives of Occupational and Environmental Health* **49**: 105–14.

Christie, M.J., Cort, J. and Venables, P.H. (1976). Individual differences is post prandial state: laboratory explorations with palmar skin potentials. *Journal of Psychosomatic Research* **20**: 501–8.

Dubowski, K.M. (1976). Human pharmacokinetics of ethanol I: Peak blood concentrations and elimination in male and female subjects. *Alcohol Technical Report* **5**: 56–63.

Dubowski, K.M. (1985). Absorption, distribution and elimination of alcohol: highway safety aspects. *Journal of Studies on Alcohol* (Supplement No. 10).

Dunbar, J.A. (1985). *A Quiet Massacre: A Review of Drinking and Driving in the United Kingdom.* London: Institute of Alcohol Studies.

Fagan, D., Tiplady, B. and Scott, D.B. (1987). Effects of ethanol on psychomotor performance. *British Journal of Anaesthesia* **59**: 961–5.

Farrimond, T. (1990). Effects of alcohol on visual constancy values and possible relation to driving performance. *Perceptual and Motor Skills* **70**: 291–5.

Fisher, M.G.P. and Atkinson, D.W. (1979). Fasting or feeding? A survey of fast-jet aircrew in the Royal Air Force Strike Command. *Aviation Space and Environmental Medicine* **51**: 1119–22.

Golby, J. (1989). Use of factor analysis in the study of alcohol-induced strategy changes in skilled performance on a soccer test. *Perceptual and Motor Skills* **68**: 147–56.

Gustafson, R. (1986a). Effect of moderate doses of alcohol on simple auditory reaction time in a vigilance setting. *Perceptual and Motor Skills* **62**: 683–90.

Gustafson, R. (1986b). Alcohol and vigilance performance: effect of small doses of alcohol on simple visual reaction time. *Perceptual and Motor Skills* **62**: 951–5.

Hammersley, R.H., Millar, K. and Finnigan, F. (unpublished). Individual differences in intoxication over time after alcohol consumption.

Hammersley, R.H., Finnigan, F. and Millar, K. (1990) *The Relationship between Alcohol Level, Ingestion of Food and Psychomotor Performance.* Report to the Alcohol Education and Research Council.

Hindmarch, I. (1982). Critical flicker fusion frequency (CFF): the effects of psychotropic compounds. *Pharmacopsychiatrica* **15** (Supplement 1): 44–8.

Hockey, R., MacLean, A. and Hamilton, P. (1981). State changes and the temporal patterning of component resources. In *Attention and Performance IX*, edited by J. Long and A. Baddeley. Hillsdale, NJ: Erlbaum.

Jones, B.M. and Jones, M.K. (1976). Alcohol effects in women during the menstrual cycle. *Annals New York Academy of Sciences* **273**: 576–87.

Jones, B.M. and Jones, M.K. (1977). Alcohol and memory impairment in male and female social drinkers. In *Alcohol and Human Memory*, edited by I.M. Birnbaum and E.S. Parker. Hillsdale, NJ: Erlbaum.

Jones, M.K. and Jones, B.M. (1980). The relationship of age and drinking habits to the effects of alcohol on memory in women. *Journal of Studies on Alcohol* **41**: 179–87.

Kent, T.A., Gunn, W.H., Goodwin, D.W., Jones, M.P., Marples, B.W. and Penick, E.C. (1986). Individual differences in state-dependent retrieval effects of alcohol intoxication. *Journal of Studies on Alcohol* **47**: 241–3.

Knight, L.J., Barabee, H.E. and Boland, F.J. (1986). Alcohol and the balanced placebo design: the role of experimenter demands in expectancy. *Journal of Abnormal Psychology*, **81**: 233–41.

Laberg, J.C. (1986). Alcohol and expectancy: subjective, psychophysiological and behavioural responses to alcohol stimuli in severely, moderately and non-dependent drinkers. *British Journal of Addiction* **81**: 797–808.

Laberg, J.C. (1990). What is presented, and what is prevented, in cue exposure and response prevention with alcohol dependent subjects? *Addictive Behaviors* **15**: 367–86.

Laberg, J.C. and Löberg, T. (1989). Expectancy and tolerance: a study of acute alcohol intoxication using the balanced placebo design. *Journal of Studies on Alcohol* **50**: 448–55.

Laberg, J.C. (1986). Alcohol and expectancy: subjective psychophysiological and behavioral responses to alcohol stimuli in severely, moderately and non-dependent drinkers. *British Journal of Addiction* **81**: 797–808.

Landauer, A.A. and Howat, P.A. (1982). Alcohol and the cognitive aspects of choice reaction time. *Psychopharmacology* **78**: 296–7.

Lawrence, N.W., Herbert, M. and Jeffcoate, W.J. (1983). Circadian variation in effects of ethanol in man. *Pharmacology, Biochemistry and Behaviour* **18** (Supplement 1): 555–8.

Levine, J.M., Kramer, J. and Levine, E. (1975). Effects of alcohol on human performance. *Journal of Applied Psychology*, **60**: 508–18.

Lin, Y.J., Weidler, D.J., Garg, D.C. and Wagner, J.C. (1976). Effects of solid food on blood levels of alcohol in man. *Research Communications in Chemistry, Pathology and Pharmacology* **13**: 713–22.

Linnoila, M., Erwin, C.W., Ramm, D. and Cleveland, W.P. (1980). Effects of age and alcohol on psychomotor performance of men. *Journal of Studies on Alcohol* **41**: 488–95.

Lipscomb, T.R. and Nathan, P.E. (1980). Blood alcohol level discrimination. *Archives of General Psychiatry* **37**: 571–6.

Lipscomb, T.R., Nathan, P.E., Wilson, T.G. and Abrams, D.B. (1980). Effects of tolerance on the anxiety-reducing function of alcohol. *Archives of General Psychiatry* **37**: 577–82.

Little, R.E., Anderson, K.W., Ervin, C.H., Worthington-Roberts, B. and Clarren, S.K. (1989). Maternal alcohol use during breast-feeding and infant mental and motor development at one year. *The New England Journal of Medicine* **321**: 425–30.

Lukas, S.E., Mendelson, J.H. and Benedikt, R.A. (1986). Instrumental analysis of ethanol-induced intoxication in human males. *Psychopharmacology*, **89**: 8–13.

MacAndrew, C. and Edgerton, R.B. (1969). *Drunken Comportment: A Social Explanation*. Chicago: Aldine.

MacCarthy, F. and Tong, J.E. (1980). Alcohol and velocity perception. II: Stimulus discrimination. *Perceptual and Motor Skills* **51**: 968–70.

Marlatt, G.A. and Rohsenow, D.J. (1980). Cognitive processes in alcohol use: Expectancy and the balanced placebo design. In *Advances in Substance Abuse: Behavioral and Biological Research*, edited by N.K. Mello. Greenwich, Conn.: JAI Press.

Maylor, E.A. and Rabbitt, P.M.A. (1987a). Effects of practice and alcohol on performance of a perceptual-motor task. *Quarterly Journal of Experimental Psychology* **39A**: 777–95.

Maylor, E.A. and Rabbitt, P.M.A. (1987b). Effects of alcohol on rate of forgetting. *Psychopharmacology* **91**: 230–5.

Maylor, E.A. and Rabbitt, P.M.A. (1988). Amount of practice and degree of attentional control have no influence on the adverse effect of alcohol in word categorization and visual search tasks. *Perception and Psychophysics* **44**: 117–26.

Maylor, E.A., Rabbitt, P.M.A., Sahgal, A. and Wright, C. (1987). Effects of alcohol on speed and accuracy in choice reaction time and visual search. *Acta Psychologica* **65**: 147–63.

Maylor, E.A., Rabbitt, P.M.A. and Connolly, S.A.V. (1989). Rate of processing and judgement of response speed: comparing the effects of alcohol and practice. *Perception and Psychophysics* **45**: 431–8.

Maylor, E.A., Rabbitt, P.M.A., James, G.H. and Kerr, S.A. (1990). Effects of alcohol and extended practice on divided-attention performance. *Perception and Psychophysics* **48**: 445–52.

McKinley, P.J., Quevedo-Converse, Y.G. and Crow, L.T. (1989). Effects of alcohol on variability—contingent reinforcement in human subjects. *Psychological Reports* **64**: 391–396.

McMillen, D.L. and Wells-Parker, E. (1987). The effect of alcohol consumption on risk-taking while driving. *Addictive Behaviours* **12**: 241–7.

McMillen, D.L., Smith, S.M. and Wells-Parker, E. (1989). The effect of alcohol, expectancy, and sensation seeking on driving risk taking. *Addictive Behaviours* **14**: 477–83.

McNamee, J.E., Tong, J.E. and Piggins, D.J. (1980). Effects of alcohol on velocity perception. I: Stimulus velocity and change in performance over time. *Perceptual and Motor Skills* **51**: 779–85.

Meuller, C.W., Lisman, S.A. and Spear, N.E. (1983). Alcohol enhancement of human memory: tests of consolidation and interference hypotheses. *Psychopharmacology* **80**: 226–30.

Millar, K. (1983). Asymmetrical transfer: an inherent weakness of repeated-measure drug experiments. *British Journal of Psychiatry* **143**: 480–6.

Millar, K., Jeffcoate, W.J. and Walder, C.P. (1987). Vasopressin and memory: improvement in normal short-term recall and reduction of alcohol-induced amnesia. *Psychological Medicine* **17**: 335–41.

Millar, K., Hammersley, R.H. and Finnigan, F. (1992). Reduction of alcohol-induced performance impairment by prior ingestion of food. *British Journal of Psychology* (in press).

Mills, K.C. and Bisgrove, E.Z. (1983a). Body sway and divided attention performance under the influence of alcohol: dose–response differences between males and females. *Alcoholism: Clinical and Experimental Research* **7**: 393–7.

Mills, K.C. and Bisgrove, E.Z. (1983b). Cognitive impairment and perceived risk from alcohol. Laboratory, self-report and field assessments. *Journal of Studies on Alcohol* **44**: 26–46.

Minocha, A., Barth, J.T., Robertson, D.G., Herold, D.A. and Spyker, D.A. (1985). Impairment of cognitive and psychomotor function by ethanol in social drinkers. *Veterinary and Human Toxicology* **27**: 533–6.

Misawa, T., Aikawa, H. and Shigeta, S. (1983). Effects of alcohol drinking on mental performance. *Sangyo-Igaku* **25**: 406–14.

Mongrain, S. and Standing, L. (1989). Impairment of cognition, risk-taking, and self-perception by alcohol. *Perceptual and Motor Skills* **69**: 199–210.

Morrow, D., Leirer, V. and Yesavage, J. (1990). The influence of alcohol and aging on radio communication during flight. *Aviation, Space, and Environmental Medicine* **61**: 12–20.

Moskowitz, H. and Murray, J.T. (1976). Alcohol and backward masking of visual information. *Journal of Studies on Alcohol* **37**: 40–5.

Moskowitz, H., Burns, M.M. and Williams, A.F. (1985). Skilled performance at low blood alcohol levels. *Journal of Studies on Alcohol* **46**: 482–5.

Nelson, T.O., McSpadden, M., Fromme, K. and Marlatt, G.A. (1986). Effects of alcohol intoxication on metamemory and on retrieval from long-term memory. *Journal of Experimental Psychology: General* **115**: 247–54.

Newlin, D.B. (1986). Conditioned compensatory response to alcohol placebo in humans. *Psychopharmacology* **88**: 247–51.

Newlin, D.B. (1989). Placebo responding in the same direction as alcohol in women. *Alcoholism: Clinical and Experimental Research* **13**: 36–9.

Niaura, R.S., Nathan, P.E., Frankenstein, W., Shapiro, A.P. and Brick, J. (1987). Gender differences in acute psychomotor, cognitive, and pharmacokinetic response to alcohol. *Addictive Behaviors* **12**: 345–56.

Niaura, R.S., Wilson, T.G. and Westrick, E. (1988). Self-awareness, alcohol consumption, and reduced cardiovascular reactivity. *Psychosomatic Medicine* **50**: 360–80.

O'Malley, S.S. and Maisto, S.A. (1984). Factors affecting the perception of intoxication: dose, tolerance, and setting. *Addictive Behaviours* **19**: 111–20.

Parker, E.S. and Noble, E.P. (1980). Alcohol and the aging process in social drinkers. *Journal of Studies of Alcohol* **41**: 170–8.

Parker, E.S., Birnbaum, I.M., Weingartner, H., Hartley, J.T., Stillman, R.C. and Wyatt, R.J. (1980a). Retrograde enhancement of human memory with alcohol. *Psychopharmacology* **69**: 219–22.

Parker, E.S., Birnbaum, I.M., Boyd, R.A. and Noble, E.P. (1980b). Neuropsychologic decrements as a function of alcohol intake in male students. *Alcoholism, Clinical and Experimental Research* **4**: 330–334.

Parker, E.S., Morihisa, J.M., Wyatt, R.J., Schwartz, B.L., Weingartner, H. and Stillman, R.C. (1981). The alcohol facilitation effect on memory: a dose-response study. *Psychopharmacology* **74**: 88–92.

Patel, R.M. (1988). Ethanol's effect on human vigilance during a simple task in the presence of an auditory stressor. *Psychological Reports* **63**: 363–6.

Pollitt, E., Lewis, N.L., Garza, C. and Schulman, R. (1982). Fasting and cognitive function. *Journal of Psychiatric Research* **17**: 169–74.

Pollock, V.E., Teasdale, T.W., Gabrielli, W.F. and Knop, J. (1986). Subjective and objective measures of response to alcohol among young men at risk for alcoholism. *Journal of Studies on Alcohol* **47**: 297–304.

Portans, I., White, J.M. and Staiger, P.K. (1989). Acute tolerance to alcohol: changes in subjective effects among social drinkers. *Psychopharmacology* **97**: 365–9.

Powell, J., Gray, J.A., Bradley, B.P., Kasvikis, Y., Strang, J., Barratt, L. and Marks, I. (1990). The effects of exposure to drug-related cues in detoxified opiate addicts: a theoretical review and some new data. *Addictive Behaviors* **15**: 339–54.

Radlow, R. and Hurst, P.M. (1985). Temporal relations between blood alcohol concentration and alcohol effect: an experiment with human subjects. *Psychopharmacology* **85**: 260–6.

Read, J.D. and Yuille, J.C. (in press). Recollections of a robbery. Effects of arousal and alcohol upon recall and person identification. *Law and Human Behavior.*

Rix, K.J.B. (1983). Predicting blood alcohol. *Nursing Times* **19** (Oct.): 68–9.

Rohrbaugh, J.W., Stapleton, J.M., Parasuraman, R., Frowein, H.W., Adinoff, B., Varner, J.L., Zubovic, E.A., Lane, E.A., Eckardt, M.J. and Linnoila, M. (1988). Alcohol intoxication reduces visual sustained attention. *Psychopharmacology* **96**: 442–6.

Rohsenow, D.J. and Marlatt, G.A. (1981). The balanced placebo design: methodological considerations. *Addictive Behaviours* **6**: 107–22.

Ross, D.F. and Pihl, R.O. (1988). Alcohol, self-focus and complex reaction-time performance. *Journal of Studies on Alcohol* **49**: 115–25.

Russ, N.W., Harwood, K.M. and Geller, S.E. (1986). Estimating alcohol impairment in the field: implications for drunken driving. *Journal of Studies on Alcohol* **47**: 237–40.

Sedman, A.J., Wilkinson, P.K., Sakmar, E., Weidler, D.J. and Wagner, J.G. (1976). Food effects on absorption and metabolism of alcohol. *Journal of Studies on Alcohol* **37**: 1197–214.

Shapiro, A.P. and Nathan, P.E. (1986). Human tolerance to alcohol: the role of Pavlovian conditioning processes. *Psychopharmacology* **88**: 90–5.

Sher, K.J. (1985). Subjective effects of alcohol: the influence of setting and individual differences in alcohol expectancies. *Journal of Studies on Alcohol* **46**: 137–46.

Shukit, M.A. (1984). Subjective responses to alcohol in sons of alcoholics and control subjects. *Archives of General Psychiatry* **41**: 879–84.

Smith, A.P. and Miles, C. (1986a). Effects of lunch on selective and sustained attention. *Neuropsychobiology* **16**: 117–20.

Smith, A.P. and Miles, C. (1986b). The effects of lunch on cognitive vigilance tasks. *Ergonomics* **29**: 1251–61.

Smith, A.P. and Miles, C. (1986c). Acute effects of meals, noise and nightwork. *British Journal of Psychology* **77**: 377–87.

Spring, B., Maller, O., Wurtman, J., Digman, L. and Cozolino, L. (1983). Effects of protein and carbohydrate meals on mood and performance: interactions with sex and age. *Journal of Psychiatric Research* **17**: 155–67.

Staiger, P.K. and White, J.M. (1988). Conditioned alcohol-like and alcohol-opposite responses in humans. *Psychopharmacology* **95**: 87–91.

Steele, C.M. and Josephs, R.A. (1990). Alcohol Myopia. Its prized and dangerous effects. *American Psychologist* **45**: 921–933.

Taberner, P.V. (1980). Sex differences in the effects of low doses of ethanol on human reaction time. *Psychopharmacology* **70**: 283–6.

Thomson, J.B. and Newlin, D.B. (1988). Effects of alcohol conditioning and expectancy on a visuo-motor integration task. *Addictive Behaviours* **13**: 73–7.

Tiplady, B. (1991). Alcohol as a comparator. In *Ambulatory Anaesthesia and Sedation: Impairment and Recovery*, edited by I.D. Keppler, L.D. Sanders and M. Rosen. Oxford: Blackwell, pp. 26–37.

Tucker, J.A. and Vuchinich, R.E. (1983). An information processing analysis of the effects of alcohol on perceptions of facial emotions. *Psychopharmacology* **79**: 215–19.

Wait, J.S., Welch, R.B., Thurgate, J.K. and Hineman, J. (1982). Drinking history and sex of subject in the effects of alcohol on perception and perceptual-motor coordination. *The International Journal of the Addictions* **17**: 445–62.

Watson, P.E., Watson, I.D. and Batt, R.D. (1981). Prediction of blood alcohol concentrations in human subjects: updating the Widmark equation. *Journal of Studies on Alcohol* **42**: 547–56.

Weingartner, H. and Murphy, D.L. (1977). State-dependent storage and retrieval of experience while intoxicated. In *Alcohol and Human Memory*, edited by I.M. Birnbaum and E.S. Parker. Hillsdale, NJ: Erlbaum.

Welling, P.G., Lyons, B.S., Elliott, M.S. and Amidon, G.L. (1977). Pharmacokinetics of alcohol following single doses to fasted and non-fasted subjects. *Journal of Clinical Pharmacology* **17**: 199–206.

Wigmore, S.W. and Hinson, R.E. (1991). The influence of setting on consumption in the balanced placebo design. *British Journal of Addiction* **86**: 205–15.

Williams, R.M., Goldman, M.S. and Williams, D.L. (1981). Expectancy and pharmacological effects of alcohol on human cognitive and motor performance: the compensation for alcohol effects. *Journal of Abnormal Psychology* **90**: 267–70.

Wilson, J.R., Erwin, G.V., McClearn, G.E., Plomin, R., Johnson, R.C., Ahern, F.M. and Cole, R.E. (1984). Effects of ethanol. II: Behavioral sensitivity and acute behavioral tolerance. *Alcoholism: Clinical and Experimental Research* **8**: 366–74.

Wilson, P. (1980). *Drinking in England and Wales*. London: HMSO.

Yesavage, J.A. and Leirer, V.O. (1986). Hangover effects on aircraft pilots 14 hours after alcohol ingestion: a preliminary report. *American Journal of Psychiatry* **143**: 1546–50.

Young, J.A. and Pihl, R.O. (1982). Alcohol consumption and response in men social drinkers. *Journal of Studies on Alcohol* **43**: 334–51.

Young, R.McD., Oei, T.P.S. and Knight, R.G. (1990). The tension reduction hypothesis revisited: an alcohol expectancy perspective. *British Journal of Addiction* **85**: 31–40.

5

Smoking, Nicotine and Human Performance

K.A. WESNES & A.C. PARROTT

INTRODUCTION

Preview

Over the past thirty-five years cigarette smoking has passed from being viewed as an acceptable social habit to a major health risk. Despite virtual universal awareness of the health risks in the Western world, with 100,000 deaths caused by smoking in the UK alone each year, it persists as a widespread habit among all age groups (Parrott, 1991d; Royal College of Physicians, 1983). Yet, of all forms of persistant drug abuse, tobacco use is clouded in the most controversy. Firstly, it is not universally accepted that nicotine is the prime motivator for the habit (Kumar et al., 1978). Secondly, there are no psychological effects of smoking which are generally accepted to form the basis for the addiction. In contrast, alcohol use for example has no such ambiguities, few would argue that widespread persistent alcohol use is unrelated to the alcohol content of drinks, nor are people unclear about the psychological effects of alcohol. Despite this difference, smoking is one of the most common forms of drug addiction, nicotine displaying all of the classical hallmarks of an addictive drug (Russell, 1989). Once begun, smoking is difficult to give up, while it is even harder to avoid relapse.

Frustratingly for the researcher, smokers themselves have a limited vocabulary for their motives for smoking. The most common is to relax or control stress, but similar in frequency are vague terms concerned with addiction, for instance craving for a cigarette, and the ensuing relief when one becomes available. What then is the basis of this addictive habit? How

HANDBOOK OF HUMAN PERFORMANCE
VOLUME 2 ISBN 0-12-650352-4

can an activity without a widely acknowledged psychological effect become so potently addictive. The chapter attempts to shed light on this problem by considering the only objective measure of psychological change which cigarette smoking has been consistently found to produce: increased mental efficiency. This is an unlikely and often unrecognized psychoactive effect, yet could be closely involved in the motivation to persist with this bizarre form of social drug use.

Pharmacokinetics of nicotine absorption

Nicotine is a naturally occurring alkaloid which is produced solely by the plant *Nicotinia tobacum*. In its unionized form nicotine freely permeates membranes including the respiratory alveoli, the skin, and buccal and nasal mucosae (Travell, 1960). When tobacco is burnt, the small amount of nicotine which is not destroyed by the heat becomes attached to the particles of tar which constitute the smoke. If the smoke is drawn into the mouth, some of the smoke particles will collide with the buccal membrane, and if the pH of the smoke is sufficiently high, as with cigar smoke, some of the nicotine will be absorbed. With cigarette smoke however, due to its generally low pH, little or no nicotine is absorbed in this manner, but if the smoke is taken into the lungs to a sufficient depth to reach the alveoli, virtually all of the nicotine will be removed from the smoke.

In terms of drug delivery systems to the CNS, cigarette smoking is unrivalled for the speed at which a bolus of nicotine is passed into the brain circulation. Following an inhaled puff of a cigarette, arterial and brain nicotine levels become very high with a substantial proportion being taken up into CNS tissue within ten seconds of the puff. This is faster than intravenous infusion and, as we see later, performance changes can be detected within a minute of a single puff. Also, a smoker can precisely titrate the puff of the cigarette to self-administer the amount of nicotine desired, the volume and lung retention time being the crucial parameters. Thereafter, brain concentrations decline rapidly as the nicotine is passed to other tissues. Plasma concentrations, however, drop more slowly, the half life of nicotine in man being 120 minutes (Benowitz et al., 1982).

Other traditional forms of tobacco use also lead to nicotine absorption. Both snuff and chewing tobacco have a sufficiently high pH to allow rapid mucosal absorption. In the case of snuff, particularly dramatic peaks of plasma nicotine have been detected (Russell et al., 1981). Indeed, one of the most persuasive arguments that tobacco use represents nicotine-seeking behaviour is that forms of use which do not result in nicotine absorption do not become popular. Gut absorption of nicotine is low due to the acidic environment of the stomach, and also because of the high first pass hepatic metabolism of nicotine. This almost certainly explains why there are no tobacco-based drinks. Primary cigar and pipe smokers rarely take the smoke into their lungs, nicotine being absorbed buccally. On the other hand, few cigarette smokers fail to take the smoke deep into the respiratory system, where nicotine absorption occurs.

THE STUDY OF THE EFFECTS OF NICOTINE ON HUMAN PERFORMANCE

To those new to the field, studying the performance effects of nicotine appears to be straightforward; surely smokers when smoking only need to be compared with smokers when not smoking? However, as is seen in the ensuing sections, this field is dogged by methodological difficulties, resulting from the complex nature of the delivery of nicotine to the CNS, and the unfortunate fact of smoking/nicotine addiction. Thus to address even basic questions, studies need to be extremely well designed. Yet the interpretation of effects obtained even from well designed studies remains a potential minefield. The ensuing sections identify some of these experimental difficulties and pitfalls while illustrating the various interpretations of the data. As will become clear, while knowledge of the effects of nicotine has advanced considerably, inadequate experimental design and shallow interpretation, are disappointingly frequent in this literature.

An archetypal study

One exemplary performance study funded by the American Committee for the study of the Tobacco Problem was entitled *The Influence of Tobacco Smoking on Mental and Motor Efficiency*. It was a placebo-controlled, single-blind, within subject repeated measures design in which the effects of tobacco smoke were assessed on twelve tests of human performance including hand tremor, tapping rate, letter cancellation, reading reaction times, rate of association learning, speed and accuracy of mental arithmetic, and digit span. Sophisticated equipment was used, which included a reaction time apparatus, accurate to $\frac{1}{300}$ second, and a voice key to facilitate the measurement of reading reaction times. A non-tobacco control was employed which prevented the eighteen volunteers realizing until after the study that there had been a tobacco-free condition. The reader may not be especially impressed with this particular study, as a number of similarly sophisticated and well controlled trials have been conducted in recent years. However, what should attract the attention of the reader is that this trial was reported by Clark Hull in 1924! Sadly for human psychopharmacology, Hull subsequently turned his efforts to animal experimentation and became famous for his work and theories on classical conditioning. Hull died in 1962, by which time no subsequent investigation had approached his classic study in terms of overall experimental excellence. A little space is devoted to this study, partly on merit as it was a truly excellent piece of work, but also because Hull identified many of the methodological problems inherent in this area of research.

The first methodological issue involved the control dose. Hull (1924) wrote: 'In modern drug experimentation, inseparably connected with the dose is the troublesome yet insistent matter of the control dose' (p. 22); and later: 'It is easy to show that without an adequate control, the results of tobacco experimentation may be almost meaningless' (p. 24). Hull gives an enjoyable description of his ingenious technique for providing a non-tobacco control condition for pipe smoking. By means of electrical induction he was able to get blindfolded pipe smokers to puff warm, slightly moistened air through a pipe (see Figure 5.1). An important part of the illusion was for one experimenter to smoke a pipe of tobacco in the same room, 'thus furnishing the indispensable odour' (p. 30). Hull assumed there was no taste to the smoke, and thus the last factor lacking was the 'occasional slight bite of the tobacco on the tongue. A little excess heat easily furnished this last necessary element of pain' (p. 30). This technique was a complete success. None of the volunteers had any idea that they were being fooled during the trial, and on being informed of the deception afterwards, several insisted that they had received nothing but tobacco smoke. Another important control concerned the motivational state of the volunteers. As part of the work up to the trial Hull extracted from each volunteer 'a solemn promise ... to keep up throughout the experiment the maximum effort that could consistently be maintained' (p. 27). Rarely do contemporary papers report any such efforts to ensure that the volunteers make reasonable efforts to perform the various performance tests.

Six further aspects of the trial design illustrate the richness of Hull's experimental procedures. Firstly, the initial experimental session was subsequently designated as a training session and excluded from data analysis. Secondly, on each study day the volunteers were given a baseline pre-smoking run through on the thirty minute test battery. This helped control for inter-individual differences and day-to-day fluctuations, and further reduced the possibility of practice effects contaminating the results. Thirdly, the volunteers took part in all stages of the trial, thus acting as their own experimental controls and reducing the influence of inter-individual differences. Fourthly, where possible, Hull measured both the speed and accuracy of task performance. Such comprehensive measurement of performance is essential if changes in information processing ability are to be unequivocally identified. Fifthly, the volunteers abstained from smoking for the three hours prior to each experimental session. Lastly, he measured heart rate and thus was able to provide evidence that nicotine was absorbed during the smoking condition. This degree of experimental control is all the more commendable when it is

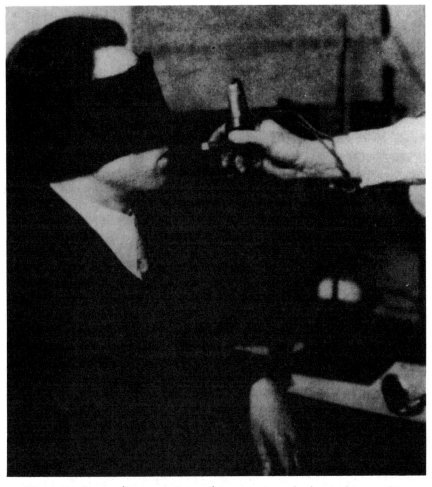

Figure 5.1 Pipe-smoking apparatus used to generate a placebo smoking condition. (After Hull, 1924.)

considered that over sixty years later, with all the technological and methodological advances which have occurred, rarely do studies attain all of these design features, while they sometimes fail to incorporate any.

By any standards this study was massive. Each of the eighteen volunteers returned on 18 consecutive days for experimental sessions lasting three hours. On half of the days the subjects received tobacco smoke, and on the other half hot, moist air. The study was thus extremely powerful in terms of the amount of data collected and the averaging over repeated days to reduce chance fluctuations.

Hull (1924) found both heart rate and hand tremor to be higher following the administration of tobacco than after hot air, which allows us to conclude that there was a difference in the amount of nicotine delivered in the two experimental conditions. The peak increase in heart rate was nine beats per minute which, while being less than that which is achieved during cigarette smoking, is consistent with the smaller amount of nicotine that is absorbed during pipe smoking. More recent work on plasma levels following different forms of nicotine administration indicates that compared with inhaled cigarette smoke, buccal absorption of nicotine from pipe and cigar smoke leads to modest, but nonetheless clearly identifiable, plasma nicotine uptake.

Besides demonstrating that hand tremor is increased by tobacco smoking, which has been subsequently replicated (Lippold et al., 1980; Wesnes and Warburton, 1983a), Hull found that smoking increased the speed of continuous mental addition for the smokers but not the non-smokers. Further, a likelihood of a gain in reading time was evidenced in both groups. Lastly, smoking disrupted rote learning and probably reduced digit span. This pattern of findings, though not dramatic, is generally consistent with our present knowledge of the effects of tobacco. The negative findings on several tasks are disappointing, but we do not know the extent to which the tasks were drug-sensitive. Further, it must be acknowledged that the amount of nicotine administered was modest, possibly similar to that produced by nicotine tablets, which can be shown to produce performance improvements only when sensitive tests are used. Also, we now know that nicotine can be absorbed via passive smoking, particularly alkaline pipe smoke which could lead to nicotine absorption via the nasal mucosa. Thus there was some possibility in Hull's study of nicotine uptake (from the experimenter smoking in the same room), on the control days. This may have served to counteract the efficacy of the control condition, the two conditions instead representing differing amounts of nicotine. Such differences are harder to detect than differences between nicotine and placebo. Despite this speculation, this was a truly exemplary study in its design and execution, and the modest performance effects could easily have reflected the unevaluated sensitivity of the tasks.

Organization of the performance sections

Despite this highly promising beginning, further research into the behavioural effects of nicotine and smoking hardly entered the literature until the 1960s. Since then, a large literature has emerged using a wide range of experimental designs, diverse forms of nicotine administration and numerous tests of performance. The literature could be organized in a number of ways: historically, by the nature of the tests, by the route and form of nicotine administration, by the study population, etc. The approach selected here is based on a general overview of the literature. Basically, nicotine, administered directly or via cigarette smoke, has a beneficial effect on a variety of tasks which require a high degree of concentration. On the other hand, if the task primarily measures the ability to learn or retrieve information, in general nicotine appears to concur no such benefit, while in some cases the drug is associated with inferior performance. The next section considers the effects of nicotine and smoking on tasks involving attention and information processing and sustained attention. This is followed by an overview of tests of learning and memory.

HUMAN PERFORMANCE: ATTENTION

The various tests discussed in the following sections cover a range of cognitive skills; they also have one thing in common in that they require high levels of attention for efficient performance. The simpler the performance requirements of a task, the greater the likelihood that changes in the efficiency of its performance will reflect alterations to the attention paid to task performance (Wesnes, 1977). Tasks which involve psychomotor skill (such as pursuit rotor) or higher levels of intellectual processing (such as logical reasoning) will reflect changes in attention together with changes in the particular skill being assessed. These considerations should be borne in mind in the following sections.

Attention and mental effort have become closely associated cognitive skills since Kahneman's (1973) seminal work, *Attention and Effort*. Attention can be measured in brief psychomotor tasks involving reaction time, where the volunteer maintains a high alertness to react rapidly to predefined stimulus events. Attention is reflected in the degree of mental effort which the volunteer puts into the task and is measured in terms of both speed and accuracy. Using another terminology, it can be said that attention is reflected in the allocation of processing resources to the task. Vigilance reflects the maintenance of such readiness to respond to simple events over extended periods. Vigilance tasks are typically simple but protracted. Tasks which require higher levels of information processing and/or more involvement of working memory can also be taxing to volunteers, particularly if the information to be processed is presented rapidly. Again, the greater the investment of mental effort, the higher will be the ensuing performance. The quality of performance on cognitive and psychomotor tasks thus depends on the degree of mental effort expended upon them, in addition to the particular skills required by the specific task. Nicotine has beneficial effects on a variety of tasks of differing complexity, difficulty and duration. One parsimonious explanation for these effects is that nicotine maximizes the attentional effort which subjects can invest in the tasks. More complex conclusions may of course be suggested, that is the advantage of such a data-rich field of research.

In the first two sections, we consider in turn the effects of nicotine and smoking on short and long tasks requiring high degrees of concentration. This is consistent with the tradition that vigilance tasks are considered as separate from short duration tests requiring concentration (e.g. simple reaction time). It may be, however, that the principal difference between these tasks will turn out to be their duration rather than the cognitive processes they test.

Short duration tests requiring sustained mental effort

Fay (1936) looked at the effects of smoking on simple and choice reaction time. A within subject design was used, with eleven smokers tested on four successive occasions, twice following smoking and twice following not smoking. Reaction times were assessed on each session immediately following smoking and 5, 15, 30 and 60 minutes later. There was no apparent effect on simple reaction time but the mean data suggested that smoking had increased the speed of choice reaction time. Surprisingly the author performed no statistics but did present the raw data, which when subjected to an analysis of variance 47 years later by Wesnes and Warburton (1983a), revealed a marginally significant favourable effect of smoking on the speed of choice reaction ($p = 0.054$).

Cotten et al. (1971) studied the effects of smoking on simple reaction time. From the brief report, the fifteen male volunteers performed reaction time testing twice while smoking and twice while not. The equipment measured reaction times to the nearest 0.01 s (contrast with Hull's 1920 equipment of 0.0033). Reaction times were assessed pre-smoking and 5, 15, 25, 40 and 55 minutes later. Contrasts were only made over time within conditions, a limitation in the generalizability of the data. Cotten et al. reported slowed reaction times 5 minutes following smoking and an increase in speed at 40 and 55 minutes.

Snyder and Henningfield (1989) used fully deprived subjects (+ 12 hours). well practised on a battery of five information processing tasks before trial commencement. The tasks included letter search, rapid arithmetic and logical reasoning. Compared with baseline, placebo gum led to: 'significant increases in rate of performance (response time) on all five of the computerized performance assessment battery tasks' (p. 21). Significant performance decrements were therefore evident following nicotine deprivation. The two active gum conditions demonstrated comparatively superior performance to placebo, on all five tasks. Placebo/2 mg gum differences were significant on three of the five tasks, while placebo/4 mg gum comparisons were significant on four tasks. Thus in this well designed study significant performance changes were noted, even with the low levels of nicotine found with 2 mg and 4 mg gum (Figure 5.2).

Three studies are covered in more detail later, but their main findings should be noted here. Williams (1980) found smoking to enhance letter cancellation performance. Keenan et al. (1989) found tobacco chewing to improve the speed of performance in a sustained stimulus evaluation task.

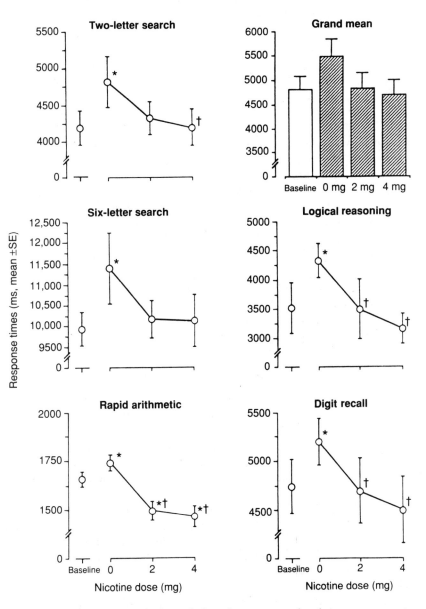

Figure 5.2 Response times for five tasks from the computerized performance assessment battery. (After Snyder and Henningfield, 1989.)

Parrott and Roberts (in press) found letter cancellation to be superior following smoking than following non-smoking.

The above studies demonstrate that there is a consistent superiority of performance on a wide variety of tasks following smoking/nicotine. The tasks all involve cognitive efficiency and the consistent finding of superiority with nicotine could be explained in terms of the drug improving the processing resources available to perform the various tasks.

Two further tasks that are frequently used in psychopharmacology are tapping and critical flicker fusion (CFF). Frith (1967) investigated the effects of nicotine upon psychomotor tapping. The data are difficult to summarize or fully understand since they were subjected to a series of *post hoc* interpretive analyses. Findings were discussed in terms of (inferred) involuntary rest pauses, the build up of reactive inhibition, and strategies hypothesized to avoid this reactive inhibition. Also, the nicotine dose was extremely small (0.1 mg chewed oral tablet), performance was only assessed for sixty-second periods, and the 2 × 2 cross-over design was analysed mainly by sign-tests and t-tests. It was suggested that nicotine increased inter-tap gap lengths (in all subjects), and delayed the appearance of reactive inhibition (in some subjects). Perhaps the clearest impression from this study was the difficulty of applying Hullian learning theory to modern psychopharmacology. This is an ironic conclusion, considering the sophistication of Hull's classic smoking and performance study. West and Jarvis (1986) investigated nasal nicotine solution on a finger-tapping task, over a series of five subtrials. Nasal nicotine significantly increased the speed of finger tapping in each trial. Furthermore, this increase was 'reduced though not obliterated by a small dose of mecamylamine', a cholinergic antagonist. Hindmarch *et al.* (1990) found a significant decrease in movement reaction time with 4 mg nicotine gum, but not with 2 mg nicotine gum.

The early 1950s saw several studies of the effects of smoking on the CFF threshold. This psychophysical threshold represents the frequency at which a flickering light source appears to be continuous. It is neither a cognitive performance task nor a direct measure of mental efficiency, although the threshold is generally correlated with the state of mental alertness, with lowered alertness associated with lowered CFF thresholds (Parrott, 1982). Two of these studies showed evidence that smoking lowered the CFF threshold (Larson *et al.*, 1950; Fabricant and Rose, 1951) while a third produced mixed results, possibly because some of the volunteers who were required to smoke were non-smokers (Garner *et al.*, 1953). A more recent study showed that three puffs from a cigarette were sufficient for the CFF to be lowered significantly over the next 20 minutes (Waller and Levander, 1980). A related measure to the CFF is the two flash fusion (TFF) threshold, which is the gap of two successive flashes at which the observed can no longer discriminate the flashes. Tong *et al.* (1974) showed that smoking lowered the TFF threshold.

Long duration tests requiring sustained attention

Three studies have investigated the effects of smoking on driving simulators. In the first, Tarriere and Hartemann (1964), used a simulated driving task in which tracking was combined with peripheral visual surveillance. The measure reported in the paper was the percentage of visual targets which were missed during the continuous $2\frac{1}{2}$ hour session. A group of twenty-four smokers performed the task on two occasions; once smoking normally before and during the session, and the other while abstaining 20 hours before and during the session. Twenty-four non-smokers also performed the task. When smoking, the smokers showed no decline in detection over the first 2 hours in marked contrast to the non-smoking condition when they declined markedly over this period. The two conditions were significantly different. The detection performance of the non-smokers fell between that of the two smoking conditions, but was not significantly different from either. The caveat in this otherwise generally commendable trial was that the authors did not report the scores on the tracking task. Obviously, the superior detection performance while smoking could be argued to reflect a strategy shift, with more attention being paid to the visual task at the expense of tracking. Without the complete data this alternative possibility confounds interpretation of the study.

Heimstra *et al.* (1967) used a more sophisticated driving task which measured four aspects of sustained performance: reaction time, steering efficiency, brake light vigilance and meter vigilance. Three groups of twenty volunteers performed the six hour task on a single occasion: smokers who were allowed *ad libitum* access to cigarettes throughout, smokers who were not allowed to smoke, and non-smokers. Both groups of smokers were allowed to smoke normally prior to arrival at the laboratory. The performance of the deprived smokers was poorest overall on all four measures of performance, this being statistically significant for tracking and brake light vigilance. The performance of the non-smokers was not significantly different from the smoking smokers at any time, though on reaction time and meter vigilance the non-smokers significantly declined over time whereas the smokers did not. Overall, the results are consistent with much subsequent work showing that smokers perform more efficiently on tasks requiring continuous attention when smoking than when not. The general failure of the smoking smokers to perform more efficiently than the non-smokers has also generally been interpreted as supporting the notion that cessation of smoking impairs performance as opposed to smoking enhancing efficiency. One issue which has been generally overlooked is that the number of cigarettes smoked during the study varied from 4 to 22 with a mean of 10. This suggests that many of the smokers in the smoking group will have gone fairly long periods without smoking during the trial, thus potentially experiencing periods of deprivation. Further, the act of smoking itself was observed physically to impair tracking control which, though non-significant, must have added to the general error variance.

Ashton et al. (1973) compared smoking-smokers and non-smokers on a car driving simulator. Stimulus conditions comprised both a driving film and light signals mounted on a display above the dashboard. The dashboard signals instructed the subject to brake, steer left, steer right, indicate left or indicate right. These often corresponded with the requirements implicit in the driving film, although it was possible to anticipate them in some situations (these fast responses were apparently often excluded from the data analysis). Three basic conditions were assessed: dashboard signals only, signals congruent with film, and signals plus film but sometimes incongruent. Further complexities were also present, e.g. different degrees of performance response being demanded. A wealth of dependent variables were also assessed. On some the non-smokers were superior, on others the smokers were superior, while on many measures there were no significant group differences. Furthermore, all group differences disappeared following cigarette extinction, suggesting that the act of smoking might have physically affected performance on some tasks. Three conclusions emerge from this study. Firstly, that non-smokers and smoking-smokers were broadly similar in complex psycho-motor performance. Secondly, deprived smokers should also have been tested. Thirdly, the whole design was over-complex. This study is, however, an example of that rare creature in human psychopharmacology, a comprehensive performance-simulator trial (Parrott, 1987).

A number of other studies have looked at the effects of smoking on sustained performance. Frankenhaeuser et al. (1971) studied simple visual reaction time. The group of twelve smokers performed the eighty-minute task twice, once smoking at twenty-minute intervals and once not. The volunteers refrained from smoking overnight prior to the two morning sessions. While smoking, the subjects were able to maintain their initial speed throughout testing while when not smoking, speed declined over time, the difference between the conditions being statistically significant. In a second study from this laboratory, the effects of smoking were again studied on sustained reaction time testing, with complex reaction time testing measured along with simple reaction time (Myrsten et al., 1971). Smoking again prevented the decline over time in the simple task while on the complex task, smoking shortened response times. In a third study, smokers who reported that they smoked in high-arousal situations were only improved by smoking in a complex and highly demanding reaction time task, while smokers who reported that they typically smoked in low-arousal situation were found to be improved only in a visual vigilance task (Myrsten et al., 1972).

Wesnes and Warburton compared the performance of three groups of ten volunteers on an 80 minute visual vigilance task (Wesnes and Warburton, 1978; Wesnes, 1979). The task used was the continuous clock task in which the subjects observed the sweep of the second hand of a clock for brief pauses which occurred on average forty times every ten minutes (Mackworth, 1965). One group were non-smokers, the other two groups comprising smokers who were requested to abstain from smoking overnight. One of the groups of smokers was required to smoke a standard cigarette to a mark a few millimetres from the filter at 20, 40 and 60 minutes into the 80 minute vigil, the other group abstained from smoking. Signal detection theory was used to derive a sensitivity index from both the correct detections of the targets as well as false positive responses. This index has the great advantage of reflecting the actual ability of the volunteers to detect the experimental targets independently of any overall biases they may have had concerning willingness to make responses. The smoking smokers maintained their initial level of performance over the 80 minute task, whereas the non-smokers and deprived smokers showed typical vigilance decrements. Unlike the findings of Heimstra *et al.*, the smokers were significantly superior to the non-smokers, although towards the later stages of the task the trend of the deprived smokers was to perform less efficiently than the non-smokers, a similar pattern to that reported by Tarriere and Hartemann.

In a second study, an 80 minute auditory vigilance task and within subject design was used, with smokers smoking regular cigarettes on one occasion and nicotine-free cigarettes on the other (Wesnes and Warburton, 1978; Wesnes, 1979). As in the previous study, cigarettes were smoked at 20, 40 and 60 minutes into the vigil. Smokers maintained their initial level of stimulus sensitivity on regular cigarettes, but showed a vigilance decrement when smoking the nicotine-free cigarettes.

To determine whether nicotine alone could have been responsible for the results obtained in the previous two studies, Wesnes and Warburton (1978; Wesnes, 1979) made nicotine tablets by titrating measured amounts of nicotine onto dextrose tablets. Placebo tablets were made equally bitter by the addition of tabasco sauce, making them indistinguishable by taste or appearance. The tablets were then administered at 20 minute intervals in the Mackworth continuous vigilance task to simulate the smoking design previously employed. A within-subjects design was employed, subjects performing the task on three occasions, once with placebo tablets and twice with active tablets (1 mg and 2 mg). Twelve non-smokers, twelve light smokers and twelve heavy smokers took part. In an initial evaluation of the hit data, the smokers detected more targets with nicotine than without, whereas there was no difference for the non-smokers (Wesnes and Warburton, 1978). However, when the false alarms were subsequently analysed, the non-smokers were found to make significantly less false alarms with nicotine (Wesnes, 1979). This prompted a reanalysis of the data combining the hit and false alarm scores using signal detection theory, which showed that all three groups (non-smokers, light and heavy smokers) showed reduced decrements in stimulus sensitivity with nicotine (Wesnes *et al.*, 1983).

The general consensus from the studies in this section is that smokers perform more efficiently on sustained tests requiring attention when smoking. This effect appears to be mediated by nicotine, and the last study suggests that non-smokers also benefit from the drug.

The rapid visual information processing (RVIP) task

The classic vigilance tasks described in the previous section had easily identifiable stimuli which, due to their infrequent presentation over time, became increasingly unlikely to be detected. This vigilance decrement could clearly be counteracted by nicotine and smoking, but as performance generally started off at a high level, these tasks were relatively insensitive to performance improvements in the absolute sense. Wesnes and Warburton therefore sought to develop a more sensitive measure. The task they developed, rapid visual information processing (RVIP), was based upon earlier tests of attention (Bakan, 1959; Talland, 1966). The earlier paradigm involved listening to a repetitive series of digits, and searching for three consecutive odd (e.g. 3, 7, 5) or three consecutive even (e.g. 2, 6, 4) numbers. The difficulty of the Talland/Bakan task was heightened by increasing the digit presentation rate from sixty to one hundred per minute. In order to measure reaction times and increase the general control over the procedures, the task was computerized, with digits presented on a visual display unit instead of headphones. Pilot testing revealed that reliable performance changes occurred over comparatively short periods (i.e. twenty minutes; Wesnes, 1979), suggesting that task was indeed more sensitive to fluctuations in efficiency than classical vigilance tasks. Subsequent work has confirmed this, showing that RVIP performance can be reliably resolved into one minute epochs (Wesnes and Warburton, 1984a; Revell, 1988). Another feature which has contributed to the sensitivity of this procedure is the constant high rate of targets (eight per minute) which ensures that even brief moments of inattention can be detected. Lastly, the ability to measure the speed of each response as well as the accuracy, permits performance improvements to be successfully differentiated from strategy changes.

Wesnes and Warburton undertook an extensive series of studies into the effects of different strength cigarettes, and other modes of nicotine administration using the RVIP task. The basic methodology used in the early studies was to obtain a ten minute performance baseline on the task prior to smoking or nicotine administration. The cigarette was then smoked or the tablet taken during a ten minute rest period, after which the subjects again performed the task, this time continuously for twenty minutes.

Wesnes and Warburton (1978, 1983b) noted significant improvements in RVIP speed and accuracy, with nicotine-deprived subjects given three strengths of cigarette. The high dose cigarette (1.65 mg nicotine), was superior to both lower dose conditions (0.27 mg, 0.7 mg nicotine). In a second study, no-smoking and nicotine-free cigarette smoking control conditions, were compared with two-strengths of cigarette (0.6 mg, 1.84 mg nicotine). Both control conditions led to a performance decline from baseline, while performance was improved to similar extents by the two cigarettes (study 2 in Wesnes and Warburton, 1983b; also Figure 5.3). In a later report, four strengths of cigarette were compared (Wesnes and Warburton, 1984a). Cigarette smoking led to significantly higher target detection and significantly faster response speed, while performance declined over time in the no-smoking control condition. The greatest performance improvement occurred with the 1.5 mg rather than the 1.7 mg nicotine cigarette. This possibly indicated an inverted-U arousal performance function: 'This supports previous findings ... which suggested that there might be a maximum delivery above and below which performance improvements tend to be smaller' (Wesnes and Warburton, 1984a, p. 341). Arousal performance relationships are further discussed later in this chapter. In each of the above studies there was evidence that besides counteracting the declines in efficiency which occurred in non-smoking/nicotine-free smoking sessions, during the first ten minutes of performance following smoking, performance was frequently significantly higher than during the pre-smoking baseline.

In a further series of studies Wesnes and Warburton repeatedly confirmed these findings and demonstrated significant RVIP changes under a wide range

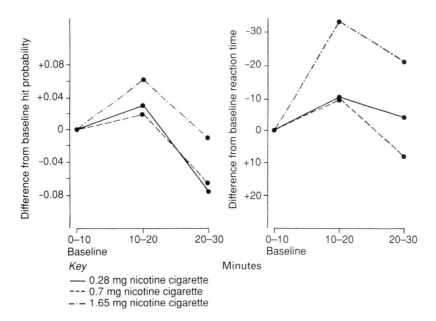

Key
—— 0.28 mg nicotine cigarette
--- 0.7 mg nicotine cigarette
—·— 1.65 mg nicotine cigarette

Figure 5.3 Group mean differences from baseline: hit probability and reaction time. (After Wesnes and Warburton, 1983b, Figure 2.)

of experimental and pharmacological conditions (Wesnes and Warburton, 1978, 1983; Wesnes, 1987). The findings from these trials were summarized as follows:

> The improvements in information processing produced by smoking occur under a wide range of conditions. Every nicotine containing cigarette we have studied improves performance. Improvements occur irrespective of the duration of testing, the speed of presentation of the digits, the density of the targets, whether or not the smokers smoke while performing, whether or not they are filmed, whether or not electrical activity is measured in another laboratory, and whether testing is carried out in the morning or afternoon. (Wesnes, 1987, p. 66)

Other research groups have confirmed the sensitivity of the RVIP task to smoking. Michel and Battig (1989) developed an adaptive version of the RVIP paradigm, where each correct detection automatically increased the rate of stimulus presentation, while a missed target led to a decrease in stimulus presentation speed. They found significantly faster processing after cigarette smoking, when compared with sham smoking. Michel et al. (1987) also noted significant performance improvements after smoking, with this adaptive RVIP task. Parrott and Winder (1989) and Parrott and Craig (in press) used the original RVIP task and found significant performance improvements in both studies when subjects smoked their own brand of cigarette. All the above studies used fully task-trained and nicotine-deprived subjects.

To confirm that nicotine was crucial to the effects of smoking on this task, Wesnes and Warburton (1984b) studied the effects of small doses of nicotine administered in tablet form (0, 0.5, 1.0 and 1.5 mg) on the performance of nine non-smokers. Dose-related performance changes were detected, with lowest performance under placebo, performance generally highest after the high dose nicotine (1.5 mg), and intermediate values for the other two doses (0.5 mg, 1.0 mg nicotine). Performance in terms of correct detections and the speed of response deteriorated significantly over time in the placebo condition, and showed a trend for the low dose of nicotine. In contrast, target hits showed a non-significant increase over baseline following the 1.5 mg dose ($p < 0.1$). Target detection after 1.5 mg tablet was significantly higher than the other three conditions in combination.

Parrott and Winder (1989) investigated RVIP performance following nicotine gum and cigarette smoking; group mean target detections are shown in Fig. 5.4. At the second post-test, a significant monotonic dose response function was present ($p < 0.01$). Furthermore, both the placebo/cigarette and placebo/4 mg gum comparisons were significant (each $p < 0.05$). In an extended replication, Parrott and Craig (in press) confirmed the general superiority of nicotine over placebo, although the pecking order among the nicotine conditions was now different. The placebo/cigarette comparison was significant during the first half of the post-test, while the placebo/2 mg gum comparison became significant during the second post-test period (immediately after smokers extinguished their cigarettes). Michel et al. (1988) found no

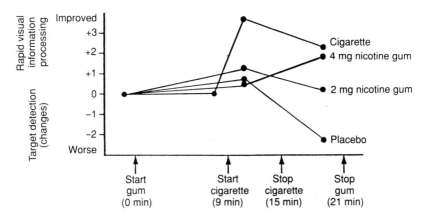

Figure 5.4 RVIP target detections following nicotine chewing gum and cigarette smoking. (After Parrott and Winder, 1989.)

effect of nicotine gum upon RVIP performance, with similar group mean scores for placebo gum and 4 mg nicotine gum. However, aspects of their design may be criticized: brief pre-trial training/practice, and only two hours of nicotine deprivation before gum administration and testing.

Another avenue of study using the RVIP was to determine the electro-cortical changes which accompany the effects of smoking on task efficiency. In a collaborative program with John Edwards and Tony Gale at Southampton University, it was demonstrated that smoking increased electrocortical arousal during the RVIP task (Warburton and Wesnes, 1979). In a subsequent study the event related potential (ERP) to the third stimulus digit in each target stimulus triad (e.g. 2−4−8) was recorded (Edwards *et al.*, 1985). High nicotine cigarettes led to significantly reduced latency of the P300 component of the ERP, together with improved speed and frequency of RVIP target detection. The reduction in the latency of the P300 to the third stimulus, was the same as the magnitude of reduction in the speed of response. This comprises a rare demonstration of concordance between electrophysiological and behavioural change with psychopharmacological research. The size and latency of P300 is thought to reflect the amount of stimulus evaluation taking place. In this context it could be argued to represent the amount of mental effort or processing resources being allocated to the task, with the reduction in latency following smoking representing the extra processing capacity made available by nicotine.

In a further research program, the RVIP task was refined to analyse the performance effects of a single inhalation. Following five minutes of baseline performance, once every minute for the next ten minutes the colour of the VDU screen changed for several seconds (or digits were not displayed); this comprised a pre-arranged signal for the subject to inhale on their cigarette.

Performance during these brief inhalation periods was ignored. Thus each one minute block represented the effects of a single inhalation (Revell, 1988; Wesnes and Warburton, 1984a; Wesnes, Simpson and Christmas, 1988a). Wesnes and Warburton (1984a) reported that, 'following the first puff, the percentage of hits in the smoking condition was significantly higher than in the non-smoking condition ... similarly ... reaction times were significantly faster'. Revell (1988) also noted significant 'puff-by-puff' improvements from the second inhalation onwards, both for response time and target detection (Figure 5.5). Wesnes *et al.* (1988a) further confirmed these puff-by-puff improvements. The above findings are consistent with those from the two previous sections. Smokers perform tests requiring high levels of concentration more efficiently when smoking than when not. Work with nicotine tablets confirms that nicotine is responsible for these effects; also, that these effects can sometimes be detected with non-smokers.

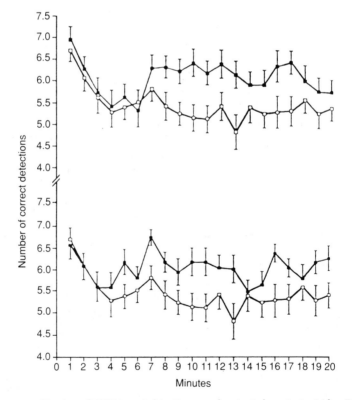

Figure 5.5 Number of RVIP target detections, made minute by minute. (After Revell, 1988.) Smoking commenced at minute 6 and continued every minute until minute 15. The two plots represent smoking of two similar cigarettes: ■, smoking; ⊟, sham-smoking.

Distractibility and width of attention

The Stroop is one of the classic human performance tests (Stroop, 1935). Numerous versions have been developed, but two conditions always need to be present: control and distraction. In the control condition, the subject scans a series of coloured blocks and names the colour of each consecutive block. In the distraction condition, the subject scans a series of colour names (e.g. blue ... green) displayed in different colours (e.g. the word blue printed in red; yellow printed in green). The subject is instructed to ignore the distracting colour name, and identify the colour in which it is printed. The Stroop effect comprises the difference in response time between the control and experimental conditions.

Wesnes and Warburton (1978) noted a significant reduction in the size of the Stroop effect following nicotine. Wesnes (1979) undertook a re-analysis of this data, and showed that the performance improvement occurred only during the second of two test periods, though the effects were indistinguishable between smokers and non-smokers. The suggestion was that nicotine improved performance only when subjects were already fatigued. Wesnes and Revell (1984) found no drug effect on the same Stroop task, although nicotine did counteract the performance decrement induced by the cholinergic antagonist scopolamine. Suter *et al.* (1983) investigated a complex variant of the Stroop task, where complementary colour names had to be identified for three aspects of each stimulus: background colour, colour of stimulus, and colour name. The authors concluded: 'No effects of smoking on Stroop performance were detected' (Suter *et al.*, 1983, p. 269). There were, however, problems with this study: it was unclear how the task generated a Stroop effect; statistical comparisons were between low-nicotine (0.2 mg) and high-nicotine (1.2 mg) cigarettes (surprisingly, the no-smoking group did not undertake the performance task); pre-test smoking abstinence was not mentioned, and subjects were only briefly trained. Parrott and Craig (in press) found no drug effect upon speed or accuracy on a computerized Stroop task, although RVIP and letter cancellation were significantly affected in this study. There was, however, evidence of a ceiling effect with the Stroop errors. To summarize, while there is no consistent evidence of altered distractibility under nicotine, the studies in this area have not been problem-free. The words of the Surgeon General (1988, p. 386) therefore remain pertinent: 'Conclusions [about nicotine and distractibility] must be tentative until the findings of Wesnes and Warburton (1978) are replicated.'

Few studies have been undertaken into selective attention, divided attention, or width of attention. Tarriere and Hartmann's (1964) study of selective attention over $2\frac{1}{2}$ hours, was described earlier. In an unpublished study (Warburton, Wesnes and Ansboro, summarized in Warburton and Walters, 1989, p. 227), two series of RVIP digits were presented simultaneously; the first series was in the visual mode, while the other series was in the auditory mode. Cigarette smoking led to significantly improved performance. However, it is difficult to gauge whether this comprised the usual improvement in sustained attention, or a reflected specific alteration in selective attention. Parrott and Craig (in press) investigated the effects of cigarette smoking and nicotine gum on a computerized width of attention task. Under all drug conditions there was a highly significant superiority in both speed and accuracy to the central visual stimuli. However, width of attention performance was not significantly affected by drug condition.

Summary

This section has described a large body of research having a consistent theme: tasks are performed more efficiently when smokers smoke than when they do not. The evidence from nicotine tablets and chewing gum is that nicotine administered alone produces comparable effects. These tasks range from basic psychomotor tapping to complex driving simulation, but all require high levels of concentration for efficient performance and involve neither the learning of novel information nor the retrieval of previously learned material. One parsimonious explanation of these effects is that nicotine enables volunteers to concentrate more efficiently through the allocation of increased processing resources to task performance. These improvements occur quickly (within one minute from the puff of a cigarette), but can then be sustained over extended periods. The general finding that smokers perform information processing tasks more efficiently when smoking than when not, has been repeatedly demonstrated. However, the mechanisms of these effects and their precise nature are the subject of much dispute (see the controversies described later in this chapter).

HUMAN PERFORMANCE: LEARNING AND MEMORY

In contrast to the work described above, the literature on the effects of cigarette smoking on learning and memory is less extensive, and the findings less clear-cut. Hull (1924) found that non-smokers when smoking had a reduced auditory memory span for series of 7–12 digits which was as evident eighty minutes following smoking to immediately after. Smokers showed a similar though slightly less marked pattern of response. Hull also studied the effects of smoking on the learning of associations between nonsense syllables and geometric shapes. For both smokers and non-smokers there was a 9 per cent loss in the rate of learning immediately after smoking which had passed by one hour. Over half a century later these two results have found general support.

Williams (1980) studied the effects of smoking three different strength cigarettes and sham smoking on the ability of forty-eight smokers to learn series of nine digits. He found that smoking increased the number of errors while the magnitude of the effect was directly related to the strength of cigarettes.

Three studies by Andersson and her co-workers have confirmed Hull's finding of impaired memory immediately following smoking. Andersson and Post (1974) gave subjects thirty successive trials in which they had to learn the order of nonsense syllables by correctly predicting the next in sequence. Twelve smokers were found to perform less efficiently immediately and up to thirty minutes after smoking a cigarette than after smoking a nicotine-free cigarette. In a second study using the same nonsense syllable learning task, Andersson (1975) again found learning to be impaired immediately after smoking. One interesting finding was that despite the early decrement, performance was superior forty-five minutes following smoking, though this was only a trend ($p < 0.10$). In the third study, Andersson and Hockey (1977) compared the effects of smoking in twenty-five smokers with that of non-smoking in twenty-five different deprived smokers, on the serial learning of eight words. There was no difference between groups in their ability to recall the words, whether scored by order of presentation or irrespective of the order. However, the individual words had been presented in different corners of a screen and without warning; the volunteers were also asked to recall their positions. The smoking smokers performed significantly worse on this aspect of the study, although the difference disappeared on a second testing when they were warned that position would be important. In another study using the learning of nonsense syllables, Carter (1974) found no difference in performance between a group of ten smoking smokers and ten non-smoking smokers.

Kleinman *et al.* (1973) tested non-smokers, smokers and 24-hour deprived smokers, on learning a list of low-association-value, nonsense syllable pairs. Three further subject groups were assessed on high association symbols. The deprived smoker group who were given the low-association syllables took more trials to criterion than the other two groups for these syllables, whereas the deprived smoker group who learned the high-association syllables took fewer trials than the other two groups. Thus, non-deprived smokers performed better than the non-smokers on the low association pairs, though as the only statistics presented were a significant interaction between smoking group and association, the extent to which this effect contributed to the interaction is unclear. The authors sought to make much of the findings in terms of deprivation effects, though chance group differences in ability might have explained these effects. It would have been more convincing had a within-subjects design been employed.

Stevens (1976) found that heavy smokers (more than 12 per day; $n = 27$) performed more poorly on three learning tasks than lighter smokers ($n = 23$)

or non-smokers ($n = 67$). Although essentially a 'smoker-type' comparison, with smokers free to smoke during testing, the results imply a negative effect of smoking on memory. Another study found evidence that smoking impaired verbal free recall. Houston *et al.* (1978) required twenty-three smokers to abstain from smoking for three hours and then to read a series of seventy-five words to them which they were then asked to recall. Eleven of the subjects then smoked a cigarette and the other twelve a nicotine-free cigarette. Following this, all subjects were then presented with the words again, and asked to recall them. The smokers who smoked the real cigarette performed significantly worse than the other smokers. Gonzales and Harris (1980), although conducting a tiny ($n = 10$) single session study, nonetheless found evidence of poorer verbal learning by smoking smokers than non-smoking smokers.

Two studies have demonstrated state-dependent effects with cigarette smoking. In the first, Peters and McGee (1982) contrasted the effects of smoking a very low nicotine delivery cigarette to a relatively high one. Half of the fifty-six smokers smoked the low delivery cigarette on the first day and the other half the high delivery cigarette. They were all then asked to learn and recall two lists of words. There was no significant difference between the two smoking conditions, although the trend was for the smokers who smoked the low nicotine cigarette to perform better. On the next day, using the classic state-dependent design, half of the subjects who smoked the high nicotine cigarette on day 1 were given the low nicotine cigarette and vice versa. Further recall and recognition testing of the material presented on day 1 was then performed. The evidence for state-dependent learning was that recall was best when the subjects smoked the same cigarette on both occasions. However, the major difference was actually inferior performance of the smokers switched from the high to the low delivery cigarette, this being significantly inferior to all three other groups. This could again be taken as evidence of poor learning with higher nicotine, particularly as recognition was also poorest in this group and there was no state dependency on this measure. Warburton *et al.* (1986) reported two studies in which cigarettes and nicotine tablets were studied for state-dependent effects. In the first, smoking was found to produce state-dependent memory effects for Chinese ideograms; in the second, nicotine tablets produced state-dependent memory effects for words. However, in the first stage of the second study, nicotine was found to improve memory immediately after administration, the only demonstration ever that the drug alone has such an effect, and thus in need of replication.

So far with the exception of one study with nicotine tablets, none of the studies has demonstrated improved learning to accompany nicotine administration via tobacco smoke. Mangan and Golding (1978) and Mangan (1983) found smoking to improve performance on difficult associations in a paired-associate task and to impair easier ones. Further in a serial learning task, the retention of the first four words of a list were improved by smoking. In a further study, however, Mangan and Golding (1983) found that when smoking occurred before paired associate learning, performance was significantly inferior at thirty minutes than that of non-smokers, and this general pattern held for one day and one week.

Overall, the general conclusion from the work above indicates that smoking and nicotine do not have beneficial effects on memory processes. Learning studies are easy to conduct and do not require the sophisticated equipment required to measure changes in attention and information processing. Thus one would have expected a beneficial effect of smoking on learning to have emerged, if one had existed. Instead the evidence suggests a negative effect of smoking on memory and learning. Since it is clear that smoking enhances attentional efficiency, this effect should summate with a potential beneficial effect of nicotine on memory to improve learning performance. Virtually none of the above studies can rule out the effects of smoking on attention as potentially contributing to any performance effects, yet as almost all report no or negative effects, it seems clear that nicotine does not have favourable effects on memory mechanisms. Furthermore, the few instances of improved memory could be explained by a greater degree of attention being paid to the experimental materials. Indeed, since the smokers should have concentrated more efficiently after smoking. the performance findings of no/negative effects, strongly suggest that nicotine may be having a negative overall effect on memory and learning.

CONTEMPORARY ISSUES AND CONTROVERSIES

In the section on attention, a consistent pattern emerged, with smokers performing a wide variety of tasks more efficiently when smoking than when not. In the section on learning and memory, no consistent pattern was evident, although the balance of data indicated that smoking has no beneficial effects on memory performance. Now it is appropriate to consider the obvious corollary, namely what happens to smokers when they are deprived of nicotine. This raises the further and more taxing questions: namely, is the important variable in the studies described in earlier sections not actually the presence of nicotine but its absence? This section first considers whether studies of smoking are simply demonstrations of the performance change which occurs when smokers are deprived of nicotine. We then consider another major issue in the cognitive psychopharmacology of nicotine: the nature of the dose response curve. Lastly, we consider the possible mechanisms which underlie the effects of nicotine and smoking on human information processing.

The smoking controversy: are smokers benefited by the presence of nicotine or compromised by its absence?

NICOTINE DEPRIVATION

Previous sections have documented that nicotine can improve attention. This raises the question of whether nicotine deprivation will impair attention. Tarriere and Hartmann (1964) found that a group of smokers showed little decrement on a $2\frac{1}{2}$ hour vigilance task when they were allowed to smoke freely, whereas the same group showed a significantly greater decline when they were barred from smoking for over 20 hours prior to testing. Further studies have generated similar findings. Heimstra et al. (1967) assessed performance in a driving simulator over a 6 hour period; Frankenhaeuser et al. (1971) measured simple visual reaction time over an 80 minute period of continuous testing; Wesnes and Warburton (1978) studied performance on the Mackworth clock test for 80 minutes. In each of the above studies, deprived smokers (more than 12 hours deprivation) showed the traditional vigilance decline over time, whereas subjects allowed to smoke maintained significantly higher levels of vigilance performance. Several other studies have confirmed the superiority of non-deprived smokers over deprived smokers, on prolonged vigilance types of task. For detailed coverage of these studies, see Wesnes and Warburton (1983a, pp. 192—4). Cigarette deprivation therefore impairs sustained attention.

The importance of tobacco deprivation, rather than cigarette deprivation, has been demonstrated by Keenan et al. (1989). Regular tobacco chewers ($n = 40$), who used at least $1\frac{1}{2}$ tins of tobacco each week (mean = 3.2 tins), were split into a 24-hour deprivation group and a non-deprived group. Non-tobacco chewers comprised a further control. The performance test was termed a 'vigilance' measure, although this may be debated (see below). The findings are summarized in Table 5.1. The authors concluded that: 'Reaction time is not different between non-chewers, and regular chewers immediately after chewing. In contrast, there was a slowing of reaction time and increased variability of reaction time with discontinuation of smokeless tobacco use in the chronic user' (Keenan et al., 1989, p. 129). Task errors were slightly more frequent following tobacco-deprivation (Table 5.1). Keenan's task may be of particular interest to human performance researchers wishing to investigate commission errors, since they were comparatively frequent, whereas omission errors were rare. Traditional measures of sustained attention (Mackworth clock test, RVIP, letter cancellation), generate high rates of omission error, but low rates of commission error. The structure of Keenan's task shows few characteristics of traditional vigilance measures. For instance, stimuli were presented regularly every two seconds for twenty-three minutes; the percentage of stimuli comprising targets was high (78 per cent); while target and non-target signals were easy to discriminate (presented at the top or

Table 5.1 Effects of chewing tobacco deprivation upon task performance: group mean values for baseline/experimental session difference scores (based upon Table 3 from Keenan *et al.*, 1989)

Measure	Performance difference from baseline
Reaction time mean (ms)[d]	
Deprived chewers	+20.1[b]
Continuous chewers	−25.6[d]
Non-chewers	−16.8[b]
Reaction time variability (ms)[d]	
Deprived chewers	+31.2[c]
Continuing chewers	−1.8
Non-chewers	−6.0
Omission errors (tot)[a]	
Deprived chewers	+11.8
Continuing chewers	−0.3
New-chewers	−2.1
Commission errors (tot)	
Deprived chewers	+6.3
Continuing chewers	−1.3
Non-chewers	−12.1

Two-tailed significance levels:
 [a] $p < 0.10$
 [b] $p < 0.05$
 [c] $p < 0.01$
 [d] $p < 0.001$
Group × session ANOVA interaction significance levels are tabulated for each assessment measure.
Paired *t*-test significance levels (i.e. baseline−experimental differences) are tabulated for each subject group.

bottom of the VDU screen). In contrast, measures of vigilance/attention have far more non-targets than targets, while stimuli are designed to be easily missed or misinterpreted. The Keenan task might best be called a repetitive reaction time task (e.g. a paced version of the Wilkinson continuous reaction time task; Wilkinson and Houghton, 1975).

NICOTINE DEPRIVATION AND NICOTINE REINSTATEMENT

The finding that smoking deprivation can impair attention causes a major difficulty for the nicotine/performance literature, since most studies use nicotine deprived subjects. What, then, is the nature of the performance change following nicotine administration; does it reflect a 'genuine' performance gain, or simply the restoration of processing capacity found prior to deprivation? The Surgeon General (1988, p. 393) has noted this problem: 'The improvement in attention ... in smokers who are allowed to smoke compared with a smoking abstinence condition ... may, in part, reflect reversal of the deleterious effects of smoking abstinence'. Wesnes and Norm (1983c, p. 228) similarly noted: 'As habitual smokers were used in the present study it would be reasonable to assume that they would normally have smoked during the period in which testing was carried out, and therefore that in the non-smoking control condition that they were in a deprived state. The crucial question here is whether their performance in this stage is suboptimal? Certainly it has been argued (Heimstra et al., 1967) that smoking in the deprived state is "below par" and that smoking simply restores it'. Several other researchers have described this dilemma (Revell, 1988; Hindmarch et al., 1990; Parrott and Roberts, in press; Surgeon General, 1990, pp. 525−6).

In order to unravel these confounding factors, performance needs to be measured at three stages: prior to nicotine deprivation, after deprivation and following nicotine reinstatement. Only then can the effects of deprivation and reinstatement be directly compared. Two trials seem to satisfy the above criteria. Snyder and Henningfield (1989) trained subjects on a computerized performance test battery until stable levels of performance were achieved (11−23 trials). This baseline performance was then compared with performance under three experimental conditions: placebo, 2 mg and 4 mg nicotine gum, following twelve hours of smoking deprivation. On all five tasks, response times were significantly impaired in the placebo gum condition (this comprised a 'deprivation' condition). On four of the five tasks, nicotine gum performance was not statistically distinguishable from baseline, while on the fifth task (rapid arithmetic), performance under both nicotine gum conditions was significantly *higher* than under baseline. Four of the five placebo/4 mg nicotine gum comparisons were significant, while three of the placebo/2 mg nicotine gum comparisons were significant. These findings show that nicotine deprivation (placebo gum) led to significantly impaired performance. Also that nicotine reinstatement (2 mg or 4 mg gum) generally led to task performance levels similar to those found during (normal smoking) baseline. The position of the fifth test is intriguing; it demonstrates that task performance was significantly higher following 2 mg and 4 mg gum, than under (cigarette smoking) baseline. One possible explanation for this could be the operation of an inverted-U function for that task.

The other study fulfilling all the above design requirements was by Parrott and Roberts (in press). Subjects were trained on a standardized letter cancellation task, then on four consecutive test days they were assessed on matched versions of the task. Either on test day 2 or 3 (counterbalanced), subjects were instructed to abstain from smoking before testing (overnight), or were allowed to remain in a non-deprived state. Pre-cigarette letter cancellation performance was assessed first. Then subjects were allowed to smoke one of their own cigarettes, and the second (post-cigarette) test was undertaken. Letter cancellation performance was significantly impaired by nicotine deprivation, when assessed both by response speed and target detection. Performance then returned near to baseline following nicotine

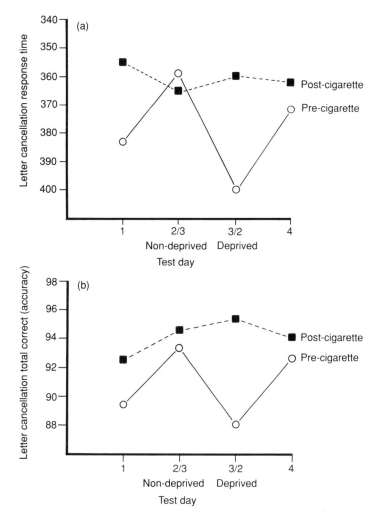

Figure 5.6 Letter cancellation response time and target detection, following smoking deprivation and cigarette reinstatement. (After Parrott and Roberts, in press.)

reinstatement (Figure 5.6). These findings are in accord with both the literature on nicotine deprivation and nicotine administration. In combination they also suggest that the apparent 'facilitation' of performance found in many nicotine administration studies may simply reflect the recovery of processing capacity lost during nicotine deprivation (see Figure 5.8). A further implication is that repetitive smoking may function to forestall the performance decrement which would occur *if* deprivation were allowed to develop. Heimstra *et al.*, (1967), and others have reached this conclusion, although others have suggested that nicotine can produce a 'real' improvement in performance.

Hindmarch *et al.* (1990) attempted to unravel the confounding effects of nicotine deprivation and reinstatement, through a different approach. Subjects were allowed to smoke normally up to the start of the test session, then a single piece of placebo or nicotine gum was given. Smoking was forbidden for the ensuing five hours of testing. The aim was to allow 'A valid comparison to be made between the nicotine condition and non-deprived placebo condition in the first instance' (Hindmarch *et al.*, 1990, p. 536). This does not, of course, solve the problem, because all subjects had nicotine in their system at the start of testing. Placebo gum did not therefore represent a genuine placebo, but rather a gradual nicotine deprivation condition. The active gum conditions similarly reflected the development of nicotine deprivation, partially slowed by the single piece of nicotine gum at the start of testing. It was thus difficult to identify the nicotine state at any performance level.

NICOTINE WITH NON-DEPRIVED SUBJECTS

Nicotine can also be administered to non-deprived volunteers. Three types of subject might be used: regular smokers, light smokers or non-smokers. The administration of nicotine to regular smokers who are *not* nicotine-deprived prior to testing is fraught with difficulty. Subjects would be in a range of nicotine states prior to further drug administration. If asked to smoke, they could also modulate their nicotine intake by altering the frequency and depth of inhalation. The whole situation would be pharmacologically uncontrolled, and this approach has therefore not generally been followed (although see West and Jarvis, 1986).

Light (social) smokers were assessed on the RVIP task in two unpublished studies, summarized in Wesnes (1987, p. 73). In the first study, subjects failed to show any significant performance change following cigarette smoking. During subsequent interviews, subjects reported that they did not normally smoke before lunch, when testing had occurred. Therefore a second study was undertaken, with performance now assessed after lunch. Improved performance was noted, although group means and significance levels were not reported (Wesnes, 1987, p. 73). One possible interpretation for these findings is that performance was improved only when subjects were in a state of nicotine deprivation. One difficulty with this proposed explanation is that subjects had not recently smoked in either study (i.e. pre-test nicotine levels were low in both studies). These findings therefore remain intriguing and difficult to explain. In another unpublished study (summarized in Parrott *et al.*, 1990), Parrott and Haines assessed eight regular smokers (more than 15 cigarettes per day), and eight light smokers (less than 5 cigarettes per day), after 4 mg nicotine or placebo gum. Both groups showed higher RVIP target detection after nicotine than placebo gum, while regular smokers showed comparatively greater performance improvements than the light smokers. Neither the main ANOVA drug effect, nor the drug × group interaction

($p = 0.065$, one-tail), were, however, significant. It had also been predicted that light smokers would not feel deprived of nicotine at testing. While the light smokers did report significantly lower cigarette-need than regular smokers ($p < 0.05$), the subjective questionnaires did indicate some desire for smoking.

Another approach is to administer nicotine to tobacco-naive subjects. Wesnes *et al.* (1983) gave nicotine tablets to thirty-six subjects: twelve heavy smokers, twelve light smokers, and twelve non-smokers. The smokers were 'instructed not to smoke for twelve hours prior to the test' (Wesnes *et al.*, 1983, p. 42). Performance on the Mackworth clock test showed a decline over time in all conditions, but the decline with placebo was significantly greater than the decline with nicotine ($p = 0.002$). There were no differences between subject groups. Thus nicotine tablets improved vigilance performance with both nicotine-deprived smokers and non-smokers. Wesnes and Warburton (1984b) gave nicotine tablets of varying strengths (0.0, 0.5, 1.0 and 1.5 mg), to nine non-smokers. Under placebo, RVIP performance showed a significant decline from baseline, both in response speed and target detection. The lower doses of nicotine tended to reduce the slope of vigilance decline, while the high-dose tablet (1.5 mg nicotine) led to higher performance than the other conditions; statistical comparisons were borderline in significance, both for response speed and target detection ($p < 0.10$, two-tailed).

One problem with nicotine tablets is that they are an inefficient way to deliver nicotine. This may be one reason why only small performance changes have generally been found. It should also be noted that information from non-smokers may be of limited relevance for regular nicotine users because of pharmacodynamic tolerance (Ashton, 1987, pp. 192–3). Potential ethical problems in the administration of nicotine to non-users may also be noted. While unlikely to lead directly to smoking, it might influence further nicotine experimentation or increase the long-term likelihood of taking up smoking. Blix (1986) described the case of a surgeon who had never smoked nor used snuff. He tried nicotine gum as an appetite suppressant, then moved to long-term snuff use because it was cheaper than the gum.

Nicotine, arousal and attention: inverted-U or linear function?

Williams (1980) found evidence for an inverted-U arousal performance function in a study assessing the effects of three strengths of cigarette on letter cancellation. Sham smoking led to a negligible performance change, while low and high strength cigarettes (0.6 mg, 1.8 mg nicotine) each led to significant performance improvements. The greatest performance gain, however, occurred with medium-strength cigarettes (1.3 mg nicotine). Overall, a significant monotonic relationship between nicotine dose and task performance improvement was present. However, 'the degree of curvature was sufficient to establish a significant inverted-U trend in gains for the low-arousal smokers'

(Williams, 1980, p. 88; note: high-arousal smokers showed a similar pattern of arousal performance relationship).

Nicotine research has generated an array of significant monotonic *and* inverted-U functions, some of these are summarized in Figures 5.7 and 5.8. Wesnes and Warburton have noted both monotonic and curvilinear trends, in their cigarette smoking studies (Wesnes and Warburton, 1983c, 1984a; Figures 5.7 and 5.8). Parrott and Winder (1989) reported a significant monotonic dose–response improvement in RVIP target detection ($p < 0.01$; Figure 5.8), while response time showed a significant curvilinear function ($p = 0.017$; Figure 5.8)

Slight (non-significant) differences in baseline values may have contributed to this effect, therefore an extended replication was undertaken (Parrott and Craig, in press). Again, a mixture of first- (monotonic) and second-order (curvilinear) polynomial functions were produced. RVIP response time showed a curvilinear trend, borderline in significance ($p < 10$, two-tail). Target detection was improved across all nicotine conditions. During the first period of testing a significant monotonic dose–response function was evident, with highest target detection performance under smoking. During the second test period a significant curvilinear function occurred, with highest performance under 2 mg nicotine gum (Figures 5.7 and 5.8). Letter cancellation was assessed in the same study and a significant monotonic function was again present (Parrott and Craig, in press).

The current picture regarding the dose–response effects of nicotine is therefore confusing, with a mixture of monotonic and curvilinear functions in evidence (Figures 5.7 and 5.8). Some degree of inconsistency might well be expected since these performance changes are quite subtle and are subjected to numerous influences (e.g. different initial arousal–performance positions; individual variation in arousability; self-modulation of nicotine intake). But there does seem to be little consistency about when and under what conditions a monotonic or curvilinear arousal–performance function will pertain. When high-nicotine cigarettes are being tested, some subjects will be given nicotine doses in excess of their normal intake. This excess nicotine might then 'upset' or 'distract' (Wesnes and Warburton, 1983, 1984). Williams (1980) noted different sized functions for low-arousal and high-arousal smokers, but the position of inverted-U peak was the same with both groups (they would be predicted to differ). Parrott and Winder (1989) and Parrott and Craig (in press) found a mixture of monotonic and curvilinear functions during single test sessions; thus between-subjects effects could not have accounted for the differences. Future studies should investigate the conditions under which the arousal–performance peak is reached. Intensive single-subject trials might provide more useful information than small group studies. They could also be combined with measures of the contingent negative variation (CNV), since Ashton *et al.* (1980) generated inverted-U functions with this EEG measure, following different doses of intravenous nicotine (see also chapter 3 in Mangan and Golding, 1984).

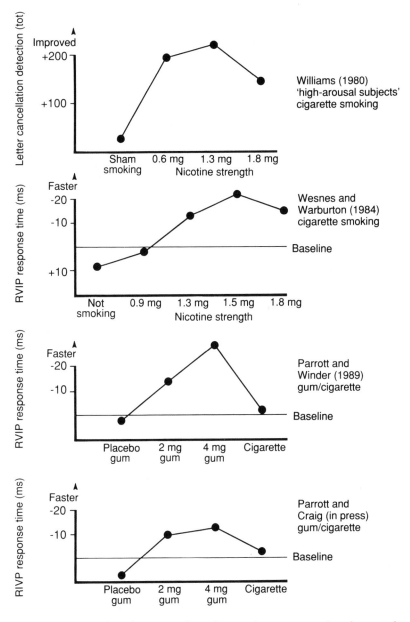

Figure 5.7 Arousal performance relationships under nicotine: selected inverted-U functions.

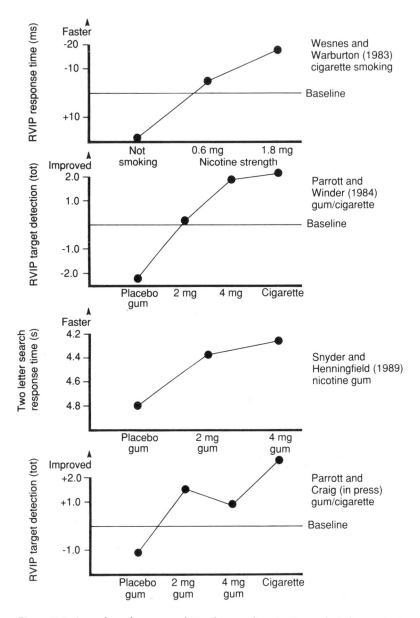

Figure 5.8 Arousal performance relationships under nicotine: selected monotonic functions.

The mechanisms via which nicotine improves information processing

A major motive underlying much of the research cited earlier by Wesnes and Warburton was to explore the hypothesis that nicotine improves human attentional efficiency via its action on central cholinergic pathways. The idea was to use nicotine as a tool to investigate the neurochemical basis of human cognitive efficiency. Nicotine is known to release the cholinergic neurotransmitter acetylcholine in the CNS (Armitage *et al.*, 1969) and to increase electrocortical arousal (Kenig and Murphree, 1973). Electrocortical arousal as measured by EEG techniques is closely related to the quality of human attentional efficiency, with low arousal being associated with poor concentration, and high arousal with high attentional efficiency. It has long been known that nicotine increases electrocortical arousal via its action on the mesencephalic reticular formation and that this effect is mediated via cholinergic neurones (Il'yutchenok and Ostrovskaya, 1962; Domino, 1967; Kawamura and Domino, 1969). The performance findings described earlier thus strongly support this hypothesis. The alternative prediction was also evaluated, namely that cholinergic blockade would lead to impaired attentional efficiency. Studies with the cholinergic receptor blocker scopolamine were conducted using the same tasks as had been used to study nicotine. Scopolamine was found to lower stimulus sensitivity on the Mackworth clock vigilance task (Wesnes and Warburton, 1983c) and to reduce correct detections of the RVIP (Wesnes and Warburton, 1984b). Further work has confirmed these effects of scopolamine (Parrott and Wesnes, 1987; Wesnes *et al.*, 1988b). Importantly, nicotine has also been found to antagonize the deleterious effects of scopolamine on the RVIP and Stroop task (Wesnes and Revell, 1984).

This work on nicotine has thus provided support for the idea that central cholinergic pathways play a role in human attention, while at the same time indicating the manner in which smoking may affect cognition. Unfortunately, although muscarinic cholinergic blockade with scopolamine disrupts memory performance (e.g. Wesnes *et al.*, 1988b), it is clear that activation of central nicotinic receptors with nicotine does not enhance memory. This work does not therefore suggest a role for nicotinic cholinergic receptors in human memory.

OVERVIEW AND RECOMMENDATIONS

Design and analysis problems

The effects of nicotine upon performance are subtle and complex. Even well controlled studies can show a variety of performance alterations. The problems of data interpretation do, however, become even more severe when the basic principles of good experimental design and appropriate statistical analysis are ignored. This section identifies some of these problems.

Hughes *et al.* (1990), in their review of the tobacco abstinence literature, included a section on human performance. They noted consistently different findings between two research groups, those of Elgerot and Henningfield: 'It is not readily apparent why one task should show positive effects and another negative effects. Perhaps a more important explanation is that the Addiction Research Centre laboratory [Henningfield] achieved stable baseline prior to testing, but the Swedish laboratory [Elgerot] did not' (Hughes *et al.*, 1990, pp.350−1). Elgerot's (1976) study, briefly summarized in the previous section, does indeed contain important errors in design and analysis. Subjects were not trained on the tasks beforehand but performed each test just twice, under the two experimental conditions. Practice effects would therefore have been large, with each test generating its own learning curve (Bittner *et al.*, 1986). Also the data should have been analysed using a 2 × 2 cross-over ANOVA. Instead *t*-tests were used, thus confounding 'time' with 'drug'. Lastly, the designation of tasks as simple or complex seems to have been *post hoc*. For instance, single-digit mental arithmetic was designated a complex task, while proof-reading was termed a simple measure. Their conclusion that: 'Abstinence from tobacco led to improved performance on the complex tests but no change on the simple ones', is empirically suspect. Nevertheless, since it is a simple message, it will probably continue to be quoted in literature reviews. In contrast, the study by Snyder and Henningfield (1989) is quite exemplary. Subjects were trained extensively beforehand, so that a statistically stable baseline was obtained for each subject. The statistical analysis procedures were appropriate and comprehensive, while other design features of the study were also excellent. Subtle findings of great interest were generated (Figure 5.2). This study can be taken as a benchmark for nicotine performance research.

One frequent design error is to test subjects who have not been adequately trained, or given adequate practice on the performance tasks. Wesnes and Warburton (1983a) recommended three ten-minute training sessions on the RVIP task, before the collection of any experimental data. Without this training, drug-induced performance change may be confounded with learning/practice. Petrie and Deary (1989) studied the effects of smoking on the RVIP, but failed to train their subjects on the tasks. Not surprisingly, their clearest finding was of significant RVIP learning effects. The ANOVA 'session' effect (i.e. smoking × order interaction) was significant both for response time and target detection. Many other studies also contain learning trends. Our own studies are certainly not free from flaw or limitation. The Wesnes and Warburton series of dose-related studies (1978, 1983c, 1984a, b; Wesnes *et al.*, 1983; Wesnes, 1987) were analysed by ANOVA, then planned comparisons or between condition comparisons. Dose−response analyses should also have been undertaken, since without the analysis of polynomial functions, firm statements about dose—response relationships cannot be made. Baseline differences in performance are another problem since non-significant baseline differences between conditions may affect the extent and significance of the small drug induced changes (Parrott and Winder, 1989; Parrott and Craig, in press; Hindmarch *et al.*, 1990).

Many of the errors in this field are quite basic. For instance, several studies have used the two-way cross-over design (e.g. smoking compared with non-smoking, with half tested in the order smoking/non-smoking, and half tested in the order non-smoking/smoking), but then analyse their data by *t*-tests (Elgerot, 1976; Frith, 1967). For the correct way to analyse a two-way cross-over design, see Hills and Armitage (1979). An unusual statistical error was present in the smoking/vigilance study of Mangan (1982). The twenty-four subjects were split into two groups and allowed to smoke either low or medium nicotine cigarettes. The experimental data from these two groups of subjects was then compared with 'control' data from the *whole* group of twenty-four subjects. It was reported: 'Clearly, improved detectability in the low nicotine group appeared due to increased detection ... with the medium nicotine group, improved vigilance was due largely to reduced false positive responses' (Mangan, 1982, p. 81). The problem resides in the use of the 'combined' control group. Each 'control/experimental' difference may have been caused by comparing the two subgroup experimental data pools with the 'combined' control group data pool (since the other twelve subjects within each each comparison will have affected the group mean baseline values, both for target detection and false positives).

Pomerleau and Pomerleau (1987) found no effect of smoking upon serial subtraction of 13s, but the sensitivity of the task was not documented nor were its references. Thus it was not possible to ascertain whether nicotine does indeed not affect repetitive mental arithmetic, or instead whether the task was insensitive. The Pomerleau study also repeats some other common design errors; subjects were apparently not nicotine-deprived before testing, nor were they trained on the task before trial commencement. In the selection of a performance test, the best advice is to choose one with established sensitivity (e.g. Mackworth clock, RVIP, letter cancellation, Wilkinson continuous reaction time). Yet despite the obvious problems and pitfalls, many researchers still attempt to design their own tasks (see: Parrott, 1991a—c).

Ignoring the pharmacokinetic/dynamic profile of smoking, can lead to suprising data interpretation. Ney *et al.* (1988) studied the timing of smoke inhalations while subjects undertook repetitive problem-solving (Ravens matrices). Interesting data were generated, but the interpretation offered by the authors reflected an ignorance of the pharmacokinetics of smoking. They found that puffing and smoke inhalation were significantly *more* frequent during the few seconds prior to presentation of each problem stimulus; whereas during the 3–10 second period following stimulus presentation, the frequency of puffing/inhalation was significantly reduced. For any researcher conversant with the pharmacokinetics of smoke inhalation (nicotine takes 7–10 seconds after inhalation to reach the brain), this study shows that smokers were self-administering a bolus of nicotine which coincided with the period of problem-solving. Ney et al. (1988), however, focused upon the low smoke intake *during* problem presentation. Thus they concluded fallaciously: 'Contrary to the view that smoking facilitates performance, we can see here that smoking is depressed at those very times when there are greatest demands upon the subject' (p. 96); also: 'While concentrating, i.e., working on the task, subjects chose not to smoke, thus showing that they did not consider smoking to be helpful' (p. 245).

General conclusions

For research to progress, a number of steps are necessary, first among which is that the quality of research needs to be improved to overcome the flaws and problems identified in previous work. Journals, for example, must become more selective about the quality of the studies they publish. All studies should at least match the experimental rigour of Hull (1924), though many studies fail that hurdle.

Nonetheless some major advances in our knowledge have taken place. We now know that, when smoking, smokers perform a wide variety of tasks with greater efficiency than when not smoking. We know that nicotine is largely responsible for this and there is some evidence from electrocortical recording that these effects are mediated via central stimulus evaluation mechanisms. Nicotine can also have beneficial effects on the mental efficiency of non-smokers. Further, it is becoming clear that there is no convincing evidence that smoking has any favourable effects on learning, despite the improvements in concentration which accompany smoking. The deleterious performance effects of nicotine/smoking deprivation are also now well established.

In terms of understanding the motives behind the addictive nature of smoking, the positive effects of nicotine on attention and information processing must certainly play an important role. For some smokers this may actually be part of the motive to smoke; certainly it is a reason frequently given by smokers for their motives (Wesnes et al., 1984). Furthermore, a 'failure to concentrate' is commonly reported after smoking cessation. One model of smoking motives is, therefore, that nicotine leads to a genuine heightening in information processing capacity, with smokers demonstrating higher performance than they would otherwise show. The alternative model is that the contrasting effects of nicotine deprivation and nicotine reinstatement lead to constant vacillation in the performance capacity of the smoker. They feel impaired (and are impaired) without their cigarettes, while they feel improved (and become comparatively improved) when smoking is restored. The prime motive for the smoker is thus to maintain their processing capacity.

Another point of view is that the reinforcement for smoking comes from the general psychological state which accompanies these changes in electrocortical arousal and attention efficiency. Thus the smoker is not motivated to aid task performance *per se*, but rather to achieve the subjective mental experience associated with an optimal state of alertness. Since this state is probably indistinguishable from naturally occurring states of arousal, it may help to explain why smokers generally have such difficulty in describing their own motives for smoking.

Somewhat surprisingly, research effort into understanding the mechanisms which govern the psychological addiction to smoking has been slight considering the enormous health risks which result from this addiction. Paradoxically, it has been the tobacco companies themselves who have funded much of this research. The general reluctance of medical and scientific research bodies to countenance that smoking may have beneficial cognitive actions has retarded the progress of research into the psychological basis of smoking addiction. Science and medicine are not best served by ignoring disquieting facts. Instead, all the facts must be addressed, put into an appropriate context, and a strategy sought to deal with the problem. Smoking is undoubtedly one of the major health hazards of the century. Smokers smoke primarily for nicotine and the particular combination of the neurochemical, electrocortical, physiological and behavioural effects it produces. A full understanding of these changes is necessary if effective strategies are to be generated.

REFERENCES

Andersson, K. (1975). Effects of cigarette smoking on learning and retention. *Psychopharmacologia (Berlin)* **41**: 1–5.

Andersson, K. and Hockey, G.R.J. (1977). Effects of cigarette smoking on incidental memory. *Psychopharmacology* **52**: 223–6.

Andersson, K. and Post, B. (1974). Effects of cigarette smoking on verbal rote learning and physiological arousal. *Scandinavian Journal of Psychology* **15**: 263–7.

Armitage, A.K., Hall, G.H. and Sellers, C.M. (1969). Effects of nicotine on electrocortical activity and acetylcholine release from the cat cerebral cortex. *British Journal of Pharmacology* **35**: 152–60.

Ashton, H. (1987). *Brain Systems, Disorders and Psychotropic Drugs.* Oxford University Press.

Ashton, H., Savage, R.D., Telford, R., Thompson, J.W. and Watson, D.W. (1973). The effects of cigarette smoking on the response to stress in a driving simulator. *British Journal of Pharmacology* **45**: 546–56.

Ashton, H., Marsh, V.R., Millman, J.E., Rawlins, M.D., Telford, R. and Thompson, J.W. (1980). Biphasic dose-related responses to the CNV to nicotine in man. *British Journal of Clinical Psychology* **10**: 579–89.

Bakan, P. (1959). Extraversion–introversion and improvement in an auditory vigilance task. *British Journal of Psychology* **50**: 325–32.

Benowitz, N.L., Jacob, P., III, Jones, R.T. and Rosenberg, J. (1982). Interindividual variability in the metabolism and cardiovascular effects of nicotine in man. *Journal of Pharmacol. Exp. Ther.* **221**: 368–72.

Bittner, A.C., Carter, R.C., Kennedy, R.S., Harbeson, M.M. and Krause, M. (1986). Performance evaluation tests for environmental research (PETER): evaluation of 114 measures. *Perceptual and Motor Skills* **63**: 683–708.

Blix, O. (1986). Misuse of nicotine gum made a smoker a snuff user. *Lakartidningen* 9 July, **83**: 2489 (Swedish).

Carter, G.L. (1974). Effects of cigarette smoking on learning. *Perceptual and Motor Skills* **39**: 1344–6.

Cotten, D.C., Thomas, J.R. and Stewart, D. (1971). Immediate effects of cigarette smoking on simple reaction time of college male smokers. *Perceptual and Motor Skills* **33**: 336.

Domino, E.F. (1967). Electroencephalographic and behavioural arousal of small doses of nicotine: a neuropsychopharmacological study. *Annals of the New York Academy of Science* **142**: 216–44.

Edwards, J.A., Wesnes, K., Warburton, D.M. and Gale, A. (1985). Evidence of more rapid stimulus evaluation following cigarette smoking. *Addictive Behaviours* **10**: 113–26.

Elgerot, A. (1976). Note on the selective effects of short-term tobacco abstinence on complex versus simple mental tasks. *Perceptual and Motor Skills* **42**: 413–14.

Fabricant, N.D. and Rose, I.W. (1951). Effect of smoking cigarettes on the flicker threshold of the normal person. *Eye, Ear and Mouth* **30**: 541–3.

Fay, P.J. (1936). The effect of cigarette smoking on simple and choice reaction time to colored lights. *Journal of Psychology* **19**: 592–603.

Frankenhaeuser, M., Myrsten, A., Post, B. and Johansson, G. (1971). Behavioural and physiological effects of cigarette smoking in a monotonous situation. *Psychopharmacology* **22**: 1–7.

Frith, C.D. (1967). The effects of nicotine on tapping: 1 and 2. *Life Sciences* **6**: 313–19 and 321–6.

Garner, L., Carl, E. and Grossman, E. (1953). Effect of cigarette smoking on flicker fusion thresholds. *American Journal of Ophthalmology* **36**: 1751–6.

Gonzales, M.A. and Harris, M.B. (1980). Effects of cigarette smoking on recall and categorization of written material. *Perceptual and Motor Skills* **50**: 407–10.

Hasenfrantz, M., Michel, C., Nil, R. and Battig, K. (1989). Can smoking increase attention in rapid information processing during noise? Electrocortical, physiological and behavioural effects. *Psychopharmacology* **98**: 75–80.

Heimstra, N.W., Bancroft, N.R. and DeKock, A.R. (1967). Effects of smoking upon sustained performance in a simulated driving task. *Annals of the New York Academy of Science* **142**: 295–307.

Hills, M. and Armitage, P. (1979). The two period crossover trial. *British Journal of Clinical Pharmacology* **8**: 7–20.

Hindmarch, I., Kerr, J.S. and Sherwood, N. (1990). Effects of nicotine gum on psychomotor performance in smokers and non-smokers. *Psychopharmacology* **100**: 535–41.

Hopkins, R., Wood, L.E. and Sinclair, N.M. (1984). Evaluation of methods to estimate cigarette smoke uptake. *Clinical Pharmacology and Therapeutics* **36**: 788–95.

Houston, J.P., Schneider, N.G. and Jarvik, M.E. (1978). Effects of smoking on free-recall and organization. *American Journal of Psychiatry* **135**: 220–2.

Hughes, J.R., Higgins, S.T. and Hasukami, D. (1990). Effects of abstinence from tobacco. In *Research Advances in Alcohol and Drug Problems*, Vol. 10, edited by L.T. Kozlowski. New York: Plenum, pp. 317–98.

Hull, C. (1924). The influence of tobacco smoking on mental and motor efficiency. *Psychological Monographs*.

Il'yutchenok, R.Yu. and Ostrovskaya, R.U. (1962). The role of mesencephalic cholinergic systems in the mechanism of nicotine activation of the electroencephalogram. *Bulletin of Experimental Biology and Medicine* **54**: 753–7.

Kahneman, D. (1973). *Attention and Effort*. Englewood Cliffs, NJ: Prentice Hall, Inc.

Kawamura, M. and Domino, E.F. (1969). Differential actions of *m* and *n* cholinergic agonists on the brain stem activating system. *International Journal of Neuropharmacology* **8**: 105—15.

Keenan, R.M., Hatsukami, D.K. and Anton, D.J. (1989). The effects of short term smokeless tobacco deprivation on performance. *Psychopharmacology* **98**: 126—30.

Kenig, L. and Murphree, M.B. (1973). Effects of intravenous nicotine in smokers and non-smokers. *Fed. Proceedings* **32**: 805.

Kleinman, K.M., Vaughn, R. and Christ, S.T. (1973). Effects of cigarette smoking and smoking deprivation on paired-associate learning of high and low meaningful nonsense syllables. *Psychological Reports* **32**: 963—6.

Kumar, R., Cooke, E.C., Lader, M.H. and Russell, M.A.H. (1978). Is tobacco smoking a form of nicotine dependence? In *Smoking Behaviour: Physiological and Psychological Influences*, edited by R.E. Thornton. London: Churchill Livingstone, pp. 224—59.

Larson, P.S., Finnegan, J.K. and Haag, H.B. (1950). Observations on the effect of cigarette smoking on the fusion frequency of flicker. *Journal of Clinical Investigation* **29**: 483—5.

Lippold, O.C.J., Williams, E.J. and Wilson, C.G. (1980). Finger tremor and cigarette smoking. *British Journal of Clinical Psychology*, **10**: 83—6.

Mackworth, J.F. (1965). The effect of amphetamine on the detectability of signals in a visual vigilance task. *Canadian Journal of Psychology* **19**: 104—9.

Mangan, G.L. (1982). The effects of cigarette smoking on vigilance performance. *Journal of General Psychology* **106**: 77—83.

Mangan, G.K. (1983). The effects of cigarette smoking on human verbal learning and retention. *Journal of General Psychology* **108**: 203—10.

Mangan, G.L. and Golding, J.F. (1978). An enhancement model of smoking maintenance. In *Smoking Behaviour: Physiological and Psychological Influences*, edited by R.E. Thornton. London: Churchill Livingstone, pp. 87—115.

Mangan, G.L. and Golding, J.F. (1983). The effects of smoking on memory consolidation. *Journal of Psychology* **115**: 65—77.

Mangan, G.L. and Golding, J.F. (1984). *The Psychopharmacology of Smoking*. Cambridge University Press.

Michel, Ch. and Battig, K. (1989). Separate and combined psychophysiological effects of cigarette and alcohol consumption. *Psychopharmacology* **97**: 65—93.

Michel, Ch., Nil, R., Buzzi, R., Woodson, P.P. and Battig, R. (1987). Rapid information processing and event related brain potentials in smokers. *Neuropsychobiology* **17**: 161—8.

Michel, Ch., Hasenfrantz, M., Nil, R. and Battig, K. (1988). Cardiovascular, electrocortical and behavioural effects of nicotine chewing gum. *Klin. Wochenscr* **66** (supplement): 72—9.

Myrsten, A-L., Frankenhaeuser, M., Post, B. and Johanssen, G. (1971). *Enhanced Behavioural Efficiency Induced by Cigarette Smoking*. Reports from the Psychological Laboratories, University of Stockholm, No. 337.

Myrsten, A-L., Frankenhaeuser, M., Andersson, K. and Mardh, A. (1972). *Immediate Effects of Cigarette Smoking as Related to Different Types of Smoking Habit*. Reports from the Psychological Laboratories, University of Stockholm, No. 378.

Ney, T., Gale, A. and Morris, H. (1989). A critical evaluation of laboratory studies of the effects of smoking on learning and memory. In *Smoking and Human Behaviour*, edited by T. Ney and A. Gale. Chichester: Wiley.

Ney, T., Gale, A. and Weaver, M. (1988). Smoking patterns during cognitive performance. *Addictive Behaviours* **13**: 291—6.

Parrott, A.C. (1982). Critical Flicker Fusion thresholds and their relationships to other measures of alertness. *Pharmacopsychiatry* **15**: 39—43.

Parrott, A.C. (1987). Assessment of psychological performance in applied situations. In *Human Psychopharmacology: Measures and Methods*, Vol. 1, edited by I. Hindmarch and P.D. Stonier. Chichester: Wiley.

Parrott A.C. (1991a). Performance tests in human psychopharmacology. I: Reliability and test standardisation. *Human Psychopharmacology* **6**: 1–9.

Parrott, A.C. (1991b). Performance tests in human psychopharmacology. II: Content, criterion and face validity. *Human Psychopharmacology* **6**: 91–8.

Parrott, A.C. (1991c). Performance tests in human psychopharmacology. III: Construct validity and overview. *Human Psychopharmacology* **6**: 197–208.

Parrott, A.C. (1991d). Social drugs: their effects upon health. In *The Psychology of Health*, edited by M. Pitts and K. Phillips. London: Routledge and Kegan Paul.

Parrott, A.C. and Craig, D. (in press). Cigarette smoking and nicotine gum (0 mg, 2 mg, 4 mg): effects upon different aspects of visual attention. *Neuropsychobiology*.

Parrott, A.C. and Roberts, G. (in press). Smoking deprivation and cigarette reinstatement: effects upon visual attention. *Journal of Psychopharmacology*.

Parrott, A.C. and Wesnes, K. (1986). Promethazine, scopolamine and cinnarazine: comparative time course of psychological performance effects. *Psychopharmacology* **92**: 513–19.

Parrott, A.C. and Winder, G. (1989). Nicotine chewing gum (2 mg, 4 mg) and cigarette smoking: comparative effects upon vigilance and heart rate. *Psychopharmacology* **97**: 257–61.

Parrott, A.C., Craig, D., Haines, M. and Winder G. (1990). *Nicotine Polacrilex Gum and Sustained Attention. Effects of Nicotine on Biological Systems*, edited by F. Adlkofer and K. Thurau. Basel: Birkhauser Press.

Peters, R. and McGee, R. (1982). Cigarette smoking and state-dependent learning. *Psychopharmacology* **76**: 232–5.

Petrie, R.A. and Deary, I. (1989). Smoking and human information processing. *Psychopharmacology* **99**: 393–6.

Pomerleau, C.S. and Pomerleau, O.F. (1987). The effect of a psychological stressor on cigarette smoking and behavioural responses. *Psychobiology* **24**: 278–85.

Revell, A.D. (1988). Smoking and performance: a puff by puff analysis. *Psychopharmacology* **96**: 563–5.

Royal College of Physicians (1983). *Health or Smoking: Follow-up Report.* London: Pitman.

Russell, M.A.H. (1988). Nicotine intake by smokers: are rates of absorption or steady state levels more important? *The Pharmacology of Nicotine*, edited by M.J. Rand and K. Thurau. Oxford: IRL, pp. 375–404.

Russell, M.A.H. (1989). The addiction research unit at the Institute of Psychiatry. II: The work of the Unit's smoking section. *British Journal of Addiction* **84**: 853–64.

Russell, M.A.H., Jarvis, M.J., Devitt, G. and Feyerabend, C. (1981). Nicotine intake by snuff users. *British Medical Journal* **283**: 814–17.

Snyder, F.R. and Henningfield, J.E. (1989). Effects of nicotine administration following 12 h of tobacco deprivation: assessment on computerised performance tasks. *Psychopharmacology* **97**: 17–22.

Stevens, H.A. (1976). Evidence that suggests a negative association between cigarette smoking and learning performance. *Journal of Clinical Psychology* **32**: 896–9.

Stroop, J.R. (1935). Studies of interference in serial verbal reactions. *Journal of Experimental Psychology* **18**: 643–61.

Surgeon General (1988). *Nicotine Addiction: The Health Consequences of Smoking.* Washington, DC: US Government Printing Office.

Surgeon General (1990). *The Health Benefits of Smoking Cessation.* Washington, DC: US Government Printing Office.

Suter, T.W., Buzzi, R., Woodson, P.P. and Battig, K. (1983). Psychophysiological correlates of conflict solving and cigarette smoking. *Activitas Nervous Sup (Praha)* **25**: 261–71.

Talland, G.A. (1966). Effects of alcohol on performance in continuous attention tasks. *Psychosomatic Medicine* **28**: 596–604.

Tarriere, H.C. and Hartmann, F. (1964). Investigations into the effects of tobacco smoking on a visual vigilance task. *Proceedings of the 2nd International Congress on Ergonomics*, 525–30.

Tong, J.E., Knott, V.J., McGraw, D.J. and Leigh, G. (1974). Alcohol, visual discrimination and heart rate; effects of dose, activation and tobacco. *Quart. J. Stud. Alc.* **35**: 1003–12.

Travell, J. (1960). Absorption of nicotine from various sites. *Annals of the New York Academy of Sciences* **90**: 13–30.

Waller, D. and Levander, S. (1980). Smoking and vigilance: the effects of tobacco on CFF as related to personality and smoking habits. *Psychopharmacology* **70**: 131–6.

Warburton, D.M. and Walters, A. (1989). *Attentional Processing in Smoking and Human Behaviour*, edited by T. Ney and A. Gale. Chichester: Wiley.

Warburton, D.M. and Wesnes, K. (1979). The role of electrocortical arousal in the smoking habit. In *Electrophysiological Effects of Nicotine*, edited by A. Remond and C. Izard. Amsterdam: Elsevier, pp. 183–200.

Warburton, D.M., Wesnes, K., Shergold, K. and James, M. (1986). Facilitation of learning and state dependency with nicotine. *Psychopharmacology* **89**: 55–9.

Wesnes, K. (1977). The effects of psychotropic drugs on human behaviour. *Modern Problems of Pharmacopsychiatry* **12**: 37–58.

Wesnes, K. (1979). The effects of nicotine and scopolamine on human attention. PhD thesis, Reading University.

Wesnes, K. (1987). Nicotine increases mental efficiency, but how? In *Tobacco Smoke and Nicotine: A Neurobiological Approach*, edited by W.R. Martin, G.R. Van Loon, E.T. Iwamoto and D.L. Davis. New York: Plenum, pp. 63–81.

Wesnes, K. and Revell, A. (1984). The separate and combined effects of scopolamine and nicotine on human information processing. *Psychopharmacology* **84**: 5–11.

Wesnes, K., Revell, A. and Warburton, D.M. (1984). Work and stress as motives for smoking. In *Smoking and the Lung*, edited by G. Cumming and G. Bonsignore. London: Plenum, pp. 233–49.

Wesnes, K., Simpson, P.M. and Christmas, L. (1988a). Puff by puff profiles of performance, mood and acceptability in low and non-low tar smokers. In *The Pharmacology of Nicotine*, edited by M.J. Rand and K. Thurau. Oxford: IRL, pp. 406–8.

Wesnes, K., Simpson, P.M. and Kidd, A.G. (1988b). An investigation of the range of cognitive impairments induced by scopolamine 0.6 mg. *Human Psychopharmacology* **3**: 27–43.

Wesnes, K. and Warburton, D.M. (1978). The effects of cigarette smoking and nicotine tablets upon human attention. In *Smoking Behaviour: Physiological and Psychological Influences*, edited by R.E. Thornton. London: Churchill Livingstone, pp. 131–47.

Wesnes, K. and Warburton, D.M. (1983a). Nicotine, smoking and human performance. *Pharmacology and Therapeutics* **21**: 189–208.

Wesnes, K. and Warburton, D.M. (1983b). The effects of smoking on rapid information processing performance. *Neuropsychobiology* **9**: 223–9.

Wesnes, K. and Warburton, D.M. (1983c). Effects of scopolamine on stimulus sensitivity and response bias in a visual vigilance task. *Neuropsychobiology* **9**: 154–7.

Wesnes, K. and Warburton, D.M. (1984a). The effects of cigarettes of varying yield on rapid information processing performance. *Psychopharmacology* **82**: 338–42.

Wesnes, K. and Warburton, D.M. (1984b). Effects of scopolamine and nicotine on human rapid information processing performance. *Psychopharmacology* **82**: 147–50.

Wesnes, K., Warburton, D.M. and Matz, B. (1983). The effects of nicotine on stimulus sensitivity and response bias in a visual vigilance task. *Neuropsychobiology* **9**: 41–4.

West, R.J. and Jarvis, M.J. (1986). Effect of nicotine on finger tapping rate in non-smokers. *Pharmacology, Biochemistry and Behaviour* **25**: 727–31.

Wilkinson, R.T. and Houghton, D. (1975). Portable four choice reaction time test with magnetic memory tape memory. *Behaviour Research Methods and Instrumentation* **2**: 441–6.

Williams, G.D. (1980). Effect of cigarette smoking on immediate memory and performance. *British Journal of Psychology* **71**: 83–90.

6

Cannabis

J.F. GOLDING

INTRODUCTION

Cannabis is obtained from the hemp plant *Cannabis sativa*, a herbaceous annual grown both for its pharmacological value and for the fine fibre of its stem (see Figure 6.1). Originally a native of Central Asia, it now has wide geographical distribution. Alternative names for cannabis include marihuana (alternative spelling: marijuana), grass, weed, pot, hashish, kif, charas, bhang, ganja, dagga.

The use of the plant for medicinal purposes and as a 'psychic liberator' was referred to in the reign of Shen Nung (Emperor of China 3rd century BC) but is thought to go back further, at least four thousand years (Emboden, 1972). Seeds of cannabis have been found in North European funerary urns dating from the 5th century BC indicating an early use in Europe.

The term hashish is said to have come from the writings of Marco Polo who in 1271 described the activities of Al-Hasan ibn-al-Sabbah, a Persian of noble descent. His followers (ashishins) conducted raids from a mountain fortress in the Persian highlands, reputedly using cannabis to heighten their valour for dastardly deeds (hence the words 'assassin' and 'hashish'). In Africa, use of cannabis pre-dated the arrival of the early Portuguese explorers, for example the people of the Zambezi valley used cannabis by breathing in the vapours of smouldering piles of hemp in a communal ritual.

The modern introduction of cannabis into Western Europe appears to have been by Napoleon's soldiers on their return from Egypt at the beginning of the nineteenth century and its hedonic properties were promoted at the Club des Hashishins in Paris in the decades of the mid-nineteenth century (Emboden,

5 cm

Figure 6.1 *Cannabis sativa* leaf, the mature plant may achieve 2 m or more in height depending on growing conditions.

1972). However, the widespread popularity of cannabis in Western societies was delayed until the 1960s and the 'flower power' movement.

It is estimated that in the USA by the 1970s, 60 per cent of young adults had experienced cannabis, 30 per cent reported monthly and less than 10 per cent daily use (Jaffe, 1985). Surveys indicate that by the late 1980s some decline had occurred in the use of cannabis in the USA (Jaffe, 1990), although minority drugs such as cocaine have increased in popularity. Among UK teenagers, 15–30 per cent have taken cannabis, and it is used by up to one million people each year in the UK (Richards, 1991). Cannabis comes third in popularity as a recreational drug (discounting caffeine) after alcohol and nicotine (Holloway, 1991; and see Figure 6.2) with which it is correlated in the individual pattern of usage (Golding *et al.*, 1983). Attempts to predict

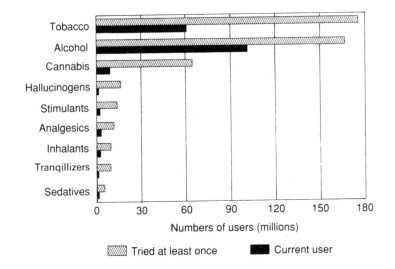

Figure 6.2 Relative usage of non-medical psychoactive drugs in the USA, caffeine excluded. Based on US household survey; not included are the homeless, prison population and military. Additional data from drug treatment centres, surveys of homeless and from law enforcement agencies suggest 2.4 million cocaine and crack addicts as well as 0.9 million heroin addicts. (Adapted from Holloway, 1991.)

which young people will use cannabis have come up with a variety of predictors. Apart from the use of alcohol and other drugs noted above, one of the strongest predictors appears to be peer influence (Hollister, 1988).

PHARMACOLOGY

Mechanisms

Cannabis contains more than sixty cannabinoids the most important in terms of its characteristic psychological effects being a highly lipophilic molecule L-delta-9-tetrahydrocannabinol (L-delta-9-THC, confusingly sometimes referred to as L-delta-1-THC) (see Figure 6.3). Most of the other cannabinoids have little or no psychoactive importance of their own but may interact with delta-9-THC to alter its effective potency.

The mechanism of action of cannabis at the neurosynaptic level has proved elusive (Jaffe, 1990). However, a specific cannabinoid receptor has been identified in the CNS recently. It raises the interesting possibility of an

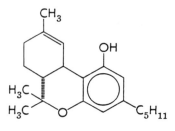

Tetrahydrocannabinol (Δ⁹-THC)

Figure 6.3 Structure of delta-9-tetrahydrocannabinol, the main active agent in cannabis; highest concentrations are found in the resin, flowering tops and leaves of the plant. (After Jaffe, 1990.)

endogenous cannabinoid synthesized by the brain, in a similar manner to the discovery of the CNS receptors for opiates and the endogenous opioid peptides (Matsuda *et al.*, 1990). In addition, the diverse pharmacological actions of THC-derivatives implies the existence of cannabinoid receptor subtypes (Snyder, 1990). The mechanisms of action at higher levels of CNS organization are still unclear, although animal studies with cannabis have implicated neurotransmitters including norepinephrine and serotonin, together with changed activity in hippocampal areas of the limbic system thought to be connected with cannabis-induced disruption of immediate memory (e.g., Murray, 1985).

Dosage

All parts of the plant contain cannabinoids but the highest concentrations are found in the resin, flowering tops and leaves. Concentrations of delta-9-THC vary widely between samples of cannabis, ranging typically between 0.5 and 11.0 per cent (Jaffe, 1990). It is difficult to give any precise figure for a 'usual' cannabis dose since this will vary according to the user. A rough idea is given by the observation that a herbal cigarette spiked with 10 mg of purified delta-9-THC will give a good 'high' when smoked by non-chronic users in the UK (Ashton *et al.*, 1981), and 20 mg is considered a 'social dose' in the USA (Leirer *et al.*, 1991). Other estimates are that $<50\ \mu$g THC kg^{-1} body weight is a low dose and $>250\ \mu$g kg^{-1} is a high dose (Johnson, 1990). An aspect of cannabinoids is that they have remarkably low lethal toxicity. Indeed, it is claimed that lethal doses in man are unknown (Hollister, 1988).

As might be expected, larger doses of cannabis produce greater impairments as assessed by a variety of tests including steadiness of balance, tracking tests, verbal tasks and short-term memory (e.g. Kiplinger and Manno, 1971;

Kiplinger *et al.*, 1971; Tinklenberg *et al.*, 1970). Absolute levels of plasma THC associated with impaired mental function are highly variable between individuals, perhaps reflecting individual variation in sensitivity and tolerance to the drug. One estimate is that only levels of 25 ng ml^{-1} or higher would be definitely associated with impairment in every case (Hollister, 1988). By contrast with blood plasma levels, urine testing is not useful for estimating mental impairment, given the extended time-course of days to weeks for elimination of THC and its metabolites following even a brief exposure to the drug.

Time-course

As with all drugs, pharmacokinetics sets limits to the actions of cannabis. This will depend on the route (smoking or ingestion — injection is rarely used) and other factors such as metabolic efficiency. Inhalation of cannabis smoke is a far more efficient method of absorption (up to say 50 per cent of presented dose absorbed and available) than ingestion (although about 95 per cent absorbed, less than 15 per cent bioavailability) (Lemberger *et al.*, 1972; Jaffe, 1990). The low efficiency for ingestion is due to first-pass degradation in the liver, which is avoided in the absorption phase with the inhalation route.

The time courses of smoking and ingestion are very different. For cannabis smoking, plasma concentrations reach a peak after seven to ten minutes, although physiological and subjective effects are not maximal until twenty to thirty minutes and last for two to three hours. Effects on performance may last longer than subjective effects, e.g. four to eight hours or more 'carry-over' (see below). For cannabis ingestion, the onset of subjective effects is delayed for a half to one hour, which correlates well with plasma concentrations; peak effects are delayed for two to three hours and last three to five hours (Jaffe, 1990). Since the onset and peak effects are delayed even with smoking, self-regulation ('self-titration') for dose is less precise than with such drugs as nicotine from tobacco. This may lead to excessive self-dosing and unwanted dysphoric effects in inexperienced users.

The systemic availability of THC from smoking varies widely depending upon the expertise of the smoker, bioavailability being less in light users (2–22 per cent range) compared with heavy users of cannabis (5–56 per cent range) (Hollister, 1988).

Inactivation and elimination is largely by metabolism in the liver, some of the initial metabolites being active also, e.g. 11-hydroxy-delta-9-THC. Very little unmetabolized THC is excreted in the urine. The initial rapid fall in plasma concentrations reflects redistribution of the lipophilic cannabinoids to lipid-rich tissues including the central nervous system. This is followed by a slower decline with a half-life of thirty hours. Traces of THC and metabolites may persist for days or weeks. Chronic cannabis users metabolize cannabinoids more rapidly, although this does not explain the tolerance to central effects.

Tolerance, physical dependence

Tolerance to cannabis develops to peripheral (e.g. heart rate rise) and central effects (e.g. mood change, psychomotor tests). Tolerance to central effects appears to be due to CNS changes rather than metabolic induction. This has been demonstrated in volunteers with repeated dosing over days. It can also be observed in chronic heavy users who consume amounts which would produce toxic effects in naive persons. No cross-tolerance has been demonstrated with LSD but some cross-tolerance has been observed with depressant drugs such as alcohol and opioids. Abrupt termination of cannabis in chronic heavy users is followed by irritability, decreased appetite, insomnia and rebound REM sleep which last several days (Jaffe, 1990). This abstinence syndrome is similar to that seen with benzodiazepine or hypnotic drug withdrawal. However, there is little evidence for physical dependence or addiction in most users (Ashton, 1987).

PHYSIOLOGY

Cannabis affects diverse peripheral and central systems of the body and has been regarded as a prime example of a pharmacologically 'dirty drug' (Ashton, 1987).

Immune system, endocrinology

Cannabinoids have been shown to depress cellular and humoral components of immune system function, most of this work having been carried out in animals. However, there is no hard clinical evidence that cannabis users are more susceptible to infection. Likewise, the teratogenicity demonstrated at high dosage levels in animals has not been shown with any certainty in humans (Jaffe, 1990). Nevertheless, cannabis is to be avoided during pregnancy since it crosses the placental barrier with possible deleterious effects on foetal development. It also enters the mother's milk. Chronic, high-dose cannabis use may lower testosterone levels and reversibly inhibit spermatogenesis. Women may be more sensitive, single doses of cannabis suppressing luteinizing hormone (LH) which may account for the observation of anovulatory cycles linked to cannabis use.

Lungs

The acute effect of cannabis on the lungs is bronchodilation. Long-term cannabis smoking has been associated with bronchitis and asthma (Jaffe, 1990). The acute bronchodilation effects represent the pharmacological actions whereas the possible asthma and bronchitic consequences of chronic cannabis smoking are caused by the general irritant actions of smoke. Cannabis smoke is carcinogenic, the tar being more carcinogenic than that found in tobacco smoke. The effective carcinogenicity is increased by the breath-holding of the cannabis smoke seen in experienced users as they attempt to increase the absorption efficiency. Breath-holding of the smoke is known to increase deposition rates of the particulate phase of smoke, be it cannabis, tobacco or combination (Golding, 1990).

Gut

Cannabis has antiemetic properties and can reduce the nausea caused by cancer chemotherapy. However, it is of unproven value as an antimotion sickness drug. By contrast, at high doses cannabis may slow gastric motility and even cause vomiting and diarrhoea (Jones, 1983).

Skin, mucosa

Cannabis will inhibit sweating and this may lead to a rise in body temperature for the user in hot climates (Jaffe, 1990). Dry mouth is a common effect. Actions on the electrodermal system measured at palmar sites (i.e. emotional/ arousal rather than thermoregulatory skin sites) are variable, perhaps reflecting the variability of CNS actions rather than any direct peripheral effects as implied by the observed inhibition of thermoregulatory sweating (Ashton *et al.*, 1981).

Heart

Heart rate is consistently increased by cannabis in a dose-related fashion (typically by twenty to fifty beats per minute (Jaffe, 1990)). If cannabis is smoked with tobacco then this rise is additive with that produced by nicotine (Ashton *et al.*, 1981). Increased myocardial oxygen demand and decreased myocardial delivery have been demonstrated as acute consequences of cannabis use. The cardiovascular effects of cannabis are doubtless deleterious to the health of persons with a pre-existing heart disease (Hollister, 1988).

Eye

Cannabis lowers intraocular pressure but does not significantly alter pupillary size. The conjuctivae are markedly reddened (Jaffe, 1990).

CNS

Effects on the CNS as observed by EEG are variable, increased alpha abundance and slowing of dominant frequency being the most common findings. Intrusion of slow waves into the waking EEG have also been observed. These observations are consistent with the view that sedative actions of cannabis are more common than stimulant effects (Jaffe, 1990). Cannabis has been demonstrated to be an anticonvulsant and to potentiate the effects of diazepam and valproic acid, the effect probably being due both to delta-9-THC and the related cannabinoid found in cannabis, cannabidiol (Ashton, 1987). Rapid eye movement (REM) sleep is reduced (Jaffe, 1990). Effects on evoked potential amplitude are variable but evoked potential latency may be slightly increased. The effects on slow event-related potentials, such as the contingent negative variation (CNV) which are thought to reflect aspects of cortical processing, are variable and personality interactions appear important in determining the direction of effect (Ashton et al., 1981). Electrodermal responses to series of irrelevant tone stimuli habituate more rapidly during cannabis intoxication, but excitation amplitude to the first stimulus remains unaffected. Responses to relevant stimuli during task performance may be elevated or depressed. Overall, such results would be consistent with stimulant and slightly more predominant depressant actions of cannabis, factors including dose, mood and personality playing an important role in modifying the outcome (Ashton et al., 1981). Diminished cerebral blood flow has been observed in chronic heavy users of cannabis as compared with controls. Such diminished blood flow was reversible upon cessation of cannabis use. Reduced brain blood flow may simply reflect decreased levels of brain activity in chronic users rather than being the mechanism by which cannabis exerts its central actions (Hollister, 1988). Initial reports of evidence for overt brain damage including cerebral atrophy and ultrastructural changes at the synaptic level consequent upon chronic cannabis use have been refuted (Hollister, 1986). However, the issue regarding more subtle effects has not been fully resolved (see below: 'Persistent effects on memory').

Potential therapeutic uses

The use of cannabis for medicinal purposes has a long history. The development of synthetic congeners of delta-9-THC and other cannabinoid constituents has been driven by the hope that some may have therapeutic usefulness. The specific drug categories in which cannabinoids may possess therapeutic potential follow the broad classes of physiological actions noted above. Possibilities which have been extensively reviewed include anti-asthmatic (bronchodilation), anticonvulsant, antiemetic, appetite stimulant, glaucoma treatment (lowering intraocular pressure), antianxiety, antidepressant, sedative–hypnotic, analgesic, anti-inflammatory, antihypertensive and anti-tumour (for more detail see Lemberger, 1980). In general terms, the practical progress to date has been slow (Ashton, 1987). For example, the development of cannabis derivatives (e.g. Nabilone) for antiemetic therapeutic use (Lemberger, 1980) has met with only limited success due to the unwanted dysphoric effects in some patients (Ashton, 1987). In spite of this setback, interest continues in the therapeutic potential of cannabinoids for a variety

Table 6.1 Summary table of principal actions of cannabis on physiology, behaviour and performance

PHYSIOLOGY	Immune system	Depressed T cell function
	Lungs	Acute bronchodilation, chronic irritation of bronchial mucosa, asthma, carcinogenic
	Mucosa, skin	Dry mouth, reduced sweating, variable effects on electrodermal activity
	Heart	Increased heart rate
	Gut	Anti-emetic for chemotherapy (CNS action?), may cause reduced motility, vomiting and diarrhoea at high dose
	Eye	Lower intraocular pressure
	CNS	Variable stimulant and depressant effects on EEG and evoked potentials; depressant effects more frequently observed
BEHAVIOUR	Mood	Enhancement of pleasure, mixed euphoria and sedation, dependent upon expectations and surroundings
	Sensation	Increased appetite, distorted time sense, intensification of mundane stimuli, hallucinogenic only in high doses
	Behaviour	Variable: loosening of thought processes and conversation, social withdrawal, uncertain existence of an 'amotivational syndrome', toxic psychosis occurs only rarely
PERFORMANCE	Physical	Reduced physical strength, impaired balance and steadiness of hand
	Simple	Little effect on simple reaction time or simple motor tasks
	Complex	Impaired: complex tracking, digit span, free recall of word-lists and prose, Stroop, sequential number subtraction and addition, most especially short-term memory
	Real world	Little effect on crude manual labour; impaired: car driving, aircraft simulator performance, smaller relative contribution to car accidents compared with alcohol, performance impairments may carry over for 24 h without subjective effects
	Interactions	Impairments exacerbated by increased task complexity and workload, by age and by concurrent use of other depressant drugs such as alcohol

These effects will be influenced by cannabis dose, e.g. the higher the dose the greater the performance deficit, the time-course will be influenced by dosage route (e.g. smoking produces faster effects than by ingestion), cannabis-induced performance deficits carry over beyond the period of subjective intoxication (e.g. for 24 hours for aircraft piloting), the development of tolerance in habitual cannabis users reduces to some extent the impairment of performance and some physiological effects (e.g. cardiovascular).

of disorders (e.g. Zuardi et al., 1991). Moreover, the recent isolation of central cannabinoid receptors (see above) may provide the basis for the future synthesis of cannabinoid drugs with more specific actions avoiding unwanted dysphoric effects.

SUBJECTIVE AND BEHAVIOURAL EFFECTS

Common effects

The hedonic properties of cannabis have long been exploited for recreational purposes. The effects of low to moderate doses include enhancement of pleasure and mixed euphoria and sedation. Anxiety or panic attacks are less often seen and psychotomimetic effects are rare except at high doses. Appetite is often increased. All of these effects depend on personality, expectations, surroundings and dose (Jones, 1971; Jaffe, 1990). Placebo effects occur, and may account for up to 50 per cent of the subjective 'high' following smoking of cannabis (Ashton et al., 1981). The intensity of subjective effects often varies in a cyclical manner over brief periods of time, so-called waxing and waning.

The myth dies hard that cannabis makes otherwise docile subjects violent. This association can be dated back as far as the twelfth century assassins (see the Introduction) and tends to be reinforced by the illegal status of the drug in most countries and consequent association with criminality (Johnson, 1990). Although it is possible that individuals with some special predisposition to violence may be triggered by cannabis, virtually every study of cannabis that has tried to measure violent or aggressive behaviour or thoughts during cannabis intoxication has concluded that these are decreased rather than increased. Moreover, in studies comparing alcohol with THC, alcohol has been found to increase aggression as a function of quantity taken whereas no such relationship was evident with THC (Hollister, 1986).

Commonly noted effects of cannabis on perception include intensification of mundane stimuli: colours, music, etc. seem more vivid, and the sensations of touch, taste and smell seem to be enhanced. However, unlike LSD, cannabis is not hallucinogenic except in high doses. Moreover, unlike LSD which has stimulant properties, cannabis usually has more sedative effects.

Distorted sense of time occurs, seconds can seem like minutes and minutes can seem like hours. Phenomena such as this have sometimes been given the label 'temporal disintegration' (e.g. Dittrich et al., 1973; Melges et al., 1970a, b). This may be due to effects on short-term memory (see below) or reflect an increase in the sensory input rate through disinhibition (on the basis that the perceived passage of time is dependent to some extent on the perceived rate of events). Social interaction, including the clarity of sequential dialogue in conversation, may be profoundly disrupted.

Weil and Zinberg (1969) described the effects in detail. Subjects had to expend more effort when high on cannabis in order to remember from moment to moment the logical thread of what they were saying. This need for increased effort when intoxicated was required whatever highly variable mood change had occurred, implying that it was not simply a motivational change. Weil and Zinberg (1969) discerned two related factors: simple forgetting by the subject of what was to be said next and a strong tendency to go off on irrelevant tangents because the line of thought was lost. In more general terms, the disruption of social interaction can be viewed as being the result of a variety of actions: simple sedative effects, short-term memory deficit, withdrawal into personal thoughts or to the effects on time perception. In particular, timing of responses is crucial for social interaction, especially for conversation. The occurrence of intrusive thoughts, the mind 'wandering off' along its own tracks, can be seen as an example of disruption of selective attention which can be especially relevant to impairment of real-life performance (see below).

An 'amotivational syndrome' has been identified with chronic cannabis consumption in which the user is less motivated to work, apathetic, dulled and has poor 'attitude'. Whether this is caused by cannabis or merely reflects the type of person who becomes a chronic cannabis user is a moot point, both factors probably being important (Jones, 1983). However, in moderate users of cannabis a variety of studies have provided only scant evidence for the existence of the 'amotivational syndrome' (for a more detailed analysis of this topic see Hollister, 1986).

Psychotoxic effects

Acute panic reaction is probably the most frequent adverse consequence of cannabis use. Although this can occur in experienced users, the conventional wisdom is that such acute panic reactions occur more commonly in inexperienced users of cannabis, with doses larger than that which experienced users may have become accustomed, and more commonly in older users who may enter the drug state with a higher level of initial apprehension. Such acute panic reactions, which often involve a fear by the user of losing control or even losing his or her mind, are usually self-limiting. They respond well to reassurance, and do not usually require sedation since the inherent sedative property of cannabis following the initial stimulation is often adequate (Hollister, 1986). Large doses of cannabis (usually $> 250\ \mu g\ kg^{-1}$ delta-9-THC by smoking) are more likely to produce psychotoxic effects. These include apprehension, paranoia, confusion, depersonalization and auditory and visual hallucinations (Isbell *et al.*, 1967; Ghodse, 1986). It has been claimed that up to 10 per cent of cannabis users may be at risk of developing acute toxic psychosis (Ghodse, 1986). Cannabis use can be a precipitating factor or proximal trigger for the development of schizophrenia, and relapse in stabilized schizophrenics (Ashton, 1987; Jaffe, 1990) although some authors take the conservative view that this effect remains unproven (Johnson, 1990). Similarly, although cannabis can be a precipitant of 'flashbacks' in former LSD users, such flashbacks often occur in the absence of cannabis (Hollister, 1986).

To summarize the position with regard to psychotoxic effects of cannabis: in most users it is only at high dose levels that any comparison can be drawn with psychotomimetic (psychedelic) drugs such as LSD, psilocin, mescaline, etc.; cannabinoids being regarded as a separate and distinct pharmacological class (see also above on cross-tolerance; Jaffe, 1990).

PERFORMANCE

Simple performance

Even low doses of cannabis impair balance and stability of stance, effects which are more apparent with the eyes closed (Kiplinger et al., 1971; Belgrave et al., 1979; Jaffe, 1990). Decreases in muscle strength and steadiness of hand can also be demonstrated (Clark et al., 1970; Jaffe, 1990). Although complex co-ordination may be impaired (Milstein et al., 1975), performance of simple motor tasks and simple reaction time are relatively unimpaired (Jaffe, 1990). To take an example, the slowing of simple reaction time following smoking of THC spiked cigarettes was non-significant at dose levels sufficient to produce significant subjective intoxication (Ashton et al., 1981). By contrast, cannabis produced significant impairments on a more complex (four-colour) reaction time test (Clark et al., 1970). Cannabis-induced impairments are generally revealed on more complex tasks (see below).

Complex motor and attentional performance

By contrast with the relatively minimal effects on simple motor performance a wide variety of effects have been shown on more complex tasks (Murray, 1986). Fine hand–eye co-ordination is impaired by cannabis. A task involving inserting small pins into holes with close aperture tolerances ('one-hole test') was disrupted by cannabis, as was rotary pursuit tracking (Salvendy, 1975). Similar results were reported by Beautrais and Marks (1976) who employed the Minnesota Rate of Manipulation test which requires the subject rapidly to extract, turn and replace into holes a number of cylindrical blocks. At 'social dose' levels, the performance deficits for an hour following dosing can be considerable on some of these fine motor co-ordination tasks, for example around 20 per cent reduction on control performance levels for the one-hole test cited above. Sometimes cannabis-induced impairment of fine hand–eye co-ordination is observed as an increase in variability of performance rather than a large overall mean impairment. Ashton *et al.* (1981) reported significantly increased variability as opposed to mean changes in time to complete a hand–eye co-ordination task involving tilting a transparent box in order simultaneously to roll a number of small balls into separate holes.

A frequently replicated observation is that cannabis impairs complex tracking performance (Manno *et al.*, 1971; Roth *et al.*, 1973; Melges, 1976) and divided-attention tracking tasks (Moskowitz *et al.*, 1981). Divided-attention tasks are particular susceptible to cannabis-induced deficits (Macavoy and Marks, 1975; Moskowitz *et al.*, 1972; Vachon *et al.*, 1974; Casswell and Marks, 1973a) although this is not to deny that 'undivided' attentional tests of performance have been demonstrated to be impaired by cannabis (e.g. Dittrich *et al.*, 1973). An example of a divided-attention task requires a subject to respond to breaks in the sequence of a light flashing in the central visual field while simultaneously being required to attend and respond to visual stimuli in any of ten lights arranged at various points away from the centre (Casswell and Marks, 1973a). Variants of this type of test require target tracking with concurrent responses to other test stimuli presented at random intervals. Such performance tests in their most developed forms take on aspects of driving or aircraft simulators (see below). The effects of cannabis on such divided-attention tasks has been interpreted as reflecting a reduction in working memory capacity (Leirer *et al.*, 1989).

The effects of cannabis have been studied on a number of other performance tests which might be termed complex but have less involvement of fine hand–eye motor co-ordination skills. Visual information processing in a tachistoscopic presentation test was significantly impaired by cannabis (Braff *et al.*, 1981). The digit-code test was significantly impaired by cannabis (Clark *et al.*, 1970). Successive alternate number addition and subtraction are impaired by cannabis (Melges *et al.*, 1970a, b; Meyer *et al.*, 1971; Casswell and Marks, 1973b; Belgrave *et al.*, 1979; Heishman *et al.*, 1990), although at very low dose levels cannabis may not significantly impair such tests (Evans *et al.*, 1973). Performance of the Stroop colour–word performance task was not impaired to a statistically significant extent at dose levels sufficient to impair recall of prose material (Miller *et al.*, 1972). The authors suggested that higher doses of cannabis would probably have achieved a significant effect on this Stroop test (Miller *et al.*, 1972). On this basis the citation by Leirer *et al.*, (1989) of the Miller *et al.* (1972) study as showing significant impairment of the Stroop test is excusable. No significant effects of cannabis were noted on a card-sorting test at a dose level sufficient, in the same experiment, to impair significantly a fine hand—eye motor skill test, the Minnesota Rate of Manipulation test (Beautrais and Marks, 1976). No significant decrement in performance was observed on a five-letter anagram test at cannabis doses which were sufficient to impair memory as assessed by recall of prose material (Abel, 1971a).

Memory

A consistent finding has been a cannabis-induced disruption of memory, short-term memory being particularly susceptible (Dornbush *et al.*, 1971; Relman, 1982). Laboratory tests have shown that cannabis impairs immediate free recall of digits (Tinklenberg *et al.*, 1970; Heishman *et al.*, 1990), free recall of prose material (Abel, 1970; Miller *et al.*, 1972, 1977a), recall of word lists (Abel, 1971a; Dittrich *et al.*, 1973) and recall of word—picture combinations (Miller *et al.*, 1977b). In studies of the effects of cannabis on free recall tasks (e.g. Miller *et al.*, 1972) it has been noted that in addition to an inability to remember specific material a frequent error was the intrusion of extraneous and totally unrelated material. The authors suggested that this might have reflected a cannabis-induced broadening of attention, and consequent failure to filter out irrelevant information during the encoding process.

An early observation concerning the effects of cannabis on memory was that impairments of immediate memory did not follow a smooth time-function but tended to be episodic, brief in duration and not under volitional control (Tinklenberg *et al.*, 1970). These episodes often simultaneously interrupted speech patterns and were associated with intrusions of extraneous perceptions and thoughts. Similar intermittent effects, so-called waxing and waning have been noted on subjective intoxication measures.

An important question (Abel, 1971b; Miller *et al.*, 1972) is whether cannabis disrupts memory at the acquisition or recall stages or both. It is now generally accepted that the cannabis-induced memory deficit appears to be preferentially on immediate memory at the encoding stage rather than disruption of retrieval of previously stored information (Leirer *et al.*, 1989). For example, Darley *et al.* (1974) failed to demonstrate a cannabis-induced deficit on free recall or recognition memory when cannabis was given shortly after encoding but well prior to retrieval. By contrast, memory disruption was caused by dosing with cannabis prior to the encoding stage. The relatively specific effect of cannabis on memory acquisition rather than consolidation or recall processes differs (in this sense) from the actions of other drugs such as nicotine or amphetamine which will affect both acquisition, consolidation and recall processes of memory (Mangan and Golding, 1984). Darley *et al.* (1977) examined the effects of cannabis using a 'common facts' recall test on college students (general information questions in humanities, sciences and current events). Recall efficiency during cannabis intoxication was the same as that with placebo. This indicated that retrieval of non-experimentally presented information is unaffected by cannabis. This was consistent with previous findings that cannabis had no effect on recall of word-lists experimentally presented prior to cannabis intoxication (Abel, 1971a, b; Darley *et al.*, 1973; Dornbush, 1974).

The effects of cannabis on memory have also been considered by several studies in the context of state-dependent memory research (Hill *et al.*, 1973; Beautrais and Marks, 1976; Darley *et al.*, 1974, 1977; Stillman *et al.*, 1974; Rickles *et al.*, 1973; Cohen and Rickles, 1974). Such studies have as their starting point the report by some cannabis users that events experienced while intoxicated are not remembered until the drug is ingested again at a later time (Darley *et al.*, 1974). It has also been argued that state-dependency may simply be one example of behavioural tolerance, i.e. the question has arisen as to whether persons who have the opportunity to practise a task while under the influence of cannabis (as with the chronic user) can learn to compensate for the drug effects (Beautrais and Marks, 1976). In a typical experimental design, subjects are trained under cannabis or placebo and retested several days later under cannabis or placebo, which yields four treatment groups: placebo—placebo, placebo—cannabis, cannabis—placebo, cannabis—cannabis. In a further elaboration for some experimental reports, contrasts are made between experienced cannabis users versus previous non-users (e.g. Beautrais and Marks, 1976). The results of this research have been far from uniform. State-dependent learning has been claimed in some reports (Hill *et al.*, 1973; Rickles *et al.*, 1973), partial or 'asymmetrical' state-dependency in another report (Darley, 1974), and no state-dependent learning effects in yet other reports (Cohen and Rickles, 1974; Beautrais and Marks, 1976). However, a fairly consistent finding has been that irrespective of any state-dependent learning effects, overall learning performance is reduced under the influence of cannabis compared with placebo.

Memory lapses or continual forgetting during cannabis intoxication appear to account at least in part, at the subjective level, for 'temporal disintegration', as they interrupt the continuity in the flow of personal time. Such 'temporal disintegration' has been invoked as an explanatory link between objective performance impairments and depersonalization phenomena, since the personal past, present and future constitute a fundamental subjective framework through which an individual identifies himself (Dittrich *et al.*, 1973).

To summarize, the major effects of cannabis on memory are on immediate memory and on acquisition processes. Cannabis has little or no effect on recall of information once it has been stored. State-dependent memory effects seem to be of relatively minor importance. The actions on immediate memory appear to account for some of the subjective temporal aspects of cannabis intoxication.

Persistent effects on memory

Much work has been carried out showing the acute impairment of short-term memory by cannabis (see above). Reductions in short-term memory performance in chronic users versus non-users have also been demonstrated (e.g. Gianutsos and Litwack, 1976). However, there is also some evidence for more persistent memory deficits in chronic cannabis users well beyond the period of acute intoxication (*Lancet*, 1989).

Five out of eight studies have detected persistent short-term memory deficits in chronic cannabis users (Souieff, 1976; Wig and Varma, 1977; Varma *et al.*, 1988; Page *et al.*, 1988; Schwartz *et al.*, 1989). The remaining three studies suggested no such deficit (Bowman and Phil, 1973; Satz *et al.*, 1976; Mendhiratta *et al.*, 1978). To take the most recent example, the Schwartz *et al.* (1989) study compared a group of chronic cannabis users with controls matched for age and IQ. Impairments were revealed in auditory and visual short-term memory which lessened over time but were still detectable some six weeks following abstinence from cannabis (confirmed by urine tests). This period is well beyond the time of any significant persistence of cannabinoids or metabolites. On this basis, it has been suggested that people who frequently smoke high-potency cannabis may be expected to manifest short-term memory deficits that continue for at least six weeks after their last puff (*Lancet*, 1989).

The observation, following weeks of abstinence from cannabis, of a slow but not complete recovery from the after-effects of chronic heavy cannabis use, leaves open the question as to whether any harmful effects on memory or other cognitive functions had been permanently damaging. The difficulty in comparing ex-chronic cannabis users with controls lies in determining what would have been the expected baseline level of performance (pre-chronic cannabis use). No amount of *post hoc* matching of controls for age, sex, socio-economic status, etc. can fully overcome this question. This limitation is especially apparent when the final observed differences are relatively small, compared with individual variation in whatever memory or performance measure is under scrutiny. Although there is no convincing evidence of gross indications of permanent cognitive or brain damage in ex-chronic users (e.g. Ashton, 1987; Johnson, 1990), the possibility remains of more subtle, enduring changes. This question is important but unresolved.

REAL-LIFE PERFORMANCE

Unskilled labour

In line with the laboratory observation that cannabis has rather minimal effects on simple performance, is the observation that crude manual labour is relatively unaffected, at least by social doses in experienced users. For example, in spite of the demonstration that the work output of Jamaican labourers was reduced immediately following smoking cannabis (Schaeffer, 1973; McGlothlin, 1975), no evidence could be found that cannabis use, as opposed to non-use by farm labourers in Jamaica, reduced overall sugar-cane cutting production rates (Comitas, 1976; Parrott, 1987). This also places into perspective the limited practical significance for such farm work of the observations made earlier, that cannabis reduces muscular strength and reduces sweating in a hot climate (Jaffe, 1990).

Operation of complex machinery

The operation of heavy machinery or driving is made hazardous by cannabis (Kvalseth, 1977; Hollister, 1986) as might be expected from the general finding that cannabis impairs performance (e.g. Manno *et al.*, 1970; Moskowitz *et al.*, 1974). At low doses few subjects show impairments, the percentage of subjects showing impairments rising above 50 per cent and the severity of the impairments increasing with increasing dosage to levels which are still realistic in terms of the cannabis doses used socially.

Driving

Cannabis has been reported to be associated with errors that might influence driving in traffic (Smart, 1974): with errors in time estimation (Hollister and Gillespie, 1970; Jones and Stone, 1970; Kaplan, 1973; Melges *et al.*, 1971; Vachon *et al.*, 1974), with errors in judgement of distance (Bech *et al.*, 1973), and with impairment of tracking tasks (Manno *et al.*, 1971; Roth *et al.*, 1973; Melges, 1976; Moskowitz *et al.*, 1981). Effects of cannabis have been investigated in driving simulators and during real driving. The effects of cannabis on simulated driving have produced mixed results. Crancer *et al.* (1969) noted that cannabis increased speedometer errors but produced no deviation from the norm on accelerator, brake, signal, steering or total errors. Alcohol had a far more deleterious effect. Rafaelsen *et al.* (1973) and Bech *et al.* (1973) demonstrated impairments of time and distance estimation and increased braking time in a driving simulator with higher doses of cannabis which were still within what can be considered a 'social dose' range. Moskowitz *et al.* (1976a) used films depicting traffic to demonstrate that alcohol disrupted visual search more than cannabis did. In another report, Moskowitz *et al.* (1976b) found no significant deviations from the norm in car control and tracking.

The effects of cannabis on driving performance in dual-control cars on closed courses and with open-street traffic was studied by Klonoff (1974) and significant impairments noted. Similar impairments with cannabis were noted by Hansteen et al. (1976) for real driving on a closed-course around bollards, this study also showing that alcohol produced greater impairments than cannabis. Reeve et al. (1985) studied driving skills on a course rigged with driving problems. Both cannabis and alcohol produced impairment of performance, the combination being worse than either alone. A similar result was found by Sutton (1983) who observed that the combination of alcohol and cannabis yielded significant impairment during a driving test but neither drug alone did.

The exact prevalence of persons who might be driving under the influence of cannabis is uncertain (Hollister, 1988). One survey found at least 5 ng ml^{-1} of THC in the blood of 14 per cent of a large random sample of drivers detained for erratic driving (Zimmerman et al., 1981). Other surveys have shown that between 4 and 37 per cent of drivers killed in road traffic accidents have cannabinoids present in their blood (Mason and McBay, 1984; Williams et al., 1985; McBay, 1986). Given the known impairments produced by cannabis on driving performance in controlled studies, such an association with fatal road accidents could be suggestive of a causal link. This has led for calls to provide cannabis testing as a road policing measure in addition to alcohol testing (Johnson, 1990). However, correlation does not prove causation. It must be noted that cannabis users tend to be risk-takers on standard personality tests and, more importantly, to use other drugs including alcohol which can impair driving (Golding et al., 1983; Hollister, 1988). Indeed, it has been noted in the largest of the above studies of drivers killed in fatal traffic accidents, that in 64 per cent of cases alcohol was present as compared with only 13 per cent where THC was present. Of the instances where THC was detected in blood, most (84 per cent) were in combination with alcohol (McBay, 1986). Moreover, the levels of THC detected were low in most instances, plasma concentrations being less than 5 ng ml^{-1} of THC. (Plasma THC concentrations would have to be closer to 25 ng ml^{-1} to indicate impaired functioning with certainty in most instances, as assessed using the USA 'roadside sobriety test' (Reeve et al., 1983).) Taken together, these statistics have led some authors to conclude that at present cannabis plays a relatively minor role in fatal traffic accidents as compared with alcohol which has been associated with fully one half of fatal car accidents in the USA (Hollister, 1988). To summarize the current imperfect state of knowledge, it has been established that cannabis can impair driving. Estimates of the extent to which it contributes to actual road accidents may be inflated by the concurrent presence of alcohol in the majority of instances.

Aircraft piloting

Aircraft piloting performance under the influence of cannabis has been studied mainly in simulators for obvious reasons. The consistent finding is that piloting is performed less accurately under the influence of cannabis (Janowsky *et al.*, 1976a, b; Yesavage *et al.*, 1985; Leirer *et al.*, 1989, 1991). Aircraft simulators enable the level of piloting difficulty to be controlled and increased, e.g. by simulating turbulent air conditions, engine malfunctions. Under such circumstances there is some evidence that the increased workload on the pilot exacerbates any cannabis-induced impairments of piloting skills. A variety of overlapping explanations have been put forward to account for the observed reduction in piloting performance. The most obvious are drawn from the impairments noted earlier, i.e. the cannabis-induced deficits in complex perceptual–motor performance, in divided and focused attention, in short-term memory: all of these cognitive activities being essential for piloting (Leirer *et al.*, 1991). In line with earlier observations concerning the disruptive actions of cannabis on various separate facets of performance (e.g. Tinklenberg *et al.*, 1970), it has been suggested that irrelevant thoughts intrude during periods when selective or divided attention are required for piloting performance (Janowski *et al.*, 1976a, b; Leirer *et al.*, 1989).

Academic

Reduced academic school performance has been associated with cannabis use (Ashton, 1987). Although it is tempting to postulate a causal relationship, it could also be argued that regular cannabis users are less interested and motivated to perform well at academic work.

Carry-over effects

Impairment of driving or flying performance after a social dose of one or two cannabis cigarettes lasts for four to eight hours (or more), well beyond the time that the user perceives the subjective effects (Yesavage *et al.*, 1985; Hollister, 1986; Ashton, 1987; Jaffe, 1990). Tinklenberg *et al.* (1970) noted that some subjects described a self-assessed residual impairment of cognitive functions which could occur up to twenty-four hours following a single dose of cannabis. Using objective measures, carry-over effects up to twenty-four hours have been demonstrated under the highly demanding conditions of aircraft simulators (Leirer *et al.*, 1991; see Figure 6.4), although this is not always a consistent finding (Leirer *et al.*, 1989). There is some evidence that twenty-four hour carry-over effects following cannabis smoking can be detected using less demanding tasks than aircraft simulators. Heishman *et al.* (1990) reported residual cannabis-induced impairments twenty-four hours later on a serial addition–subtraction test and on a digit recall test, these effects occurring in the absence of any subjective symptoms of cannabis.

Such residual impairments can produce a particularly dangerous situation in which the operators of complex machinery may not be subjectively aware

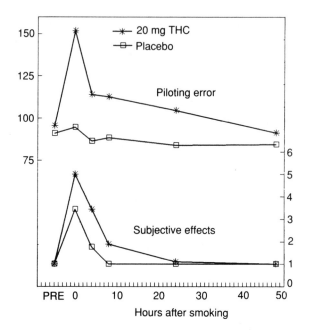

Figure 6.4 Effects of smoking cannabis or placebo on piloting performance (top) and concomitant subjective ratings (bottom). Note that piloting performance deficits are maximal at the time of peak subjective effects of cannabis. However, whereas subjective effects last for only a few hours and are not significant by 24 hours post-smoking, performance deficits carry-over and performance is still significantly impaired at 24 hours. Note also the transient subjective effects following smoking placebo which are not accompanied by any performance deficit. (Graphical presentation of data drawn from Leirer *et al.*, 1991.)

of the impairment produced by cannabis and cannot rely on their judgement concerning their ability to perform (Leirer *et al.*, 1991). The reason that these carry-over effects occur is not known. They could be due to the slow time-course of elimination of delta-9-THC and active metabolites from the CNS (see earlier, 'Pharmacology'). Alternatively, some disruption may be caused by THC or metabolites to neurotransmitters levels or receptor function which has a long recovery time.

OTHER FACTORS AND INTERACTIONS

Alcohol

Alcohol magnifies the impairments produced by cannabis on complex performance (Manno *et al.*, 1971; Sutton, 1983; Reeve *et al.*, 1985; Jaffe,

1990). Such additive interactions are reminiscent of the exacerbated performance decrements produced by concurrent intake of alcohol with commonly used medications possessing sedative effects such as antihistamines or minor tranquillizers.

Age

Older age groups appear more susceptible to the performance deficits produced by cannabis. Leirer *et al.* (1989) demonstrated that older pilots (30–48 years) were more impaired by cannabis than younger pilots (18–29 years). The two age groups were similar on such factors as flight hours and previous experience of cannabis, suggesting that the greater cannabis-induced impairment of the older fliers was attributable to the age factor. It can be suggested that the older pilots have less 'spare mental capacity' which only becomes relevant at high workload rates in the face of a drug which is reducing the mental resources available.

Tolerance

Tolerance produced by repeated use of cannabis may critically modify the severity of performance impairment produced by cannabis. Casual cannabis smokers usually experience more impairment of cognitive and psychomotor performance than do habitual cannabis users in response to a given dose of cannabis (Caldwell *et al.*, 1969; Meyer *et al.*, 1971; Murray, 1985; Jaffe, 1990; Johnson, 1990).

SUMMARY DISCUSSION

Discounting caffeine, cannabis is the third most popular 'recreational' drug after alcohol and tobacco. The main psychoactive constituent is delta-9-THC. It is smoked or ingested for its hedonic actions of mixed euphoria and sedation which typically last for two to three hours. Cannabis shares some of the sedative properties of depressant drugs such as alcohol and, at very high doses, the hallucinogenic but not stimulant actions of psychedelics such as LSD. However, it has a distinctive pattern of effects and it is conventionally regarded as being in a pharmacological class of its own.

As with most pleasures, a price has to be paid. Penalties (apart from legal or financial) include deleterious effects on health, mental well-being and performance. The main health risks are to the lungs and are related to smoking as opposed to ingesting cannabis. Chronic cannabis smoking is associated with asthma and may increase the chances of lung cancer, the carcinogenicity of cannabis smoke being greater than smoke from tobacco with which it is frequently mixed. Unwanted effects on mental function include dysphoria and reduced performance. However, in spite of the development of some degree of tolerance with repeated use, and minor 'rebound' symptoms upon cessation in heavy chronic users, there is little evidence for 'addiction' as seen with narcotics.

Dysphoric actions such as anxiety or panic reaction are relatively infrequent as compared with hedonic effects, a balance of outcome which accounts for the drug's popularity. These and more severe psychotoxic effects are observed at high dose levels and/or with individuals with some prior susceptibility including emotional stress. Only at high dose levels, which the user will usually try to avoid, can any comparison be made with psychedelic drugs such as LSD.

Reduced motor and mental performance occurs at dose levels used socially. In general, the larger the dose of cannabis and the more complex the task, the greater is the performance deficit. The time-course of maximum performance impairment is associated with the typical two to three hour duration period of subjective intoxication. However, some degree of performance impairment may 'carry-over' beyond the period of subjective intoxication. Under the highly demanding conditions of flight simulators, such 'carry-over' has been shown to occur up to twenty-four hours later.

Although crude motor performance and responses are relatively spared, fine motor skills are impaired, including fine hand–eye co-ordination and balance. Immediate and short-term memory is impaired and this action appears to be at the acquisition or encoding stage rather than retrieval. Recall of established memory is relatively unaffected by cannabis. Over and above this main effect on memory, there is some limited evidence for a state-dependent memory effect but this is relatively unimportant by comparison. Control of attention is handicapped by cannabis, tasks involving divided-attention being particularly vulnerable. Such a pattern of effects on attention and memory has been conceptualized by some researchers as a reduction of 'working memory capacity'. Memory lapses or continual forgetting during cannabis intoxication appear to account at least in part, for some subjective effects: a so-called temporal disintegration, including slowing of the perceived passage of time and depersonalization experiences.

Performance deficits shown in the laboratory have the practical implication of reduced performance and increased risk of accidents for many real-life tasks during cannabis intoxication. Most research has concentrated on two practical skills: car driving and aircraft piloting. Doses of cannabis at levels likely to be used socially have been demonstrated to impair such skills. However, 'social doses' of alcohol by comparison appear to produce greater impairments than cannabis. There is some evidence that the combination of the two drugs may cause greater impairments than either alone. The evidence from blood samples taken from drivers involved in fatal car crashes indicates that at present the overall contribution of cannabis to such accidents is relatively minor in comparison with that of alcohol.

The recent discovery of a specific cannabinoid receptor in the brain, if confirmed, will lead to a clearer understanding of the mechanism of action of cannabis. It may also enable the synthesis of cannabinoids with more selective actions for therapeutic uses (e.g. cannabinoid anti-emetics) which have enjoyed only limited success to date because of unwanted dysphoric side-effects.

REFERENCES

Abel, E.L. (1970). Marijuana and memory. *Nature, London* **227**: 1151–2.

Abel, E.L. (1971a). Effects of marihuana on the solution of anagrams, memory and appetite. *Nature, London* **231**: 260–1.

Abel, E.L. (1971b). Marijuana and memory: acquisition or retrieval? *Science, New York* **173**: 1038–40.

Ashton, C.H. (1987). Cannabis: dangers and possible uses. *British Medical Journal* **294**: 141–2.

Ashton, H., Golding, J.F., Marsh, V.R., Millman, J.E. and Thompson, J.W. (1981). The seed and the soil: effect of dosage, personality and starting state on the response to delta-9-tetrahydrocannabinol in man. *British Journal of Clinical Pharmacology* **12**: 705–20.

Beautrais, A.L. and Marks, D.F. (1976). A test of state dependency effects in marihuana intoxication for the learning of psychomotor tasks. *Psychopharmacologia* **46**: 37–40.

Bech, P., Rafaelsen, L. and Rafaelsen, O.J. (1973). Cannabis and alcohol: effects on estimation of time and distance. *Psychopharmacologia* **32**: 373–81.

Belgrave, B.E., Bird, K.D., Chesler, G.B., Jackson, D.M., Lubbe, K.E., Starmer, G.A. and Teo, R.K.C. (1979). The effect of (−)trans-delta-9-tetrahydrocannabinol alone and in combination with ethanol, on human performance. *Psychopharmacology* **62**: 53–60.

Bowman, M. and Phil, R.O. (1973). Cannabis: psychological effects of chronic heavy use: a controlled study of intellectual functioning in chronic users of high potency cannabis. *Psychopharmacologia*, **29**: 159–70.

Braff, D.L., Silverton, L., Saccuzzo, D.P. and Janowsky, D.S. (1981). Impaired speed of visual information processing in marijuana intoxication. *American Journal of Psychiatry* **138**: 613–17.

Caldwell, D.F., Myers, S.A., Domino, E.F. and Merriam, P.E. (1969). Auditory and visual threshold effects of marihuana in man. *Perceptual and Motor Skills* **29**: 755–9.

Casswell, S. and Marks, D.F. (1973a). Cannabis-induced impairment of performance on a divided attention task. *Nature, London* **241**: 60–1.

Casswell, S. and Marks, D.F. (1973b). Cannabis and temporal disintegration in experienced and naive subjects. *Science, New York* **179**: 803–5.

Clark, L.D., Hughes, R. and Nakashima, E.N. (1970). Behavioural effects of marihuana. *Archives of General Psychiatry* **23**: 193–8.

Cohen, M.J. and Rickles, W.H. (1974). Performance on a verbal learning task by subjects of heavy past marijuana usage. *Psychopharmacologia* **37**: 323–30.

Comitas, L. (1976). Cannabis and work in Jamaica: a refutation of the amotivational syndrome. *Annals of the New York Academy of Sciences* **282**: 24–32.

Crancer, A., Dille, J.M., Delay, J.C., Wallace, J.E. and Haykin, M.D. (1969). Comparison of the effects of marihuana and alcohol on simulated driving performance. *Science, New York* **164**: 851–4.

Darley, C.F., Tinklenberg, J.R., Roth, W.T., Hollister, L.E. and Atkinson, R.C. (1973). Influence of marihuana on storage and retrieval processes in memory. *Memory and Cognition* **1**: 196–200.

Darley, C.F., Tinklenberg, J.R., Roth, W.T. and Atkinson, R.C. (1974). The nature of storage deficits and state-dependent retrieval under marijuana. *Psychopharmacologia* **37**: 139–49.

Darley, C.F., Tinklenberg, J.R., Roth, W.T., Vernon, S. and Kopell, B.S. (1977). Marijuana effects on long-term memory assessment and retrieval. *Psychopharmacology* **52**: 239–41.

Dittrich, A., Battig, K. and von Zeppelin, I. (1973). Effects of (−)-delta-9-tetrahydrocannabinol (delta-9-THC) on memory, attention and subjective state. *Psychopharmacologia* **33**: 369–76.

Dornbush, R.L. (1974). Marijuana and memory: effects of smoking on storage. *Transactions of New York Academy of Sciences* **36**: 94–100.

Dornbush, R.L., Fink, M. and Freedman, A.M. (1971). Marijuana, memory and perception. *American Journal of Psychiatry* **128**: 194–7.

Emboden, W. (1972). *Narcotic Plants*. London: Studio Vista.

Evans, M.A., Martz, R., Brown, D.J., Rodda, B., Kiplinger, G.F., Lemberger, L. and Forney, R.B. (1973). Impairment of performance with low doses of marihuana. *Clinical Pharmacology and Therapeutics* **14**: 936–40.

Ghodse, H.A. (1986). Cannabis psychosis. *British Journal of Addiction* **81**: 473–8.

Gianutsos, R. and Litwack, A.R. (1976). Chronic marijuana smokers show reduced coding into long-term storage. *Bulletin of the Psychonomic Society* **7**: 277–9.

Golding, J.F. (1990). Smoking. In *Textbook of Respiratory Medicine*, edited by R.A.L. Brewis, G.J. Gibson and D.M. Geddes, London: Baillière Tindall, pp. 445–60.

Golding, J.F., Harpur, T. and Brent-Smith, H. (1983). Personality, drinking and drug-taking correlates of cigarette smoking. *Personality and Individual Differences* **4**: 703–6.

Hansteen, R.W., Miller, R.D., Lonero, L., Reid, L.D. and Jones, B. (1976). Effects of cannabis and alcohol on automobile driving and psychomotor tracking. *Annals of the New York Academy of Sciences* **282**: 240–56.

Heishman, S.J., Huestis, M.A., Henningfield, J.E. and Cone, E.J. (1990). Acute and residual effects of marijuana: profiles of plasma THC levels, physiological, subjective, and performance measures. *Pharmacology, Biochemistry and Behavior* **37**: 561–5.

Hill, S.Y., Schwin, R., Powell, B. and Goodwin, D.W. (1973). State-dependent effects of marijuana on human memory. *Nature, London* **243**: 241–2.

Hollister, L.E. (1986). Health aspects of cannabis. *Pharmacological Reviews* **38**: 1–20.

Hollister, L.E. (1988). Cannabis: 1988. *Acta Psychiatrica Scandinavica* **78** (Supplement 345): 108–18.

Hollister, L.E. and Gillespie, H.K. (1970). Marihuana, ethanol, and dextroamphetamine. *Archives of General Psychiatry* **23**: 199–207.

Holloway, M. (1991). Rx for addiction. *Scientific American* **264**: 70–9.

Isbell, H., Gorodetzsky, C.W., Jasinski, D., Clausen, V., von Spulak, F. and Korte, F. (1967). Effects of (−)delta 9-trans-tetrahydrocannabinol in man. *Psychopharmacologia* **11**: 184–8.

Jaffe, J.H. (1985). Drug addiction and drug abuse. In *The Pharmacological Basis of Therapeutics* (7th edn), edited by A. Goodman Gilman, L.S. Goodman, T.W. Rall and F. Murad. New York: Macmillan, pp. 532–81.

Jaffe, J.H. (1990). Drug addiction and drug abuse. In *The Pharmacological Basis of Therapeutics* (8th edn), edited by A. Goodman Gilman, L.S. Goodman, T.W. Rall, A.S. Nies and P. Taylor. New York: Pergamon Press, pp. 522–73.

Janoswsky, D.S., Meacham, M.P., Blaine, J.D., Schoor, M. and Bozzetti, L.P. (1976a). Marijuana effects on simulated flying ability. *American Journal of Psychiatry* **133**: 384–8.

Janoswsky, D.S., Meacham, M.P., Blaine, J.D., Schoor, M. and Bozzetti, L.P. (1976b). Simulated flying performance after marihuana intoxication. *Aviation, Space and Environmental Medicine* **47**: 124–8.

Johnson, B.A. (1990). Psychopharmacological effects of cannabis. *British Journal of Hospital Medicine* **43**: 114−22.

Jones, R.T. (1971). Marihuana-induced 'high': influence of expectation, setting and previous drug experience. *Pharmacological Reviews* **23**: 359−69.

Jones, R.T. (1983). Cannabis and health. *Annual Review of Medicine* **34**: 247−58.

Jones, R.T. and Stone, G.C. (1970). Psychological studies of marijuana and alcohol in man. *Psychopharmacologia* **18**: 108−17.

Kaplan, J. (1973). Review of marihuana: a signal of misunderstanding. *Science, New York,* **179**: 167−8.

Kiplinger, G.F. and Manno, J.E. (1971). Dose−response relationships to cannabis in human subjects. *Pharmacological Reviews* **23**: 339−47.

Kiplinger, G.F., Manno, J.E., Rodda, B.E. and Forney, R.B. (1971). Dose-related analysis of the effects of tetrahydrocannabinol in man. *Clinical Pharmacology and Therapeutics* **12**: 650−7.

Klonoff, H. (1974). Marijuana and driving in real-life situations. *Science, New York* **186**: 317−24.

Kvalseth, T.O. (1977). Effects of marijuana on human reaction time and motor control. *Perceptual and Motor Skills* **45**: 935−9.

Lancet (1989). Short-term memory impairment in chronic cannabis users. *Lancet* (editorial) **ii**: 1254−5.

Leirer, V.O., Yesavage, J.A. and Morrow, D.G. (1989). Marijuana, aging, and task difficulty effects on pilot performance. *Aviation, Space and Environmental Medicine* **60**: 1145−52.

Leirer, V.O., Yesavage, J.A. and Morrow, D.G. (1991). Marijuana carry-over effects on aircraft pilot performance. *Aviation, Space and Environmental Medicine* **62**: 221−7.

Lemberger, L. (1980). Potential therapeutic usefulness of marijuana. *Annual Review of Pharmacology and Toxicology* **20**: 151−72.

Lemberger, L., Weiss, J.L., Watanabe, A.M., Galanter, I.M., Wyatt, R.J. and Cardon, P.V. (1972). Delta-9-Tetrahydrocannabinol: temporal correlation of the psychologic effects and blood levels after various routes of administration. *New England Journal of Medicine* **286**: 685−8.

Macavoy, M.G. and Marks, D.F. (1975). Divided attention performance of cannabis users and non-users following cannabis and alcohol. *Psychopharmacologia* **44**: 147−52.

Mangan, G.L. and Golding, J.F. (1984). *The Psychopharmacology of Smoking.* Cambridge University Press.

Manno, J.E., Kiplinger, G.E., Haine, S.E., Bennett, I.F. and Forney, R.B. (1970). Comparative effects of smoking marihuana or placebo on human motor and mental performance. *Clinical Pharmacology and Therapeutics* **11**: 808−15.

Manno, J.E., Kiplinger, G.F., Scholz, N., Forney, R.B. and Haine, S.E. (1971). The influence of alcohol and marihuana on motor and mental performance. *Clinical Pharmacology and Therapeutics* **12**: 202−11.

Mason, A.P. and McBay, A.J. (1984). Ethanol, marihuana and other drug use in 600 drivers killed in single-vehicle crashes in North Carolina 1978−81. *Journal of Forensic Sciences* **29**: 788−792.

Matsuda, L.A., Lolait, S.J., Brownstein, M.J., Young, A.C. and Bonner, T.J. (1990). Structure of a cannabinoid receptor and functional expression of the cloned cDNA. *Nature, London* **346**: 561−4.

McBay, A.J. (1986). Drug concentrations and traffic safety. *Alcohol, Drugs, Driving* **2**: 51−60.

McGlothlin, W.H. (1975). Drug use and abuse. *Annual Review of Psychology* **26**: 45−64.

Melges, F.T. (1976). Tracking difficulties and paranoid ideation during hashish and alcohol intoxication. *American Journal of Psychiatry* **133**: 1024−8.

Melges, F.T., Tinklenberg, J.R., Hollister, L.E. and Gillespie, H.K. (1970a). Marihuana and temporal disintegration. *Science, New York* **168**: 1118−20.

Melges, F.T., Tinklenberg, J.R., Hollister, L.E. and Gillespie, H.K. (1970b). Temporal disintegration and depersonalization during marihuana intoxication. *Archives of General Psychiatry* **23**: 204−10.

Melges, F.T., Tinklenberg, J.R., Hollister, L.E. and Gillespie, H.K. (1971). Marihuana and the temporal span of awareness. *Archives of General Psychiatry* **24**: 564–7.

Mendhiratta, S.S., Wig, N.N. and Varma, S.K. (1978). Some psychological correlates of long-term heavy cannabis users. *British Journal of Psychiatry* **132**: 482–6.

Meyer, R.E., Pillard, R.C., Shapiro, L.M. and Mirin, S.M. (1971). Administration of marijuana to heavy and casual marijuana users. *American Journal of Psychiatry* **128**: 198–203.

Miller, L., Drew, W.G. and Kiplinger, G.F. (1972). Effects of marijuana on recall of narrative material and Stroop colour–word performance. *Nature, London* **237**: 172–3.

Miller, L.L., Cornett, T.L., Brightwell, D.R., McFarland, D.J., Drew, W.G. and Wikler, A. (1977a). Marijuana: effects on storage and retrieval of prose materials. *Psychopharmacology* **51**: 311–6.

Miller, L.L., McFarland, D.J., Cornett, T.L., Brightwell, D.R. and Wikler, A. (1977b). Marijuana: effects on free recall and subjective organization of pictures and words. *Psychopharmacology* **55**: 257–60.

Milstein, S.L., MacCannell, K., Karr, G. and Clark, S. (1975). Marijuana-produced impairments in coordination. Experienced and non-experienced subjects. *Journal of Nervous and Mental Disease* **161**: 26–31.

Moskowitz, H., Sharma, S. and McGlothlin, W. (1972). Effect of marijuana upon peripheral vision as a function of the information processing demands in central vision. *Perceptual and Motor Skills* **35**: 875–82.

Moskowitz, H., Shea, R. and Burns, M. (1974). Effect of marihuana on the psychological refractory period. *Perceptual and Motor Skills* **38**: 959–62.

Moskowitz, H., Zieman, K. and Sharma, S. (1976a). Visual search behavior while viewing driving scenes under the influence of alcohol and marihuana. *Human Factors* **18**: 417–32.

Moskowitz, H., Hulbert, S. and McGlothlin, W. (1976b). Marihuana: effect on simulated driving performance. *Accident Analysis Prevention* **8**: 45–50.

Moskowitz, H., Sharma, S. and Zieman, K. (1981). Duration of skills performance impairment. *Proceedings of the 25th Conference of the American Association for Automotive Medicine, San Francisco*, pp. 87–96.

Murray, J.B. (1985). Marijuana's effects on human cognitive functions, psychomotor functions, and personality. *Journal of General Psychology* **113**: 23–55.

Page, J.B., Fletcher, J. and True, W.R. (1988). Psychosociocultural perspectives on chronic cannabis use: the Costa Rican follow-up. *Journal of Psychoactive Drugs* **20**: 57–65.

Parrott, A.C. (1987). Assessment of psychological performance in applied situations. In *Human Psychopharmacology. Measures and Methods*, edited by I. Hindmarch and P.D. Stonier. Chichester: Wiley, pp. 93–112.

Rafaelsen, O., Bech, P., Christiansen, H., Christrup, H., Nyboe, J. and Rafaelsen, L. (1973). Cannabis and alcohol: effects on simulated car driving. *Science, New York* **179**: 920–3.

Reeve, V.C., Grant, J.D., Robertson, W., Gillespie, H.K. and Hollister, L.E. (1983). Plasma concentrations of delta-9-tetrahydrocannabinol and impaired motor function. *Drug and Alcohol Dependence* **11**: 167–75.

Reeve, V.C., Peck, R., Boland, P. and Mallory, C. (1985). Marijuana–alcohol driving performance study: a summary of preliminary findings. *Proceedings of the Ninth International Conference on Alcohol, Drugs, and Traffic Safety.*

Relman, A.S. (1982). Marihuana and health. *New England Journal of Medicine* **306**: 603–4.

Richards, T. (1991). Drug abuse increasing. (Drug misuse in Britain, national audit of drug misuse statistics 1990, published by: Institute for the Study of Drug Dependence, 1 Hatton Place, London EC1N 8ND). *British Medical Journal* **302**: 132.

Rickles, W.H., Cohen, M.J., Whitaker, C.A. and McIntyre, K.E. (1973). Marijuana induced state-dependent verbal learning. *Psychopharmacologia* **30**: 349–54.

Roth, W.T., Tinklenberg, J.R., Whitaker, C.A., Darley, C.F., Kopell, B.S. and Hollister, L.E. (1973). The effect of marihuana on tracking task performance. *Psychopharmacologia* **33**: 259–65.

Salvendy, G. (1975). Marijuana and human performance. *Human Factors* **17**: 229–35.

Satz, P., Fletcher, J.M. and Sutker, L.L.S. (1976). Neuropsychologic, intellectual and personality correlates of chronic marijuana use in native Costa Ricans. *Annals of the New York Academy of Sciences* **282**: 266–306.

Schaeffer, J.H. (1973). *Cannabis sativa* and agricultural work in a Jamaican hill community. In *Effects of Chronic Smoking of Cannabis in Jamaica*, edited by V. Rubin and L. Comitas. New York: Research Institute for the Study of Man.

Schwartz, R.H., Gruenewald, P.J., Klitzner, M. and Fedio, P. (1989). Short-term memory impairment in cannabis-dependent adolescents. *American Journal of Diseases of Children* **143**: 1214–19.

Smart, R.G. (1974). Marijuana and driving risk among college students. *Journal of Safety Research* **6**: 155.

Snyder, S.H. (1990). Planning for serendipity. *Nature, London* **346**: 508.

Souief, M.I. (1976). Differential association between chronic cannabis use and brain function deficits. *Annals of the New York Academy of Sciences* **282**: 323–43.

Stillman, R.C., Weingartner, H., Wyatt, R.J., Gillin, J.C. and Eich, J. (1974). State-dependent (dissociative) effects of marihuana on human memory. *Archives of General Psychiatry* **31**: 81–5.

Sutton, L.R. (1983). The effects of alcohol, marihuana and their combination on driving ability. *Journal of Studies on Alcohol* **44**: 438–45.

Tinklenberg, J.R., Melges, F.T., Hollister, L.E. and Gillespie, H.K. (1970). Marijuana and immediate memory. *Nature, London* **226**: 1171–2.

Vachon, L., Sulkowski, A. and Rich, E. (1974). Marihuana effects on learning, attention and time estimation. *Psychopharmacologia* **39**: 1–11.

Varma, V.K., Malhotra, A.K., Dang, R., Das, K. and Nehra, R. (1988). Cannabis and cognitive functions: a prospective study. *Drug and Alcohol Dependence* **21**: 147–52.

Weil, A.T. and Zinberg, N.E. (1969). Acute effects of marihuana on speech. *Nature, London* **222**: 434–7.

Wig, N.N. and Varma, V.K. (1977). Patterns of long-term heavy cannabis use in North India and its effects on cognitive functions: a preliminary report. *Drug and Alcohol Dependence* **2**: 211–19.

Williams, A.F., Peat, M.A., Crouch, D.J., Wells, J.K. and Finkle, B.S. (1985). Drugs in fatally injured young male drivers. *Public Health Reports* **100**: 19–25.

Yesavage, J.A., Leirer, V.O., Denari, M. and Hollister, L.E. (1985). Carry-over effects of marijuana intoxication on aircraft pilot performance: a preliminary report. *American Journal of Psychiatry* **142**: 1325–9.

Zimmerman, E.G., Yeager, E.P., Soares, J.R., Hollister, L.E. and Reeve, V.C. (1981). Measurement of delta-9-tetrahydrocannabinol (THC) in whole blood samples from impaired motorists. *Journal of Forensic Sciences* **28**: 957–62.

Zuardi, A.W., Rodrigues, J.A. and Cunha, J.M. (1991). Effects of cannabidiol in animal models predictive of antipsychotic activity. *Psychopharmacology* **104**: 260–4.

7

Colds, Influenza and Performance

A.P. SMITH

SOCIO-ECONOMIC EFFECTS OF RESPIRATORY ILLNESSES

It has been estimated that respiratory disease consumes 20 per cent of general practitioner services and that it costs over £25 million per year. Similarly, hospital expenditure related to such illnesses (calculated in terms of cost per hospital bed) amounts to about £1 billion per year. The term 'respiratory disease' covers many different illnesses and it is always a good idea to provide estimates for specific illnesses as well as respiratory disease in general. Influenza accounts for 25–75 per cent of the GP services mentioned above. These figures are based on inter-epidemic years and when there is an epidemic the hospitalization rates for adults with high risk medical conditions increase fivefold. All of these figures are approximations, but they show we are dealing with illnesses which have a large impact on the health services.

Absenteeism figures also show that these illnesses have large economic consequences. For example, in the Hong Kong epidemic of 1968 it was estimated that over 26 million working days were lost due to incapacity from influenza. Even in inter-epidemic years this figure can be as high as 7–10 million days. In economic terms it has been estimated that in the 1974–5 influenza outbreaks over £100 million was lost in productivity and in the amount paid out in sickness benefits. The impact of influenza can be highlighted by comparing it with other disorders. For example, influenza accounts for 10–12 per cent of all absences from work, which is about the same as those due to musculo-skeletal disorders and twice the number due to psychiatric disorders.

Colds and influenza affect most of the population (it has been estimated that we have between one and three colds a year), and we spend over £100 million per year on medication for them. It is highly desirable, therefore, that we increase our knowledge of these illnesses, with the practical aims of lowering health care costs, decreasing absenteeism from work, and improving the quality of life. This involves considering the effects of such illnesses on performance efficiency and safety, which is the central theme of this chapter.

ANECDOTAL EVIDENCE OF EFFECTS OF COLDS AND INFLUENZA

Tye (1960) produced a report on the relationship between influenza and accidents. This report was based largely on anecdotal reports of influenza being the cause of many different types of accident. Indeed, the impetus for the report was the following account given by a man who had slammed the door of his car and trapped the fingers of his small son, permanently damaging two of them.

> 'I wasn't thinking', he said. 'Normally I always watch for that sort of thing, but my head was a bit muzzy at the time. I had a touch of flu coming on....'

Tye considers that 'influenza IS an invisible factor in many accidents; it DOES cost the nation millions of pounds when the judgement of individuals is "off-peak" due to an approaching influenza attack; and it CAN wipe out in one instant the safety sense in individuals which has taken years to develop.' This conclusion was based largely on case histories, two of which are summarized below.

The first report comes from a man on a construction site.

> You've got to be absolutely 100 per cent at this job. Nothing else'll do, We work hundreds of feet up. You can kill not only yourself, but if you drop a tool you can kill one of your mates down below. I always keep an eye open for anyone with flu coming on and I keep clear of 'em.

The second report comes from a police inspector with many years of experience in road safety.

> I'm convinced that people who drive on the roads when they've got flu coming on are accident prone. ... I investigated an accident between two cars that collided head-on at a dangerous set of crossroads. The accident was caused because one of the drivers sneezed. He explained to me, 'Sorry, officer. I oughtn't to be driving at all. I think I've got flu. I've been sneezing all day but I thought it was just a cold when I went to work this morning.'

These case histories are supported by statistics on road accidents. Table 7.1 shows the number of accidents involving ill drivers. It can be seen that this figure increased dramatically in 1957, the year of the Asian influenza epidemic.

It is interesting that Tye's report cites cases where performance was impaired just before the illness started. It is often assumed that when an

Table 7.1 The number of road
accidents involving
illness in influenza
epidemic and non-
epidemic years

Year	Number of accidents
1954	742
1955	816
1956	779
[a]1957	1024
1958	873

[a] Epidemic year.

individual has influenza he or she will retire to bed and the question of impaired efficiency will not arise. However, prior to the onset of the illness, performance efficiency may be reduced and other reports suggest that impaired performance may extend into the period after the symptoms have gone. Grant (1972) states that the evidence for influenzal encephalopathy (drowsiness, confusion and epileptiform events) is well established. He also argues that post-influenzal effects may occur and that these can influence the judgements of highly skilled professional staff. Grant cites eleven case histories to support this view and the general features of these can be illustrated by considering the following case.

> The individual concerned was responsible for calibration of a spectrophotometer before commencing a day's work. ... He had previously been off work for two days with influenza and returned alleging health. ... During the first part of the morning he made eleven attempts ... to correctly prepare the instrument. On six occasions he stated his opinion that all the preparative procedures had been completed, and that the instrument was ready for use. Each time, however, elementary faults were observed. Despite the incorrectness of the last calibration, the individual commenced work, compiling results which were finally discarded by himself three weeks later.

The outstanding features of these case histories are that individuals who had been ill with influenza but no longer had the primary symptoms frequently made technical errors which went unnoticed. There was firm rejection of advisory comments by colleagues, yet the mistakes could not be attributed to poor motivation or general lack of ability.

Overall, these results suggested that experimental studies of illness and performance should be carried out. The case for these appears stronger for influenza than for colds. Indeed, many individuals would claim that the effects of the common cold are too slight or transitory to be of any practical importance, and people are often chided by colleagues for staying off work with a cold. However, many influenza-like illnesses are produced by viruses similar to those which lead to the common cold. Indeed, the term influenza often refers to the systemic effects (fever, myalgia and malaise) which may accompany a variety of viral infections, and early experimental studies examined infections such as sandfly fever, which is rare but has certain similarities to influenza. These studies will now be briefly reviewed.

EXPERIMENTAL STUDIES OF INFECTION

Warm and Alluisi (1967) concluded that 'data concerning the effects of infection on human performance are essentially non-existent'. Since their review studies of the effects of very severe illnesses (e.g. rabbit fever, a febrile disease characterized by headache, photophobia, nausea, myalgia and depression) on performance have been carried out (Alluisi *et al.*, 1971, 1973; Thurmond *et al.*, 1971). In one study, those who became ill showed an average drop in performance of about 25 per cent and after recovery they were still 15 per cent below the level of the control group (Alluisi *et al.*, 1971). There was some evidence that active tasks such as arithmetic computation showed a greater decrement than passive tasks such as watchkeeping.

The illnesses studied in the above experiments were very severe and analogous effects rarely occur in everyday life. In contrast to this, colds and influenza are widespread and it is of great importance to know more about their effects on performance. There are few studies of this topic and the reasons for this will be discussed in the next section. In one of the few reports of a controlled experiment on naturally occurring colds, Heazlett and Whaley (1976) tested 120 thirteen-year-olds when they were well. Thirty pupils subsequently developed colds and they were retested during their illness. Thirty healthy controls were then randomly selected and retested. The children carried out three tasks and the results showed that reading comprehension was unimpaired whereas auditory and visual perception were worse when the children had colds. The tasks used in this experiment were crude (auditory perception was measured by four sets of nonsense syllables being pronounced to the subject and the subject repeating them; and visual perception was measured by the subject repeating the sequential lighting pattern of four numbered bulbs in a box). Yet even these tasks were able to pick up some form of decrement in the group of subjects who reported having a cold. Such results clearly require replication and yet there has been little attempt to carry out further research in this area. Reasons for this, and difficulties encountered in this type of study, are discussed in the next section.

DIFFICULTIES ENCOUNTERED IN STUDYING THE EFFECTS OF UPPER RESPIRATORY VIRUS ILLNESSES

One possible reason for the lack of research is that people feel that they already know about the behavioural effects of such illnesses, and it is, therefore, a waste of time carrying out experiments. Another reason that there has been little research in this area is that it is difficult to study naturally-occurring illnesses. These illnesses are hard to predict and it is unclear whether a virus produced the symptoms, and if so which virus was the infecting agent (there are over two hundred viruses that produce colds). The study of naturally occurring illnesses only enables one to examine the effects of clinical illnesses, and it is often difficult to obtain objective measures of the symptoms. It is also possible that subclinical infections may influence behaviour and these can only be identified using the appropriate virological techniques. Such problems have been overcome by examining the effects of experimentally induced colds and influenza at the MRC Common Cold Unit, Salisbury. Before describing the routine of this Unit it is necessary to discuss briefly the causes of colds and influenza in more detail.

THE CAUSES AND SYMPTOMS OF UPPER RESPIRATORY VIRUS ILLNESSES

Higgins (1984) characterized a cold as 'an increase in nasal discharge, often accompanied by nasal stuffiness, sore throat, coughing and sneezing, but usually lacking the constitutional symptoms of fever, headache, myalgia and malaise which are features of influenza.'

Up to the 1950s only the influenza A and B viruses had been identified. Subsequently, over two hundred viruses producing upper respiratory tract infections have been identified. The majority of colds are thought to be caused by rhinoviruses (over one hundred different types have now been identified) or coronaviruses. However, about one-third of colds are produced by other viruses, such as parainfluenza virus and respiratory syncytial virus, which cause severe illnesses in children but produce symptoms in adults which are indistinguishable from the common cold. While the agents which produce infection are well documented, it is still unclear exactly how they are transmitted and what lies between infection and the appearance of symptoms.

Influenza is caused mainly by influenza A and B viruses. Influenza A is antigenically unstable (Chakraverty et al., 1986) and new subtypes are constantly appearing. Certain base changes in its DNA sequence alter the viral-specific proteins that are recognized by the host immune system, thus changing the viruses' antigenic properties. This means that previously immune populations are once again vulnerable, which gives rise to epidemics. Epidemics occur at infrequent intervals, usually after an absence of several years. However, virological surveillance of the UK by the Public Health Laboratory has shown that over the past thirty years strains of influenza A and B circulate widely each winter (Chakraverty et al., 1986).

A.P. Smith

THE ROUTINE OF THE COMMON COLD UNIT

Volunteers aged 18–50 years came to the MRC Common Cold Unit* for a ten-day stay, during which they agreed to receive an infecting virus inoculation. The volunteers were housed in groups of one to three and isolated from outside contacts (to minimize the chances of infection with other viruses and to reduce the possibility of cross-infection between volunteers). Prior to coming to the Unit the volunteers sent a self-reported medical history. Anyone with serious medical conditions or taking current medication (e.g. sleeping pills, tranquillizers or anti-depressants) was not allowed to take part in the trial, and neither were pregnant women.

On the first day of the trial the volunteers were given a medical examination, chest X-ray, and biochemical assays performed on a blood sample. Any volunteers with abnormal results were excluded from the trial. The blood sample was also necessary to enable assessment of the initial antibody levels for the virus they were to be given. Isolation began in the afternoon of the first day and the volunteers were observed during a three-day quarantine period so that any individuals who were incubating a cold could be excluded. A nasal washing was obtained on the third day of the trial and if the virus was isolated at this time (i.e. if the individual had a subclinical infection) then the person was also excluded.

Volunteers were then given either the virus (or on some trials two viruses) or a saline placebo on the fourth day. The trials were conducted double-blind with neither the volunteers, the Unit's clinician, nor any of the staff who interacted with the subjects knowing which volunteers received virus or placebo. About one-third of the volunteers given a virus remained uninfected (i.e. the virus could not be detected in the person's body). This meant that very few subjects were given placebo in order to maximize infection rates (typically two or three volunteers out of thirty were given saline).

The most frequently used viruses were rhinoviruses types 2, 9 and 14, coronavirus type 229E, and respiratory syncytial virus. A few studies involved challenge with influenza A or influenza B viruses. Starting two days before virus challenge and continuing six days after challenge, each volunteer was examined daily by the Unit's clinician and any signs/symptoms of respiratory illness recorded using a standard protocol (see Beare and Reed, 1977). Examples of items on the protocol include sneezing, watering of the eyes, nasal stuffiness, nasal obstruction, sinus pain, sore throat, hoarseness, cough and fever. Objective measures of illness were taken, the most important in the case of colds being the number of tissues used daily and the weight of nasal secretion. Sublingual temperatures were also recorded in the early morning and evening.

---

* All procedures of the Common Cold Unit were approved by the Harrow District Ethical Committee and carried out with the consent of the volunteers.

The following assays were carried out to isolate viruses and identify changes in viral-specific antibody levels. The nasal wash samples were mixed with broth and stored in aliquots at $-70°C$. Rhinoviruses were detected in O-Hela cells, respiratory syncytial virus in Hep2 cells and coronavirus in C-16 strain of human fibroblast cells. When a characteristic cytopathic effect was observed the tissue culture fluids were passaged into further cultures and identity tests on the virus performed. Rhinoviruses and coronaviruses were confirmed by neutralization tests (with specific rabbit immune serum) and respiratory syncytial virus by immunofluorescent staining of culture cells. Levels of neutralizing antibodies (rhinoviruses only) and of specific antiviral IgA and IgG (all viruses) were determined from the initial blood sample and one returned to the Unit twenty-eight days after challenge. A fourfold rise in neutralizing antibodies was regarded as significant evidence of infection. An IgG or IgA increase of two standard deviations greater than the mean of non-challenged volunteers was also taken as a measure of infection.

Approximately two-thirds of the volunteers became infected with the virus. About half of these infected volunteers developed a significant cold approximately 24–96 hours after challenge (depending on the type of virus). The significance of a cold was based on the clinician's judgement (using data from the symptom/sign protocol). At the end of the trial the clinician judged the severity of each volunteer's cold on a scale ranging from nil (0) to severe (4). Ratings of a mild cold (2) or greater were considered positive clinical diagnoses. Volunteers also judged the severity of their colds on the same scale, and clinical diagnosis and self-diagnosis agreed about 90 per cent of the time.

PERFORMANCE TESTING: RESEARCH STRATEGY AND METHODOLOGY

The clinical trials at the Common Cold Unit were designed for purposes other than examining the effects of respiratory virus infections on performance. This imposed certain limitations on the type of task and length and frequency of testing. Similarly, portable tests had to be used because the volunteers were in isolation and could only be tested in their flats.

As already mentioned, there is little information on the effects of naturally occurring illnesses on performance. It was decided, therefore, initially to examine the effects of a variety of different viruses on many different aspects of performance, the aim being to draw up a profile of the effects of the different illnesses. Following this 'broad-band strategy' (see Hockey and Hamilton, 1983) it was envisaged that a hypothesis-driven approach with more focused test selection would be adopted. Unfortunately, the closure of the Unit meant that this second stage was not completed. However, the initial studies greatly increased our knowledge of the effects of colds and influenza on performance and the methods used are described below.

Two main methods of performance testing were used. The first involved administration of paper and pencil tests measuring logical reasoning, visual search and semantic processing. Subjects also rated their mood and performed a simple motor task involving the transfer of pegs from a full solitaire set to an empty one. These tests were carried out at four times of day (8.00 a.m., 12 noon, 5.00 p.m. and 10 p.m.) on every day of the trial. It was important to examine performance at several times of day for two reasons. Firstly, it has been shown that performance changes over the day and, secondly, there is diurnal variation in the severity of symptoms of colds and influenza (see Smith et al., 1988a) with nasal secretion and temperature being highest in the early morning. This first method of assessing performance was used only in a small number of trials, largely because it was unpopular with the volunteers and because it interfered with the routine of the Unit.

The second method of assessing performance used computerized performance tasks, with volunteers being tested once in the pre-challenge quarantine period (the baseline measurement) and again when symptoms were apparent in some volunteers. In a few trials, performance testing was also carried out in the incubation period, and in one trial performance was assessed after the symptoms had gone. Subjects were always tested at the same time of day on all occasions (although some subjects were tested in the morning and others in the afternoon, which meant that a between-subjects comparison allowed diurnal variation of any effects to be measured). The computerized tasks were selected to assess a range of functions (memory, attention, motor skills) and most of the tests have been widely used to study abnormal states or stressful environments. In most trials the volunteers could be subdivided into those with colds, those with subclinical infections and those who remained uninfected (or were given placebos). In some trials, however, there were no volunteers in certain categories. Analyses of covariance were carried out on the data using the pre-challenge scores as covariates. This statistical technique takes account of baseline differences when assessing the effects of the illness.

The following section describes the effects of influenza on performance.

INFLUENZA AND PERFORMANCE

Smith et al. (1987a) examined the effects of influenza illnesses on three tasks. Two of the tasks required subjects to detect and respond quickly to targets appearing at irregular intervals (a variable fore-period simple reaction time task and a '5s' detection task where subjects were shown single digits and had to respond as quickly as possible when they saw a 5). The other was a pursuit tracking task designed to test hand—eye co-ordination.

Influenza B increased reaction times in both detection tasks (results are shown in Figure 7.1). Analysis of the tracking task showed no significant difference between those with influenza and those who remained healthy.

It should be pointed out that the effects of influenza on the simple reaction time task were very large (a 57 per cent impairment). This can be illustrated by comparing the magnitude of the effect with that produced by a moderate dose of alcohol or by having to perform at night. In both of these latter cases the impairment is typically in the range of 5—10 per cent.

Smith *et al.* (1988b) examined the effects of influenza B on performance of the paper and pencil tests and pegboard test at four times of day. Volunteers with influenza B illnesses were impaired on a visual search task with a high-memory load (subjects had to search for the presence of five target

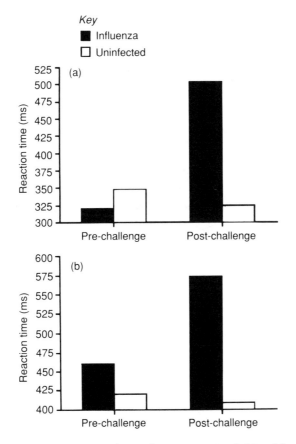

Figure 7.1 Mean reaction time in the simple reaction time task (a) and fives detection task (b) for influenza B and uninfected groups.

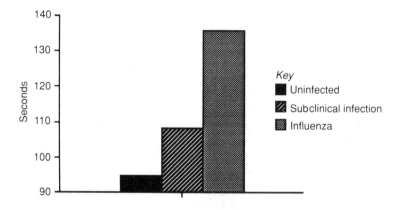

Figure 7.2 Effects of influenza B and infection on the search and memory task.

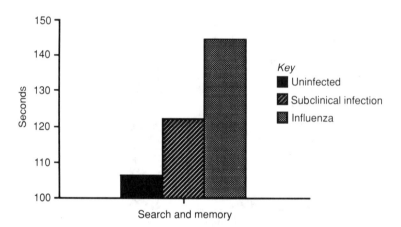

Figure 7.3 Performance of the search and memory task in the incubation period of influenza B illnesses.

letters at the start of a line and the speed and accuracy of searching a twelve-line block was recorded). In contrast to this, volunteers with influenza were not impaired on the pegboard task. These results are shown in Figure 7.2.

The study also showed that influenza did not impair the speed or accuracy of logical reasoning. However, it did show that even subclinical infections can impair performance (see Figure 7.2) and it also demonstrated that effects may be apparent in the incubation period prior to the onset of symptoms. This last effect is shown in Figure 7.3.

It has already been mentioned that influenza is produced by either influenza A or influenza B viruses. The only study of the effects of influenza A on

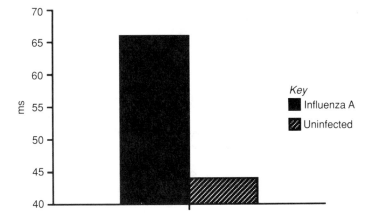

Figure 7.4 Effects of influenza A illnesses on the difference between search and focused attention tasks.

performance is reported by Smith *et al.* (1989). They examined the effects of influenza on two types of selective attention, one involving focused attention and the other categoric search. Broadbent *et al.* (1989) have argued that the distinction between the two types of task is a fundamental one for models of selective attention. This view is supported by several pieces of evidence, one of which is that factors which change the state of the person have selective effects on measures from the two tasks. The results from the influenza study showed that performance of the search task was impaired by influenza but not performance on the focused attention task. The difference between reaction times for the two tasks is shown for subjects with and without influenza in Figure 7.4.

The error data also confirmed that influenza impaired search tasks but not those involving focused attention. Unfortunately, no further influenza trials were carried out at the Common Cold Unit. An attempt was, however, made to examine the mechanisms underlying the effects of influenza on performance and this study is described below.

INTERFERON ALPHA AND PERFORMANCE

In influenza, interferon α can be found in the circulation and it is now clear that such peptide mediators have an effect on the CNS. It was, therefore, postulated that the performance deficits observed in influenza may be due to interferon or some similar molecule. This was tested by injecting volunteers with different doses of interferon α and it was predicted that those who

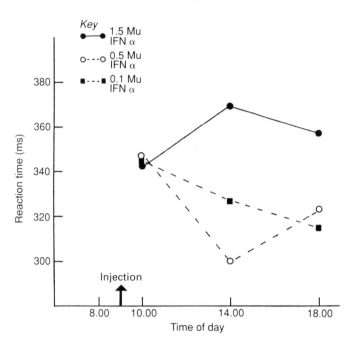

Figure 7.5 Effects of three doses of interferon α on performance of the variable fore-period simple reaction time task.

received a dose which produced the symptoms of influenza would show comparable performance impairments. The results of this study are described in detail in Smith et al. (1988c) and Smith et al. (1991a). The data from the simple reaction time task showed that an injection of 1.5 Mu produced an identical change to that seen in subjects with influenza. This is shown in Figure 7.5.

However, there were two problems with the interferon–influenza hypothesis. Firstly, the search and memory task was not impaired by IFN, whereas influenza B infections led to slower performance of this task. Secondly, performance on the pegboard task was impaired by interferon, and yet this has not been found in studies of influenza. These discrepant results could reflect differences between virally-induced interferon production and direct challenge, or it could be that other peptide mediators (e.g. interleukin 1) are also responsible for the influenza effects. While it is clear, therefore, that the interferon explanation of the effects of influenza is too simplistic, the results of the study show that cytokines do produce CNS effects and that further research is now needed to map out in detail which effects reflect the actions of given peptide mediators.

EXPERIMENTALLY-INDUCED INFLUENZA AND PERFORMANCE: SOME CONCLUSIONS

These preliminary studies of the effects of experimentally induced influenza infections and illnesses confirm the view that influenza may impair performance efficiency. The effects appear to be selective with tasks requiring response to targets presented at uncertain times or in unknown locations being most impaired. The absence of more global effects may reflect the small numbers of subjects tested (i.e. the methodology picked up only the biggest effects) and this must now be examined by studying naturally occurring influenza. The results do confirm some other points raised by the case histories reported earlier in the chapter. For example, they show that a person does not have to be symptomatic to be impaired, for those with subclinical infections and volunteers incubating illnesses were also impaired. Such results have been obtained in studies of other illnesses (see Elsass and Henriksen, 1984) and they raise the interesting possibility that performance changes may be used as indicators of subsequent illness.

The studies of experimentally induced influenza are also important for the area of psychoneuroimmunology, in that they show that a virally-induced immune response influences the brain and behaviour. Initially, we believed that the mediator involved was interferon α, but this alone cannot account for all of the performance effects of influenza. Further studies must, therefore, determine whether the results we obtained at the Common Cold Unit generalize to naturally occurring illnesses, and they must also assess the functional significance of such effects. At the same time, we must continue to study the mechanisms by which influenza affects the CNS, as these are likely to be common to many other viral infections.

The next section reviews studies of the effects of experimentally-induced colds on performance.

EXPERIMENTALLY-INDUCED COLDS AND PERFORMANCE

Smith *et al.* (1987a) examined the effects of colds produced by rhinoviruses and coronaviruses on the same three tests used in the influenza trials. These results are shown in Figure 7.6, and it can be seen that they are very different from those found with influenza.

Subjects with colds were not impaired on the two detection tasks but they were worse at the tracking task than those who remained well. Separate analyses of the rhinovirus and coronavirus groups showed similar effects, although the impairment on the tracking task was greater in those with rhinovirus colds. The rhinovirus group had greater nasal secretion than those

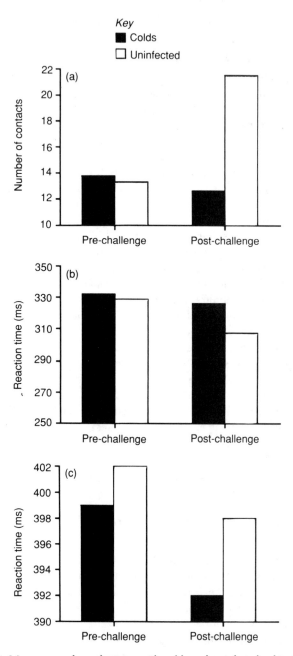

Figure 7.6 Mean scores for volunteers with colds and uninfected subjects on three performance tasks: (a) tracking; (b) simple reaction time; (c) fives detection.

challenged with the coronavirus, and this suggested that there may be a direct link between the severity of the symptoms and the performance decrement. However, when correlations were calculated between objective measures of illness and performance (for subjects with significant colds only) no significant relationship was obtained.

Smith *et al.* (1988b) compared the effects of influenza with colds following challenge with respiratory syncytial virus. Again, the volunteers with colds showed a different pattern of impairment to those with influenza, and in the case of colds it was performance of the pegboard task which was impaired, not the search and memory task. This is shown in Figure 7.7.

Volunteers with colds also differed from those with influenza in that no impairments were observed during the incubation period and neither did volunteers with subclinical infections show significant changes. However, results from another study (Smith *et al.*, 1987b) did show that both those with colds and those with subclinical infections were slower than uninfected subjects on another task (the five-choice serial reaction time task) involving hand–eye co-ordination. These results are shown in Figure 7.8.

Anecdotal evidence suggests that the effects of upper respiratory tract illnesses may persist after the primary symptoms have gone. This was examined by Smith *et al.*, (1989) in a trial where volunteers stayed at the Unit for three weeks and where it was possible to test them not only when they were symptomatic but when symptoms were no longer observable. The results are shown in Figure 7.9 and confirm the findings of Alluisi *et al.* (1971) in that the effects of viral illnesses continued into convalescence. At

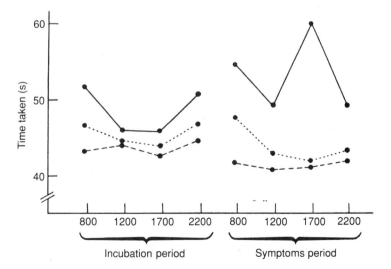

Figure 7.7 Effects of colds on performance of the pegboard task at four times of day during the incubation and symptoms period.

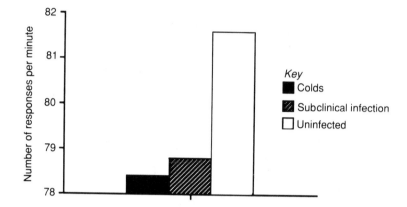

Figure 7.8 Effects of infection and illness following challenge with a respiratory syncytial virus on the speed of performing the five-choice serial reaction time task.

the moment it is unclear why such after-effects occur. One possibility is that the performance tests are sensitive to the immunological changes that occur after symptoms have gone. Another possibility is that subjects continue to perform at a lower level because they 'learnt' the task when they were ill. Further experiments are required to resolve this issue.

These initial studies showed that experimentally-induced colds impair tasks involving hand–eye co-ordination but have little effect on detection tasks. It is unclear which mechanisms underlie these effects. There is considerable evidence that certain types of virus (e.g. enteroviruses) have a strong affinity for muscle and may produce muscle damage. Recent evidence (Mier-Jedrzejowicz *et al.*, 1988) confirms that upper respiratory tract infections can influence muscle function and this provides a plausible explanation for some of the effects on performance. Another possibility is that some other cytokine (e.g. interleukin 2) is involved. Indeed, it is well known that these mediators have an effect on the muscles which could account for the impaired hand–eye co-ordination. Alternatively, the impairments could be due to changes in sensory stimulation via the trigeminal nerves in the nose. Lastly, they could represent a 'distraction effect', produced by sneezing or other nasal irritations. The main difficulty for all these possible explanations is in accounting for why the effects are selective (observed in some tasks but not others). These selective effects were examined in further detail by considering the effects of colds on a range of memory tasks and also different aspects of vision. The following sections summarize these two topics.

COLDS AND MEMORY

Most of the early studies used simple psychomotor tasks and more recent experiments looked at the effects of experimentally-induced colds on memory

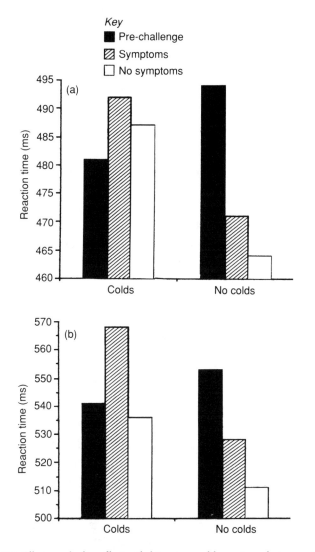

Figure 7.9 Effects and after-effects of rhinovirus colds on two-choice reaction time tasks: (a) focused attention; (b) search.

(Smith *et al.*, 1990a). Many aspects of memory, such as the ability to recall a string of digits in order, or to recall a list of words, appeared to be unaffected by having a cold. Similarly, there was little evidence that colds impair retrieval of information from semantic memory. However, having a cold did produce difficulties in learning and recall of more complex material such as the information presented in a story. Here the effect was not that recall was reduced but rather that people with a cold had more difficulty following the theme of a story and instead focused on detail which was less relevant to the overall theme. In contrast to this, colds did not impair retrieval of material learnt before the cold. Indeed, there was some evidence that reminiscence, the ability to recall information which was not retrievable immediately after learning, was better when the person had a cold. This may reflect the decreased arousal produced by the cold.

COLDS AND VISION

Smith *et al.* (in press) examined the effects of infection and illness on pattern sensitivity and contrast sensitivity. Results from two studies involving challenge with respiratory syncytial viruses showed that volunteers with subclinical infections reported more illusions when shown a figure like Figure 7.10 than did those who were uninfected or who had colds.

This effect was not replicated when volunteers were challenged with either a coronavirus or rhinovirus. However, contrast sensitivity improved in volunteers with a subclinical coronavirus infection. These studies were also important in that they showed that pre-challenge measures can be used to indicate susceptibility to infection and illness. These effects are reviewed in the following section.

Figure 7.10 The pattern with spatial characteristics that produces illusions and visual discomfort.

PRE-CHALLENGE PERFORMANCE AND SUSCEPTIBILITY TO INFECTION AND ILLNESS

There has been considerable interest in investigating whether psychological factors are important in determining susceptibility to infection and illness. Studies carried out at the Common Cold Unit (e.g. Totman *et al.*, 1980; Broadbent *et al.*, 1984; Cohen *et al.*, 1991) have shown that factors such as personality and stress influence vulnerability to infection. Smith *et al.* (1990b) showed that performance measures taken prior to virus challenge may also be related to the likelihood of developing a cold. In other words, volunteers who get a cold may be worse than those who remain uninfected even before they are given the virus. Smith *et al.* (in press) found that volunteers who developed colds following respiratory syncytial virus challenge were more sensitive to a visually disturbing pattern prior to challenge than individuals who remained symptom-free. This effect could not be attributed to different stress levels or personality characteristics of the two groups of subjects.

DRUGS, COLDS AND PERFORMANCE

Many trials at the Common Cold Unit were designed to assess the efficacy of prophylactic and therapeutic drugs. It was possible to determine not only the clinical efficacy of the drugs but to examine whether they removed the performance impairments associated with a cold. One study demonstrated that sodium nedocromil (a drug thought to suppress mediators such as histamine) reduced cold symptoms and the extent of the cold-induced performance decrement (Barrow *et al.*, 1990). Similarly, Smith *et al.* (1991b) showed that sucking zinc gluconate lozenges can eliminate the slower reaction times associated with having a cold. Unfortunately, the mode of action of these drugs is unclear, and they provide little information about the mechanisms underlying the effects of colds on performance.

CONCLUSIONS ABOUT EXPERIMENTALLY-INDUCED UPPER RESPIRATORY VIRAL ILLNESSES AND PERFORMANCE

The research carried out at the Common Cold Unit showed that upper respiratory virus infections and illnesses can reduce performance efficiency. The effects were selective in that they depended on the nature of the activity being carried out and the type of virus. The impairments were not restricted to times when the person was symptomatic but also occurred before and after the illness. Subclinical infections also reduced performance, although again the effect was selective. The research also showed that performance measures taken before virus challenge were related to susceptibility of developing a cold.

Unfortunately, we have little knowledge of the mechanisms underlying these effects, although it does appear that peptide mediators may be involved. It must now be asked what implications these studies have for safety and efficiency.

FUTURE STUDIES: NATURALLY OCCURRING UPPER RESPIRATORY VIRAL ILLNESSES AND PERFORMANCE

The major achievement of the Common Cold Unit research was that it provided a basis for future research on the effects of upper respiratory viral illnesses. Indeed, the results show that such a study is now warranted, although one should bear in mind that it would be a mistake to assume that analogous effects will necessarily be observed with real-life illnesses and tasks. Naturally occurring illnesses are typically more severe than those examined at the Common Cold Unit and one could argue that they should produce far greater effects. However, many real-life tasks are well practised and one could suggest that this will make them less susceptible to the effects of these illnesses. One should also note that many other factors influence performance efficiency and it would be wrong to continue to study the effects of these illnesses in isolation. Indeed, it is possible that viral illnesses not only have direct effects on performance but may indirectly influence it by making the person more susceptible to other factors.

One great advantage of the Common Cold Unit studies has been that they have shown which methodological features are essential. The selective effects of different viruses means that one must use virological techniques to attempt to discover which virus was responsible for the illness. This is difficult to do at the moment and only about 30 per cent of samples yield a positive viral identification, which means large numbers of subjects must be tested to obtain enough subjects in each virus condition. Ideally, one also wants to carry out prospective studies with pre-illness baselines for subjects. This technique is much more sensitive than cross-sectional methodologies. One also wants to use tasks which are not susceptible to the effects of compensatory effort, which can reduce the apparent effect of other low arousal states such as sleep-deprivation. In other words, research on the functional significance of upper respiratory illnesses will have both problems which are specific to the topic and those which are common to the study of other possible influences on performance. Nevertheless, the anecdotal case histories and results from the controlled Common Cold Unit studies suggest that more research is needed in this area to address applied questions and also to provide further information on the underlying mechanisms which link infections to the brain and behaviour.

REFERENCES

Alluisi, E.A., Thurmond, J.B. and Coates, G.D. (1971). Behavioral effects of infectious disease: respiratory *Pasteurella tularensis* in man. *Perceptual and Motor Skills* **32**: 647−88.

Alluisi, E.A., Beisel, W.R., Bartelloni, P.J. and Coates, G.D. (1973). Behavioral effects of tularensis and sandfly fever in man. *Journal of Infectious Diseases* **128**: 710−17.

Barrow, G.I., Higgins, P.G., Al-Nakib, W., Smith, A.P., Wenham, R.B.M. and Tyrrell, D.A.J. (1990). The effect of intranasal nedocromil sodium on viral upper respiratory tract infections in human volunteers. *Clinical Allergy* **20**: 45−51.

Beare, A.S. and Reed, S.E. (1977). The study of antiviral compounds in volunteers. In *Chemoprophylaxis and Virus Infections*, vol. 2, edited by J.S. Oxford. Cleveland: CRC Press.

Broadbent, D.E., Broadbent, M.H.P., Phillpotts, R. and Wallace, J. (1984). Some further studies on the prediction of experimental colds in volunteers by psychological factors. *Journal of Psychosomatic Research* **28**: 511−23.

Broadbent, D.E., Broadbent, M.H.P. and Jones, J.L. (1989). Time of day as an instrument for the analysis of attention. *European Journal of Cognitive Psychology* **1**: 69−94

Chakraverty, P., Cunningham, P., Shen, G.Z. and Pereira, M.S. (1986). Influenza in the United Kingdom 1982−1985. *Journal of Hygiene* **97**: 347−58

Cohen, S., Tyrrell, D.A.J. and Smith, A.P. (1991). Psychological stress in humans and susceptibility to the common cold. *New England Journal of Medicine* **325**: 606−612.

Elsass, P. and Henriksen, L. (1984). Acute cerebral dysfunctions after open heart surgery: a reaction time study. *Scandinavian Journal of Thoracic Surgery* **18**: 161−5.

Grant, J. (1972). Post-influenzal judgement deflection among scientific personnel. *Asian Journal of Medicine* **8**: 535−9.

Heazlett, M. and Whaley, R.F. (1976). The common cold: its effect on perceptual ability and reading comprehension among pupils of a seventh grade class. *Journal of School Health* **46**: 145−7.

Higgins, P.G. (1984). The common cold. *International Medicine* **4**: 15−17.

Hockey, R. and Hamilton, P. (1983). The cognitive patterning of stress states. In *Stress and Fatigue in Human Performance*, edited by G.R.J. Hockey. Chichester: Wiley.

Mier-Jedzrejowicz, A., Brophy, C. and Green, M. (1988). Respiratory muscle weakness during upper respiratory tract infections. *American Review of Respiratory Disease* **138**: 5−7.

Smith, A.P. (1990). Respiratory virus infections and performance. *Philosophical Transactions of the Royal Society of London* **B327**: 519−28.

Smith, A.P., Tyrrell, D.A.J., Coyle, K.B. and Willman, J.S. (1987a). Selective effects of minor illnesses on human performance. *British Journal of Psychology* **78**: 183−8.

Smith, A.P., Tyrrell, D.A.J., Al-Nakib, W., Coyle, K.B., Donovan, C.B., Higgins, P.G. and Willman, J.S. (1987b). Effects of experimentally-induced respiratory virus infections on psychomotor performance. *Neuropsychobiology* **18**: 144−8.

Smith, A.P., Tyrrell, D.A.J., Coyle, K.B., Higgins, P.G. and Willman, J.S. (1988a). Diurnal variation in the symptoms of colds and influenza. *Chronobiology International* **5**: 411−16.

Smith, A.P., Tyrrell, D.A.J., Al-Nakib, W., Coyle, K.B., Donovan, C.B., Higgins, P.G. and Willman, J.S. (1988b). The effects of experimentally-induced respiratory virus infections on performance. *Psychological Medicine* **18**: 65−71.

Smith, A.P., Tyrrell, D.A.J., Coyle, K.B. and Higgins, P.G. (1988c). Effects of interferon alpha on performance in man: a preliminary report. *Psychopharmacology* **96**: 414–16.

Smith, A.P., Tyrrell, D.A.J., Al-Nakib, W., Barrow, G.I., Higgins, P.G., Leekam, S. and Trickett, S. (1989). Effects and after-effects of the common cold and influenza on human performance. *Neuropsychobiology* **21**: 90–3.

Smith, A.P., Tyrrell, D.A.J., Barrow, G.I., Coyle, K.B., Higgins, P.G., Trickett, S. and Willman, J.S. (1990a). Effects of experimentally-induced colds on aspects of memory. *Perceptual and Motor Skills* **71**: 1207–15.

Smith, A.P., Tyrrell, D.A.J., Coyle, K.B., Higgins, P.G. and Willman, J.S. (1990b). Individual differences in susceptibility to infection and illness following respiratory virus challenge. *Psychology and Health* **4**: 201–11.

Smith, A.P., Tyrrell, D.A.J., Coyle, K.B. and Higgins, P.G. (1991a). Effects and after-effects of interferon alpha on human performance, mood and physiological function. *Journal of Psychopharmacology* **5**: 243–50.

Smith, A.P., Tyrrell, D.A.J., Al-Nakib, W., Barrow, G.I., Higgins, P.G. and Wenham, R. (1991b). The effects of zinc gluconate and nedocromil sodium on performance deficits produced by the common cold. *Journal of Psychopharmacology* **5**: 251–4.

Smith, A.P., Tyrrell, D.A.J., Barrow, G.I., Higgins, P.G., Bull, S., Trickett, S. and Wilkins, A.J. (in press). The common cold, pattern sensitivity and contrast sensitivity. *Psychological Medicine*.

Thurmond, J.B., Alluisi, E.A. and Coates, G.D. (1971). An extended study of the behavioral effects of respiratory *Pasteurella tularensis* in man. *Perceptual and Motor Skills* **33**: 439–54.

Totman, R., Kiff, J., Reed, S.E. and Craig, J.W. (1980). Predicting experimental colds in volunteers from different measures of recent life stress. *Journal of Psychosomatic Research* **24**: 155–63.

Tye, J. (1960). *The Invisible Factor: An Inquiry into the Relationship between Influenza and Accidents.* London: British Safety Council.

Warm, J.S. and Alluisi, E.A. (1967). Behavioral reactions to infections: review of the psychological literature. *Perceptual and Motor Skills* **24**: 755–83.

8

HIV and AIDS

V. EGAN & G. GOODWIN

INTRODUCTION

It is only ten years since a cluster of rare illnesses in young homosexual men led to the description of a new disease: the acquired immune deficiency syndrome (AIDS). Until the emergence of AIDS, these illnesses (pneumocystis carinii pneumonia and Kaposi's Sarcoma) were only seen in patients who were immuno-suppressed, for example following transplant surgery or treatment for lymphomas, or who were significantly malnourished. Immunological assessment of men with AIDS subsequently demonstrated a characteristic lack of CD4 lymphocytes, white blood cells vital for their immune response, and which rendered them vulnerable to pathogens normally well controlled by the immune system. The cause of AIDS was eventually traced to the human immunodeficiency virus (HIV), a retrovirus which can integrate itself into the genome of the host (Gallo et al., 1984). HIV enters the macrophages and lymphocytes of an individual's immune system, providing blood-borne entry into all the organ systems and accounting for the diverse manifestations of HIV infection (Fauci et al., 1984).

Though, in Western countries at least, HIV is relatively rare outside defined populations, HIV can be easily transmitted. This was first recognized for sexual transmission among homosexual males, but other groups have experienced epidemic infections, notably haemophiliacs and intravenous drug users. The spread of HIV can be very rapid; 51 per cent of one sample of HIV positive drug users in Edinburgh acquired the virus in one year (Robertson

We thank Dr Ray Brettle for his comments on this manuscript. We would also like to thank the doctors, nurses and patients of the City Hospital, Edinburgh, for assisting in our study of neuropsychological changes in HIV-infected drug users. This work was funded by MRC Special Project Grant 69006357.

et al., 1986). In Africa, South America and South East Asia heterosexual transmission of HIV appears to be common and sometimes even epidemic (Piot *et al.*, 1988).

HIV can affect the nervous system in two general ways. Firstly, a range of illnesses can occur when the immunocomprised host becomes vulnerable to opportunistic infections of the nervous system. These diseases usually have a short history and are more or less treatable. Secondly, and of more direct concern to the present account, it appears that HIV penetrates the brain early in the course of infection and can have a direct effect on its function. The latter complications of HIV infection threaten chronic impairment of intellectual performance. This chapter discusses HIV illness and the AIDS dementia complex (ADC), with special reference to neuropsychological measures and processes. Neuropsychiatric aspects of HIV infection are also briefly reviewed.

THE CLASSIFICATION OF HIV ILLNESS

HIV infection is staged according to the clinical criteria set by the American Center for Disease Control (CDC) (Centers for Disease Control, 1986); Table 8.1 presents a summary. This staging system accommodates a broad range of possible clinical events in the medical history of the HIV-infected patient. It should be noted that only three categories of disease define frank AIDS; these are 4C.1, 4D, or a diagnosis of AIDS dementia complex, i.e. stage IV disease is not synonymous with AIDS. There is an alternative staging system for HIV based on clinical measures and CD4 lymphocyte counts known as the Walter Reed staging system (Redfield *et al.*, 1986). Though the Walter Reed system is probably more sensitive to the graduations of difference between stages of HIV illness, it requires regular assessment of the patient's

Table 8.1 Center for Disease Control classification of HIV infection

Group 1	Acute HIV seroconversion
Group 2	Asymptomatic infection
Group 3	Persistent generalized lymphadenopathy
Group 4	Other disease (chronic/severe expression of HIV illness)

Subgroup:
4A	Constitutional disease
4B	Neurological disease
4C	Secondary infectious diseases
	1 As defined for AIDS
	2 Other infectious diseases
4D	Secondary cancers
4E	Other conditions

blood cell population: an expensive and intensive facility. By contrast, CDC staging only needs a clinical assessment, and has consequently become standard.

CDC stage 1 can present with a glandular-fever-like syndrome and is associated with sero-conversion to positive HIV antibody status. Patients at CDC stage 2 are asymptomatic for symptoms of HIV, but are HIV positive, and HIV antigen is detectable in blood. CDC stage 3 is characterized by persistent generalized lymphadenopathy, i.e. lymph node enlargement of 1 cm or more, at two or more non-contiguous extra-inguinal sites persisting for more than three months with no other explanation.

Stage 4 disease is a broadly inclusive category covering a range of clinical symptoms and signs of HIV infection other than, or in addition to, lymphadenopathy; stage 4 illness thus includes patients who are minimally symptomatic and those who are severely ill. Subgroups 4A and 4C.2 comprise what is known as 'AIDS-related complex' (ARC). In the case of subgroup 4A, the HIV-infected patient has one or more of the following symptoms: fever for more than a month; involuntary loss of more than 10 per cent of their body weight, and diarrhoea persisting for more than one month with no explanation other than HIV infection. The diagnosis of these features in HIV positive intravenous drug users is problematic. Stage 4C.2 categorizes systemic or invasive diseases, such as oral hairy leukoplakia, multi-dermatomal herpes zoster, recurrent salmonella bacteria, nocarditis, tuberculosis and oral candidiasis. These illnesses have little ambiguity and can be diagnosed objectively.

Subgroup 4B represents the various neurological diseases seen in people with severe HIV infection (see Table 8.2). Subgroup 4C subsumes the various secondary infectious diseases so characteristic of full blown AIDS and

Table 8.2 Opportunistic neurological illnesses seen in HIV infection

Brain
    Cytomegalovirus encephalitis
    Toxoplasmosis
    Central nervous system lymphoma
    Progressive multifocal leukoencephalopathy
    Other viral encephalitis (e.g. herpes encephalitis)

Spinal cord
    Myelitis (from cytomegalovirus, herpes simplex virus)

Meninges
    Cryptococcal meningitis
    Mycobacterial infections
    Bacterial meningitis

Nerve roots
    Shingles
    Cytomegalovirus

indicative of a defect in cell-mediated immunity. Category 4C.1 includes pneumocystis carinii pneumonia; toxoplasmosis; candidiasis of the oesophagus, bronchial or pulmonary system; cryptococcosis; mycobacterial infection; cytomegalovirus infection; chronic mucocutaneous or disseminated herpes simplex virus infection, and progressive multi-focal leukoencephalopathy. Category 4C.2 has been described above. Subgroup 4D involves various secondary cancers such as Kaposi's sarcoma, non-Hodgkin's lymphoma or primary lymphoma of the brain. Subgroup 4E contains the various other conditions of HIV infection, clinical findings and diseases not in other groups, but indicative of defective cell-mediated immunity (e.g. thrombocytopaenia), constitutional symptoms not meeting criteria for CDC stage 4A, infectious diseases not classified in 4C, or patients with neoplasms not in subgroup 4D.

THE AIDS DEMENTIA COMPLEX

Clinical features

HIV is neurotropic and enters the brain early in infection (Resnick *et al.*, 1988). The main neuropsychiatric manifestation of HIV infection emerges later in the illness, when a progressive cognitive/motor impairment may become manifest. AIDS dementia complex (ADC) was first described and so named by Navia *et al.* (1986a). Patients with ADC have neurological and neuropsycho-logical symptoms not accounted for by systemic illness, opportunistic infections of the CNS, neoplasms such as Hodgkin's disease, or encephalopathy due to severe renal, pulmonary or hepatic disease (Price and Brew, 1988). The exclusion of other causes of cognitive/motor impairment may require medical investigations such as lumbar puncture and brain-imaging to exclude illnesses such as toxoplasmosis, meningitis or herpes encephalitis.

Patients with advanced ADC have motor dysfunction such as inco-ordination, ataxia and slowness; behavioural disturbances such as social withdrawl, reduced spontaneity and apathy not attributable to significant depression; and cognitive changes such as poor attention, slowed information-processing speed, and impaired memory (Tross *et al.*, 1988). The Price staging system (Price and Brew, 1988) provides a threshold for the diagnosis of ADC based on a description of the level of functional disability and impaired activities of daily living seen in the patient. This encompasses a range from mild to end-stage severity, and incorporates both clinical observations and objective measures (see Table 8.3).

Cognitive slowing is particularly characteristic of ADC. Studies using simple and choice reaction time paradigms have shown that while simple reaction time does not progressively discriminate patients who are HIV negative, asymptomatic, or have ARC or AIDS, choice reaction time is significantly

Table 8.3 Price staging for the AIDS dementia complex (ADC)

Stage	
0	**Normal mental functioning**
1	**Mild ADC**
	A change in *one* of the following:
	Impaired work or social activity
	Impaired activities of daily living
	Abnormal central nervous system neurology
	Decline of neuropsychology/neurophysiology
2	**Moderate ADC**
	Obvious deterioration in performance in all areas; requires some support from others for activities of daily living
	Impaired work or social activity
	Impaired activity of daily living
	Abnormal central nervous system neurology
	Decline of neuropsychology/neurophysiology
3	**Major ADC**
	Slowing and dementia obvious
	Cannot follow news, personal events or conduct complex conversation
	Obvious slowing of thinking
	Impaired activities of daily living requiring constant assistance
	Motor slowing and ataxia
	Gross decline in neuropsychology and neurophysiology
4	**End stage ADC**
	Cognitive function rudimentary: mute
	No independence in activities of daily living
	Paraparesis and incontinence

slower for ARC and AIDS patients compared with control or asymptomatic patients (Perdices and Cooper, 1989a). This slowing is clinically obvious and appears to determine performance in most domains of observed neuropsychological abnormality in HIV-infected patients. Delayed performance time appears related to impaired ability in quick and fluent mental processing rather than to altered elementary cognitive functions *per se* (Poutianen *et al.*, 1988). This reflects the current view that the speed of basic information processing is an important correlate of intellectual function (*cf.* Vernon, 1987). The slowing of cognitive and motor processes suggests that the overall character of ADC is that of a 'subcortical dementia' in which slowing of motor and mental function predominates over memory loss, aphasia, agnosia or apraxia (Cumming and Benson, 1988). One piece of evidence that supports such a clinical classification is that a major focus of HIV pathology is observed in subcortical structures such as the basal ganglia (Navia *et al.*, 1986b).

The clinical resemblance between AIDS dementia and other dementing diseases was demonstrated by a study that directly compared the neuropsychological function of patients with AIDS to patients with Alzheimer's disease (a cortical dementia), Huntington's disease (a subcortical dementia), or a control group matched on age and estimated full-scale IQ. Discriminant function analysis correctly identified 90 per cent of the AIDS sample, 85 per cent of the Huntington's and Alzheimer's disease patients, and all of the controls. Seventy-one per cent of the AIDS patients were classified as normal, while the remaining 29 per cent showed a profile similar to that of Huntington's disease. Subjective measures of mood did not discriminate the groups as effectively as tests of memory and information processing speed. The study thus confirmed that the neuropsychological profile of AIDS patients with cognitive impairment was closer to a subcortical than to a cortical dementing illness (Brouwers et al., 1989).

Clinically obvious ADC (Price stages 2–4) presents little diagnostic difficulty and is often accompanied by motor symptoms due to myelopathy (the involvement of white matter tracts in the spinal cord and brain stem). Much more contentious is the point at which any patient or group of patients can first be said to show cognitive impairment alone. This problem is addressed at length later in the chapter.

The incidence of ADC

The incidence of ADC depends on the population being described. Of a series of autopsy cases seen by neurologists, 66 per cent had previously had dementia (Price et al., 1988a). This figure is due to the sampling bias of the population; the patients would not have been referred to a neurologist unless brain involvement was already suspected. In another study, 31.3 per cent of patients with AIDS had neurological complications (Snider et al., 1983). This study was based on an audit of fifty consecutive inpatients from New York with AIDS; however, in 1983 HIV positive patients tended to present when they were already severely immunocompromised, and how long they had lived with AIDS was difficult to ascertain. The incidence of ADC has thus been influenced by their source, their stage of infection and their criteria for diagnosis. The most comprehensive study of ADC incidence involved assessing all the cases of AIDS reported to the CDC from 1 September 1987 to 31 December, 1988. ADC was defined as a disabling cognitive/motor dysfunction, in the absence of any condition other than HIV to account for this finding. Of the adults, 6.5 per cent had ADC, with only 3 per cent having it as the only early manifestation of AIDS; it was slightly more common (around 10 per cent) in children and elderly patients with AIDS (Janssen et al., 1989). This gives a more conservative estimate of the incidence of ADC, and one that may better reflect the overall contribution to morbidity in ambulant groups. There is little doubt that cognitive impairment is common in the terminal stages of the illness, but the clinical significance of this may become overshadowed by a variety of debilitating complications of the infection.

The pathology of ADC

Computerized tomography and magnetic resonance imaging (MRI) scans of the brain in AIDS have shown widened cortical sulci and enlarged ventricles. This cerebral atrophy demonstrates that ADC is a chronic condition, and suggests that it may take some time to reach a threshold for clinical impairment. MRI scans are particularly useful as they show the differential density of white and grey matter. Patients with ADC show patchy or diffusely increased signals from MRI scans, in keeping with increased water content in the hemispheric white matter, basal ganglia and thalamus (Price et al., 1988a). Lumbar punctures enable samples of cerebro-spinal fluid (CSF) to be taken, and confirmation that HIV is active within the brain of the patient is provided by the identification of p24 HIV-1 core protein antigen, and the HIV virus itself, in the CSF (Price et al., 1988b).

The neuropathology seen at post mortem and associated with ADC is predominantly subcortical, although there may also be neuronal loss in the frontal cortex (Everall et al., 1991). The most common finding is pallor of the white matter, which is more severe in central and periventricular regions than in the immediately subcortical fibres. A reactive astrocytosis may accompany this white matter pallor and extend into subcortical grey structures. Diffuse microscopic lesions and multi-nucleated giant cells containing HIV particles are also observed (Lantos et al., 1989). Price has suggested that two pathological mechanisms can be distinguished in the pathogenesis of ADC: gliosis and pallor of the subcortical nuclei (present in individuals with mild ADC), and viral-induced cell fusion leading to multi-nucleated cell encephalitis (with focal white matter rarefaction) in more severe cases (Price, 1990). Price suggests that these events are caused by the loss of immune system control over HIV replication. The initial immune response protects the brain from infection, but as immune control declines, cytokines (mediators of cellular immunity) are either poorly broken down or found in excessive quantities. Consequently, other serological markers of cell-mediated immune reactions such as neopterin and quinolinic acid appear to increase in patients with AIDS (Melmed et al., 1989; Heyes et al., 1989). Studies of CSF from ninety-seven HIV-infected patients with neurological illnesses found that the highest CSF neopterin concentrations were in those patients with opportunistic infections of the CNS, CNS lymphomas, and ADC (Brew et al., 1990). CSF neopterin concentrations correlate with the severity of ADC, and decrease in conjunction with clinical improvement following treatment with AZT. In a similar fashion, CSF quinolinic acid levels correlate positively with slower reaction time in AIDS patients; higher levels of CSF quinolinic acid have been seen in macaques with an analogous cognitive impairment attributable to their infection with Simian immunodeficiency virus; and levels of CSF quinolinic acid decrease following treatment with AZT (Martin et al., 1990; Heyes et al., 1990, 1991). This suggests that both CSF neopterin and quinolinic acid are surrogate markers of neurological involvement, and can be used to monitor the response of the patient to antiviral treatments.

Neuropsychological testing of brain function

ADC is a neurological disease in which the brains of predominantly young people are damaged by a specific pathology. By the use of standard clinical tests, the effect of HIV on domains of cognitive function can be systematically described. These results may also provide insights into more general neuropsychological processes. Table 8.4 presents a summary of the most commonly used tests and the functions they measure. (An excellent general reference covering the practical application of neuropsychological tests is found in Lezak, 1983.) Tests of pre-morbid IQ such as the WAIS-R vocabulary scale (Wechsler, 1981) or the National Adult Reading Test (Nelson, 1981) are useful in that they enable the tester to estimate the previous intellectual level of the patient and to compare this with currently observed function.

In some cases, it has been suggested, the cognitive abnormalities seen in HIV positive people are due to 'pseudodementia': impaired neuropsychological performance actually attributable to depressive illness (Caine, 1986; Rubinow *et al.*, 1988). Pseudodementia is a poorly defined and often ambiguous term sometimes used to describe the impaired performance on cognitive function tests in psychiatric patients with functional (non-dementing) illness. In elderly

Table 8.4 Neuropsychological tests commonly used with HIV-positive patients

Function	Test
Memory	WAIS-R digit span
	Wechsler logical memory test
	Auditory–verbal learning test
	Bushke selective reminding test
Attention	Trail-making test (parts A and B)
	Paced auditory serial addition task
Pre-morbid IQ	WAIS-R vocabulary
	National adult reading test
Current IQ	WAIS-R block design
Mood	Beck depression inventory
	Hospital anxiety and depression scale
	Speilberger state–trait anxiety scale
Information processing speed	Auditory evoked potential
	Two-choice reaction time
	WAIS-R digit symbol
	Controlled word fluency test
	Two and seven letter cancellation task
	Sternberg memory scanning task
	Stroop test
Psychomotor speed	Perdue grooved pegboard
	Halstead–Reitan tapping test
	Pursuit rotor

patients, depressive pseudodementia is normally believed to reflect an underlying subclinical cognitive impairment with an irreversible organic basis (Lishman, 1978). Depression reveals the underlying impairment. Neuropsychological studies have confirmed incomplete recovery in such patients (Abas *et al.*, 1990).

However, hysterical or dissociative pseudodementia can also be associated with depression and is fully reversible. The number of patients with prominent evidence of both cognitive impairment and depression presents an important challenge to clinicians. Whether there are parallels between clinical experience in the elderly and what might be expected in younger patients with a rather different dementia is unclear. This situation is demonstrated in Figure 8.1.

The most complicated picture that can be envisaged is where a patient develops a depressive illness and an hysterical pseudodementia. The golden clinical rule must be always to seek and treat depressive symptoms. Self-rating mood scales such as the Beck depression inventory (BDI) and the hospital anxiety and depression (HAD) scale (Beck *et al.*, 1961; Zigmond and Snaith, 1983) provide a simple way of estimating clinically significant levels of subjective anxiety or depression, prior to a clinical interview. Clinicians should be aware that depressive illness is sometimes associated with impaired attention and memory (Caine, 1986).

A range of memory tests is presented in Table 8.4; one of the most sensitive being the auditory–verbal learning test (AVLT; Rey, 1964). The AVLT enables a number of memory functions to be evaluated: short-term memory, learning rate, pro- and retro-active interference, long-term memory, forgetting rate, and recognition and incidental memory (Peaker and Stewart,

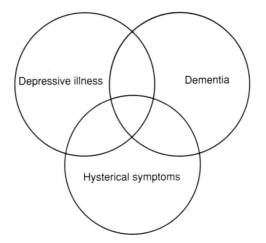

Figure 8.1 The possible overlap between three distinct diagnoses accounting for pseudodementia in the elderly and which may also apply in younger people with AIDS.

1989). The AVLT is more versatile than the Wechsler logical memory test, and parallel AVLT forms are also available (Shapiro and Harrison, 1990). The AVLT is sensitive to HIV-related memory impairment, possibly because it measures the individual's ability spontaneously to organize unstructured material for learning. This would be consistent with reports that the burden of HIV disease falls on frontal and subcortical brain regions (Wilkins *et al.*, 1990a).

Information processing speed and psychomotor tasks are central to the assessment of possible ADC. For practical purposes, most use the trail-making (Reitan and Wolfson, 1985) or WAIS-R digit symbol tests (Wechsler, 1981). Though these are both sensitive to psychomotor slowing, repeated testing of the same patient is likely to lead to practice effects, which may initially mask progressive decline in cognitive function. One solution is to reverse the order of the numbers and characters on the trail-making test, so that number 1 (to be joined to number 2) is in the position previously held by number 25, and so on. A parallel form of the WAIS-R digit symbol task is provided by the earlier WAIS digit symbol substitution test.

Performance scores on these different measures are a function of the population under consideration. Thus, samples of well educated homosexual men tend to score very well on most neuropsychological measures, when compared with the mediocre performance of drug users (Wilkins *et al.*, 1990b). (Grant *et al.* (1978) found that 37 per cent of the multiple drug users tested on the Halstead–Reitan neuropsychological battery had cognitive impairment. This pre-dates HIV infection as a possible contributory cause.) More recently, the performance of HIV-infected drug users on WAIS-R block design, digit symbol, arithmetic and digit span subtests was found to be significantly below the scores predicted by population models that combined measures of pre-morbid IQ and demographic factors. The differences were so large that there was an obvious risk that drug-related cognitive impairment would be attributed instead to the effects of HIV infection *per se* (Egan *et al.*, 1990; see Figure 8.2). In our view, the interpretation of neuropsychological results from drug users should remain highly empirical and conservative (Egan, 1992).

The WAIS-R and its various subtests have the advantage that they are sensitive, have population norms and span some of the appropriate functional domains. However, the WAIS-R does not measure long-term memory, fluency or information processing speed uncontaminated by psychomotor speed. It is, therefore, advisable to combine WAIS-R subtests with tests that measure these attributes. The pre-morbid IQ of the patient should also be estimated to give an idea of their expected function. The impact of HIV disease on the brain may, to some extent, be a function of pre-morbid cognitive ability, as is the case for alcohol consumption (Grant, 1987). The implication is that drug-using populations may be more incapacitated by cognitive impairment: a prediction which has yet to be confirmed empirically.

Some clinical investigations are largely unsuitable for investigating patients

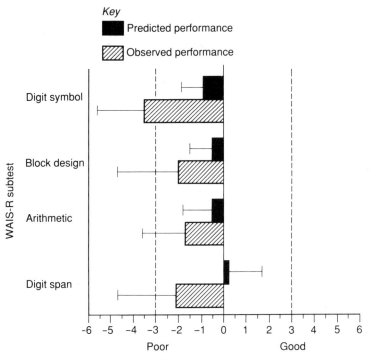

Figure 8.2 The difference between mean predicted and observed scaled scores for a sample of HIV positive drug users for selected WAIS-R subtests. Zero on the horizontal axis represents the average scaled score (10) for the normal population; dotted lines represent one standard deviation from the population mean. Histogram error bars represent standard deviations for the four tests. All differences between predicted and observed means were significant at $p < 0.001$. (Data from Egan *et al.*, 1990.)

with suspected ADC. The mini mental state examination (Folstein *et al.*, 1975), though brief and sensitive to the gross abnormalities seen in cortical dementias such as Alzheimer's disease, only minimally assesses psychomotor function; it is therefore, not surprisingly, insensitive to ADC (Dilley *et al.*, 1989). The Luria–Nebraska tests examine language at the expense of more basic mental functions. Some assessments are generally valuable but impractical: for example, tests of general intelligence such as the standard progressive matrices (Raven, 1962), which do not specify different mental functions. The paced auditory serial addition task is sensitive to closed head injury and abnormalities of attention (Gronwall, 1977); however, it is also stressful and strongly related to IQ (Egan, 1988).

Neurophysiological assessment of brain function

If brain pathology determines cognitive decline, one might expect physiological measures to be useful collateral evidence of brain involvement. A number of physiological measures appear sensitive enough to detect the effects of HIV infection and have the advantage of being free of any influence the subject's intelligence may have on the task. For example, the use of infra-red oculography to record eye movements in a group of AIDS patients with and without ADC found that abnormalities of saccades, smooth pursuit and fixational instability correlated with the severity of dementia (Currie *et al.*, 1988). This result presumably reflects the subcortical pathology of HIV and its non-specific effect on the distributed high performance system controlling eye movements.

Electrophysiological measures have been used to evaluate patients with a range of neuropsychiatric illnesses. One of the simplest tasks to involve a cognitive component involves averaging the amplified electrical potentials recorded from the brain in response to expected and unexpected events. These are known as event-related potentials. In the auditory domain, two tones of different pitch are presented as expected and unexpected stimuli. A typical waveform from an auditory evoked potential (AEP) has peaks and

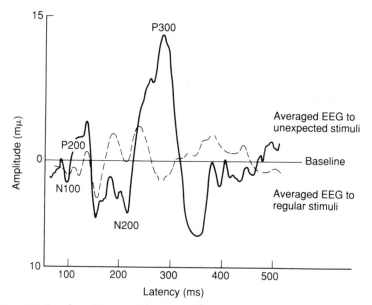

Figure 8.3 Sample auditory evoked potential from an HIV positive patient. Peaks N_1, N_2, P_2 and P_3 labelled as N100, N200, P200 and P300. The solid line is the brain's response to the unexpected 'pip' stimulus; dotted line represents the brain's response to a regular 'tone' stimulus.

troughs which are assumed to correspond to different processes involved in the identification and discrimination of the sounds. This waveform has distinctive positive peaks about 200 and 300 ms post-stimulus (P_2, P_3); and a negative peak potential approximately 100 ms after stimulus onset (N_1) (see Figure 8.3; Donchin, 1981).

These potentials appear to correspond to brain function: thus the P_3 wave is only recorded after the unexpected tone. P_3 appears to be related, therefore, to a simple form of cognition. It is now well established that P_3 latency slows progressively in patients with cortical dementias (Polich *et al.*, 1986), while P_2 and N_1 also slow in patients with subcortical dementia (Goodin and Aminoff, 1986). The latter changes presumably reflect impaired conduction and registration of stimuli that are expected, as well as unexpected. It is of considerable interest, therefore, that P_3 is slowed in homosexual men with ADC, and similar, but less marked alterations of AEP have been observed in HIV positive (but otherwise asymptomatic) men. This suggests that some individuals with low-grade HIV-infection have subclinical encephalopathy (Goodin *et al.*, 1990). However this study did not prove this, as there was no comparison to a matched HIV negative control group. Nor were additional factors, particularly drug and alcohol use, adequately controlled.

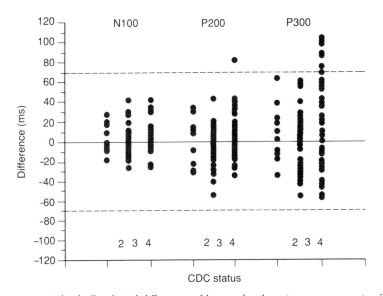

Figure 8.4 Individually plotted differences of latency for the primary components of the AEP for 100 HIV positive drug users tested twice on the same task. CDC status 2, 3 and 4 corresponds to the stage of HIV-disease for the patient at second test. The dotted line represents the point two standard deviations from the mean P300 difference for the sample. The significant slowing of AEP is apparent for P_3 latency amongst patients with stage 4 HIV disease. (Data from Goodwin *et al.*, 1990.)

The AEP paradigm has also been applied successfully to drug users with HIV (Goodwin et al., 1990). Drug users introduce additional pharmacological variance into measurement of P_3 latency, as the continued use of opiates and benzodiazepines may artificially slow the AEP. In addition, drug users tend to be poorly educated and have eventful medical histories. Despite these problems, neurophysiological testing is feasible in drug users, and the inherent difficulties with cross-sectional comparisons can be largely overcome by having drug users act as their own controls in prospective assessments. P_3 latency is reproducible, and correlates at 0.49 ($p < 0.001$) with itself over one year. Stepwise multiple regression models combining the effect of variables such as medical history, current drug use and subjective complaints predicted a maximum of about 14 per cent of P_3 latency variance, indicating that P_3 is not systematically affected by confounding variables. An increase in P_3 latency occurs for patients moving to, or progressing within CDC stage 4 HIV disease (see Figure 8.4). Drug users with ADC have particularly slowed AEP latarcies (Maxwell et al., 1991).

In addition it has been found that P_3 latency correlates with the WAIS-R digit symbol subtest, and with parts A and B of the trail-making test (Egan et al., 1989) but not so highly with WAIS-R block design. This suggests that P_3 latency measures some version of mental speed rather than non-verbal intelligence per se.

DOES ADC HAVE AN EARLY ONSET?

If frank ADC is common in the late stages of AIDS (Navia et al., 1986a), the following questions arise. When can it first be detected? When does it become clinically significant? When should it be treated? These issues became controversial following an early study which reported that asymptomatic HIV positive patients may already have cognitive abnormalities (Grant et al., 1987). The study took a sample of fifty-five homosexual men who were either HIV asymptomatic, or had ARC or AIDS, and compared them with a control group of eleven seronegative men on eight neuropsychological tests. Each subject's performance on these tests was rated as 'unimpaired', 'probably impaired' or 'definitely impaired'. A person was classed as abnormal if either two tests were probably impaired or one test was definitely abnormal. Using these criteria, seven (44 per cent) of the sixteen in the seropositive group were abnormal, compared to one (9 per cent) of the eleven in the control group. The result was interpreted as meaning that people with asymptomatic HIV infection may have early neuropsychiatric impairment without severe immuno-suppression. Furthermore, such neuropsychiatric impairment was interpreted as dementia. The disadvantage of using the term 'AIDS dementia complex' for the full spectrum of neuropsychological impairment came into focus around this finding, as the press reported that HIV positive individuals were poor risks in responsible jobs. The US Department of Defense first removed (but then had to replace) HIV positive individuals from sensitive or stressful positions, irrespective of actual neuropsychological function or health. The initial confusion was considerable: Did a positive HIV serology imply cognitive impairment or not?

Neuropsychological studies have now been conducted on thousands of HIV positive individuals, and large control groups matched for life-style. The strongest evidence against the early and insidious onset of ADC comes from the Multicentre AIDS Cohort Study (MACS). No differences in neuro-psychiatric symptoms or psychological performance were found between 727 asymptomatic HIV positive patients, compared with 769 controls. However, using the same measures, the performance of CDC stage 4 symptomatic patients with HIV was significantly worse than that for the HIV seronegative group (Miller *et al.*, 1990). Prospective studies have also provided evidence against early progression towards neuropsychological abnormality; 132 HIV asymptomatic patients (and 132 controls) from the MACS were tested four times on a neuropsychological test battery (Selnes *et al.*, 1990). There was no reduction in test performance over time for the HIV positive group, as compared with HIV seronegative controls.

Nevertheless, it is possible that the failure to detect a main group effect in the larger studies is too reassuring. Grant (1990) has argued that the MACS study has a number of limitations, including sampling error, poorly matched control groups, superficial testing of neuropsychological function, and differential recruitment rates between centres. In addition, individuals who felt that their cognitive function was impaired had the option of withdrawing from the follow-up, which would have the effect of selectively excluding most of those individuals who developed cognitive impairment. These may be valid points which subsequent studies should consider. However, the overall impression is clear: though some asymptomatic HIV positive individuals have unexpected neuropsychological impairment, the number of such persons is not appreciably higher than would be seen in seronegative subjects, and is probably more often due to factors such as drug use than HIV infection alone. Even when significant cognitive impairment is detected in an HIV positive individual, it does not imply inevitable progression to severe dementia.

In any case, cognitive impairment may be more common than is appreciated in other chronic diseases, such as renal failure, liver disease or viral disease, as described in the other chapters of this book. Some of the neuropsychological impairment in AIDS may be a simple manifestation of, for example, elevated levels of interferon or other cellular products associated with chronic infection. It appears prudent to distinguish relatively minor cognitive/motor impairment (Price stages 0.5 and 1), from more serious cognitive/motor impairment (Price stages 2 to 4). Price stages 2 to 4 merit the use of the emotive term 'dementia'; the more minor impairment does not.

PSYCHOLOGICAL AND PSYCHIATRIC ABNORMALITIES IN HIV POSITIVE INDIVIDUALS

Diagnosis of HIV seropositivity is highly stressful for a person; they have to cope with an illness which is infectious, unpredictable in its complications, and ultimately terminal. The psychiatric disturbances of people with HIV can be broadly grouped into the following categories: adjustment reactions, affective disorders and psychoses. While a full description of the differences in emphasis distinguishing the ICD-9 (European) and DSM-IIIR (American) approach to psychiatric diagnosis is beyond the current discussion, it is worth emphasizing the similarities between adjustment reactions (ICD-9) and adjustment disorders (DSM-IIIR). These are by far the most common psychiatric problems associated with HIV infection.

Adjustment reactions

An adjustment reaction of some degree usually follows the diagnosis of HIV seropositivity; it would be surprising if this news were without psychological impact. Individuals with adjustment reactions may express despair, guilt, grief, anxiety, protest, depression and hypochondria (Miller and Riccio, 1990). The phenomenology, severity and duration of these reactions are similar to those after other major crises or disease diagnoses, and do not generally lead to chronic impairment of day-to-day functioning; counselling, psychosocial support and mild anxiolytics often help a patient cope with their initial distress. Adjustment reactions may, however, be more chronic and intense. Other problems may contribute to the maintenance of a more prolonged reaction. Thus in one study, the psychosocial factors associated with elevated depression, anxiety, and anger—hostility symptom scores were a history of psychiatric disorder before HIV diagnosis, a family history of psychiatric illness, low educational attainments, poor social support, an external locus of control, and the recent experience of life events involving some loss (Dew et al., 1990). These characteristics are risk factors for aggravated psychological distress irrespective of HIV infection.

It is important that chronic or severe adjustment reactions with depressive symptoms are carefully observed for the development of a more complete depressive syndrome requiring active pharmacological treatment. This is particularly likely to be problematic where a counsellor or psychologist has little experience of psychiatric illness. The most important common sense indication for psychiatric referral is when symptoms, especially suicidal thoughts, continue or begin to worsen rather than showing gradual resolution.

Affective disorders

Although HIV-infected patients sometimes (Jacobsen *et al.*, 1988) but not always (Perry *et al.*, 1990) report depressed mood as an accompaniment to their adjustment reaction, the depressive episode rarely meets the formal criteria for depressive illness (or major depression, as diagnosed by DSM-III criteria (American Psychiatric Association, 1980)). The onset of depressive illness in HIV-infected patients is likely to be facilitated by factors such as poor social support, poor social or health care, and problems involving poor accommodation, finances or employment, as well as a personal or familial predisposition to affective illness. The risk of suicide in these individuals should be carefully assessed in relation to the usual socio-demographic risk factors and the current mental state (Rundell *et al.*, 1988).

Self-rating scales are not sufficient for the diagnosis of depressive illness, which should always be based on a diagnostic interview. Premorbid personality affects self-rating scales in a pervasive fashion, with neurotic individuals reporting poor mood states even without diagnosed affective illnesses (Meites *et al.*, 1980). Thus, a study of 192 HIV positive outpatients (of whom 95 per cent were homosexual) found that almost half of the 31 per cent who reported significant psychiatric problems reported emotional problems *before* HIV infection (King, 1989). Lastly, early reports of cognitive impairment were attributed to depressive illness in patients with AIDS. The subcortical pathology in HIV dementia results in retardation and slowing that is essentially organic in its aetiology. Although subjective complaints of cognitive impairment are highly associated with depressive symptoms in HIV infection (Hearn *et al.*, 1989), objective cognitive impairment is not (Kovner *et al.*, 1989).

Psychoses

Psychotic episodes in individuals with HIV could indicate some underlying organic brain involvement, because 'symptomatic psychoses' are seen in, for example, Huntington's chorea. A search of the literature up to March 1988, having excluded reactive cases, patients with recent drug use and those with a previous psychiatric disorder, found only nine patients with psychosis as part of their initial presentation of HIV infection (Vogel-Scibilia *et al.*, 1988). The authors concluded that it was not possible to distinguish whether these psychotic episodes were due to organic or coincidental factors, though the long-term outcome of these cases was poor, in that four of their nine cases died within six months. They calculated that by chance alone, there should be about 750 cases a year in the USA of HIV-infected patients with a first episode of a schizophrenia-like illness.

Similar considerations apply to affective psychoses. Patients with advanced HIV illness have developed manic illnesses in the absence of a previous psychiatric history (Boccellari *et al.*, 1988). The clinical presentation of the mania appears typical, with prominent hyperactivity, euphoria and grandiose delusions, and patients appear to respond readily to lithium (Dauncey, 1988). Once stable, a residual state of increasing cognitive impairment associated with ADC may follow the acute manic state (Smith, 1990).

It is difficult to see how adequately controlled studies will be possible to establish the relationship, if any, between HIV infection and psychotic illness. It appears unlikely that rates of psychosis are substantially increased in HIV positive individuals (Halstead *et al.*, 1988). Severe psychotic illness is not especially rare, and its occurrence in the HIV positive population is to be expected by chance.

Lastly, an important distinction needs to be drawn between the functional psychoses and delirium, in which psychotic features may be florid. Delirium can accompany the flu-like illness that can characterize initial HIV infection and seroconversion (CDC stage 1), or it may complicate other systemic infections. It should normally be self-limiting with resolution of the underlying cause. Some early reports of 'AIDS psychosis' may have been confusional episodes better classified as delirium.

Psychopathology involving beliefs and delusions about HIV infection

While not strictly related to HIV infection, some individuals may suffer irrational fears about having the disease. These will range from the worried well (Miller *et al.*, 1988) to patients with obsessional beliefs requiring outpatient treatment, or even frank psychosis (which will often require hospital admission). Patients who appear to be deluded should be referred to a psychiatrist. The delusion that one has AIDS may be the main symptom of a depressive psychosis: this carries a substantial risk of suicide. The more irrationally that help is sought, the more a counsellor should suspect mental illness.

THE TREATMENT OF ADC WITH AZT

The main treatment for severe HIV-related disease is currently zidovudine (AZT). AZT is an anti-viral drug that blocks the reproduction of the HIV virus, and for a short while (typically three to six months) increases the CD4 count of the individual. Though AZT reduces the mortality, severity and frequency of opportunistic infections in immunocompromised patients, it also has some toxicity, and higher doses in ill patients can cause anaemia. Anecdotal evidence originally suggested that AZT may improve the symptoms of ADC (Yarchoan *et al.*, 1987). This has been confirmed by a double-blind, placebo-controlled trial of oral AZT, in which 281 patients with advanced ARC or AIDS were tested over sixteen weeks to assess changes in neuropsychological function following drug treatment. Patients on AZT, in particular AIDS patients, had improved mental function compared to patients on placebo (Schmitt *et al.*, 1988). Though these results suggest that HIV-related cognitive abnormalities may be partially ameliorated by AZT, the sample tested did not include any patients with frank dementia.

Another study has argued that severe ADC has declined in incidence following the introduction of AZT; of the 196 patients with AIDS seen in an Amsterdam hospital over six years, 40 (20 per cent) had ADC. One hundred and seven patients did not take AZT, either because they developed AIDS before the drug was available, or because they refused treatment with the drug; 38 of these 107 patients developed ADC, compared to 2 of the 89 taking AZT. Thus, as AZT entered the pharmacopoeia, ADC declined (Portegies *et al.*, 1989). The problem with this observation is that the initial high incidence of ADC may have been a cohort effect, with a peak of ADC being seen in patients who had developed AIDS quickly. These promising results should therefore be evaluated cautiously.

The improving effects of AZT on neuropsychological function should also be considered in conjunction with the equally improving effects on per-formance provided by practice. An Australian study tested forty-seven homosexual men about to be placed on AZT, retested them six months later, and found that their performance improved across the two tests, as did performance for an untreated HIV negative control group. As ever, the use of parallel forms when retesting patients may reduce the effect of task practice or familiarity (Perdices and Cooper, 1989b). Overall, though aggressive treatment with AZT may prevent at least early ADC, the ethical difficulties with clinical trials in this area mean that controlled evaluations may not be possible.

The benefit of treatment with AZT has to be measured against its possible costs. The long-term effects of AZT have yet to be established, and the recent extension of the AZT licence to incorporate treatment of asymptomatic HIV disease may limit its use in the phase when HIV illness is more severe. AZT can stop being clinically useful for several reasons: the patient may develop dangerous side-effects (for example, by becoming anaemic and transfusion-dependent), or the virus may become resistant to the drug, perhaps because of virus mutation.

The treatment of opportunistic infections in patients with AIDS has progressed substantially in the past ten years, so that, for example, pneumo-cystis carinii pneumonia is now rarely a cause of death. As the treatment of previously fatal infections improves, AIDS patients will live longer. It is possible that the longer the AIDS patient survives, the greater their probability of acquiring ADC. However, the apparent reversibility of the ADC, even if only partial, means that it can be made a reason for therapeutic intervention; and this is likely to assume an increasing importance.

CONCLUSIONS AND COMMENTS

Unless neuropsychological performance suggests otherwise, there is no reason that people with HIV and AIDS should be excluded from the workplace, provided they remain in passable physical health. A positive HIV test is an unreliable guide to the level of cognitive function. Severe neuropsychological impairment is a late, and, perhaps, not especially common, manifestation of HIV illness. Its treatment is an important current challenge. The psychiatric disorders that HIV positive patients have are probably governed by the same factors that cause psychiatric illness in the general population. Less severe emotional disturbance can be managed by trained counsellors supported by clinical psychology and psychiatry, depending on special interest. Some specialized knowledge of medical and social aspects of HIV, and the populations it affects, is necessary for such help to be effective (Sno et al., 1989).

Over the past ten years the face of AIDS in the developed world has gradually changed: drug users and heterosexuals, often female, are now more likely to be newly diagnosed as HIV positive than homosexual or haemophiliac men. Opportunistic infections are now treated more effectively, and are consequently less likely to be fatal. People live with AIDS for longer than ever before, and anti-viral treatments other than AZT, such as DDI and soluble CD^4 are being developed. These changes will shape the clinical definition of HIV infection and its impact on mental function. Neuropsychological assessment promises to occupy an unusually prominent place in the evaluation of treatment efficacy and outcome.

REFERENCES

Abas, M.A., Sahakian, B.J. and Levy, R. (1990). Neuropsychological deficits and CT scan changes in elderly depressives. *Psychological Medicine* **20**: 507–20.

American Psychiatric Association (1980). *Diagnostic and Statistical Manual of Mental Disorders III*. Washington, DC: American Psychiatric Associations.

Beck, A.T., Ward, C.H., Mendelson, M., Mock, J.M. and Erbaugh, J.K. (1961). An inventory for measuring depression. *Archives of General Psychiatry* **4**: 561–71.

Boccellari, A., Dilley, J.W. and Shore, M.D. (1988). Neuropsychiatric aspects of AIDS dementia complex: a report on a clinical series. *Neurotoxicology* **9**: 381–90.

Brew, B.J., Bhalla, R.B., Morris, P., Gallardo, H., McArthur, J., Schwartz, M.K. and Price, R.W. (1990). Cerebrospinal fluid neopterin in human immunodeficiency virus type 1 infection. *Annals of Neurology* **28**: 556–60.

Brouwers, P., Mohr, E., Hendricks, M., Claus, M., Young, M. and Pierce, P. (1989). Multivariate statistical determination of incidence and character of cognitive impairments in HIV patients. *Fifth International Conference on AIDS, Montreal*, June (abstract Th BP208).

Caine, E. (1986). The neuropsychology of depression: the pseudodementia syndrome. In *The Neuropsychological Assessment of Neuropsychiatric Disorders*, edited by I. Grant and K.M. Adams. New York: Oxford University Press.

Centers for Disease Control (1986). Classification system for human T-lymphotropic virus type III/lymphadenopathy-associated virus infection. *MMWR* **35**: 334–9.

Cumming, J.L. and Benson, D.F. (1988). Psychological dysfunction accompanying subcortical dementia. *Annual Review of Medicine* **39**: 53–61.

Currie, J., Benson, E., Ramsden, B., Perdices, M. and Cooper, D. (1988). Eye movement abnormalities as a predictor of the Acquired Immunodeficiency Syndrome Dementia Complex. *Archives of Neurology* **45**: 949–53.

Dauncey, K. (1988). Mania in the early stages of AIDS. *British Journal of Psychiatry* **152**: 716–17.

Dew, M.A., Ragni, M.V. and Nimorwicz, P. (1990). Infection with human immunodeficiency virus and vulnerability to psychiatric distress. *Archives of General Psychiatry* **47**: 737–44.

Dilley, J.W., Boccellari, A. and Davis, A. (1989). The use of the mini mental status examination as a cognitive screen in patients with AIDS. *Fifth International Conference on AIDS, Montreal* (abstract WBP 193).

Donchin, E. (1981). Surprise! ... Surprise? *Psychophysiology* **18**: 493–513.

Egan, V. (1988). PASAT: Observed correlations with IQ. *Personality and Individual Differences* **9**: 179–80.

Egan, V. (1992). Editorial: Neuropsychological aspects of HIV infection. *AIDS Care* **4**: 1–10

Egan, V., Chiswick, A., Goodwin, G., St Clair, D., Brettle, R. and Deary, I. (1989). P300 correlates with neuropsychological testing in HIV-positive drug users at CDC status 2 and 3. *Neurological and Neuropsychological Complications of HIV Infection Conference, Quebec City, Canada* (abstract NP-6).

Egan, V., Crawford, J., Brettle, R.P.B. and Goodwin, G. (1990). The Edinburgh cohort of HIV positive drug users: current impaired intellectual function is due to drug use rather than early AIDS dementia complex. *AIDS* **4**: 651–6.

Everall, I.P., Luthert, P.J. and Lantos, P.L. (1991). Neuronal loss in the frontal cortex in HIV infection *The Lancet* **337**: 1119–21.

Fauci, A.S., Macher, A.M., Longo, D.L., Lane, H.C., Rook, A.H., Masur, H. and Gelmann, E.P. (1984). Acquired immunodeficiency syndrome: epidemiologic, clinical, immunologic and therapeutic considerations. *Annals of Internal Medicine* **100**: 92–106.

Folstein, M.F., Folstein, S.E. and McHugh, P.R. (1975). The Mini Mental State Examination. *Journal of Psychiatric Research* **12**: 189–98.

Gallo, R.C., Salahuddin, S.Z., Popovic, M., Shearer, G.M., Keplan, M., Haynes, B.F., Palker, T.J., Redfield, R., Oleske, J. and Safai, B. (1984). Frequent detection and isolation of cytopathic heteroviruses (HTLV-III) from patients with AIDS and at risk for AIDS. *Science, New York* **224**: 500–2.

Goodin, D.S. and Aminoff, M.J. (1986). Electrophysiological differences between subtypes of dementia. *Brain* **109**: 1103–13.

Goodin, D.S., Aminoff, M.J., Chernoff, D.N. and Hollander, H. (1990). Long latency event-related potentials in patients infected with human immunodeficiency virus. *Annals of Neurology* **27**: 414–19.

Goodwin, G.M., Chiswick, A., Egan, V., St Clair, D. and Brettle, R.P. (1990). The Edinburgh cohort of HIV positive drug users: prospective testing of brain function using auditory event-related potentials shows progressive slowing in patients with CDC stage IV disease. *AIDS* **12**: 1237–44.

Grant, I. (1987). Alcohol and the brain: neuropsychological correlates. *Journal of Consulting and Clinical Psychology* **55**: 310–24.

Grant, I. (1990). A critical overview: point. Oral presentation to the *Neurological and Neuropsychological Complications of HIV Infection: Update 1990, Monterey, CA*.

Grant, I., Adams, K.M., Carlin, A.S., Rennick, P.M., Judd, L.L. and Schoof, K. (1978). The collaborative neuropsychological study of polydrug users. *Archives of General Psychiatry* **35**: 1063–74.

Grant, I., Atkinson, J.H., Hampton, J., Hesselink, J.R., Kennedy, C.J., Richman, D.D., Spector, S.A. and McCutchan, J.A. (1987). Evidence for early central nervous system involvement in the acquired immunodeficiency syndrome (AIDS) and other human immunodeficiency virus (HIV) infections. *Annals of Internal Medicine* **107**: 828–36.

Gronwall, D. (1977). Paced auditory serial addition task: a measure of recovery from concussion. *Perceptual and Motor Skills* **44**: 367–73.

Halstead, S., Riccio, M., Harlow, P., Ovetti, R. and Thompson, C. (1988). Psychosis associated with HIV infection. *British Journal of Psychiatry* **153**: 618–23.

Hearn, M., Newman, S., McAllister, R., Weller, I. and Harrison, M. (1989). Mood state, neuropsychology and self-reported cognitive deficits in HIV infection. *Fifth International Conference on AIDS, Montreal* (abstract WBP-185).

Heyes, M.P., Brew, B.J., Martin, A., Price, R.W., Rubinow, D. and Salazar, A.M. (1989). Quinolinic acid concentrations are increased in plasma and cerebrospinal fluid in AIDS and correlate with AIDS dementia complex. *Fifth International Conference on AIDS, Montreal* (abstract ThBP-232).

Heyes, M.P., Saito, J., Gravell, M., London, W.T., Johnson, P., Lackner, A., Smith, M., Quearry, B.J. and Markey, S.P. (1990). Increased CSF quinolinic acid and brain indolamine-3-dioxygenase activity in simian immunodeficiency virus-infected macaques. *Neurological and Neuropsychological Complications of HIV Infection: Update 1990, Monterey, CA* (abstract BS-3).

Heyes, M.P., Brew, B.J., Martin, A., Price, R.W., Salazar, A.M., Sidtis, J.J., Yergey, J.A., Mouradian, M., Sadler, A.E., Keilp, J., Rubinow, D. and Markey, S.P. (1991). Quinolinic acid in cerebrospinal fluid and serum in HIV-1 infection: relation to clinical and neurological status. *Annals of Neurology* **29**: 202–9.

Jacobsen, P.B., Perry, S.W., Hirsch, D.A., Scavuzzo, D. and Roberts, R.B. (1988). Psychological reactions of individuals at risk for AIDS during an experimental drug trial. *Psychosomatics* **29**: 182–7.

Janssen, R.S., Sterh-Green, J. and Starcher, T. (1989). Epidemiology of HIV encephalopathy in the United States. *Fifth International Conference on AIDS, Montreal* (abstract MAO-31).

King, M.B. (1989). Psychosocial status of 192 out-patients with HIV infection and AIDS. *British Journal of Psychiatry* **154**: 237–42.

Kovner, R., Perecman, E., Lazar, W., Hainline, B., Kaplan, M.H., Lesser, M. and Beresford, R. (1989). Relation of personality and attentional factors to cognitive deficits in human immunodeficiency virus-infected subjects. *Archives of Neurology* **46**: 274–7.

Lantos, P.L., McLaughlin, J.E., Scholtz, C.L., Berry, C.L. and Tighe, J.R. (1989). Neuropathology of the brain in HIV infection. *Lancet* **333**: 309–311.

Lezak, M. (1983). *Neuropsychological Testing*. New York: Oxford University Press.

Lishman, W.A. (1978). *Organic Psychiatry: The Psychological Consequences of Cerebral Disorder*. Oxford: Blackwell Scientific.

Martin, A., Heyes, M., Sclazar, A., Williams, J.W.L., Roller, T., Kampen, D., Coats, M. and Markey, S. (1990). Progressive motor and cognitive slowing in HIV positive subjects: possible relation to quinolinic acid. *Neurological and Neuropsychological Complications of HIV Infection: Update 1990, Monterey, CA* (abstract NPS-5).

Maxwell, J., Egan, V., Chiswick, A., Burns, S., Gordon, A., Kean, D., Brettle, R.P. and Pullen, I. (1991). HIV-1 associated cognitive/motor complex in an injecting drug user. *AIDS Care* **3**: 373–81.

Melmed, R.N., Taylor, J.M.G., Detels, R., Bozorgmehri, M. and Fahey, J.L. (1989). Serum neopterin changes in HIV-infected subjects: indicator of significant pathology, CD4 T cell changes and the development of AIDS. *Journal of the Acquired Immune Deficiency Syndrome* **2**: 70–6.

Meites, K., Lovallo, W. and Pishkin, V. (1980). A comparison of four scales for anxiety, depression, and neuroticism. *Journal of Clinical Psychology* **36**: 427–32.

Miller, D. and Riccio, M. (1990). Non-organic psychiatric and psychosocial syndromes associated with HIV-1 infection and disease. *AIDS* **4**: 381–8.

Miller, D., Acton, T.M.G. and Hedge, B. (1988). The worried well: identification and management. *Journal of the Royal College of Physicians in London* **22**: 158–65.

Miller, E.N., Selnes, O.A., McArthur, J., Satz, P., Becker, J.T., Cohen, B.A., Sheridan, K., Machando, A.M., Van Gorp, W.G. and Visscher, B. (1990). Neuropsychological performance in HIV-1 infected homosexual men: the multicentre AIDS cohort study (MACS). *Neurology* **40**: 197–203.

Navia, B.A., Jordan, B.D. and Price, R.W. (1986a). The AIDS dementia complex I: clinical features. *Annals of Neurology* **19**: 517–24.

Navia, B.A., Cho, E.S., Petito, C.K. and Price, R.W. (1986b). The AIDS dementia complex II: neuropathology. *Annals of Neurology* **19**: 525–35.

Nelson, H.E. (1982). *The National Adult Reading Test: Test Manual*. Windsor: NFER–Nelson.

Peaker, A. and Stewart, L.E. (1989). Rey's Auditory Verbal Learning Test: a review. In *Developments in Clinical and Experimental Neuropsychology*, edited by J.R. Crawford and D.M. Parker. New York: Plenum.

Perdices, M. and Cooper, D.A. (1989a). Simple and choice reaction time in patients with human immunodeficiency virus. *Annals of Neurology* **25**: 460–7.

Perdices, M. and Cooper, D.A. (1989b). Preliminary report on the neuropsychological performance of patients with ARC before and after treatment with zidovudine. *Neurological and Neuropsychological Complications of HIV Infection Conference, Quebec City* (abstract NP-25).

Perry, S.W., Jacobsberg, L.B., Fishman, B., Weiler, P.H., Gold, J.W.M. and Frances, A.J. (1990). Psychological responses to serological testing for HIV. *AIDS* **4**: 145–52.

Piot, P., Plummer, F., Mhalu, F.S., Lamboray, J-L., Chin, J. and Mann, J.M. (1988). AIDS: an international perspective. *Science, New York* **239**: 573–9.

Polich, J., Ehlers, C.E., Otis, S., Mandell, A.J. and Bloom, F.E. (1986). P300 reflects the degree of cognitive decline in dementing illness. *Electroencephalography and Clinical Neurophysiology* **63**: 138–44.

Portegies, P., de Gans, J., Lange, J.M.A., Derix, M.M.A., Speelman, H., Bakker, M., Danner, S.A. and Goudsmit, J. (1989). Declining incidence of AIDS dementia complex after introduction of zidovudine treatment. *British Medical Journal* **299**: 819–21.

Poutianen, E., Iivanainen, M., Elovaara, I., Valle, S-L. and Lahdevirta, J. (1988). Cognitive changes as early signs of HIV infection. *Acta Neurologica Scandinavica* **78**: 49–52.

Price, R.W. (1990). Pathogenesis of HIV related dementia. Oral presentation to the *Neurological and Neuropsychological Complications of HIV Infection: Update 1990, Conference, Monterey, CA*.

Price, R.W. and Brew, B.J. (1988). The AIDS dementia complex. *Journal of Infectious Diseases* **158**: 1079–83.

Price, R.W., Sidtis, J.J., Navia, B.A., Rosenblum, M., Scheck, A.C. and Cleary, P. (1988a). The brain in AIDS: central nervous system HIV-1 infection and AIDS dementia complex. *Science, New York* **239**: 586–92.

Price, R.W., Sidtis, J.J., Navia, B.A., Pumarola-Sune, T. and Ornitz, D.B. (1988b). The AIDS dementia complex. In *AIDS and the Nervous System*, edited by M.L. Rosenblum, R.M. Levy and D.E. Breseden. New York: Raven Press, pp. 203–19.

Raven, J. (1962). *Manual for the Standard Progressive Matrices and Vocabulary Scales*. London: Lewis.

Redfield, R.R., Wright, D.C. and Tramont, E.C. (1986). The Walter Reed staging classification for HTLV III/LAV infection. *New England Journal of Medicine* **314**: 131–2.

Reitan, R.M. and Wolfson, D. (1985). *The Halstead–Reitan Neuropsychological Test Battery:*

Theory and Clinical Interpretation. Tucson, Arizona: Neuropsychology Press.

Resnick, L., Berger, J.R., Shapshak, R. and Tourtellotte, W.W. (1988) Early penetration of the blood–brain barrier by HIV. *Neurology* **38**: 9–14.

Rey, A. (1964). *L'examen Clinique en Psychologie.* Paris: Presses Universitaires.

Robertson, J.R., Bucknall, A.B.V., Welsby, P.D., Roberts, J.J., Inglis, J.M., Peutherer, F. and Brettle, R.P. (1986). Epidemic of AIDS-related virus (HTLV-III/LAV) among intravenous drug abusers. *British Medical Journal* **292**: 527–30.

Rubinow, D.R., Berretini, C.H., Brouwers, P. and Lane, H.C. (1988). Neuropsychiatric consequences of AIDS. *Annals of Neurology* **23** (Supplement): S24–26.

Rundell, J., Thompson, J., Zajac, R. and Beatty, R. (1988). Psychiatric diagnosis and attempted suicide in HIV-infected USAF personnel. *Fourth International Conference on AIDS. Stockholm* (abstract 8595).

Schmitt, F.A., Bigley, J.W., McKinnis, R., Logue, P.E., Evans, R.W., Drucker, J.L. and the AZT Collaborative Working Group (1988). Neuropsychological outcome of zidovudine (AZT) treatment of patients with AIDS and AIDS-related complex. *New England Journal of Medicine* **319**: 1573–8.

Selnes, O.A., Miller, E., McArthur, J.C., Gordon, B., Munoz, A., Sheridan, K., Fox, R. and Saah, A.J. (1990). HIV-1 infection: no evidence of cognitive decline during the asymptomatic stages *Neurology* **40**: 204–8.

Shapiro, D.M. and Harrison, D.W. (1990). Alternative forms of the AVLT: a procedure and test of form equivalency. *Archives of Clinical Neuropsychology* **5**: 405–10.

Smith, J. (1990). Manic psychosis as a neuropsychiatric complication of HIV infection. *Neurological and Neuropsychological Complications of HIV infection: Update 1990, Monterey, CA* (abstract PSY-3).

Snider, W.D., Simpson, D.M., Neilsen, S., Gold, J.M.W., Metroka, C.E. and Posner, J.B. (1983). Neurological complications of AIDS: analysis of 50 patients. *Annals of Neurology* **14**: 403–14.

Sno, H.N., Storosum, G. and Swinkels, J.A. (1989). HIV infection: psychiatric findings in the Netherlands. *British Journal of Psychiatry* **155**: 814–17.

Tross, S., Price, R.W., Navia, B., Thaler, H.T., Gold, J., Hirsch, D.A. and Sidtis, J.J. (1988). Neuropsychological characterisation of the AIDS dementia complex: a preliminary report. *AIDS* **2**: 81–8.

Vernon, P.E. (ed.) (1987). *Intelligence and Speed of Information Processing.* New Jersey: Ablex.

Vogel-Scibilia, S.E., Mulsant, B.H. and Keshavan, M.S. (1988). HIV presenting as a psychosis: a critique. *Acta Psychiatrica Scandinavica* **78**: 656.

Wechsler, D. (1981). *Wechsler Adult Intelligence Scale: Revised.* New York: Psychological Corporation.

Wilkins, J., Robertson, K., Robertson, W. and Hall, C. (1990a). Characterization of HIV-related memory impairment. *Neurological and Neuropsychological Complications of HIV Infection: Update 1990, Monterey, CA* (abstract NPS-30).

Wilkins, J.W., Robertson, K.R., van der Horst, C., Robertson, W.T., Fryer, J.G. and Hall, C.D. (1990b). The importance of confounding factors in the evaluation of neuropsychological changes in patients infected with human immunodeficiency virus. *Journal of the Acquired Immune Deficiency Syndrome* **3**: 938–42.

Yarchoan, R., Brouwers, P., Spitzer, A.R., Grafman, J., Safai, B., Perno, C.F., Larson, S.M., Berg, G., Fischl, M.A., Wichman, A., Thomas, R.V., Brunetti, A., Schmidt, P.J., Myers, C.E. and Broder, S. (1987). Response of human immunodeficiency virus-associated neurological disease to 3'-azido-3'-deoxythymidine. *The Lancet* **333**: 132–5.

Zigmond, A.S. and Snaith, R.P. (1983). The Hospital Anxiety and Depression Scale. *Acta Psychiatrica Scandinavica* **67**: 361–70.

9

Diabetes, Hypoglycaemia and Cognitive Performance

IAN J. DEARY

INTRODUCTION

Diabetes mellitus is an illness characterized by a lack of insulin, which may be total or partial, or ineffectiveness of insulin. Insulin is a hormone which is responsible for the uptake of glucose from the bloodstream to the metabolizing cells of the body. Therefore, lack of insulin leads to disordered metabolism, whereby there is a high glucose concentration in the blood (hyperglycaemia) with reduced cellular levels. The illness is treated by diet, oral hypoglycaemic agents or by injections of animal or human insulin. The form of the illness that will be of primary concern in this chapter is often referred to as insulin-dependent or type I diabetes. The treatment of this form, by definition, requires insulin injections and tends to affect younger individuals; it typically has an onset at any time from infancy to young adulthood.

Because treatment with insulin must be geared towards attaining a relatively normal level of blood glucose, and because blood glucose levels are dependent upon several factors, such as food ingestion, exercise and illness, there is a persistent danger of accidental insulin overdosage and a resulting hypoglycaemic (i.e. low blood glucose level) attack. These are not uncommon and may be divided, somewhat arbitrarily, into two types: mild and severe. In mild attacks there are two sets of symptoms (Hepburn et al., 1991, 1992): autonomic, such as sweating, trembling and palpitation, as a result of the autonomic nervous system's activation by hypoglycaemia; and neuro-glycopenic, such as difficulty concentrating, confusion and drowsiness, as a result of low blood glucose availability in the cerebral cortex. Severe attacks typically involve unconsciousness or behaviour so deranged that the help of

HANDBOOK OF HUMAN PERFORMANCE
VOLUME 2 ISBN 0-12-650352-4

another person is required to administer oral or intravenous glucose or a glucagon injection to facilitate recovery.

The brain is particularly vulnerable to hypoglycaemia because it cannot use any other fuel except glucose. Therefore, when blood glucose levels fall, derangement of mental function soon follows. It is the impairment of brain functioning as a result of hypoglycaemia that is the subject of this chapter. Research in this area is aimed at answering two questions: What are the cognitive consequences of acute hypoglycaemia, i.e. at what blood glucose levels do particular cognitive processes begin to deteriorate? And, are there permanent cognitive impairments following repeated or single attacks of severe hypoglycaemia?

COGNITIVE IMPAIRMENTS ASSOCIATED WITH ACUTE HYPOGLYCAEMIA

Treatment of diabetes mellitus with injections of exogenous insulin was introduced at the beginning of the 1920s, and it was shortly thereafter that the consequences of excess insulin were noted. Central nervous system symptoms and signs of hypoglycaemia were documented (Fletcher and Campbell, 1922); indeed Wilder (1943) observed that, 'the symptoms produced by a drop in blood sugar are *mainly mental and neurological*' (italics in the original), and anticipated later psychological research by stating that the brain's dependence on blood glucose offered a 'unique opportunity for the objective study of mental functions ... enhanced by the fact that we can restore these functions almost immediately'. Wilder's observations were unsystematic and based upon accidental insulin overdoses, experiments by medical staff upon themselves, insulin shock therapy for schizophrenia (Spencer, 1948) and other spontaneous hypoglycaemic attacks. However, early accounts of hypoglycaemia did have the advantages of including subjects' own impressions of hypoglycaemia and of mentioning the associated mood and personality changes, which tend not to be documented in more recent studies (Fineberg and Altschul, 1952).

Before the advent of studies involving well controlled, experimentally induced hypoglycaemia in humans in the laboratory, two studies attempted to examine the effects of low blood glucose on cognitive functioning. Using bolus injections of insulin to reach blood glucoses at a mean of 1.6 mmol l^{-1}, Russell and Rix-Trot (1975) noted that fine motor co-ordination, word-list recall and the rate of solving reasoning problems were reduced, whereas spatial ability, recognition and reasoning accuracy were maintained. Flender and Lifshitz (1976) reported that, in children at blood glucoses between 2.9 and 3.6 mmol l^{-1}, fine motor co-ordination, memory performance and concentration deteriorated.

Controlled hypoglycaemia studies by Holmes *et al.*

Holmes and colleagues introduced research on various aspects of cognitive functioning in response to low glucose levels using well controlled insulin and glucose infusion techniques (Holmes, 1987; Holmes *et al.*, 1983, 1984, 1986). In this type of experiment, typically, a constant infusion of insulin is begun and the desired glucose level is obtained by intermittent intravenous infusions of 20 per cent glucose. The normal adult human range (± 2 SD from the mean) of fasting blood glucose concentration is 3.6 to 5.8 mmol l^{-1}, and such experiments usually involve blood glucose levels below the lower end of this range.

Holmes *et al.* (1983) found that, in twelve type I diabetic patients maintained at a blood glucose of 3.3 mmol l^{-1}, reaction time and speed of simple mathematical calculation was slowed versus a euglycaemia condition, whereas accuracy of calculation and memory function remained intact. Using another twelve diabetic subjects and a similar design, Holmes *et al.* (1984) reported that verbal fluency and those conditions of the Stroop task that involved generating word labels to colour stimuli were impaired during mild hypoglycaemia, whereas word recognition was not. Investigating how mild hypoglycaemia (3.1 versus 6.1 mmol l^{-1}) affected tasks of different complexity in twenty-four type I diabetic patients, Holmes *et al.* (1986) found that choice and discrimination visual reaction times were slowed, but that simple reaction time, tachistoscopic recognition and finger tapping were not, i.e. it appeared that more complex tasks were impaired, while simpler sensory intake and motor functions remained intact (Figure 9.1). These findings were only partially replicated by Holmes (1987), where simple and choice auditory reaction times were slowed, but finger tapping and auditory go/no-go reaction time were unaffected by glucose levels of 3.1 mmol l^{-1}.

Studies following on from the pioneering work of Holmes and colleagues may be divided into those utilizing broad psychological test batteries and those which have concentrated on reaction times.

Induced hypoglycaemia and psychological test batteries

Hoffman *et al.* (1989) examined the performance of eighteen patients with type I diabetes at blood glucose levels of 2.7 and 5.6 mmol l^{-1} and noted that pursuit rotor and trail-making B performances were significantly impaired during hypoglycaemia. Simple reaction time and performance on a 'driving simulator' remained intact, although the validity of the latter instrument is doubtful (D'Auria, 1991). Pramming *et al.* (1986) induced hypoglycaemia in sixteen subjects with IDDM and discovered significant impairment in digit span at 3 mmol l^{-1} and, by 2 mmol l^{-1}, additional impairments in letter cancellation, verbal fluency, trail-making B, story recall and serial sevens. Only

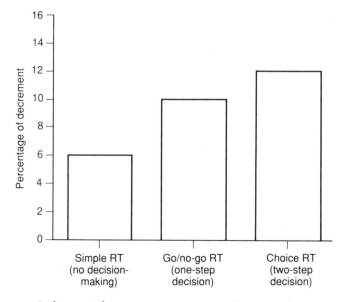

Figure 9.1 Performance decrement in reaction time latency at low glucose level (3.1 mmol l^{-1}) compared with control gucose level (6.1 mmol l^{-1}). (From Holmes *et al.*, 1986.)

finger tapping was unimpaired at a glucose level of 2 mmol l^{-1}. The majority of patients began to show cognitive decline before there were any warning symptoms of hypoglycaemia. Significant reductions in trail making performance and in digit symbol substitution test scores (DSST) were recorded by Stevens *et al.* (1989) in twelve non-diabetic subjects whose blood glucose was lowered to 3.4 mmol l^{-1} versus a control condition of 4.9 mmol l^{-1}. Repeated DSST testing in the two conditions indicated that there was a less steep learning curve and a lower asymptote for performance in the hypoglycaemia condition (Figure 9.2). Simple and choice reaction time, critical flicker fusion and finger tapping were not affected.

Widom and Simonson (1990) investigated type I diabetic patients and non-diabetics during hypoglycaemia and found that the blood glucose thresholds for impairments in letter cancellation, digit symbol and trail making tests were 2.4–2.7, 2.6–2.8 and 2.3–2.7 mmol l^{-1}, respectively. There were no differences in thresholds between the groups, but there were large individual differences with some subjects' performances beginning to decline at 4.0 mmol l^{-1}, while others' scores were maintained at normal levels when blood glucose was below 2.2 mmol l^{-1}. The sources of these individual differences are unknown and their discovery must be a priority in future research. However, some indication was given by Snorgaard *et al.* (1991), who reported that non-diabetic subjects with food-relieved symptoms of

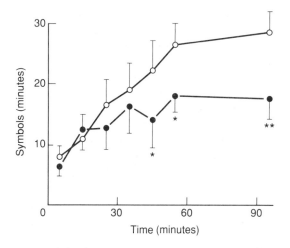

Figure 9.2 Digit symbol substitution test scores (means ± SE) during euglycaemic (open symbols) and hypoglycaemic (closed symbols) study periods. * $p < 0.005$, ** $p < 0.003$. (From Stevens *et al.*, 1989.)

hypoglycaemia tend to have cognitive dysfunction at higher glucose levels than controls.

Kerr *et al.* (1991) confirmed that, at a blood glucose level of 2.8 mmol l^{-1} in IDDM patients, DSST scores are impaired, as are semantic processing and grooved pegboard test scores. They also noted that insulin concentration *per se* had no effect on cognitive function. Mitrakou *et al.* (1991), in a study involving ten non-diabetic subjects, reported that a blood glucose level of 2.4 was sufficient to impair performance on verbal fluency, trail-making B, Stroop, simple and choice reaction time, digit cancellation, delayed verbal memory and backward digit span, but not forward digit span or trail-making A. However, there were no significant impairments at 3.1 mmol l^{-1}. In their study, hypoglycaemic warning symptoms and awareness of cognitive dysfunction appeared before demonstrable cognitive decline.

Reaction times during acute hypoglycaemia

The findings of Holmes *et al.* (1986) and Holmes (1987) are complemented by those of a study by Herold *et al.* (1985) where fourteen controls and twelve type 1 diabetic subjects were tested under conditions of euglycaemia and at a glucose concentration of 2.5 mmol l^{-1}. Not only was reaction time longer and more variable during hypoglycaemia, the longest reaction times occurred as much as sixty minutes after the glucose nadir and some subjects had not returned to baseline reaction times after forty minutes spent at euglycaemic levels in recovery. This delayed recovery of psychological function after hypoglycaemia has important practical applications for diabetic people returning to complex tasks after an attack. Blackman et al. (1990) found a similar delay of recovery of reaction time in ten non-diabetic subjects whose blood glucose was taken to 2.6 mmol l^{-1}. P300 latencies of the auditory and visual evoked potentials were equally slow to recover, and P300 latency and reaction time were correlated at 0.44 ($p < 0.001$) during hypoglycaemia. Similar impairments on reaction times during hypoglycaemia (glucose at 2.5 mmol l^{-1}) in normals and diabetic subjects and subjects with food-relieved hypoglycaemia symptoms may be found in the studies by Heller et al. (1987) and Snorgaard et al. (1991), respectively. The former is equivocal with respect to the possibility of delayed recovery and both have clinical groups that are poorly matched to their respective control groups.

Two studies have produced somewhat anomalous results. Simple reaction time was slower and more variable during hypoglycaemia as mild as 3.0 mmol l^{-1} in seven non-diabetic subjects (Kerr et al., 1989). In other studies simple reaction time was unimpaired (e.g. Holmes et al., 1986) at about this level. Further, Stevens et al. (1989) found that choice reaction time was not impaired at a blood glucose of 3.4 mmol l^{-1}, although this is a mild degree of hypoglycaemia. Apart from reaction time, another 'simple' psychological task that appears to be impaired by hypoglycaemia is colour discrimination. Harrad et al. (1985) found that glucose levels of 2.5 mmol l^{-1} and 1.5 mmol l^{-1} led to impairments in performance on the Farnsworth 100 hue test, but not on a digit span test.

Hormone responses, symptoms and cognitive changes during acute hypoglycaemia

The hormonal response to hypoglycaemia involves increases in the circulating concentrations of adrenalin, noradrenalin, glucagon, growth hormone, cortisol and pancreatic polypeptide. Since these effect changes in metabolism that raise blood glucose once more, and since the onset of awareness of the physical symptoms of hypoglycaemia is also protective, it is of interest to discover the temporal relationships between these sets of variables. Ipp and Forster (1987) reported that adrenalin concentration increased sharply without a change in trail-making test performance in non-diabetic subjects at a blood glucose of 3.0 mmol l^{-1}. Stevens et al. (1989) discovered that in non-diabetic subjects the hormonal response to hypoglycaemia began at higher glucose levels than the onset of warning symptoms, which occurred before there were signs of cognitive dysfunction: somewhat contrary to the findings of Pramming et al. (1986). Kerr et al. (1989) and Jones et al. (1990) confirmed that a rise in adrenalin was detectable before other hormones, and before a change in P300 latency, respectively.

One of the most detailed studies in this field (Mitrakou et al., 1991) has shown that, in non-diabetic subjects, adrenalin and other hormones rise at glucose levels around 3.7 mmol l^{-1}, autonomic symptoms occur at 3.0, neuroglycopenic symptoms at 3.0 and significant cognitive impairment begins at about 2.4 mmol l^{-1}. Therefore, there is some indication that normal subjects are well protected from the deleterious cognitive effects of hypoglycaemia. However, Hoffman *et al.* (1989) reported that diabetic patients might experience cognitive impairments before the onset of warning symptoms, and at about the same time as the counter-regulatory hormonal response. Widom and Simonson (1990) and Amiel *et al.* (1991) have suggested that patients whose diabetes was particularly well controlled were the most vulnerable to the late development of warning symptoms.

Brain electrophysiology and acute hypoglycaemia

A rise in the latency of the P300 wave of the averaged brain electrical evoked potential to oddball stimuli was reported to occur at glucose levels as high as 4.0 mmol l^{-1} in non-diabetic individuals (De Feo *et al.*, 1988). Cognitive changes at such a mild level of hypoglycaemia, in fact such a glucose level could hardly be considered hypoglycaemic, have not been replicated by others, and the result is an interesting anomaly. Blackman *et al.* (1990) suggested that P300 latencies were intact at 3.3 mmol l^{-1} glucose, but slowed at 2.6 mmol l^{-1} (Figure 9.3); Kiss *et al.* (1989) found no increase in P300 latency in non-diabetics at 3.7 mmol l^{-1}; and Jones *et al.* (1990), studying non-diabetics, obtained delayed P300 latencies at 3.0 but not at 3.4 mmol l^{-1}.

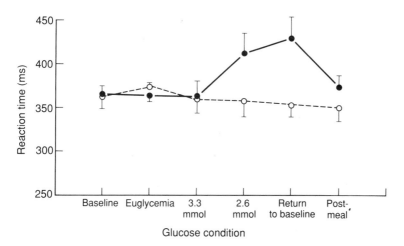

Figure 9.3 Mean ± SE reaction time during euglycaemic (open symbols) and hypo-glycaemic (closed symbols) conditions. $p < 0.01$ between conditions at 2.6 mmol l^{-1} glucose; $p < 0.0001$ at return to baseline. (From Blackman *et al.*, 1990.)

There does not appear to be any effect of moderately severe hypoglycaemia on the P100 wave of the averaged evoked potential in non-diabetics (Tamburanno et al., 1988). Again, there is remarkable between-subjects variability in the brain's response to hypoglycaemia; some subjects appear to develop evoked potential changes only at very low blood glucose levels, and there are large differences in recovery times (Kiss et al., 1989; Koh et al., 1988). Delayed recovery of the P300 latency after hypoglycaemia has been found in the studies of De Feo et al. (1988), Harrad et al. (1985), Blackman et al. (1990; Figure 9.3) and Tallroth et al. (1990).

There is good agreement that alpha activity decreases in the electroencephalogram during hypoglycaemia, but not the area of the brain which is most affected: frontal, parieto-occipital and temporal areas have all appeared to be the most sensitive areas in different studies (Tamburanno et al., 1988; Harrad et al., 1985; Pramming et al., 1988; Tallroth et al., 1990).

PERMANENT COGNITIVE IMPAIRMENT AFTER SEVERE HYPOGLYCAEMIA?

About 10 per cent of patients with diabetes will have a severe attack of hypoglycaemia about once a year. Is this an acceptable side-effect of diabetic control with insulin? Hypoglycaemic attacks can lead to death (Kalimo and Olsson, 1980), but it is not known whether most subjects recover from recurrent severe hypoglycaemic attacks without permanent alteration of cognitive function (Ryan, 1988). This lack of knowledge exists in spite of the fact that there is a large number of studies which have compared psychological test performances in diabetic patients and matched controls. Although such studies tend to show that patients do under-perform when compared with controls, they rarely suggest what the aetiological factor(s) might be (see Richardson, 1990, for a useful review of this research). Candidate factors for causing mild brain dysfunction in diabetes are: peripheral and central neuropathy, persistent hyperglycaemia, vascular changes, the broader psychological effects of having a chronic illness, missed education because of the illness and, of course, repeated severe hypoglycaemia. It is this latter, putative cause of cognitive impairment that is examined here.

The effects of recurrent severe hypoglycaemia are of particular interest because two large-scale studies have shown that diabetic subjects who receive intensive insulin regimes, aimed at maintaining their blood glucose concentrations near to normal physiological levels for as much of the time as possible, have up to three times as many severe hypoglycaemic attacks compared with those patients on more conventional regimes (DCCT Research Group, 1991; Reichard et al., 1988). Prevention of these attacks is made more difficult because they often occur during sleep (Caspaire and Elving, 1985).

Cognitive effects of severe hypoglycaemia during childhood

There is general agreement that the human brain is particularly sensitive to the deleterious effects of severe hypoglycaemia during early development (Haworth and McRae, 1965; Ingram *et al.*, 1967; Hirabyashi *et al.*, 1980; Ryan, 1988), and it is suggested that neonatal hypoglycaemia may cause a lowering of later IQ scores and difficulties with mental and motor development (Pildes *et al.*, 1974; Lucas *et al.*, 1988). Not only is the child's brain more sensitive to hypoglycaemia, children whose diabetes begins before the age of three years tend to suffer more episodes of severe hypoglycaemia (Ternand *et al.*, 1982).

The work of Ack *et al.* (1961) suggested that children whose diabetes started before the age of five were significantly lower in IQ than their siblings, by about ten points, and that episodes of hypoglycaemia and/or acidosis severe enough to require hospitalization might have an aetiological role in this difference. Ryan *et al.* (1984) found that adolescents with diabetes were poorer on tests of verbal intelligence, visuo-motor co-ordination and critical flicker threshold than matched controls. Factors other than severe hypoglycaemia were thought to be responsible for the differences. The following year, Ryan and colleagues (1985) found that it was only adolescents whose diabetes had begun before five years of age who were cognitively disadvantaged when compared with controls; this group had lower scores on tests of intelligence, visuo-spatial ability, learning and memory, attention and school achievement and mental and motor speed. Although there was no direct supporting evidence, the authors suggested that multiple episodes of hypoglycaemia were likely to be responsible for the differences in test scores. Similar results, concerning the relationship between early hypoglycaemia-related convulsions and later lower mental test performance, were reported by Rovet *et al.* (1987, 1988). Golden *et al.* (1989) have suggested that the incidence of relatively mild hypoglycaemia episodes in children might be related to lower reasoning performance.

Severe hypoglycaemia in the neonatal period and in early childhood have been related to physical CNS pathology and abnormal EEG findings (Koivisto *et al.*, 1972; Eeg-Olofsson, 1977). Cortical evoked potential abnormalities have been found in about 30 per cent of diabetic adolescents (Cirillo *et al.*, 1984), but hypoglycaemia has not been established as the cause of these.

Cognitive effects of severe hypoglycaemia in adulthood

Several studies have indicated that there is some degree of cognitive impairment in type II, or non-insulin-dependent, diabetes (Perlmuter *et al.*, 1984; Robertson-Tchabo *et al.*, 1986; Tun *et al.*, 1987; Reaven *et al.*, 1990; Mooradian *et al.*, 1988) but, because hypoglycaemia is less prevalent in this type of diabetes where other factors might be responsible for cognitive effects, they are not considered further here. Other studies examining the effects of diabetes on cognition are either lacking in a control group (Kubany et al., 1956), or were conducted when patients suffered derangements of glucose metabolism rarely found today (Miles and Root, 1920).

Bale (1973) discovered that an excess of diabetic patients over controls tended to score in the 'brain damaged' range of a word-learning test. Those diabetic patients with low word-learning test scores tended to be those with a history containing more episodes of severe hypoglycaemia. One patient had a difference of twenty-eight points between verbal and performance IQ on the Wechsler adult intelligence scale (WAIS) and, on average, diabetics with low word-learning scores were 5 points lower on performance versus verbal IQ. Skenazy and Bigler (1984) reported that adult type I diabetic patients had lower WAIS performance IQ scores than either chronically ill or healthy controls, and that there was a significant correlation ($r = 0.44$, $p < 0.04$) between performance IQs and the numbers of 'insulin reactions'. The correlation between insulin reactions and verbal IQ was near to zero.

Wredling et al. (1990) compared seventeen insulin-dependent diabetic patients with and without a history of repeated attacks of severe hypo-glycaemia on various cognitive tests. Patient groups were matched for age, age at onset of diabetes, illness duration, insulin regime, education, employment and diabetic complications. Those having had severe hypoglycaemia were poorer on some tapping tests, had more reversals on the Necker cube test, had reduced forward digit span and were slower on the digit symbol test, but appeared equally able on trail-making and reaction time tests, and were superior on a maze learning test.

Langan et al. (1991) found a correlation of -0.33 ($p < 0.001$, corrected for potentially confounding variables) between 'IQ impairment', measured by subtracting WAIS-revised performance IQ scores from estimates of pre-morbid IQ derived from the national adult reading test (NART), and the frequency of severe hypoglycaemia obtained from patients' histories. Severe hypoglycaemia frequency correlated significantly with performance IQ and reaction time speed and variability, but not with verbal fluency or auditory verbal learning test scores. Further study involving the same group of diabetic subjects showed that: patients with a history of more than five severe hypoglycaemia episodes, but not those without such a history, were lower in WAIS-R IQ than matched healthy controls (Deary et al., 1991) and had current IQ levels that were significantly lower than their premorbid IQ estimates (Figure 9.4); and that unawareness of the symptoms of hypoglycaemia was a risk factor for increased incidence of hypoglycaemia and, perhaps, for cognitive impairment (MacLeod et al., 1991). In the same group there appeared to be an increasing size of correlation between frequency of severe hypo-glycaemia and reaction time in the Hick and Sternberg memory scan techniques as the complexity of the task increases (Deary et al., in press). In a small

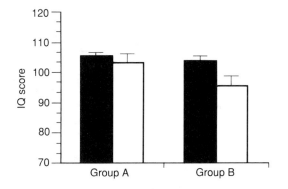

Figure 9.4 Pre-morbid (black bars) and present IQ level (white bars) for patients with no history of severe hypoglycaemia (group A) and patients with at least five episodes of severe hypoglycaemia (group B). Pre-morbid versus present IQ comparison for group A is non-significant, comparison for group B is significant at $p < 0.01$. (From Langan *et al.*, 1991.)

study, Holmes *et al.* (1988) found tentative evidence for a link between slower reaction times and episodes of severe hypoglycaemia, linked to low glycosylated haemoglobin levels.

Not all studies have confirmed the impression that severe hypoglycaemia causes cognitive impairment. One of the few prospective studies was conducted by Reichard *et al.* (1991a), in which forty-four intensively treated and fifty-three conventionally treated insulin-dependent diabetic patients were followed up for three years, and their experiences of hypoglycaemia were documented. The group being treated on an intensive insulin regime suffered more severe hypoglycaemia but were not significantly different on cognitive testing, including reaction time, digit span, maze learning and the Necker cube test. However, the two groups were not completely separated with respect to their experience of hypoglycaemia and the test battery is rather limited. Additionally, the follow-up time was brief, although the short report of the five-year follow-up of these patients still finds no cognitive differences between the groups in spite of their increasingly disparate experiences of hypoglycaemia (Reichard *et al.*, 1991b).

Two reports contained in short abstracts failed to find a relationship between history of severe hypoglycaemia and cognitive impairment indexed by trail-making and P300 latency (Grimm *et al.*, 1991) and paired associate learning (Lichty and Klachko, 1985).

There are other putative causes of any cognitive impairment that is found to be present in patients with type I diabetes. Holmes (1986) indicated that poor glycaemic control, suggestive of sustained hyperglycaemia, might be associated with poor performance on vocabulary and reaction time tests. Franceschi *et al.* (1984) and Lawson *et al.* (1984) provide some evidence consistent with a relationship between neuropathy in insulin-treated diabetic patients and poor memory test performance. Poor memory test performance and slowed speed of reaction in adult diabetic patients was demonstrated by Meuter et al. (1980) but no cause for these deficits was explored. Duration of illness has been associated with poor memory test scores (Prescott et al., 1990), and with abnormal brain stem auditory evoked responses and abnormalities in subcortical and/or brainstem regions as revealed by magnetic resonance imaging (Dejgaard et al., 1990). Others have suggested that hypo- or hyperglycaemia, rather than duration of illness, are likely causes of abnormal brain stem evoked potentials in diabetic patients (Khardori et al., 1986). However, there is no general agreement about the existence of neurophysiological abnormalities in diabetic patients (Algan et al., 1989) and what evidence exists suggests that neurophysiological and cognitive effects do not necessarily co-exist or correlate (Pozzessere et al., 1991; Donald et al., 1984).

An exception to the lack of correlation between detectable brain changes and alterations of psychological performance is the case report by Chalmers et al. (1991) in which a diabetic man suffered a severe hypoglycaemic attack and sustained deficits in immediate and delayed memory performance despite intact 'general cognitive functioning'. Immediate memory performance improved with time but, several months later, the delayed memory deficit remained. Magnetic resonance imaging of the brain revealed an abnormality in the left temporal area which the authors believed was consistent with the psychological performance deficit.

CONCLUDING REMARKS

Experimental research on the impairments associated with acute hypoglycaemia is less than ten years old and many issues remain unresolved. What are the sources of the individual differences in susceptibility to mental impairment? Do the impairments in psychological test performance predict deficits in driving, occupational tasks, etc? Can newer dynamic brain scanning techniques illuminate the relationships between brain metabolism changes and deficits in performance? What are the detailed relationships among the hormonal responses, warning symptoms, cognitive impairments and neurophysiological changes? And so on.

Children who experience severe hypoglycaemia before the age of five years are at increased risk of having poorer than expected cognitive ability. Psychological performance research on the question of the effects of repeated severe hypoglycaemia during adulthood has met with severe methodological problems, e.g. those concerned with obtaining valid estimates of hypoglycaemia experience and estimates of pre-morbid mental ability levels and performance decrements. Despite increasingly persuasive evidence that there is permanent, but probably modest, cognitive decline after several severe hypoglycaemia attacks, the jury is still out. Large-scale prospective studies, such as the DCCT (DCCT Research Group, 1991), have still to report their cognitive findings but it is unlikely that a single study will be definitive.

REFERENCES

Ack, M., Miller, I. and Weil, W.B. (1961). Intelligence of children with diabetes mellitus. *Pediatrics* **28**: 764–70.

Algan, M., Ziegler, O., Gehin, P., Got, I., Raspiller, A., Weber, M., Genton, P., Saudax, E. and Drouin, P. (1989). Visual evoked potentials in diabetic patients. *Diabetes Care* **12**: 227–9.

Amiel, S.A., Pottinger, R.C., Archibald, H.R., Chusney, G., Cunnah, D.T.F., Prior, P.F. and Gale, E.A.M. (1991). Effect of antecedent glucose control on cerebral function during hypoglycaemia. *Diabetes Care* **14**: 109–18.

Bale, R.N. (1973). Brain damage in diabetes mellitus. *British Journal of Psychiatry* **122**: 337–41.

Blackman, J.D., Towle, V.L., Lewis, G.F., Spire, J.P. and Polonsky, K.S. (1990). Hypoglycaemic thresholds for cognitive dysfunction in humans. *Diabetes* **39**: 828–35.

Caspaire, A.F. and Elving, L.D. (1985). Severe hypoglycaemia in diabetic patients: frequency, causes, prevention. *Diabetes Care* **8**: 141–5.

Chalmers, J., Risk, M.T.A., Kean, D.M., Grant, R., Ashworth, B. and Campbell, I.W. (1991). Severe amnesia after hypoglycaemia: clinical, psychometric and magnetic resonance imaging correlations. *Diabetes Care* **14**: 922–5.

Cirillo, D., Gonfiantini, E., De Grandis, D., Bongiovanni, L., Robert, J.J. and Pinelli, L. (1984). Visual evoked potentials in diabetic children and adolescents. *Diabetes Care* **7**: 273–5.

D'Auria, D. (1991). An occupational physician's view. In *Ambulatory Anaesthesia and Sedation: Impairment and Recovery*, edited by I.D. Klepper, L.D. Sanders and M. Rosen. Oxford: Blackwell Scientific.

DCCT Research Group (1991). Epidemiology of severe hypoglycaemia in the diabetes control and complications trial. *American Journal of Medicine* **90**: 450–9.

Deary, I.J., Crawford, J.R., Hepburn, D.A., Langan, S.J., Graham, K.S. and Frier, B.M. (1991). Is severe recurrent hypoglycaemia a cause of cognitive impairment in diabetes? Paper presented to the Scottish Society of Physicians, Dumfries.

Deary, I.J., Langan, S.J., Graham, K.S., Hepburn, D.A. and Frier, B.M. (in press). Severe hypoglycaemia, intelligence and speed of information processing. *Intelligence*.

De Feo, P., Gallai, V., Mazzotta, G., Crispino, G., Torlone, E., Periello, G., Ventura, M., Santeusanio, F., Brunetti, P. and Bolli, G. (1988). Modest decrements in plasma glucose concentration cause early impairment in cognitive function and later activation of glucose counterregulation in the absence of hypoglycaemic symptoms in normal man. *Journal of Clinical Investigation* **82**: 436–44.

Dejgaard, A., Gade, A., Larsson, H., Balle, V., Parving, H. and Parving, H-H. (1990). Evidence for diabetic encephalopathy. *Diabetic Medicine* **8**: 162–7.

Donald, M.W., Williams Erdahl, D.L., Surridge, D.H.C., Monga, T.N., Lawson, J.S., Bird, C.E. and Letemendia, F.J.J. (1984). Functional correlates of reduced central conduction velocity in diabetic subjects. *Diabetes* **33**: 627–33.

Eeg-Olofsson, O. (1977). Hypoglycaemia and neurological disturbances in children with diabetes mellitus. *Acta Paediatrica Scandinavica* **270** (Supplement): 91–5.

Fineberg, S.K. and Altschul, A. (1952). The encephalography of hyperinsulinism. *Annals of Internal Medicine* **36**: 536–50.

Flender, J. and Lifshitz, F. (1976). The effects of fluctuations of blood glucose levels on the psychological performance of juvenile diabetics. *Diabetes* **25**: 334 (abstract).

Fletcher, A.A. and Campbell, W.R. (1922). The blood sugar following insulin administration and the symptom complex – hypoglycaemia. *Journal of Metabolic Research* **2**: 637–49.

Franceschi, M., Cecchetto, R., Minicucci, F., Smizne, S., Baio, G. and Canal, N. (1984). Cognitive processes in insulin-dependent diabetes. *Diabetes Care* **7**: 228–31.

Golden, M.P., Ingersoll, G.M., Russell, B.A., Wright, J.C. and Huberty, T.J. (1989). Longitudinal relationship of asymptomatic hypoglycaemia to cognitive function in IDDM. *Diabetes Care* **12**: 89–93.

Grimm, G., Damjancic, P., Fasching, P., Madl, C., Kramer, L. and Waldhausl, W. (1991). Einfluss schwerer, anamnestisch erhebbarer hypoglykamischer Episoden auf die kognitive Hirnfunktion bei Patienten mit Diabetes mellitus Typ-I. *Aktuelle Endokrinologie und Stoffwechsel* **12**: 113 (abstract).

Harrad, R.A., Cockram, C.S., Plumb, A.P., Stone, S., Fenwick, P. and Soncksen, P.H. (1985). The effect of hypoglycaemia on visual function: a clinical and electrophysiological study. *Clinical Science* **69**: 673–9.

Haworth, J.C. and McRae, K.N. (1965). The neurological and developmental effects of neonatal hypoglycaemia. *Canadian Medical Association Journal* **92**: 861–5.

Heller, S.R., MacDonald, I.A., Herbert, M. and Tattersall, R.B. (1987). Influence of sympathetic nervous system on hypoglycaemic warning symptoms. *Lancet* **2**: 359–63.

Hepburn, D.A., Deary, I.J., Frier, B.M., Patrick, A.W., Quinn, J.D. and Fisher, B.M. (1991) Symptoms of acute insulin-induced hypoglycaemia in humans with and without type 1 (insulin-dependent) diabetes: a factor analytic approach. *Diabetes Care* **14**: 949–57.

Hepburn, D.A., Deary, I.J. and Frier, B.M. (1992). Classification of symptoms of hypoglycaemia in insulin-treated diabetic patients using factor analysis: relationship to hypoglycaemia unawareness. *Diabetic Medicine* **9**: 70–5.

Herold, K.C., Polonsky, K.S., Cohen, R.M., Levy, J. and Douglas, F. (1985). Variable deterioration in cortical function during insulin-induced hypoglycaemia. *Diabetes* **34**: 677–85.

Hirabyashi, S., Kitahara, T. and Hishida, T. (1980). Computed tomography in perinatal hypoxic and hypoglycaemic encephalopathy with emphasis on follow-up studies. *Journal of Computer Assisted Tomography* **4**: 451–6.

Hoffman, R.G., Speelman, D.J., Hinnen, D.A., Conley, K.L., Guthrie, R.A. and Knapp, R.K. (1989). Changes in cortical functioning with acute hypoglycaemia and hyperglycaemia in Type 1 diabetes. *Diabetes Care* **12**: 193–7.

Holmes, C. (1986). Neuropsychological profiles in men with insulin-dependent diabetes. *Journal of Consulting and Clinical Psychology* **54**: 386–9.

Holmes, C.S. (1987). Metabolic control and auditory information processing at altered glucose levels in insulin-dependent diabetes. *Brain and Cognition* **6**: 161–74.

Holmes, C.S., Hayford, J.T., Gonzalez, J.L. and Weydert, J.A. (1983). A survey of cognitive functioning at different glucose levels in diabetic persons. *Diabetes Care* **6**: 180–5.

Holmes, C.S., Koepke, K.M., Thompson, R.G., Gyves, P.W. and Weydert, J.A. (1984). Verbal fluency and naming performance in type 1 diabetes at different blood glucose concentrations. *Diabetes Care* **7**: 454–9.

Holmes, C.S., Koepke, K.M. and Thompson, R.G. (1986). Simple versus complex impairments at three blood glucose levels. *Psychoneuroendocrinology* **11**: 353–7.

Holmes, C.S., Tsalikian, E. and Yamada, T. (1988). Blood glucose control and visual and auditory attention in men with insulin-dependent diabetes. *Diabetic Medicine* **5**: 634–9.

Ingram, T.T.S., Stark, G.D. and Blackburn, I. (1967). Ataxia and other neurological disorders as sequels of severe hypoglycaemia in childhood. *Brain* **90**: 851–62.

Ipp, E. and Forster, B. (1987). Sparing of cognitive function in mild hypoglycaemia: dissociation from the neuroendocrine response. *Journal of Clinical Endocrinology and Metabolism* **65**: 806–10.

Jones, T.W., McCarthy, G., Tamborlane, W.V., Caprio, S., Roessler, E., Kraemer, D., Starick-Zych,

K., Allison, T., Boulware, S.D. and Sherwin, R.S. (1990). Mild hypoglycaemia and impairment of brainstem and cortical evoked potentials in healthy subjects. *Diabetes* **39**: 1550–5.

Kalimo, H. and Olsson, Y. (1980). Effects of severe hypoglycaemia on the human brain. *Acta Neurologica Scandinavica* **62**: 345–56.

Kerr, D., MacDonald, I.A. and Tattersall, R.B. (1989). Adaptation to mild hypoglycaemia in normal subjects despite sustained increases in counter-regulatory hormones. *Diabetologia* **32**: 249–54.

Kerr, D., Reza, M., Smith, N. and Leatherdale, B.A. (1991). Importance of insulin in subjective, cognitive and hormonal responses to hypoglycaemia in patients with IDDM. *Diabetes* **40**: 1057–62.

Kiss, I., Ryan, C.M., Mitrakou, A., Jenssen, T., Durrant, J. and Gerich, J.E. (1989). The effects of experimentally induced hypoglycaemia on neuropsychological and electrophysiological indices of cognitive function. *Journal of Clinical and Experimental Neuropsychology* **11**: 77 (abstract).

Khardori, R., Sloer, N.G., Good, D.C., Devlesc-Howard, A.B., Broughton, D. and Walbert, J. (1986). Brainstem auditory and visual evoked potentials in Type 1 (insulin-dependent) diabetic patients. *Diabetologia* **29**: 362–5.

Koh, T.H.H.G., Aynsley-Green, A., Tarbit, M. and Eyre, J.A. (1988). Neural dysfunction during hypoglycaemia. *Archives of Disease in Childhood* **63**: 1353–8.

Koivisto, M., Blanco-Sequeiros, M. and Krause, U. (1972). Neonatal symptomatic and asymptomatic hypoglycaemia: a follow-up study of 151 children. *Developmental Medicine and Child Neurology* **14**: 603–14.

Kubany, A.J., Danowsky, T.S. and Moses, C. (1956). The personality and intelligence of diabetics. *Diabetes* **5**:462–7.

Langan, S.J., Deary, I.J., Hepburn, D.A. and Frier, B.M. (1991). Cumulative cognitive impairment following recurrent severe hypoglycaemia in adult patients with insulin-treated diabetes mellitus. *Diabetologia* **34**: 337–44.

Lawson, J.S., Williams Erdahl, D.L., Monga, T.N., Bird, C.E., Donald, M.W., Surridge, D.H.C. and Letemendia, F.J.J. (1984) Neuropsychological function in diabetic patients with neuropathy. *British Journal of Psychiatry* **145**: 263–8.

Lichty, W. and Klachko, D. (1985). Memory in Type I diabetes. *Diabetes* **34** (Supplement 1): 19A (abstract).

Lucas, A., Morley, R. and Cole, T.J. (1988). Adverse neurodevelopmental outcome of moderate neonatal hypoglycaemia. *British Medical Journal* **297**: 1304–8.

MacLeod, K.M., Deary, I.J., Graham, K.S., Hepburn, D.A. and Frier, B.M. (1991). Hypoglycaemia unawareness: a risk factor for severe hypoglycaemia and cognitive impairment in insulin-treated diabetes. *Diabetologia* **34** (Supplement 2): A186 (abstract).

Meuter, F., Thomas, W., Gruneklee, D., Gries, F.A. and Lohmann, R. (1980. Psychometric evaluation of performance in diabetes mellitus. *Hormone and Metabolic Research Supplement* **9**: 9–17.

Miles, W.R. and Root, H.F. (1920). Psychological tests applied to diabetic patients. *Archives of Internal Medicine* **30**: 767–77.

Mitrakou, A., Ryan, C., Veneman, T., Mokan, M., Jenssen, T., Kiss, I., Durrant, J., Cryer, P. and Gerich, J. (1991). Hierarchy of glycaemic thresholds for counterregulatory hormone secretion, symptoms and cerebral dysfunction. *American Journal of Physiology (Endocrinology and Metabolism)* **23**: E67–E74.

Mooradian, A.D., Perryman, K., Fitten, J., Kavonian, G.D. and Morley, J.E. (1988). Cortical function in elderly non-insulin dependent diabetic patients. *Archives of Internal Medicine* **148**: 2369–72.

Perlmuter, L.C., Hakami, M.K., Hodgson-Harrington, C., Ginsberg, J., Katz, J., Singer, D.E. and Nathan, D.M. (1984). Decreased cognitive function in aging non-insulin-dependent diabetic patients. *American Journal of Medicine* **77**: 1043–8.

Pildes, R.S., Cornblath, M., Warren, I., Page-El, E., di Menza, S., Merritt, D.M. and Peeva, A.

(1974). A prospective controlled study of neonatal hypoglycaemia *Pediatrics* **54**: 5–14.

Pozzessere, G., Valle, E., De Grinis, S., Cordischi, V., Fattapposta, F., Rozzo, P.A., Pietravalle, P., Cristina, G., Morano, S. and Di Mario, U. (1991). Abnormalities of cognitive functions in IDDM revealed by P300 event-related potential analysis: comparison with short-latency evoked potentials and psychometric tests. *Diabetes* **40**: 952–8.

Pramming, S., Thorsteinsson, B., Theilgaard, A., Pinner, E.M. and Binder, C. (1986). Cognitive function during hypoglycaemia in Type 1 diabetes mellitus. *British Medical Journal* **292**: 647–50.

Pramming, S., Thorsteinsson, B., Stigsby, B. and Binder, C. (1988). Glycaemic threshold for changes in electroencephalograms during hypoglycaemia in patients with insulin dependent diabetes. *British Medical Journal* **296**: 665–7.

Prescott, J.H., Richardson, J.T.E. and Gillespie, C.R. (1990). Cognitive function in diabetes mellitus: the effects of duration of illness and glycaemic control. *British Journal of Clinical Psychology* **29**: 167–75.

Reaven, G.M., Thompson, L.W., Nahum, D. and Haskins, E. (1990). Relationship between hyperglycaemia and cognitive function in older NIDDM patients. *Diabetes Care* **13**: 16–21.

Reichard, P., Britz, A., Cars, I., Nilsson, B.Y., Sobocinsky-Olsson, B. and Rosenqvist, U. (1988). The Stockholm Diabetes Intervention Study (SDIS): 18 months' results. *Acta Medica Scandinavica* **224**: 115–22.

Reichard, P., Berglund, A., Britz, A., Levander, S. and Rosenqvist, U. (1991a). Hypoglycaemic episodes during intensified insulin treatment: increased frequency but no effect on cognitive function. *Journal of Internal Medicine* **229**: 9–16.

Reichard, P., Britz, A., Levander, S. and Rosenqvist, U. (1991b). No neuropsychological deficits after five years of intensified insulin treatment: the Stockholm Diabetes Intervention Study (SDIS). *Diabetes* **40** (Supplement 1): 549A (abstract).

Richardson, J.T.E. (1990). Cognitive function in diabetes mellitus. *Neuroscience and Behavioral Reviews* **14**: 385–8.

Robertson-Tchabo, E.A., Arenberg, A., Tobin, J.D. and Plotz, J.B. (1986). A longitudinal study of cognitive performance in noninsulin dependent (Type II) diabetic men. *Experimental Gerontology* **21**: 459–57.

Rovet, J.F., Ehrlich, R.M. and Hoppe, M. (1987). Intellectual deficits associated with early onset of insulin-dependent diabetes mellitus in children *Diabetes Care* **10**: 510–15.

Rovet, J.F., Ehrlich, R.M. and Hoppe, M. (1988). Specific intellectual deficits in children with early onset diabetes mellitus. *Child Development* **59**: 226–34.

Russell, P.N. and Rix-Trot, H.M. (1975). An exploratory study of some behavioural consequences of insulin induced hypoglycaemia. *New Zealand Medical Journal* **81**: 337–40.

Ryan, C.M. (1988). Neurobehavioural complications of Type I diabetes: examination of possible risk factors. *Diabetes Care* **11**: 86–93.

Ryan, C., Vega, A., Longstreet, C. and Drash, A. (1984). Neuropsychological changes in adolescents with insulin-dependent diabetes. *Journal of Consulting and Clinical Psychology* **52**: 335–42.

Ryan, C., Vega, A. and Drash, A. (1985). Cognitive deficits in adolescents who developed diabetes early in life. *Paediatrics* **75**: 921–7.

Skenazy, J.A. and Bigler, E.D. (1984). Neuropsychological findings in diabetes mellitus. *Journal of Clinical Psychology* **40**: 246–58.

Snorgaard, O., Lassen, L.H., Rosenfalck, A.M. and Binder, C. (1991). Glycaemic thresholds for hypoglycaemic symptoms, impairment of cognitive function, and release of counter-regulatory hormones in subjects with functional hypoglycaemia. *Journal of Internal Medicine* **229**: 343–50.

Spencer, A.M. (1948). Post-hypoglycaemic encephalopathy in Sakel's insulin treatment. *Journal of Mental Science* **94**: 513.

Stevens, A.B., McKane, W.R., Bell, P.M., Bell, P., King, D.J. and Hayes, J.R. (1989). Psychomotor performance and counterregulatory responses during mild hypoglycaemia in healthy volunteers. *Diabetes Care* **12**: 12–17.

Tallroth, G., Lindgren, M., Stenberg, G., Rosen, I. and Agardh, C.D. (1990). Neurophysiological changes during insulin-induced hypoglycaemia and in the recovery period following glucose infusion in Type I (insulin-dependent) diabetes mellitus and in normal man. *Diabetologia* **33**: 319–23.

Tamburanno, G., Lala, A., Locuratolo, N., Leonetti, F., Sbraccia, P., Giaccari, A., Busco, S. and Porcu, S. (1988). Electroencephalography and visually evoked potentials during moderate hypoglycaemia. *Journal of Clinical Endocrinology and Metabolism* **66**: 1301–6.

Ternand, C., Go, V.L.W. and Gerich, J.E. (1982). Endocrine pancreatic response of children with onset of insulin-requiring diabetes before age 3 and after age 5. *Journal of Pediatrics* **101**: 36–9.

Tun, P.A., Perlmuter, L.C., Russo, P. and Nathan, D.M. (1987). Memory self-assessment and performance in aged diabetics and non-diabetics. *Experimental Aging Research* **13**: 151–7.

Widom, B. and Simonson, D.C. (1990). Glycaemic control and neuropsychologic function during hypoglycaemia in patients with insulin-dependent diabetes mellitus. *Annals of Internal Medicine* **112**: 904–12.

Wilder, J. (1943). Psychological problems in hypoglycaemia. *American Journal of Digestive Diseases* **10**: 428–35.

Wredling, R., Levander, S., Adamson, U. and Lins, P.E. (1990). Permanent neuropsychological impairment after recurrent episodes of severe hypoglycaemia in man. *Diabetologia* **33**: 152–7.

10

Chronic Fatigue Syndrome and Performance

A.P. SMITH

THE CHRONIC FATIGUE SYNDROME

A number of clinical syndromes have been described which refer to similar groups of patients who present with the principal complaint of disabling fatigue. Various names have been used and these include epidemic neuromyasthenia, idiopathic chronic fatigue and myalgia syndrome, benign myalgic encephalomyelitis, chronic infectious mononucleosis, Royal Free disease, post-viral fatigue syndrome, fibrositis-fibromyalgia and chronic fatigue syndrome. The term 'chronic fatigue syndrome' (CFS) is the one now most frequently used because it is descriptive and free from aetiological implications.

Symptoms of chronic fatigue syndrome are:

1. Muscle fatigue, often made worse by exercise.
2. Mental fatigue.
3. Psychiatric symptoms such as depression may often be present.
4. CFS often follows an apparent viral infection and immunological abnormalities have been reported.
5. Behavioural problems such as impairments of attention, motor function, memory, language, increased visual and auditory sensitivity and sleep disturbance are often present.

The main aim of this chapter is to review the evidence relating to the behavioural problems. However, before this is done a brief history of the syndrome and a summary of current knowledge of neuromuscular disorders, psychiatric symptoms, viral infections and immunological abnormalities associated with CFS is given.

HISTORY

A detailed account of the history of CFS is given by Wessely (1991a), to which the reader is referred for a more extensive coverage of the points made here.

First of all it should be noted that there are many similarities between the above description of chronic fatigue and neurasthenia (see Komaroff, 1988; White, 1989). Indeed, Cobb (1920) defined neurasthenia as 'a condition of nervous exhaustion, characterized by undue fatigue on slightest exertion, both physical and mental, with which are associated symptoms of abnormal functioning, mainly referrable to disorders of the vegetative nervous system. The chief symptoms are headache, gastrointestinal disturbances and subjective sensations of all kinds'. However, by the 1920s neurasthenia was replaced by new psychiatric diagnoses and the dominant view was that all neurasthenic states were, in reality, depression.

Even early descriptions of neurasthenia linked it with febrile disease, especially with influenza. However, other agents such as alimentary bacteria, typhoid, streptococcus and brucellosis were also implicated. Indeed, there was some success in linking mysterious clinical conditions to infective agents and in the USA it became popular to link chronic fatigue with the Epstein Barr virus. In the UK, more attention was devoted to the enterovirus family, starting with the alleged association between poliovirus and Royal Free disease, and continuing with Scottish research linking the coxsackie virus to epidemic myalgic encephalomyelitis. However, it should also be noted that other researchers (e.g. McEvedy and Beard, 1970) claimed that epidemic myalgic encephalomyelitis was an example of mass hysteria.

This brief historical account shows that one of the major issues in studying CFS has been aetiology. However, there has also been considerable disagreement over case definition and an attempt to resolve this is described in the next section. Following this the evidence for peripheral, central and psychiatric explanations of the syndrome will be reviewed.

CASE DEFINITION

Holmes et al. (1988) attempted to address the problem of case definition; although this was a welcome advance, the definition proved to be unsatisfactory in practice (see Manu et al., 1988; Komaroff and Geiger, 1989). Other definitions have proved to be unsatisfactory and have not been widely accepted (Lloyd et al., 1988). In an attempt to produce guidelines for research on the chronic fatigue syndrome a meeting was held in Oxford in 1990 (see Sharpe et al., 1991). Two broad syndromes were identified, the first being the chronic fatigue syndrome characterized as follows:

1. Fatigue is the principal symptom and this is severe, disabling, and affects physical and mental functioning. The symptom of fatigue must be present for at least six months, during which it occurs at least 50 per cent of the time.
2. Other symptoms may be present such as myalgia, mood and sleep disturbance.
3. The syndrome has a definite onset which is not lifelong.
4. Patients with established conditions known to produce fatigue (e.g. severe anaemia) should be excluded. Similarly, patients with a current diagnosis of schizophrenia, manic depressive illness, substance abuse, eating disorder or proven organic brain disease should also be excluded.

The second syndrome, the post-infectious fatigue syndrome (PIFS) is a subtype of CFS which either follows or is associated with a current infection. PIFS patients must fulfil the criteria for CFS and there should also be definite evidence of infection. The syndrome should also be present for a minimum of six months after the onset of infection.

The meeting also produced guidelines for conducting research; these are described later in the chapter.

The next sections consider CFS and neuromuscular disorder, psychiatry, infection and the immune system. The reader is referred to Wessely (1991b) for more detailed coverage of the points made here.

CFS and neuromuscular disorder

It is now quite clear that neuromuscular abnormalities cannot alone account for the features of CFS. Indeed, nerve conduction studies are invariably normal and studies of dynamic muscle function have demonstrated no abnormalities, except for those which are a consequence of physical inactivity. Jamal and Hansen (1985) found that single fibre EMG confirmed prolonged muscle jitters in 75 per cent of the patients tested. However, an attempted replication (Roberts, 1990) only demonstrated abnormal jitter values in four out of thirty cases. Arnold *et al.* (1984) demonstrated that CFS patients have a derangement in muscle energy metabolism with abnormally early intracellular acidosis, out of proportion to the associated changes in high-energy phosphates. However, the significance of these abnormalities on nuclear magnetic spectroscopy remains disputed (Lewis and Haller, 1991).

CFS and psychiatry

Many chronic fatigue patients fulfil operational criteria for psychiatric disorder. However, this does not mean that the symptoms are fictitious or that psychiatric disorder is the cause of the CFS. It is quite likely that in some patients psychiatric disorder has been misdiagnosed as CFS. In others both the CFS and psychopathology may be due to an underlying condition, and in others the psychiatric symptoms may be a consequence of physical disorder. However, it should be noted that CFS cannot be explained either directly in terms of psychiatric disorder nor in terms of a psychological reaction to physical disease.

CFS, infection and the immune system

It will be recalled that CFS has been linked with the Epstein Barr virus in the USA, coxsackie viruses in the UK, and now with the Human Herpes Virus 6. However, enthusiasm for these views has now subsided and even the more sophisticated virological studies (e.g. Gow *et al.*, 1991) are open to criticism that they used highly selected samples and that the results may not generalize to other groups of patients. Indeed, premature claims of detection of viruses may just reflect the neglect of basic research principles. Only longitudinal studies following a proven infective episode will provide clear information about the post-infectious fatigue syndrome.

Immunological abnormalities in CFS are now attracting increasing attention. There is clear evidence of abnormalities, such as raised circulating immune complexes and decreased natural killer cell function, but the effects are often inconsistent, non-specific, and not related to clinical findings (see Buchwald and Komaroff, 1991; Strauss, 1988). More recent studies, using sophisticated methodology, have yet to report their findings formally, but Wessely (1991b) suggests that these preliminary results support the idea of non-specific dysregulation of immune function in a minority of CFS patients, and that this occurs irrespective of psychiatric status.

One may summarize by saying that there is evidence that *some* CFS patients have a chronic viral infection, muscle damage and immune system abnormalities. Many CFS patients also report psychiatric symptoms. The next section describes recent research on performance impairments observed in the CFS. This research has the advantage that it follows research in other disciplines and there are established guidelines for carrying out such research. Indeed, it is now clear that greater emphasis must be placed on reliability and generalizability, and that appropriate controls must also be studied. Similarly, routine psychiatric assessments must be included.

GUIDELINES FOR RESEARCH

At the Oxford meeting (see Sharpe *et al.*, 1991) the following guidelines were agreed:

1. *Sampling.* The way in which the sample was obtained should be clearly described. In particular, it is essential to know whether the sample was recruited from primary care or from secondary referral centres.

2. *Comparison groups.* In the current state of knowledge, multiple comparison groups may be required. These may include healthy controls, patients with neuromuscular disorder, patients with conditions causing inactivity, patients with depressive disorder, and patients with known infectious diseases.
3. *Study design.* Both cross-sectional and longitudinal designs may be useful.
4. *Measurements.* All measures should be reliable, valid and reproducible between centres.
5. *Reporting of studies.* It should be clearly stated whether CFS or PIFS is being studied. The degree of disability should be measured and stated. The exclusion criteria described and the degree of investigation specified. All patients should be assessed for associated psychiatric disorder and the results of this assessment reported.

CFS AND PERFORMANCE

The Sussex programme

This involved a questionnaire study of over two hundred CFS patients aimed at assessing subjective reports of problems of memory, attention and motor function. Subjects from the above sample then carried out objective tests of memory, attention and perceptual–motor skills. The CFS subjects were a community sample who volunteered to participate in the research. They were compared with matched healthy controls and also with patients recovering from acute respiratory viral illnesses (influenza-like illnesses) and those with AIDS. The intention was also to compare the CFS group with depressed patients and also with those with muscle damage (e.g. patients with poliomyositis). However, this was not possible and is being undertaken as part of the new Cardiff programme. It was possible to retest some patients six months later which meant that the reliability of any findings could be assessed.

The Glasgow study

In collaboration with Professor Behan, Glasgow University, a similar study to the Sussex one was carried out on a selected sample of the patients referred to the Neurology Department at the Southern General Hospital, Glasgow. This study allowed us to determine whether results obtained with a community sample were also obtained with a sample at a tertiary referral centre. Fifty-seven patients were compared with nineteen matched healthy controls. The patients were selected according to the following criteria:

1. Presence of severe fatigue for six months or more which reduced the patient's premorbid level of activity by 50 per cent or more.

2. The presence of at least three of the following symptoms: myalgia, nocturnal sweating, fever, hot flushes or feeling cold, fluctuations in body weight, changes in appetite and bowel habit, depression, anxiety, poor memory and concentration.

Chronic infections, malignancy and other conditions which may cause fatigue were excluded by clinical examination and appropriate laboratory investigations. None of the patients had a past medical or family history of depression or any other major psychiatric illness, and all patients had a good work record and a well-adjusted premorbid personality. Patients on medication (e.g. anti-depressants) were excluded from the study.

Assessment of the nature of the illness, current symptoms and psychopathology

In order to assess the characteristics of the illness and current symptoms we have developed our own questionnaire. This provides information on: (1) demographics; (2) history of the illness; (3) information on diagnoses, tests for presence of viruses, tests for muscle damage; (4) current state of health; (5) factors which change the person's condition. In addition to this patients filled in a revised version of the Middlesex Hospital Questionnaire (Crown and Crisp, 1966) which measures anxiety, depression, somatic symptoms and obsessional symptoms over the last six weeks. The subjects also filled in the Cognitive Failures Questionnaire (Broadbent et al., 1982) which measures failures of attention, memory and motor function.

Sussex study: results of the survey

Two hundred and thirty-two CFS subjects returned questionnaires and they were compared with one hundred controls. Thirty-six per cent of the CFS sample reported that they had received a positive result regarding the presence of a viral infection. Table 10.1 shows the cognitive failures scores and the anxiety, depression and somatic symptoms scores for the CFS subjects (split into those with a positive virus identification and those who had not) and the controls. The results showed that the CFS subjects reported more cognitive failures than the control subjects (this was true for both the virus positive and negative groups). Certain types of problem were more frequently reported by the CFS patients than others; these are shown in Table 10.2.

These results confirm anecdotal reports which have suggested that CFS patients have concentration problems, memory impairments and suffer from anomia.

The CFS patients had higher levels of anxiety, somatic symptoms and depression than the controls. One of the problems of using questionnaires

Table 10.1 Mean scores from the Middlesex Hospital Questionnaire and Cognitive Failures Questionnaire for controls, patients who had a positive virus identification (CFS+) and those who had a negative result or no assay (CFS−)

	Anxiety	*Somatic symptoms*	*Depression*	*Cognitive failures*
Controls	4.3	3.3	3.3	42.2
$n = 100$	(2.9)	(2.3)	(2.5)	(11.7)
CFS+	6.4	6.3	7.7	54.9
$n = 83$	(2.8)	(2.9)	(2.6)	(15.7)
CFS−	7.0	7.1	8.1	52.7
$n = 149$	(3.4)	(3.4)	(2.8)	(19.3)

High scores = high levels of anxiety, etc.
Standard deviations in parentheses.

Table 10.2 Types of cognitive failure reported by CFS group

Do you read something and find you haven't been thinking about it and must read it again?

Do you find you forget why you went from one part of the house to the other?

Do you fail to notice signposts on the road?

Do you find you forget whether you've turned off a light or a fire or locked the door?

Do you fail to listen to people's names when you are meeting them?

Do you fail to hear people speaking to you when you are doing something else?

Do you find yourself suddenly wondering whether you've used a word correctly?

Do you have trouble making up your mind?

Do you forget where you put something like a newspaper or a book?

Do you daydream when you ought to be listening to something?

Do you find you forget people's names?

Do you start doing one thing at home and get distracted into doing something else unintentionally?

Do you find you can't quite remember something although it's on the tip of your tongue?

Table 10.3 Cognitive failures scores for CFS patients with high and low neuroticism scores

	High neuroticism	*Low neuroticism*
CFS+	62.6	47.7
	(14.0)	(16.7)
CFS−	61.0	46.1
	(18.4)	(17.4)

CFS+ patients who have had a positive result from a test for the presence of a virus; CFS−, a negative result or no test.
Standard deviations in parentheses.

to assess behavioural impairments is that subjects with high CFQ scores also tend to have high neuroticism scores. The subjects in the present CFS sample were subdivided into those with high and low neuroticism scores (on the basis of a median split) and it was found that only those with high levels of psychopathology were significantly different from the controls. These results are shown in Table 10.3.

These results suggest that the higher CFQ scores of the CFS subjects reflect the higher levels of psychopathology in this group. The next stage in the research was to determine whether the reported deficits would be verified using objective measures of performance.

Sussex study: objective measures of performance

On the basis of the questionnaire results it was possible to select eighteen CFS patients who had received a positive result on the VP1 test (see Mowbray, 1991) or who had been shown to have high levels of EBV antibodies. These patients were compared with nine matched healthy control subjects. The

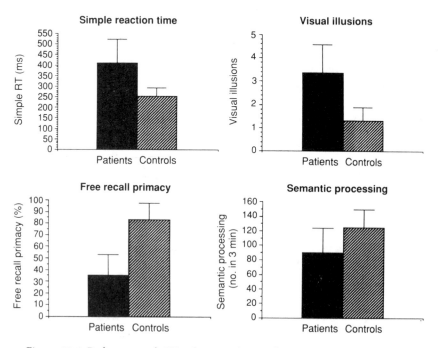

Figure 10.1 Performance of CFS subjects and controls on a range of tasks. (After Smith, 1991. Standard deviations shown as bars)

results from the study are described in detail in Smith (1991) and may be briefly summarized as follows:

1. There was clear evidence of slower motor performance, increased visual sensitivity and memory deficits in the CFS group. These effects are shown in Figure 10.1.
2. It is unlikely that these reflect a general impairment of intellectual function as the digit span performance of the two groups was very similar.
3. There was little evidence of the performance impairments being related to the levels of depression of the patients.

The first question one must ask about the data presented here is whether it is replicable. This was examined by repeating the procedure using a sample of CFS patients in Glasgow.

The Glasgow study: a replication and extension of the original Sussex study (Smith *et al.*, submitted)

The patients and controls did not differ significantly in age or education level. The average length of the patients' illness was five years, with a range of one to thirty-one years. Forty per cent of the patients reported that their illness was preceded by an influenza-like illness, 10 per cent glandular fever, 28 per cent high levels of stress, and the remainder could not recall any specific event. Eighty-five per cent of the patients had received a diagnosis of CFS from a doctor. Five per cent of the patients reported that their present condition was worse than at any stage of the illness, 26 per cent regarded it as bad, 35 per cent bad with some recovery, 28 per cent felt they were recovering with some relapses, and 5 per cent felt that they had recovered. Thirty per cent of the patients reported that the previous month had been a bad one with regard to their illness, 44 per cent thought it was average, and 26 per cent reported that it had been a good month. Sixty-three per cent stated that exercise made the condition worse, with 40 per cent reporting that even gentle walking led to a deterioration. Forty-six per cent reported that drinking alcohol increased the severity of the symptoms. Mental effort contributed to a worsening of the condition of 77 per cent of the sample, and 81 per cent reported that stress made their illness worse.

The CFS subjects completed a symptom checklist and the percentage of subjects with the following symptoms are shown in Table 10.4.

The results from the questionnaires showed that the CFS patients reported significantly higher levels of depression, anxiety, physical symptoms and cognitive failures than the controls. These effects are shown in Figure 10.2.

Mood was assessed at the time of testing and the CFS patients rated themselves less alert, more feeble, less clear-headed, more clumsy, more

Table 10.4 Percentage of CFS subjects reporting various symptoms. (After Smith *et al.*, submitted)

Physical weakness	82%	Excessive fatigue	75%
Legs feeling heavy	58%	Muscle pain	84%
Pain in chest	40%	Pain in joints	63%
Nausea	42%	Indigestion	33%
Bloated stomach	49%	Wind	44%
Sore throat	37%	Headache	75%
Earache	17%	Sore eyes	49%
Sensitive to noise	54%	Sensitive to light	60%
Feeling hot/cold	70%	Sweating	51%
Shivering	37%	Swollen glands	19%
Racing heart	30%	Insomnia	51%
Depression	47%	Anxiety	51%
Loss of concentration	84%	Loss of memory	68%
Allergies	21%		

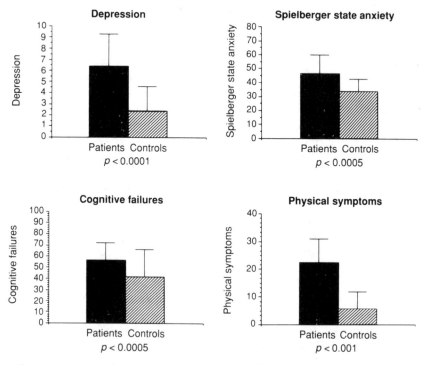

Figure 10.2 Mean depression, anxiety, physical symptoms and cognitive failures scores of CFS and control groups. Standard deviations shown as bars. (After Smith *et al.*, submitted.)

lethargic, more discontented, more mentally slow, more dreamy, more incompetent, sadder and more depressed than the controls.

The performance data showed that the CFS group were slower on simple reaction time and five-choice serial response tasks. The patients were also more visually sensitive than the controls (i.e. they reported more illusions of movement, colour, etc. when shown a visually disturbing figure). The CFS group were worse at sustaining attention and were more easily distracted by irrelevant stimuli. Semantic processing, speed of logical reasoning and recognition memory were also impaired but digit span and free recall performance did not differ significantly from the controls. In other words, the results generally replicated the findings obtained in the initial Sussex study.

Further analyses were carried out to determine whether the performance impairments were related to levels of depression. The results showed that none of the performance impairments could be attributed to psychopathology. Laboratory data on damage of muscle mitochondria and the presence of enteroviral genomic RNA sequences was available for some of the CFS subjects. However, the results showed no difference between those with positive scores on these assays and other CFS subjects.

Overall, this study confirmed the results of Smith (1991) which shows that the motor impairments, attentional problems and memory deficits are present in different samples of CFS patients. The data also demonstrate that these effects do not reflect depression and are not related to measures of infection or muscular damage. Before considering possible explanations of the effects some other studies will be described. These had two aims, the first being to look at the reliability of the performance impairments over time, the second being to compare the impairments with those found in viral illnesses.

RELIABILITY OF THE PERFORMANCE IMPAIRMENTS ASSOCIATED WITH CFS

Smith *et al.* (in preparation, a) compared the performance of eight CFS subjects with twenty-three healthy controls on a variety of pencil and paper tests of performance. They then retested the subjects approximately six months later. The two groups of subjects were matched with regard to age and education. As usual, the CFS subjects had higher scores for depression, somatic symptoms and cognitive failures and this was true on both occasions. The CFS subjects were slower on a motor task (involving transferring pegs from a full solitaire set to an empty one), and performed attention tasks (search and memory tasks), logical reasoning tasks and semantic memory tasks more slowly and less accurately. These effects were obtained on both occasions which shows that the performance impairments associated with the CFS are reliable over time. These data are shown in Figure 10.3.

Smith *et al.* (in preparation, b) carried out a similar study using a computerized battery of performance tests measuring motor skills, attention and aspects of memory. Nine CFS patients were retested six months later as were nineteen matched healthy controls. The controls were slightly younger and better educated than the CFS subjects but when these factors were included in the analysis they did not modify any of the differences between controls and CFS subjects. The patients were more depressed than the controls, although there were some patients with low levels of psychopathology and some controls with quite high levels. When depression was included as a factor in the analyses none of the differences between the CFS subjects and controls disappeared. Indeed, depression had little effect on performance which makes it difficult to account for any of the CFS-performance effects in terms of psychopathology.

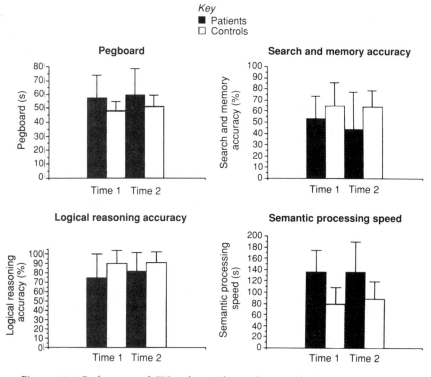

Figure 10.3 Performance of CFS and controls on a battery of tests. T_2 approximately six months after T_1. Standard deviations shown as bars. (Smith *et al.*, in preparation, a.)

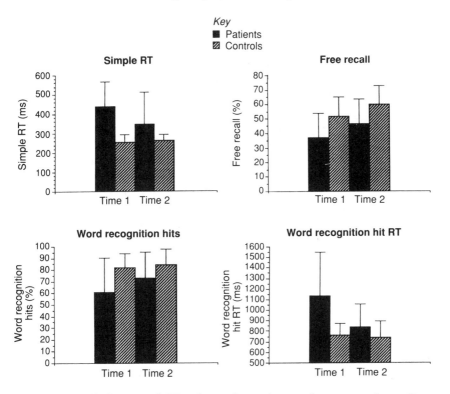

Figure 10.4 Performance of CFS and controls on a battery of computerized tests. T_2 approximately six months after T_1. Standard deviations shown as bars. (Smith *et al.*, in preparation, b.)

The CFS patients were slower on motor tasks (simple reaction time, two-choice reaction time and number matching reaction time). The results from the memory tasks showed that there was no difference between the groups on digit span, memory scanning or picture recognition. However, free recall and delayed word recognition accuracy were impaired and the CFS subjects took longer than the controls to decide whether words or pictures were shown before. All of these effects were still present on retest (both positive and negative results). In many tasks the patients showed a greater practice effect than the control subjects but they still performed at a lower level than the controls. These effects are shown in Figure 10.4.

Again, these results show that the selective impairments observed in the performance of CFS subjects are reliable and cannot be accounted for by depression. The next set of studies addressed the question of whether the effects seen in CFS resembled those seen in viral illnesses.

VIRAL ILLNESSES AND CFS

Smith *et al.* (in preparation, c) compared the performance of twenty-five CFS patients with thirty-two healthy controls and ten patients with a prolonged illness following influenza (diagnosed by a clinician). The groups did not differ significantly in age or education level. Both the CFS subjects and influenza subjects had higher levels of depression than the controls. In terms of psychomotor performance the CFS subjects were slower than the influenza subjects who were slower than the controls. However, the influenza subjects were more impaired on tests of sustained attention and selective attention than the CFS subjects or controls. Both influenza and CFS subjects were impaired on free recall, recognition memory and semantic memory tasks compared to the control group. These results are shown in Figure 10.5.

Overall, the results show a remarkable similarity between the impairments observed in patients with CFS and those who have had a prolonged

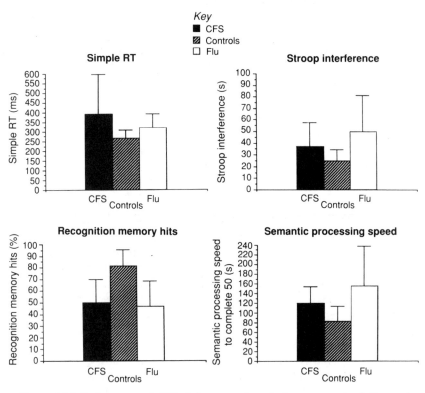

Figure 10.5 Performance of CFS, influenza and control groups on a battery of performance tests. Standard deviations shown as bars. (Smith *et al.*, in preparation, c.)

illness after influenza. Indeed, one of the characteristics of the influenza group was that they all reported that they were atopic (had a large number of allergies, or were asthmatic) and this is also common in CFS.

Smith *et al.* (in preparation, b) compared the CFS subjects with three patients with AIDS. The results showed that the impairments were very similar in the two groups. Indeed, if anything, the CFS subjects were more impaired on psychomotor tasks than were the AIDS patients.

CONFIRMATION FROM THE USA

A recent paper from the USA (Daugherty *et al.*, 1991) reports data on the psychological performance of a group of patients with CFS. The clinical characteristics of this group are summarized in Table 10.5.

Cognitive function tests were carried out on nineteen of the twenty patients and these revealed evidence of significant dysfunction. These results are summarized in Table 10.6.

Table 10.5 Clinical characteristics of the Nevada CFS patients. (After Daugherty *et al.*, 1991)

Acute onset of influenza-like symptoms, including myalgia, with subsequent extreme fatigue of several months' duration

Recurrent upper respiratory tract infection

Tender, enlarged lymph nodes

Night sweats and / or low-grade temperature

Difficulty concentrating, trouble with memory, and signs of depression

Absence of evidence for endocrine, neoplastic or collagen vascular disease

Table 10.6 Performance impairments in the Nevada CFS patients. (After Daugherty *et al.*, 1991)

Test	Mean percentage points below T-score norms
Psychometric intelligence (full-scale IQ)	74
Attention	74
Sequencing ability	32
Problem solving	58
Kinesthetic deficit (actual performance test)	53
Motor skills	
Grip strength, dominant	47
Grip strength, non-dominant	63
Tapping, dominant	32
Tapping, non-dominant	26
Verbal memory	68
Visual memory	37

While most patients scored in the pathological range on one or more of the functions measured the most pronounced and frequent deficits were found in tests of attention–concentration, problem-solving, kinaesthetic ability and verbal memory. These results confirm the general view obtained from the Sussex and Glasgow studies and show that the performance impairments observed in CFS generalize to different populations and may be detected using different methodologies.

MECHANISMS INVOLVED IN THE PERFORMANCE IMPAIRMENTS IN CFS

The results from the Sussex and Glasgow studies show that the performance impairments do not reflect the depression often reported by CFS patients. Several possible explanations of the impairments must now be considered. The first is that the impairments reflect structural damage to the brain. Evidence for this view comes from the Daugherty *et al.* (1991) study which included MRI scans of the patients. These showed two patterns of abnormality, the more frequent showing tiny punctate foci with abnormally increased signal intensity in the upper central semiovale and bilaterallly in the high parasagittal convolution white matter tracts. The second pattern showed multiple bilateral patchy areas of abnormally increased signal intensity in the white matter tracts of the brain. These were located in the deep frontal white matter and peripherally in the white matter and were not periventricular. The authors state that the observed patterns are consistent with an atypical organic brain syndrome and are not the same as seen in Alzheimer's disease, focal head injuries, multiple sclerosis, systemic lupus erythematosus, personality disorders, depression, psychosis, anxiety or stress. Indeed, the most similar condition is HIV infection, which fits in with the results obtained by Smith *et al.* (in preparation, b).

Alternatively, the effects could be due to an imbalance of neurotransmitter function. Results from a study measuring evoked potentials do show that the effects observed in CFS patients are very similar to those produced by the cholinergic antagonist scopolamine (Prasher *et al.*, 1990). If this is the case it may be possible to reverse any impairments by suitable pharmacological interventions.

Other factors may also underline some of the impairments. For example, the slower motor performance may be a peripheral effect that reflects inactivity or direct damage to the muscles. Now that performance impairments have been demonstrated, we are in the position where we can consider the precise nature of the neurological dysfunction underlying these effects. Similarly, we can examine how this may be induced by viral infections and/or by immune system abnormalities. One can then use a prospective, longitudinal method-ology to look at the aetiology of the various effects.

CONCLUSIONS

The studies reviewed in this chapter demonstrate that CFS patients show impaired performance in a number of domains. Typically, they are slower at psychomotor tasks, have impaired selective and sustained attention, impaired recall and recognition memory, and are slower and less accurate when performing working memory and semantic memory tasks. These results have been obtained in different laboratories using different populations of subjects, and appear to be reliable over time. Although no direct comparison with depressed patients has been carried out, it appears unlikely that the effects can be attributed to depression as comparable results have been obtained in the CFS subjects with high and low levels of depression. Indeed, the most comparable groups of patients tested to date appear to be those with a prolonged influenza-like illness and those with AIDS. However, it should be noted that there is considerable heterogeneity in the clinical profile and aetiology of CFS and it is unlikely that *all* CFS patients will show identical performance impairments. Indeed, it is likely that several mechanisms underlie the effects reported here and further research is clearly needed to clarify the incidence of different forms of neurological dysfunction and the aetiology that led to the different conditions. It should be noted, however, that the performance impairments observed here may be of some diagnostic value, and they may also be useful indicators of changes in the patient's condition and the efficacy of treatment. They may also be of occupational relevance in that it is clearly not desirable or safe for impaired individuals to carry out certain activities. Objective assessment of performance is the best way to address this issue rather than assuming that we can infer the ability to perform efficiently and safely from a clinical examination.

REFERENCES

Arnold, D.I., Radda, G.K., Bore, P.I., Styles, P. and Taylor, D.I. (1984). Excessive intracellular acidosis of skeletal muscle on exercise in a patient with a post-viral exhaustion/fatigue syndrome. *Lancet* 1367–9.

Broadbent, D.E., Cooper, P.J., FitzGerald, P.F. and Parkes, K.R. (1982). The cognitive failures questionnaire (CFQ) and its correlates. *British Journal of Clinical Psychology* 21: 1–6.

Buchwald, D. and Komaroff, A. (1991). Review of laboratory findings for patients with chronic fatigue syndrome. *Review of Infectious Diseases* 13 (Supplement 1): 12–18.

Cobb, I.A. (1920). *Manual of Neurasthenia (Nervous Exhaustion)*. London: Baillière, Tindall & Cox.

Crown, S. and Crisp, A.H. (1966). A short clinical diagnostic self-rating scale for psychoneurotic patients. *British Journal of Psychiatry* 112: 917–23.

Daugherty, S.A., Henry, B.E., Peterson, D.L., Swarts, R.L., Bastien, S. and Thomas, R.S. (1991). Chronic fatigue syndrome in Northern Nevada. *Reviews of Infectious Diseases* **13**: 39–44.

Gow, J.W., Behan, W.M.H., Clements, G.B., Woodall, C., Riding, M. and Behan, P.O. (1991). Enteroviral RNA sequences detected by polymerase chain reaction in muscle of patients with postviral fatigue syndrome. *British Medical Journal* **302**: 692–6

Holmes, G.P., Kaplan, J.E., Gantz, N.M., Komaroff, A.L., Schonberger, L.B., Straus, S.E., Jones, J.F., Dubois, R.E., Cunningham-Rundles, C., Pahwa, S., Tosato, G., Zegans, L.S., Purtilo, D.T., Brown, N., Schooley, R.T. and Brus, I. (1988). Chronic fatigue syndrome: a working case definition. *Annals of Internal Medicine* **308**: 387–9.

Jamal, G.A. and Hansen, S. (1985). Electrophysiological studies in the post-viral fatigue syndrome. *Journal of Neurology, Neurosurgery and Psychiatry* **48**: 691–4.

Komaroff, A. (1988). Chronic fatigue syndromes: relationship to chronic viral infections. *Journal of Virological Methods* **21**: 3–10.

Komaroff, A. and Geiger, A. (1989). Does the CDC working case definition of chronic fatigue syndrome (CFS) identify a distinct group? *Clinical Research* **37**: 778A.

Lewis, S. and Haller, R. (1991). Physiologic measurement of exercise and fatigue with special reference to chronic fatigue syndrome. *Reviews of Infectious Diseases* **13** (Supplement 1): 98–108.

Lloyd, A.R., Wakefield, A., Boughton, C. and Dwyer, J. (1988). What is myalgic encephalo-myelitis? *Lancet* 1286–7.

Manu, P., Lane, T.J. and Matthews, D.A. (1988). The frequency of the chronic fatigue syndrome in patients with symptoms of persistent fatigue. *Annals of Internal Medicine* **109**: 554–6.

McEvedy, C.P. and Beard, A.W. (1970). Royal Free epidemic of 1955: a reconsideration. *British Medical Journal* **1**: 7–11.

Mowbray, J. (1991). Enterovirus and Epstein-Barr virus in M.E. In *Post-viral Fatigue Syndrome (M.E.)*, edited by R. Jenkins and J. Mowbray. Chichester: Wiley, pp. 61–74.

Prasher, D., Smith, A. and Findley, L. (1990). Sensory and cognitive event-related potentials in myalgic encephalomyelitis. *Journal of Neurology, Neurosurgery and Psychiatry* **53**: 247–53.

Roberts, L. (1990). Single fibre EMG studies on the chronic fatigue syndrome. *Journal of Neurological Sciences* **98** (Supplement): 97.

Sharpe, M., Archard, L., Banatvala, J., Behan, P., Booth, R., Borysiewicz, L., Clare, A., Clifford Rose, R., David, A., Edwards, R., Hawton, K., Lambert, H., Lane, R., Mann, A., McDonald, L., Mowbray, J., Pearson, D., Pelosi, A., Peters, T., Peto, T., Preedy, V., Smith, A., Smith, D., Taylor, D., Tyrrell, D., Wallace, P., Warrell, D., Wessely, S., White, P., Wood, C. and Wright, D. (1991). A report. Chronic fatigue syndrome: guidelines for research. *Journal of the Royal Society of Medicine* **84**: 118–21.

Smith, A.P. (1991). Cognitive changes in myalgic encephalomyelitis. In *Post-viral Fatigue Syndrome (M.E.)*, edited by R. Jenkins and J. Mowbray. Chichester: Wiley, pp. 179–94.

Smith, A.P., Behan, P.O., Bell, W., Millar, K. and Bakheit, M. (submitted). Behavioural problems associated with the post-viral fatigue syndrome.

Smith, A.P., Smith, B.A. and Armer, L. (in preparation, a). The chronic fatigue syndrome: performance and mood effects.

Smith, A.P., Smith, B.A., Armer, L., Christmas, L., Simpson, P. and Wesnes, K. (in preparation, b). Performance deficits associated with HIV infection and the chronic fatigue syndrome.

Smith, A.P., Smith, B.A. and Watkins, J. (in preparation, c). Chronic fatigue syndrome, influenza and performance.

Straus, S. (1988). The chronic mononucleosis syndrome. *Journal of Infectious Diseases* **157**: 405–12.

Wessely, S. (1991a). History of postviral fatigue syndrome. *British Medical Bulletin* **47**.

Wessely, S. (1991b). Chronic fatigue syndrome. *J. Neurology, Neurosurgery and Psychiatry* **54**.

White, P. (1989). Fatigue syndrome: neurasthenia revived. *British Medical Journal* **298**: 1199–200.

11

Prescribed Psychotropic Drugs: the Major and Minor Tranquillizers

L.R. HARTLEY

INTRODUCTION

Over the past few years there has been growing interest in the effects drugs such as tranquillizers have on performance, and in accounting for their effects on human information processing and cognition. This interest has arisen because the classes of drugs termed tranquillizers are some of the most potent and successful drugs available and they have been used increasingly widely to treat people with a range of problems in many different situations. In the past it was assumed that administration of any drug was detrimental to performance and that this precluded their use in settings outside the strict clinical environment. In part, this was because the therapeutic effect of drugs has traditionally been assessed by global ratings of the personal and clinical conduct and behaviour of patients to whom they have been administered. However, the specific effects of drugs on information processing and cognition is not revealed by global surveys. Recent developments in pharmacology have shown that psychoactive medications such as tranquillizers operate upon complex chemical and physical processes in the nervous system. Indeed, theoretical advances in understanding the nervous system and the effect drugs have on it, have emphasized their complex role in determining behaviour. Accordingly, it has come to be appreciated that these many and complex effects of drugs on information processing and cognition can only be understood by detailed studies of their impact.

These recent developments in pharmacology have rendered unnecessary any severe restrictions on the widespread use of tranquillizers, so that the benefits of tranquillizers are available to most people. Indeed, many of the people now receiving these drugs are daily employed in highly skilled and

HANDBOOK OF HUMAN PERFORMANCE
VOLUME 2 ISBN 0-12-650352-4

demanding jobs such as flying aircraft, navigating ships, making complex decisions or dealing with difficult human relationships. Nevertheless, it is quite likely that some dosages of particular tranquillizers impair some of the cognitive processes required in people's daily jobs and private lives. It is, therefore, important to identify the drugs and their doses which put their recipients at increased risk of accident or poor decision-making.

Generally speaking, the potentially adverse effects of drugs upon performance can be grouped into three classes. Most drugs, tranquillizers included, not only have a specific benefit on the symptoms for which they are prescribed but also often have other concurrent and unwanted side-effects such as causing drowsiness or mental confusion. A second adverse effect can occur in the form of residual after-effects of drugs taken earlier. For example, some tranquillizing hypnotics, administered to induce sleep, can impair performance on the following day. Thirdly, prolonged administration of drugs can lead to forms of dependence on them. Withdrawal of the drug could then be accompanied by a range of adverse effects, many of which would be the augmented symptoms for which the drugs were administered in the first place, such as insomnia or anxiety. In evaluating the potential beneficial and adverse effects of drugs on performance it is important to characterize the profile of desirable and undesirable effects from these perspectives. Furthermore, the impact of dose and duration of action of the drugs upon performance must be considered.

This chapter first presents some elementary pharmacological considerations in the use and choice of drugs. A brief description of the clinical use of tranquillizers and related compounds is then given. The main part of the chapter is a consideration of the impact of drugs on information processing and cognition, and a framework for this is provided by a discussion of their effect within stage and hierarchical models of cognitive processes. Particular attention is given to studies of the effects of drugs on tasks of occupational importance such as driving-related skills. Lastly, the implications of stage and hierarchical models of information processing and cognition for countermeasures to the impact of drugs on performance are considered. These considerations suggest several strategies to counter the adverse effects of drugs on driving.

GENERAL CONSIDERATIONS IN DRUG ADMINISTRATION

A large number of factors, many beyond the scope of the present chapter, determine how a drug produces its characteristic effect. A full discussion of these factors can be found in Goodman and Gilman (1976). The following summarizes these considerations.

To achieve its effect, a drug must reach an adequate concentration at its sites of action in the nervous system, and particularly in the brain in the case of tranquillizers. Although this is obviously a function of the amount of drug administered, the concentrations reached at the sites will also depend upon the drug's potential for absorption from the place of administration, distribution in the tissues of the body, binding and localization in particular tissues, metabolic inactivation and excretion from the body. At any time the concentration of the drug at its target site represents an equilibrium between these factors and the physio-chemical form in which the drug is administered, and an individual's physical chemistry (Figure 11.1).

By way of example, changes in the physical chemistry of the drug can change its duration of action and potency many-fold. Correspondingly, differences in the physical chemistry between individuals, and within individuals from day to day, as a consequence of weight, diet, fitness, stress, time of day, activity and fatigue, can modify the impact of a drug.

Cellular mechanisms of action

Most tranquillizers are thought to act by chemically affecting cell enzymes or combining with nerve cells (Figure 11.2). Accordingly, the actions of drugs are directly related to their chemical structure. This understanding has been utilized by drug manufacturers who, by making changes in the chemistry of, for example, the benzodiazepine minor tranquillizers, have produced a range of similar drugs differing in longevity, potency and therapeutic potential. To accomplish their action most tranquillizers combine with receptor sites on one or more specific types of cell in the nervous system. By doing so the drug affects the action of the neurotransmitters by which those nerve cells communicate.

Thus, the action of most tranquillizers can be localized to the known neurotransmitters. Often, the effect of a drug can be understood because it augments or antagonizes the action of the neurotransmitters, or indeed of other drugs, by competing with them to combine with the receptor sites on cells. There is little doubt that the efficiency of a drug depends upon some function of the number or rate of occupation of specific receptor sites on the nerve cells.

Drug variability and selectivity of action

To understand, evaluate and compare drugs, their effects must be related to dosage and characterized in terms of efficiency, variability, selectivity and time course of action following single or multiple administrations. Although all drugs are named according to their most obvious effect, such as tranquillization, this should not obscure the fact that all drugs have multiple

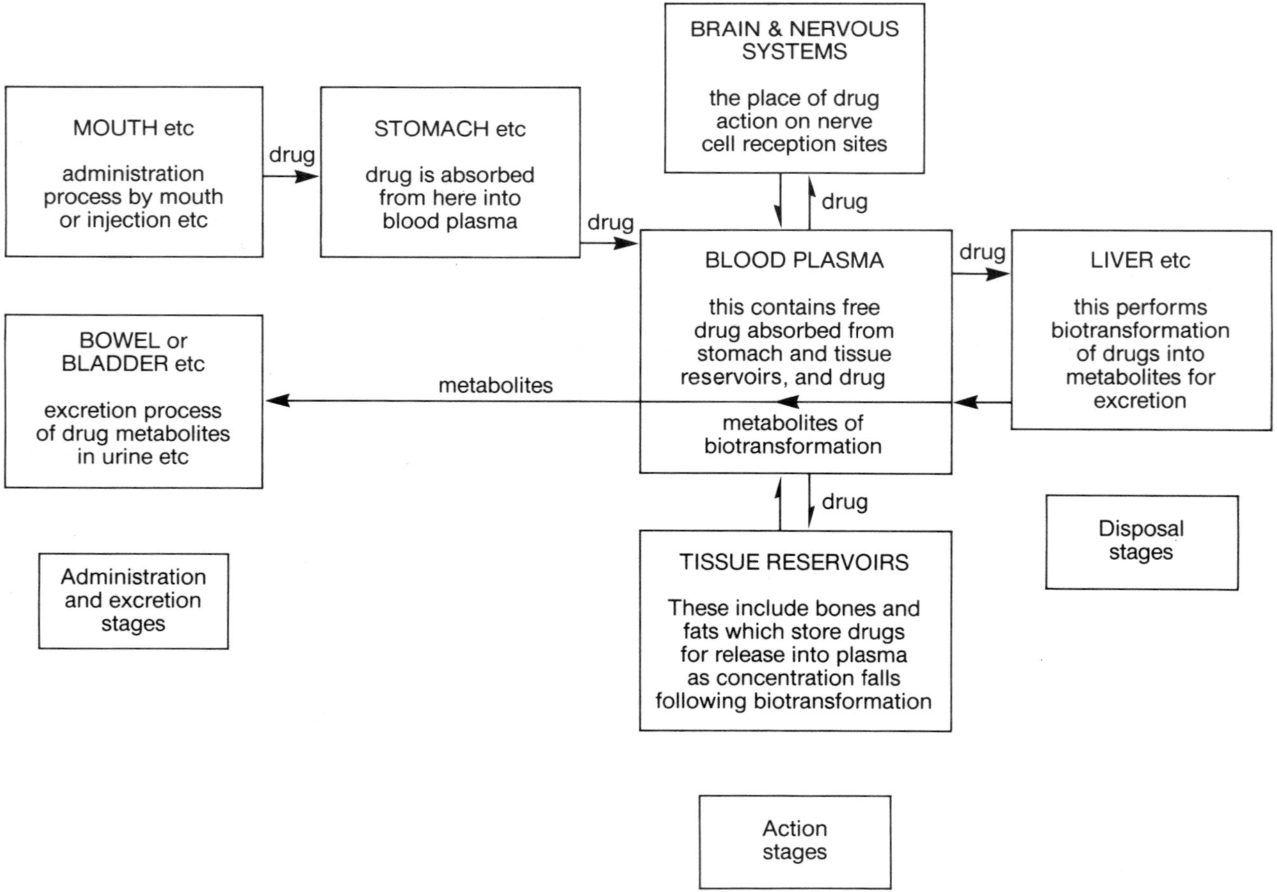

Figure 11.1 Schematic of the equilibrium reached by a drug in different compartments of the body.

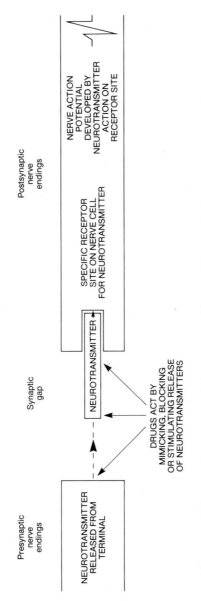

Figure 11.2 Schematic representation of the many possible sites of action of a drug at a synapse in the nervous system.

physiological and psychological actions. Some actions are desirable and beneficial, such as tranquillization, and usually dictate the name and so choice of drug. However, some actions of otherwise beneficial drugs may be adverse, such as the depression of respiration produced by some minor tranquillizers. Ideally, the drug chosen for a condition should have a highly selective, beneficial or therapeutic effect with few adverse and unwanted side-effects. Evaluations of a drug's clinical benefit take account of the relationship between the dose administered and the individual's response to each of the drug's several effects.

A further complication in the choice of a drug to administer is that the several effects of a drug such as a tranquillizer, may not follow the same time course. Each of the several actions of a drug can be described by their latency to onset, time to peak effect and duration. These factors are largely determined by the route of administration, pharmaco-dynamics and individual chemistry as discussed above. It is usual to characterize the duration of a drug's effect by the relationship between the dose and effects of the drug. These relationships are often complex and may be the composite of several effects of the tranquillizers. However, several important facts can be determined from these relationships:

1. The potency or dose of drug required to produce a given effect.
2. The margin of safety of the drug, or ratio between the dose that is clinically useful and that which is toxic.
3. The efficiency of the drug or maximum benefit that can be attained without undesirable effects.
4. The variability of the drugs or the range of effects produced within a population.

Some of the factors affecting the variability of a drug's effect are relatively easy to control. Thus, heavier individuals require larger doses to achieve the same effects. Children and the aged are often more sensitive to the effects of drugs and there are small gender differences. The manner and time of drug administration influence the variability of effect, as does the speed of its inactivation.

Tolerance and dependence to drugs

A major advantage to some tranquillizers is that little tolerance is developed to them. Tolerance can be understood at several levels, ranging from the efficiency of metabolism to behavioural adaptation to the effects of drugs. Once tolerance to a drug has developed, cross-tolerance to chemically related drugs is likely to occur. Interactions between the effects of drugs occur for a variety of reasons including the development of tolerance, cross-tolerance, competition for the receptors on cells, alterations in the absorption and distribution of the drugs or from combinations of these factors. Accordingly, drugs may act synergistically when administered together if their combined effect is greater than the sum of each administered separately; and they may act antagonistically if the converse occurs.

Lastly, dependence of psychoactive drugs is always possible, and dependence on tranquillizers is no exception, for a variety of reasons. Dependence can range from repeating administration of a drug to provide satisfaction irrespective of relief of specific symptoms, to the appearance of specific physical and mental symptoms when administration is withheld. These signs may coexist to some degree when minor tranquillizers or hypnotics are repeatedly administered for insomnia.

GENERAL CONSIDERATIONS IN TESTING DRUGS

Clinical testing

The use of global rating scales and behavioural inventories to assess drugs has provided useful clinical information but little or no information on which to base models and theories of their effects on psychological processes such as attention, memory and allocation of mental resources. Thus, traditional techniques have provided little evidence to complement developing psychological models of clinical states such as schizophrenia and anxiety. Nor have these techniques illuminated many of the specific benefits of administration of tranquillizers which are, nevertheless, the most important treatment for these conditions. Only recently have more contemporary approaches to studying the specific action of drugs, such as major tranquillizers, in normal people and patients permitted the development of psychological models of schizophrenia. The simplest of models assumes that psychological over-arousal results in heightened sensitivity to external stimulation (Kornetsky and Eliasson, 1969; see also Figure 11.3).

It is possible that such heightened sensitivity may be associated with selective neuropsychological imbalance in the clinical patient. Clinical symptoms may thus reflect imperfect processes of sustained and selective attention. Understanding the clinical benefit of major and minor tranquillizers in ameliorating these symptoms is important to developing the models further. These psychological theories are compatible with, and complement, contemporary biochemical and neurological views drawn from treatment of psychoses and neuroses by tranquillizers.

Still less do the traditional techniques provide information about the occupational significance of drugs despite the overwhelming recent evidence of the impact of major and minor tranquillizers on human performance such

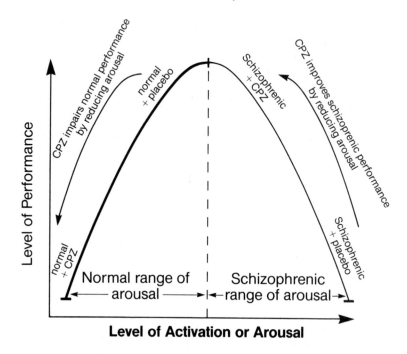

Figure 11.3 The effects of chlorpromazine (CPZ) on arousal as hypothesized by Kornetsky and Eliasson.

as driving and flying (O'Hanlon and de Gier, 1986). Testing the effects of drugs such as tranquillizers on psychological processes in clinical patients and normal people has become a major part of recent research. However, such testing presents many difficulties of design and interpretation. Some of the difficulties arise from the many considerations of administration, dynamics and multiplicity of effect of a drug, as discussed above. Some of the problems are, however, unique to testing human performance. Differences between studies in administration, dose, subject selection and testing, and limitations in the parameters investigated, make comparisons and interpretations of a drug's effect on human performance difficult.

Problems of clinical tests

In most clinical settings patients are administered a drug frequently and for a lengthy duration, but psychological studies are usually constrained to investigate the effect of a single acute dose. The significance of the psychological testing of drugs administered to normals may be limited because the clinical benefit of major tranquillizers usually takes some time to develop and clinical patients may develop tolerance to some effects of the drugs in the meantime.

Some of the problems when testing for psychological effects, raised by differences of drug administration and dynamics, can be illustrated by considering dose, time and duration parameters. As discussed above two similar drugs may show differences in potency, and in the slope and shape of their relationship between dose and physiological effect. The comparable relationships between drug dose and human performance on psychological tests have been largely ignored. Most studies of drug effects on performance have been constrained to a single acute, moderate and ethically justifiable dose. Yet quite different effects of two drugs may be observed on the selected performance variables according to the doses chosen for the study.

Similar difficulties are encountered when studying performance at different points in time following administration of the drug. Most performance is examined at the time when the drug is assumed to have reached its peak plasma concentration. However, not only do differences between people, and in what they have recently done, affect the timing of the peak but also the psychological variables under study may be affected differently by different plasma concentrations. Lengthy, as opposed to brief, performance testing following drug administration may assist interpretation of this problem, but any changes in effect of the drug on performance over time may confound differences in plasma level with differences in psychological response to the drug.

Selection of subjects for drug studies

The selection of subjects for studies of drugs and performance is open to the problems common to other branches of psychology but, in addition, drug studies are often conducted for their theoretical or practical relevance to clinical populations although only non-clinical normals may be used in the study. Since drugs such as tranquillizers are usually prescribed to people with diagnosed clinical problems, it may be that patients can be psychologically distinguished from the normals on whom many psychological drugs studies are often conducted. Such considerations are common in personality research and in some drug studies (Humphreys and Revelle, 1984). For example, if anxiety has effects on psychological processes then the results from studies of the effect of anxiolytic minor tranquillizers on normals may be only partially relevant to the clinically anxious. These drugs might benefit performance of the anxious but handicap the normal. Such considerations would be even more important in the case of major tranquillizers used to treat more severe clinical states (Hartley *et al.*, 1989).

Choice of psychological test

A major issue is the choice of psychological test or dependent variable in drug studies. In order to provide information about a drug's psychological effect the chosen dependent variables must firstly be sensitive to, and selectively affected by different drugs and, secondly, be of importance in current psychological theory. Meta-analyses of studies of minor tranquillizers have revealed many studies use insensitive dependent variables. Insensitivity may arise either from real independence of the psychological process from a drug's action or from the ability of individuals to compensate for the drug's effect by redistributing their cognitive resources under executive control. Studies of prolonged performance following drug administration are of importance in distinguishing these alternatives.

Comparisons of findings from studies of different drugs often reveal great similarity in their effects on performance. Few of the many tranquillizers have not been shown to slow responding in some way. Accordingly, there is an increasing need to find tests that distinguish between the different drugs. Contemporary theories of cognition provide a framework for the choice of selective measures that are at the same time meaningful within those theories. The history of studies into performance under the major tranquillizer chlorpromazine illustrates this need (Mirsky and Kornetsky, 1964). A brief test of coding performance, the digit symbol substitution test, was shown to be little affected by the drug. However, a test of sustained attention, the continuous performance test, was severely impaired in normals but improved in clinical schizophrenics by chlorpromazine. Comparable studies of the minor tranquillizers, such as diazepam, revealed it affected coding performance more than prolonged attention.

Such findings as these, based on theoretical understanding at that time, permitted the development of psychological models of schizophrenia and of the benefit of chlorpromazine. These studies allowed the development of the recent theoretical and empirical studies described below.

CLINICAL CONCLUSIONS ON TRANQUILLIZER USE

Some attention is given here to the clinical justification and generalizations about major and minor tranquillizer administration. Part of the reason for attending to this is because it is of occupational and practical importance. Furthermore psychological understanding and theories of tranquillizer action have reached the point where some integration with clinical knowledge can be attempted.

Major tranquillizers

Drugs belonging to the class called major tranquillizers are mainly, but not exclusively, used for the treatment of psychoses, mania, alcoholism and agitated senility. Studies of clinical benefit of the tranquillizers have usually agreed that they are effective in schizophrenia, schizo-affective disorders, of use initially in the treatment of mania, of some benefit to Gilles de la Tourette syndrome and to age-related disorders, or occasional use in toxic states induced by other drugs, of occasional use in anxiety and related states but of no benefit in depression.

BENEFITS AND USAGE

All of the major tranquillizers have been examined in double-blind tests for their benefit in schizophrenia. Nearly all such studies have shown that the major tranquillizers are superior to placebo in the treatment of the disorder. For example, in one large-scale study, 75 per cent of drug-treated patients improved by comparison with 25 per cent of patients treated by non-drug means (Goldberg *et al.*, 1965). The drugs alleviate many of both the primary symptoms such as thought disorder and secondary symptoms such as agitation, hostility, delusions and hallucinations associated with the condition. They also normalize psychomotor behaviour (Goldberg and Mattsson, 1967). Since these drugs enable many patients to live normal lives they are of considerable practical importance.

The first such drug, chlorpromazine, a phenothiazine, was introduced in the 1950s when it was found therapeutically beneficial and permitted a dramatic reduction in the number of hospitalized patients, many of whom were able to lead satisfactory lives on maintenance doses of the drug. Since that time many new phenothiazines have been synthesized and other classes of major tranquillizer, such as the butyrophenones and thioxanthenes have been developed. More recently still, atypical major tranquillizers such as clopazine, unrelated to the existing classes, have been found to have useful therapeutic effects.

For practical purposes the main features distinguishing between the different drugs are their potency, longevity of action and specific side-effects associated with administration. Studies of the comparative therapeutic benefit of the major tranquillizers in schizophrenia have shown them roughly equivalent in efficiency, in producing similar changes on similar symptoms dimensions (Davis and Garver, 1978). Many years of study have failed to provide a completely rational system for the choice of a drug for an individual's symptoms. Indeed differences in the response to various drugs may reflect differences in optimal dosage and metabolism as much as specific effects of the drug. Accordingly the choice of drug administered is often left to the clinicians' judgement which, apart from considerations of potency and longevity, will be based on the degree of sedation and side-effects produced by the drug.

Few other drugs have such discretion in dosage as that of the major tranquillizers, and it may vary 100-fold. Indeed, upper limits on dose may be dictated more by avoidance of unwanted side-effects, such as Parkinson-like or dyskinesic symptoms, than by demonstrable clinical effectiveness. Treatment may often begin by administering two moderate doses and continue with a single larger dose administered in the evening for several weeks. A failure of symptom amelioration would usually signify that a differnt drug should be tried. If symptoms ameliorate then the dose is progressively reduced to a maintenance level for an indefinite period. Hogarty and Goldberg (1973) studied patients over twelve months following discharge from hospital. About 70 per cent of those without maintenance drug treatment relapsed whereas only about 30 per cent on maintenance treatment relapsed.

EFFECTS

Nearly all major tranquillizers share two unique effects: their ability to ameliorate the symptoms of psychoses and their ability to evoke extra-pyramidal motor disorders such as Parkinsonian like side-effects. Both probably arise from the effect of the drug on the several branches of the nervous system which utilize the neurotransmitter, dopamine (see Figure 11.4). From studies of the distribution of dopamine and of the site of

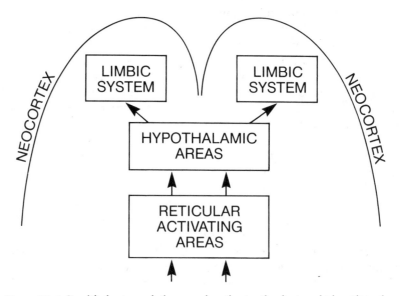

Figure 11.4 Simplified view of the neural paths in the brain which utilize the neurotransmitter dopamine.

action of chlorpromazine, it is clear that major tranquillizers could have widespread effects in the nervous system (Snyder, 1974; Snyder *et al.*, 1977). They affect the reticular activating system, the limbic system and the hypothalamus and other regions in the forebrain innervated by dopamine.

On the basis of these findings, generalizations describing their effects would be that they reduce the role of distracting stimuli and the emotional impact of, and somatic responses to, stimuli. These effects can be loosely described as sedative and this generalization is captured by the term 'tranquillizer' to indicate that doses of these drugs reduce some but not all activity. Indeed, some tranquillizers have little sedative effect and can mildly activate motor behaviour. This often subtle pattern of effects of the drugs is apparent in the following detailed review of drug studies.

DISADVANTAGES

The major tranquillizers have occupational significance for people prescribed maintenance doses of the drugs for the clinical states described above and for those on shorter-term treatment for anxiety and related symptoms. Long-term maintenance, use of major tranquillizers is associated with the occasional occurrence of motor disorders or dyskinesias and dystonias. These can include reversible conditions such as tremor, involuntary motor activities, rigidity, ataxia including Parkinson-like symptoms. Irreversible conditions include abnormalities of oral movements and sometimes of the limb extremities. These states have serious implications for people operating complex equipment whilst driving and flying for example. However, it is quite likely that the performance of patients with severe clinical conditions is improved by these drugs and that they develop tolerance to some of the drug effects associated with acute use.

Short-term, or acute, use of the major tranquillizers is not likely to be associated with any motor disorders. Rather, acute use is associated with a number of changes in attentional and other behaviours, especially in externally paced tests, as described below. However, it is not easy to infer an increase in accident risk or other indices of impairment from these results, and indeed there is a lack of evidence of involvement of major tranquillizers in road accidents (Judd, 1985).

Minor tranquillizers

These agents encompass several different classes of drugs including the: benzodiazepines, propanediols, antihistaminics, beta-andrenergic blockers and some barbiturates. This large group includes several drugs, such as some of the benzodiazepines and barbiturates, which are also termed hypnotics to emphasize their similar, but nocturnal, use. There are several reasons for grouping these classes together, including similarities in their use and benefit, and possibly action since some may modulate post synaptic responses to GABA (Olsen, 1981). Specific receptors for benzodiazepines have been found in many areas of the nervous system but are most concentrated in the cortex and where they support a facilitatory action on GABAergic synapses (Haefely, 1978; Mohler and Okada, 1978).

BENEFITS AND USAGE

These are compounds that not only help tranquillize or alleviate daytime problems, but also nocturnal problems such as the many causes of insomnia associated with changes in time zone or muscle spasms (myoclonus), for example. Although sharing the title 'tranquilliizer' with the antipsychotic drugs just discussed, the minor tranquillizers differ clinically, chemically and pharmacologically from them. Historically, the first of the minor tranquillizing drugs introduced was meprobamate, developed from compounds which were observed to produce muscle relaxation and quieting. Currently, the most widely used minor tranquillizers are the benzodiazepines, which were developed in the 1950s from compounds synthesized years earlier but not tested. Screening showed many similarities between the action of meprobamate and the benzodiazepines but with much greater potency of the new compounds. So successful were the new compounds that they have become one of the most widely administered drugs.

The minor tranquillizers have shown themselves effective in a number of areas. In particular, they are beneficial in the treatment of fear or anxiety (Rickels et al., 1978). Most studies show that benzodiazepines exceed the barbiturates, which are themselves of benefit compared with placebo, in alleviating global symptoms of axiety.

In contrast to fear, anxiety can be characterized as feelings of apprehension which may not be associated with the presence of a stressful or fearful event. Although fear is often a brief response to the presence of a threatening event, anxiety can be a long-lasting response without an obvious physical stimulus. Such states may accompany broad situations such as occupational uncertainty, domestic conflict and bereavements or more specific situations such as flying in aircraft and examinations. Anxiety may often be associated with other identifiable disorders such as depression or ill health, accompany the response to drug abuse such as alcohol, or may sometimes have no identifiable concomitant.

In severe cases deserving treatment, the dysphoric feeling of anxiety may be accompanied by physical signs such as heightened muscle tension, palpitations, headaches, dizziness, abdominal and thoracic pains, which may contribute to impaired performance and sleep. The minor tranquillizers are beneficial in temporarily reducing not only the dysphoric feeling, but also the physical signs, of anxiety and may thus facilitate better performance and sleep. Clinical evaluations conclude that approximately 50 per cent of anxious patients improve globally following benzodiazpeine administration (Rickels *et al.*, 1978). The drugs significantly benefit both anxiety and its somatic consequences but have little effect on any other associated symptoms such as depression.

The minor tranquillizers have an important role to play, not only in alleviating daytime problems of anxiety and fearfulness, but they are also of benefit in sleep disorders (Nicholson, 1986). Sleep disorders can be categorized into three, approximately equal classes. These include: insomina or reported nocturnal sleeplessness; excessive daytime sleepiness or partial narcolepsy; and abnormal nocturnal behaviours such as somnabulism. The minor tranquillizers have a role only in the first of these classes.

SLEEP AND HYPNOTICS

Although insomnia is regarded as less frequent and severe than it is self-reported to be, nevertheless many events do interfere with quality and quantity of sleep. These events include: changes in time zone and the consequential jet lag; changes in working shift or circadian cycle and the consequential sleep loss; drug-dependent insomnia associated with continued noctural use of a mild tranquillizer or hypnotic; chronic anxiety and its associated somatic symptoms, and a range of other problems including apnea and myoclonus of the limbs.

Recordings of the electroencephalograph, eye movement and muscle tone permit precise, reliable and objective measurements of the quality and quantity of sleep. However, the relationship between these objective and self-reported measures of sleep quality and quantity are controversial and equivocal. A significant group of insomniacs deny sleeping despite objective measurement of sleep onset and duration. This fact suggests caution in administration of minor tranquillizers and hypnotics when there is not sufficient cause for a diagnosis of insomnia, such as would be warranted by a change in time zone.

Since the rhythm of sleeping follows the normal twenty-four hour cycle, disturbance in quality and quantity of sleep is likely when people are expected to change or reverse their normal cycle on arrival in a different time zone. Furthermore, the feelings of drowsiness likely to be experienced during newly scheduled hours of wakefulness may be compounded by poor sleep in the new time zone. Workers on rotating shift systems, such as nurses, are subject to similar stresses and experience corresponding sleep difficulties. The short acting minor tranquillizers have been found effective in reducing sleep latency in these settings, without significantly impairing subsequent day time performance (Nicholson, 1986).

A closely related setting is that of 'phase lag' in sleep, often occasioned by prematurely inducing sleep by taking daytime naps or longer acting minor tranquillizers or hypnotics. After taking such drugs the person may feel drowsy during the day, take a nap, then have difficulty getting to sleep at a normal time in the evening and so take another drug dose, and then repeat the cycle later each day.

Anxiety and its symptoms may intefere with the onset of sleep. Many minor tranquillizers are effective hypnotics which reduce sleep latency and increase its duration in the anxious. Another factor, inducing insomnia, and alleviated by these drugs is nocturnal myoclonus or repetitive jerking and the experience of uncomfortable sensations, in the limbs during sleep. People experiencing these problems suffer both more subjective and objective arousals and poorer sleep. The longer acting benzodiazepines have been found to reduce these arousals.

DISADVANTAGES

The administration of minor tranquillizers may produce unwanted side-effects and therefore they are usually inappropriate for chronic administration. Indeed, their chronic use may lead to dependence following their termination. Such unwanted effects include drowsiness, confusion, mild ataxia, memory and cognitive impairment. These are important considerations in many occu-pational settings, even following acute use. The impact of these side-effects on the skills required in driving performance has been reviewed by Hindmarch (1986). He concluded that these side-effects impair steering, reaction time and road positioning skills in laboratory simulation and real driving. Navigational performance at route-finding and map reading may also be impaired. The general conclusions have been endorsed by Betts et al. (1986) who also stress that personality, experience and gender may interact with the drug's effect on driving.

It is not surprising, therefore, that there have been some reports of the possible involvement of minor tranquillizers in road accidents (Linnoila, 1976). Ellinwood and Heatherley (1985) concluded that some benzodiazepines approximately doubled car accident risk. MacPherson et al. (1984) calculated the odds of a car crash for different classes of drug and found them to be significantly increased by some, but not all, minor tranquillizers (O'Hanlon and Volkerts, 1986). After-effects of hypnotics taken the previous night on daytime driving performance are not uncommon (Schmidt et al., 1986). Furthermore, the adverse effect of minor tranquillizers on driving and related performance is increased by alcohol use.

Chronic use of the minor tranquillizers is appropriate when these drugs replace others demonstrating more severe unwanted effects or when the physical accompaniments to the state of axiety have themselves become a significant health or performance problem.

The benzodiazepines are the most frequent choice of minor tranquillizer since they have been demonstrated to show little loss of effectiveness, by adaptation or tolerance to their continued use, and great tolerance to overdoses. By contrast, considerable adaptation or tolerance develops to administration of the barbiturates and meprobamate. Thus, they lose effectiveness rapidly and have a much smaller margin between clinical and lethal doses.

Although short-acting benzodiazepines are available, as measured by the half-life of the drug and its active metabolites in the body, many benzodiazepines remain active in the body for days. By contrast the barbiturates, for example, have half-lives measured in hours. The half-life of a drug and its metabolites is of importance in its appropriate choice and in the rapidity of onset of any withdrawal symptoms following prolonged high dosage. Diazepam or Valium has a half-life of twenty to fifty hours and its metabolism produces active compounds. Thus, if administered daily , a steady level of drug in the plasma is reached within a few days; in relatively chronic anxiety this would be desirable.

By contrast oxazepam or Serax has a half-life well inside a day and produces no important active metabolites. Thus it is appropriate for, brief, acute use where rapid termination of drug action is required to minimize its impact on demanding operations such as flying, driving or operating complex, dangerous equipment. When anxiety is relatively limited and situation specific, such as in panic attacks, phobias or anticipatory fearfulness of events, then short half-life benzodiazepines are appropriate. Treatment of insomina may require a drug with a moderate half-life in order to promote and maintain sleep.

The choice of benzodiazepines to be administered should reflect a subtle balance between the extent to which the drug's side-effects interfere with the requirement on the person for optimal performance and reduction of the target symptoms, which may themselves interfere with optimal performance.

By contrast, the other members of the family of minor tranquillizers have less to offer, with the possible exception of the beta-adrenergic blockers. The propanediols, exemplified by meprobamate, are relatively unpopular because of their low potency, small margin between clinical and lethal doses, susceptibility to adaptation or the development of tolerance, and their liability to produce dependence to their use. These problems are even more serious in the use of barbiturates and severely limit their administration. Use of the sedative antihistaminics suffers from similar reservations.

The beta-adrenergic blocking drugs exemplified by propanolol or Inderal, have been increasingly used for their beneficial action in anxiety-provoking settings. The beta receptors of the adrenergic synapses in the sympathetic branch of the autonomic nervous system are stimulated in anxiety and fear. Reducing their activity in some anxiety provoking settings is beneficial, for reasons similar to the use of these drugs in hypertension and related disorders (see Figure 11.5).

Accordingly, these drugs are often employed when, for example, muscle tremor, tachycardia and respiratory spasms may interfere with optimal performance, as they may in oratory, skilled sport and musical performance

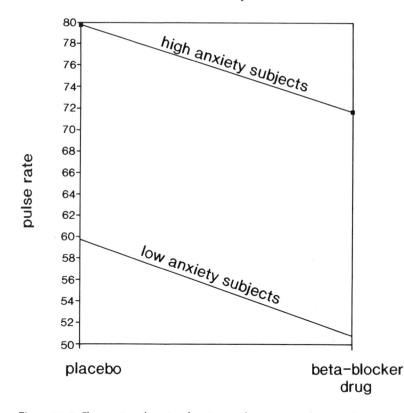

Figure 11.5 Changes in pulse rate of anxious and non-anxious human subjects under the drug propanolol. (After Hartley *et al.*, 1983.)

(Hartley *et al.*, 1983). Conversely, by preventing some responses that are adaptive in competitive field sports, their use is limited to highly skilled performance.

EXPERIMENTAL STUDIES OF TRANQUILLIZERS: MAJOR AND MINOR TRANQUILLIZERS COMPARED

Attention

As noted earlier, an important series of studies of tranquillizers was carried out by Mirsky and colleagues (e.g. Mirsky and Rosvold, 1960 and Mirsky and Kornetsky, 1964). They concluded that, like sleep-loss, the major tranquillizer chlorpromazine caused a dramatic impairment of performance on an externally-paced test of vigilance or sustained attention, the continuous performance test (CPT). In this task each stimulus is given at a time fixed externally, and without reference to the participant; so good performance is dependent on the adequacy and orientation of attention to the brief, temporally uncertain events in the test. Any attentional or motor response that is too slow must lead to an error of commission or omission because there is no opportunity to correct those errors by, later, adjustment of performance.

The digit symbol substitution test (DSST), with which the CPT compared, is a self-paced test of speed at encoding symbols. Each stimulus is presented following the response to the previous problem. In this test, the only adverse consequence of imperfect attentional or motor performance is momentary slowing of the average speed of performance, which can be compensated for by faster performance later. The test was little affected by chlorpromazine but considerably impaired by barbiturates and other minor tranquillizers. Since it was a self-paced task, stimuli and responses could be selected without incurring any disadvantage, whenever a participant's orientation and preparation was adequate. This test of average speed would be relatively immune to temporary inefficiencies caused by a drug such as chlorpromazine but still be sensitive to drugs, such as minor tranquillizers, which slowed all reactions.

These studies were important at the time because they revealed that major tranquillizers such as chlorpromazine induced momentary inefficiencies in performance requiring simple responses but did not impair the complex cognitive processes required in encoding and developing the representation of stimuli. By contrast the minor tranquillizers investigated did not induce momentary inefficiency but impaired the complex cognitive process involved in stimulus coding. These findings were developed and elaborated by Mirsky and Kornetsky (1964), who compared schizophrenic and normal performance on the tasks. They found schizophrenics performed worse than normals on the CPT but that their performance improved to near normal levels with chlorpromazine. These findings have been repeatedly confirmed (Nuechterlein and Dawson, 1984).

Mirsky and Kornetsky explained these observations, using theories current at that time, by suggesting that schizophrenics were over-aroused compared with normals, and their over-arousal caused momentary inefficiencies in performance. Hypothetical arousal was thought to have an inverted-U relationship with performance. Performance on any task was supposed to be best at intermediate levels of arousal. Without the drug, normals might be at their optimal arousal for the CPT; but their arousal might be reduced below optimum by the drug. Schizophrenics, on the other hand, might be over their peak of optimum arousal without the drug, but reduced to their optimal point of arousal following drug administration.

These findings were used by Broadbent (1971) as partial support for a dual mechanism of arousal in which the lower mechanism is responsible for automatic and well established actions whilst the upper mechanism monitors and alters the parameters of the lower system to maintain optimal performance. The lower mechanism was accordingly thought to be impaired by major tranquillizers and sleep loss, and the upper mechanism impaired by minor tranquillizers and hypnotics.

Hartley (1983) reviewed a number of studies of similar tasks which enabled the effects of major and minor tranquillizers and a number of other related drugs to be contrasted. It was noted that Loeb et al. (1965) had found a steeper fall in detections and sensitivity on a paced vigilance task under chlorpromazine compared to placebo. In a similar setting Hartley (1977) had also found an accelerated decline in detections after subjects had been administered chlorpromazine (see Figure 11.6).

The conditions of temporal uncertainty and receptor orientation may have made this test quite sensitive to the adverse effect of chlorpromazine. Further findings in this study were the specific antagonism between the actions of chlorpromazine and noise to be seen in some measures of performance.

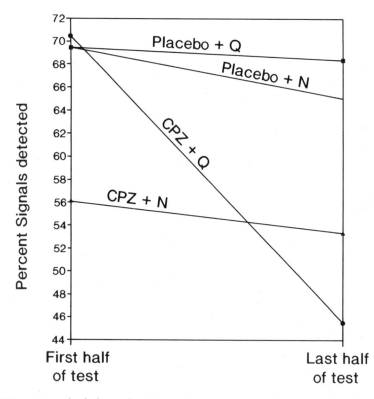

Figure 11.6 The decline in detections under chlorpromazine (CPZ) found in a vigilance task by Hartley et al. (1977).

Accordingly it was suggested that this antagonism reflected a common site of action of chlorpromazine and noise.

Hartley (1983) noted that stimulants such as amphetamine, which pharmacologically and psychologically have an opposing action to chlorpromazine, improve performance on paced tasks like the CPT and do so most when temporal or spatial uncertainty impairs performance. These conclusions about amphetamine also seem appropriate to studies of reaction time employing temporally uncertain as contrasted to fixed-foreperiod warnings (Trumbo and Gaillard, 1974). In contrast to these results on stimulants, Arnold and Hartley (1990) found that chlorpromazine slowed simple reactions most under conditions of temporal uncertainty. Chlorpromazine, compared with placebo, generally slowed responses but the effect was least when subjects had been warned of an impending signal and greatest when they were not warned.

In a study of choice serial reaction time it was found that errors of commission and omission, which cannot be compensated for by later performance, was increased by chlorpromazine (Hartley *et al.*, 1978). Following chlorpromazine speed on the task was at first slightly faster, and on average similar to placebo (see Figure 11.7). Interestingly, Trumbo and Gaillard (1974) showed that a minor tranquillizer slowed speed of response unselectively following both variable and constant warning intervals.

Many other studies have supported the contrast between the effects of minor and major tranquillizers on average speed as compared to variability and errors in performance. Neither Linnoila and Mattila (1973) nor Jones *et al.* (1978) found that diazepam impaired a paced auditory vigilance task. However, indications of impairment of the DSST, and other tests requiring cognitive processing, have been observed under diazepam (Salkind *et al.*, 1979; Zimmerman *et al.*, 1979; Wittenborn, 1979). These tasks have in common a greater emphasis on the acquisition and manipulation of fresh information in comparison with the requirements of the CPT. This interpretation is consistent with the many reports that diazepam impairs the acquisition of information for recall later.

Memory

Clarke *et al.* (1970) carried out an early study of the effect of diazepam on memory. They found that diazepam did not impair recall memory of materials acquired before drug injection. Recall of material acquired after injection was significantly impaired. They concluded that intravenous diazepam produces dense anterograde amnesia but little, if any, retrograde impairment of memory. Interestingly, they found no evidence that diazepam impaired vigilance, intelligence and simple decisions. Grove-White and Kelman (1971) also found minor tranquillizers such as diazepam, impaired immediate recall of fresh information acquired after, but not before, drug administration. But this

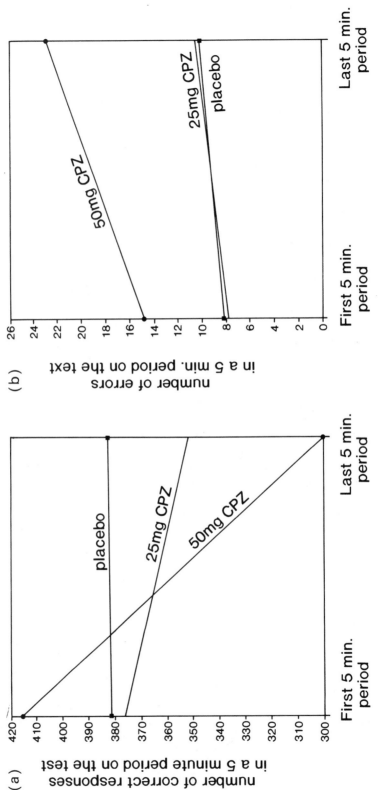

(a)

number of correct responses
in a 5 minute period on the test

420
410
400
390
380
370
360
350
340
330
320
310
300

placebo

25mg CPZ

50mg CPZ

First 5 min.
period

Last 5 min.
period

(b)

number of errors
in a 5 min. period on the text

26
24
22
20
18
16
14
12
10
8
6
4
2
0

50mg CPZ

25mg CPZ
placebo

First 5 min.
period

Last 5 min.
period

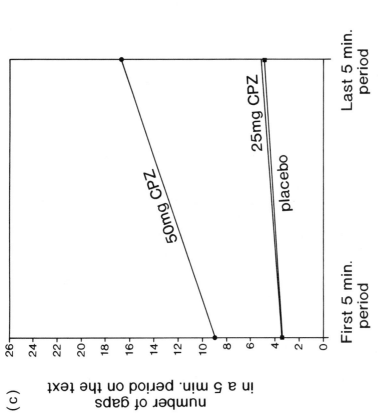

Figure 11.7 Changes in speed and errors of commission and omission on a serial reaction task found by Hartley *et al.* (1978). (a), Effect of placebo and CPZ on the number of correct serial reactions; (b), effect of placebo and CPZ on errors in serial reaction performance; (c), effect of placebo and CPZ in serial reaction performance.

impairment occurred only when recall was required after a delay of twenty seconds. They suggest that minor tranquillizers do not affect acquisition as such, but impair the processes involved in retention and development of the stimulus representation, and accelerate its decay.

This conclusion has been confirmed several times by Ghoneim, Jones and co-workers (Ghoneim and Mewaldt, 1975; Jones et al., 1978). The latter report is interesting in finding no effect of minor tranquillizer on mental arithmetic, nor on the recall of early and later items in lists learned under diazepam. Only the recall of items presented in the middle of the lists was impaired by minor tranquillizers. This contrast may support the conclusion that minor tranquillizers do not impair acquisition but rather impair the effortful processes involved in developing the representation of the stimuli required by recall.

Contrasts between the effect of diazepam and chlorpromazine on immediate memory are important for several reasons. The absence of an effect of chlorpromazine on memory would, firstly, be consistent with the present view that the drug does not affect memory but impairs preparation of attention and responses, and secondly confirms that memory impairment is not a function of simple tranquillization. Liljequist et al. (1975) failed to find any effect of chlorpromazine on learning even after prolonged administration. Liljequist et al. (1978) compared the effects of diazepam and chlorpromazine on acquisition and recall of paired associate material. They found diazepam, but not chlorpromazine, impaired acquisition of information. Similarly, chlor-promazine has not been found to impair the acquisition of iconic information from brief visual presentations (Stone et al., 1969).

In a comprehensive study Brosan et al. (1986) examined performance on serial reaction, syntactic reasoning and semantic processing before, during and after a three week administration of the minor tranquillizer diazepam. They concluded that any harmful effects of diazepam were on average speed in all three tests, but were not upon variability and errors in performance which tended to improve under the drug. This was a pattern of results quite different from that expected for chlorpromazine. Under diazepam the syntactic reasoning test showed increasing impairment with more complex material, suggesting minor tranquillizers impair more complex cognitive operations, rather than affecting well established responses as chlorpromazine does. Since response speed was slower in more difficult syntactic reasoning, this suggests that the effect of diazepam is not on acquisition but on the rehearsal and manipulation processes required to develop stimulus representations in order to answer questions. No evidence of habituation or tolerance to diazepam was found and its effects continued after administration ceased.

Emotion and other measures

Other recent studies indicate that some actions of major tranquillizers observed in laboratory tasks reflect some clinical generalizations about their action.

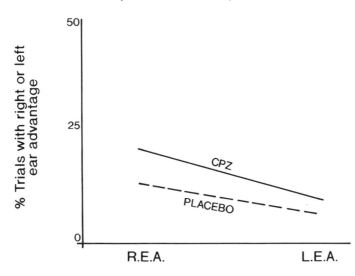

Figure 11.8 The change in ear advantage under chlorpromazine on a dichotic task. R.E.A. is the right ear advantage, L.E.A. the left ear advantage. (Hartley *et al.*, 1988.)

They also suggest that active processes of attention and response are uniquely influenced by the major tranquillizers, and the processes leading to stimulus representation are left relatively unaffected. These studies, conducted on normal volunteers who received a single 50 mg dose of chlorpromazine, are reported more fully in Hartley (1991) and summarized below.

Hartley *et al.* (1988) found that, in a dichotic listening task, accuracy was higher on the right than on the left ear and that chlorpromazine increased the accuracy or selectivity of each ear (Figure 11.8).

If any active processes of attention and preparation, irrelevant to the task, interfered with development of the perceptual representation chlorpromazine could benefit perceptual selectivity if it diminishes these active processes. Interestingly, similar observations have been made under conditions of sleep loss.

Natural facial expressions were studied under chlorpromazine whilst subjects related positive and negative emotional experiences (Hartley *et al.*, 1989). Natural facial expressions are almost exclusively under the control of the extrapyramidal nervous system, are highly dopamine dependent and therefore might be very sensitive to major tranquillizers affecting the dopamine system. If chlorpromazine reduced the somatic impact of emotion then facial expressions might be reduced during emotional experiences. It was found that negative expressions were more frequent and intense on the left side of the face. Chlorpromazine reduced this left lateralization and slightly increased the occurrence of negative expressions on the right side of the face. Positive expressions were bilaterally represented and their intensity and frequency was bilaterally reduced by chlorpromazine (Figure 11.9).

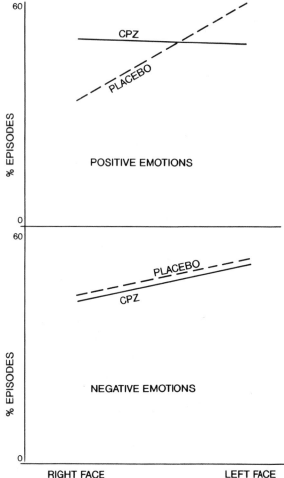

Figure 11.9 The change in intensity of facial expression under chlorpromazine found by Hartley *et al.* (1989).

Ratings of the valence of pleasant and unpleasant narrations showed chlorpromazine made these narratives more pleasant, indicating that chlorpromazine had central effects on the process of emotion as well as effects upon the peripheral expression of emotion.

A further experiment examined the impact of word emotionality in a task requiring a lexical decision between words and non-words (Hartley and Ireland, 1991; Hartley 1992). If chlorpromazine reduced the emotional impact of stimuli then it would be expected that any beneficial effect of emotion on speed of decisions would be attenuated by chlorpromazine. Emotionally

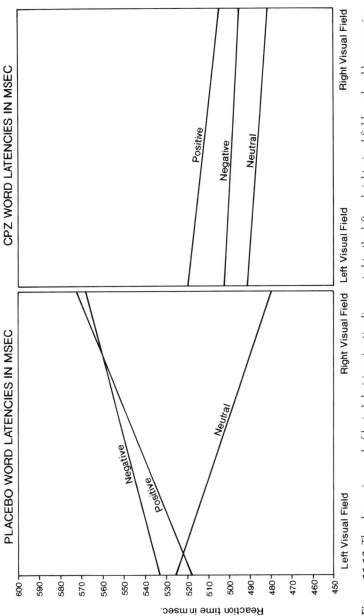

Figure 11.10 The change in speed of lexical decisions to stimuli presented to the left and right visual fields under chlorpromazine found by Hartley and Ireland (1991).

positive, negative or neutral words were unilaterally presented to the left and right visual hemi-fields. Under placebo, lexical decisions in the right visual field were faster for neutral than affective words. Right visual field responses were slowed, but left visual field decisions were not influenced, by affect. Emotionality, therefore, adversely affects only responses in the right visual field under placebo. The impairment in speed of decision to emotional words was accordingly lateralized to the left hemisphere (Figure 11.10).

Following chlorpromazine the speed of lexical decisons, in both right and left visual field, was equal in all affect conditions. This suggests that chlorpromazine speeded the slow processing of affective material in the left hemisphere, by reducing the interference of emotionality with lexical decisions. The left cerebral hemisphere is more specialized for words than is the right hemisphere and may extract more meaning and hence emotion from words. Word-related arousal may therefore not be so great in the right as in the left hemisphere, and so the time taken to process information in the right hemisphere may be greater. Possibly emotion over-arouses the left hemisphere and impairs its word recognition performance. Following chlorpromazine, left hemisphere performance may be improved through reduced emotional activation, but the right hemisphere may be little affected by chlorpromazine because the initial level of word and emotion related arousal is lower.

ADVANCES IN PSYCHOLOGICAL THEORY OF
TRANQUILLIZER ACTION

Recent work of Sanders and colleagues (Sanders, 1983, 1986; Sanders and Reitsma, 1982a, b; Sanders et al., 1982) have combined stage models of information processing with energy models of resource allocation. Stage models are based on Sternberg's proposal of several processing steps intervening between stimulus preprocessing and motor response and adjustment. Energy models are based on Kahneman's (1973) resource concept of attention in which he proposed that a pool of resources is available to all tasks under an allocation policy and that arousal can increase the pool to cope with demand.

Sanders (1983) proposes that processing a signal to the point of response requires resources or energy from a phasic arousal system modulating perception, and from a tonic activation system modulating motor preparation and execution. This is related to the distinction Pribram and McGuiness (1975) draw between phasic arousal and tonic activation mechanisms. Phasic arousal is thought to modulate perceptual processing associated with the information characteristics of the environment and is augmented by novelty and increasing complexity of stimuli. Tonic activation influences the subjects' readiness or preparedness to respond and may modulate processes of active attention and maintain the organism's set for ongoing behaviour. While phasic arousal may be partly governed by stimulus information, tonic activation may be internally controlled and characteristic of vigilant rather than orienting behaviour. Both systems draw separately on the pool of effort resources. More phasic arousal resources are required if perceptual demands are increased by poor signal quality, for example. More phasic activation resources are required if motor response demands increase under time uncertainty.

Frowein (1981) contrasted the effects of a barbiturate minor tranquillizer with the stimulant amphetamine, a major tranquillizer antagonist, on processing stages. Frowein found that the effect of a minor tranquillizer interacted only with the perceptual stage of processing signal quality. The effects of amphetamine interacted with the response stages processing time uncertainty and motor adjustment. Sanders (1986) explains these findings by proposing that minor tranquillizers inhibit phasic arousal and thus impair resource allocation to perceptual processing. The stimulant, amphetamine, a major tranquillizer antagonist, is supposed to promote tonic activation and thus facilitate resources allocated to response processing.

Sander's view is compatible with the distinction drawn here between the effects of minor and major tranquillizers. Minor tranquillizers do not seem to impair the processes of preparation, adjustment and response choice involved in memory retrieval, serial reaction, vigilance and detection. However, they do impair the perceptual processes involved in rehearsal, elaboration and manipulation of the stimulus code up to the point of decision or choice between stimulus representations. By contrast, major tranquillizers appear to impair processes of preparation, adjustment and response choice in vigilance, serial reaction and some motor tasks. They do not, however, appear to cause any impairment of perceptual processes in rehearsal, elaboration and code manipulation.

CLINICAL DRUG BENEFIT AND PSYCHOLOGICAL THEORY

Major tranquillizers and response modulation

The previous section outlined a case for major tranquillizers affecting preparation, adjustment and response choice by their impact upon tonic activation mechanisms. Generalizations about the clinical benefit of major tranquillizers emphasize that schizophrenics are, in some sense, over-aroused by stimulation. Recent reviews of the clinical state (Dawson and Nuechterlein, 1984) suggest greater autonomic responsiveness coupled with high tonic arousal during presentation of innocuous stimuli and hyper-responsiveness to mildly aversive loud noise. Moreover, drug benefits include reducing susceptibility to distracting stimuli, the emotional impact of stimuli and their somatic consequences. However, a reconciliation between the clinical and psychological theories could propose that the clinical benefits of major tranquillizers are to reduce tonic activation.

Reviews of information processing and attentional functioning in schizophrenia are broadly consistent with a state of heightened tonic activation. In a comprehensive review of these deficits in populations at risk or with active symptoms of the disorder, or in remission, Nuechterlein and Dawson (1984) draw several conclusions. Deficits occur in all populations on vigilance tasks, span of apprehension tests, and in serial recall tasks where high processing loads are imposed.

A specific interpretation of these deficits by Shakow (1979) proposes that the clinical state is characterized by an inability to sustain appropriate preparation and readiness for stimuli and responses required in a task. In studies of reaction time, patients show an inability to take advantage of the predictability or regularity of events in tests. The deficit in vigilance tasks appears to be in handling high moment-to-moment demands on attention. In studies of selective listening, patients make errors of omission of relevant stimuli and show more irrelevant intrusions. In studies of recall from immediate memory, patients are most deficient when they cannot control the rate and duration of stimuli presented and their recall is particularly vulnerable to distraction. It is possible that patients engage in rehearsal or other activities irrelevant to the task of recall.

Nuechterlein and Dawson (1984) conclude that a reduction in amount of processing capacity available for task-relevant cognitive operations underlies the variety of deficits reported above. The reduction in available capacity could occur for several reasons: firstly, the total pool of resources is reduced in patients; secondly, there is mismanagement of the allocation of resources; thirdly, more resources are required by patients for cognitive operations that are normally accomplished automatically; lastly, more resources are allocated to task-irrelevant external and internal stimulus processing. A consideration of the possible benefits of major tranquillizers to the patients may discriminate between these options.

Some experimental studies, such as those of Mirsky and Kornetsky (1964) suggest that the benefit of major tranquillizers could be to reduce the active processes of attention and response rather than to influence the relatively passive processes of elaboration of the stimulus representation. This would be consistent with an effect of major tranquillizers on tonic activation mechanisms and resources.

The perceptual mechanisms discussed in Sander's (1983) model take little account of the many active processes of attentional response, such as preparation and adjustment, that are adjuncts to normal perception outside the laboratory. These processes range from adjustment and preparation of sense organs and attention to motor responses. Over-facilitation of these active mechanisms of adjustment and preparation, by excessive tonic activation, might present part of the picture of clinical symptoms in schizophrenia. Indeed, the excessive deployment of these active processes might interfere with the effective use of the more passive processes that normally lead to development of the stimulus representation. The excessive deployment of superfluous and irrelevant process of preparation and adjustment might certainly give rise to a picture of agitation, distractibility, over-responsiveness and poor performance in clinical cases.

The clinical benefit of major tranquillizers might derive from their action on the tonic activation mechanism discussed by Sanders. If the resources available for tonic activation were reduced by major tranquillizers then attention and other aspects of poor clinical performance might improve. More specifically, it might be expected that if major tranquillizers reduced tonic activation of preparation, attention and response adjustment processes, then less information irrelevant to current performance would be processed. Conversely, the drug by permitting only the occurrence of preparation and attention appropriate to the task, might encourage more relevant information to be processed.

This benefit could occur by reducing the vicious circle of inattention and poor performance. If major tranquillizers reduced inappropriate preparation, attention and response then relevant stimuli might be selected for longer intervals. This mechanism would permit the more passive and automatic processes of perception to develop adequate stimulus representations for ensuing decisions and responses. This is not dissimilar to Easterbrook's (1959) suggestion that emotion and motivation affect the range of cues utilized in performance. Major tranquillizers might thus control inappropriate and irrelevant attention and response and by doing so would allow more appropriate perceptual representations to guide cognition and behaviour.

Minor tranquillizers and perceptual bias

As noted above, one of the principal uses of minor tranquillizers has been in the treatment of anxiety and fear. A clinical generalization characterizing the anxious is that their perception of threats in the environment induces unpleasant mental and somatic consequences. Minor tranquillizers seem to inhibit anxiety, and this benefit could arise from controlling the perception and/or consequences of threat. Clinically, there is little doubt that many minor tranquillizers, such as the benzodiazepines relieve some of the consequences of perceived threat, such as heightened muscle tension. The previous discussion of the psychological theory of the action of minor tranquillizers also suggests that they might have an effect on the resources provided by phasic arousal for perceptual processing. If this were the case, then minor tranquillizers could benefit anxiety by also inhibiting the perception of threat. Thus, it is of interest that a number of studies of the effect of anxiety on perceptual information processing have been reported recently (Eysenck et al., 1987).

A most impressive finding has been that anxious patients develop a perceptual bias towards the brief visual presentation of emotionally threatening words (Macleod et al., 1986). The words included physical and social threats, and each threatening word was paired with a matched neutral item. After a word-pair had been briefly shown to patients, one of the words was sometimes replaced with a dot requiring a simple response. When the dot replaced a threatening rather than non-threatening word anxious patients reacted relatively faster than the non-anxious. A similar relationship with trait anxiety has been found in the normal population (Broadbent and Broadbent, 1988). The results suggest the potential to develop a perceptual bias to threats is an enduring feature of the individual and the bias seems to increase the longer the anxious are exposed to presentations of threatening words.

These findings suggest that the highly trait-anxious become rapidly sensitive to the presence of threats in the environment, even if the threats are not restricted to a specific subject of anxiety, such as spiders. This is apparent since none of the words, patients or normals were so specifically selected by investigators. So the rise in perceptual bias seems quite general to any unpleasant threat, although it might be greater if threats were specifically matched to groups of patients. Furthermore, since the perceptual bias seems to develop with increasing length of exposure to threatening words, it seems that the anxious normal subject has a permanent and selective feature detector for threats. Rather, the pattern suggests that initial recognition of threats increases the bias, and resources deployed, to attend to any threat in the future.

If these conclusions are justified, they are not inconsistent with the role of minor tranquillizers in current psychological theory. If minor tranquillizers act to diminish the resources provided by the phasic arousal mechanism for perceptual processes, as suggested by Sanders, they would be of benefit in inhibiting the development of anxiety by this means. More specifically, they would inhibit the increasing effort and resources that the trait-anxious devote to attending selectively to further threats once a threat has been recognized. The drug-induced inhibition of perceptual activation would slow down, if not control, the development of the vicious circle of threat perception, followed by increasing attention to further threats, that the anxious pursue. The unpleasant consequences of the perception of such threats would accordingly be less likely.

Minor tranquillizers could, then, be of benefit not only in controlling some of the symptoms of anxiety such as increased muscle tension, but also in preventing the causes of that anxiety being given so much attention so often.

Of course, minor tranquillizers seem to be of more general benefit than for alleviating anxiety. It remains to be seen whether perceptual biases similar to those found in anxiety operate in conditions of anger and hostility, for example. If so, then parallel benefits of minor tranquillizers might be found in controlling the development of these emotions too.

The inhibition of the growth of perceptual bias towards anxiety-evoking events seems to distinguish the mode of action of minor tranquillizers clearly from that of the major tranquillizers. The benefit of the latter, by reducing the inappropriate preparation and employment of attention and motor responses, could favour the use of normal perceptual processes.

Hierarchical models of performance and tranquillizer action

Can this contrast in the effects of major and minor tranquillizers be integrated more closely with empirical studies of their action? The action of tranquillizers has been presented in terms of their adjustment of the tonic activation resources available for preparation and responding, and of the phasic arousal resources available for perception. Their benefit arises from controlling inappropriate levels, or distribution, of these resources in clinical states. Broadbent's (1971) proposal of two arousal mechanisms, described above, provides a framework for integration. The parameters of performance of the lower level, responsible for execution of appropriate established responses, are monitored and adjusted by the upper-level mechanism. Only when monitoring by the upper was impaired would resources normally allocated by the lower arousal mechanism be inappropriate or insufficient. Clinical states, such as anxiety and schizophrenia, might reflect the failure in the upper mechanism, either to monitor for or to impose optimal resource allocation, or to select an appropriate criterion. Failures could thus arise not only from inappropriate action by the upper mechanism but also from deviations in the lower mechanism. Transquillizers may act at one or more of these points.

Contemporary views of cognitive mechanisms (e.g. Rasmussen, 1986) distinguish several levels of control corresponding roughly to familiarity with the task and its environment. Some descriptions of driving distinguish between the strategic, manoeuvring and control levels of performance (e.g. Janssen, 1979; Goodstein *et al.*, 1988). This classification is similar to hierarchical descriptions of action from goal selection through formulation of an action plan to programme implementation (Pew, 1984). Strategic levels of driving describe, for example, the skills employed in navigation, and when driving under speed and accuracy constraints. The manoeuvring level of control describes tactical management, for example in overtaking, intersection behaviour and acquisition of traffic information. Most of the skills executed by the higher strategic and manoeuvring levels of the hierarchy would be discrete in nature and called into play voluntarily by the driver. Subordinate to the strategic and manoeuvring levels is the control level of the hierarchy. Control-level behaviours are mainly continuous in nature and include the relatively automatic, attention-free processes in vehicle handling, such as course-keeping and velocity control.

A major benefit of being able to carry out operations such as vehicle handling at the control level is that few cognitive resources would be required by those attention-free operations. By contrast, vehicle control which involved the higher strategic and manoeuvring levels of the hierarchy would require cognitive resources. An important implication of this distinction in resource requirements of the upper and lower levels is that skills executed by the control level would be less vulnerable to disruption than would be the case at higher levels. Disruption of the strategic and manoeuvring levels of skill could occur when insufficient resources were allocated to their operations. It is clear that most drivers typically allocate insufficient resources to driving. Johansson and Backlund (1970) demonstrated this point by unexpectedly stopping drivers about 700 m past a road sign, and found that only a minor proportion of the signs could be correctly reported in comparison with occasions when drivers were looking for the signs. If drugs, such as minor tranquillizers diminished either the resources available or the motivation to allocate resources to driving activities, then it would be expected that skills at the manoeuvring and strategic levels of the hierarchy would be degraded, if not disappear. For this reason the relatively resource-independent skills of the control level will tend to be more resistant to the effects of some drugs than are those executed by higher levels. That is not to say, however, that control-level skills are unaffected by all drugs. As discussed, major tranquillizers seem to have their major impact on the well established decision processes of the lower control level of the hierarchy, and indeed some mechanisms required by all levels of the hierarchy, such as fine motor control, are impaired by some drugs.

In hierarchical descriptions of performance, the higher levels of control regulate the parameters of lower levels when either the performance of the latter departs from optimality or when it is inadequate to meet the demands on it. Involvement of higher levels of control in a task, although permitting slower, more flexible processing, requires more resources. Training, and thus practice, enables control of a skill to be passed from higher to lower levels in the hierarchy. Practice is beneficial in permitting resources to be utilized more efficiently.

Descriptions of driving, such as this hierarchical model provides, will be fruitful in providing the theoretical orientation necessary to understand the effects of drugs on driving. As noted, previous laboratory tests of drugs have been unsuccessful in achieving sensitivity to, and discrimination between, the different effects that the many available drugs can have on driving-related performance. This is hardly surprising in view of the foregoing analysis. Most of those studies have employed tests requiring only one, often unrepresentative skill of the many involved in driving. The skill under investigation might also be chosen from a level of the hierarchy unaffected by the drug.

The findings from some laboratory and clinical tests of the effects of drugs may permit a hierarchical classification of major and minor tranquillizers, Some drugs may affect one level of the hierarchy more than the others; and within any level of the hierarchy a drug may impair the control of certain skills more than other skills. Major tranquillizers most probably impair well established decision selection and execution processes of the type represented mainly at the lower control level and possibly at the manoeuvring level of the hierarchy.

Minor tranquillizers, on the other hand, appear to have their impact on the more complex processes of elaborating the stimulus representation to the point of decision selection. Thus, minor tranquillizers would impair skills represented mainly in the higher manoeuvring level of control and possibly at the strategic level of the hierarchy. Since impairment of the operating parameters of a lower level of the hierarchy by a drug or other stress can be compensated for by involvement of a higher level of the hierarchy, it is important to establish the level of the hierarchy of driving skills affected by a drug.

Major tranquillizers are potent drugs. If they impair the well established and automatic decision processes, their effect on driving has the potential to be quite hazardous. For example, the continuous operation of course-keeping during driving could be impaired. Yet research shows their adverse effect on driving and accidents seems slight. If, however, major tranquillizers only affected processes represented in the lower control level of the hierarchy, then their detrimental effect on the lower control level may be compensated by involvement of higher levels unaffected by the drug. For example, operators making discrete manoeuvres to correct poor continuous course-keeping illustrates the involvement of the manoeuvring level of the hierarchy to maintain a constant level of driving competence, despite impairment of the lower control level.

By contrast, minor tranquillizers are widely used recreationally and prescriptively because of their benign effect; yet many of them appear to raise significantly the risk of driving accidents. This adverse impact on driving could be understood if minor tranquillizers affected skills represented in a high level of control in the hierarchy as they would impair performance in two ways. Minor tranquillizers would degrade the skills controlled by the higher level of the hierarchy such as at the manoeuvring level (Janssen, 1979): overtaking manoeuvres might, for example, be impaired. Indeed, the process of subjective risk assessment might be degraded. In addition, if performance controlled by a lower level of the hierarchy fell short of optimum, or was beyond its capabilities, drug impairment of the higher level would have serious consequences. Minor tranquillizers would reduce the ability of the higher level to compensate for the poor performance of the lower level. For example, discrete corrections to poor continuous course-keeping would be impaired. In summary, the higher the level of the hierarchy affected by the drug, the more potentially serious is the drug's effect on complex tasks such as driving.

TRAINING AND COUNTER-MEASURES TO DRUG EFFECTS

The viewpoint that the higher the level of the hierarchy affected by the drug, the more potentially serious the drug's effect on complexities has some implications for training in general, but for young driver training especially. It is clear from epidemiological studies that young drivers are particularly at risk of driving accidents. One view of this problem is that young drivers have not acquired perceptual–cognitive expertise in hazard assessment characteristic of mature drivers (Milech et al., 1989). Almost certainly they will not have had the opportunity to practise those skills to the point at which they can be automatically employed at the control level of the hierarchy. For the reasons discussed above, the relatively resource-demanding driving skills of the young may therefore be especially vulnerable to disruption by certain classes of drug such as those of the minor tranquillizer type, whether taken for prescriptive or recreational purposes. Minor tranquillizers and similar hypnotics are, of course, widely taken for recreational purposes, often in combination with other agents, such as alcohol. It would, therefore, be expected that the driving of the young is most likely to be impaired by such drugs.

An important aim of training would be to attempt to reduce the adverse impact of drugs and other stresses on young driver performance. One consequence of practice is that it enables operators automatically to execute skills that would otherwise require the resources of controlled processing. A widely held view of the benefit of training is that it provides some immunity to drugs and stress by enabling the operator to execute as many skills as possible automatically. This training would undoubtedly be of benefit, and would achieve its ends in two ways. Firstly, it would free up the resources that the equivalent, non-automatic processes require when they are executed under the control of higher levels. More importantly, practice at a skill would enable its control to be passed from a higher to a lower level of the hierarchy. Were a drug to impair a lower level of the hierarchy, any inefficiencies in performance at that level would be compensated, at least in part, from a higher level unaffected by the drug. Consequently, the more practised and automatic a skill is, the more invulnerable would a young driver be to the adverse impact of some drugs.

As discussed previously, drugs of recreational importance, such as the minor tranquillizers and hypnotics, appear to impair the more resource-demanding skills of the manoeuvring and strategic levels of the hierarchy.

Extensive practice or training at simulated driving tasks would permit the young to acquire many driving skills at the resource-independent control level of the hierarchy. It would be expected, therefore, that such training would reduce the vulnerability of the young to driving skill impairments following the use of prescriptive or recreational drugs.

These considerations also suggest a second approach to training to combat the adverse effect of drugs and stress. Although training is beneficial, it takes time and effort to acquire the appropriate skills and to automate and pass them to lower levels of control. In the meantime young drivers are out on the road. The second, and more important approach to training must also be to provide training in the compensatory skills executed from levels of the hierarchy above those affected by drugs and stresses. For example, were the manoeuvring level of skill impaired by minor tranquillizers (as well it might be), training would aim to provide strategical level compensatory skills. In practice, these compensatory skills could include the adoption of a more conservative speed-error constraint during driving; emphasis of the role of selective and safe route navigation; utilization of selective and safe lower-level control strategies under high-level compensation. Such an approach will be successful only if the level of the hierarchy affected by a drug can be identified and the way in which the drug adversely affects those skills is understood.

The primary focus of training compensatory skills at upper levels of the hierarchy could be on the acquisition and practice of self-monitoring strategies by young drivers. As far as we are aware, little or no research has been conducted on identifying successful self-monitoring strategies in driving or other areas. Some recent data suggest that such self-monitoring strategies may be quite powerful predictors of driving accident risk (O''Toole, 1990). Drivers may develop these skills in the course of their education but quite possibly some acquire them autonomously. Clearly, these skills need to be identified and a training programme developed for them to combat the adverse effects of some drugs on operational performance.

REFERENCES

Arnold, P.K. and Hartley, L.R. (1990). Drug effects on cued reaction time, lateralisation and dichotic listening. *Current Psychological Reviews and Research* **8**: 273–86.

Betts, T., Mortiboy, D., Nimmo, J. and Knight, R. (1986). A review of research: the effects of psychotropic drugs on actual driving performance. In *Drugs and Driving*, edited by J.F. O'Hanlon and J.J. de Gier. London: Taylor and Francis.

Broadbent, D.E. (1971). *Decision and Stress.* New York and London: Academic Press.

Broadbent, D. and Broadbent, M. (1988). Anxiety and attentional bias: state and trait. *Cognition and Emotion* **2**: 165–83.

Brosan, L., Broadbent, D.E., Nutt, D. and Broadbent, M. (1986). Performance effects of diazepam during and after prolonged administration. *Psychological Medicine* **16**: 561–71.

Clarke, P.R.F., Eccersley, P.S., Frisby, J.P. and Thornton, J.A. (1970). The amnesic effects of diazepam (valium). *British Journal of Anaesthesia* **42**: 690–7.

Davis, J.M. and Garver, D.L. (1978). Neuroleptics: clinical use in psychiatry. In *Handbook of Psychopharmacology*, Vol. 10, edited by L.L. Iversen, S.D. Iversen and S.H. Snyder. New York: Plenum.

Dawson, M.E. and Nuechterlein, K.H. (1984). Psychophysiological dysfunctions in the developmental course of schizophrenic disorders. *Schizophrenia Bulletin* **10**: 204–32.

Easterbrook, J.A. (1959). The effect of emotion on cue utilisation and the organisation of behaviour. *Psychological Review* **66**: 183–210.

Ellinwood, E.H. and Heatherley, D.G. (1985). Benzodiazepines, the popular minor tranquilizers: dynamics of effect on driving skills. *Accident Analysis and Prevention* **17**: 283–90.

Eysenck M.W., Macleod, C. and Mathews, A. (1987). Cognitive functioning and anxiety. *Psychological Research* **49**: 189–95.

Frowein, H.W. (1981). Selective effects of barbiturate and amphetamine on information processing and response execution. *Acta Psychologica* **47**: 105–19.

Ghoneim, M.M. and Mewaldt, S.P. (1975). Effects of diazepam and scopolamine on storage, retrieval and organisational processes in memory. *Psychopharmacologia,* **44**: 257–62.

Goldberg, S.C., Klerman, G.L. and Cole, J.O. (1965). Changes in schizophrenic psychopathology and ward behaviour as a function of phenothiazine treatment. *British Journal of Psychiatry* **111**: 120–33.

Goldberg, S.C. and Mattsson, N. (1967). Symptom changes associated with improvements in schizophrenia. *Journal of Consulting Psychology* **31**: 175–80.

Goodman, L.S. and Gilman, A. (1976). *The Pharmacological Basis of Therapeutics.* London: Macmillan.

Goodstein, L.P., Andersen, H.B. and Olssen, S.E. (eds) (1988). *Tasks, Errors and Mental Models.* London: Taylor and Francis.

Grove-White, I.G. and Kelman, G.R. (1971). The effect of methohexitone, diazepam and sodium 4-hydroxybutyrate on short-term memory. *British Journal of Anaesthesia* **43**: 113–16.

Haefely, W.E. (1978). Central actions of benzodiazepines: general introduction. *British Journal of Psychiatry* **133**: 2231–8.

Hartley, L.R. (1983). Arousal, temporal and spatial uncertainty and drug effects. *Progress in Neuropsychopharmacology, Biology and Psychiatry* **7**: 29–37.

Hartley, L.R. (1992). Behavioural asymmetry and chlorpromazine. Thiazines and structurally related compounds. In *Proceedings of the Sixth International Conference on Phenothiazines and Structurally Related Psychotropic Compounds*, edited by H. Keyzer. Los Angeles: Krieger.

Hartley, L.R., Couper-Smartt, J. and Henry, T. (1977). Behavioural antagonism between chlorpromazine and noise in man. *Psychopharmacology* **55**: 97–102.

Hartley, L.R., Henry, T. and Couper-Smartt, J. (1978). Serial reaction performance and chlorpromazine. *British Journal of Psychology* **69**: 271–6.

Hartley, L.R., Ungapen, S., Davie, I. and Spencer, J. (1983). The effect of beta blocking drugs on speakers' performance and memory. *British Journal of Psychiatry,* **142**: 512–17.

Hartley, L.R., Coxon, L. and Spencer, J. (1988). Pharmacological effects on lateralized behaviour. *Current Psychological Review and Research* **6**: 301–13.

Hartley, L.R., Morrison, D.L. and Arnold, P.K. (1989a). Stress and skill in acquisition and performance of cognitive skill, edited by A. Colley and R. Beech. New York: Wiley.

Hartley, L.R., Strother, N., Arnold, P.K. and Mulligan, B. (1989b). Lateralisation of emotion under a neuroleptic drug. *Physiology and Behaviour* **45**: 917–21.

Hartley, L.R., Serna, P., Arnold, P.K. and Mulligan, B. (1990). Listening, priming and emotion under a neuroleptic drug. *Physiology and Behaviour* **47**: 837–41.

Hartley, L.R. and Ireland, L. (1991). Priming, lateralisation and chlorpromazine. *Physiology and Behaviour* **50**: 101–19.

Hindmarch, I. (1986). The effects of psychoactive drugs on car handling and related psychomotor ability: a review. In *Drugs and Driving*, edited by J.F. O'Hanlon and J.J. de Gier. London: Taylor and Francis.

Hogarty, G.E. and Goldberg, S.C. (1973). Drugs and sociotherapy in the aftercare of schizophrenic patients. *Archives of General Psychiatry* **28**: 54–64.

Humphreys, M.S. and Revelle, W. (1984). Personality, motivation and performance: a theory of the relationship between individual differences and information processing. *Psychological Review* **91**: 153–84.

Janssen, W.H. (1979). *Route planning en geleiding: een literatuurstudie*. Rapport IZF 1979-C13, Institute for Perception TNO Soesterberg.

Johansson, L.C. and Backlund, F. (1970). Drivers and road signs. *Ergonomics* **13**: 749–60.

Jones, D.M., Lewis, M.J. and Spriggs, T.L.B. (1978). The effects of low doses of diazepam on human performance in group administered tasks. *British Journal of Clinical Pharmacology* **6**: 333–7.

Judd, L.L. (1985). The effects of antipsychotic drugs on driving and driving related psychomotor functions. *Accident Analysis and Prevention* **17**: 319–22.

Kahneman, D. (1973). *Attention and Effort*. Englewood Cliffs, NJ: Prentice Hall, Inc.

Kornetsky, C. and Eliasson, M. (1969). Reticular stimulation and chlorpromazine: an animal model for schizophrenic overarousal. *Science, New York,* **165**: 1273–4.

Liljequist, R., Linnoila, M., Saario, I., Sappala, T. and Mattila, M.J. (1975). Effect of two weeks treatment with chlorpromazine and bromazepam alone or in combination. *Psychopharmacology* **40**: 205–8.

Liljequist, R., Linnoila, M. and Mattila, M.J. (1978). Effects of diazepam and chlorpromazine on memory function in man. *European Journal of Clinical Pharmacology* **13**: 339–43.

Linnoila, M. (1976). Tranquilizers and driving. *Accident Analysis and Prevention* **8**: 15–19.

Linnoila, M. and Mattila, M.J. (1973). Drug interactions in psychological skills related to driving: diazepam and alcohol. *European Journal of Clinical Pharmacology* **5**: 186–94.

Loeb, M. (1965). Influence of d-amphetamine, benactyzine and chlorpromazine on performance in an auditory vigilance task. *Psychonomic Science* **3**: 29–30.

MacLeod, C., Mathews, A. and Tata, P. (1986). Attentional bias in emotional disorders. *Journal of Abnormal Psychology* **95**: 15–20.

MacPherson, R.D., Perl, J. and Starmer, G.A. (1984). Self-reported drug-usage and crash incidence in breathalyzed drivers. *Accident Analysis and Prevention* **16**: 139–48

Milech, D., Glencross, D. and Hartley, L.R. (1989). *Skills Acquisition by Young Drivers: Perceiving, Interpreting and Responding to the Driving Environment*. Report MR4, Canberra: Federal Office of Road Safety.

Mirsky, A.F. and Kornetsky, C. (1964). On the dissimilar effects of drugs on the digit symbol substitution and continuous performance tests. *Psychopharmacologia* **5**: 161–77.

Mirsky, A.F. and Rosvold, H.E. (1960). The use of psychoactive drugs as a neuropsychological tool in studies of attention in man. In *Drugs and Behaviour*, edited by L. Uhr and J.G. Miller. New York: Wiley.

Mohler, H. and Okada, T. (1978). The benzodiazepine receptor in normal and pathological human brain. *British Journal of Psychiatry* **133**: 261–8.

Nicholson, A.N. (1986). Hypnotics in transient insomnia. In *Drugs and Driving*, edited by J.F. O'Hanlon and J.J. de Gier. London: Taylor and Francis.

Nuechterlein, K.H. and Dawson, M.E. (1984). Information processing and attentional functioning in the developmental course of schizophrenic disorders. *Schizophrenia Bulletin* **10**: 160–203.

O'Hanlon, J.F. and de Gier, J.J. (eds) (1986). *Drugs and Driving*. London: Taylor and Francis.

O'Hanlon, J.F. and Volkerts, E.R. (1986). Hypnotics and actual driving performance. *Acta Psychiatrica Scandinavica* **74**: 95–104.

Olsen, R.W. (1981). GABA–benzodiazepine–barbiturate receptor interactions. *Journal of Neurochemistry* **37**: 1–13.

O'Toole, B.I. (1990). Intelligence and behaviour and motor vehicle accident mortality. *Accident Analysis and Prevention* **22**: 211–21.

Pew, R.W. (1984). A distributed processing view of human motor control. In *Cognition and Motor Behaviour,* edited by W. Prinz and A.F. Sanders. Heidelberg: Springer.

Pribram, K.H. and McGuiness, D. (1975). Arousal, activation and effort in the control of attention. *Psychological Review* **82**: 116–49.

Rasmussen, J. (1986). *Information Processing and Human–Machine Interaction: An Approach to Cognitive Engineering.* Amsterdam: North-Holland.

Rickels, K., Downing, R.W. and Winokur, A. (1978). Antianxiety drugs: clinical use in psychiatry. In *Handbook of Psychopharmacology,* Vol. 13, edited by L.L. Iversen, S.D. Iversen and S.H. Snyder. New York: Plenum.

Salkind, M.R., Hanks, G.W. and Silverstone, J.T. (1979). Evaluation of the effects of clobazam, a 1,5 benzodiazepine on mood and psychomotor performance in clinically anxious patients in general practice. *British Journal of Clinical Pharmacology* **7**: 113S–118S.

Sanders, A.F. (1983). Towards a model of stress and performance. *Acta Psychologica* **53**: 61–97.

Sanders, A.F. (1986). Drugs, driving and measurement of human performance. In *Drugs and Driving,* edited by J.F. O'Hanlon and J.J. de Gier. London: Taylor and Francis.

Sanders, A.F. and Reitsma, W.D. (1982a). Lack of sleep and covert orienting of attention. *Acta Psychologica* **52**: 137–45.

Sanders, A.F. and Reitsma, W.D. (1982b). The effect of sleep loss on processing information in the functional visual field. *Acta Psychologica* **51**: 149–62.

Sanders, A.F., Wijnen, J.L.C. and van Arkel, A.E. (1982). An additive factor analysis of the effects of sleep loss on reaction processes. *Acta Psychologica* **51**: 41–59.

Schmidt, U., Brenemuhl, D. and Ruther, E. (1986). Aspects of driving after hypnotic therapy with particular reference to temazepam. *Acta Psychiatrica Scandinavica* **74**: 112–18.

Shakow, D. (1979). *Adaptations in Schizophrenia: The Theory of Segmental Set.* New York: Wiley.

Snyder, S.H. (1974). Catecholamines as mediators of drug effects in schizophrenia. In *The Neurosciences Third Study Program,* edited by F.O. Schmitt and F.G. Worden. Cambridge, Mass.: MIT Press.

Snyder, S.H., Cresse, I. and Burt, D.R. (1977). Dopamine receptor binding in mammalian brain: relevance to psychiatry. In *Neuroregulators and Psychiatric Disorders,* edited by E. Usdin, D.A. Hambrug and J.D. Barches. New York: Oxford University Press.

Sternberg, S. (1969). On the discovery of processing stages: some extensions on Donder's method. *Acta Psychologica* **30**: 276–91.

Stone, G.C., Callaway, E., Jones, R.T. and Gentry, T. (1969). Chlorpromazine slows decay of visual short term memory. *Psychonomic Science* **16**: 229–30.

Trumbo, D.A. and Gaillard, A.W.K. (1974). Drugs, time-uncertainty, signal modality and reaction time. In *Attention and Performance IV,* edited by P.M.A. Rabbitt and S. Dornic. New York and London: Academic Press.

Wittenborn, J.R. (1979). Effects of benzodiazepines on psychomotor performance. *British Journal of Clinical Pharmacology* **7**: 61S–67S.

Zimmerman Tansella, C., Tansella, M. and Lader, M. (1979). A comparison of the clinical and psychological effects of diazepam and amylobarbitone in anxious patients. *British Journal of Clinical Pharmacology* **7**: 605–11.

12

Antidepressant Drugs, Cognitive Function and Human Performance

H.V. CURRAN

INTRODUCTION

For most people, depression refers to a mild and transient mood which is often a response to upsetting events in life. For some people, however, depression can be so severe and prolonged that psychiatric treatment may be warranted. Because of its relative prevalence, depression has been dubbed the common cold of mental illness (Miller and Seligman, 1973). At any one time, about 8 per cent of women and 4 per cent of men in the general population are clinically depressed (Boyd and Weissman, 1982). Although the effectiveness of psychological treatments for depression, especially cognitive–behavioural therapies, is now widely accepted, most depressed people who seek treatment will receive medication in the form of anti-depressant drugs.

The number of antidepressants available has increased markedly over the years. However, there is little to choose between them in terms of their antidepressant effects. A major criterion for selecting which antidepressant is appropriate is, therefore, the extent to which each causes unwanted side-effects, including impairments of cognition and performance. Such impairments could have serious consequences for people taking antidepressants, most of whom will continue the activities of their normal lives such as driving, looking after children and making decisions.

Given the widespread use of antidepressants, and given that these drugs are usually prescribed for periods of months or even years, one might reasonably expect that their effects on cognition and performance are well established. However, this is not the case. Certainly, doctors in Britain are advised to warn patients beginning treatment with antidepressants that they

HANDBOOK OF HUMAN PERFORMANCE
VOLUME 2 ISBN 0-12-650352-4

may experience drowsiness which may affect their ability to drive or operate machinery (British National Formulary, 1990). Caution is also given that antidepressants may increase the effects of alcohol. The basis of these cautions appears to rest on the results of relatively few studies. Antidepressants have received little attention in the research literature compared with other types of mood-altering drug such as stimulants, tranquillizers and sleeping pills (Curran, 1986, 1991).

In reviewing the literature on antidepressants and cognitive function a decade ago, Thompson and Trimble (1982) bemoaned the fact that the few studies which had been carried out had often produced inconsistent findings. Today there are more studies to draw upon but, with some notable exceptions, methodological inadequacies and conceptual confusions are rife. It is probably fair to say that advances in the field have stemmed more from a clearer understanding of the role of cognitive factors in depression than of the effects of antidepressants drugs.

In this chapter, an overview is presented of what we know about the effects of antidepressants on cognition and performance. It begins by outlining a simple, conceptual framework for understanding how an antidepressant may affect performance both directly and indirectly (via its effects on depressed mood). Subsequent sections examine the results of studies firstly with normal, volunteer subjects, and secondly with depressed patients. Lastly, implications are drawn for the prescribing physician, for the depressed patient and for future research needs. The focus throughout this chapter is on antidepressants in terms of their most widespread use: the treatment of depression. It should be noted, however, that there are other clinical indications for some anti-depressants including nocturnal enuresis and certain anxiety disorders (especially obsessive–compulsive disorder and panic disorder; see Leibowitz et al., 1988, for review). The performance effects of antidepressants in these diverse groups are very poorly researched and will not be considered separately here.

DEPRESSION, COGNITION AND ANTIDEPRESSANTS: A CONCEPTUAL FRAMEWORK

Depression and cognition

When people are very depressed they often complain of having problems in concentrating and in remembering things. Objective evidence also indicates that depressed states may be associated with both quantitative and qualitative differences in performance and cognitive processing.

Quantitative aspects include what is often referred to as psychomotor retardation: a slowness of reactions, of speech and of movements reflected in performance deficits across a range of psychometric tests (Miller, 1975; Raps *et al.*, 1980; Nelson and Charney, 1980). Measurement of speech rate, using a polygraph, is one simple and fairly sensitive index of retardation. One study showed that depressed patients paused longer in speaking than healthy controls, and that speech rate returned to normal on recovery from depression (Szbadi *et al.*, 1976). Marked individual variations occur in which particular aspects of psychomotor function are retarded, and this in turn contributes to the variation in the results of studies (Blackburn, 1988). Not all diagnostic subgroups of depressed patients show retardation, and large differences are found between unipolar and bipolar depressives Furthermore, whereas some depressed individuals may have speech retardation, others may instead show retardation in motor speed or in rates of information processing.

Concentration, learning and memory are often impaired (Weingartner *et al.*, 1981). Indeed, with elderly depressed patients, such impairments can be so pronounced that care is needed to differentiate depression from dementia. Early studies of cognition produced ambiguous findings which could be interpreted along the lines that depressed people performed poorly on tests simply because of their lack of motivation to perform well (Miller, 1975). Later studies have indicated that reduced motivation alone is not a sufficient explanation, as depression does not affect all aspects of functioning equally. For instance, short-term memory is preserved relative to episodic memory (Weingartner *et al.*, 1981). Further, within episodic memory tasks, a differential pattern of deficit is observed with, for example, details of a story being retained well but its central themes being poorly remembered by depressed people compared with others (e.g. Watts and Cooper, 1989). Weingartner *et al.* (1981) found no difference between depressed patients and healthy controls in remembering well structured information. However, unstructured information was poorly retained by the depressed group, implying that depression is associated with less elaborate encoding and processing of information.

Performance impairments in depression appear more evident on tasks which require active and sustained cognitive processing than those requiring simpler, more automatic processes. Weingartner and Silberman (1982) suggest that the degree of cognitive impairment in depression will vary with the degree of sustained effort required in a task. In a similar vein, Ellis and Ashbrook (1988) argue that depression is associated with a reduction in processing resources.

Qualitative differences in information processing between depressed and non-depressed mood states have attracted considerable research interest in the past decade (for reviews see Blaney, 1986; Segal, 1988). A number of studies consistently indicate that depression is associated with a bias towards recollecting negative information about oneself rather than positive information. For example, Clark and Teasdale (1982) carried out a study of depressed inpatients whose mood-states showed marked diurnal variation. They demonstrated that in response to neutral cue words, memories rated as pleasant tended to be retrieved on the less depressed occasion and memories rated as unpleasant on the more depressed occasion. Such findings give experimental support to major theories such as Beck's (1967, 1976) which conceptualize cognitive factors as central to the maintenance of depressed mood-states.

Depression, cognition and antidepressants

Given the interdependence between depressed mood and cognition, it follows that an antidepressant can influence performance in two main ways as illustrated in Figure 12.1. Firstly, through acting centrally on the brain, an antidepressant could affect cognitive and psychomotor performance *directly*. Secondly, it could act *indirectly* by elevating depressed mood and thus enhancing performance. In this way, it can be seen how an antidepressant may impair performance in normal (non-depressed) subjects via its central effects. In depressed subjects, however, the same antidepressant may improve performance, have no effect or impair performance depending on the relative contributions of its mood-elevating and central effects.

Types of antidepressant drug

Which central effects are important for cognition and performance? Rather than produce a lengthy list of different antidepressants evaluating what is

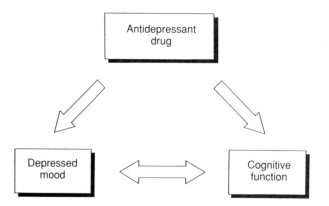

Figure 12.1 A simple model of how an antidepressant may affect cognitive function directly and/or indirectly via mood effects.

known about the effects of each, it would clearly be helpful to categorize them in terms of actions which are relevant to performance. Two actions which are thought to be of particular importance are the anticholinergic (antimuscarinic) and sedative effects of antidepressants.

Learning and memory are thought to involve cholinergic mediation so that anticholinergic antidepressants may produce impairments in subjects' ability to learn and remember (Deutsch, 1971; Drachman, 1978). There is a wide literature on the amnesic effects of the anticholinergic (non-anti-depressant) drug scopolamine and decreased cerebral cholinergic activity has been linked to dementia in Alzheimer's disease (e.g. Zornetzer, 1978; Bartus *et al.*, 1982; Collerton, 1986).

Sedative compounds can impair psychomotor speed and attentional functions, and generally produce 'blanket impairments', lowering performance levels across a wide range of tasks. Such global effects have to be considered when interpreting impairments in performance on cognitive tasks.

The most widely prescribed antidepressants are a large group of drugs called *tricyclics*. Within this group, the main difference between individual tricyclics is the extent to which each produces sedative and anticholinergic effects. For instance, the commonly used antidepressant amitriptyline has marked sedative and anticholinergic properties, whereas imipramine is less sedative but similarly anticholinergic. Newer antidepressants are generally lower in anticholinergic effects but vary considerably in sedative properties.

Table 12.1 Types of antidepressant

Tricyclics	Amitriptyline
	Imipramine
	Lofepramine
	Protriptyline
	Trimipramine
	Dothiepin
	Doxepin
	Amoxapine
	Clomipramine
	Desipramine
	Nortriptyline
	Butriptyline
	Maprotiline
Related compounds	Mianserin
	Iprindole
	Trazodone
	Viloxazine
Selective serotonin uptake inhibitors	Fluvoxamine
	Fluoxetine
	Sertraline
	Paroxetine
MAOIs	Phenelzine
	Isocarboxid
	Tranylcypromine

Many of these compounds are thought to have major actions on the neurotransmitter, serotonin, the role of which in terms of performance and cognition is little understood (Altman et al., 1987). Monoamine oxidase inhibitors (MAOIs) are older compounds which are not widely prescribed as they can interact dangerously with some foods and drugs. Early research suggested that MAOIs impaired concentration and performance, but these drugs have received virtually no research attention in the past ten years or so, and they are not considered further in this chapter. Table 12.1 provides a list of the main antidepressants available.

STUDIES WITH NORMAL, HEALTHY SUBJECTS

Most studies on the performance effects of antidepressants have been carried out with normal, healthy subjects, and more than half of such studies have assessed the effects of only a single dose of a drug. In assessing the effects of antidepressants in this way, one is in effect looking at just one side of the triangle (refer to Figure 12.1). Depression itself is not a factor in that antidepressants do not have a mood-elevating effect in people who are not depressed.

Effects of single doses

In healthy subjects, antidepressants produce a range of psychomotor and cognitive effects which depend on:

1. The particular antidepressant.
2. Its dosage.
3. The time(s) post-drug when performance is tested.
4. The performance tests used.
5. The characteristics of the subjects tested.

Despite considerable variations between studies in these factors, it is possible to infer some generalizations.

Following a single dose, sedative antidepressants such as amitriptyline produce a wide range of dose-related performance impairments on psychomotor tasks (e.g. finger tapping speeds, reaction time tasks), attentional tasks (e.g. vigilance, digit cancellation), and cognitive tasks (e.g. free recall, recognition, problem-solving) (Matilla et al., 1978; Chan et al., 1980; Hindmarch et al., 1983; Linnoila et al., 1983). Indeed, in their earlier review, Thompson and Trimble (1982) point out that amitriptyline and mianserin are generally associated with impairments of performance, whereas viloxazine and nomifensine are associated with beneficial or few detrimental effects. These two sets of antidepressants represent two extremes of the sedative/non-sedative spectrum, and thus their performance effects may simply reflect differences in global sedative effects.

Less sedative tricyclics generally produce fewer impairments at normal clinical doses (Ferris *et al.*, 1981; Thompson and Trimble, 1982). Among the non-tricyclics, sedation also appears to be a key factor in determining performance effects of single doses. For example, trazodone and mianserin have little anticholinergic effects but are sedative and produce a range of performance impairments (Warrington *et al.*, 1984; Curran and Lader, 1986). In contrast, fluoxetine, viloxazine and fluvoxamine appear non-sedative and are not associated with performance impairments (Bayliss and Duncan, 1974; Kirby and Turner, 1974; Curran and Lader, 1986; Moscovitz and Burns, 1986).

Given the apparent importance of an antidepressant's sedative effects, and given the link between anticholinergic effects and learning and memory, an experiment was designed to investigate the relationship between anti-depressants' sedative and anticholinergic profiles and their effects on memory and psychomotor performance (Curran *et al.*, 1988). The aim was to do this both by a discriminating drug design and by task discrimination. Drugs were selected on the basis of previous evidence to represent extreme ends of the anticholinergic/non-anticholinergic and sedative/non-sedative spectra. Amitriptyline and protriptyline were selected from the table in Richelson (1984) as having the highest affinities for muscarinic acetylcholine receptors of the human brain caudate nucleus. The two 'low' anticholinergic compounds, viloxazine and trazodone, have the lowest affinities reported in the same table. The sedating properties of amitriptyline and trazodone are well documented (Bye *et al.*, 1978; Matilla *et al.*, 1978; Gershon, 1984). Protriptyline and viloxazine have been found to be relatively non-sedating and may have slight stimulant effects (Turner *et al.*, 1975; Bye *et al.*, 1978; Greenwood, 1982).

Amitriptyline (37.5, 70 mg), trazodone (100, 200 mg), viloxazine (100, 200 mg), protriptyline (10, 20 mg) or placebo were administered in a double-blind, independent groups design. Ninety healthy volunteers participated as subjects and completed a battery of tests before, and two and four hours after drug administration.

Different profiles of cognitive and psychomotor effects were produced by the different antidepressants. The most discriminating factor was the sedative effect of each drug. The less sedating antidepressants, protriptyline and viloxazine, produced similar effects across the range of measures used. Neither of these compounds impaired performance on memory or psychomotor tasks. If anything, the lower doses – especially of protriptyline – had a slight stimulant effect on performance and slightly increased feelings of alertness. The high dose of viloxazine produced an increase in subjective ratings of drowsiness at two hours, but, nevertheless, did not impair objective measures of performance. This lack of cognitive effects accords with the few other studies of the lower dose levels of both protriptyline (Bye et al., 1978) and viloxazine (Bayliss and Duncan, 1974; Kirby and Turner, 1974).

In contrast, the two sedating antidepressants produced global impairments on virtually every task. The impairments produced by amitriptyline and trazodone were virtually identical on a wide range of measures: symbol copying, symbol substitution, cancellation, choice reaction time, digit span and visuo-spatial span. Thus manual motor speed, attention, recoding skills and primary memory were equally affected by both sedative antidepressants and equally unaffected by both non-sedative antidepressants. Although amitriptyline depressed CFFT more than trazodone, both compounds produced similar levels of subjective sedation and physical tiredness.

The tasks on which the effects of the two sedative compounds significantly differed were those involving episodic memory. Amitriptyline produced impairments on these tasks which were generally larger than those produced by trazodone, with the difference between the higher doses being greater than the difference between the lower doses. This greater effect of amitriptyline on episodic memory may have reflected its additional anticholinergic action, operating over and above its sedative effects.

Antidepressants and the elderly

Depression occurs at a high rate in the elderly population (Gurland et al., 1980) who thus form a substantial proportion of people prescribed anti-depressants. Elderly people metabolize drugs more slowly and so may experience more accentuated performance impairments. Branconnier et al. (1982) assessed the effects of 50 mg of amitriptyline on just six volunteers aged over sixty years. Like the results of Curran et al. (1988), they found clear impairments on episodic memory tasks. Moscovitz and Burns (1986) compared the effects of amitriptyline (50 mg) with trazodone (100 mg) on fifteen elderly subjects (over 60 years) and found that amitriptyline produced more attentional impairments than trazodone.

It is likely that any performance decrements are more debilitating for elderly groups, given that a degree of slowering is due to ageing per se. A modest decline in the cognitive or psychomotor abilities of a young person may be compensated for and impinge relatively little on their daily lives. However, the same loss in an older person who is already performing at a lower baseline may have more serious subjective and clinical consequences.

The problem may be compounded by 'polydrug therapy' as many elderly people may be concomitantly taking other drugs, such as sleeping pills or various over-the-counter drugs. In clinical practice, it is not that unusual to see an elderly patients displaying some signs of dementia, such as poor concentration and memory, but who, when later taken off their antidepressants, hypnotics and tranquillizers, no longer show such signs.

Alcohol and antidepressants

The results of studies which have assessed the effects of alcohol in combination with antidepressants are fairly consistent. Even small amounts of alcohol may increase the detrimental effects of antidepressants on performance or cause additional deficits to emerge (Seppala, 1977; Matilla *et al.*, 1978; Landauer *et al.*, 1969; Bayliss and Duncan, 1974).

Effects of repeated doses

Repeated doses of a drug can have one or more of three main effects. Firstly, as the drug and its active metabolites accumulate in the system, its acute effects may be aggravated and increase over the treatment period. Secondly, repeated dosing may lead to tolerance whereby the effects of a single dose lessen or are absent over days or weeks of treatment. Thirdly, repeated dosing may not lead to any accumulation of effect in that baseline (pre-dosage) measures remain stable, but for a time following each daily dose, performance is impaired.

Few studies have looked at the effects of repeated doses of antidepressants, but in general these have not found evidence of accumulation of performance impairments over time. Rather, decrements tend to be most pronounced in the initial days of repeated dosing although residual impairments may be detectable after one or two weeks. For example, at the end of two weekly treatments with amitriptyline (60 mg per day) reaction times were found to be slowed down, and these impairments were exaggerated with the addition of alcohol (Seppala *et al.*, 1975; Seppala, 1977; Matilla *et al.*, 1978). Allen *et al.* (1991) found that although there was no accumulation of impairment over a ten day treatment with clomipramine, volunteers were impaired at three to four hours after a dose on days 5 and 10, implying a lack of tolerance to the acute effects of the drug.

Where studies have monitored both levels of sedation and levels of performance, the two tend to covary over time. For example, Curran and Lader (1986) compared the effects of mianserin with fluvoxamine and a placebo over an eight day treatment period. Unlike fluvoxamine, the sedative antidepressant mianserin produced marked impairments following the first dose: reaction times and motor speeds were slower, CFFT was depressed and voltages in the slow EEG wavebands increased. These sedative effects, however, lessened over the treatment period. A single dose of mianserin also produced impairments on a word recall task (free recall of forty-nine categorizable words presented over three trials), as shown in Figure 12.2, which were no longer evident at the end of the eight day treatment (Curran *et al.*, 1986). Analyses showed that the initial impairments of episodic memory correlated significantly with levels of subjective sedation, with motor

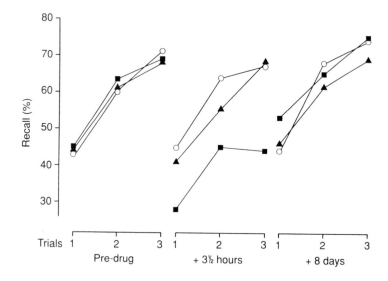

Figure 12.2 Effects of fluvoxamine (▲), mianserin (■) and placebo (○) on percentage of words recalled pre-drug, $3\frac{1}{2}$ hours post-drug and on day 8 of treatment. (From Curran *et al.*, 1986; reprinted with permission.)

speed (finger tapping rate), and with simple reaction times, as depicted in Figure 12.3. Thus it appeared that impairments in memory, as well as psychomotor impairments were global effects due, in a large part at least, to the sedative effect of mianserin, and that tolerance to sedation built up over an eight day period.

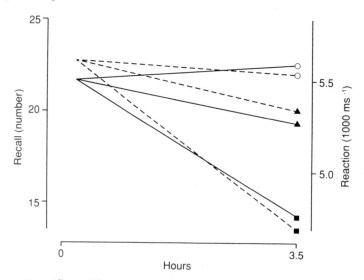

Figure 12.3 Effects of fluvoxamine (▲), mianserin (■) and placebo (○) on number of words recalled (*broken line*) and (*solid line*): (a) reaction times.

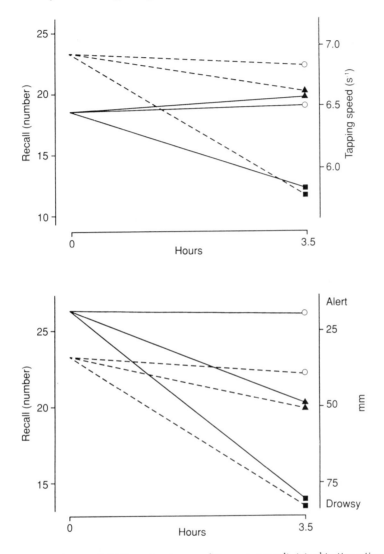

Figure 12.3 *Continued.* (b) finger tapping speed (taps per second); (c) subjective ratings of alertness. (From Curran *et al.*, 1986; reprinted with permission.)

Following on from the study of single doses of antidepressants with differing sedative and anticholinergic profiles, an attempt was made to assess the extent to which tolerance developed to the performance effects of amitriptyline and trazodone (Sakulsripong *et al.*, 1991). Amitriptyline (37.5 mg), trazodone (100 mg) and placebo were administered for the first seven days and in double-dosage for the next seven days.

Lack of tolerance to the effects of a daytime dose of both amitriptyline and trazodone was found on psychomotor measures. Both antidepressants produced similar levels of sedation which were as high after the morning dose on day 14 as they were on day 1. Subjective sedation and psychomotor measures generally revealed large effects of hour of testing but not of day of testing, showing a lack of tolerance to acute effects over treatment. When measures of sedation were covaried from psychomotor measures there were no significant drug effects, indicating that psychomotor impairments were by-products of changes in arousal.

However, significant differences between amitriptyline and trazodone on most measures of memory performance remained after covarying sedation. Further, these results implied that tolerance built up to the memory-impairing effects of a daytime dose of amitriptyline over the treatment period for measures of immediate memory but that delayed memory performance showed residual impairments at the end of the two weeks.

Few studies have assessed the effects of antidepressants on real-life activities such as operating machinery, cooking or driving. However, if reaction times, vigilance and psychomotor skills are impaired in laboratory tasks, it is likely that a skill such as driving a car, which involves all those abilities, will also be impaired. Indeed, Clayton et al. (1977) report deficits on tests of car driving ability after seven days of imipramine (150 mg per day), but no impairment by viloxazine (75 mg per day). Compared with both placebo and an untreated control group, subjects given imipramine hit more bollards when weaving a car through a series of bollards. Further, people given imipramine had poorer scores on a measure of risk-taking when parking the vehicle.

EFFECTS OF ANTIDEPRESSANTS ON DEPRESSED PATIENTS

When antidepressants are prescribed, they are given for a minimum of two to three weeks as it generally takes this time before they begin to have an antidepressant effect, and full efficacy may take six to eight weeks. Often, these drugs are prescribed for periods of several months or more. The development of tolerance restricts the relevance of studies with volunteers which assess effects over short time periods. Further, in patient studies, one is necessarily assessing the effects of all possible dynamics represented in Figure 12.1. Over the time course of a normal treatment period, the interactions depicted within the triangle may also change substantially.

An overview of studies shows that cognitive function may either sometimes improve in parallel with mood elevation, or sometimes show no change or impairments, despite improvement in depressed mood, or sometimes improve over a time course quite different from that of mood changes. Improvements in both mood and cognition have been reported in some studies of imipramine (Sternberg and Jarvik, 1976; Glass et al., 1981), amitriptyline (Sternberg and

Jarvik, 1976), clovoxamine (Lamping *et al.*, 1984), trazodone and fluvoxamine (Fudge *et al.*, 1990). Impairments in cognition despite elevated mood have also been reported in studies of imipramine (Amin *et al.*, 1980; Legg and Stiff, 1976) and amitriptyline (Lamping *et al.*, 1984; McNair *et al.*, 1984). Where studies have employed a variety of cognitive and psychomotor measures, a differential pattern of effects has often emerged with some aspects of performance being impaired while other aspects show no change.

For example, Calev *et al.* (1989) found a twenty-one day treatment with imipramine had no effect on short-term verbal memory or on the retrieval of information acquired before drug treatment began, but did produce significant anterograde impairments of episodic memory (as assessed by paired-associate learning). During the three week duration of that study, performance changes were not accompanied by significant changes in depressed mood. Improvements in paired-associate learning were reported by Fudge *et al.* (1990) over a six week treatment of depressed outpatients with either trazodone or fluoxetine. These improvements, however, paralleled significant mood changes such that covarying out depression scores on the Hamilton left no significant memory effects.

Lamping *et al.* (1984) used a range of cognitive assessments in a study of forty patients administered either amitriptyline or clovoxamine for four weeks. Amelioration of depressed mood was similar in both drug groups, and there were no changes in performance on a prose recall task or a ten-word recall task. To examine the extent to which changes in memory performance over treatment were due to changes in response bias rather than retention, Lamping *et al.* used a signal detection analysis of performance on a word recognition task. Response bias was unchanged but retention showed a significant difference between the two drug groups. Lamping *et al.* concluded that amitriptyline impaired memory compared with clovoxamine, but this interpretation is questionable because:

1. Recognition performance was near ceiling levels initially.
2. Other verbal memory tasks showed no drug difference.
3. There was evidence that amitriptyline produced improved performance relative to clovoxamine on a test of visual retention.

A different time course of changes in varied aspects of mood, cognition and psychomotor performance was apparent in a study by Lader *et al.* (1987) of seventy depressed inpatients prescribed a variety of antidepressants, often with other psychotropic drugs. Lader *et al.* conclude:

> Marked differences emerged in the *severity* and *rate* of response of various components of depressed illness. Sad affect, lack of interest, hopelessness, helplessness, suicidal thinking and somatic dysfunction rapidly recovered. An intermediate rate was observed for low self esteem, sleep disturbances, cognitive slowing ... and subjective memory complaints. Specific features like guilt ... and anxiety remitted slowly. (p. 98)

The clear inconsistencies in the findings of studies with depressed patients are attributable to marked methodological differences between them. Patient samples involved have been highly heterogeneous, varying from chronically hospitalized cases to depressed subjects recruited from newspaper adverts. Treatment regimes have also been diverse, and even where the same antidepressant has been used, dosages have varied considerably. Allocation to treatment groups has not always been random. Further, practice effects on performance tasks can be confounded with improvements in function where studies do not have placebo controls. Assessments of cognitive function and psychomotor performance have also varied, and, in some cases, the same version of a test has been administered repeatedly such that practice effects render results largely uninterpretable. The timing of assessments during a treatment period is also crucial in view of the need to monitor both tolerance and the interrelationship between changes in mood and changes in cognition.

CONCLUSIONS

The effect of antidepressants on cognition and performance remains a neglected field of research, and little progress has been made in the decade since Thompson and Trimble (1982) reviewed the literature. The widest gap in our knowledge remains that of how these drugs affect the functioning of those people who are most likely to be taking them: depressed people who are prescribed antidepressants either by their general practitioner or as a hospital outpatient. Major methodological differences between studies, as well as the general dearth of research, renders most conclusions tentative.

Evidence from normal volunteer studies suggests that there are differences between the performance effects of different antidepressants. Single dose studies indicate that one major determinant of those differences is the sedative properties of an antidepressant. Sedative compounds produce blanket impairments across a wide range of performance tests such that conclusions are precluded about a drug's effects on specific aspects of cognitive or psychomotor functioning. Those impairments appear to be exacerbated by even small amounts of alcohol, and one would predict that concurrent use of other sedative psychotropics, such as benzodiazepines, would similarly exaggerate performance decrements. Studies from our own laboratory indicate that anticholinergic antidepressants may produce additional attentional or mnemonic decrements.

How tolerance may develop to these effects when an antidepressant is taken repeatedly remains to be fully assessed. Evidence from studies with volunteer subjects suggests that tolerance develops differentially to the various effects, and that the pattern of differential tolerance depends on the particular antidepressant. There is some indication that tolerance to sedative effects develops more rapidly than tolerance to cognitive impairments. Further, after repeated dosing, performance impairments may be evident for a period of time following individual, daily doses.

Results of volunteer studies cannot be generalized to predict effects in patient populations, where baseline deficits in functioning appear associated with depressed mood itself and where the interaction of performance, drug and mood-state is complex. However, erring on the side of caution, such results would reinforce good clinical practice of prescribing sedative anti-depressants in a single, night-time dose, not only to promote sleep but also so that performance decrements related to that dose may be largely 'slept off' although some residual effects may be detectable the following day. Further, cautioning patients about exacerbating such effects with alcohol is clearly warranted.

Evidence from studies with depressed patients has not produced a consistent picture of effects. Antidepressants have been reported to impair, improve or have no effect on the performance of depressed subjects. Further, the covariance between changes in mood and performance has shown similar inconsistencies across the few studies where a reasonable attempt has been made to assess this interrelationship.

Future research must clearly address the issue of possible impairments in the ability of depressed people to function optimally while taking anti-depressants over normal treatment periods. It should also follow up patients to assess whether any impairments found while an antidepressant was being taken are ameliorated when the drug is withdrawn. Repeated assessments of both performance and mood within and beyond the treatment period will enable researchers to assess the interrelationships between those variables and how this may change over time. Assessments themselves should be carefully selected such that they do not merely detect global sedative effects of drugs but also tap the kinds of performance impairment associated with depression, such as in tasks requiring mental effort.

A further criterion in selecting assessments should be their ecological validity or relevance to everyday task demands. Showing a drug-induced impairment in a laboratory task such as substituting symbols for digits clearly says little about how that drug may affect real-life activities. Few studies have assessed effects on day-to-day tasks, but the evidence implies that at least some antidepressants have deleterious effects on real-life skills such as driving.

Lastly, on a more theoretical note, antidepressants are potential tools in the study of mood and cognition. One question we are currently addressing in a longitudinal study is whether these drugs, by elevating depressed mood, may also change the negative bias in cognitive processing associated with depression. The answer to such questions require methodologically sound research with depressed patients over extended periods of treatment, with its associated problems of recruitment, drop-outs and so on. Only by undertaking such time-consuming studies can we begin to claim that research is relevant to those patients who are taking antidepressants.

REFERENCES

Allen, D., Curran, H.V. and Lader, M. (1991). The effects of repeated doses of clomipramine and alprazolam on physiological, psychomotor and cognitive functions in normal subjects. *European Journal of Clinical Pharmacology* **40**: 355–62.

Altman, H.J., Normile, H.J. and Gershon, S. (1987). Non-cholinergic pharmacology in human cognitive disorders. In *Cognitive Neurochemistry*, edited by S.M. Stahl, S.D. Iversen and E.C. Goodman. Oxford University Press, pp. 346–71.

Amin, M.M., Khan, P. and Lehmann, H.E. (1980). The differential effects of viloxazine and imipramine on performance tests: their relationship to behavioural toxicity. *Psychopharmacology Bulletin* **16**: 57–60.

Bartus, R.T., Dean, R.L., Beer, B. and Lippa, A.S. (1982). The cholinergic hypothesis of geriatric memory dysfunction. *Science, New York* **217**: 408–17.

Bayliss, P.F. and Duncan, S.M. (1974). The clinical pharmacology of viloxazine hydrochloride: a new antidepressant of novel chemical structure. *British Journal of Clinical Pharmacology* **1**: 431–7.

Beck, A.T. (1967). *Depression: Clinical, Experimental and Theoretical Aspects*. New York: Hoeber.

Beck, A.T. (1976). *Cognitive Therapy and the Emotional Disorders*. New York: International Universities Press.

Blackburn, I.M. (1988). Psychological processes in depression. In *Adult Abnormal Psychology*, edited by E. Miller and P.J. Cooper. London: Churchill Livingstone.

Blaney, P.H. (1986). Affect and memory: a review. *Psychological Bulletin* **99**: 229–46.

Boyd, J.H. and Weissman, M.M. (1982). Epidemiology. In *Handbook of Affective Disorders*, edited by E.S. Paykel. New York: Guildford Press, pp. 109–25.

Branconnier, R.J., Devitt, D.R., Cole J. and Spera, K.F. (1982). Amitriptyline selectively disrupts verbal recall from secondary memory of the normal aged. *Neurobiology of Aging* **3**: 55–9.

British National Formulary (1990). *British Medical Association and Royal Pharmaceutical Society of Great Britain*. London: The Pharmaceutical Press.

Bye, C., Clubley, M. and Peck, A.W. (1978). Drowsiness, impaired performance and tricyclic antidepressant drugs. *British Journal of Clinical Pharmacology* **6**: 155–62.

Calev, A., Ben-Tzvi, E., Shapira, B., Drexler, H., Carasso, R. and Lerer, B. (1989). Distinct memory impairments following electroconvulsive therapy and imipramine. *Psychological Medicine* **19**: 111–19.

Chan, M., Ehsanullah, R., Wadsworth, J. and McEwen, J. (1980). A comparison of the pharmacodynamic properties of nomifensine and amitriptyline in normal subjects. *British Journal of Clinical Pharmacology* **9**: 247–53.

Clarke, D.M. and Teasdale, J.D. (1982). Diurnal variation in clinical depression and accessibility of memories of positive and negative experiences. *Journal of Abnormal Psychology* **91**: 87–95.

Clayton, A.B., Harvey, P.G. and Betts, T.A. (1977). Effects of two antidepressants, imipramine and viloxazine, upon driving performance. *Psychopharmacology* **55**: 9–12.

Collerton, D. (1986). Cholinergic function and intellectual decline in Alzheimer's disease. *Neuroscience* **19**: 1–28.

Curran, H.V. (1986). Tranquillising memories: a review of the effects of benzodiazepines on human memory. *Biological Psychology* **23**: 179–213.

Curran, H.V. (1991). Benzodiazepines, mood and memory: a review. *Psychopharmacology*, **105**: 1–8.

Curran, H.V. and Golombok, S. (1985). *Bottling It Up*. London: Faber and Faber.

Curran, H.V. and Lader, M. (1986). The psychopharmacological effects of repeated doses of fluvoxamine, mianserin and placebo in healthy human subjects. *European Journal of Pharmacology* **29**: 601–7.

Curran, H.V., Sakulsriprong, M. and Lader, M. (1988). Antidepressants and human memory:

an investigation of four drugs with different sedative and anticholinergic profiles. *Psychopharmacology* **95**: 520–7.

Curran, H.V., Shine, P. and Lader, M. (1986). Effects of repeated doses of fluvoxamine, mianserin and placebo on memory and measures of sedation, *Psychopharmacology* **89**: 360–3.

Deutsch, J. (1971). The cholinergic synapse and the site of memory. *Science, New York* **174**: 788–94.

Drachman, D.A. (1978). Central cholinergic system and memory. In *Psychopharmacology: A Generation of Progress*, edited by M.A. Lipton *et al.* New York: Raven Press. Based on Drachman and Leavitt (1974). *Archives of Neurology* **30**: 113–21.

Ellis, H.C. and Ashbrook, P.W. (1988). Resource allocation model of the effects of depressed mood states on memory. In *Affect, Cognition and Social Behaviour*, edited by K. Fielder and J. Forgas. Toronto: Hogrefe, pp. 25–43.

Ferris, S.H., McCarthy, M., Reisberg, B., Gershon, S. and Bush, D. (1980). Influence of zimeldine and imipramine on psychomotor skill and cognitive function *Acta Psychiatrica Scandinavica* **63** (Suppl. 290): 302

Fudge, J.L., Perry, P.J., Garvey, M.J. and Kelly, M.W. (1990). A comparison of the effect of fluoxetine and trazodone on the cognitive functioning of depressed patients. *Journal of Affective Disorders* **18**: 275–80.

Gershon, S. (1984). Comparative side effect profiles of trazodone and imipramine: special reference to the geriatric population. *Psychopathology* **17**: 39–50.

Glass, R.M., Uhlenhuth, E.H., Hartel, F.W., Matuzas, W. and Fischman, N.W. (1981). Cognitive dysfunction and imipramine in outpatient depressives. *Archives of General Psychiatry* **38**: 1048–51.

Greenwood, D.T. (1982). Viloxazine and neurotransmitter function. In *Typical and Atypical Antidepressants: Molecular Mechanisms*, edited by E. Costa and G. Racagni. New York: Raven Press.

Gurland, B., Dean, L. and Cross, P. (1980). The epidemiology of depression and dementia in the elderly: the use of multiple indicators of the conditions. In *Psychopathology in the Aged*, edited by D. Cole and M. Barrett. New York: Raven Press.

Hindmarch, I., Subhan, Z. and Stoker, M.J. (1983). The effects of zimeldine and amitriptyline on car driving and psychomotor performance, *Acta Psychiatrica Scandinavica* **68** (Supplement 308): 141–6.

Kirby, M. and Turner, P. (1974). Some preliminary observations on ICI 58,834, a new psychotropic agent in man. *British Journal of Clinical Pharmacology* **1**: 169.

Lader, M., Lang, R. and Wilson, G. (1987). *Patterns of Improvement in Depressed In-patients.* Maudsley Monographs 30, Oxford University Press.

Lamping, D.L., Spring, B. and Gelenberg, A.J. (1984). Effects of two antidepressants on memory performance in depressed outpatients: a double-blind study. *Psychopharmacology* **84**: 254–61.

Landauer, A., Milner, G. and Patman, J. (1969). Alcohol and amitriptyline effects on skills related to driving behaviours. *Science, New York* **163**: 1467–8.

Legg, J.F. and Stiff, M.P. (1976). Drug related patterns of depressed patients. *Psychopharmacology* **50**: 205–10.

Leibowitz, M.R., Fyer, A., Gorman, J., Campeas, R., Sandberg, D., Hollander, E., Lazlo, A. and Klein, D. (1988). Tricyclic therapy of the DSM-III anxiety disorders: a review with implications for further research. *Journal of Psychiatric Research* **22** (Supplement 1): 7–31.

Linnoila, M., Johnson, J., Dubyoski, T., Ross, R., Buchsbaum, M., Potter, W.Z. and Weingartner, H. (1983). Effects of amitriptyline, desipramine and zimeidine alone and in combination with ethanol, on information processing, and memory in healthy volunteers. *Acta Psychiatrica* **68** (Suppl. 308): 175–181.

Matilla, M.J., Liljequist, R. and Seppala, T. (1978). Effects of amitriptyline and mianserin on psychomotor skills and memory in man. *British Journal of Clinical Pharmacology* **55**: 53–5.

McNair, D.M., Kahn, R.J., Frankenthaler, L.M. and Faldetta, L.L. (1984). Amoxapine and amitriptyline II specificity of cognitive effects during brief treatment of depression. *Psychopharmacology* **83**: 134–139.

Miller, W.R. (1975). Psychological deficit in depression. *Psychological Bulletin* **82**: 238–60.

Miller, W.R. and Seligman, M.E.P. (1973). Depression and the perception of reinforcement. *Journal of Abnormal Psychology*, **82**: 62–73.

Moscovitz, H. and Burns, M.M. (1986). Cognitive performance in geriatric subjects after acute treatment with antidepressants. *Neuropsychobiology* **15**: 18–43.

Nelson, J.C. and Charney, D.S. (1980). Primary affective disorder criteria and the endogenous–reactive distinction. *Archives of General Psychiatry* **37**: 787–93.

Raps, C.S., Reinhard, K.E. and Seligman, M.E.P. (1980). Reversal of cognitive and affective deficits associated with depression and learned helplessness by mood elevation in patients. *Journal of Abnormal Psychology* **89**: 342–9.

Rickelson, E. (1984). The newer antidepressants: structures, pharmacokinetics, pharmacodynamics and proposed mechanisms of action. *Psychopharmacology Bulletin* **20**: 213–23.

Sakulsripong, M.Q., Curran, H.V. and Lader, M.H. (1991). Does tolerance develop to the sedative and amnesic effects of antidepressants.? A comparison of amitriptyline, trazodone and placebo. *European Journal of Clinical Pharmacology* **40**: 43–8.

Segal, Z.V. (1988). Appraisal of the self-schema construct in cognitive models of depression. *Psychological Bulletin* **103**: 147–62.

Seppala, T. (1977). Psychomotor skills during acute and two week treatment with mianserin (ORG GB94) and amitriptyline, and their combined effects with alcohol. *Annals of Clinical Research* **9**: 66–72.

Seppala, T., Linnoila, M., Elonen, F., Matilla, M.J. and Maki, M. (1975). Effect of tricyclic antidepressants and alcohol on psychomotor skills related to driving. *Clinical Pharmacology and Therapeutics* **17**: 515–22.

Seppala, T., Stromberg, C. and Bergman, I. (1984). Effects of zimeldine, mianserin and amitriptyline on psychomotor skills and their interaction with ethanol: a placebo controlled cross-over study. *European Journal of Clinical Pharmacology* **27**: 181–9.

Sternberg, D.E. and Jarvik, M.E. (1976). Memory functions in depression. *Archives of General Psychiatry* **33**: 219–24.

Szbadi, E., Bradshaw, C.M. and Besson, J.A. (1976). Elongation of pause time in speech: a simple objective measure of motor retardation in depression. *British Journal of Psychiatry* **129**: 592–7.

Thompson, P.J. and Trimble, M.R. (1982). Non-MAOI antidepressant drugs and cognitive functions: a review. *Psychological Medicine* **12**: 539–48.

Turner, P., Bayliss, P.F. and Ghose, K. (1975). Clinical pharmacology of viloxazine (vivalan). *Journal of International Medical Research* **3** (Supplement 3): 41–9.

Warrington, S.J., Ankier, S.I. and Turner, P. (1984). An evaluation of possible interactions between ethanol and trazadone or amitriptyline. *British Journal of Clinical Pharmacology* **18**: 549–557.

Watts, F.N. and Cooper, Z. (1989). The effects of depression on structural aspects of the recall of prose. *Journal of Abnormal Psychology* **98**: 150–3.

Weingartner, H., Cohen, R., Murphy, D.L., Martello, J. and Gerdt, C. (1981). Cognitive processes in depression. *Archives of General Psychiatry* **38**: 42–7.

Weingartner, H. and Silberman, E. (1982). Models of cognitive impairment: cognitive changes in depression. *Psychopharmacology Bulletin* **18**: 27–42.

Zornetzer, S.F. (1978). Neurotransmitter modulation and memory: a new neuropharmacological phrenology. In *Psychopharmacology: A Generation of Progress*, edited by L.A. Lipton, A. Di Marcio and K.F. Killam. New York: Raven Press.

13

The Effects of Anaesthetic and Analgesic Drugs

K. MILLAR

INTRODUCTION: AN EARLY STUDY OF RECOVERY

The effects of anaesthetic and related drugs have long been of interest to psychologists. The early indulgences of William James in the 'ether frolics' of Victorian times may not have been particularly edifying for their insights, but they no doubt provided James at least with temporary relief from his chronic hypochondriasis (Knight, 1950). This was, perhaps, more relief than that granted to early surgical patients for, as Mostert (1975) points out, contemporary reports noted that it was common for the surgeon to enquire during 'anaesthesia' whether the patient was experiencing pain (*Lancet*, 1847). Indeed, conversation between the surgical team and the patient was as common then with so-called general anaesthesia as it is today with local or regional anaesthesia.

The after-effects of anaesthesia upon cognitive or skilled performance was, understandably, less of an issue in those early years. Far greater concern was attached to simple survival, not only from the trauma of surgery but also from wound infection and over-enthusiastic application of ether or chloroform during the operation itself. With the passage of time, anaesthetic techniques became more refined and new volatile and intravenous agents were introduced to ensure that most patients would be oblivious to surgical events (see Millar, 1989).

An experiment by William McDougall during his time at the Psychological Laboratory in Oxford must stand as one of the earliest objective assessments of the influence of an anaesthetic upon the time course of its cognitive after-effects (McDougall and Smith, 1920: a report of a study conducted in 1914). McDougall studied the effects of chloroform and other drugs, including alcohol, strychnine and opium, upon psychomotor and perceptual performance. Inclusion of the latter drugs suggests that ethical committees had little jurisdiction in those days, and it is a credit to McDougall's determination – and certainly to his constitution – that he himself acted as a subject in the study.

Of particular note was McDougall's use of a 'windmill test' to detect drug effects upon CNS processes. The test, which involved the subject reporting the perception of phase reversals in the apparent direction of motion of the rotating vanes of a model windmill, was apparently sensitive to the depressant effects of alcohol and fatigue in that both conditions resulted in a reduction in the number of reported reversals. The concept behind the test would seem to bear considerable similarity to the critical flicker fusion test which enjoys considerable application in present-day studies of anaesthetics (Hindmarch, 1988).

The effect of chloroform on the windmill test is shown in Table 13.1 with McDougall's subjective sensations. As McDougall pointed out, the effect of chloroform appeared to reach a maximum after some one to two minutes of inhaling the vapour, with recovery being progressive over a period of ten minutes. His assistant, Miss Smith, whose baseline phase rate was seven reversals per minute, experienced a reduction to five phases in two minutes following chloroform. Another volunteer whose normal phase rate was five per two minutes, seemed to be particularly affected by the chloroform, reporting a change in phase only some three minutes following the vapour.

McDougall's study was undoubtedly crude but it will be seen that his

Table 13.1 Recovery of performance and subjective impressions of a single subject on the windmill test (a progenitor of the critical flicker fusion threshold) as measured by the number of perceived phase reversals of apparent motion of the rotating vanes in sixty seconds; note the use of a baseline measure and the monitoring of performance over time until recovery to baseline functioning. (Adapted from McDougall and Smith, 1920.)

Recovery of chloroform

February 2nd, 1914   Subject: W. McD.

Time	Observations
3.55 p.m.	11 phase reversals in 60 s (baseline)
3.57 p.m.	'Four deep breaths of vapour from a piece of lint sprinkled with chloroform and held over the face. This was sufficient to cause giddiness, with buzzing in the ears, and a sense of swelling in the face.'
Immediately thereafter	2 phase reversals in 60 s
4.00 p.m.	4 phase reversals in 60 s
4.02 p.m.	7 phase reversals in 60 s
	'Feeling almost normal'
4.03 p.m.	9 Feeling almost normal
4.05 p.m.	10 Feeling almost normal
4.08 p.m.	12 Feeling almost normal

basic design is similar to that employed in present-day studies. In fact, McDougall's inclusion of a baseline session to establish pre-drug performance levels renders his study superior to some recent research which has committed the serious error of omitting any baseline measure.

While studies such as McDougall's confirmed that an anaesthetic agent had the potential to disrupt cognitive processes, in the 1920s the result would have been of little practical importance. Patients would spend a quite lengthy period in hospital following surgery, and certainly long enough for any after-effects of the anaesthetic to wear off. That is not the case today. In recent years there has been an increasing trend for surgical procedures and anaesthesia to be administered on a 'day-case' or 'day-care' basis. In other words, patients are admitted to the day-case unit early in the morning (or, occasionally, the preceding evening), are prepared for and undergo surgery, and then when recovered they return home the same afternoon or evening. The same is true of dental patients who may have general anaesthesia or deep sedation and then return home a short time after the procedure.

Such routines have much to offer in terms of cost saving and reduced disruption to patients' lives, but it is of vital importance that, when discharged, patients have recovered their psychomotor and cognitive faculties. The real-life issue of whether patients are 'street-fit' after anaesthesia is central to the assessment of recovery and is the focus of the present chapter.

In order to understand the difficulties inherent in this kind of research, it is useful firstly to consider the typical design of a recovery study. The example will concern the design applied to hospitalized patient populations. There are also laboratory studies of anaesthetic effects upon fit volunteers, but the special problems which attach to such studies are discussed later when issues of methodology are under consideration.

THE TYPICAL STUDY OF RECOVERY FROM ANAESTHESIA

The time course of a typical recovery study would be as follows. After admission, patients would normally practise the battery of performance tasks to establish a baseline level of performance. They might then receive premedication which serves the dual purpose of sedation and reducing anxiety (a benzodiazepine may be used for this purpose), and of drying up secretions which may be undesirable during surgery (an anticholinergic drug such as atropine might be employed here). Anaesthesia would then be induced by intravenous injection and might be maintained for the duration of the procedure by repeated intravenous bolus or by inhalation of a volatile agent such as halothane or nitrous oxide in oxygen.

Initial recovery would be established by the simple 'wake-up' test which requires the patient to give his or her correct name, date of birth and address.

Then if the patient were physically capable, he or she would again perform the test battery at regular intervals until, as judged by the level of performance or by physical signs, the patient were considered fit to be discharged.

The above describes an ideal situation. But the very nature of a recovery study means that it is beset by problems which afflict the reliability and validity of its conclusions. These problems are best considered now as a prelude to the review of results from recovery studies. It is important to refer back to these problems when discussing the uncertain results of many studies.

Methodological and conceptual problems

GENERAL

Testing conditions in hospital settings are often far from ideal because of noise distraction, patient discomfort and the fact that psychological testing must inevitably give precedent to the often inflexible nature of the medical routine. Secondly, baseline performance measures are influenced by the fact that most patients are anxious prior to anaesthesia. As it is well established that anxiety can adversely affect performance (Eysenck, 1981), the baseline level of performance partially reflects the adverse effect of this emotion and is then not directly comparable with post-anaesthetic performance where anxiety levels are considerably reduced (Wallace, 1987).

Moreover, while many studies set out ostensibly to examine the effects of particular anaesthetic agents upon recovery, their results are confounded with the effects of the premedicative drugs. However, some studies are notable for having employed unpremedicated patients in order to give a clearer impression of the anaesthetic effects (e.g. Herbert et al., 1983) or have controlled the premedication condition so as to demonstrate its interaction with the anaesthetic (Baillie et al., 1989). Patients may also be administered antibiotic drugs to treat pre- and post-surgical infections. Such drugs inhibit protein synthesis and are known to have an adverse effect upon human learning (Idzikowski and Oswald, 1983), thus further confounding the effects of anaesthetic agents.

Furthermore, the post-anaesthetic test routine may not follow an orderly time sequence. Whilst most papers would give the impression that all patients were tested at very regular intervals in the post-anaesthetic period, experience of the practical realities suggest that this is unlikely. The implications of this for data presentation and analysis are considered below.

THE CONCEPTS OF 'IMPAIRMENT' AND 'RECOVERY'

Impairment. Implicit in the concept of impaired performance is the notion that one has a reliable measure of unimpaired performance with which the anticipated adverse effect of an anaesthetic can be compared. But it has already been pointed out above that the pre-anaesthetic baseline or control conditions are contaminated with the effects of anxiety and of inadequate practice. There is, then, no absolute or standard level of performance from which one can infer impairment.

It is evident that most investigators equate the term 'impairment' with a mean difference between control and treatment conditions which lies beyond the $p < 0.05$ level of significance; there are two problems with this criterion. The first is that a statistically significant difference may be so small as to have no practical or clinical relevance. The second problem is that it neglects the fact that the effect of the anaesthetic may be to make performance *more variable*. The mean difference between control and treatment may be small and non-significant, the effect of the anaesthetic being to make performance more erratic. To take the example of choice reaction time, some fast responses may be offset by some much slower responses which might indicate lapses of attention. Such lapses may have serious consequences in the case of a post-surgical patient who has been discharged following day-case surgery.

Equally, the effect of an anaesthetic may be to cause performance variability in only a few individuals. This selective vulnerability is masked when the data are expressed as group mean values, and the misleading impression is given that the anaesthetic in question has no overall adverse effect. An example of this problem is seen in the tabular results of Nightingale *et al.* (1988) in their study of single-breath halothane for short procedures. None of the tasks showed any significant differences from baseline but the mean choice reaction time is shown to be 635 ms with a standard deviation of 995 ms. This would imply that several patients were particularly adversely affected; a fact that is hidden by the mean alone.

To cope with this problem, Gardner and Altman (1986) and Matthews *et al.* (1990) suggest that patients whose performance profiles are similar might be graphed within the same subpanel of a multi-panel figure in order to illustrate common performance trends within subgroups of the sample.

Matthews *et al.* (1990) also draw attention to the conventional presentation and analysis of data from psychomotor recovery studies where performance is measured at several different time points following the recovery of consciousness. Commonly, the data are plotted as group mean values at each time point to produce a curve describing the recovery of performance over time. The first problem with this approach is that individual variation is masked by the group performance curve. Secondly, separate significance tests are often conducted at each time point but without correction for the multiple comparisons in order to take account of the enhanced probability of type 1 error. The time points are often quite close together (perhaps less than thirty minutes) so that the tests are not independent and the value at one time point will probably influence succeeding points. If a test at one time is significant, then it is likely that tests at adjacent times will also be significant.

There are two ways of dealing with this problem. The first is to follow the advice of Gardner and Altman (1986) and Matthews *et al.* (1990) and adopt the confidence interval approach to significant differences in preference to hypothesis testing. Figure 13.1 illustrates this technique applied by Hickey *et al.* (1991) in their study of semantic recognition memory performance after propofol anaesthesia. Impairment is assumed to occur only when the confidence interval does not encompass the baseline level (Hickey *et al.* had first established that practice effects were absent). The second is to calculate a summary measure of performance for each subject so that instead of the repeated measurements over several time points being entered as an individual subject's data, performance is described by the single value of the area of the graph under the individual subject's performance curve (Matthews *et al.*, 1990, provide a simple formula to calculate the area). Hickey *et al.* (1991) applied the approach to the data shown in Figure 13.1; the transformed data is shown in Table 13.2. Note that the table reveals the marked inter-individual variability which is not immediately evident from the figure.

The summary measure has several virtues. It copes much better with missing data than does a conventional analysis. It is also the only measure that can be relied upon if the time points of assessment vary between subjects as may commonly occur when the requirements of methodology must take second place to the often rigid nature of ward life and post-operative care. A potential drawback is, however, that the summary measure employed alone will tend to mask the time of maximal impairment which may be of clinical or practical importance. It is important also to map out performance over time.

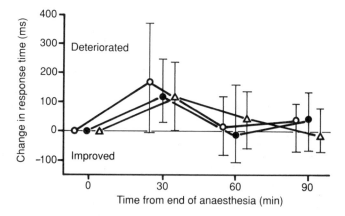

Figure 13.1 Median (95% CI) change in semantic recognition time from baseline (○) after outpatient anaesthesia illustrated by the confidence interval approach. △ = High-dominance word recognition, ● = low-dominance word recognition, ○ = neutral word recognition. (From Hickey *et al.*, 1991; reproduced with permission of the *British Journal of Anaesthesia*.)

Table 13.2 Transformed semantic recognition time data from Figure 13.1 to show expression of performance over time as an 'area under the curve', and to indicate marked inter-individual variation in performance. (Adapted from Hickey *et al.*, 1991; reproduced with permission of the *British Journal of Anaesthesia.*)

Patient	High dominance	Low dominance	Neutral
1	−82	252	650
2	508	−260	580
3	326	−188	−64
4	164	374	396
5	−232	116	−525
6	−302	140	−174
7	435	675	391
8	212	222	168
9	190	−288	630
10	335	528	448

Recovery. Just as the concept of impairment is difficult to define, so is the nature of recovery. Herbert (1991) has observed that the criterion of recovery in many studies is that the patient's performance should have returned to the baseline (pre-anaesthetic) performance level. But this criterion is flawed because few investigators provide patients with sufficient pre-operative exposure to the tasks to overcome practice effects and establish stable baseline performance. As Herbert (1991) states: 'If performance on a given test does improve with repeated exposure to it, then to adopt a return to pre-operative baseline as a criterion of recovery will artificially bias the data towards showing relatively fast recovery'.

The difficulty is compounded by the common omission of any control group which, assuming that it was exposed to similar amounts of practice as the anaesthetic group in order to establish baseline performance, would give an indication of the extent to which performance changed over time due to practice alone. Studies by Herbert *et al.* (1983) and Scott *et al.* (1983) were notable for including control groups in their assessment of recovery of CRT performance. The data from Scott *et al.* are shown in Figure 13.2 where they illustrate very clearly Herbert's criticism of the criterion of recovery to baseline performance. It can be seen that there is a gross practice effect. Examination of the performance profiles shows that when the post-anaesthetic groups have returned to the equivalent of their baseline performance, the parallel performance of the control group shows considerable improvement relative to their baseline: In other words, the fact that the post-anaesthetic group are performing at baseline level does not imply recovery; on the contrary, they

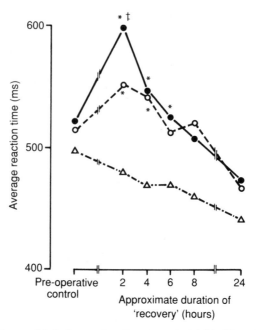

Figure 13.2 Mean serial choice reaction time in control (△), thiopentone (○) and methohexitone (●) conditions before and after anaesthesia and surgery. * denotes mean value significantly greater than control; † denotes mean significantly greater than thiopentone condition (both $p < 0.05$). The figure illustrates the importance of a control measure to reveal the non-stability of performance due to practice. (From Scott *et al.*, 1983; reproduced with permission of Academic Press.)

are still impaired relative to the change shown in the control group's performance.

It is important to be aware that the majority of tasks employed in recovery research may have appreciable practice components. Few investigators provide sufficient practice for performance to stabilize, and in some cases this may be unrealistic. For instance, Millar and Wilkinson (1981) showed that even with extensive pre-training, practice effects could be lengthy and influenced by individual variation. One of their subjects showed continued improvement in serial choice reaction time over a three-week period.

It is a credit to some authors that they draw attention to the presence of practice effects in their data and caution that the sensitivity of the assessment of recovery may be reduced as a consequence (e.g. Sanders *et al.*, 1989). On the other hand, the claim that performance has stabilized after a period of practice should not be taken to imply that practice effects are absent. In a trial of three performance tasks applied to anaesthetic recovery research, Denis *et al.* (1984) assumed that the one test which showed 'stable' performance over time in a control condition was the only 'reliable and valid' task. However, Millar (1986) showed that invariant performance is *not* a reliable indication of the absence of practice effects, citing File and Lister's 1983 study which showed that even where control performance was stable over time, the adverse effect of lorazepam still varied in inverse proportion to the amount of prior training on the task. In other words, a drug could interact with a so-called masked practice effect which was undetected by control performance to give a misleading impression of the adverse effect of the drug.

THE LACK OF A TAXONOMY OF PERFORMANCE TASKS

M. Jones (1988) and Zuurmond *et al.* (1989) observe that a primary failing in recovery research is that the tests used to evaluate recovery have not been standardized. Furthermore, they often tend to measure several psychological functions simultaneously so that when performance shows impairment it may be unclear which of the functions is affected.

Wilkinson (1969) drew attention to this problem more than twenty years ago, and Hindmarch (1989) has commented, appropriately, that the rationale for many tasks has been a matter of whimsy rather than an attempt to develop an accurate and sensitive instrument. However, some systematic attempts are being made to develop a comprehensive taxonomy. In a series of important articles, Parrott (1990, 1991a, b) has described the method of establishing the reliability and validity of performance tasks applied in clinical settings. Parrott's critical and objective stance marks an important step forward. A further advance is found in the establishment of the Recovery Interest Group (RIG, 1990) whose aim is to establish sensitive tasks for assessment of recovery from anaesthesia.

TIME ON TASK

It has long been known that the length of time spent working on a task is one of the most important determinants of whether a stressor will impair its performance or not. Wilkinson (1969) has reviewed considerable evidence to show that stress effects upon performance might be missed if the work period is too short. Poulton and Edwards (1974) provided a good example of this in a study of the interaction of hyoscine with heat. In the first five minutes of tracking performance there was little difference between the various conditions of the experiment. On the basis of a five-minute performance, therefore, one might have assumed that neither stressor had any adverse effect upon performance. Only as time on the task continued did the adverse effects of sleep deprivation and heat become evident. Millar and Standen (1982) have shown a similar effect with the antihistamine brompheniramine. Performance impairment was shown only in the later stages of the twenty minute session, hence refuting the conclusion of earlier studies based on short tasks that the drug had no adverse effect.

In the short term, a subject can muster resources to maintain performance at a satisfactory level even when severely sleep-deprived. With extended performance, however, this coping strategy cannot be sustained. The implication, then, is that when short tasks are employed, a quite misleading impression may be given of the effects of a stressor such as a drug upon performance.

Herbert (1987) has observed the relevance of this fact to recovery research where it is common to apply extremely short tasks. For instance, Raybould and Bradshaw (1987) employed a one minute digit symbol substitution task in their study of midazolam premedication; Zuurmond et al. (1989) measured only twenty reactions on a CRT task in their study of methohexitone; Reitan et al. (1986) assessed only a thirty second performance on the pegboard test in their study of midazolam and thiopentone.

The studies above are examined in greater detail in the review below. At this stage, it is simply relevant to note that they tend to show a common performance pattern whereby, following an initial impairment, performance returns quite quickly to 'normal' levels. It is then concluded that any residual impairment has dissipated. Clearly, however, given the evidence above, such a conclusion may be invalid. Just as in the case of sleep-deprived volunteers, patients are quite capable of pulling themselves together to do their best and perform adequately on a task which they know from their experience of the pre-anaesthetic baseline measure will not last long. They may do so in response to a personal challenge or in the belief that it will help the investigation if they perform as well as possible. The conclusion to be drawn from such results is, then, that patients who may still be suffering sedation can rouse themselves to perform adequately in the short term. This gives the misleading impression that performance has returned to normal although a quite opposite conclusion might be reached if the work period were extended.

Failure to be aware of the importance of the factor of time-on-task is potentially serious. Herbert (1991) has castigated the inadequacies of short test routines by observing the irony that 'the major concern of post-anaesthetic performance testing is to present analogues of real life. But it is highly probable that most patients drive their cars for longer than a few seconds or even minutes. Prolonging the performance measures for a relatively long time would seem to reflect real-life situations to a clearer extent.'

THE LEVEL OF MEASUREMENT

Broadbent (1984) has pointed out that in assessing the effect of a drug upon cognitive and psychomotor efficiency, it is important to examine performance at the level of the subfunction if the mechanism of the drug effect is to be understood. The demonstration of gross impairment of a memory task performance could, for instance, imply interference with attention, encoding or retrieval; it is therefore necessary to employ experimental designs which provide much finer assessment of performance.

Unfortunately, many performance studies of anaesthetics have involved gross assessments and therefore leave the precise mechanism of impairment unclear. A good example is that of memory, where reduction in digit span by certain drugs has been taken to imply a global impairment of memory function. Other empirical evidence shows such a conclusion to be totally unfounded.

THE EFFECTS OF ANAESTHESIA ON COGNITIVE AND PSYCHOMOTOR PERFORMANCE

Normally, in embarking upon a description of clinical and experimental studies of drug effects upon performance, the intention would be to recruit evidence to identify differential, dose-dependent effects of drugs upon specific sub-functions of cognition. However, this approach is difficult to achieve in the anaesthetic literature. For example, while many studies have been conducted with different doses of the intravenous agent propofol, it is difficult or impossible to establish dose-related effects because the studies also differ in other methodological details such as the time on task, amount of practice (if any), control group (if any), patients' ages and surgical treatments, and other drugs administered prior to, during and after surgery. Such confounding variables obscure the precise effects of the drug ostensibly under investigation.

For this reason, in the review that follows, drug doses are rarely given for the simple reason that they are not particularly illuminative. It can be assumed in the case of anaesthetic and analgesic drugs employed in clinical trials with patients undergoing surgery, doses in the normal clinical range – subject to the discretion of the anaesthetist – were employed.

Table 13.3 lists the anaesthetic drugs commonly employed in the UK and which are mentioned in this chapter. The reader may find it useful to refer to this table as the drugs and their effects are discussed.

Reaction processes

SIMPLE REACTION TIME (SRT)

The SRT task has the virtue that it is undemanding to learn, and therefore tends to require little practice to establish a stable baseline level of performance. This is important in recovery research where practical conditions may not afford much time for practice. Conversely, the undemanding nature of the

Table 13.3 Inhalational and intravenous/intramuscular anaesthetic agents in current use in the UK

Name	Route of administration	Use
Nitrous oxide	Inhalational	I (M)
Halothane	Inhalational	I (M)
Enflurane	Inhalational	I (M)
Isoflurane	Inhalational	I (M)
Propofol	Intravenous	(I) M
Thiopentone	Intravenous	(I) M
Methohexitone	Intravenous	(I) M
Etomidate	Intravenous	(I) M
Ketamine	Intravenous/muscular	(I, M)

I = induction. M = maintenance. ( ) = most common use.

task may blunt its sensitivity to performance impairment. It then becomes important to ensure that performance is examined in detail in order to detect possibly small effects.

The importance of such fine analysis is shown in a study by Ghoneim *et al.* (1975) where median SRT was not found to vary significantly between diazepam and fentanyl. However, the standard deviations revealed that response variability was significantly increased with diazepam. Why the authors examined the standard deviation when their summary measure was non-parametric remains unclear. Nonetheless, the result implies that patients were more prone to make the occasional long reaction during recovery from diazepam, perhaps indicating transient lapses in attention which would have important real-life implications.

More recently, Ghoneim *et al.* (1988) have reported no influence of thiopentone induction and nitrous oxide with isoflurane/enflurane anaesthesia on visual SRT. It is unclear whether response variability was assessed, but some difficulty may arise from the fact that only twenty reactions were examined at each test period during recovery. Moreover, there was inter-patient variability of one to seven days in the interval between recovering consciousness from the anaesthetic and the first test period. Patients tested seven days after anaesthesia would be less likely to show impairment and would affect the mean performance of the group in a favourable way.

Forrest and Galletly (1987) and Galletly *et al.* (1988) employed test sessions of thirty-five trials of visual SRT, termed somewhat inappropriately 'reflex time', in their studies of the after-effects of different anaesthetic techniques. The earlier study compared propofol and midazolam anaesthesia and concluded that propofol caused less performance impairment, recovery to baseline occurring within sixty minutes. With midazolam, recovery took some four hours. The reliability of the baseline measure is, however, in doubt because of evidence of unresolved practice effects in their figure 3.

The later study employed eight volunteers in a cross-over design to compare intravenous diazepam and midazolam sedation at intervals up to three hours from injection. However, performance was expressed as a 'composite sedation score' in terms of the number of psychomotor tests which had returned to baseline levels (SRT, letter deletion and various memory tasks). The approach is entirely uninformative and cannot be recommended for recovery research because it gives no indication of which aspects of performance are impaired or, indeed, which functions recover more quickly.

A more recent study by Boysen *et al.* (1989) suggested that recovery of auditory SRT (fifty reactions at each test session) after propofol was complete within about sixty minutes, hence confirming the results of Forrest and Galletly (1987) and indicating that the recovery characteristics of propofol were superior to those of thiopental and etomidate. In fact, performance after propofol was substantially better than baseline performance: a result also observed by Forrest and Galletly, and which may be ascribed to practice. Although the authors suggest that the effect may be due to propofol inducing 'facilitative CNS excitation', it is more plausibly interpreted as a practice effect.

A further study by Boysen *et al.* (1990) compared recovery of the same auditory SRT after propofol with that of methohexitone. The results are not directly comparable with the authors' earlier study because performance is expressed in milliseconds rather than percentage change from baseline. The results indicate that recovery is superior with methohexitone over the first thirty minutes from recovery but it is notable that their data table (see Boysen *et al.*, 1990, table 5, p. 214) shows the statistically significant advantage for methohexitone to be of the order of only 1 ms (213 ms versus 214 ms for propofol). At sixty minutes, propofol is then shown to be significantly better at 200 ms against 206 ms with methohexitone. It seems most unlikely that such small differences have any real-life significance. They simply reflect the misleading impression that can sometimes be gained from non-parametric data analysis (in this case the Wilcoxon test) due to the ranking procedures involved in assessing differences between treatments.

Finally, Cashman and Power (1989) employed visual SRT to examine recovery from brief nitrous oxide and halothane anaesthesia with two doses of zolpidem as premedication (including placebo). Simple reaction time was impaired in a dose-related manner during recovery in all conditions, but had recovered by three hours for placebo and low dose. The authors noted the importance of monotonous and boring tasks in detecting residual impairment, but their claim that their own tests fell within this category is unconvincing in view of the short task duration.

Clearly, none of the studies above employed the SRT task for time periods that would be likely to induce boredom and monotony. For this reason, and the inherent simplicity of the task, it may not be surprising that variable results have been obtained. It would seem that SRT may be of value only in situations where relatively gross post-anaesthetic impairment may be expected.

CHOICE REACTION TIME (CRT)

Studies have employed tests of both *serial* and *discrete* choice reaction time. One might anticipate that the demand for continuous performance inherent in the serial task might make it the more sensitive because the patient is given no opportunity for respite. The discrete task, on the other hand, permits the patient to prepare for each trial. Unfortunately, no study has been conducted to compare performance on the two tasks in order to establish whether they are differentially sensitive.

Serial performance. Three studies are of particular note: all have used the four-choice serial reaction time apparatus devised by Wilkinson and Houghton (1975). The device is a portable and electronic version of the original electromechanical five-choice machine developed by Leonard (1959) and employed in many important studies of factors affecting human performance through the 1960s and early 1970s.

Herbert *et al.* (1983) examined recovery of four-choice performance (five-minute test sessions) after anaesthesia induced with thiopentone and maintained with halothane and nitrous oxide, or where halothane was used for induction and maintenance. The design also included a control group of hospitalized orthopaedic patients who had undergone surgery some two weeks beforehand. The results are shown in Figure 13.3 and reveal that recovery was most impaired after halothane induction and maintenance. However, the most important aspect of the results was the demonstration of a previously unanticipated biphasic recovery pattern. Herbert *et al.* extended their assessment of recovery over two days, in contrast to the majority of studies which restrict testing to the few hours following surgery. Performance profiles indicated that the halothane group was still impaired by lunchtime on the day after surgery, while the other groups had apparently returned to normal. However, on the second day after surgery, performance impairment re-emerged for all but the group whose respiration was controlled during surgery.

Herbert *et al.* point out that:

> This re-emergence of impaired reaction time two days after the operation emphasizes the importance of extending the testing beyond the point where patients have apparently recovered. Without such testing, results of the present study would have concurred with those of earlier reports showing that the psychomotor consequences of general anaesthesia are fairly short-lived. The present data, however, suggest that *it would seem wise to extend the warning not to drive to at least 48 hours post-operatively.* (my italics)

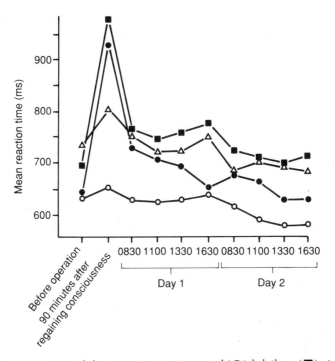

Figure 13.3 Mean serial choice reaction time in control (○), halothane (■), standard
anaesthesia with controlled ventilation (●) and with spontaneous
ventilation (△) before and after surgery. The results show re-emergence
of impairment on day 2. (From Herbert *et al.*, 1983; reproduced with
permission of the *British Medical Journal*.)

The warning above is salutary in view of the fact that most studies examine
only the first few hours of recovery from anaesthesia, and often with short
tasks whose sensitivity may be questionable.

Scott *et al.* (1983) compared the effects of thiopentone and methohexitone
anaesthesia on four-choice performance (five minutes per session) for
twenty-four hours after recovery. A hospitalized control group was included.
Again the task was shown sensitive in discriminating not only overall
impairment, but particularly in the case of methohexitone in the first two
hours after surgery.

Given that few patients would be discharged within two hours, this would
seem of little practical significance. The data are of particular importance,
however, in demonstrating the dangers of employing the 'return to baseline
function' as a criterion of recovery. The data of Scott *et al.* (1983) were
shown in Figure 13.2 where it was clear from the control group's performance
that there was a considerable practice effect. Considering the experimental
groups, while their performance at eight hours from surgery was equivalent

to their baseline performance, it was evident that the control group's performance relative to baseline had improved considerably (the authors provide no SE data, hence making it impossible to establish whether particular differences may be significant). The implication then is that, equivalent to baseline or not, the experimental group were still impaired at eight hours from recovery.

The four-choice task was also used by Barker *et al.* (1986) to compare the after-effects of diazepam or midazolam administered intravenously for sedation during dental surgery. As each of the fifty patients was required to make at least two visits for surgery, the authors were able to employ a cross-over design whereby each patient received both drugs on separate occasions, the order of administration being balanced across patients. Unfortunately, the authors provided only thirty seconds of practice to 'familiarize' the patients with the task, and the baseline score was then derived from only two minutes of performance. Clearly, such brief exposure is quite insufficient in a task which has been shown to have a very extensive practice component (Millar and Wilkinson, 1981). Moreover, neither a placebo condition nor a control group was included.

The results provided no evidence of a differential effect of the two treatments, performance in both conditions showing a marked practice effect which, in the absence of a control group, made it impossible to establish whether any general impairment had occurred. There was also evidence of a sequence effect due to the cross-over design whereby the (non-significantly) faster performance with midazolam was enhanced when subjects experienced diazepam first followed by midazolam at their second visit. These problems were compounded by use of inappropriate statistical tests; the chi-square was based on 'independent' groups which in fact were composed of the same individuals.

Discrete choice performance. The Leeds psychomotor performance tester has had wide application in the assessment of discrete choice performance. The task is basically a six-choice RT task with the facility to measure both decision time and motor speed. The task is effectively subject-paced because each trial can only begin when subjects have returned their hand from the response key to a 'home' key to signal readiness for the next trial. Thus subjects can prepare themselves to respond optimally on each trial.

Most studies using discrete CRT have shown positive results. The study by Mackenzie and Grant (1985) in Figure 13.4 is a typical example in showing superior recovery after propofol than methohexitone or thiopentone. Their study included a control group which showed that practice effects were probably absent or minimal, no doubt due to the fifty practice trials provided beforehand. One reservation might apply to their conclusion that performance had recovered to normal after some ninety minutes: each test session comprised only twenty trials, hence providing scope for patients to motivate

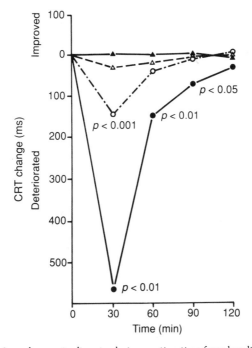

Figure 13.4 Mean changes in discrete choice reaction time from baseline as a function of control (▲), thiopentone (●), propofol (△) and methohexitone (○) anaesthesia. Note the stable control performance, implying an absence of practice effects. But has performance really returned to normal at 90 minutes? (From Mackenzie and Grant, 1985; reproduced with permission of the *British Journal of Anaesthesia.*)

themselves to perform well in the short term even if feeling the worse for the anaesthetic.

Moreover, the conclusions of Mackenzie and Grant contrast with those of the more recent study by Sanders *et al.* (1989) which showed no pattern of superior recovery after propofol when compared with thiopentone. Both anaesthetics caused equal impairment of recovery in the post-surgical period. Impairment (relative to baseline performance) was still present at three hours from surgery and the authors observed that many patients might still be 'significantly impaired in psychomotor function at the time they are customarily discharged from hospital'.

This conclusion is alarming, particularly since it echoes the similar warning from Herbert *et al.* (1983) mentioned above. One must be further concerned by the fact that, since Sanders *et al.* did not include a control group which would probably have shown the common practice effect in CRT performance, their data may *under-estimate* the degree of residual performance impairment because their criterion of recovery was that of return to baseline functioning.

The study by Baillie et al. (1989) provides further uncertainty about the time course of CRT impairment. A two-choice task was employed to assess recovery from propofol anaesthesia preceded either by temazepam or placebo premedication. The results indicated that maximal impairment occurred at thirty minutes from recovery, and particularly where premedication had been with temazepam, hence confirming the point made in a previous section that, when uncontrolled, premedicative drugs may obscure the absolute effects of an anaesthetic upon performance. The authors concluded that recovery, regardless of premedication, was largely complete but gave the *caveat* that in the 'absence of a control group and an opportunity to conduct practice sessions ... it is not possible to specify whether these apparent recoveries ... were solely a recovery from drug-induced impairments or were partially the result of improvement in efficiency resulting from repeated performance of the task.' To this might be added the observation that the CRT task lasted seventy-five seconds: hardly a demanding requirement for patients, and one that might reduce the sensitivity of the task to residual impairment.

A recent study by Hickey et al. (1991) showed no effect of propofol anaesthesia on six-choice RT. Although the authors provided practice data to suggest that baseline performance had been stabilized, the result is difficult to evaluate because only twenty reactions were measured at each test time and no control group was included.

While the intravenous agent propofol has gained a reputation for being relatively free of residual psychomotor effects, from the five studies above it would appear rash to conclude that impairment of discrete CRT performance by propofol anaesthesia may be a relatively transient phenomenon. The methodological difficulties make it uncertain precisely what the specific effect might be.

The results of studies of other agents are not particularly illuminative. Nightingale et al. (1988) compared the effects of halothane and thiopentone as induction agents on recovery of five-choice performance. Practice was not specified and only twenty reactions were measured at each test session. The data showed great variability in performance (e.g. a standard deviation of 995 ms for a mean of 635 ms: see Nightingale et al., table 3, p. 555) and it is, then, no surprise to find that recovery did not vary between the two anaesthetic conditions. The criterion for recovery was that of return to baseline performance, but as no control group was included, it was impossible to establish the extent to which practice had affected the performance profiles.

Similar problems afflicted the study by Zuurmond et al. (1989) which, ironically, had set out to evaluate the relative sensitivities of various psychomotor tasks to post-anaesthetic impairment. The five-choice task was administered for twenty seconds to minimal effect. There was no control group. In their discussion, Zuurmond et al. made the surprising recommendation that 'recovery tests should be as simple as possible, practical, and cause the patient minimal strain'. Such a recommendation would seem quite counter to the evidence of three decades of performance assessment. It also contrasts with that of Jones (1988) in his review of psychomotor recovery where he cautions that problems may arise from the use of short tasks, and that situation-specific motivational factors may act to mask impairment.

Vigilance and attention

Several tasks have been employed to assess the effects of anaesthetics upon attentional processes. These range from the simple, and most commonly used, letter deletion task, through digit symbol substitution to more complex dual tasks. While many tasks have the potential to be sensitive to residual impairment, the methodological problems outlined above often conspire to reduce their efficiency.

LETTER DELETION

The task is simple to administer and commonly requires the patient to scan pages of random letters for particular targets which have to be circled or deleted. Performance is scored in terms of the number of letters deleted within a given time and, more rarely, the number of errors.

A common feature of all the studies to be reported here is their use of short tasks: usually of the order of two or three minutes. Several can be discounted immediately because they suffer from one or more of the following methodological problems: they provide no information on task duration, show clear between-treatment differences at baseline, suffer from unresolved practice effects or have excess inter-patient variability in the time between anaesthesia and test of recovery (Ghoneim *et al.*, 1988; Kashtan *et al.*, 1990; Nightingale *et al.*, 1988; Sinclair and Cooper, 1983).

More reliable studies provide a reasonably clear picture of impairment. Two-minute letter deletion performance showed impairment for between three and four hours after midazolam for day-case surgery, while little if any impairment was associated with propofol (Forrest and Galletly, 1987; Vuyk *et al.*, 1990). While neither of the latter studies employed a control group, the results seem to support the view that impairment of vigilance after propofol is quite brief, while that from midazolam takes considerably longer.

Cashman and Power (1989) have shown a broadly similar pattern of recovery of three-minute deletion performance after nitrous oxide and halothane anaesthesia whereby performance had returned to baseline levels within some three hours. Zuurmond *et al.* (1989) have reported impairment of a three-minute deletion task to last only some ninety minutes when anaesthesia was induced by methohexitone and maintained with NO_2 and isoflurane. The non-significant effect of nitrous oxide when used for sedation reported by Conry *et al.* (1989) may be a straightforward consequence of the very low dose of the drug, or a side-effect of their cross-over design, already described above.

While one might question whether the preceding studies would have revealed greater or longer-lasting impairment if they had used longer tasks, the study by Baillie *et al.* (1989), shown in Figure 13.5, reveals that brief task duration need not be a handicap if a high rate of information presentation is employed. The authors presented the 'number matching task' (Wesnes, 1985) which requires the patient to detect a target number in a stream of digits presented at eighty digits per minute. Although the task is only seventy-five seconds in duration, the demands on the patient's attention are considerable and provide no opportunity for respite. Performance was shown still to be impaired some four hours after propofol anaesthesia, a result that confirms the evidence of Sanders *et al.* (1989) and demands a reappraisal of the conclusion above that recovery from propofol might be rapid. This result seems much more consistent with the findings from reaction time performance which suggest that recovery from propofol is still not complete some three hours after anaesthesia, and that patients are at risk of being discharged while still impaired (Sanders *et al.*, 1989).

While one should not make too much of a single study, it seems that a simple task which is highly demanding of attention because of the rate of information presentation, and which affords patients no opportunity to collect

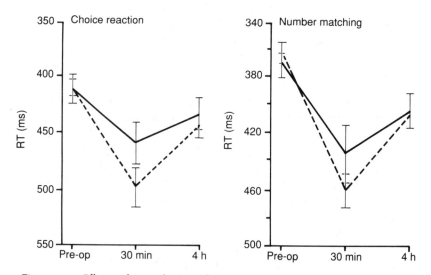

Figure 13.5 Effects of anaesthesia with (– – –) and without (———) temazepam premedication on discrete choice reaction time and the number matching task. Number matching remains impaired at 4 hours, perhaps implying greater sensitivity. (From Baillie *et al.*, 1989; reproduced with permission of the *British Journal of Anaesthesia*.)

their thoughts, may be sensitive to long-lasting impairment of attentional processes which go undetected by longer, subject-paced tasks.

DIGIT SYMBOL SUBSTITUTION TASK (DSST)

The task is more demanding than simple letter deletion because it requires the patient gradually to memorize or constantly to refer back to the defined pairing between digits and symbols in order to carry out the substitution task.

A sixty second DSST has been shown sensitive to dose-related impairment following midazolam (7.5 mg / 15 mg) for premedication prior to thiopentone anaesthesia, the impairment lasting in excess of two hours (the limit of the testing schedule: Raybould and Bradshaw, 1987). Similarly, Philip *et al.* (1990) have shown impairment of ninety second DSST for some three hours after midazolam for general anaesthesia. Rather uncertain evidence from Barker *et al.* (1986) indicates that such impairment might endure for some fifteen to twenty-four hours, but as noted above, their cross-over design and lack of control group renders the effects uncertain.

There is evidence that ninety second DSST performance may be impaired for some two to three days after thiopentone and nitrous oxide anaesthesia (Chung *et al.*, 1990). However, the absolute nature of the duration of the impairment is uncertain because of the lack of a control group which would have shown to what extent the baseline measure had 'shifted' due to practice. If anything, therefore, the study may under-estimate the degree of impairment.

The results from these simple deletion and DSST tests of attentional processes indicate that impairment may in some cases last several days. The implication is that patients who are discharged a few hours after day-case surgery may be significantly less vigilant than in their 'normal' state. Moreover, it is possible that the undemanding nature of some tasks may result in undetected impairment as shown in the contrast between simple deletion and the rapid information presentation of the number matching task.

MAZE-DRAWING, TRACING, CO-ORDINATION AND DEXTERITY

Maze-drawing has been supposedly shown sensitive to premedication with hyoscine and atropine: hyoscine was shown still to impair performance speed (but not accuracy) at three hours from anaesthesia (Anderson *et al.*, 1985). However, the lack of a control group makes it difficult to judge the absolute nature of the impairment, a difficulty that also afflicts the demonstration by Azar *et al.* (1984) that the anaesthetics fentanyl, enflurane and isoflurane were equivalent in impairing maze-drawing for only one or two hours.

Sanders *et al.* (1980) found no effect of thipentone or propofol upon tracing at three or twenty-four hours after surgery. Co-ordination and dexterity showed similar impairment with both drugs at some three hours from surgery. The presence of practice effects makes it difficult to draw firm conclusions from the study.

PURSUIT ROTOR

Performance has been shown to be markedly impaired at one hour from both diazepam sedation and halothane anaesthesia (Gale, 1976). While the study employed a control group whose performance was assessed over twenty-four hours, the anaesthetized groups provided data only for the first hour, a curious methodological aspect which leaves the long-term effects quite unclear. However, using different anaesthetic agents, Denis *et al.* (1984) have shown that pursuit rotor performance is still impaired at three-and-a-half hours from surgery after nitrous oxide with isoflurane or enflurane anaesthesia. Some criticisms were made of this study in the methodological section at the beginning of this chapter, and it seems likely that the results under-estimate impairment because performance is probably affected by a masked practice effect.

TRACKING, DUAL TASKS AND DRIVING SIMULATION

Moss *et al.* (1987) employed a dual task involving primary tracking and secondary visual reaction time to compare recovery from halothane and alfentanil anaesthesia. The results indicated that tracking accuracy was impaired at two hours after alfentanil, but by the following morning both groups of patients had improved on their baseline scores. Secondary task performance was largely equivalent between the groups, with both showing impairment at two hours. However, there was clear evidence of a practice effect because, as noted above, dual task performance was significantly better than baseline · by the following day. There was no control group and the task lasted only four minutes at each test period. It is therefore difficult to accept that recovery might really be complete within two hours.

'Skills related to driving' were examined by Korttila and Linnoila (1974) in their study of the residual effects of intravenous diazepam, flunitrazepam and droperidol. Separate groups of volunteers received one of the above drugs and performed a simple tracking task for between thirty and eighty seconds, and a ten-minute attention task requiring detection of changes on dials presented in the centre or periphery of vision. All the drugs were associated with impaired tracking for some eight to ten hours. The attentional task showed more mixed effects. Signals on the central dials were detected more readily over time, indicating a practice effect, although this was less marked for the benzodiazepines. On the peripheral dials, performance was worse with droperidol over ten hours but improved with flunitrazepam, implying an enhanced attentional field.

Unfortunately, Korttila and Linnoila did not include a control group and the authors themselves suggested that the results might be biased by insufficient training leading to masked practice effects. While the results imply a lengthy recovery period for these quite complex attentional processes, the absolute duration cannot be determined reliably.

In subsequent superior research, Korttila *et al.* (1975a) included a control group in their study of volunteers' performance in a driving simulator after anaesthesia with thiopentone, methohexitone, propanidid and althesin. The driving task lasted for thirty minutes and therefore gives a closer approximation to the demands of real life than many other studies. Volunteers who received thiopentone or methohexitone were still significantly impaired (more likely to collide, drive off the road, neglect instructions) at some six to eight hours when compared with the control group. Similarly, braking reaction times were significantly impaired at six to eight hours with the latter anaesthetics (see Figure 13.6).

An alarming aspect of the results was the volunteers' subjective impression of their driving ability. At eight hours from recovery, 90 per cent of those receiving methohexitone, and 70 per cent of those having thiopentone, rated their driving as normal. Given the objective evidence of their significant impairment at this time, the authors point to the risk that patients might face in emergency situations if they elect to drive soon after anaesthesia. The authors also drew attention to the fact that their volunteers were young and healthy, and that greater decrements might be seen in older individuals who were in poor health.

The study by Kortilla *et al.* (1975a) may reflect the value of employing a 'real-life' task for a 'real-life' period of time where, as the authors point out, its lengthy and monotonous nature may have helped to detect impairment. Hart *et al.* (1976) also followed this rationale when employing the lengthy

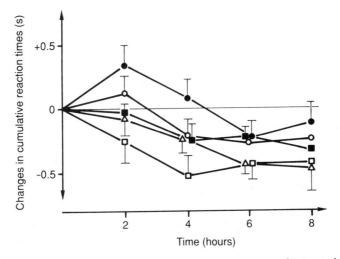

Figure 13.6 Changes in braking reaction time on a 30 minute driving task after thiopentone (●), methohexitone (○), propanidid (△), althesin (□), and for a control condition (■). (From Korttila *et al.*, 1975a; reproduced with permission of *Anesthesiology*.)

and monotonous Wilkinson auditory vigilance task (Wilkinson, 1970) in their
study of two doses of diazepam and amylobarbitone sodium. The drugs were
examined for their sedative, rather than anaesthetic, effects. However, the
study is worth considering here for its implications as to the relative merits
of long versus brief tasks because the authors also included a fifteen minute
multi-target deletion task and a ninety second digit symbol task.

The one-hour vigilance task showed performance with both drugs to be
impaired relative to placebo at $1\frac{3}{4}$ hours but no difference was detected at
4−5 hours from treatment. While the fifteen minute deletion task showed no
impairment at any time, the ninety second DSST task detected drug
impairment relative to placebo for $2\frac{3}{4}$ hours. It would therefore appear that
the shortest attention task remained sensitive to impairment of attention for
a longer period than the ostensibly more demanding one-hour task. The
authors suggested that the memory demands of the DSST task rendered it
more vulnerable and cited the parallel impairment of a short-term memory
task. However, this explanation seems less compelling given that the
multi-target deletion task also had a memory component but was not affected
by the drugs.

General interpretation of the results is made difficult by the fact that low
doses had a greater adverse effect upon vigilance performance than did high
doses. This may reflect an effect of the cross-over design which can cause
asymmetries in treatment effects. It is then uncertain whether a between-groups
design would have shown a similar effect and, in particular, whether the DSST
would have been more sensitive.

Simple motor skills

Motor performance is inherent in the tasks above. The effects of anaesthetics
upon simple aspects of motor performance and dexterity have also been
examined in isolation and they are considered briefly here.

TAPPING

After unspecified anaesthesia for various surgical procedures, Edwards *et al.*
(1981) showed impairment of tapping, for three to seven *days*. The conclusion
differs markedly from those of other studies which reported no effect upon
tapping (Ghoneim *et al.* 1988) or resolved impairment within two hours
(Zuurmond *et al.*, 1989), and recovery within some 5 to 15 minutes from brief
exposure to nitrous oxide (Herwig *et al.*, 1984).

PEGBOARD AND POSTBOX TESTS

The pegboard test was introduced to recovery research by Vickers (1965)
and requires the patient to transfer pegs as quickly as possible from one side

of a board to another, or measures the number of pegs transferred in a set time. Vickers (1965) employed no significance tests but concluded that performance remained impaired for some 45–90 minutes after methohexitone, and some 120 minutes after thiopentone. Denis *et al.* (1984) concluded that pegboard performance was impaired for $3\frac{1}{2}$ hours after nitrous oxide with isoflurane or enflurane, but it has been noted above that their study was afflicted with masked practice effects. Reitan *et al.* (1986) concluded that pegboard performance returned to baseline levels at $5\frac{1}{2}$ hours after midazolam and 4 hours after thiopentone. Given the problems of baseline measurement and the lack of a control group, the conclusion is probably an under-estimate.

The results of Weightman and Zacharias (1987) provide an important insight concerning the all-important factor of individual variation in recovery. At three hours after propofol anaesthesia, all patients had returned to baseline levels in contrast to 68 per cent of a group receiving thiopentone. However, at six hours from surgery, three thiopentone patients had still not returned to baseline pegboard performance.

Nielsen *et al.* (1991) conducted a largely similar study to the latter but found no difference in pegboard performance between propofol and thiopentone anaesthesia. They concluded that, 'on average', patients' performance had recovered to baseline levels after two hours. The term 'on average' indicates that a sizeable proportion of patients had presumably *not* recovered at this stage.

The postbox test employs a child's postbox toy ('Kiddicraft') which requires different plastic shapes to be posted through the appropriately shaped aperture in the box as rapidly as possible. The reader will sense that the very nature of the 'task' must introduce considerable variability in the performance measure. Recovery of postbox performance has been shown to be rapid (twenty-five minutes) after methohexitone and althesin anaesthesia (Sinclair and Cooper, 1983) and after thiopentone, nitrous oxide and halothane (Sear *et al.*, 1983; 35–40 minutes). However, Hindmarch and Bhatti (1987) have pointed out general methodological inadequacies in the above and other studies using the postbox test, and it should be noted that the recent study by Nielsen *et al.* (1991) concluded that recovery required at least two hours. The task would seem to fall within the province of those which Hindmarch (1989) has appropriately described as 'whimsy' and which offer no serious or reliable measure of performance impairment and recovery.

Critical flicker fusion threshold (CFFT)

While not formally a performance task, the CFFT has been used widely in recovery research. It is useful for completion to discuss it here, not least for the reason that McDougall and Smith's (1920) successful use of the 'windmill test' mentioned at the beginning of the chapter foreshadowed this modern equivalent.

CFFT employs the psycho-physical method of limits to determine the presence or absence of flicker in a light source as the time between onset and offset of the light is decreased (descending threshold) or increased (ascending threshold). The ability to resolve the time difference between flashes is impaired in sedated states (low threshold) and may be facilitated in states of high arousal.

Hindmarch (1988) has provided an extensive review of CFFT applied to drug studies including anaesthetic recovery (see also Hindmarch and Bhatti, 1987). While it is certainly the case that the task has apparently been shown sensitive to drug-induced arousal changes, there are many negative findings (e.g. Fagan et al., 1987; Manner et al., 1987; Millar et al., 1991; Valtonen et al., 1989) and some inconsistent results. For example, Korttila et al. (1981) found that CFFT was enhanced by nitrous oxide − implying increased arousal. − while psychomotor performance was impaired − implying sedation. Nitrous oxide is generally assumed to have a sedative effect.

Korttila et al. (1975a) have suggested that impairment of CFFT has no clinical relevance when assessment has failed to check whether other aspects of visual function are impaired. In other words, the assumption that depression of the CFFT indicates sedation is unwarranted unless it is shown to be unconfounded with the effect of the drug upon peripheral visual processes such as the pupillary response to light.

Memory function

Studies of the recovery of memory function suffer from the same methodological difficulties outlined above for psycho-motor tasks. Ghoneim et al. (1990) have reviewed the anaesthetic literature from January 1978 to May 1988 to identify common deficiencies in designs and methodologies. They report that, within the sampled ten-year span, only 42 per cent of studies employed a control group, only 47 per cent were double-blind, and only 23 per cent included pre- and post-treatment measurements of memory. This leaves only a very small proportion of studies which might provide reliable data.

These conclusions are very similar to those of Idzikowski (1988) who conducted a review of the general literature of drug effects on memory and drew an equally bleak picture. Both reviews remarked upon the tendency of investigators to regard memory as 'a unitary process or as an all-or-none phenomenon'. For instance, if digit span were found to be impaired then it would often be concluded that this implied a global impairment of memory. It will be shown below that such a conclusion is quite inconsistent with other evidence (e.g. Jones et al., 1978, 1979).

The issue of individual difference in the amnesic effects of drugs is also rarely addressed. This is unfortunate because Netter (1988) has shown that drugs may have quite different effects – sometimes quite opposite effects – depending upon the nature of the individual concerned.

Recovery research has tended to be characterized by studies which give patients visual or verbal stimuli to remember, and then test their recall quite soon thereafter. The finer points of recent theorizing on the properties of working memory have yet to make their mark in anaesthesia research (Baddeley, 1986).

The reader should also refer to a recent excellent review by Ghoneim and Mewaldt (1990) which examines the effects of benzodiazepines on memory in the specific context of anaesthesia. The authors conclude that the drugs have an anterograde, but no retrograde amnesic effect; they do not impair short-term or semantic memory, but do impair episodic memory. These effects are detailed in the discussion of a number of studies below where the benzodiazepines have been adminstered alone or in conjunction with anaesthetic drugs.

DIGIT SPAN

Span has been shown to be reduced for some three hours after nitrous oxide (Ogg *et al.*, 1979), while midazolam and thiopental have been associated with an impairment of only forty-eight minutes and two hours respectively (Reitan *et al.*, 1986). Selective impairment of digit span by hyoscine, but not atropine, has been reported by Anderson *et al.* (1985), the impairment resolving itself within some three hours. Sanders *et al.* (1989) report span being impaired for one hour after propofol and thiopentone while Kestin *et al.* (1990) found no impairment due to propofol and only thirty-minute impairment after midazolam. None of the preceding studies employed a control group.

In volunteers, diazepam has been shown to impair the recall of digit strings, a task that is quite similar to that of digit span (Jones *et al.*, 1978, 1979), although Brown *et al.* (1982) found no effect of either diazepam or lorazepam on a span-type task. The role of individual variation in determining vulnerability was suggested in the further study of Brown *et al.* (1983) which showed that lorazepam only impaired the memory of a sub-group of their sample.

Cohen and MacKenzie (1982) found no effect of atropine, thiopentone or a mixture of nitrous oxide, oxygen and halothane upon a complex series of digit span tasks performed some two hours after recovering consciousness. In fact, the patients performed as well as a control group and a group having local anaesthesia. Nightingale *et al.* (1988) also found no signficant effect of halothane or thiopental upon span, and a similar lack of effect of nitrous oxide has been reported by Conry *et al.* (1989) and Chung *et al.* (1990). Sanders *et al.* (1989) reported impairment of span at one hour after thiopentone or propofol, but performance had returned to baseline by three hours.

Despite the popularity of the digit span task (probably because it is easy and quick to administer), it is clear that there is little evidence of consistent drug effects. The possibility that attentional, rather than memory, impairment might underlie span reduction is rarely entertained by investigators. Overall, there must be doubts over the sensitivity of the task and therefore its value in assessing recovery.

One can also query what aspects of real-life memory are represented by span-type performance other than those of learning and recalling telephone numbers. In this regard it is relevant to note that while Jones et al. (1978, 1979) found impaired span performance after diazepam, they found no effect upon mental arithmetic (Jones et al., 1978), a task which is also highly dependent upon the retention of numerical information. Nor did they find an effect upon the recall of lists of words (Jones et al., 1979). The latter tasks are much more akin to the sort of information that a patient may encounter in real life. The fact that such complex tasks may be unaffected in a study which shows drug-impairment of digit span must detract from the conclusions to be drawn about the practical implications of the impairment (Millar, 1991).

LEARNING LISTS OF VERBAL INFORMATION

In practical terms, such tasks would seem useful in recovery research because patients are often given verbal instructions regarding their behaviour after discharge. This information may involve instructions for self-medication and activities to be avoided. It is important to know whether the ability to remember such information is impaired. However, few studies examine recall over a sufficiently long period, or for relevant information, to mimic real-life circumstances.

Korttila et al. (1981) have reported impairment in the immediate recall of twelve-word lists in volunteers breathing 30 per cent nitrous oxide. Impairment developed within two minutes of beginning to inhale the gas and continued throughout inhalation. Performance recovered to baseline level within twelve minutes of breathing room air. The result leaves it uncertain which process or processes in memory might have been affected. However, Adam et al. (1974) reported a similar effect to the above and showed it to be a state-dependent memory effect. Information was presented while patients breathed subanaesthetic concentrations of isoflurane; they were subsequently shown to be incapable of retrieving the material when recovered from the drug. However, when the drug was reinstated, and patients restored to the 'subanaesthetized state', they were able to show good recall of the material presented during initial exposure to the isoflurane. State-dependent effects may be important during the recovery phase and illustrate the fact that material may be available in memory, but not be readily accessible. In other words, the anaesthetic need not have precluded learning of the material: the limiting factor is the sensitivity of the assessment of its retrieval.

Hyoscine premedication has been shown to impair immediate recall of verbal lists for up to three hours after surgery (Anderson *et al.*, 1985). In the same study, atropine was associated with impairment only at thirty minutes after drug administration, and prior to the induction of anaesthesia.

With lorazepam 2 mg, Scharf *et al.* (1983) have found significant impairment of long-term recall (eight and twenty-four hours after drug administration) for sixteen-word lists learned two hours after drug ingestion. Mac *et al.* (1985) and Scharf *et al.* (1984) have replicated these results for lorazepam.

Pomara *et al.* (1985) have also shown a significant amnesic action of diazepam upon the verbal memory of healthy elderly subjects. However, their patients also reported increased feelings of sedation following diazepam, and the amnesic effect may therefore have been due to the non-specific sedative effects of the drug affecting attention to the material to be learned, rather than impairing learning or retrieval of the information itself.

Kumar *et al.* (1987) showed that chronic administration of lorazepam and alprazolam did not affect immediate recall of sixteen-word lists, but both drugs impaired delayed recall, the impairment being greater after alprazolam. In a comparison between diazepam and oxazepam, Mewaldt *et al.* (1986) have shown both drugs to impair the immediate recall of twenty-word lists for some three hours after treatment. Impairment was greater overall after oxazepam. In the case of delayed recall, both drugs were associated with impaired performance for four hours after treatment.

These results replicate the earlier findings of Mewaldt *et al.* (1983) where diazepam impaired the recall of post-treatment lists as an increasing function of the length of the word list.

In a subsequent study by the same group (Ghoneim *et al.*, 1984), memory impairment due to diazepam was again shown to increase as the dosage increased from 0.1 to 0.3 mg kg^{-1}. Recovery of normal function following the 0.3 mg kg dose occurred after some $5\frac{1}{2}$ hours.

While the adverse effects of diazepam have been interpreted as evidence for a fundamental impairment of long-term learning by the drug (Ghoneim *et al.*, 1984), this must be viewed in the context of inconsistent results. Desai *et al.* (1983) have shown that diazepam (5 mg) may *improve* memory in highly anxious patients, probably due to diazepam exerting a normalizing effect, but the result still creates difficulties for theories which attempt to implicate diazepam in some impairment of a basic mechanism of memory. The role of individual differences has also been emphasized by Brown *et al.* (1983) who have shown marked differences in vulnerability to the amnesic effects of lorazepam. Equally, however, File *et al.* (1982) found that amnesia due to lorazepam (2.5 mg) was equivalent for subjects high or low in state and trait anxiety.

It is difficult to make a reliable comparison between the latter studies because of their different designs. Two employed separate-groups designs (Brown *et al.*, Desai *et al.*) while the other employed a within-subjects design where all volunteers met all drug treatments. The latter designs often carry the penalty of reducing the magnitude of the difference between treatment conditions (Armitage and Hills, 1982).

VISUAL MEMORY

A veil will be drawn over those studies which have assessed visual memory by showing patients single and familiar objects prior to, or shortly after recovery from, anaesthesia and then testing their recall. One study involved holding up a dollar bill to patients before induction of anaesthesia. On recovery, a dollar bill was again shown to the (American) patients and they were asked if they 'had ever seen one of these before'. Surprisingly, they all had. Irrefutable evidence for a lack of retrograde amnesia? Perhaps not.

In a relatively early study, Ogg et al. (1979) showed the recall of picture card information to be impaired for an hour in the recovery period after both fentanyl and methohexitone with nitrous oxide in patients having minor gynaecological surgery. A similar finding has been reported by Studd and Eltringham (1980) after surgery preceded by lorazepam 2.5 mg or diazepam 10 mg premedication. Although greater impairment was seen for lorazepam premedication, neither drug impaired recall of recorded music or, more crucially, transfer to the operating room. This 'sparing' of the memory of a significant event is important, as is shown in the later discussion of this section.

Liu et al. (1984) showed that there was no retrograde amnesia for visual objects presented prior to diazepam (2.5–15 mg) administered to thirty-six endoscopy patients. However, the control group consisted of only nine subjects. As the groups were very different in size, they cannot have been properly matched on salient features. Given that no previous studies had shown any retrograde amnesia due to diazepam, it would seem unlikely that this design would have detected it.

A similar problem of interpretation due to differences between treatment groups is seen in the study by Juhl et al. (1984) of flurazepam and triazolam (currently unavailable in the UK). Flurazepam was associated with greatest impairment of recall of pictures but patients who experienced amnesia also reported greatest sleepiness. The supposed memory deficit may, therefore, have been one of impaired attention due to reduced arousal, rather than an effect upon visual memory. In this regard, it is worth observing the suggestion of File and Lister (1982) that the supposed effects of lorazepam upon memory may be due to the non-specific sedative effects of the drug, although sedation itself need not be associated with memory impairment (Millar and Wilkinson, 1981).

A further difficulty due to lack of pre-operative baseline measures is found in a study of midazolam and diazepam used alone or with fentanyl for outpatient dentistry by Ochs et al. (1986). Pictures of common objects were shown at 15, 30, 60, 120 and 180 minutes after achievement of sedation. Greatest amnesia was found for objects presented early in the sedation period and particularly for midazolam alone or in combination with fentanyl.

However, the lack of baseline measures makes it uncertain whether the groups differed anyway – regardless of drug treatment – in their ability to recall visual information. Moreover, contrary to the authors' conclusions, it is evident from their published data that amnesia lasted longer overall with diazepam. Tucker *et al.* (1984) also reported amnesia for visual stimuli when diazepam and ketamine were involved in dental outpatient sedation but no statistical tests were applied to the data so the significance remains unclear.

Pre-operative baseline measures were taken by Reitan *et al.* (1986) who tested the recognition memory of two groups of thirty-four patients at hourly intervals for six hours after induction with midazolam or thiopental. Midazolam was associated with 'complete amnesia' for 84 per cent of patients but for only 31 per cent of the thiopental group. Simpson *et al.* (1987) also employed baseline measures with which to contrast visual short-term memory performance (the 'object learning test') during recovery after premedication with papaveretum and either atropine or glycopyrrolate, and a standard anaesthetic. Atropine produced a significant decrement in memory when patients were tested *two days* after surgery but no impairment was associated with glycopyrrolate.

SEMANTIC MEMORY

Semantic memory seems relatively unaffected by drugs employed during anaesthesia. Ghoneim *et al.* (1984) found an overall slowing in semantic classification time after $0.1-0.3$ mg kg^{-1} of diazepam but there was no differential effect as a function of retrieval dominance. Millar *et al.* (1980) have pointed out that where no differential dominance effects occur it is difficult to determine whether a drug has impaired retrieval or simple reaction processes.

More recently, Roy-Byrne *et al.* (1987) reported no effect of 10 mg of diazepam on a semantic generation task (naming as many category exemplars within ninety seconds). Moss *et al.* (1987) also found no effect of anaesthesia with methohexitone induced by either halothane or alfentanil on a semantic classification task: the authors did not manipulate retrieval dominance. Hickey *et al.* (1991) did manipulate dominance but, while they found significant slowing in classification time in the first thirty minutes after propofol anaesthesia, found no differential effects due to this factor. Overall, these results would seem to confirm the conclusion of Ghoneim and Mewaldt (1990) that semantic memory is unaffected by drugs used during anaesthesia.

REAL-LIFE IMPLICATIONS: RETROGRADE ENHANCEMENT OF A MEMORY;
MEMORY FOR SIGNIFICANT EVENTS; REVERSING THE EFFECTS OF SEDATION

Retrograde enhancement. In none of the studies reported above was there any evidence of *retrograde amnesia*. For example, Brown *et al.* (1982) observed that intravenous diazepam and lorazepam caused severe anterograde amnesia lasting several hours but had no effect on the eventual recall of lists learned ten minutes prior to the injection. The authors suggest that this implies that the drugs do not affect retrieval mechansims. A number of studies have shown that not only may information presented prior to a drug be spared its amnesic effects, but also recall of such material may be considerably *enhanced* when followed, for example, by administration of lorazepam.

Mewaldt *et al.* (1986) have shown that the delayed recall of lists learned *prior* to administration of diazepam and oxazepam was significantly better for the drug than placebo conditions. The earlier study by Mewaldt *et al.* (1983) was also notable for the fact that delayed retrieval of words learned in a pre-treatment baseline session was enhanced in those subjects who had an active drug treatment with diazepam. Ghoneim *et al.* (1984) have shown that as the dose of diazepam increased, so the retrieval of words learned prior to drug administration also increased.

The above effects are evident with benzodiazepines and a similar result has been shown for anaesthetic agents in Noble's (1987) study of propofol and methohexitone. Both agents were associated with anterograde amnesia for some twenty-four hours after surgery but recall of information given in the baseline session was significantly improved, particularly for methohexitone. A control group did not show similar benefit.

This retrograde enhancement of material presented prior to an amnesic drug has been investigated with respect to alcohol (Mueller *et al.*, 1983; Parker *et al.*, 1980) where a similar pattern of poor recall of post-drug information contrasts with the enhanced recall of pre-drug material. It has been shown that the post-drug information, being poorly learned and difficult to retrieve, exerts little *retroactive interference* to impede the retrieval of information learned prior to drug administration. Retrieval of the latter information is then enhanced due to reduced interference effects.

Such results have important implications for the timing of information-presentation to patients about their medication, self-care and post-operative behaviour after discharge from day-case anaesthesia. Jones and Rosen (1991) and Millar (1991) have suggested that it might be more effective to give such information to patients before, rather than after, the anaesthetic (as is the common procedure). It has been well demonstrated that, even when unexposed to amnesic drugs, patients may forget more than 50 per cent of the information given to them in a medical consultation (Ley, 1979); the effects of drug-induced anterograde amnesia would presumably exacerbate the problem.

Memory for significant events. One should also exercise caution in drawing firm conclusions from studies which apparently show amnesic effects of peri-operative and anaesthetic drugs in the light of an important method-ological issue raised by O'Boyle *et al.* (1987) in their study of midazolam and diazepam in dental outpatients. Both drugs produced significant amnesia for photographs of common objects and of items relevant to dentistry, with amnesia being most marked at forty minutes following midazolam and in the first five minutes following diazepam. However, an important finding was that amnesia was relatively *less* marked for significant surgical events than for the 'artificial' stimuli presented as visual objects. This observation has also been made by Clyburn *et al.* (1986), O'Boyle (1988) and Studd and Eltringham (1980). O'Boyle *et al.* (1987) point out that as surgical events are probably more significant to patients, they may receive greater attention and elaboration. The consequence is that patients retain a reasonably intact memory for such significant events. The implication, then, is that memory tests which rely upon artificial stimuli having little relevance or meaning to the patient must have limited sensitivity to post-anaesthetic amnesia.

Reversing the effects of sedation. It is possible to reverse the subjective sedative effects of the benzodiazepines by administering the antagonist flumazenil. Andrews *et al.* (1990) have suggested that in addition to reducing subjective sedation, flumazenil can also reduce the adverse effects of the benzodiazepines on performance.

Clearly, the ability to reverse the effect of a sedative drug is of considerable clinical and practical importance: it would seem to imply that it may be possible to render a patient fit for discharge more quickly than would otherwise be the case. However, Philip *et al.* (1990) and Sanders *et al.* (1991) have

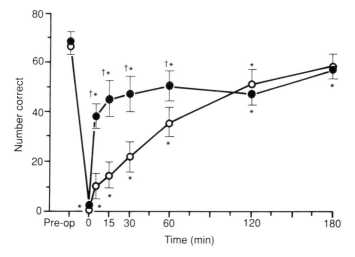

Figure 13.7 Digit symbol substitution with flumazenil (●) vs placebo (○). † = $p < 0.05$ flumazenil vs placebo; * = $p < 0.05$ flumazenil vs pre-operative control. (From Philip *et al.*, 1990; reproduced with permission of the International Anesthesia Research Society.)

shown that the beneficial effects of flumazenil seem to extend only to the initial sixty to ninety minutes of recovery; thereafter, the psychomotor performance of groups receiving flumazenil or placebo to reverse midazolam and diazepam sedation remained the same. The data from Philip *et al.* (1990) are shown in Figure 13.7. Sanders *et al.* (1991) noted that psycho-motor recovery had still not returned to baseline at three hours from surgery. They concluded that reversal of sedation with flumazenil 'would not hasten the safe discharge of patients'.

ANALGESICS

Analgesic drugs control pain. Some have a primarily peripheral action (e.g. aspirin, paracetamol) but others act centrally and may have sedative effects that would be predicted to impair performance (e.g. the opioids). The local anaesthetics such as lignocaine act to block the conduction of nerve impulses by impeding ionic flow across the nerve membrane.

Table 13.4 shows the commonly used analgesics and their classification: the reader will find it useful to refer to this table as the drug effects are discussed. An excellent description of the clinical use of such drugs is to be found in the review by Bond (1984).

There are fewer studies of the performance effects of analgesic drugs when compared with the anaesthetics literature. In considering their effects, the discussion adheres to the routine of the earlier part of the chapter where each subsection discusses the effects of various drugs upon specific cognitive or

Table 13.4 Analgesic drugs, as mentioned in the text, subdivided according to classification

Local anaesthetics
Bupivocaine, etidocaine, lignocaine, lidocaine, meprivocaine, prilocaine

Antipyretic analgesics and anti-inflammatory drugs
Aspirin, indomethacin, paracetamol, phenylbutazone

Narcotic analgesics
Buprenorphine, codeine, dextropropoxyphene, morphine, oxycodone, pentazocine

Narcotic analgesic agents commonly used in theatre

Name	Route of administration	Use
Alfentanil	Intravenous	IV (B) I
Buprenorphine	Intravenous / muscular	IV (B)
Diamorphine	Intravenous / muscular	IV (B)
Fentanyl	Intravenous / muscular	IV (B) I
Morphine	Intravenous / muscular	IV (B)
Phenoperidine	Intravenous	IV (B)

IV = intravenous. B = bolus. I = induction. ( ) = most common use.

psycho-motor processes. As in the case of anaesthetics, discussion of their effects will consider each class of performance tasks in turn.

Reaction processes

The study by Bruera *et al.* (1989) serves as an interesting and salutary starting point because it indicates the ethical problems that can affect studies of drugs whose action is to relieve pain. Bruera *et al.* examined the effects of the narcotic agents morphine, oxycodene and codeine on simple tapping per-formance of cancer patients. None had brain metastases which might affect performance.

In such a study it would be unthinkable to give patients placebo, but the lack of control creates difficulties in interpreting the results. Patients on steady-state analgesic therapy showed no adverse effect of treatment, while those who experienced an increase in the analgesic dose did suffer slowing in tapping speed until the new dose was stabilized after one week. Given the absence of placebo, and that higher doses of narcotic agents can cause drowsiness and nausea (confirmed by subjective measures taken by Bruera *et al.*, 1989), it is difficult to establish what effects, if any, there might be upon cognitive processes. Cognitive disorders are, in any case, a frequent psychiatric complication of advanced cancer (Massie and Holland, 1987): a fact which further confounds the issue.

The alternative research strategy is to examine analgesic side-effects in fit volunteers (who are predominantly young males) but this is equally problematic. Such people may, by virtue of their good physical condition, be less susceptible to drug effects and their performance may not be an accurate reflection of how older, less fit individuals might fare (Korttila *et al.*, 1975a). These difficulties should be borne in mind when considering the research which follows.

Korttila and his co-worders have conducted a series of studies with volunteers treated with local anaesthetic agents. The first of these involved thirty subjects allocated to separate groups to receive placebo, lidocaine or lidocaine and adrenaline (Korttila, 1974). Choice reaction time was impaired for $\frac{1}{2}-1$ hour after injection with lidocaine but no effects were seen for the other conditions. The length of the test was not specified and practice effects were observed. The combination of adrenaline with lidocaine abolished the decrement in performance, the author suggesting that this might have been due to a sympathomimetic effect. Overall, Korttila (1974) concluded that driving should be avoided for $1-1\frac{1}{2}$ hours after injection of lidocaine.

In a subsequent study, Korttila *et al.* (1975b) found no effect of bupivocaine or etidocaine on choice reaction time (thirty-two trials). The result is, of course, contrary to the previous finding but cannot be taken to imply that the two drugs simply have no effect relative to lidocaine. Firstly, lidocaine should have been used as a positive control; one would expect replication of the previous impairment. Secondly, the authors employed a cross-over design with eleven volunteers in contrast to the previous separate groups study. The former designs are well known to reduce the magnitude of difference between treatment effects (Poulton, 1982). The fact that the design may have corrupted the data form is further implied by the fact that performance was faster with the drugs than with placebo.

The later study of prilocaine, meprivocaine and placebo in a cross-over trial with ten volunteers also failed to include a positive control and found no effect upon choice reaction time (Korttila, 1977). The same criticisms as above apply, and the author himself observed that the short tasks may have blunted sensitivity.

Bradley and Nicholson (1987) conducted a comparison of aspirin and paracetamol, whose action is considered to be mainly peripheral, with the centrally acting analgesics meptazinol and pentazocine. A complicated cross-over design involved seven female volunteers, five of whom encountered ten treatment conditions. The authors describe the use of a particular statistical adjustment to attempt to correct the inevitable learning and adaptation effects that would occur with such a design. The study included placebo and a positive control in the form of the antihistamine triprolidine.

None of the treatment drugs was found to impair choice reaction time (performance was assessed from the latter twenty trials out of a total of thirty) and indeed aspirin was seen to *reduce* response time. One might be tempted to ascribe the lack of effect to the influence of the design, particularly given that the positive control triprolidine caused no impairment.

More recently, MacDonald *et al.* (1989) employed a cross-over design with twelve volunteers to study the opioid buprenorphine and the non-opioid keterolac (see Figure 13.8). Only buprenorphine impaired choice reaction time, the peak occurring at $1\frac{1}{2}$–4 hours from injection, and performance had still not returned to baseline at 8 hours. Psychomotor impairment was paralleled by marked subjective feelings of incapacitation such that nine of the volunteers felt at some stage unable to perform all the tests.

Divided attention; tracking; vigilance

Several studies have examined the effects of analgesic drugs on activities which may be relevant to driving. The studies by Korttila and co-workers (mentioned above) examined attention and tracking, and provide a rather discrepant picture.

Lidocaine impaired divided attention, but the addition of adrenalin caused facilitation relative to the placebo control group (Korttila, 1974), a result which again the author ascribed to the sympatho-mimetic action of the drug. In a later study (Korttila *et al.*, 1975b) employing a tracking task, bupivocaine

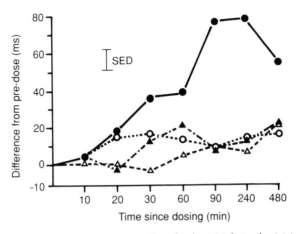

Figure 13.8 Discrete choice reaction time after placebo (○), keterolac (▲), diclofenac (△) and buprenorphine (●). (From MacDonald *et al.*, 1989; reproduced with permission of the *British Journal of Clinical Pharmacology*.)

was associated with more, and etidocaine with fewer, errors. The problems due to the cross-over design and practice effects have been noted above, but it remains unclear why the drugs should have quite opposite effects. The authors' suggestion that the effect might be due to etidocaine causing greater tiredness leading to 'temporary arousal' which facilitated performance hardly seems credible.

In the further crossover study of prilocaine, mepivacaine and placebo in ten volunteers, an attentional task showed obvious practice effects (see Korttila, 1977, figure 1). The thirty second co-ordination task showed no difference between placebo and prilocaine but mepivocaine significantly impaired performance.

Some similar difficulties occur in interpreting the effects of centrally acting opioid analgesics meptazinol and pentazocine when compared with aspirin and paracetamol (Bradley and Nicholson, 1987). The complicated design of this study has already been noted. None of the drugs had any effect on tracking (visuo-motor co-ordination). The task lasted six hundred seconds, the last five hundred of which were taken as the performance score. In contrast to the results for choice reaction time above, the fact that the positive control condition was impaired for some $\frac{3}{4}$–2 hours would imply that the task had the potential to be sensitive to impairment of attentional processes.

However, as remarked earlier, *dual tasks* may offer the potential for greater sensitivity in that a drug may not affect primary tracking performance but might impair a simultaneous secondary reaction task. Saarialho-Kere *et al.* (1989; see also 1988) showed just this effect in their cross-over study of the opioid analgesic oxycodene which included a positive control with the antihistamine diphenhydramine whose sedative effects are well-known to impair performance (Mattila *et al.*, 1986). Neither drug impaired a tracking task but both impaired secondary reaction time at $1\frac{1}{2}$ hours. Clearly, therefore, although tracking may demand attention, it may be insensitive when employed alone. Again it is relevant to note that Saarialho-Kere *et al.* (1989) found little evidence for a drug effect on an attentional task (monitoring four VDUs for critical signals), any effect being obscured by a main effect of experimental session which indicates a practice effect 'despite proper pretraining'.

MacDonald *et al.* (1989) also showed the opioid buprenorphine to impair dual task tracking and secondary reaction time for some four to eight hours, while the non-opioid analgesic keterolac had no adverse effect. A vigilance task requiring the subject to detect repeated presentations of visual patterns showed both drugs to impair correct detections at four hours, but only buprenorphine was also associated with increased false alarms for some four to eight hours after treatment.

Dershwitz *et al.* (1991) employed the Halstead trail-making test and Treiger dot test (both simple analogies of tracking and co-ordination) to show that the opioid butorphanol caused equivalent impairment to a sedative dose of midazolam. The drugs were also examined in combination because they are often administered together in clinical practice, but the impairment remained equivalent to single administration, implying no synergistic effect.

From the above, a tentative conclusion would be that the simple, peripherally acting analgesics cause little impairment of attentional processes, while the centrally acting opioids are more likely to have adverse effects. There may be some merit in employing dual tasks to detect finer aspects of impairment.

Memory; digit symbol substitution (DSST)

Bradley and Nicholson (1987) reported that 25 mg of pentazocine impaired two-minute DSST performance for some three-quarters to two hours, as did a positive control triprolidine condition. Their results are difficult to interpret because, surprisingly, 50 mg of pentazocine had no effect. Moreover, Saarialho-Kere *et al.* (1986, 1988, 1989) have shown no effect of 70 mg pentazocine upon three-minute DSST performance. Both studies employed cross-over designs (the complexity of the Bradley and Nicholson design has already been remarked upon above) and it may be that this introduced some distortions to the data form. The further claim by Bradley and Nicholson (1987) that aspirin and paracetamol had no effect on DSST must therefore also be viewed with caution.

MacDonald *et al.* (1989) showed the opioid buprenorphine to impair DSST for four to eight hours, but the non-opioid keterolac had no effect. In contrast, there was no effect of either drug upon digit span.

Dershwitz *et al.* (1991) found the opioid butorphanol to have relatively minor anterograde amnesic effects upon a visual memory task (picture cards). This contrasted with the pronounced dose-dependent amnesic effects of midazolam. Interestingly, when combined, the amnesic effects of the two drugs were, if anything, less than for midazolam alone, probably because the dose of midazolam was reduced in the combination condition.

GENERAL VERSUS REGIONAL ANAESTHESIA

The research discussed above must raise the question in the reader's mind as to the relative effects of general, compared with regional, anaesthesia. The question is of both practical and theoretical interest. At the practical level, many patients would prefer to be conscious during surgery; fear of death under anaesthetic is common. There are also certain clinical advantages in having an awake patient in terms of physical recovery, and if it were shown that psycho-motor performance were also less impaired, then this would be an argument for increasing the number of procedures conducted under regional anaesthesia.

Theoretical interest would attach to the insights that a carefully controlled comparison might provide as to the mechanism of impairment after general anaesthesia. While many investigators have followed Davison *et al.* (1975) in ascribing cognitive changes directly to the effect of anaesthetic drugs on higher brain centres, others (e.g. Kehlet, 1979) have suggested that impairment may arise from increased metabolic demands induced by the endocrine stress response to surgery (see Riis *et al.*, 1983).

There are three studies worth considering, the first being by Riis *et al.* who examined immediate and long-term (three months) cognitive functioning after general or regional anaesthesia in elderly patients undergoing hip replacement. Patients were allocated at random to one of three groups to receive general anaesthesia, epidural anaesthesia or general anaesthesia *plus* epidural anaesthesia. The latter condition is critical because epidural anaesthesia involves regional blockade which prevents the endocrine–metabolic stress response. The design therefore permits separate examination of the respective role of control and metabolic processes in causing impairment.

A battery of attentional and memory tasks was employed: trail-making, digit symbol, digit span, story recall and picture recognition. All groups showed equivalent short-term impairments and similar improvement in the long-term. Levels of plasma glucose and cortisol were lower in patients having regional blockade (general and epidural) indicating the effectiveness with which the 'trauma' response was reduced. Overall, the study produced no evidence of differential cognitive impairment between the two anaesthetic techniques.

These results have been replicated by Ghoneim *et al.* (1988; but see criticisms above) and by Neilson *et al.* (1990), although the latter authors considered performance only three months after anaesthesia and therefore leave uncertain whether differential effects might have been present in the short-term.

The studies above were principally concerned with potential adverse effects of general anaesthesia upon elderly patients who may be at greater risk of impairment (Chung *et al.*, 1990). However, it might seem reasonable to conclude that other age groups would show similar lack of difference between conditions.

THE EFFECTS OF ANAESTHETIC GASES UPON THEATRE PERSONNEL

The final section of this chapter addresses the issues of whether the performance efficiency of the anaesthetist and other personnel in the operating theatre might be impaired by the atmospheric pollution by anaesthetic gases. There is a considerable literature concerning the 'ergonomics of anaesthesia' and much of this emphasizes the monitoring function of the anaesthetist which demands lengthy periods of sustained attention while the patient is maintained in steady-state anaesthesia (DeAnda and Gaba, 1990; Gaba, 1984; Gaba and Lee, 1990; Weinger and Englund, 1990). As noted above, attentional deficits certainly characterize patient impairment after anaesthesia and it would seem important to consider whether the anaesthetists themselves fall victim to their own treatment.

Anaesthetists are exposed to anaesthetic gases which escape from the delivery mask and the unabsorbed gases which are exhaled by the patient. The problem has been well recognized and so-called scavenging equipment can be employed to remove such gases from the theatre atmosphere. By comparing anaesthetists' cognitive functioning after working in scavenged and unscavenged theatres it is, then, possible to determine whether such pollution has any adverse effect.

Early studies by Bruce and colleagues (1974, 1975, 1976) suggested that exposure to atmospheric concentrations of 14 ppm halothane and 550 ppm nitrous oxide impaired anaesthetists' vigilance performance. However, these results have not been replicated in subsequent research. Smith and Shirley (1978) and Stollery *et al.* (1988) found no effect of typical atmospheric concentrations of halothane and nitrous oxide upon either naive volunteers (who might be expected to be more vulnerable) or upon experienced anaesthetists.

To end on an unsavoury note, it is useful to record Weinger and Englund's (1990) observation that other 'malodorous' pollution of the theatre environment by faecal matter and discharge from abscesses is associated with a significant adverse effect on vigilance. They cite the research by Rotton (1983). One would predict that this is an area that is unattractive for further research.

CONCLUSIONS

The preceding review has shown that general anaesthesia and some forms of analgesia can cause significant impairment of psycho-motor and attentional processes, and that the duration of impairment may be considerable. However, it was also shown that it is difficult to make specific statements about impairment and recovery because the methods employed in research studies are not equivalent and thus the results are discrepant. Rather than list the problems as factors which obscure the effects of anaesthetics and analgesics, it may be more productive to conclude by setting each difficulty in the context of the future research which might resolve it.

The direction for future research

INDIVIDUAL VARIATION

Too little is known about individual variation in recovery. It is evident from the results of many studies that while mean differences between anaesthetic conditions may not differ after, say three hours, some patients — as judged by the standard deviation of the performance measure — are probably still impaired. Research is needed to establish what factors might underlie such variation and how potentially vulnerable individuals might be detected *prior* to anaesthesia. Hickey *et al.* (1991) have shown how the use of individual performance analysis can be applied to recovery from propofol anaesthesia and its effects upon choice reaction time and semantic memory. More studies should follow this example with the aim to make a more detailed analysis of the physiological and psychological characteristics of the patient which might interact with specific anaesthetics to produce individual recovery profiles.

CRITERIA OF IMPAIRMENT AND RECOVERY

The criteria for impairment and recovery are not well defined. It has been shown that insufficient practice and the use of a 'return to baseline' criterion of recovery leads to an underestimation of the degree and duration of post-anaesthetic impairment.

Resolution of the problem depends upon better appreciation of practice effects: many investigators seem unaware of their enduring nature and the need to establish a plateau in performance. Failing that, since one has to recognize that the time to establish stable performance is often lacking in a recovery study, then at least proper control measures should be employed. Untreated control groups, placebo and positive control conditions should be employed to establish reliable effects. The problem also depends upon the nature of the tasks themselves, as described below.

TASKS: TAXONOMY, DURATION AND COMPLEXITY

The lack of a taxonomy of performance tasks has long been lamented (Fleishman, 1959; Wilkinson, 1969; Zuurmond et al., 1989). Without such a taxonomy, it is difficult to see how research can further the present understanding of anaesthetic and other drugs upon human performance. However, some recent initiatives give hope for the future. Parrott, (1990, 1991a, b) has published an excellent series of papers describing the method of assessing the reliability and validity of tasks employed in clinical settings. Furthermore, the Recovery Interest Group (RIG, 1990) has been established in the UK with the aim of defining sensitive tasks for assessing recovery from anaesthesia.

Among the issues to be resolved by such research are those of task duration and complexity. It has long been accepted that, by and large, lengthy and monotonous tasks may be more sensitive than simple tasks. But in the real-life recovery setting, it is often not feasible to administer lengthy tasks, nor, as noted above, is it possible to provide sufficient practice to stabilize performance on complex tasks. It would therefore seem important to invest effort in determining the extent to which short and simple tasks can be devised to provide similar sensitivity to more complex assessments. Some evidence reviewed above gives rise to optimism where it was shown that a short and simple task could offer considerable sensitivity provided that a high rate of information processing was required and where the patient had no opportunity for respite (Wesnes, 1985).

RECOVERY AND REAL LIFE

Studies of recovery employ contrived tasks which are performed by patients in the unfamiliar environment of a hospital ward or recovery room. Even if performance on such tasks does show impairment – or the lack of it – does this really have implications for patients when they are discharged? Some of the evidence reviewed above would suggest that the conclusions drawn from many studies may be misleading: some may underestimate the duration of impairment while others, by the unfamiliar and unimportant nature of the stimulus materials presented, may erroneously imply an adverse effect. In the latter regard, it will be recalled that O'Boyle et al. (1987) showed much reduced amnesic effects of midazolam for information and events that had real-life relevance to the patient when compared with the 'irrelevant' stimuli of a memory task.

Such results may question whether other abilities, apparently shown to be impaired or spared in conventional recovery studies, would show similar effects in a truly real-life context. In other words, what is the ecological validity of the typical recovery study?

There would seem to be a need to follow discharged patients into the real world to observe how they cope with their everyday routine. This might be done both objectively by assessing their performance on everyday tasks, and subjectively by having them, or a relative, rate their subjective performance. There are a number of reasonably well validated questionnaires that might be employed to assess any cognitive and memory deficits that might be present (Broadbent *et al.*, 1982; for review see Herrmann, 1984).

Baddeley and Wilkins (1984) have shown the benefits of taking experimentation out of the laboratory in order to understand the functioning of human memory. The same must be equally true of understanding not only memory but also other cognitive processes when their efficiency has been compromised by anaesthetic or analgesic drugs. At present, studies of recovery largely provide evidence which permits one to speculate as to whether a patient is fit for discharge: that individual needs to be followed into his or her own domestic and work environment in order to establish that recovery is indeed fully and reliably complete.

REFERENCES

Adam, N., Castro, A.D. and Clark, D.L. (1974). State-dependent learning with a general anesthetic (isoflurane) in man. *Journal of Life Sciences* **4**: 125–34.

Anderson, S., McGuire, R. and McKeown, D. (1985). Comparison of the cognitive effects of premedication with hyoscine and atropine. *British Journal of Anaesthesia* **57**: 169–73.

Andrews, P.J.D., Wright, D.J. and Lamont, M.C. (1990). Flumazenil in the outpatient. *Anaesthesia* **45**: 45–8.

Armitage, P. and Hills, M. (1982). The two-period crossover trial. *The Statistician* **31**: 119–31.

Azar, I., Karambelkar, D.J. and Lear, E. (1984). Neurologic state and psychomotor function following anesthesia for ambulatory surgery. *Anesthesiology* **60**: 347–9.

Baddeley, A.D. (1986). *Working Memory*. Oxford: Clarendon.

Baddeley, A.D. and Wilkins, A.J. (1984). Taking memory out of the laboratory. In *Everyday Memory, Actions and Absent-mindedness*, edited by J.E. Harris and P.E. Morris. New York and London: Academic Press, pp. 1–17.

Baillie, R., Christmas, L., Price, N., Restall, J., Simpson, P. and Wesnes, K. (1989). Effects of temazepam premedication on cognitive recovery following alfentanil–propofol anaesthesia. *British Journal of Anaesthesia* **63**: 68–75.

Barker, I., Butchart, D.G.M., Gibson, J., Lawson, J.I.M. and Mackenzie, N. (1986). IV Sedation for conservative dentistry. *British Journal of Anaesthesia* **58**: 371–7.

Bond, M.R. (1984). *Pain: Its Nature, Analysis and Treatment*. London: Churchill Livingstone.

Boysen, K., Sanchez, R., Krintel, J.J., Hansen, M., Haar, P.H. and Dyrberg, V. (1989). Induction and recovery characteristics of propofol, thiopental and etomidate. *Acta Anaesthesiologica Scandinavica* **33**: 689–92.

Boysen, K., Sanchez, R., Ravn, J., Pedersen, E., Krintel, J.J. and Dyrberg, V. (1990). Comparison of induction with and first hour of recovery from brief propofol and methohexital anesthesia. *Acta Anaesthesiologica Scandinavica* **34**: 212–15.

Bradley, C.M. and Nicholson, A.N. (1987). Studies on performance with aspirin and paracetamol and with the centrally acting analgesics meptazinol and pentazocine. *European Journal of Clinical Pharmacology* **32**: 135–9.

Broadbent, D.E. (1984). Performance and its measurement. *British Journal of Clinical Pharmacology* **18**: 5S–9S.

Broadbent, D.E., Cooper, P.F., Fitzgerald, P. and Parkes, K.R. (1982). The Cognitive Failures Questionnaire (CFQ) and its correlates. *British Journal of Psychology* **21**: 1–16.

Brown, J., Lewis, V., Brown, M., Horn, G. and Bowes, J.B. (1982). A comparison between transient amnesias produced by two drugs (diazepam and lorazepam) and amnesia of organic origin. *Neuropsychologica* **20**: 55–70.

Brown, J.J., Brown, M.M. and Bowes, J.B. (1983). Effects of lorazepam on rate of forgetting, on retrieval from semantic memory and on manual dexterity. *Neuropsychologia* **21**: 501–12.

Bruce, D.L. and Bach, M.J. (1975). Psychological studies of human performance as affected by traces of enflurane and nitrous oxide. *Anesthesiology* **42**: 194–6.

Bruce, D.L. and Bach, M.J. (1976). Effects of trace anaesthetic gases on behavioural performance of volunteers. *British Journal of Anaesthesia* **48**: 871–5.

Bruce, D.L., Bach, M.J. and Arbit, J. (1974). Trace anesthetic effects on perceptual, cognitive and motor skills. *Anesthesiology* **40**: 453–8.

Bruera, E., Macmillan, K., Hanson, J. and MacDonald, R.N. (1989). The cognitive effects of the administration of narcotic analgesics in patients with cancer pain. *Pain* **39**: 13–16.

Cashman, J.N. and Power, S.J. (1989). An evaluation of tests of psychomotor function in assessing recovery following a brief anaesthetic. *Acta Anaesthesiologica Scandinavica* **33**: 693–7.

Chung, F., Seyone, C., Dyck, B., Chung, A., Ong, D., Taylor, A. and Stone, R. (1990). Age-related cognitive recovery after general anesthesia. *Anesthesia and Analgesia* **71**: 217–24.

Clyburn, P., Kay, N.H. and McKenzie, P.J. (1986). Effects of diazepam and midazolam on recovery from anaesthesia in outpatients. *British Journal of Anaesthesia* **58**: 872–5.

Cohen, R.L. and MacKenzie, A.I. (1982). Anaesthesia and cognitive functioning. *Anaesthesia* **37**: 47–52.

Conry, J.P., Feigal, R.J. and Beniak, T.E. (1989). Assessment of recovery from nitrous oxide–oxygen sedation using neuropsychometry. *Anesthesia Progress* **36**: 15–20.

Davison, L.A., Steinhelber, J.C., Eger, E.I. and Stevens, W.C. (1975). Psychological effects of halothane and enflurane anaesthesia. *Anesthesiology* **43**: 313–24.

DeAnda, A. and Gaba, D.M. (1990). Unplanned incidents during comprehensive anesthesia simulation. *Anesthesia and Analgesia* **71**: 77–82.

Denis, R., Letourneau, J.E. and Londorf, D. (1984). Reliability and validity of psychomotor tests as measures of recovery from isoflurane or enflurane anesthesia in a day-care surgery unit. *Anesthesia and Analgesia* **63**: 653–6.

Dershwitz, M., Rosow, C.E., DiBiase, P.M. and Zaslavsky, A. (1991). Comparison of the sedative effects of butorphanol and midazolam. *Anesthesiology* **74**: 717–24.

Desai, N., Taylor-Davies, A. and Barnett, D.B. (1983). The effects of diazepam and oxprenolol on short-term memory in individuals of high and low state anxiety. *British Journal of Clinical Pharmacology* **15**: 197–202.

Edwards, H., Rose, E.A., Schorow, M. and King, T.C. (1981). Postoperative deterioration in psychomotor function. *Journal of the American Medical Association* **245**: 1342–3.

Eysenck, M.W. (1981). *Attention and Arousal: Cognition and Performance*. Berlin: Springer.

Fagan, D., Tiplady, B. and Scott, B. (1987). Effects of ethanol on psychomotor performance. *British Journal of Anaesthesia* **59**: 961–5.

File, S.E., Bond, A.J. and Lister, R.G. (1982). Interaction between effects of caffeine and lorazepam in performance tests and self-ratings. *Journal of Clinical Psychopharmacology* **2**: 102–6.

File, S.E. and Lister, R.G. (1982). Do lorazepam-induced deficits in learning result from impaired rehearsal, reduced motivation or increased sedation? *British Journal of Clinical Pharmacology* **14**: 545–50.

File, S.E. and Lister, R.G. (1983). Does tolerance to lorazepam develop with once weekly dosing? *British Journal of Clinical Pharmacology* **16**: 645−50.

Fleishman, E.A. (1959). Primary abilities in the space environment. In *What Needs Doing about Man in Space?* edited by R.M. Chambers and B.J. Smith. Philadelphia: General Electric.

Forrest, P. and Galletly, D.C. (1987). Comparison of propofol and antagonized midazolam anaesthesia for day-case surgery. *Anaesthesia and Intensive Care* **15**: 394−401.

Gaba, D.M. (1989). Human error in anesthetic mishaps. *International Anesthesiology Clinics* **27**: 137−47.

Gaba, D.M. and Lee, T. (1990). Measuring the workload of the anesthesiologist. *Anesthesia and Analgesia* **71**: 354−61.

Gale, G.D. (1976). Recovery from methohexitone, halothane and diazepam. *British Journal of Anaesthesia* **48**: 691−7.

Galletly, D., Forrest, P. and Purdie, G. (1988). Comparison of the recovery characteristics of diazepam and midazolam. *British Journal of Anaesthesia* **60**: 520−4.

Gardner, M.J. and Altman, D. (1986). Confidence intervals rather than *P* values: estimation rather than hypothesis testing. *British Medical Journal* **292**: 746−50.

Ghoneim, M.M. and Mewaldt, S.P. (1990). Benzodiazepines and human memory: a review. *Anesthesiology* **72**: 926−38.

Ghoneim, M.M., Mewaldt, S.P. and Thatcher, J.W. (1975). The effect of diazepam and fentanyl on mental, psychomotor, and electroencephalographic functions and their rate of recovery. *Psychopharmacology* **44**: 61−6.

Ghoneim, M.M., Hinrichs, J.V. and Mewaldt, S.P. (1984). Dose−response analysis of the behavioral effects of diazepam. 1: Learning and memory. *Psychopharmacology* **82**: 291−5.

Ghoneim, M.M., Hinrichs, J.V., O'Hara, M.W., Mehta, M.P., Pathak, D., Kumar, V. and Clark, C.R. (1988). Comparison of psychologic and cognitive functions after general or regional anesthesia. *Anesthesiology* **69**: 507−15.

Ghoneim, M.M., Ali, M.A. and Block, R.I. (1990). Appraisal of the quality of assessment of memory in anaesthesia and psychopharmacology literature. *Anesthesiology* **73**: 815−20.

Hart, J., Hill, H.M., Bye, C.E., Wilkinson, R.T. and Peck, A.W. (1976). The effects of low doses of amylobarbitone sodium and diazepam on human performance. *British Journal of Clinical Pharmacology* **3**: 289−98.

Herbert, M. (1987). The duration of post-anaesthetic mental impairment. In *Aspects of Recovery from Anaesthesia*, edited by I. Hindmarch and J.G. Jones. Chichester: Wiley, pp. 103−12.

Herbert, M. (1992). Psychomotor effects of anaesthesia. In *Psychology, Pain and Anaesthesia*, edited by R.J. Smith. London: Chapman and Hall, in press.

Herbert, M., Healy, T.E.J., Bourke, J.B., Fletcher, I.R. and Rose, J.M. (1983). Profile of recovery after general anaesthesia. *British Medical Journal* **286**: 1539−42.

Herrmann, D.J. (1984). Questionnaires about memory. In *Everyday Memory, Actions and Absent-mindedness*, edited by J.E. Harris and P.E. Morris. New York and London: Academic Press, pp. 133−52.

Herwig, L.D., Milam, S.B. and Jones, D.L. (1984). Time course of recovery following nitrous oxide administration. *Anesthesia Progress* **31**: 133−5.

Hickey, S., Asbury, A.J. and Millar, K. (1991). Psychomotor recovery after outpatient anaesthesia: individual impairments may be masked by group analysis. *British Journal of Anaesthesia* **66**: 345−52.

Hindmarch, I. (1988). Information processing, critical flicker fusion threshold and benzo-diazepines: results and speculations. In *Benzodiazepine Receptor Ligands, Memory and Information Processing*, edited by I. Hindmarch and I. Ott. Berlin: Springer, pp. 79−89.

Hindmarch, I. (1989). Editorial: Psychometrics and psychopharmacology. *Human Psychopharmacology* **4**: 79−80.

Hindmarch, I. and Bhatti, J.Z. (1987). Recovery of cognitive and psychomotor function following anaesthesia: a review. In *Aspects of Recovery from Anaesthesia*, edited by I. Hindmarch and J.G. Jones. Chichester: Wiley, pp. 113−66.

Idzikowski, C.J. (1988), The effects of drugs on memory. In *Practical Aspects of Memory*, edited by M.M. Gruneberg, P.E. Morris and R.N. Sykes. Chichester: Wiley, pp. 193–8.

Idzikowski, C.J. and Oswald, I. (1983). Interference with human memory by an antibiotic. *Psychopharmacology* 79: 108–10.

Jones, D.M., Lewis, M.J. and Spriggs, T.L.B. (1978). The effects of low doses of diazepam on human performance in group administered tasks. *British Journal of Clinical Pharmacology* 6: 333–7.

Jones, D.M., Jones, M.E.L., Lewis, M.J. and Spriggs, T.L.B. (1979). Drugs and human memory: effects of low doses of nitrazepam and hyoscine on retention. *British Journal of Clinical Pharmacology* 7: 479–83.

Jones, J.G. and Rosen, M. (1991). Conclusion. In *Ambulatory Anaesthesia and Sedation*, edited by I.D. Klepper, L.D. Sanders and M. Rosen. Oxford: Blackwell, pp. 285–8.

Jones, M.J.T. (1988). The influence of anesthetic methods on mental function. *Acta Chirurgica Scandinavica* 550 (Supplement): 169–76.

Juhl, R.P., Daugherty, V.M. and Kroboth, P.D. (1984). Incidence of next-day anterograde amnesia caused by flurazepam hydrochloride and triazolam. *Clinical Pharmacology* 3: 622–5.

Kashtan, H., Edelist, G., Mallon, J. and Kapala, D. (1990). Comparative evaluation of propofol and thiopentone for total intravenous anaesthesia. *Canadian Journal of Anaesthesia* 37: 170–6.

Kehlet, H. (1979). Stress-free surgery and anesthesia. *Acta Anesthesiologica Scandinavica* 23: 503–4.

Kestin, I.G., Harvey, P.B. and Nixon, C. (1990). Psychomotor recovery after three methods of sedation during spinal anaesthesia. *British Journal of Anaesthesia* 64: 675–81.

Knight, M. (1950). *William James*. London: Penguin Books.

Korttila, K. (1974). Psychomotor skills related to driving after intramuscular lidocaine. *Acta Anaesthesiologica Scandinavica* 18: 290–6.

Korttila, K. (1977). Lack of impairment in skills related to driving after intramuscular administration of prilocaine or mepivicaine. *Acta Anaesthesiologica Scandinavica* 21: 31–6.

Korttila, K. and Linnoila, M. (1974). Skills related to driving after intravenous diazepam, flunitrazepam or droperidol. *British Journal of Anaesthesia* 46: 961–9.

Korttila, K., Linnoila, M., Ertama, P. and Hakkinen, S. (1975a). Recovery and simulated driving after intravenous anesthesia with thiopental, methohexital, propanidid, or alphadione. *Anesthesiology* 43: 291–9.

Korttila, K., Hakkinen, S. and Linnoila, M. (1975b). Side effects and skills related to driving after intramuscular administration of bupivicaine and etidocaine. *Acta Anaesthesiologica Scandinavica* 19: 384–91.

Korttila, K., Ghoheim, M.M., Jacobs, L., Mewaldt, S.P. and Petersen, R.C. (1981). Time course of mental and psychomotor effects of 30 per cent nitrous oxide during inhalation and recovery. *Anesthesiology* 54: 220–6.

Kumar, R., Mac, D.S., Gabrielli, W.F., Jr and Goodwin, D.W. (1987). Anxiolytics and memory: a comparison of lorazepam and alprazolam. *Journal of Clinical Psychiatry* 48: 158–60.

Lancet (1847). Operations under the influence of ether (anonymous case reports). *Lancet* 77–80.

Leonard, J.A. (1959). *Five Choice Serial Reaction Apparatus*. Report no. 326, Medical Research Council Applied Psychology Unit, Cambridge.

Ley, P. (1979). Memory for medical information. *British Journal of Social and Clinical Psychology* 18: 245–55.

Liu, S., Miller, N. and Waye, J.D. (1984). Retrograde amnesia effects of intravenous diazepam in endoscopy patients. *Gastrointestology and Endoscopy* 30: 340–2.

MacDonald, F.C., Gough, K.J., Nicoll, R.A.G. and Dow, R.J. (1989). Psychomotor effects of keterolac in comparison with buprenorphine and diclofenac. *British Journal of Clinical Pharmacology* 27: 453–9.

Mac, D.S., Kumar, R. and Goodwin, D.W. (1985). Anterograde amnesia with oral lorazepam. *Journal of Clinical Psychiatry* 46: 137–8.

Mackenzie, N. and Grant, I.S. (1985). Comparison of the new emulsion formulation of propofol with methohexitone and thiopentone for induction of anaesthesia in day cases. *British Journal of Anaesthesia* **57**: 725−31.

Manner, T., Kanto, J. and Salonen, M. (1987). Use of simple tests to determine the residual effects of the analgesic component of balanced anaesthesia. *British Journal of Anaesthesia* **59**: 978−82.

Massie, M. and Holland, J. (1987). The cancer patient with pain. Psychiatric complications and their management. *Medical Clinics of North America* **71**: 243−58.

Matthews, J.N.S., Altman, D.G., Campbell, M.J. and Royston, P. (1990). Analysis of serial measurements in medical research. *British Medical Journal* **300**: 230−5.

Mattila, M.J., Mattila, M. and Konno, K. (1986). Acute and subacute actions on human performance and interaction with diazepam of temelastine and diphenhyramine. *European Journal of Clinical Pharmacology* **31**: 291−8.

McDougall, W, and Smith, M. (1920). Effects of alcohol and some other drugs during normal and fatigued conditions. *Medical Research Council Special Report Series* **56**: 5−34.

Mewaldt, S.P., Hinrichs, J.V. and Ghoneim, M.M. (1983). Diazepam and memory: support for a duplex model of memory. *Memory and Cognition* **11**: 557−64.

Mewaldt, S.P., Ghoneim, M.M. and Hinrichs, J.V. (1986). The behavioral effects of diazepam and oxazepam are similar. *Psychopharmacology* **88**: 165−71.

Millar, K. (1986). Psychomotor tasks and recovery from anesthesia. *Anesthesia and Analgesia* **65**: 543−4.

Millar, K. (1989). Recall, recognition and implicit memory for intra-anaesthetic events. In *Clinical Anaesthesiology*, edited by J.G. Jones. London: Baillière Tindall, pp. 487−510.

Millar, K. (1991). Memory function. In *Ambulatory Anaesthesia and Sedation*, edited by I.D. Klepper, L.D. Sanders and M. Rosen. Oxford: Blackwell, pp. 140−57.

Millar, K. and Standen, P.J. (1982). Differences in performance impairment due to brompheniramine maleate as a function of the sustained release system. *British Journal of Clinical Pharmacology* **14**: 49−55.

Millar, K. and Wilkinson, R.T. (1981). Effects upon vigilance and reaction speed of the addition of ephedrine hydrochloride to chlorpheniramine maleate. *European Journal of Clinical Pharmacology* **20**: 351−7.

Millar, K., Styles, B.C. and Wastell, D.G. (1980). Time of day and retrieval from long-term memory. *British Journal of Psychology* **71**: 407−14.

Millar, K., Hammersley, R.H. and Finnigan, F. (1992). Reduction of alcohol-induced performance impairment by prior ingestion of food. *British Journal of Psychology* **83**: 261−278.

Moss, E., Hindmarch, I., Pain, A.J. and Edmonson, R.S. (1987). A comparison of recovery after halothane or alfentanil in anaesthesia for minor surgery. *British Journal of Anaesthesia* **59**: 970−7.

Mostert, J.W. (1975). States of awareness during general anaesthesia. *Perspectives in Biology and Medicine* **19**: 68−76.

Mueller, C., Lisman, S.A. and Spear, N.E. (1983). Alcohol enhancement of human memory: tests of consolidation and interference hypotheses. *Psychopharmacology* **80**: 226−30.

Netter, P. (1988). Individual differences in benzodiazepine-induced changes of memory. In *Benzodiazepine Receptor Ligands, Memory and Information Processing*, edited by I. Hindmarch and I. Ott. Berlin: Springer, pp. 90−113.

Neilson, W.R., Gelb, A.W., Casey, J.E., Penny, F.J., Merchant, R.N. and Manninen, P.H. (1990). Long-term cognitive and social sequelae of general versus regional anesthesia during arthroplasty in the elderly. *Anesthesiology* **73**: 1103−9.

Nightingale, J.J., Stock, J.G.L., McKiernan, E.P. and Wilton, N.C.T. (1988). Recovery after single-breath halothane induction of anaesthesia in day-case patients. *Anaesthesia* **43**: 554−6.

Noble, J. (1987). Day case anaesthesia and memory: a comparison of methohexitone and propofol. In *Aspects of Recovery from Anaesthesia*, edited by I. Hindmarch, J.G. Jones and E. Moss. Chichester: Wiley, pp. 93−101.

Norton, A.C. and Dundas, C.R. (1990). Induction agents for day-case anaesthesia. *Anaesthesia*

45: 198–203.

O'Boyle, C.A. (1988). Benzodiazepine-induced amnesia and anaesthetic practice: a review. In *Benzodiazepine Receptor Ligands, Memory and Information Processing*, edited by I. Hindmarch and I. Ott. Berlin: Springer, pp. 146–65.

O'Boyle, C.A., Barry, H., Fox, E., Harris, D. and McCreary, C. (1987). Benzodiazepine-induced event amnesia following a stressful surgical procedure. *Psychopharmacology* **91**: 244–7.

Ochs, M.W., Tucker, M.R. and White, R.P., Jr (1986). A comparison of amnesia in outpatients sedated with midazolam or diazepam alone or in combination with fentanyl during oral surgery. *Journal of the American Dental Association* **113**: 894–7.

Ogg, T.W., Fischer, H.B., Bethune, D.W. and Collins, J.M. (1979). Day case anaesthesia and memory. *Anaesthesia* **34**: 784–9.

Parker, E.S., Birnbaum, I.M., Weingartner, H., Hartley, J.T., Stillman, R.C. and Wyatt, R.J. (1980). Retrograde enhancement of human memory with alcohol. *Psychopharmacology* **69**: 219–22.

Parrott, A.C. (1990). Performance tests in human psychopharmacology. 1: reliability and standardisation. *Human Psychopharmacology* **5**: 1–9.

Parrott, A.C. (1991a). Performance tests in human psychopharmacology. 2: content validity, criterion validity, and face validity. *Human Psychopharmacology* **6**: 91–8.

Parrott, A.C. (1991b). Performance tests in human psychopharmacology. 3: construct validity and test interpretation. *Human Psychopharmacology* **6** (in press).

Philip, B.K., Simpson, T.H., Hauch, M.A. and Mallampati, S.R. (1990). Flumazenil reverses sedation after midazolam-induced general anesthesia in ambulatory surgery patients. *Anesthesia and Analgesia* **71**: 371–6.

Pomara, N., Stanley, B., Block. R., Berchou, R.C., Stanley, M., Greenblatt, D.J., Newton, R.E. and Gershon, S. (1985). Increased sensitivity of the elderly to the central depressant effects of diazepam. *Journal of Clinical Psychiatry* **4**: 185–7.

Poulton, E.C. (1982). Influential companions: effects of one strategy on another in the within-subject designs of cognitive psychology. *Psychological Bulletin* **91**: 673–90.

Poulton, E.C. and Edwards, R.S. (1974). Interactions, range effects and comparisons between tasks in experiments measuring performance with pairs of stresses: mild heat and 1 mg of L-hyoscine hydrobromide. *Aviation, Space and Environmental Medicine* **45**: 735–41.

Raybould, D. and Bradshaw, E.G. (1987). Premedication for day-case surgery. *Anaesthesia* **42**: 591–5.

Reitan, J.A., Porter, W. and Braunstein, M. (1986). Comparison of psychomotor skills and amnesia after induction of anaesthesia with midazolam or thiopental. *Anesthesia and Analgesia* **65**: 933–7.

RIG (1990). *Recovery Interest Group: Newsletter Number 1.* Department of Anaesthetics, University of Wales College of Cardiff.

Riis, J., Lomholt, B., Haxholdt, O., Kehlet, H., Valentin, N., Danielsen, U. and Dyrberg, V. (1983). Immediate and long-term mental recovery from general versus epidural anesthesia in elderly patients. *Acta Anaesthesiologica Scandinavica* **27**: 44–9.

Rotton, J. (1983). Affective and cognitive consequences of malodorous pollution. *Basic Applied Social Psychology* **4**: 171–91.

Roy-Byrne, P.P., Uhde, T.W., Holcomb, H., Thompson, K., King, A.K. and Weingartner, H. (1987). Effects of diazepam on cognitive processes in normal subjects. *Psychopharmacology* **91**: 30–3.

Saariahlo-Kere, U., Mattila, M.J. and Seppala, T. (1986). Pentazocine and codeine: effects on human performance and mood and interactions with diazepam. *Medical Biology* **64**: 293–9.

Saarialho-Kere, U., Julkunen, H., Mattila, M.J. and Seppala, T. (1988). Psychomotor performance of patients with rheumatoid arthritis: cross-over comparison of dextropropoxyphene, dextropropoxyphene plus amitriptyline, indomethacin, and placebo. *Pharmacology and Toxicology* **63**: 286–92.

Saarialho-Kere, U., Mattila, M.J. and Seppala, T. (1989). Psychomotor, respiratory and neuroendocrinological effects of a μ-opioid receptor antagonist (oxycodone) in healthy volunteers. *Pharmacology and Toxicology* **65**: 252–7.

Sanders, L.D., Isaac, P.A., Yeomans, W.A., Clyburn, P.A., Rosen, M. and Robinson, J.O. (1989). Propofol-induced anaesthesia. *Anaesthesia* **44**: 200–4.

Sanders, L.D., Piggott, S.E., Isaac, P.A., Okell, R.W., Roberts, B., Rosen, M. and Robinson, J.O. (1991). Reversal of benzodiazepine sedation with the antagonist flumazenil. *British Journal of Anaesthesia* **66**: 445–53.

Scharf, M.B., Khosla, N., Lysaght, R., Brocker, N. and Moran, J. (1983). Anterograde amnesia with oral lorazepam. *Journal of Clinical Psychiatry* **44**: 362–4.

Scharf, M.B., Khosla, N., Brocker, N. and Goff, P. (1984). Differential amnestic properties of short- and long-acting benzodiazepines. *Journal of Clinical Psychiatry* **45**: 51–3.

Scott, A.W.C., Whitwam, J.G. and Wilkinson, R.T. (1983). Choice reaction time: a method of measuring postoperative psychomotor performance decrements. *Anaesthesia* **38**: 1162–8.

Sear, J.W., Cooper, G.M. and Kumar, V. (1983). The effect of age on recovery. *Anaesthesia* **38**: 1158–61.

Simpson, K.H., Smith, R.J. and Davies, L.F. (1987). Comparison of the effects of atropine and glycopyrrolate on cognitive function following general anaesthesia. *British Journal of Anaesthesia* **59**: 966–9.

Sinclair, M.E. and Cooper, G.M. (1983). Alfentanil and recovery. *Anaesthesia* **38**: 435–7.

Smith, G. and Shirley, A.W. (1978). A review of the effects of trace concentrations of anaesthetics on performance. *British Journal of Anaesthesia* **50**: 701–12.

Stollery, B.T., Broadbent, D.E., Lee, W.T., Keen, R.J., Healey, T.E.J. and Beatty, P. (1988). Mood and cognitive functions in anaesthetists working in actively scavenged operating theatres. *British Journal of Anaesthesia* **61**: 446–55.

Studd, C. and Eltringham, R.J. (1980). Lorazepam as night sedation and premedication: a comparison with diazepam. *Anaesthesia* **35**: 60–4.

Tucker, M.R., Hann, J.R. and Phillips, C.L. (1984). Subanesthetic doses of ketamine, diazepam, and nitrous oxide for adult outpatient sedation. *Journal of Oral and Maxillofacial Surgery* **42**: 668–72.

Valtonen, M., Salonen, M., Forssel, H., Scheinin, M. and Viinamaki, O. (1989). Propofol infusion for sedation in outpatient surgery. *Anaesthesia* **44**: 730–4.

Vickers, M.D. (1965). The measurement of recovery from anaesthesia. *British Journal of Anaesthesia* **37**: 296–302.

Vuyk, J., Hennis, P.J., Burm, A.G.L., de Voogt, J-W.H. and Spierdijk, J. (1990). Comparison of midazolam and propofol in combination with alfentanil for total intravenous anesthesia. *Anesthesia and Analgesia* **71**: 645–50.

Wallace, L.M. (1987). Trait anxiety as a predictor of adjustment to and recovery from surgery. *British Journal of Clinical Psychology* **26**: 73–4.

Weightman, W.M. and Zacharias, M. (1987). Comparison of propofol and thiopentone anaesthesia (with special reference to recovery characteristics). *Anaesthesia and Intensive Care* **15**: 389–93.

Weinger, M.B. and Englund, C.E. (1990). Ergonomic and human factors affecting anesthetic vigilance and monitoring performance in the operating room environment. *Anesthesiology* **73**: 995–1021.

Wesnes, K. (1985). A fully automated psychometric test battery for human psychopharmacology. *Abstracts of Fourth World Congress of Biological Psychiatry, Philadelphia*, p. 153.

Wilkinson, R.T. (1969). Some factors influencing the effect of environmental stressors upon performance. *Psychological Bulletin* **72**: 260–72.

Wilkinson, R.T. (1970). Methods for research in sleep deprivation and sleep function. In *Sleep and Dreaming, International Psychiatry Clinics*, edited by E. Hartmann, Boston: Little, Brown, pp. 369–82.

Wilkinson, R.T. and Houghton, D. (1975). Portable four-choice reaction time test with magnetic tape memory. *Behavioral Research Methods and Instrumentation* **7**: 441–6.

Zuurmond, W.W.A., Balk, V.A., Van Dis, H., Van Leeuwen, H. and Paul, E.A.A. (1989). Multidimensionality of psychological recovery from anaesthesia. *Anaesthesia* **44**: 889–92.

Subject Index

Acetylcholine 159
Acrodermatitis 37
Addiction and caffeine 67, 68
Addiction and cannabis 174
Adrenalin and cognition 248, 249
Adenosine 53, 54
AIDS 219–238
AIDS 265, 275
   and neuropsychological testing 226, 227, 228, 229
   history of 219, 220
   nature of 222, 223, 224
   onset of 232, 233
   pathology of 225
   prevalence of 219, 220, 224
   Price's staging of 223
   stages of 220, 221, 222
   treatment of 236, 237, 238
AIDS dementia complex (ADC) 222–233
AIDS related complex (ARC) 221
Alcohol 73–121, 327
   and age 118, 119
   and aggression 178
   and anxiety 113
   and behaviour 85
   and blackouts 116
   and body sway 91, 104, 105
   and cannabis 188, 189
   and central nervous system 85, 86
   and co-ordination 91, 92
   and driving 92, 93
   and environment of consumption 115
   and flight simulators 107
   and food 106
   and heart rate 112, 113
   and learning 97, 98
   and maternity 118
   and mediators of 85–89, 106–109
   and memory 95, 96, 97, 98
   and metabolic rates 75, 76, 116, 117

   and perception 94, 95
   and personality 114, 115
   and practice 103, 104
   and reaction-time 98–106
   and reasoning 103
   and self awareness 111, 112
   and self control 112
   and semantic processing 103
   and signal detection 98, 99, 100
   and task impairments 86–106
   and tracking 89, 90, 91, 92
   expectation of 110, 111, 112
   experimental approaches to 74–85
   individual differences 115–119
   intake 77
   measurement of 74, 75, 76
   methodological problems of 78, 83, 84, 85
   physiology 112, 113
   prevalence of use 171
   psychopharmacological models 85–89
   sex differences 117, 118
Alcohol dependence 113
Alcohol myopia 88
Alcoholism 113
Altitude tolerance, and meals 4
Alzheimer's Disease 223, 224, 229, 323
Amino acids 14, 15
Amitriptyline 324
Amotivational syndrome 179
Amnesia 367, 368
Amphetamines 299
Anaemia 40
Anaesthetic drugs 337–370, 375–379
   and attention 355–360
   and co-ordination 357
   and cognition 347–370
   and critical flicker fusion 361, 362
   and digit span 263, 264
   and driving 358, 359, 360
   and dual-task performance 358, 359, 360

Anaesthetic drugs *continued*
  and learning 364, 365, 366
  and letter detection 355, 356, 357
  and levels of 375, 376
  and memory 362–370
  and motor skills 360, 361
  and reaction-time 343, 344, 346
  and reaction-time, choice 350–355
  and reaction-time, simple 347–350
  and semantic memory 367
  and state dependent learning 364, 365, 366
  and task taxonomy 345
  and theatre personnel 376, 377
  and tracking 358, 359, 360
  and visual memory 366, 367
  early studies 337, 338, 339
  future research 377, 378, 379
  impairments 340, 341, 342
  methodological issues 339–347
  recovery 343, 344, 345, 346
Analgesic drugs 370–375
  and attention 372, 373, 374
  and dual task performance 373, 374
  and memory 374, 375
  and reaction-time 371, 372, 373, 374
  and side effects 371
  and tracking 373, 374
  classification of 370
Anorexia nervosa 37, 38
Anti depressant drugs 319–333
  and alcohol 327
  and cognition 322–332
  and critical flicker fusion 326, 327
  and EEG 327
  and elderly 326
  and memory 327, 328, 329, 330
  and nondepressed subjects 324–330
  and reaction-time 328, 329, 330
  and sedation 325, 326
  repeated doses 327, 328, 329, 330
  tolerance 329, 330
  types of 322, 323, 324
Anticholingeric drugs and memory 323
Antihistamine bropheniramine 345
Anxiety 7
  and alcohol 113
  and caffeine 62, 66, 67, 68
  and psychotropic drugs 293, 295, 296, 309, 310
Arousal and nicotine 155, 156, 157, 158, 159
Arousal and psychotropic drugs 285, 286, 297, 298, 307, 308
Asthma 174
Attention and anaesthetic drugs 355, 356, 357, 358, 359, 360
  and analgesic drugs 372, 373, 374
  and influenza 206, 207
  and nicotine 133–146
  and psychotropic drugs 296, 297, 298, 299
Auditory evoked potential (AEP) 230, 231, 232

Auditory-verbal learning test (AVLT) 227, 228
AZT 236, 237, 238
  long-term effects 237

Beck Depression Inventory 227
Benzodiazapines 65, 174, 176
Beri-beri amnesia 33, 34
Beta-adrenergic blockers 295
Breakfast 16–20
  and caffeine 19, 20
  and memory 19, 20
  and school performance 17
  size of 17, 19
  habitual eating of 18
British ability scale 28
Bronchodilation 174, 176

Caffeine 49–70
  action of 53, 54
  and addiction 67, 68
  and age 62, 63
  and alertness 62, 63
  and anxiety 62, 66, 67, 68
  and behaviour 55–65
  and benzodiazapines 65
  and contraception 55, 66
  and driving 63, 64
  and marksmanship 64
  and mood changes 62, 63
  and motor performance 67
  and personality 65, 66
  and public health 69, 70
  and reaction-time 58, 59
  and short-term memory 61
  and sleep 64, 65
  and smoking 57
  and vigilance 59, 60, 61
  and vision 58
  experimental approaches to 55, 56
  history of 50
  metabolism 54, 55
  natural doses of 51, 52, 53
  tolerance 57
Calcium pantothenate 31
Calvert non-verbal test 27
Cannabis 169–191
  and academic performance 187
  and age 189
  and aircraft piloting 186, 187
  and alcohol 188, 189
  and behaviour 178, 179, 180
  and central nervous system 176
  and driving 185, 186
  and eye 175
  and flashbacks 180
  and heart rate 175
  and immune system 174

and lungs 174
and memory 179, 182, 183, 184
and mucosa 175
and panic attacks 179
and pregnancy 174
and reaction-time 180
and schizophrenia 180
and self-regulation 173
and skin 175
and stomach 175
and subjective effects 178, 179, 180
and tasks, complex 180, 181, 182
and tasks, simple 180
and violence 178
and work output 184, 185
dependence 174
leaf 170
metabolism 173, 174
methods of use 173
molecular structure 172
origins 169, 170
physiology 174, 175, 176, 177, 178
practical uses 176, 177, 178
prevalence of use 170, 171
psychoactive doses 172, 173
psychopharmacology 171, 172
rate of effect 173
tolerance 174, 189
withdrawals 174
Carcinogenics 175
Catecholamines 15
Cerebral atrophy 176
Chloroform 337, 338
Chloropromazine and arousal 285, 286, 298
Choline 15
Chronic fatigue syndrome 261–277
and cognition 265–273, 275, 276
and memory 268, 269
and mood 269, 270, 271, 274
and neurotransmitters 263, 276
and psychiatry 263, 264
and psychophysiology 276
and reaction-time 268, 269, 271, 273
and visual sensitivity 268, 269
associated illnesses 269, 270
Cardiff Programme 265
case definition of 262, 263
duration of 269
Glasgow study 265, 266, 269
history of 262
immunology 264
influenza 274, 275
research design 264, 265
Sussex programme 265, 266, 267, 268, 269
symptoms of 261
Circadian rhythms 4, 7, 102, 107
Cognition and hypoglycaemia 243–255
Cognitive failures questionnaire 266, 267

Colds 197–217
and influenza 209, 210, 211
and memory 212, 213, 214
and muscle function 212
and performance testing 203, 204
and reaction-time 209, 210, 211
and reading ability 200
and road accidents 198, 199, 200
and stress 215
and vision 214
causes of 201
economic consequences of 197, 198
experimentation on 200, 201
length of effects 211, 212
prevalence of 197
susceptibility to 215
Common Cold Unit 201, 202, 203, 215–217
experimental procedures 202, 203
Coronaviruses 201, 202, 203, 209, 214
Coxsackie virus 262, 264
Critical flicker frequency 13
Critical flicker fusion 95, 246
and anaesthetic drugs 361, 362
and anti depressant drugs 326, 327
and nicotine 136
Critical flicker vision 58
Cytokines 212

Decision making and alcohol 98–106
Delirium 236
Depression 319–333
and cognition 320, 321, 322
and memory 321
and prevalence of 319
and selective recall 321, 322
and speech rate 321
Depressive pseudodementia 226, 227
Diabetes Mellitus 243–255
age of onset 243
treatment of 243, 244
type II 251, 252
Dichotic listening 303
Dietary deficiencies 41, 42
Divided attention 104, 105, 106
Dopamine 290, 303
Drugs, prevalence of use 170, 171
DSMIII–R 234, 235
Dual task performance 13, 90, 104, 105, 358, 359, 360, 373, 374
Dyslexia 38

Electrical Evoked Potential 249
Epstein–Barr virus 262, 264
Eysenck personality inventory 7, 65, 66

Facial expressions 303, 304
Febrile disease 262
Folate 33, 35

Glucose 243
Gottschaldt hidden shapes test 66

Hangovers 106, 107, 108
Herpes virus 264
Hippocampus 37
HIV 219–238
 and auditory evoked potential 230, 231, 232
 and cognitive impairment 232, 233
 and depression 235
 and eye movements 230
 and psychological abnormalities 234, 235, 236
 and psychoses 235
 classification of 220, 221, 222
 fears of 236
 neurophysiology 230, 231, 232
 reaction of diagnosis to 234
Hodgkin's disease 222
Hormone responses and hypoglycaemia 248, 249
Huntington's disease 223, 224
Hyoscine 345
Hyperkinetic children 32
Hypoglycaemia 15, 243–255
 adulthood 251, 252, 253, 254
 and childhood affects 251
 and cognition 244–255
 and controlled studies of 245
 and driving 245
 and hormone responses 248, 249
 and induced studies of 245, 246, 247
 and IQ 251, 252, 253, 254
 and memory 254
 and permanent cognitive impairment 250, 251, 252, 253, 254
 and reaction-time 245, 247, 248
 brain electrophysiology 249, 250

Immune system 174
Influenza 197–217
 and attention 206, 207
 and reaction-time 204, 205
 and tracking 205
 and reasoning 205, 206
Information processing models 306, 307
Insomnia 293, 294
Insulin 243
 overdoses of 243, 244
Intelligence and vitamins 26–31
Interferon alpha 207, 208
 and reaction-time 208
Intoxification and subjective judgements of 108, 109
Iron 40, 41

Korsakoff's dementia 34

LSD 174, 178, 180
Luria-Nebraska tests 229

Magnetic Resonance Imaging (MRI) 225
Meals 1–21
 and calorific content 9, 10
 and carbohydrates 8, 9
 and circadian rhythms 4, 6, 7
 and cognition 3, 4, 5, 6, 7
 and personality factors 7
 and protein 8, 9
 size of 9, 10, 11
Memory and alcohol 95, 96, 97, 98
 and breakfast 19, 20
 and cannabis 179, 182, 183, 184
 and colds 212, 213, 214
Menstruation 117
Meprobamate 292
Methylphenidate 32
Methylxanthines 50, 51, 54
Middlesex Hospital questionnaire 266, 267
Minerals 25–43
Minnesota multiphasic personality inventory 34, 36
Monoamine oxidase inhibitors (MAOI) 324
Multicentre AIDS Cohort Study (MACS) 233
Myocardial oxygen 175
Myoclonus 292

Nabilone 177
Neurasthenia 262
Niacinamide 31
Nicotine 127–163
 and arousal 155, 156, 157, 158, 159
 and attention 133–146
 and auditory memory span 146
 and auditory vigilance 139
 and central nervous system 159
 and cognition 132–159
 and control dose 130
 and critical flicker fusion 136
 and death rates 127
 and driving 137, 138
 and EEG measurements 159
 and event related potential (ERP) 143
 and experimental measures 129
 and heart rate 131, 132
 and learning 146, 147, 148, 149
 and light smokers 154, 155
 and memory 146, 147, 148, 149
 and non-smokers 154, 155
 and rapid visual information processing (RVIP) 140–144, 154, 156
 and reaction-time 134, 138, 150, 151
 and selective attention 134, 135, 136, 145, 146
 and serial learning 148, 149
 and state dependent learning 148

and strength of cigarette 141, 147, 155
and stroop test 145
and sustained attention 137, 138, 139, 140
and two flash fusion threshold 136
and visual vigilance 138, 139
absorption 128, 129
methodological problems 129–133, 159–162
neurochemistry 159
Nicotine deprivation 150–155
and attention 150, 151

O-Hela cells 203

Panic anxiety disorder 66
Panic attacks 179
Perceptual bias 309, 310, 311
Placebo 130
Pneumocystis carinii pneumonia (PCP) 237
Post infectious fatigue syndrome (PIFS) 263
Post-lunch performance 1–16
and alcohol 12, 13, 14
and arousal 11, 12
and caffeine 12
and noise 11, 12
and sex differences 8
and sleep deprivation 14
and time of day 5
and type of task 6
Prophylactic drugs 215
Psychopharmacological models 85, 86, 87, 88, 89
Psychoses 235, 236
Psychotropic drugs 279–315
and anxiety 293, 295, 296, 309, 310
and appropriate tests 289
and arousal 285, 286, 297, 298, 307, 308
and attention 296, 297, 298, 299
and cell enzymes 281
and dependence 284, 285
and dichotic listening 303
and driving 311, 312, 313, 314
and emotion 304, 305, 306
and facial expressions 303, 304
and information processing models 306, 307
and memory 299, 302
and perceptual bias 309, 310, 311
and reaction-time 299, 300, 301, 305, 308
and road accidents 294
and schizophrenia 289, 290, 297, 307, 308
biological action 280–285
counter-measures 314, 315
experimental studies 296–306
half-life 295
methodological issues 285, 286, 287, 288
models of action 311, 312, 313, 314
neurochemistry 281, 290, 291
side effects 291, 294, 295, 296

tolerance 284, 285
variability of 281, 282, 283, 284
Pyridoxine 32

Reaction-time and alcohol 98–106
and anaesthetic drugs 343, 344, 346, 347-355
and analgesic drugs 371, 372, 373, 374
and anti depressant drugs 328, 329, 330
and breakfast 17
and cannabis 180
and chronic fatigue syndrome 268, 269, 271, 273
and colds 209, 210, 211
and hypoglycaemia 245, 247, 248
and influenza 204, 205
and interferon alpha 208
and nicotine 134, 138, 150, 151
and psychotropic drugs 299, 300, 301, 305, 308
Reaction-time choice 101, 102, 103
Reaction-time complex 103, 104
Reaction-time simple 100, 101
Reasoning and alcohol 103
and influenza 205, 206
REM sleep 174, 176
Retrograde amnesia 367, 368
Rhinoviruses 201, 203, 209, 214
Riboflavin 32, 33, 41
Risk taking behaviour 92, 93, 114, 115

Schizophrenia 180, 289, 290, 297, 307, 308
Scurvy 36
Selenium 38, 39, 40
and geriatric patients 39
Serotonin 324
Smoking (see nicotine) 127–163
Sodium nedocromil 215
State dependent learning 98, 148, 183
Stress and colds 215
Stroop test 5, 145, 245

Temporal disintegration 178
Thiamin 32–35
and children 35
Tobacco (see nicotine) 127–163
Tomography 225
Toxic psychosis 180
Tracking and alcohol 89, 90, 91, 92
and anaesthetic drugs 358, 359, 360
and analgesic drugs 371, 372, 373, 374
and cannabis 181
and colds 209
and influenza 205
Tranquillisers (see psychotropic drugs) 279–315
Tricyclic drugs 323, 324

Tryptophan   14, 15
Tyrosine   15

Violence and alcohol   178
    and cannabis   178
Vision, and caffeine   58
    and colds   214
Vitamin B12 and psychiatric syndromes   35
Vitamin C   35, 36
Vitamins   25–43
    and elderly   32, 33
    and intelligence   26, 27, 28
    and learning difficulties   31, 32

    and memory   33
    and mood   33
    supplementation of in children   25, 26, 27

Weschler Adult Intelligence Scale (WAIS)   28,
    226, 228, 252

Zidovudine   236, 237, 238
    and long-term effects   237
Zinc   36, 37, 38
    and anorexia nervosa   37, 38
    and dyslexia   38
    and speed of growth   36
Zinc gluconate   215

Author Index

Aamoot, R.L.   37, 43
Abas, M.A.   227, 238
Abbash, A.   37, 46
Abel, E.L.   182, 183, 191
Abou-Saleh, M.T.   35, 43
Abrams, D.B.   80, 91, 113, 123
Ack, M.   251, 255
Acton, T.M.G.   236, 240
Adam, N.   364, 379
Adams, C.E.A.   38, 44
Adams, K.M.   228, 239
Adamson, U.   252, 259
Adinoff, B.   82, 99, 100, 125
Agaroh, C-D 250, 259
Ahern, F.M.   82, 90, 91, 92, 94, 95, 97, 100,
   104, 112, 126
Aikawa, H.   81, 95, 102, 124
Aitken, P.P.   77, 121
Al-Nakib, W.   205, 207, 211, 215, 217, 218
Alderrice, J.T.   38, 44
Algan, M.   254, 255
Ali, M.A.   362, 381
Allen, D.   327, 334
Allison, T.   248, 249, 257
Alluisi, E.A.   200, 211, 217, 218
Altman, D.G.   341, 342, 381, 383
Altman, H.J.   324, 334
Altschul, A.   244, 255
Amedee-Manesme, O.   42, 46
Amiel, S.A.   249, 255
Amin, M.M.   331, 334
Aminoff, M.J.   231, 239
Amldon, G.L.   106, 126
Amos, S.P.   26, 28, 30, 46
Andersen, H.B.   311, 316
Anderson, K.J.   65, 72
Anderson, K.W.   118, 123
Anderson, S.   357, 363, 365, 379
Andersson, K.   138, 147, 163, 165
Andrews, P.J.D.   369, 379

Ankier, S.I.   325, 336
Annau, Z.   54, 72
Anton, D.J.   134, 150, 151, 165
Arab, L.   41, 43
Arbit, J.   376, 380
Archard, L.   262, 264, 278
Archibald, H.R.   249, 255
Arenberg, A.   251, 258
Armer, L.   271, 272, 273, 275, 276, 278
Armitage, A.K.   159, 163
Armitage, P.   161, 164, 366, 379
Arnold, D.I.   263, 277
Arnold, P.K.   287, 299, 303, 304, 315, 316
Aruffo, C.   34, 44
Asbury, A.J.   342, 343, 354, 381
Ashbrook, P.W.   321, 335."
Ashton, C.H.   138, 155, 156, 163, 172, 174, 175,
   176, 177, 178, 180, 181, 184, 187, 191
Ashworth, B.   254, 255
Atkinson, D.W.   106, 122
Atkinson, J.H.   232, 239
Atkinson, R.C.   182, 183, 192
Attwood, D.A.   74, 79, 93, 121
Aynsley-Green, A.   250, 257
Azar, I.   357, 379

Bach, M.J.   376, 380
Bachevalier, J.   35, 44
Backlund, F.   312, 317
Baddeley, A.D.   363, 379
Baer, K.   4, 7, 9, 22, 106, 122
Baid, G.   253, 256
Baillie, R.   340, 354, 356, 379
Bakan, P.   140, 163
Baker, S.J.   79, 94, 95, 121
Bakheit, M.   269, 270, 278
Bale, R.N.   252, 255
Balk, V.A.   345, 346, 354, 355, 360, 385
Balle, V.   254, 255

Banatvala, J. 262, 264, 278
Bancroft, N.R. 137, 150, 152, 153, 164
Barabee, H.E. 110, 122
Barclay, L. 34, 45
Barclay, M.I. 39, 43
Barker, I. 352, 357, 379
Barnett, D.B. 365, 380
Barone, J.J. 51, 72
Barrat, L. 110, 125
Barrow, G.I. 207, 211, 213, 214, 215, 218
Barry, H. 368, 369, 384
Bartelloni, P.J. 200, 217
Barth, J.T. 81, 91, 96, 102, 124
Bartus, R.T. 323, 334
Batt, R.D. 74, 126
Battig, K. 61, 66, 70, 178, 142, 145, 165, 166, 178, 182, 183, 192
Bayliss, P.F. 325, 326, 327, 334, 336
Baylor, A.M. 79, 86, 100, 101, 121
Beard, A.W. 262, 278
Beare, A.S. 202, 217
Beatty, P. 376, 385
Beatty, R. 235, 241
Beautrais, A.L. 180, 182, 183, 191
Bech, P. 185, 191, 194
Beck, A.T. 227, 238, 322, 334
Beckwith, B. 61, 66, 70
Beer, B. 323, 334
Behan, P.O. 262, 264, 269, 270, 278
Behan, W.M.H. 264, 278
Behstune, D.W. 363, 366, 384
Beisel, W.R. 200, 217
Belgrave, B.E. 180, 181, 191
Bell, I.R. 35, 43."
Bell, P.M. 246, 247, 248, 258
Bell, W. 269, 270, 278
Ben-Tzvi, E. 331, 334
Bender, A.E. 16, 18, 19, 22
Benedikt, R.A. 108, 123
Beniak, T.E. 355, 363, 380
Bennett, I.F. 185, 188, 193
Benowitz, N.L. 128, 164
Benson, E. 230, 239
Benton, D. 18, 20, 22, 26, 27, 28, 29, 30, 36, 38, 40, 43, 44
Berchou, R.C. 365, 384
Beresford, R. 235, 240
Berg, C.J. 57, 65, 72
Berg, G. 113, 121
Berg, R. 51, 70
Berger, J.R. 222, 241
Berger, R.S. 79, 91, 115, 121
Berglund, A. 253, 258
Berretini, C.H. 226, 241
Besson, J.A. 321, 336
Betts, T.A. 294, 315, 330, 334
Bhagavan, H.N. 32, 44
Bhalla, R.B. 225, 239
Bhatti, J.Z. 361, 362, 381

Bickerman, H.A. 4, 17, 22
Bierness, D. 79, 89, 114, 121
Bigler, E.D. 252, 258
Bigley, J.W. 237, 241
Binder, C. 245, 246, 248, 250, 258
Bird, C.E. 253, 254, 255, 257
Bird, K.D. 180, 181, 191
Birnbaum, I.M. 81, 98, 124, 367, 384
Bisgrove, E.Z. 81, 91, 104, 105, 109, 117, 124
Bittner, A.C. 160, 164
Blackburn, I.M. 251, 256, 321, 334
Blackman, J.D. 248, 249, 255
Blaine, J.D. 186, 192
Blake, M.J.F. 3, 22
Blanco-Sequeiros, M. 251, 257
Blaney, P.H. 321, 334
Bleyl, H. 33, 44
Blix, O. 155, 164
Block. R.I. 362, 365, 381, 384
Bloom, F.E. 231, 241
Blouin, A.G. 18, 22
Boccellari, A. 229, 236, 238, 239
Boggs, U.R. 25, 30, 44
Boland, F.J. 110, 122
Boland, P. 186, 188, 194
Bolli, G. 250, 255
Bonati, M. 55, 70
Bond, A.J. 58, 61, 65, 70, 365, 380
Bond, M.R. 370, 379
Bongiovanni, L. 251, 255
Bonner, T.J. 172, 193
Booth, R. 262, 264, 278."
Bore, P.I. 263, 277
Borson, W.F. 116, 121
Borysiewicz, L. 262, 264, 278
Botez, M.I. 35, 44
Botez, T. 35, 44
Boulenger, J.P. 66, 67, 70
Boulware, S.D. 248, 249, 257
Bourguignon, J. 54, 71
Bourke, J.B. 340, 343, 350, 351, 353, 381
Bouvet, W. 4, 17, 22
Bowden, S.C. 79, 107, 121
Bowes, J.B. 363, 365, 382
Bowman, M. 184, 191
Boyd, J.H. 319, 334
Boysen, K. 349, 379
Bozzetti, L.P. 186, 192
Bradley, B.P. 110, 125
Bradley, C.M. 372, 373, 374, 380
Bradshaw, C.M. 321, 336
Braff, D.L. 181, 191
Branconnier, R.J. 326, 334
Brass, J. 34, 45
Braunstein, M. 346, 361, 363, 367, 384
Braverman, E.R. 37, 46
Breckenridge, R.L. 79, 91, 115, 121
Brenemuhl, D. 294, 318
Brent-Smith, H. 170, 186, 192

Brettle, R.P.B. 228, 229, 231, 232, 239
Brew, B.J. 222, 225, 239, 240, 241
Brewer, N. 79, 93, 121
Brick, J. 81, 89, 91, 96, 118, 124
Brightwell, D.R. 182, 194
Britz, A. 250, 253, 258
Broadbent, D.E. 8, 22, 207, 215, 217, 266, 277, 297, 302, 310, 311, 315, 316, 346, 376, 379, 380, 385
Broadbent, M.H.P. 8, 22, 207, 215, 217, 302, 310, 315
Brocker, N. 365, 385
Bronzert, D.A. 37, 45
Brophy, C. 212, 217
Brosnan, L. 302, 315
Broughton, D. 254, 257
Brouwers, P. 226, 241
Brown, D.J. 181, 192
Brown, J. 363, 365, 380
Brown, M. 363, 365, 380
Brown, N. 262, 278
Browne, R.C. 1, 22
Brownstein, M.J. 172, 193
Brozek. J. 4, 8, 22, 32, 34, 44
Bruera, E. 371, 380
Brunetti, P. 250, 255
Bruns, R.F. 53, 54, 55, 70
Brus, I. 262, 278
Bryce, D.L. 376, 380
Bryce-Smith, D. 38, 44, 47."
Buchsbaum, M. 324, 335
Buchwald, D. 264, 277
Bucknall, A.B.V. 219, 241
Bull, S. 214, 218
Burg, A.W. 51, 54, 70
Burger, P.C. 34, 46
Burk, R.F. 38, 44
Burley, V. 27, 29, 46
Burm, A.G.L. 355, 385
Burns, M.M. 81, 90, 94, 99, 124, 325, 335
Burt, D.R. 291, 318
Burton, J.R. 35, 45
Busco, S. 250, 259
Bush, D. 325, 335
Busija, D.W. 67, 71
Buss, D.H. 39, 47
Butchart, D.G.M. 352, 357, 379
Buts, J.P. 27, 28, 29, 30, 44
Buzzi, R. 61, 66, 70, 142, 145, 165, 166
Bye, C.E. 58, 59, 61, 62, 70, 325, 326, 334, 359, 381

Caces, P. 42, 45
Caine, E. 226, 227, 239, 240
Caldwell, D.F. 38, 44, 189, 191
Calev, A. 331, 334
Callaway, E. 302, 318
Cameron, O.G. 66, 71

Campbell, I.W. 254, 255
Campbell, J.A. 41, 46
Campbell, M.E. 41, 46
Campbell, M.J. 341, 342, 383
Campbell, S.S. 3, 6, 22
Campbell, W.R. 244, 256
Campeas, R. 320, 335
Canal, N. 253, 256
Caprio, S. 248, 249, 256
Carasso, R. 331, 334
Cardon, P.V. 173, 193
Carl, E. 136, 164
Carlier, C. 42, 45
Carlin, A.S. 228, 239
Carney, M.W.P. 35, 42, 44
Carpenter, J.A. 74, 121
Cars, I. 250, 258
Carter, G.L. 147, 164
Carter, J.P. 42, 46
Carter, R.C. 160, 164
Casey, J.E. 361, 383
Cashman, J.N. 349, 355, 380
Caspaire, A.F. 250, 255
Castro, A.D. 364, 379
Caswell, S. 181, 191
Cattell, R.B. 30, 44, 66, 70
Cecchetto, R. 253, 256
Chakaverty, P. 201, 217
Chalmers, J. 254, 255
Chan, M. 324, 334."
Chanarin, I. 35, 46
Charney, D.S. 321, 335
Chasty, H. 38, 45
Chesler, G.B. 180, 181, 191
Childs, J. 58, 72
Chiles, W.D. 74, 79, 107, 121
Chin, J. 220, 241
Chiswick, A. 231, 232, 239
Cho, E.S. 223, 240
Chome, J. 33, 44
Christ, S.T. 147, 165
Christiansen, H. 185, 194
Christie, M.J. 8, 15, 22, 106, 122
Christmas, L. 144, 167, 272, 273, 275, 276, 278, 340, 354, 356, 379
Christrup, H. 185, 194
Chrzan, G.J. 79, 94, 95, 121
Chung, A. 357, 363, 380
Chung, F. 357, 380
Chusney, G. 249, 255
Cirillo, D. 251, 255
Clare, A. 262, 264, 278
Clark, C.R. 348, 355, 360, 381
Clark, D.L. 364, 379
Clark, D.M. 321, 334
Clark, L.D. 180, 181, 191
Clark, S. 180, 194
Clarke, P.R.F. 299, 316
Clarren, S.K. 118, 123

Clausen, J. 39, 44
Clausen, V. 179, 192
Clayton, A.B. 330, 334
Clements, G.B. 264, 278
Cleveland, W.P. 80, 90, 99, 101, 103, 118, 123
Clifford Rose, R. 262, 264, 278
Clubley, M. 58, 59, 61, 62, 70, 325, 326, 334
Clyburn, P.A. 344, 353, 356, 363, 369, 380, 385
Coates, G.D. 200, 211, 217, 218
Coats, M. 225, 246
Cobb, I.A. 262, 277
Cockram, C.S. 248, 250, 256
Cohen, M.J. 183, 191, 194
Cohen, R. 321, 336
Cohen, R.L. 363, 380
Cohen, R.M. 247, 256
Cohen, S. 215, 218
Cohn, C. 15, 22
Cole, J. 326, 334
Cole, J.O. 35, 43, 62, 70, 289, 316
Cole, R.E. 82, 90, 91, 92, 94, 95, 97, 100, 104, 112, 126.
Cole, T.J. 251, 257
Coleman, M. 32, 44
Collerton, D. 323, 334
Collins, J.M. 363, 384
Collins, W.E. 74, 79, 107, 121.¨
Colquhoun, W.P. 4, 22
Colton, T. 65, 70
Combs, G.F. 40, 44
Combs, S.B. 40, 44
Comholt, B. 375, 384
Comitas, L. 185, 191
Cone, E.J. 181, 182, 192
Conley, K.L. 245, 249, 256
Connelly, S.A.V. 80, 84, 87, 102, 103, 123
Connors, C.K. 18, 22
Connors, G.J. 79, 89, 101, 104, 112, 121
Conry, J.P. 355, 363, 380
Cook, R. 27, 29, 30, 38, 40, 44
Cooke, E.C. 127, 165
Cooper, D.A. 223, 230, 237, 239, 241
Cooper, G.M. 355, 385
Cooper, P.F. 379, 380
Cooper, P.J. 266, 277
Cooper, Z. 321, 336
Cooperman, J.M. 41, 45
Coppen, C. 35, 43
Cordischi, V. 254, 258
Cornblath, M. 251, 257
Cornett, T.L. 182, 194
Corrigan, F.M. 39, 47
Cort, J. 106, 122
Cott, A. 31, 44
Cotten, D.C. 134, 164
Couper-Smartt, J. 299, 300, 301, 316
Coursin, D.B. 32, 44
Coviella, I.L.G. 51, 58, 59, 60, 61, 63, 67, 71
Coxon, L. 303, 316

Coyle, K.B. 204, 205, 208, 209, 211, 213, 215, 217, 218
Cozolino, L. 8, 14, 15, 23, 106, 125
Craig, A. 4, 7, 9, 11, 22, 106, 122
Craig, D. 142, 145, 146, 156, 161, 166
Craig, J.W. 215, 218
Crawford, J.R. 228, 229, 232, 239, 252, 255
Cresse, I. 291, 318
Crisp, A.H. 266, 277
Crispino, G. 250, 255
Cristina, G. 254, 258
Crombie, I.K. 27, 29, 44
Cross, M. 32, 44
Cross, P. 326, 335
Crouch, D.J. 186, 195
Crown, S. 266, 277
Cryer, P. 247, 248, 249, 250, 257
Cunha, J.M. 178, 195
Cunnah, D.T.F. 249, 255
Cunningham, P. 201, 217
Cunningham-Rundles, C. 262, 278
Curran, H.V. 320, 325, 327, 328, 329, 334, 335, 336
Currie, J. 230, 239.¨

Daly, J.W. 53, 54. 55, 70
Damhancic, P. 253, 256
Damsgaard, E. 40, 45
Dang, R. 184, 195
Danielsoen, U. 375, 384
Danowsky, T.S. 252, 257
Darley, C.F. 181, 182, 183, 194
Das, K. 184, 195
Daugherty, S.A. 275, 276, 278
Daugherty, V.M. 366, 382
Daum, K. 17, 23
Dauncey, K. 236, 239
David, A. 262, 264, 278
Davie, I. 296, 316
Davies, L.F. 367, 385
Davies, S. 38, 45
Davis, A. 229, 239
Davis, J.M. 289, 316
Davison, L.A. 375, 380
Dawson, M.E. 297, 307, 308, 316, 317
De Gans, J. 237, 241
De Gier, J.J. 286, 317
De Grandis, D. 251, 255
De Grinis, S. 254, 258
De Kock, A.R. 137, 164
De Veau, L. 32, 44
De Wardener, H.E. 33, 44
De-Voogt, J.W.H. 355, 385
DeAnda, A. 376, 380
DeKock, A.R. 150, 152, 153, 164
Dean, L. 326, 335
Dean, R.L. 323, 334
Deary, I.J. 160, 166, 243, 252, 253, 255, 256, 257

Debiasg, P.M. 374, 375, 380
Defeo, P. 250, 255
Dejg∼ard, A. 254, 255
Demmel, U. 40, 45
Denari, M. 187, 195
Denis, R. 344, 358, 361, 380
Dershwitz, M. 374, 375, 380
Desai, N. 365, 380
Detels, R. 225, 240
Deutsch, J. 323, 335
Devitt, D.R. 326, 334
Devlesc-Howard, A.B. 254, 257
Dew, M.A. 234, 239
Dews, P.B. 55, 65, 70
Di Mario, U. 254, 258
Di Menza, S. 251, 257
Dickie, N.H. 16, 18, 22
Dickins, Q.S. 64, 65, 72
Diekmann, A. 4, 7, 9, 22, 106, 122
Digman, L. 8, 14, 15, 23, 106, 125
Dilley, J.W. 229, 236, 238, 239
Dinsmore, W.W. 38, 44
Dittrich, A. 178, 181, 182, 183, 192.
Domino, E.F. 159, 164, 165, 189, 191
Donald, M.W. 253, 254, 255, 257
Donchin, E. 231, 239
Donovan, C.B. 205, 211, 217
Doraz, W.E. 26, 30, 44
Dornbrush, R.L. 182, 183, 192
Dostalova, L. 42, 45
Douglas, F. 247, 256
Dow, R.J. 372, 373, 374, 382
Downing, R.W. 293, 318
Drachman, D.A. 323, 335
Drash, A. 251, 258
Dreier, T. 35, 43
Drew, W.G. 181, 182, 194
Drexler, H. 331, 334
Droppleman, L.F. 63, 72
Drouin, P. 254, 255
Du, V. 27, 29, 44
Dubois, R.E. 262, 278
Dubos, R. 40, 44
Dubowski, K.M. 116, 117, 121
Dubyoski, T. 324, 335
Dunbar, J.A. 92, 122
Duncan, S.M. 325, 326, 327, 334
Dungan, J. 61, 66, 70
Durrant, J. 247, 248, 249, 250, 257
Dyck, B. 357, 380
Dyk, R.B. 66, 72.
Dyrberg, V. 349, 375, 379, 384

Eadie, D.R. 77, 121
Easterbrook, J.A. 309, 316
Eaton-Williams, P. 12, 13, 23
Eccersley, P.S. 299, 316
Eckardt, M.J. 82, 125

Edelist, G. 355, 382
Edgerton, R.B. 77, 123
Edman, J.S. 35, 43
Edmonson, R.S. 358, 367, 383
Edwards, H. 360, 380
Edwards, J.A. 143, 164
Edwards, R. 262, 264, 278
Edwards, R.S. 345, 384
Eeg-Olofsson, O. 251, 255
Egan, V. 228, 229, 231, 232, 239
Eger, E.I. 375, 380
Ehlers, C.E. 231, 241
Ehlrich, R.M. 251, 258
Ehsanullah, R. 324, 334
Eich, J. 183, 195
Elgerot, A. 161, 164
Eliasson, M. 285, 286, 317
Ellinwood, E.H. 294, 316
Elliot, M.S. 106, 126
Ellis, H.C. 321, 335
Elconen, F. 327, 336
Elovaara, I. 223, 241
Elsass, P. 209, 217.¨
Eltringham, R.J. 366, 369, 385
Elving, L.D. 250, 255
Emboden, W. 169, 192
Emde, G.G. 51, 58, 59, 60, 61, 63, 67, 71
Englund, C.E. 376, 381
Erbaugh, J.K. 227, 238
Erikson, G.C. 61, 66, 70
Ertama, P. 359, 362, 382
Ervin, C.H. 118, 123
Erwin, C.W. 80, 90, 99, 101, 103, 118, 123
Erwin, G.V. 82, 90, 91, 92, 94, 95, 97, 100,
   104, 112, 126
Escobar, A. 34, 44
Evans, M.A. 181, 192
Evans, S.M. 51, 62, 71
Exton-Smith, A.N. 32, 45
Eyre, J.M. 250, 257
Eysenck, H.J. 28, 30, 46, 65, 70
Eysenck, M.W. 310, 316, 340, 380
Eysenck, S.B.G. 65, 70

Fabricant, N.D. 136, 164
Fagan, D. 79, 91, 95, 99, 101, 103, 122, 362, 380
Faldetta, L.L. 331, 335
Farmer, C.J. 36, 45
Farrimond, T. 79, 94, 122
Fasching, P. 253, 256
Faterson, H.F. 66, 72
Fauci, A.S. 219, 239
Fay, P.J. 134, 164
Fedio, P. 184, 195
Feierabend, J.M. 61, 70
Feigal, R.J. 355, 380
Feinendegen, L.E. 40, 45
Fenwick, P. 248, 250, 256

Ferris, S.H. 325, 335
Fiegal, R.J. 363, 380
File, S.A. 58, 61, 65, 70.
File, S.E. 345, 365, 380, 381
Findley, L. 276, 278
Fine, B.J. 66, 70
Fineburg, S.K. 244, 255
Fink, M. 182, 192
Finkle, B.S. 186, 195
Finnegan, J.K. 136, 165
Finnigan, F. 6, 12, 22, 81, 95, 96, 101, 102, 104, 106, 108, 109, 116, 124, 362, 383
Fischer, H.B. 363, 366, 384
Fischman, N.W. 330, 335
Fisher, B.M. 243, 256
Fisher, M.G.P. 106, 122
Fishman, B. 235, 241
Fitten, J. 251, 257
Fitzgerald, P.F. 266, 277, 379, 380
Fleishman, E.A. 378, 381.¨
Flender, J. 244, 256
Fletcher, A.A. 244, 256
Fletcher, I.R. 340, 343, 350, 351, 353, 381
Fletcher, J. 184, 195
Florey, C. 27, 29, 44
Folkard, S. 1, 2, 6, 7, 22
Folstein, M.F. 229, 239
Folstein, S.E. 229, 239
Fontaine, F. 35, 44
Forbes, A.L. 41, 46
Forney, R.B. 173, 180, 181, 185, 188, 193
Forrest, P. 348, 349, 355, 381
Forssel, H. 362, 385
Forster, B. 248, 256
Fox, E. 368, 369, 384
Frances, A.J. 235, 241
Franceschi, M. 253, 256
Frankenhaeuser, M. 138, 150, 164, 165
Frankenstein, W. 81, 89, 91, 96, 118, 124
Frankenthaler, L.M. 331, 335
Freedman, A.M. 182, 192
Frier, B.M. 243, 252, 253, 255, 256, 257
Frisby, J.P. 299, 316
Frith, C.D. 136, 161, 164
Fromme, K. 81, 96, 124
Frowein, H.W. 82, 99, 100, 125, 307, 316
Fryer, A. 320, 335
Fryer, J.G. 228, 242
Fudge, J.L. 331, 335

Gaba, D.M. 376, 380, 381
Gabrieli, J.D.E. 66, 71
Gabrielli, W.F. 82, 90, 109, 124, 365, 382
Gade, A. 254, 255
Gaillard, A.W.K. 299, 318
Galanter, I.M. 173, 193
Galbraith, J. 38, 45
Gale, A. 143, 161, 162, 164, 165

Gale, E.A.M. 249, 255
Gale, G.D. 358, 381
Gallai, V. 250, 255
Gallardo, H. 225, 239
Galleti, F. 55, 70
Galletly, D. 348, 349, 355, 381
Gallo, R.C. 219, 239
Gantz, N.M. 262, 278
Garattini, S. 55, 70
Gardner, M.J. 341, 342, 381
Garfield, G.S. 56, 71
Garg, D.C. 76, 106, 123
Garner, L. 136, 164
Garry, P.J. 32, 45
Garver, D.L. 289, 316
Garvey, M.J. 331, 335
Garza, C. 17, 22, 106, 124
Gatenby, S. 27, 29, 46
Gehin, P. 254, 255
Geiger, A. 262, 278.¨
Gelb, A.W. 361, 383
Gelenberg, A.J. 331, 335
Geller, S.E. 77, 109, 125
Genton, P. 254, 255
Gentry, T. 302, 318
Gerdt, C. 321, 336
Gerich, J.E. 247, 248, 249, 250, 251, 257, 259
Gershon, S. 324, 325, 334, 335, 365, 384
Ghadirian, M. 42, 47
Ghodse, H.A. 179, 180, 192
Ghoneim, M.M. 61, 72, 302, 316, 348, 355, 360, 362, 363, 364, 365, 367, 368, 381, 382, 383
Ghose, K. 325, 336
Giacarri, A. 250, 259
Gianutsos, R. 184, 192
Gibson, G. 34, 45
Gibson, J. 352, 357, 379
Gilbert, R.M. 51, 70
Gillespie, C.R. 254, 258
Gillespie, H.K. 173, 178, 181, 182, 185, 187, 192, 193, 195
Gilliland, K. 65, 72
Gillin, J.C. 183, 195
Gilman, A. 280, 316
Ginsberg, J. 251, 257
Glass, R.M. 330, 335
Glencross, D. 314, 317
Go, V.L.W. 251, 259
Goddes, N. 27, 29, 46
Goff, P. 365, 385
Golberg, S.C. 289, 290, 316, 317
Golby, J. 79, 91, 95, 101, 122
Gold, J.W.M. 235, 241
Golden, M.P. 251, 256
Golding, J.F. 148, 149, 156, 165, 170, 172, 175, 176, 178, 180, 181, 182, 186, 191, 192, 193
Goldman, M.S. 82, 111, 126
Goldstein, A. 57, 71
Goldstein, L. 36, 46

Gomez, S.Z.   65, 71
Gonfiantini, E.   251, 255
Gonzales, M.A.   148, 164
Gonzalez, J.L.   245, 256
Good, D.C.   254, 257
Goodenough, D.R.   66, 72.
Goodin, D.S.   231, 239
Goodman, L.S.   280, 316
Goodstein, L.P.   311, 316
Goodwin, D.W.   79, 98, 103, 116, 122, 183, 192, 365, 382
Goodwin, G.M.   228, 229, 232, 239
Goodwin, J.M.   32, 45
Goodwin, J.S.   32, 45
Gorman, J.   320, 335
Gorodetzsky, C.W.   179, 192."
Gorsuch, R.E.   7, 23
Gosselin, R.E.   65, 70
Got, I.   254, 255
Gough, K.J.   372, 373, 374, 382
Gourley, J.K.   67, 71
Gow, J.W.   264, 278
Graham, D.M.   51, 71
Graham, K.S.   252, 255, 257
Grant, E.C.G.   38, 45
Grant, I.S.   228, 232, 233, 239, 352, 353, 382
Grant, J.   199, 217
Grant, J.D.   186, 194
Grant, R.   254, 255
Gravell, M.   225, 240
Gray, J.A.   110, 125
Greden, J.F.   66, 71
Green, G.   31, 45
Green, M.   212, 217
Greenblatt, D.J.   365, 384
Greenfield, D.   17, 22
Greenwood, C.T.   41, 45
Greenwood, D.T.   325, 335
Griebel, G.   54, 71
Gries, F.A.   254, 257
Griffiths, R.R.   51, 58, 61, 62, 65, 68, 71, 72
Grimm, G.   253, 256
Gronwall, D.   229, 240
Grossman, E.   136, 164
Grove-White, I.G.   299, 316
Gruenewald, P.J.   184, 195
Gruneklee, D.   254, 257
Gunn, W.H.   79, 98, 103, 116, 122
Gurland, B.   326, 335
Gustafon, R.   79, 100, 122
Guthrie, R.A.   245, 249, 256
Gyves, P.W.   245, 256

Haag, H.B.   136, 165
Haar, P.H.   349, 379
Haefely, W.E.   292, 316
Hager, L.   61, 66, 70
Haine, S.E.   181, 185, 188, 193

Hainline, B.   235, 240
Hakami, M.K.   251, 257
Hakkinen, S.   359, 362, 371, 382
Hall, C.D.   228, 242
Hall, G.H.   159, 163
Haller, R.   263, 278
Hambridge, K.M.   36, 37, 47
Hamilton, E.   37, 45
Hamilton, P.   79, 95, 103, 122, 203, 217
Hammersley, R.H.   6, 12, 22, 81, 95, 96, 101, 102, 104, 106, 108, 109, 116, 124, 362, 383
Hanks, G.W.   299, 317
Hansen, M.   349, 379
Hansen, S.   263, 278."
Hanson, J.   371, 380
Hansteen, R.W.   185, 192
Harbeson, M.M.   160, 164
Harpur, T.   170, 186, 192
Harrad, R.A.   248, 250, 256
Harrell, R.F.   35, 45
Harrer, C.J.   4, 17, 22
Harris, D.   368, 369, 384
Harris, M.B.   148, 164
Harrison, D.W.   228, 241
Hart, J.   359, 381
Hartel, F.W.   330, 335
Hartemann, F.   137, 166
Hartley, J.T.   81, 98, 124, 367, 384
Hartley, L.R.   287, 296, 298, 299, 300, 301, 303, 304, 305, 314, 315, 316, 317
Hartmann, F.   150, 166
Harvey, P.B.   363, 382
Harvey, P.G.   330, 334
Harwood, K.M.   77, 109, 125
Hasenfrantz, M.   142, 165
Haskins, E.   251, 258
Hasukami, D.   160, 164
Hatsukami, D.K.   134, 150, 151, 165
Hauch, M.A.   357, 369, 370, 384
Hawke, W.   31, 45
Haworth, J.C.   251, 256
Hawton, K.   262, 264, 278
Haxholdt, O.   375, 384
Hayes, J.R.   246, 248, 258
Hayford, J.T.   245, 256
Hazzard, W.R.   32, 47
Healey, T.E.J.   340, 343, 350, 351, 353, 376, 381, 385
Hearn, M.   235, 240
Heatherley, D.G.   294, 316
Heazlett, M.   200, 217
Hector, M.   35, 45
Hedge, B.   236, 240
Hehra, R.   184, 195
Heimstra, N.W.   137, 150, 152, 153, 164
Heishman, S.J.   181, 182, 192
Heisman, S.J.   51, 62, 71
Heistad, D.D.   67, 71
Heller, S.R.   248, 256

Henkin, R.I. 37, 45
Henningfield, J.E. 134, 135, 152, 160, 166, 181, 182, 192
Hennis, P.J. 355, 385
Henriksen, L. 209, 217
Henry, R.S. 275, 276, 278
Henry, T. 299, 300, 301, 316
Henson, T.A. 58, 59, 61, 62, 70
Hepburn, D.A. 243, 252, 253, 255, 256, 257
Herbert, M. 80, 102, 103, 123, 248, 256, 340, 343, 346, 350, 351, 353, 381
Herberth, B. 41, 45."
Herold, D.A. 81, 91, 96, 124
Herold, K.C. 247, 256
Herrman, D.J. 379, 381
Herwig, L.D. 360, 381
Heseker, H. 30, 33, 44, 45
Hesselink, J.R. 232, 239
Heydorn, K. 40, 45
Heyes, M.P. 225, 240
Hickey, S. 342, 343, 354, 381
Higgins, P.G. 201, 205, 207, 208, 211, 213, 214, 215, 217, 218
Higgins, S.T. 160, 164
Hill, M.M. 359, 381
Hill, S.Y. 183, 192
Hills, M. 161, 164, 366, 379
Hindmarch, I. 95, 122, 136, 154, 161, 164, 294, 316, 324, 335, 345, 358, 361, 362, 367, 381, 383
Hineman, J. 74, 82, 91, 94, 117, 125
Hinnen, D.A. 245, 249, 256
Hinrichs, J.V. 61, 72, 348, 355, 360, 365, 367, 368, 381, 383
Hinson, R.E. 115, 126
Hirabyashi, S. 251, 256
Hirsch, D.A. 235, 240
Hirsh, K. 51, 53, 54, 67, 68, 71
Hishida, T. 251, 256
Hock, A. 40, 45
Hockey, G.R.J. 79, 95, 103, 122, 147, 163, 203, 217
Hodgson-Harrington, C. 251, 257
Hoffman, R.G. 245, 249, 256
Hogarty, G.E. 290, 317
Holcomb, H. 367, 384
Holland, J. 371, 383
Hollander, E. 320, 335
Hollister, L.E. 171, 172, 173, 175, 176, 178, 179, 180, 181, 182, 185, 186, 187, 192, 194, 195
Holloway, M. 170, 171, 192
Holmes, C.S. 245, 246, 247, 248, 253, 256
Holmes, G.P. 262, 278
Holtzman, S.G. 67, 68, 71
Hood, J. 32, 36, 45
Hoppe, M. 251, 258
Horn, G. 363, 380
Horne, J.A. 66, 71
Hornsby, B. 38, 45
Horton, K.B. 42, 46

Houghton, D. 151, 167, 350, 385
House, F.R. 42, 46
Houseworth, C. 61, 66, 70
Houston, J.P. 148, 164
Howard, J.M. 38, 45
Howat, P.A. 79, 86, 102, 123
Huberty, T.J. 251, 258
Huestis, M.A. 181, 182, 192."
Hughes, J.R. 160, 164
Hughes, R. 180, 181, 191
Hulbert, S. 185, 194
Hull, C. 129, 130, 131, 146, 162, 164
Humm, T.M. 64, 65, 72
Humphreys, M.S. 65, 72, 287, 317
Hunter, R. 35, 45
Huppe, R. 33, 44
Hurst, P.M. 108, 125

Idzikowski, C.J. 340, 362, 382
Il'Yutchenok, R.Yu. 159, 164
Imig, C.J. 17, 23
Ingersoll, G.M. 251, 256
Ingram, T.T.S. 251, 256
Ionescu-Pioggia, M. 62, 70
Ipp, E. 248, 256
Ireland, L. 304, 305, 316
Isaac, P.A. 344, 353, 356, 363, 385
Isbell, H. 179, 192
Ismond, D.R. 57, 65, 72

Jackson, D.M. 180, 181, 191
Jacob, P. 128, 164
Jacobs, L. 362, 382
Jacobsberg, L.B. 235, 241
Jacobsen, P.B. 235, 240, 241
Jaffe, J.H. 170, 171, 172, 173, 174, 175, 176, 178, 180, 185, 187, 188, 189, 192
Jamal, G.A. 263, 278
James, G.H. 84, 90, 101, 123
James, M. 148, 167
Janowsky, D.S. 181, 186, 191, 192
Janseen, R.S. 224, 240
Janssen, W.H. 311, 313, 317
Jarvik, M.E. 148, 164, 331, 336
Jarvis, M.J. 136, 154, 167
Jasinski, D. 179, 192
Jeffcoate, W.J. 80, 81, 96, 102, 103, 123, 124
Jenssen, T. 247, 248, 249, 250, 257.
Johansson, G. 138, 150, 164, 165
Johansson, L.C. 312, 317
Johnson, B.A. 178, 180, 184, 186, 189, 193
Johnson, J. 324, 335
Johnson, L.C. 65, 71
Johnson, R.C. 82, 90, 91, 92, 94, 95, 97, 100, 104, 112, 126
Johnson, R.F. 64, 71
Johnston, G.S. 37, 43

Jones, B.   185, 192
Jones, B.M.   95, 96, 117, 122
Jones, D.L.   8, 22, 360, 381
Jones, D.M.   299, 317, 362, 363, 364, 382
Jones, J.F.   262, 278
Jones, J.G.   368, 382
Jones, J.L.   207, 217
Jones, M.   35, 45
Jones, M.E.L.   362, 363, 364, 382
Jones, M.J.T.   345, 355, 382
Jones, M.K.   95, 96, 117, 122
Jones, M.P.   79, 98, 103, 116, 122
Jones, R.T.   128, 164, 175, 178, 179, 185, 193
Jones, R.T.   302, 318
Jones, T.G.   35, 45
Jones, T.W.   248, 249, 256
Jordan, B.D.   222, 240
Josephs, R.A.   88, 125
Judd, L.L.   228, 239, 291, 317
Juhl, R.P.   366, 382
Julia, H.L.   55, 72
Julkenen, H.   373, 374, 384

Kahn, R.J.   331, 335
Kahneman, D.   133, 165, 306, 317
Kaizer, S.   57, 71
Kalimo, H.   250, 257
Kampen, D.   225, 240
Kang, K.   36, 46
Kanto, J.   362, 383
Kapala, D.   355, 382
Kaplan, I.   185, 193
Kaplan, J.E.   262, 278
Kaplan, M.H.   235, 240
Karambelkar, D.J.   357, 379
Karlan, S.C.   15, 22
Karp, S.A.   66, 72
Karr, G.   180, 194
Kashtan, H.   355, 382
Kasperek, K.   40, 45
Kasvikis, Y.   110, 125
Katima, J.J.   54, 72
Katz, J.   251, 257
Katz, M.M.   36, 45
Kavonian, G.D.   251, 257
Kawamura, M.   159, 164
Kay, N.H.   369, 380
Kayaalp, S.O.   36, 45
Kean, D.M.   254, 255
Keen, R.J.   376, 385
Keenan, R.M.   134, 150, 151, 165
Kehlet, H.   375, 382
Keiper, C.G.   59, 63, 72.
Keller, M.A.   26, 30, 44
Kelly, M.W.   331, 335
Kelman, G.R.   299, 316
Kendrick, A.M.   14, 19, 23
Kenig, L.   159, 165

Kennedy, R.A.   27, 29, 44
Kennedy, R.S.   160, 164
Kent, T.A.   79, 98, 103, 116, 122
Kerr, D.   247, 248, 257
Kerr, J.S.   136, 154, 161, 164
Kerr, S.A.   84, 90, 101, 123
Kershner, J.   31, 45
Keshavan, M.S.   235, 242
Kestin, I.G.   363, 382
Keys, A.   4, 8, 22.¨
Khan, P.   331, 334
Khardori, 254, 257
Khosla, N.   365, 385
Kidd, A.G.   159, 167
Kiff, J.   215, 218
Kim, I.   40, 46
King, A.K.   367, 384
King, C.G.   4, 17, 22
King, D.J.   246, 247, 248, 258
King, M.B.   235, 240
King, T.C.   360, 380
Kinsman, R.H.   32, 36, 45
Kiplinger, G.F.   172, 173, 180, 181, 185, 188, 193
Kirby, M.   325, 326, 335
Kiss, I.   247, 248, 249, 250, 257
Kitahara, T.   251, 256
Klachko, D.   253, 257
Klein, D.   320, 335
Kleinman, K.M.   147, 165
Klerman, G.L.   289, 316
Klitzner, M.   184, 195
Klonoff, H.   185, 193
Knapp, R.K.   245, 249, 256
Knight, L.J.   110, 122
Knight, M.   337, 382
Knight, R.   294, 315
Knight, R.G.   77, 126
Knop, J.   82, 90, 109, 124
Knott, V.J.   136, 166
Koepke, K.M.   245, 246, 247, 248, 256
Koh, T.H.H.G.   250, 257
Koivisto, M.   251, 257
Komaroff, A.   262, 264, 277, 278
Konno, K.   374, 383
Kopell, B.S.   181, 182, 183, 192, 194
Kornetsky, C.   285, 286, 288, 296, 297, 308, 317
Korte, F.   179, 192
Korttila, K.   358, 359, 362, 364, 371, 372, 382
Kovner, R.   235, 240
Kraemer, D.   248, 249, 256
Kramer, J.   74, 123
Kramer, L.   253, 256
Krause, M.   160, 164
Krause, U.   251, 257
Krintel, J.J.   349, 379
Kristensen, M.   39, 44
Kroboth, P.D.   366, 382
Kubala, A.L.   36, 45
Kubany, A.J.   252, 257

Kubler, W.   30, 33, 44, 45
Kumar, R.   127, 165, 365, 382
Kumar, V.   348, 355, 360, 381
Kuznicki, J.T.   58, 67, 71
Kvalseth, T.O.   185, 193

LaBrie, R.   62, 70
Laberg, J.C.   79, 109, 110, 113, 121, 122, 123
Lader, M.   127, 165, 299, 318, 325, 326, 327, 328, 329, 331, 334, 335, 336
Lahdevirta, J.   223, 241
Lala, A.   250, 259
Lambert, H.   262, 264, 278
Lamboray, J-L 220, 241
Lamont, M.C.   369, 379
Lamping, D.L.   331, 335
Landauer, A.A.   79, 86, 102, 123, 327, 335
Lane, R.   262, 264, 278
Lane, T.J.   262, 278
Lang, R.   331, 335
Langan, S.J.   252, 253, 255, 257
Lange, J.M.A.   237, 241
Lantos, P.L.   225, 240
Larsen, N.A.   40, 45
Larsen, R.   17, 23
Larson, G.E.   38, 46
Larson, P.S.   136, 165
Larsson, H.   254, 255
Lassen, L.H.   246, 248, 258
Latini, R.   55, 70
Lawrence, N.W.   80, 102, 103, 123
Lawson, J.I.M.   352, 357, 379
Lawson, J.S.   253, 254, 257
Layne, C.S.   79, 86, 100, 101, 121
Lazar, W.   235, 240
Lazlo, A.   320, 335
Le Devehat, C.   41, 45
Lear, E.   357, 379
Leathar, D.S.   77, 121
Leatherdale, B.A.   247, 257
Leathwood, P.   12, 13, 23, 62, 63, 71
Lee, M.A.   66, 71
Lee, T.   376, 381
Lee, W.T.   376, 385
Leekam, S.   8, 9, 10, 23, 207, 211, 218
Legg, J.F.   331, 335
Lehmann, H.E.   331, 334
Leibel, R.L.   40, 46
Leibowitz, M.R.   320, 335
Leigh, G.   58, 72, 136, 166
Leirer, V.O.   81, 82, 107, 124, 126, 172, 181, 182, 187, 188, 189, 193, 195
Lemberger, L.   173, 177, 181, 193
Lemoine, A.   41, 45
Lennox, B.   33, 44
Leonard, J.A.   350, 382
Leonetti, F.   250, 259
Lerer, B.   331, 334

Lesser, M.   235, 240
Letemendia, F.J.J.   253, 254, 255, 257
Letourneau, J.E.   344, 358, 361, 380
Levander, S.   136, 167, 252, 253, 258, 259,
Levine, J.M.   74, 123
Leving, E.   74, 123
Levy, J.   247, 256
Levy, M.   65, 71.
Levy, R.   227, 238
Lewis, C.   32, 44
Lewis, G.F.   248, 249, 255
Lewis, M.J.   299, 317, 362, 363, 364, 382
Lewis, N.L.   17, 22, 106, 124
Lewis, S.   263, 278
Lewis, V.   363, 380
Ley, P.   368, 382
Lezak, M.   226, 240
Li, T-K 116, 121
Lichman, W.A.   227, 240
Lichty, W.   253, 257
Liebel, R.L.   17, 22
Lieberman, H.R.   51, 56, 58, 59, 60, 61, 63, 66, 67, 71
Lifshitz, F.   244, 256
Liljequist, R.   302, 317, 324, 325, 327, 335
Lin, Y.J.   76, 106, 123
Lindgren, M.   250, 259
Linnoila, M.   80, 82, 90, 99, 101, 103, 118, 123, 125, 294, 299, 302, 315, 317, 324, 327, 335, 358, 359, 362, 371, 382
Lins, P.E.   252, 259
Lippa, A.S.   323, 334
Lippold, O.C.J.   132, 165
Lipscomb, T.R.   80, 91, 113, 123
Liptzin, B.   35, 43
Lisman, S.A.   81, 98, 124, 368, 383
Lister, R.G.   58, 61, 65, 70, 345, 365, 380, 381
Little, R.E.   118, 123
Litwack, A.R.   184, 192
Liu, S.   366, 382
Livanainen, M.   223, 241
Lobban, M.C.   1, 22
Loberg, T.   79, 113, 122
Locuratolo, N.   250, 259
Lohmann, R.   254, 257
Loke, W.H.   59, 61, 62, 71, 72
Lolait, S.J.   172, 193
Londorf, D.   344, 358, 361, 380
Lonero, L.   185, 192
Longo, D.L.   219, 239
Longstreet, C.   251, 258
Lonsdale, D.   42, 45
Lopez, C.   41, 45
Lorr, M.   63, 72
Lovallo, W.   235, 240
Love, A.H.G.   38, 44
Lubbe, K.E.   180, 181, 191
Lucas, A.   251, 257
Lukas, S.E.   108, 123

Lushene, R.E.   7, 23
Lyons, B.S.   106, 126
Lysaght, R.   365, 385

Maag, U.   35, 44.¨
Maben, A.   14, 19, 23
Mac, D.S.   365, 382
MacAndrew, C.   77, 123
MacCannell, K.   180, 194
MacCarthy, F.   80, 94, 123
MacDonald, F.C.   372, 373, 374, 382
MacDonald, I.A.   248, 256
MacDonald, R.N.   371, 380
MacLean, A.   79, 95, 103, 122
MacPherson, A.   39, 43
MacPherson, R.D.   294, 317
Macavoy, M.G.   181, 193
Macher, A.M.   219, 239
Machotra, A.K.   184, 195
Mackenzie, A.I.   363, 380
Mackenzie, M.   352, 357, 379
Mackenzie, N.   352, 353, 382
Mackworth, J.F.   139, 165
Macleod, C.   310, 316, 317
Macleod, K.M.   252, 257
Macmillan, K.   371, 380
Madill, H.D.   74, 79, 93, 121
Madl, C.   253, 256
Maisto, S.A.   79, 89, 91, 101, 104, 112, 121, 124
Maki, M.   327, 336
Mallampati, S.R.   357, 369, 370, 384
Maller, O.   8, 14, 15, 23, 106, 125
Mallon, J.   355, 382
Mallory, C.   186, 188, 194
Malvy, J.M.D.   42, 45
Mandell, A.J.   231, 241
Mangan, G.L.   148, 149, 156, 161, 165, 182, 193
Mann, A.   262, 264, 278
Mann, J.M   220, 241
Mann, J.R.   367, 385
Manner, T.   362, 383
Manninen, P.H.   361, 383
Manno, J.E.   172, 173, 180, 181, 185, 188, 193
Manu, P.   262, 278
Marby, D.W.   35, 43
Marcus, M.L.   67, 71
Mardh, A.   138, 165
Markey, S.   225, 240
Marks, D.F.   180, 181, 182, 183, 191, 194
Marks, I.   110, 125
Marlatt, G.A.   81, 96, 110, 124, 125
Marples, P.W.   79, 98, 103, 116, 122
Marsh, V.R.   172, 175, 176, 178, 180, 181, 191
Marshman, J.A.   51, 70

Martello, J.   321, 336
Martin, A.   225, 240
Martin, C.   17, 23
Martin, J.R.   61, 70
Martz, R.   181, 192
Masito, S.A.   81, 124
Mason, A.P.   186, 193.¨
Massie, M.   371, 383
Mathews, A.   310, 316, 317
Matilla, M.J.   324, 325, 327, 335
Matsuda, L.A.   172, 193
Matthews, D.A.   262, 278
Matthews, D.M.   35, 45
Matthews, J.N.S.   341, 342, 383
Mattila, M.J.   299, 302, 317, 373, 374, 383, 384
Mattsson, N.   289, 316
Matuzas, W.   330, 335
Matz, B.   139, 155, 167
Mayfield, R.D.   79, 86, 100, 101, 121
Maylor, E.A.   80, 84, 87, 90, 97, 99, 100, 101, 102, 103, 105, 123
Mazzotta, G.   250, 255
McAllister, R.   235, 240
McArthur, J.   225, 233, 239, 240, 241
McBay, A.J.   186, 193
McBrearty,   8, 15, 22
McCarthy, G.   248, 249, 256
McCarthy, M.   325, 335
McClearn, G.E.   82, 90, 91, 92, 94, 95, 97, 100, 104, 112, 126
McConnell, F.   42, 46
McCord, L.   66, 70
McCreary, C.   368, 369, 384
McDonald, L.   262, 264, 278
McDougall, W.   337, 338, 361, 383
McEvedy, C.P.   262, 278
McEwen, J.   324, 334
McFarland, D.J.   182, 194
McGee, R.   148, 166
McGlothlin, W.   181, 185, 194
McGraw, D.J.   136, 166
McGuiness, D.   306, 318
McGuire, R.   357, 363, 365, 379
McHugh, P.R.   229, 239
McIntyre, K.E.   183, 194
McKane, W.R.   246, 247, 248, 258
McKelvey, R.K.   59, 63, 72
McKenzie, P.J.   369, 380
McKeown, D.   357, 363, 365, 379
McKiernan, E.P.   341, 354, 355, 363, 383
McKinnis, R.   237, 241
McLaughlin, J.E.   225, 240
McMaster, D.   38, 44
McMillen, D.L.   80, 81, 92, 114, 122, 123
McNair, D.M.   63, 72, 331, 335
McNamee, J.E.   80, 94, 123
McNeill, G.   8, 9, 10, 23, 27, 29, 44
McNeill, R.E.J.   77, 121

McRae, K.N.   251, 256
McSpadden, M.   81, 96, 124
Meacham, M.P.   186, 192
Mehta, M.P.   348, 355, 360, 381
Meites, K.   235, 240
Melges, F.T.   173, 178, 181, 182, 185, 187, 193, 195
Meliska, C.J.   59, 71
Melmed, R.N.   225, 240
Mendelson, J.H.   108, 123
Mendelson, M.   227, 238
Mendhiratta, S.S.   184, 194
Menzies, I.   27, 29, 44
Merchant, R.N.   361, 383
Merriam, P.E.   189, 191
Merritt, D.M.   251, 257
Mewaldt, S.P.   302, 316, 348, 362, 363, 364, 365
Mewaldt, S.P.   367, 368, 381, 382, 383
Meyer, R.E.   181, 189, 194
Mhalu, F.S.   220, 241
Michel, Ch.   142, 165
Mier-Jedzrejowicz, A.   212, 217
Milam, S.B.   360, 381
Milech, D.   314, 317
Miles, C.   4, 5, 6, 7, 9, 11, 12, 20, 23, 106, 125.
Miles, W.R.   252, 257
Millar, K.   6, 12, 22, 81, 83, 95, 96, 101, 102, 104, 106, 108, 109, 116, 123, 124, 269, 270, 278, 337, 342, 343, 344, 345, 352, 354, 362, 364, 366, 367, 368, 381, 383
Miller, D.   234, 236, 240
Miller, E.N.   233, 240, 241
Miller, I.   251, 255
Miller, J.Z.   36, 46
Miller, L.L.   181, 182, 194
Miller, N.   366, 382
Miller, R.D.   185, 192
Miller, W.R.   319, 321, 335
Millman, J.E.   172, 175, 176, 178, 180, 181, 191
Mills, K.C.   81, 91, 104, 105, 109, 117, 124
Mills, L.   31, 47
Milner, G.   327, 335
Milstein, S.L.   180, 194
Minicucci, F.   253, 256
Minocha, A.   81, 91, 96, 102, 124
Mirin, S.M.   181, 189, 194
Mirsky, A.F.   288, 296, 297, 308, 317
Misawa, T.   81, 95, 102, 124
Misslin, R.   54, 71
Mitrakou, A.   247, 248, 249, 257
Mock, J.M.   227, 238
Mohler, H.   292, 317
Mokan, M.   247, 248, 257
Monga, T.N.   253, 254, 255, 257
Mongrain, S.   81, 92, 99, 115, 124
Monk, T.H.   1, 2, 6, 7, 22
Montagnon, B.   42, 45
Mooradian, A.D.   251, 257

Moran, J.   365, 385
Morano, S.   254, 258
Morihisa, J.M.   81, 98, 124.¨
Morley, J.E.   251, 257
Morley, R.   251, 257
Morris, P.   225, 239
Morrow, D.   81, 107, 124
Morrow, D.G.   172, 181, 182, 187, 188, 189, 193
Mortiboy, D.   294, 315
Moscovitz, H.   325, 335
Moses, C.   252, 257
Moskowitz, H.   81, 90, 94, 95, 99, 124, 181, 185, 194
Moss, E.   358, 367, 383
Mostert, J.W.   337, 383
Mourey, M.S.   42, 45
Mowbray, J.   262, 264, 268, 278
Muechterlein, K.H.   297, 307, 308, 316, 317
Muehlbach, M.J.   64, 65, 72
Mueller, C.   37, 45, 368, 383
Mueller, C.W.   81, 98, 124
Mueter, F.   254, 257
Mulligan, B.   287, 303, 304, 316
Mulsant, B.H.   235, 242
Murphree, H.B.   36, 46
Murphree, M.B.   159, 165
Murphy, D.L.   95, 126, 321, 336
Murray, J.B.   172, 180, 189, 193, 194
Murray, J.T.   95, 124
Myers, L.   17, 23
Myers, S.A.   189, 191
Myrsten, A.   138, 150, 164, 165

Nadel, A.   34, 46
Nader, T.   66, 71
Nahum, D.   251, 258
Naismith, D.J.   27, 29, 46
Nakashima, E.N.   180, 181, 191
Nance, W.E.   36, 46
Nathan, D.M.   251, 257, 259
Nathan, P.E.   80, 81, 82, 89, 91, 96, 110, 112, 113, 118, 123, 124, 125
Navia, B.A.   222, 223, 224, 225, 240, 241, 242
Naylor, G.J.   36, 46
Neff, N.H.   36, 45
Neilsen, S.   224, 241
Neilsen, S.A.   39, 44
Neims, A.   57, 65, 72
Nelson, H.E.   226, 240
Nelson, J.C.   321, 335
Nelson, M.   27, 29, 46
Nelson, T.O.   81, 96, 124
Netter, P.   362, 383
Newlin, D.B.   90, 110, 112, 124, 125
Newman, S.   235, 240
Newton, R.E.   365, 384
Ney, T.   161, 162, 165

Niaura, R.S.   81, 89, 91, 96, 105, 118, 124
Nicholson, A.M.   372, 373, 374, 380
Nicholson, A.N.   293, 318
Nicoll, R.A.G.   372, 373, 374, 382."
Nicols, R.C.   36, 46
Nielsen, W.R.   361, 383
Nightingale, J.J.   341, 354, 355, 363, 383
Nil, R.   142, 165
Nilsson, B.Y.   250, 258
Nimmo, J.   294, 315
Nimorwicz, P.   234, 239
Nixon, C.   363, 382
Noble, E.P.   81, 118, 124
Noble, J.   368, 383
Normile, H.J.   324, 334
Nutt, D.   302, 315
Nyboe, J.   185, 194

O'Boyle, C.A.   368, 369, 384
O'Hanlon, J.F.   286, 294, 317
O'Hara, M.W.   348, 355, 360, 381
O'Malley, S.S.   81, 91, 124
O'Toole, B.I.   315, 317
Oberleas, D.   38, 44
Ochs, M.W.   366, 384
Oei, T.P.S.   77, 126
Ogg, T.W.   363, 366, 384
Ohman, A.   113, 121
Okada, T.   292, 317
Olsen, R.W.   292, 317
Olssen, S.E.   311, 316
Olsson, Y.   250, 257
Ong, D.   357, 363, 380
Ornitz, D.B.   224, 241
Osborne, L.   79, 86, 100, 101, 121
Ostberg, O.   66, 71
Ostrovskaya, R.U.   159, 164
Oswald, I.   340, 382
Otis, S.   231, 241
Oyler, J.R.   4, 17, 22

Page, J.B.   184, 194
Page-El, E.   251, 257
Pahwa, S.   262, 278
Pain, A.J.   358, 367, 383
Pakkenberg, H.   40, 45
Parasuraman, R.   82, 99, 100, 125
Park, C.N.   79, 94, 95, 121
Parker, E.S.   81, 98, 118, 124, 367, 384
Parkes, K.R.   266, 277, 379, 380
Parrott, A.C.   127, 136, 138, 142, 143, 145, 146,
   152, 153, 156, 159, 161, 165, 166, 185, 194,
   345, 384
Pascoe, P.A.   36, 46
Patel, R.M.   81, 99, 124
Pathak, D.   348, 355, 360, 381
Patman, J.   327, 335

Patrick, A.W.   243, 256
Patten, B.M.   37, 45
Paul, E.A.A.   345, 346, 354, 355, 360, 385
Paul, T.   33, 44
Peaker, A.   227, 240
Pearson, D.   262, 264, 278."
Peat, M.A.   186, 195
Peck, A.W.   58, 59, 61, 62, 70, 325, 326, 334,
   359, 381
Peck, R.   186, 188, 194
Pedersen, E.   349, 379
Peeva, A.   251, 257
Pelosi, A.   262, 264, 278
Penick, E.C.   79, 98, 103, 116, 122
Penny, F.J.   361, 383
Perceman, E.   235, 240
Perdices, M.   223, 230, 237, 239, 241
Pereira, M.S.   201, 217
Periello, G.   250, 255
Peritz, E.   28, 30, 46
Perl, J.   294, 317
Perlmuter, L.C.   251, 257, 259
Perry, P.J.   331, 335
Perry, S.W.   235, 240
Perryman, K.   251, 257
Persson, L.   62, 72
Peters, R.   148, 166
Peters, T.   262, 264, 278
Petersen, R.P.   362, 382
Petito, C.K.   223, 240
Peto, T.   262, 264, 278
Petrie, R.A.   160, 166
Petros, T.   61, 66, 70
Pew, R.W.   311, 317
Pfeiffer, C.C.   36, 37, 46
Phil, R.O.   184, 191
Philip, B.K.   357, 369, 370, 384
Phillips, C.L.   367, 385
Phillpots, R.   215, 218
Pietravalle, P.   254, 258
Piggins, D.J.   80, 94, 123
Pihl, R.O.   82, 104, 111, 112, 125, 126
Pildes, R.S.   251, 257
Pillard, R.C.   181, 189, 194
Pinelli, L.   251, 255
Pinner, E.M.   245, 248, 258
Piot, P.   220, 241
Pishkin, V.   235, 240
Plomin, R.   82, 90, 91, 92, 94, 95, 97, 100, 104,
   112, 126
Plotz, J.B.   251, 258
Plumb, A.P.   248, 250, 256
Plummer, F.   220, 241
Polich, J.   231, 241
Pollet, P.   62, 63, 71
Pollitt, E.   17, 22, 40, 46, 106, 124
Pollock, V.E.   82, 90, 109, 124
Polonsky, K.S.   247, 248, 249, 255, 256
Pomara, N.   365, 384

Pomerleau, C.S.   161, 166
Pomerleau, O.F.   161, 166
Pope, H.G.   62, 70
Popovic, M.   219, 239."
Porcu, S.   250, 259
Portans, I.   108, 125
Porte, D.   15, 23
Portegies, P.   237, 241
Porter, W.   346, 361, 363, 367, 384
Post, B.   138, 147, 150, 163, 164, 165
Post, R.M.   66, 67, 70
Potter, W.Z.   324, 335
Pottinger, R.C.   249, 255
Poulton, E.C.   345, 372, 384
Poutianen, E.   223, 241
Powell, B.   183, 192
Powell, J.   110, 125
Power, S.J.   349, 355, 380
Pozzessere, G.   254, 258
Pramming, S.   245, 248, 250, 258
Prasad, A.S.   37, 38, 44, 46
Prasher, D.   276, 278
Preedy, V.   262, 264, 278
Prescott, J.H.   254, 258
Preston, K.L.   51, 62, 71
Pribram, K.H.   306, 318
Price, N.   340, 354, 356, 379
Price, R.W.   32, 46, 222, 223, 224, 225, 239, 240, 241, 242
Prior, C.A.   39, 47
Prior, P.F.   249, 255
Pudel, V.   30, 33, 44, 45
Pumarola-Sune, T.   224, 241
Purdie, G.   348, 381
Purtilo, D.T.   262, 278

Quinn, J.D.   243, 256

Rabbani, P.   37, 46
Rabbitt, P.M.A.   80, 84, 87, 90, 97, 99, 100, 101, 102, 103, 105, 123
Radda, G.K.   263, 277
Radlow, R.   108, 125
Rafaelsen, L.   185, 191, 194
Rafaelsen, O.J.   185, 191, 194
Ragni, M.V.   234, 239
Rall, T.W.   51, 54, 55, 72
Ralph, A.   8, 9, 10, 23
Ramm, D.   80, 90, 99, 101, 103, 118, 123
Ramsden, B.   230, 239
Randall, B.   17, 23
Rapoport, J.L.   57, 65, 72
Raps, C.S.   321, 335
Rasmussen, J.   311, 318
Raspiller, A.   254, 255
Raun, J.   349, 379
Raven, J.   229, 241

Ravindran, A.   42, 44
Re, P.K.   37, 45
Read, J.D.   82, 97, 125
Reaven, G.M.   251, 258
Redfield, R.R.   220, 241
Reed, S.E.   202, 215, 217, 218."
Reeve, V.C.   186, 188, 194
Regina, E.G.   59, 63, 72
Reichard, P.   250, 253, 258
Reid, L.D.   185, 192
Reinhard, K.E.   321, 335
Reisberg, B.   325, 335
Reitan, J.A.   346, 361, 363, 367, 384
Reitan, R.M.   228, 241
Reitsman, W.D.   306, 318
Relman, A.S.   182, 194
Remmy, D.   54, 71
Rennick, P.M.   228, 239
Resnick, L.   222, 241
Restall, J.   340, 354, 356, 379
Revell, A.D.   140, 144, 145, 152, 159, 162, 166, 167
Revelle, W.   65, 72, 287, 317
Rey, A.   227, 241
Reynolds, E.H.   35, 46
Reza, M.   247, 257
Riccio, M.   234, 240
Rich, E.   181, 185, 195
Richards, M.M.K.   18, 22
Richards, T.   170, 194
Richardson, D.P.   41, 45
Richardson, J.T.E.   250, 254, 258
Rickels, K.   293, 318
Rickles, W.H.   183, 191, 194
Riddington, C.J.   58, 59, 61, 62, 70
Riding, M.   264, 278
Riis, J.   375, 384
Rimland, B.   38, 46
Rinsler, M.   42, 44
Risk, M.T.A.   254, 255
Ritzman, R.   25, 30, 44
Rix, K.J.B.   116, 125
Rix-Trot, H.M.   244, 258
Roache, J.D.   58, 61, 62, 65, 72
Robert, J.J.   251, 255
Roberts, C.   51, 59, 60, 61, 63, 67, 71
Roberts, D.   26, 27, 30, 44, 136, 152, 153, 166
Roberts, H.R.   51, 72
Roberts, L.   263, 278
Robertson, D.G.   81, 91, 96, 102, 124
Robertson, J.   39, 47
Robertson, J.R.   219, 241
Robertson, K.R.   228, 242
Robertson, W.   186, 194
Robertson, W.T.   228, 242
Robertson-Tchabo, E.A.   251, 258
Robinson, J.O.   344, 353, 356, 363, 385
Rodda, B.E.   173, 180, 181, 193
Rodrigues, J.A.   178, 195

Rodriguez-Carbajal, J.   34, 44
Roessler, E.   248, 249, 256
Rohrbaugh, J.W.   82, 99, 100, 125."
Roller, T.   225, 240
Roloff, L.   17, 23
Root, H.F.   252, 257
Rose, E.A.   360, 380
Rose, I.W.   136, 164
Rose, J.M.   340, 343, 350, 351, 353, 381
Rosen, I.   250, 259
Rosen, M.   344, 353, 356, 363, 368, 382, 385.
Rosenberg, J.   128, 164
Rosenfalck, A.M.   246, 248, 258
Rosenhow, D.J.   110, 125
Rosenquist, U.   250, 253, 258
Rosow, C.E.   374, 375, 380
Ross, D.F.   82, 104, 111, 125, 126
Ross, R.   324, 335
Rosvold, H.E.   296, 317
Roth, W.T.   181, 182, 183, 194
Rotton, J.   377, 384
Rovet, J.F.   251, 258
Roy-Byrne, P.P.   367, 384
Royston, P.   341, 342, 383
Rozzo, P.A.   254, 258
Rubenstein, J.S.   36, 45
Rubinow, D.R.   226, 241
Rumble, W.F.   37, 43
Rundell, J.   235, 241
Russ, N.W.   77, 109, 125
Russell, B.A.   251, 256
Russell, M.A.H.   127, 128, 165, 166
Russell, P.N.   244, 258
Russo, P.   251, 259
Rusted, J.M.   12, 13, 23
Ruther, E.   294, 318
Ryan, C.   247, 248, 257
Ryan, C.M.   250, 251, 258

Saarialho-Kere, U.   373, 374, 384
Sacahuddin, S.Z.   219, 239
Saccuzzo, D.P.   181, 191
Saczano, J.   17, 23
Saffroy-Splitter, M.   54, 71
Sahakian, B.J.   227, 238
Sahgal, A.   80, 84, 99, 123
Saito, J.   225, 240
Sakmar, E.   76, 106, 125
Sakulsriprong, M.   325, 326, 327, 328, 329, 334, 336
Salkind, M.R.   299, 318
Salonen, M.   362, 383, 385
Salvendy, G.   180, 194
Sanchez, R.   349, 379
Sandberg, D.   320, 335
Sanders, A.F.   306, 307, 308, 318
Sanders, L.D.   344, 353, 356, 363, 385
Sandow, B.   79, 93, 121

Sandstead, H.H.   37, 38, 42, 46, 47
Sannerud,C.A.   51, 62, 71
Santeusanio,F.   250, 255
Santoro,D.   25, 30, 44."
Sarby, Z.I.   41, 46
Sargent, J.   18, 20, 22
Satlin, A.   35, 43
Satz, P.   184, 194
Saudax, E.   254, 255
Saunders, J.H.   79, 94, 95, 121
Savage, R.D.   138, 156, 163
Savory, M.   12, 13, 23
Sawyer, D.A.   55, 72
Sbraccia, P.   250, 259
Scalzar, A.   225, 240
Schaeffer, J.H.   185, 195
Scharf, M.B.   365, 385
Scheaf, A.   25, 30, 44
Scheider, N.G.   148, 164
Scheinin, M.   362, 385
Schelenburg, B.   41, 43
Schicha, H.   40, 45
Schlierf, G.   41, 43
Schmidt, U.   294, 318
Schmitt, F.A.   237, 241
Schneider, N.G.   148, 164
Schoenthaler, S.J.   26, 28, 30, 33, 46
Scholtz, C.L.   225, 240
Scholz, N.   181, 193
Schonberger, L.B.   262, 278
Schoof, K.   228, 239
Schooley, R.T.   262, 278
Schoor, M.   186, 192
Schorow, M.   360, 380
Schulman, R.   106, 124
Schumacher, M.T.   17, 23
Schwartz, B.L.   81, 98, 124
Schwartz, J.V,   41, 45
Schwartz, M.K.   225, 239
Schwartz, R.H.   184, 195
Schweitzer, P.K.   64, 65, 72
Schwieder, M.   51, 70
Schwin, R.   183, 192
Scott, A.C.   77, 121
Scott, A.W.C.   343, 344, 351, 385
Scott, B.   362, 380
Scott, D.B.   79, 91, 95, 99, 101, 103, 122
Scott, D.L.   32, 45
Sedman, A.J.   76, 106, 125
Segal, Z.V.   321, 336
Seitz, C.P.   4, 17, 22
Seligman, M.E.P.   319, 321, 335
Sellers, C.M.   159, 165
Selnes, O.A.   233, 240, 241
Seppala, T.   324, 325, 327, 335, 336, 373, 374, 384
Serna, P.   304, 316
Seyone, C.   357, 380
Shakow, D.   308, 318
Shapira, B.   331, 334

Shapiro, A.P. 81, 82, 89, 91, 96, 110, 112, 118, 124, 125
Shapiro, D.M. 228, 241
Shapiro, L.M. 181, 189, 194
Shapshak, R. 222, 241
Sharma, S. 181, 185, 194
Sharpe, M. 262, 264, 278
Sheffield, M.T. 35, 44
Shen, G.Z. 201, 217
Sher, K.J. 117, 125
Shergold, K. 148, 167
Sherwin, R.S. 248, 249, 257
Sherwood, N. 136, 154, 161, 164
Shigeta, S. 81, 95, 102, 124
Shirley, A.W. 376, 385
Shore, M.D. 236, 238
Shorvon, S.D. 35, 46
Shukit, M.A. 109, 125
Shulman, R.J. 17, 22
Sidtis, J.J. 224, 225, 241
Silberman, E. 321, 336
Silverstone, J.T. 299, 317
Silverton, L. 181, 191
Simon, L. 65, 72
Simonson, D.C. 246, 249, 259
Simonson, E. 4, 8, 22
Simpson, D.M. 224, 241
Simpson, K.H. 367, 385
Simpson, P. 272, 273, 275, 276, 278, 340, 354, 356, 379
Simpson, P.M. 144, 159, 167
Simpson, R.I.D. 38, 44
Simpson, T.H. 357, 369, 370, 384
Sinclair, M.E. 355. 385
Singer, D.E. 251, 257
Sjoberg, L. 62, 72
Skenazy, J.A. 252, 258
Skutle, A. 113, 121
Sloer, N.G. 254, 257
Smith, A.H.W. 36, 46
Smith, A.P. 4, 5, 6, 7, 8, 9, 10, 11, 12, 13, 14, 19, 20, 22, 23, 106, 125, 204, 205, 207, 208, 209, 211, 213, 214, 215, 217, 218, 262, 264, 268, 269, 270, 271, 272, 273, 274, 275, 276, 278
Smith, B.A. 271, 272, 273, 274, 275, 276, 278
Smith, D. 262, 264, 278
Smith, D.L. 58, 72
Smith, G. 376, 385
Smith, G.M. 59, 63, 72
Smith, J. 236, 241
Smith, M. 337, 338, 361, 383
Smith, N. 247, 257
Smith, R.J. 367, 385
Smith, R.P. 65, 70
Smith, S.M. 81, 92, 114, 122, 123
Smizne, S. 253, 256.˝
Snaith, R.P. 227, 242
Snider, W.D. 224, 241
Sno, H.N. 238, 242

Snorgaard, O. 246, 248, 258
Snyder, F.R. 134, 135, 152, 160, 166
Snyder, S.H. 53, 54, 55, 70, 72, 291, 318
Soares, J.R. 186, 195
Sobocinsky-Olsson, B. 250, 258
Sobotka, T.J. 68, 72
Sommer, B.R. 35, 46
Soncksen, P.H. 248, 250, 256
Souieff, M.I. 184, 195
Spear, N.E. 81, 98, 124, 367, 383
Speelman, D.J. 245, 249, 256
Spencer, A.M. 244, 258
Spencer, J. 296, 303, 316
Spera, K.F. 326, 334
Spielberger, C.D. 7, 23
Spierdijk. J. 355, 385
Spinweber, C.L. 65, 71
Spirduso, W.W. 79, 86, 100, 101, 121
Spire, J.P. 248, 249, 255
Spriggs, T.L.B. 299, 317, 362, 363, 364, 382
Spring, B. 8, 14, 15, 23, 56, 71, 106, 125, 331, 335.
Spyker, D.A. 81, 91, 96, 124
St.Clair, D. 231, 232, 239
Staiger, P.K. 108, 113, 125
Standen, P.J. 345, 383
Standing, L. 81, 92, 99, 115, 124
Stanley, B. 365, 384
Stanley, M. 365, 384
Stapleton, J.M. 82, 99, 100, 125
Starcher, T. 224, 240
Starick-Zynch, K. 248, 249, 256
Stark, G.D. 251, 256
Starmer, G.A. 180, 181, 191, 294, 317
Steele, C.M. 88, 125
Steinberg, G. 32, 44
Steinhelber, J.C. 375, 380
Sterh-Green, J. 224, 240
Sternberg, D.E. 330, 336
Sternberg, G. 250, 259
Sterner, R.T. 32, 46
Stevens, A.B. 246, 247, 248, 258
Stevens, H.A. 147, 166
Stevens, W.C. 375, 380
Stewart, D. 134, 164
Stewart, L.E. 227, 240
Stiff, M.P. 331, 335
Stigsby, B. 250, 258
Stillman, R.C. 81, 98, 124, 183, 195, 367, 384
Stock, J.G.L. 341, 354, 355, 363, 383
Stoker, M.J. 324, 335
Stollery, B.T. 376, 385
Stone, B.M. 36, 46
Stone, G.C. 185, 302, 318.˝
Stone, R. 357, 363, 380
Stone, S. 248, 250, 256
Storosum, G. 238, 242
Strang, J. 110, 125
Straus, S.E. 262, 264, 278

Stroop, J.R.   145, 166
Strother, N.   287, 303, 304, 316
Studd, C.   366, 369, 385
Styles, B.C.   367, 383
Styles, P.   263, 277
Subhan, Z.   324, 335
Sugermen, J.L.   64, 65, 72
Sulkowski, A.   181, 185, 195
Surridge, D.H.C.   253, 254, 255, 257
Suter, T.W.   145, 166
Sutker, L.L.S.   184, 194
Sutton, L.R.   186, 188, 195
Svensson, E.   62, 72
Swift, C.G.   58, 62, 72
Swinkels, J.A.   238, 242
Szbadi, E.   321, 336

Taberner, P.V.   82, 101, 117, 125
Talland, G.A.   140, 166
Tallroth, C.   250, 259
Tamborlane, W.V.   248, 249, 256, 259
Tamburanno, G.   250, 259
Tannahill, R.   50, 71
Tansella, C.   299, 318
Tarbit, M.   250, 257
Tarriere, H.C.   137, 150, 166
Tata, P.   310, 317
Tattersall, R.B.   248, 256
Taylor, A.   357, 363, 380
Taylor, D.I.   262, 263, 264, 277, 278
Taylor, G.F.   33, 46
Taylor, J.M.G.   225, 240
Taylor-Davies, A.   365, 380
Teasdale, J.D.   321, 334
Teasdale, T.W.   82, 90, 109, 124
Telford, R.   138, 156, 163
Teo, R.K.C.   180, 181, 191
Ternard, C.   251, 259
Thatcher, J.W.   348, 381
Theilgaard, A.   245, 248, 258
Thiessen, I.   31, 47
Thomas, J.R.   134, 164
Thomas, W.   254, 257
Thompson, J.   235, 241
Thompson, J.B.   90, 125
Thompson, J.W.   138, 156, 163, 172, 175, 176, 178, 180, 181, 191
Thompson, K.   367, 384
Thompson, L.W.   251, 258
Thompson, P.J.   320, 324, 325, 332, 336
Thompson, R.G.   245, 246, 247, 248, 256
Thomson, J.B.   112, 125.
Thorn, J.   39, 47.¨
Thornton, J.A.   299, 316
Thorsteinsson, B.   245, 248, 250, 258
Thurgate, J.K.   74, 82, 91, 94, 117, 125
Thurmond, J.B.   200, 211, 217, 218
Tinklenberg, J.R.   173, 178, 181, 182, 183, 185, 187, 193, 194, 195,

Tiplady, B.   58, 62, 72, 79, 84, 91, 95, 99, 101, 103, 122, 125, 362, 380
Tippett, J.   32, 44
Tobin, J.D.   251, 258
Todman, J.   27, 29, 44
Tognoni, G.   55, 70
Tong, J.E.   58, 72, 80, 94, 123, 136, 166
Torlone, E.   250, 255
Tosato, G.   262, 278
Totman, R.   215, 218
Tourtelle, W.W.   222, 241
Towle, V.L.   248, 249, 255
Tramont, E.C.   220, 241
Travell, J.   128, 167
Trickett, S.   207, 211, 213, 214, 218
Trimble, M.R.   320, 324, 325, 332, 336
Tross, S.   222, 242
True, W.R.   184, 195
Trumbo, D.A.   299, 318
Tsalikian, E.   253, 256
Tucker, D.M.   38, 47
Tucker, J.A.   82, 94, 110, 111, 125
Tucker, M.R.   366, 367, 384
Tun, P.A.   251, 259
Turin, A.C.   55, 72
Turner, L.S.   58, 67, 71
Turner, P.   325, 326, 335, 336
Tuttle, W.W.   17, 23
Tye, J.   198, 218
Tyrrell, D.A.J.   204, 205, 207, 208, 209, 211, 213, 214, 215, 217, 218, 262, 264, 278

Uhde, T.W.   66, 67, 70, 367, 384
Uhlenhuth, E.H.   330, 335
Ungapen, S.   296, 316
Uuchinich, R.E.   94, 110, 111, 125

Vachon, L.   181, 185, 195
Valentin, N.   375, 384
Valle, E.   254, 258
Valle, S.L.   223, 241
Valtonen, M.   362, 385
Van Arkel, A.E.   306, 318
Van Der Horst, C.   228, 242
Van Der Zwaag, R.   42, 46
Van Dis, H.   345, 346, 354, 355, 360, 385
Van Doornick, W.J.   37, 47
Van Leeuwen, H.   345, 346, 354, 355, 360, 385
Van Rhijn, A.G.   39, 47
Varma, S.K.   184, 194
Varma, V.K.   184, 195
Varner, J.L.   82, 99, 100, 125
Vattapposta, F.   254, 258.¨
Vaughn, R.   147, 165
Vega, A.   251, 258
Venables, P.H.   106, 122
Veneman, T.   247, 248, 257

Ventura, M.   250, 255
Vernon, P.E.   223, 242
Vernon, S.   182, 183, 192
Vickers, M.D.   360, 361, 385
Viinamaki, O.   362, 385
Vogel, E.   54, 71
Vogel-Scibilia, S.E.   235, 242
Vogel-Sprott, M.   79, 89, 114, 121
Volkerts, E.R.   294, 317
Von Borstel, R.W.   55, 57, 66, 72
Von Spulak, F.   179, 192
Von Zeppelin, I.   178, 181, 182, 183, 192
Vuchinich, R.E.   82, 125
Vuyk, J.   355, 385

Wadsworth, J.   324, 334
Wagner, J.C.   76, 106, 123, 125
Wait, J.S.   74, 82, 91, 94, 117, 125
Wakefield, J.   26, 30, 44
Walbert, J.   254, 257
Walder, C.P.   81, 96, 124
Waldhausl, W.   253, 256
Wallace, J.   215, 218
Wallace, L.M.   340, 380
Wallace, P.   262, 264, 278
Waller, D.   136, 167
Walravens, P.A.   36, 37, 47
Walsh, J.K.   64, 65, 72
Walsh, K.W.   79, 107, 121
Walters, A.   145, 167
Walton, N.H.   79, 107, 121
Warburton, D.M.   11, 23, 132, 138, 139, 140,
   141, 142, 143, 144, 145, 148, 150, 155, 156,
   159, 160, 162, 167
Ward, C.H.   227, 238
Ward, N.I.   38, 47
Warm, J.S.   200, 218
Warrell, D.   262, 264, 278
Warren, I.   251, 257
Warrington, S.J.   325, 336
Wastell, D.G.   367, 383
Watanabe, A.M.   173, 193
Watkins, J.   274, 278
Watson, D.W.   138, 156, 163
Watson, I.D.   74, 126
Watson, P.E.   74, 126
Watson, R.   38, 47
Watts, F.N.   321, 336
Waye, J.D.   366, 382
Weaver, M.   161, 162, 165
Weber, M.   254, 255
Wechsler, D.   226, 228, 242
Weidler, D.J.   76, 106, 123, 125
Weightman, W.M.   361, 385.¨
Weil, A.T.   179, 195
Weil, W.B.   251, 255
Weiler, P.H.   235, 241
Weingartner, H.   81, 95, 98, 124, 126, 183, 195,
   321, 324, 336, 367, 384

Weinger, M.B.   376, 381
Weiss, J.L.   173, 193
Weissman, M.M.   319, 334
Welch, R.B.   74, 82, 91, 94, 117, 125
Welling, P.G.   106, 126
Wells, J.K.   186, 195
Wells-Parker, E.   80, 81, 92, 114, 122, 123
Welsby, P.D.   219, 241
Wenham, R.   215, 218
Wesnes, K.   11, 23, 132, 133, 138, 139, 140,
   141, 142, 143, 144, 145, 148, 150, 152, 155,
   156, 159, 160, 162, 167, 272, 273, 275, 276,
   278, 340, 354, 356, 379, 385
Wessely, S.   262, 263, 264, 278
West, R.J.   136, 154, 167
Westenhofer, J.   30, 33, 45
Wever, R.A.   7, 23
Weydert, J.A.   245, 256
Whaley, R.F.   200, 217
Whitaker, C.A.   181, 183, 194
Whitby, O.   57, 71
White, J.M.   108, 113, 125
White, P.   262, 264, 278
White, R.P.   366, 384
Whitwarm, J.G.   343, 344, 351, 385
Widom, B.   246, 249, 259
Wig, N.N.   184, 194, 195
Wigmore, S.W.   115, 126
Wijnen, J.L.C.   306, 318
Wikler, A.   182, 194
Wilder, J.   244, 259
Wilkins, A.J.   214, 218, 379
Wilkins, J.   228, 242
Wilkinson, P.K.   76, 106, 125
Wilkinson, R.T.   59, 72, 151, 167, 343, 344, 345,
   350, 351, 352, 359, 360, 366, 381, 383, 385
William, J.S.   204, 205, 209, 211, 213, 215, 217,
Williams Erdahl, P.L.   253, 254, 255, 257
Williams, A.F.   81, 90, 94, 99, 124, 186, 195
Williams, D.G.   42, 44
Williams, D.L.   82, 111, 126
Williams, E.J.   132, 165
Williams, G.D.   134, 147, 155, 156, 167
Williams, J.W.L.   225, 240
Williams, R.D.   74, 79, 93, 121
Williams, R.M.   82, 111, 126
Willman, J.S.   218
Wilson, C.G.   132, 165
Wilson, G.   331, 335
Wilson, J.R.   82, 90, 91, 92, 94, 95, 97, 100,
   104, 112, 126
Wilson, M.   17, 23
Wilson, P.   117, 119, 126
Wilson, T.G.   80, 91, 113, 123
Wilton, N.C.T.   341, 354, 355, 363, 383
Winder, G.   142, 143, 156, 161, 166
Winokur, A.   293, 318
Witkin, H.A.   66, 72
Wittenborn, J.R.   299, 318

Wolf, B.   51, 62, 71
Wolf, R.   37, 45
Wolff, E.A.   66, 67, 70
Wolfson, D.   228, 241
Wolkowitz, O.M.   35, 46
Wood, C.   262, 264, 278
Woodall, C.   264, 278
Woods, S.C.   15, 19, 23
Woodson, P.P.   51, 62, 68, 71, 142, 145, 165, 166
Worthington-Roberts, B.   32, 47, 118, 123
Wredling, R.   252, 259
Wright, C.   80, 84, 99, 123
Wright, D.   262, 264, 278
Wright, D.C.   220, 241
Wright, D.J.   369, 379
Wright, J.C.   251, 258
Wurtman, J.   8, 14, 15, 23, 106, 125
Wurtman, R.J.   51, 58, 59, 60, 61, 63, 66, 67, 71
Wyatt, R.J.   81, 98, 124, 173, 183, 193, 195, 367, 384.

Yamada, T.   253, 256
Yeager, E.P.   186, 195
Yehuda, S.   40, 47
Yeomans, W.A.   344, 353, 356, 363, 385

Yesavage, J.A.   81, 82, 107, 124, 126, 172, 181, 182, 187, 188, 189, 193, 195
Youdim, M.B.H.   40, 47
Young, A.C.   172, 193
Young, J.A.   82, 112, 126
Young, J.F.   55, 70
Young, R.   77, 126
Young, S.N.   42, 47
Yudkin, J.   28, 30, 46
Yuille, J.C.   82, 97, 125

Zacharias, M.   361, 385
Zahn, T.P.   57, 65, 72
Zajac, R.   235, 241
Zaslavsky, A.   374, 375, 380
Zegans, L.S.   262, 278
Ziegler, O.   254, 255
Zieman, K.   181, 185, 194
Zigmond, A.S.   227, 242
Zimmerman, Tansella, C.   299, 318
Zimmerman, E.G.   186, 195
Zinberg, N.E.   179, 195
Zornetzer, S.F.   323, 336.¨
Zuaroi, A.W.   178, 195
Zubovic, E.A.   82, 125
Zuurmond, W.W.A.   345, 346, 354, 355, 360, 385
Zylber-Katz, E.   65, 71